BUILDING

DMZs for Enterprise Networks

Robert J. Shimonski

Will Schmied

Dr. Thomas W. Shinder

Victor Chang

Drew Simonis

Damiano Imperatore

KEY	SERIAL NUMBER
001	TH3H7GYV43
002	QUCK7T6CVF
003	8BRWN5TX3A
004	Z2FXX3H89Y
005	UJMPT3D33S
006	X6B7NCVER6
007	TH34EPQ2AK
008	9BKMLAZYD7
009	CAN7N3V6FH
010	5BBABY339Z

PUBLISHED BY
Syngress Publishing, Inc.
800 Hingham Street
Rockland, MA 02370

Building DMZs for Enterprise Networks

Printed in the United States of America

1 2 3 4 5 6 7 8 9 0

ISBN: 1-931836-88-4

Technical Editor: Robert J. Shimonski   Cover Designer: Michael Kavish
Acquisitions Editor: Jonathan E. Babcock   Page Layout and Art by: Patricia Lupien
Indexer: Rich Carlson   Copy Editor: Darlene Bordwell

Distributed by Publishers Group West in the United States and Jaguar Book Group in Canada.

Acknowledgments

We would like to acknowledge the following people for their kindness and support in making this book possible.

Karen Cross, Meaghan Cunningham, Kim Wylie, Harry Kirchner, Kevin Votel, Kent Anderson, Frida Yara, Jon Mayes, John Mesjak, Peg O'Donnell, Sandra Patterson, Betty Redmond, Roy Remer, Ron Shapiro, Patricia Kelly, Kristin Keith, Jennifer Pascal, Doug Reil, David Dahl, Janis Carpenter, and Susan Fryer of Publishers Group West for sharing their incredible marketing experience and expertise.

The incredibly hard working team at Elsevier Science, including Jonathan Bunkell, AnnHelen Lindeholm, Duncan Enright, David Burton, Rosanna Ramacciotti, Robert Fairbrother, Miguel Sanchez, Klaus Beran, and Rosie Moss for making certain that our vision remains worldwide in scope.

David Buckland, Wendi Wong, Daniel Loh, Marie Chieng, Lucy Chong, Leslie Lim, Audrey Gan, and Joseph Chan of STP Distributors for the enthusiasm with which they receive our books.

Kwon Sung June at Acorn Publishing for his support.

Jackie Gross, Gayle Voycey, Alexia Penny, Anik Robitaille, Craig Siddall, Darlene Morrow, Iolanda Miller, Jane Mackay, and Marie Skelly at Jackie Gross & Associates for all their help and enthusiasm representing our product in Canada.

Lois Fraser, Connie McMenemy, Shannon Russell, and the rest of the great folks at Jaguar Book Group for their help with distribution of Syngress books in Canada.

David Scott, Tricia Wilden, Marilla Burgess, Annette Scott, Geoff Ebbs, Hedley Partis, Bec Lowe, and Mark Langley of Woodslane for distributing our books throughout Australia, New Zealand, Papua New Guinea, Fiji Tonga, Solomon Islands, and the Cook Islands.

Winston Lim of Global Publishing for his help and support with distribution of Syngress books in the Philippines.

Contributors

Thomas W. Shinder M.D. (MVP, MCSE) is a computing industry veteran who has worked as a trainer, writer, and a consultant for Fortune 500 companies including FINA Oil, Lucent Technologies, and Sealand Container Corporation. Tom was a Series Editor of the Syngress/Osborne Series of Windows 2000 Certification Study Guides and is author of the best selling books *Configuring ISA Server 2000: Building Firewalls with Windows 2000* (Syngress Publishing, ISBN: 1-928994-29-6) and *Dr. Tom Shinder's ISA Server & Beyond* (ISBN: 1-931836-66-3). Tom is the editor of the *Brainbuzz.com Win2k News* newsletter and is a regular contributor to TechProGuild. He is also content editor, contributor, and moderator for the World's leading site on ISA Server 2000, www.isaserver.org. Microsoft recognized Tom's leadership in the ISA Server community and awarded him their Most Valued Professional (MVP) award in December of 2001.

Will Schmied (BSET, MCSE, CWNA, TICSA, MCSA, Security+, Network+, A+) is the President of Area 51 Partners, Inc., a provider of wired and wireless networking implementation and security services to businesses in the Hampton Roads, VA area. Will holds a bachelors degree in mechanical engineering technology from Old Dominion University in addition to his various IT industry certifications and is a member of the IEEE and ISSA. Will has previously authored or contributed to several other publications by Syngress Publishing including *Implementing and Administering Security in a Microsoft Windows 2000 Network Study Guide and DVD Training System (Exam 70-214)* (ISBN: 1-931836-84-1), *Security+ Study Guide & DVD Training System* (ISBN: 1-931836-72-8), and *Configuring and Troubleshooting Windows XP Professional* (ISBN: 1-928994-80-6).

Will lives in Newport News, Virginia with his wife, Chris, and their children Christopher, Austin, Andrea, and Hannah. Will would like to thank his family for believing in him and giving him the support and encouragement he needed during all of those late nights in "the lab." Will would also like to say thanks to the entire team of professionals at Syngress Publishing—you make being an author easy. Special thanks to Jon Babcock for having a sense of humor that never seems to go out of style.

Norris L. Johnson, Jr. (Security+, MCSA, MCSE, CTT+, A+, Linux+, Network +, CCNA) is a technology trainer and owner of a consulting company in the Seattle-Tacoma area. His consultancies have included deployments and security planning for local firms and public agencies, as well as providing services to other local computer firms in need of problem solving and solutions for their clients. He specializes in Windows NT 4.0, Windows 2000 and Windows XP issues, providing consultation and implementation for networks, security planning, and services. In addition to consulting work, Norris provides technical training for clients and teaches for area community and technical colleges. He is co-author of *Security+ Study Guide & DVD Training System* (Syngress Publishing, ISBN: 1-931836-72-8), *Configuring and Troubleshooting Windows XP Professional* (ISBN: 1-928994-80-6), and *Hack Proofing Your Network, Second Edition* (ISBN: 1-928994-70-9). Norris has also performed technical edits and reviews on *Hack Proofing Windows 2000 Server* (ISBN: 1-931836-49-3) and *Windows 2000 Active Directory, Second Edition* (ISBN: 1-928994-60-1). Norris holds a bachelor's degree from Washington State University. He is deeply appreciative of the support of his wife, Cindy, and three sons in helping to maintain his focus and efforts toward computer training and education.

Michael Sweeney (CCNA, CCDA, CCNP, MCSE) is the owner of the network consulting firm Packetattack.com. His specialties are network design, network troubleshooting, wireless network design, security, and network analysis using NAI Sniffer and Airmagnet for wireless network analysis. Michael's prior published works include *Cisco Security Specialist's Guide to PIX Firewalls* (Syngress Publishing, ISBN: 1-931836-63-9).

Michael is a graduate of the University of California, Irvine, extension program with a certificate in Communications and Network Engineering. Michael resides in Orange, CA with his wife Jeanne and daughter Amanda.

Ido Dubrawsky (CCNA, SCSA) has been working as a UNIX/Network Administrator for over 10 years. He has experience with a variety of UNIX operating systems including Solaris, Linux, BSD, HP-UX, AIX, and Ultrix. He was previously a member of Cisco's Secure Consulting Service providing security posture assessments to Cisco customers and is currently a member of the SAFE architecture team. Ido has written articles and papers on topics in network security such as IDS, configuring Solaris virtual private networks, and wireless security. Ido is a contributing author for *Hack Proofing Sun Solaris 8* (Syngress, ISBN: 1-928994-44-X) and *Hack Proofing Your Network, Second Edition* (ISBN: 1-928994-70-9) When not working on network security issues or traveling to conferences, Ido spends his free time with his wife and their children.

Victor Chang (CCSA, CCSE, CCNA CCSE+, NSA) is the Product Line Support Team Lead for IPSO and Hardware with Nokia. He currently provides Product Line Escalation Support for the Nokia IP Series Appliances and assists Product Management in new product development. Victor lives in Fremont, CA. He would like to thank his parents, Tsun San and Suh Jiuan Chang, Ricardo and Eva Estevez, as well as the rest of his family and friends. Without their love and support none of this would have been possible.

Hal Flynn is a Senior Vulnerability Analyst for Symantec. He is also the UNIX Focus Area Manager of the SecurityFocus website, and moderator of the Focus-Sun and Focus-Linux mailing lists. Hal is a Veteran of the United States Navy, where he served as a Hospital Corpsman with 2nd

Marine Division. He has worked in a wide range of roles such as systems administration, systems analysis, and consulting in both the commercial and government environments. Hal lives in Calgary, Alberta, Canada and is a certified Wreck Diver, Ice Diver, and Rescue Diver.

Damiano Imperatore (CCIE #9407, CCNP, CCNA, CCDA, MCSA) is a Systems Engineer for Verizon's Enterprise Solutions Group (ESG). Damiano is responsible for designing networking solutions for several of New York's government agencies and large enterprises. Damiano has over 8 years of experience in the data networking field with strengths in designing, building, and securing large complex enterprise networks. Prior to Verizon, Damiano worked for the Cendant Corporation as a Lead Network Architect where he designed, managed and supported Cendant's very large global network. At Cendant, he was also tasked with designing and supporting DMZ infrastructures for several major websites including Avis Rent-A-Car, Century 21 and websites related to Cendant's hospitality unit. Damiano holds a bachelor's degree in Computer Science from Hofstra University.

Daniel Kligerman (CCSA, CCSE, Extreme Networks GSE, LE) is a Consulting Analyst with TELUS Enterprise Solutions Inc., where he specializes in routing, switching, load balancing, and network security in an Internet hosting environment. Daniel is a contributing author for *Check Point Next Generation Security Administration* (Syngress, ISBN: 1-928994-74-1). A University of Toronto graduate, Daniel holds an honors bachelor's of Science degree in Computer Science, Statistics, and English. Daniel currently resides in Toronto, Canada. He would like to thank Robert, Anne, Lorne, and Merita for their support.

Drew Simonis (CCNA, SCSA, SCNA, CCSA, CCSE, IBM CS) is a Senior Network Security Engineer with the RL Phillips Group, LLC. He provides senior level security consulting to the United States Navy, working on large enterprise networks. He considers himself a security generalist, with a strong background in system administration, Internet application development, intrusion detection and prevention and response, and penetration testing. Drew's background includes a consulting position with Fiderus, serving as a security architect with AT&T and as a Technical Team Lead with IBM. Drew has a bachelors degree from the University of South Florida and is also a member of American MENSA. Drew has contributed to several Syngress publications, including the best selling *Check Point Next Generation Security Administration* (ISBN: 1-928994-74-1). Drew lives in Suffolk, VA with his wife Kym and daughters Cailyn and Delany.

Tod Beardsley began geek life in the mid-'80s as a pre-teen Commodore Vic-20 hacker and BBS sysop in the San Francisco East Bay. Since then, he has administered several networks of varying scale and flavor, has earned MCSE and GCIA certifications, and is presently employed at Dell Computer Corporation in Round Rock, Texas. Tod is Dell's Subject Matter Expert for security on the Windows NT/2000 server platform, with a focus on Dell's Internet-exposed site operations. In addition to performing the duties of a paid Windows dork, Tod is a Debian GNU/Linux enthusiast, a grader for the GIAC GCIA certification, and holds the esteemed distinction of 2000's runner-up Sexiest Geek Alive.

Technical Editor and Contributor

Robert J. Shimonski (TruSecure TICSA, Cisco CCDP, CCNP, Symantec SPS, NAI Sniffer SCP, Nortel NNCSS, Microsoft MCSE, MCP+I, Novell Master CNE, CIP, CIBS, CNS, IWA CWP, DCSE, Prosoft MCIW, SANS.org GSEC, GCIH, CompTIA Server+, Network+, Inet+, A+, e-Biz+, Security+, HTI+) is a Lead Network and Security Engineer for a leading manufacturing company, Danaher Corporation. At Danaher, Robert is responsible for leading the IT department within his division into implementing new technologies, standardization, upgrades, migrations, high-end project planning and designing infrastructure architecture. Robert is also part of the corporate security team responsible for setting guidelines and policy for the entire corporation worldwide. In his role as a Lead Network Engineer, Robert has designed, migrated, and implemented very large-scale Cisco and Nortel based networks. Robert has held positions as a Network Architect for Cendant Information Technology and worked on accounts ranging from the IRS to AVIS Rent a Car, and was part of the team that rebuilt the entire Avis worldwide network infrastructure to include the Core and all remote locations. Robert maintains a role as a part time technical trainer at a local computer school, teaching classes on networking and systems administration whenever possible.

Robert is also a part-time author who has worked on over 25 book projects as both an author and technical editor. He has written and edited books on a plethora of topics with a strong emphasis on network security. Robert has designed and worked on several projects dealing with cutting edge technologies for Syngress Publishing, including the only book dedicated to the Sniffer Pro protocol analyzer. Robert has worked on the following Syngress Publishing titles: *Building DMZs for Enterprise Networks* (ISBN: 1-931836-88-4), *Security+ Study Guide & DVD Training System* (ISBN: 1-931836-72-8), *Sniffer Pro Network Optimization & Troubleshooting Handbook* (ISBN: 1-931836-57-4), *Configuring and Troubleshooting Windows XP Professional* (ISBN: 1-928994-80-6), *SSCP Study Guide & DVD Training System* (ISBN: 1-931836-80-9), *Nokia Network Security Solutions*

Handbook (ISBN: 1-931836-70-1) and the *MCSE Implementing and Administering Security in a Windows 2000 Network Study Guide & DVD Training System* (ISBN: 1-931836-84-1).

Robert's specialties include network infrastructure design with the Cisco product line, systems engineering with Windows 2000/2003 Server, NetWare 6, Red Hat Linux and Apple OSX. Robert's true love is network security design and management utilizing products from the Nokia, Cisco, and Check Point arsenal. Robert is also an advocate of Network Management and loves to 'sniff' networks with Sniffer-based technologies. When not doing something with computer related technology, Robert enjoys spending time with Erika, or snowboarding wherever the snow may fall and stick.

Contents

Foreword

One of the most complicated areas of network technology is designing, planning, implementing, and constantly maintaining a demilitarized zone (DMZ) segment. The basic concept of the DMZ comes from the U.S./Korean conflict, which ended in 1953 with an armistice signed by North Korea, China, and the United States. The armistice terms included the establishment of what would be called the *Demilitarized Zone,* or DMZ, between North and South Korea. The DMZ was a wide strip of land where no weapons heavier than an infantry soldier's machine gun would be allowed. The intention was to prevent further conflict, since no formal peace resolution had been reached (and has not been reached to this day, although North and South Korea signed a nonaggression treaty in 1991). In short, the DMZ's purpose was to keep the North Koreans in North Korea and out of South Korea. Over time, however, the DMZ rules were modified to allow traffic to pass between the two countries, albeit not exactly freely.

In today's computer networks, the concept of a DMZ has been borrowed from the Korean peninsula with the same basic idea: to keep people out of the protected network segment, typically referred to as the *private network* or the *intranet.* Usually, however, a DMZ presents certain network services to the public network while protecting the private network. If all you wanted to do was protect the internal network, you could easily (and with far less risk and effort) accomplish the task through the judicious use of routers and firewalls. The fact that you actually want to segregate network traffic into two groups is what necessitates the implementation and use of a DMZ solution. You need your public servers (Web, SMTP, and FTP servers and the like) to be accessible to the public network but still afforded some basic measure of protection. By the same token, you want to tightly control who and what type of access is allowed to enter the private protected network.

The building of a DMZ can seem very complicated because you need to be a network engineer (and a good one at that), a systems engineer (to build up the services running on the DMZ and around it), and a highly skilled security analyst (to harden and test the DMZ segment). Due to the need for such a diverse skill set, it is common for most companies to have a team of designers and even some consultants perform this work. Until now, no book was dedicated to even looking at this area of network design. With this book, all that changes—and we believe it is long overdue.

The other issue that always arises when you're designing and building DMZs is choice of vendor product line. Since there are so many to choose from, we decided to look at the most common systems and hardware utilized in most DMZ segments. This book covers (in great detail) the planning and design of DMZ segments with products and tools from Cisco, Check Point, Nokia, Sun Solaris, Microsoft, and many other vendors. We chose to cover many vendors because it is important that you learn to configure DMZs with many vendors' products. More important, we want the reader to realize that although the various vendors' products are different from one another, all the underlying concepts are the same!

After reading this book, you will be able to understand, design, plan, implement, maintain, secure, and test a DMZ segment using a variety of technologies. It is suggested that you read the chapters in order, although more experienced readers might want to jump ahead at certain points to chapters that hold particular interest to them. Remember: In reading this book, you are learning how to become a DMZ architect. If you are new to DMZs, you will be best served by reading this book straight through once to learn all the little tips and tricks in the design and implementation phases, and then go back and concentrate on the chapters dealing with whatever products or systems you are using.

This book follows a natural progression that is broken into four steps:

1. Learn the concepts and major design principles of all DMZs.
2. Learn how to configure the actual hardware that makes up DMZs.
3. Learn how to securely populate the DMZs with systems and services.
4. Learn how to troubleshoot, maintain, test, and implement security on your DMZ.

Let's take a look at the actual chapter breakdown. Part I of the book focuses on design and consists of the first four chapters. Design is critical to building DMZs, and you should have a good understanding of design concepts when you are done reading this section. The chapters in Part 1 are:

- **Chapter 1: DMZ Concepts, Layout, and Conceptual Design** This chapter takes a steppingstone approach to the concept of a DMZ. The DMZ can be (and usually is) different every time it's implemented. Each company or business has its own needs and requirements; for this reason, each DMZ could be different from others in some way, shape, or form. For instance, the fact that your DMZ terminates the Internet connection with a private T1 instead of a VPN-based Internet connection changes your DMZ ever so slightly in the design and configuration—hence creating an automatic difference. Still other DMZs are designed to provide different services and so on. The number of differences can be overwhelming, so it's very important to at least understand all the terminology, underlying concepts, and general issues you will deal with. This chapter highlights all these issues for you. You will learn not only DMZ concepts, layout, and conceptual design but also how to plan your network security (and why), the history of the DMZ, design fundamentals, basic and advanced risks from the DMZ, and strategies you can implement for advanced DMZ design. All in all, this chapter represents Level 1 of your DMZ education, and even the most highly skilled techs are encouraged to read it because it contains everything you will need to build on in later chapters.

- **Chapter 2: Windows 2000 DMZ Design** This chapter covers all the details you need to plan a Windows 2000 DMZ. This chapter focuses only on the conceptual design. Later chapters cover the hardware and services ends of the Windows 2000 DMZ, but by the time you are done reading Chapter 2, you will be able to lay out a plan to set up any Windows 2000 DMZ scenario you need. It is recommended that you read Chapter 1 first so that you are familiar with the terminology and the concepts are clear.

- **Chapter 3: Sun Solaris DMZ Design** This chapter is identical to Chapter 2 except it examines Sun Solaris, one of the most popular and hottest Internet technologies today, instead of Windows 2000. Solaris, made for secure Internet-based services, is covered here in the same format as Chapter 2 with one exception: Chapter 3 shows you how to build a DMZ from a Sun Solaris server.

- **Chapter 4: Wireless DMZs** This chapter covers the planning, layout, and design of a wireless DMZ. As of this writing of this book, no other publication goes into the detail you see on this topic in Chapter 4. Wireless DMZs are a growing phenomenon as more and more wireless ISPs (WISPs) and other wireless systems are used. You will learn why we need wireless DMZs as well as how to plan and design the wireless DMZ. You are shown multiple wireless DMZ examples and a down-and-dirty wireless LAN security best-practices list, since the most disturbing issues revolving around wireless technology is its somewhat questionable security. This chapter will answer your questions on this cutting-edge area.

Part II covers the buildup of hardware that creates the network segment known as the DMZ. You will learn how to build infrastructure with Cisco PIX firewalls, Check Point NG, Nokia solutions, and Microsoft ISA 2000. After reading the four chapters in Part II, you will know how to implement one of four different firewall vendor products with an internal, external, and DMZ segment (or multiple DMZ segments) for just about any situation. No matter your firewall choice, you will learn how to configure it properly for use with a DMZ segment. You might question why you would want to read all these chapters if you were only interested in one technology. There are several answers to this question. You might be planning a DMZ and not know what solution best fits your organization. In this case, reading these chapters will allow you to see the options that are and are not available with each of the technologies. You can also get some idea of the cost of various solutions. You could come to the conclusion that ISA is too complicated for your needs or that the Check Point NG system has too many bells and whistles you simply don't need. Reading all the chapters in Part II will better prepare you to decide on the best fit for your needs. The chapters that make up Part II are as follows:

- **Chapter 5: Firewall Design: Cisco PIX** This chapter covers the essentials through highly advanced topics you'll need to configure a DMZ-based solution with the Cisco PIX firewall, one of the most popular systems. You will learn how to plan which PIX you will need, how to plan and design the PIX, how to make a DMZ and control the traffic to and from it, and many other things you will need to know to put this solution in place.

- **Chapter 6: Firewall and DMZ Design: Check Point NG** This chapter covers essentially the same information as Chapter 5 except utilizing the Check Point NG product. In Chapter 6, you will learn the fundamentals of planning what you need, the design of the Check Point NG system with a DMZ, how to secure your perimeters, and how to make a DMZ segment and control its traffic.

- **Chapter 7: Firewall and DMZ Design: Nokia Firewall** This chapter has the same fundamental structure as Chapters 5 and 6 except the focus is on the Nokia product line. Nokia runs Check Point, but the configuration and planning can be different in some aspects, as described in detail in Chapter 7. The chapter covers the basics of the Nokia firewall, securing your network perimeter, a Nokia firewall and DMZ design checklist, and other important details you will need to know to build your DMZ.

- **Chapter 8: Firewall and DMZ Design: ISA Server 2000** The last chapter in this section again covers building DMZs, this time with the Microsoft ISA Server. In this chapter you will learn how to configure a tri-homed DMZ; how to publish DMZ SMTP servers, Web servers, and FTP servers; and how to build a trihomed DMZ. If you have never worked with ISA before, you will see that it is a little tricky.

Part III of the book covers all the essentials of DMZ population and security. The chapters in this part are:

- **Chapter 9: DMZ Router and Switch Security** Chapter 9 takes a hard look at securing the most commonly forgotten pieces of the DMZ: the connecting hardware. Routers and switches need to be considered for security as well; the material in Chapter 9 will be all you need to completely harden your edge systems. The coverage is biased toward Cisco, but that is because Cisco products are most commonly used. However, you can apply the same concepts and theory to your Nortel, 3Com, or any other devices. In this chapter you will learn about securing routers, switches, and their protocols used in and around the DMZ. Because the chapter is Cisco based, you will also learn how to completely harden the Cisco IOS, get updates on IOS bugs and security advisories, and other crucial Cisco-based issues.

- **Chapter 10: DMZ-Based VPN Services** This chapter covers one of the hottest, most widely used solutions today: the virtual private network, or VPN. Known for its flexibility in design and ease of use, the VPN is one of the most commonly implemented solutions in networks, but where do you place this service in the DMZ? What about differences between site-to-site VPNs and others? Where do the devices go? All this information is covered in Chapter 10. Chapter 10 also focuses on designing VPN services in the DMZ, designing an IPSec solution, and connecting business-to-business (B2B) sites.

- **Chapter 11: Implementing Wireless DMZs** This chapter covers the actual configuration details you need to implement wireless DMZs. The chapter material relates to coverage in Chapter 4 (the design chapter for wireless DMZs), so that you can set up a freeware or Cisco-based solution. You will be surprised at how easy it is to build a wireless DMZ, as this chapter shows. You will learn about implementing a wireless Gateway with Reef Edge Dolphin and implementing RADIUS with Cisco LEAP.

- **Chapter 12: Sun Solaris Bastion Hosts** This chapter covers Sun Solaris (one of the most common DMZ host systems today) as it would be used in the DMZ. You learn to harden the base operating system as well as services it provides. It is critical that you read this section if you place Sun systems on your DMZ. You will learn that the DMZ is publicly accessible, so failing to harden these systems almost guarantees your network will be hacked and exploited. In this chapter we look at Sun Solaris bastion hosts, configuring the fundamentals, controlling access to resources, auditing access to resources, authentication, and all the hardening you need to lock down your systems.

- **Chapter 13: Windows 2000 Bastion Hosts** This chapter covers the same concepts as Chapter 12 but with a focus on Windows 2000. This chapter can be partnered with Chapter 2 to guide you in building Windows 2000 bastion hosts on your DMZ. The chapter covers the hardening details as well as showing you how to configure security, set up remote administration of DMZ hosts, vulnerability-scan your hosts, and implement advanced host security.

Part IV of this book consists of two very important chapters on security. Now that your DMZ is in place, is designed properly, is working well, and is populated with services, you need to ask yourself: How secure is my network? Was it done right? In this final installment of this book, you will learn just that:

- **Chapter 14: Hacking the DMZ** This chapter takes you into the mind of the hacker—how a hacker sees your DMZ and what you need to do to secure the DMZ before hackers tear into it and cause problems. This lengthy chapter covers many assessment tests and techniques that hackers use to exploit your systems. You will learn how to hack the DMZ, perform reconnaissance and penetration testing, execute specific attacks on DMZ hosts, and follow a DMZ hardening checklist.

- **Chapter 15: Intrusion Detection in the DMZ** This chapter covers intrusion detection systems (IDS) in the DMZ—basically, all there is to know about placement and setup, giving you the options to look at Cisco IDS as well as Snort. In this chapter you will learn how to set up a honeypot, configure IDS, use CiscoSecure IDS and Snort, and set up a "poor man's IDS" on a small budget.

Finally, we have included a bonus appendix for registered readers that covers how to harden IIS, Microsoft's flagship Web server. To Access the bonus appendix, go to www.syngress.com, click on the "Solutions" link on the bottom left of the screen and register your book as per the instructions. Web servers are common on the DMZ, so it is important that you know exactly how to harden these systems. This appendix shows you how, step by step.

The DMZ is a critical segment found in many networks (any network that has a WAN link or Internet connection could build a DMZ). Until now, there was not enough information available on DMZs. That's where *Building DMZs for Enterprise Networks* comes in. We think that you'll find this book your one-stop guide to planning, designing, deploying, and maintaining a secure and viable DMZ segment on your production network.

—Robert J. Shimonski
Lead Network and Security Engineer, Danaher Corporation
June 2003

## Chapter 1

DMZ Concepts, Layout, and Conceptual Design

Solutions in this chapter:

- Planning Network Security
- DMZ Definitions and History
- DMZ Design Fundamentals
- Advanced Risks
- Advanced Design Strategies

☑ Summary

☑ Solutions Fast Track

☑ Frequently Asked Questions

Introduction

During the course of the last few years, it has become increasingly evident that there is a pronounced need for protection of internal networks from the outside world. As machine technologies have improved and extensive shifts in the functions that a user can accomplish through more user-friendly interfaces have occurred, many more attacks have been mounted against enterprise and nonenterprise systems. Unlike the patterns in the past, when networks were primarily attacked and probed by "professional" attackers, the systems you protect are now routinely scanned by individuals and groups ranging from pre-teens "just trying it out" to organized groups of criminals seeking to abridge your systems or utilize information that is stored within your enterprise that can give them identities, disclose trade information, allow them access to funds, or disrupt critical services that your organization provides.

This book is designed to be a definitive work for your use in understanding the concepts of protection, the terminology and pieces of the demilitarized zone (DMZ) structure, and design of the DMZ for the enterprise. A DMZ is a method of providing segregation of networks and services that need to be provided to users, visitors, or partners through the use of firewalls and multiple layers of filtering and control to protect internal systems.

Along the way, the authors will provide you with the information you need to appropriately design, implement, monitor, and maintain an efficient and useful DMZ structure. The book contains not only the theory but the "how to" information that you will need in order to be successful in protecting your internal networks from attack. Information is available about different hardware and software implementations (including Cisco PIX, Nokia, Check Point, Microsoft ISA Server, and others) that you will find useful in planning and implementing your DMZ.

Chapter 1 gives you a great deal of background information and refreshes your knowledge of security concepts, defines DMZ terminology to improve understanding and create a common ground for discussion, and explores DMZ design basics before expanding into advanced risks and the advanced designs that might be used to better protect your networks. After looking at these basic concepts, Chapter 2 discusses the procedures and placement for Windows-based services within the DMZ and internal networks, and Chapter 3 covers UNIX-based services within the DMZ and internal networks. It is imperative that you read this first section of the book because it will give you the underlying fundamentals and concepts you need to accurately design a DMZ.

Planning Network Security

To implement security for your network and systems, a base plan must be written and evaluated by all the stakeholders in your organization. This initial plan will be used to define the starting parameters for security policies and direction for your protection plan. The plan will contain the decisions that will lead to the design of a functional DMZ to meet the needs and level of protection that your organization determines are necessary.

Planning for network security requires an evaluation of the risks involved with loss of data, unauthorized access to data, and information compromise. The plan must also consider cost factors, staff knowledge and training, and the hardware and platforms currently in use, as well as helping with the estimations of future need. As we will see, the DMZ plan and concept provide a multilayered security capability, but as with anything that involves multiple components, administration costs and equipment costs increase with the complexity of the system.

It should be understood that no security plan is ever a final plan. Instead, we work continuously to revise and update the plan in an ongoing effort to provide the best possible coverage that minimizes the risk of intrusion and damage. Of course, before we can provide a meaningful and effective evaluation of the areas we need to protect, we must understand the components that have to be protected. In the next few sections of this chapter, we look more closely at the fundamentals of security and define more precisely what exactly we are trying to protect.

Security Fundamentals

When discussing the fundamentals of security in our networks, we use the *confidentiality, integrity, and availability (CIA)* triad model as a starting point. This CIA triad provides security professionals with the paths they needed to evaluate their security and a set of rules that make it somewhat easier to group tools and procedures to try to ensure that the conditions are met. While using CIA as an evaluation method is still a good practice and sound methodology today, we must consider a number of other factors that weren't covered at the time that the CIA concept was developed.

For instance, CIA calls for *confidentiality*. As recently as a few years ago, one of the methods that could be used to provide confidentiality for network resources simply involved using a proxy server or a firewall, or even something as simple as Network Address Translation (NAT), between the outside (untrusted) network and our internal (trusted) network. At that time, it served the purpose that it was designed for; it separated the two types of networks from each other and limited users from the untrusted network in their attempts to view our internal networks. Figure 1.1 illustrates the original configuration we might have used.

Figure 1.1 Original Basic Firewall Configuration

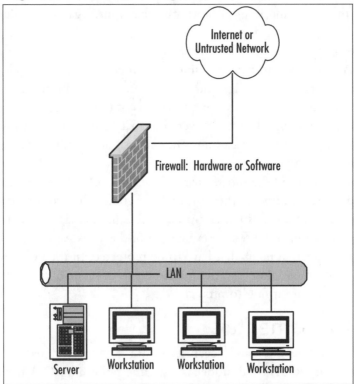

Since those days, however, we've greatly expanded the role of our network infras-tructure and our resources to provide information in response to both public requests and those of our employees and customers or partners. Additionally, the freely available tools and relative ease with which spoofing attacks and other attacks can be mounted against us have increased the requirements that we isolate our networks and protect the information that is contained on them. That same growth in the availability of tools and attack methodologies has necessitated the expansion of the CIA concepts that were originally handled through a single-firewall type of plan to a greatly expanded multi-layer approach to try to ensure that we are providing that protection. This is where we begin to consider the use of the DMZ concept, allowing us to better segregate and divide our networks. Figure 1.2 demonstrates a generic DMZ configuration.

Figure 1.2 Generic DMZ Configuration

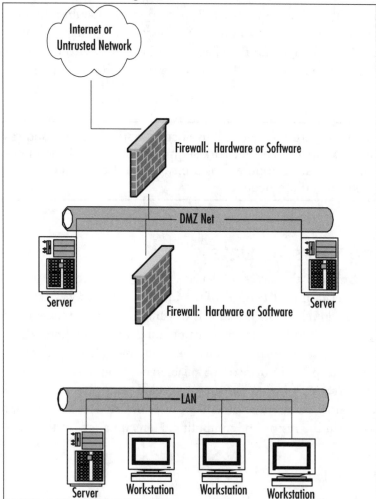

One of the reasons for this shift in coverage is our need to provide services to some employees and others outside of the local area network (LAN) environment when we might not want to allow those services to be available to everyone. A single-method protection option (firewall, NAT, packet filtering) requires the administrator to completely allow or block a service or protocol to all connections and doesn't have granularity or flexibility in its operation. This inflexible arrangement meant that the third part of the triad, *availability*, was not always possible. The addition of the extra layer of filtering provided by the second firewall (or more) in the control environment allows us to more finely control access to the data and servers hosting that data. This in turn allows us to more fully implement the second part of the triad, *integrity*. If we can control these access points more closely through access control lists and user accounts, for instance, it is much more likely that we will succeed in maintaining the integrity of the data and keeping it in a protected and undamaged state. As we'll see through our study in this book, the DMZ design and flexibility contribute greatly to the administrator's ability to provide CIA and still provide services to those who need them.

> **NOTE**
>
> The firewall configurations we will use act primarily to route and restrict traffic flow to and from particular network segments. As we will see in later sections of the chapter, those configurations are varied and depend on the protections we have determined are needed.

Identifying Risks to Data

As we continue to review the basics of security, it is necessary to review some of the risks that occur in relation to data. One of the important things we have learned as systems operators and administrators is that it is of paramount importance to protect the data that we are charged with controlling, maintaining, and providing. We understand that there is a necessity to perform backup operations, provide disaster recovery services, and generally keep the information available and intact 24 hours a day, seven days a week, 365 days a year. While you prepare to develop your plan for protection, consider that there are now many more potential causes of data loss and corruption than at any time previously in the history of computing. Here are a few of the ways data can be lost:

- Hardware failure
- Power disruption
- Outside attacks
    - Enumeration of your network
    - Access to confidential data
    - Modification of critical data
    - Destruction of data

- Internal attacks
  - Unauthorized access
  - Theft of information
  - Disclosure of information to others
  - Destruction of data

- Natural disasters
  - Water, flooding
  - Fire
  - Ground movement
  - Weather disasters (hurricane, tornado, ice storms, others)

- Human failures
  - Inadvertent deletion of data
  - Disregard for physical security of equipment/network
  - Configuration errors

Are all these situations relevant to the DMZ? Obviously, not all relate directly to the consideration of the DMZ and its implementation. However, we'll see as we continue that the overall planning that is done for the DMZ and its design must incorporate the overall security planning that is done systemwide. Thus, we must consider all these potential problem areas as we create the part of the plan to provide for retention and protection of the data sources in our systems.

Identifying Risks to Services

Maintaining the security of services being provided to partners, employees, and customers can be a difficult task. The continued growth of shared information and availability of technologies to provide network-based information and services to an ever-growing user base outside our internal networks generates a number of risks to the information being provided. Additional sources of risk are created through the services we provide to the end user. Today, it is quite normal to provide e-mail, Web, secure online purchasing, and other services directly to individuals and companies outside our LAN. Some of the things that can be classified as risks to services are:

- Denial of Service (DoS) attacks
- Unauthorized use of services

- E-mail relaying ("spam")
- Compromise of systems through misconfiguration of services, such as:
  - DNS server zone transfer misconfiguration
  - Telnet service active and unprotected
  - File Transfer Protocol (FTP) server file root unsecured or not otherwise protected
- Interception or diversion of services or service information
- Unauthorized remote control of systems

As you can see, the risks of service disruption are not limited to failure of our systems; they also incorporate the risks of attack and lack of availability of services provided to us by others that could impact our operation. We must anticipate those risks as we design our security plans.

Identifying Potential Threats

As you prepare your overall security plan and DMZ, it is important that you identify and evaluate the potential risks and threats to your network, systems, and data. You must evaluate your risks thoroughly during the identification process to assign some sort of value to the risks in order to determine priorities for protection and likelihood of loss resulting from those risks and threats if they materialize. In this vein, you should be looking at and establishing a risk evaluation for anything that could potentially disrupt, slow, or damage your systems, data, or credibility. In this area, it is important to assign these values to potential threats such as:

- Outside hacker attacks
- Trojans, worms, and virus attacks
- DoS or Distributed Denial of Service (DDoS) attacks
- Compromise or loss of internal confidential information
- Network monitoring and data interception
- Internal attacks by employees
- Hardware failures
- Loss of critical systems

This identification process creates the basis for your security plan, policies, and implementation of your security environment. You should realize that this is an ongoing evaluation that is subject to change as conditions within your company and partners, as well as employee need for access, change and morph over time. We have learned that security is a process and is never truly "finished." However, a good basic evaluation goes a long way toward creating the most secure system that we can achieve.

Introducing Common Security Standards

Security and network professionals use a number of currently accepted procedures and standards to conduct our business and ensure that we are following the accepted practices for security and access. Although we have a responsibility as network and systems administrators to try to attain perfection in the availability and integrity of our data, we also have constraints placed on us in accomplishing those conditions. Those constraints include budgets, physical plant capability, and training of users and technicians to maintain the security and integrity of the data. These constraints do not relieve us of our responsibility for maintaining the data safely and securely. To that end, we currently employ some accepted standards for security that help us perform our tasks to the best possible level. In this section, we remind you of the common security standards and briefly discuss them:

- **Authentication, authorization, and auditing (AAA)** AAA use is required in security operations for creating and maintaining the method of authenticating users and processes and validating their credentials prior to allowing access to resources. It is also the method we use to grant access or deny access to the resource. Auditing of activity is a crucial part of this function.

- **Confidentiality, integrity, and availability (CIA)** CIA is the originally defined process that established the goals that we have used to try to protect our data from unauthorized view, corruption, or unauthorized modification and to provide constant availability. Over the past few years, the CIA processes have expanded to include a more comprehensive guideline that also includes the process of defining risk and use of risk management tools to provide a more complete method of protection.

- **Least privilege** This concept is used by the security planner and team to define the levels of access to resources and the network that should be allowed. From a security standpoint, it is always preferable to be too restrictive with the capability to relax the access levels than to be too loose and have a breach occur.

Remember, too, that the security process involves a three-tiered model for security protection:

- **Computer security**, including the use of risk assessment, the expanded CIA goals, and enterprise planning that extends throughout the entire enterprise, rather than to just a portion of it

- **Physical security**, in which we must build and include physical access systems and coordinate them with our network access systems

- **Trusted users,** who become an important cog in maintaining the integrity of our security efforts

Policies, Plans, and Procedures

Earlier in this chapter, we mentioned that it is important to provide and conduct an initial baseline security audit and institute a security plan for the organization. Along with this practice, it is equally important to provide adequate information not only to the individuals in charge of security but to everyone in the organization who must cooperate to achieve the desired goal in relation to the security and integrity of the information and services provided in your environment. To that end, we must provide additional service beyond the security evaluation and plan. This includes working with a planning team that includes legal, human resource, and management input along with our security planning and administration and evaluation by this team to prepare the documentation. At a minimum, your security plan should provide documentation and supporting work that includes:

- Acceptable-use policies

- Permitted activities

- Disciplines for infractions

- Auditing policies

- Disaster recovery plans

- Reporting hierarchy and escalation paths

- Overall security policy

  - What needs protection and from what type of attack?

  - What methodologies will be utilized for protection?

  - Who is responsible for implementation, monitoring, and maintenance?

  - Risk analysis—what is vulnerable and what is the cost if lost/damaged/compromised?

- Growth and service needs projections
- User training and education plans

These documents are necessary for the proper implementation and enforcement of policy after delivery of your overall security plan. Figure 1.3 provides a brief pictorial view of what is involved in your security policy design. This design process is necessary and must be completed and in force prior to proceeding to the tasks of designing the DMZ. Without the security policy in place, DMZ design will be ineffective and not cost-effective, because it will have to be reconfigured to fit with the organization's overall security needs.

Figure 1.3 The Path to Completion of a Security Policy Document

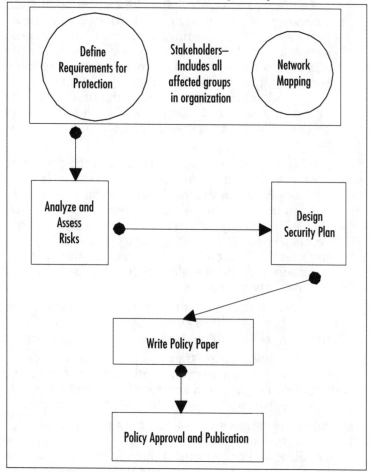

DMZ Definitions and History

In the security fundamentals section, we began to discuss some of the terminology and definitions that are related to our work with DMZ structure and its components. Before we proceed to a more in-depth discussion of the DMZ, we need to go over some definitions of the components and a brief history of the DMZ and the philosophy that has led to the implementation of the technologies for protection. To begin, we define some common terms that we will use throughout the book as we discuss DMZs. Table 1.1 details and defines these terms.

Table 1.1 DMZ Definitions

Term	Definition or Description
DMZ	In computer networks, a demilitarized zone, or DMZ, is a computer host or small network inserted as a "neutral zone" between a company's private network and the outside public network. The DMZ prevents outside users from getting direct access to a server that has company data. (The term comes from the geographic buffer zone that was set up between North Korea and South Korea following the United Nations "police action" in the early 1950s.) A DMZ is an optional and more secure approach to a firewall and effectively acts as a proxy server.
Bastion host (untrusted host)	A machine (usually a server) located in the DMZ with strong host-level protection and minimal services. It is used as a gateway between the inside and the outside of networks. The bastion host is normally *not* the firewall but a separate machine that will probably be sacrificial in the design and expected to be compromised. The notation "untrusted host" may be used because the bastion host is always considered to be potentially compromised and therefore should not be fully trusted by internal network clients.
Firewall	A hardware device or software package that provides filtering and/or provision of rules to allow or deny specific types of network traffic to flow between internal and external networks.
Proxy server	An application-based translation of network access requests. Provision for local user authentication for access to untrusted network. Logging and control of port/protocol access may be possible. Normally used to connect two networks.
Network Address Translation (NAT)	Application-based translation of requests for service or connection to an external network. No user authentication is possible, and port/protocol filtering is not usually performed here. Used to redirect requests through one interface. Requests for connection at outside interface must have originated from inside host or they are dropped.

Continued

Table 1.1 DMZ Definitions

Term	Definition or Description
Packet filtering	The use of a set of rules to open or close ports to specific protocols (such as allowing Transmission Control Protocol (TCP) or User Datagram Protocol (UDP) packets) or protocol ID(s) such as allowing or blocking Internet Control Message Protocol (ICMP).
Stateful packet filtering	The use of a process to inspect packets as they reach the firewall and maintain the state of the connection by allowing or disallowing packets to pass based on the access policy.
Screened subnet	This is an isolated network containing hosts that need to be accessible from both the untrusted external network and the internal network. An example is the placement of a bastion host in a dual-firewall network, with the bastion host in the network between the firewalls. A screened subnet is often a part of a DMZ implementation.
Screening router	An often-used initial screening method to limit traffic to and from a protected network. It may employ various methods of packet filtering and protocol limitation and act as a limited initial firewall device.

DMZ use has become a much more necessary method of providing the multilayer approach to security that has become a popular method of providing security. The use of DMZ structures developed as evolving business environments required the provision of increasing numbers of services and connectivity to accomplish the desired tasks for the particular business. New technologies and designs have provided a higher level of protection for the data and services we are charged with protecting.

DMZ Concepts

The use of a DMZ and its overall design and implementation can be relatively simple or extremely complex, depending on the needs of the particular business or network system. The DMZ concept came into use as the need for separation of networks became more acute when we began to provide more access to services for individuals or partners outside the LAN infrastructure. One of the primary reasons that the DMZ has come into favor is the realization that a single type of protection is subject to failure. This failure can arise from configuration errors, planning errors, equipment failure, or deliberate action on the part of an internal employee or external attack force. The DMZ has proven to be more secure and to offer multiple layers of protection for the security of the protected networks and machines. It has also proven to be very flexible, scalable, and relatively robust in its ability to provide the protection we need. DMZ design now includes the ability to use multiple products (both hardware- and software-based) on multiple plat-forms to achieve the level of protection necessary, and DMZs are often designed to pro-vide failover capabilities as well.

When we are working with a DMZ, we must have a common ground to work from. To facilitate understanding, we examine a number of conceptual paths for traffic flow in the following section. Before we look at the conceptual paths, let's make sure that we understand the basic configurations that can be used for firewall and DMZ location and how each of them can be visualized. In the following figures, we'll see and discuss these configurations. Please note that each of these configurations is useful on internal networks needing protection as well as protecting your resources from net-works such as the Internet. Our first configuration is shown in Figure 1.4.

Figure 1.4 A Basic Network With a Single Firewall

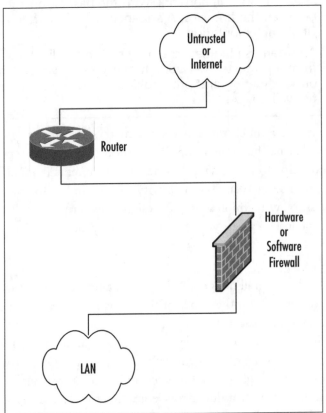

In Figure 1.4, we can see the basic configuration that would be used in a simple network situation in which there was no need to provide external services. This config-uration would typically be used to begin to protect a small business or home network. It could also be used within an internal network to protect an inner network that needed to be divided and isolated from the main network. This situation could include payroll, finance, or development divisions that need to protect their information and keep it away from general network use and view.

Figure 1.5 details a protection design that would allow for the implementation and provision of services outside the protected network. In this design, it would be absolutely imperative that rules be enacted to not allow the untrusted host to access the internal network. Security of the bastion host machine would be accomplished on the machine itself, and only minimal and absolutely necessary services would be enabled or installed on that machine. In this design, we might be providing a Web presence that did not involve e-commerce or the necessity to dynamically update content. This design would not be used for provision of virtual private network (VPN) connections, FTP services, or other services that required other content updates to be performed regularly.

Figure 1.5 Basic Network, Single Firewall and Bastion Host (Untrusted Host)

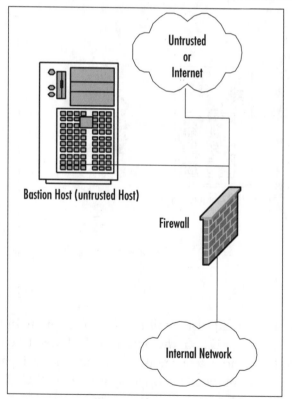

Figure 1.6 shows a basic DMZ structure. In this design, the bastion host is partially protected by the firewall. Rather than the full exposure that would result to the bastion

host in Figure 1.5, this setup would allow us to specify that the bastion host in Figure 1.6 could be allowed full outbound connection, but the firewall could be configured to allow only port 80 traffic inbound to the bastion host (assuming it was a Web server) or others as necessary for connection from outside. This design would allow connection from the internal network to the bastion host if it was necessary. This design would potentially allow updating of Web server content from the internal network if allowed by firewall rule, which could allow traffic to and from the bastion host on specific ports as designated. (There is more on that topic later in the chapter.)

Figure 1.6 A Basic Firewall With a DMZ

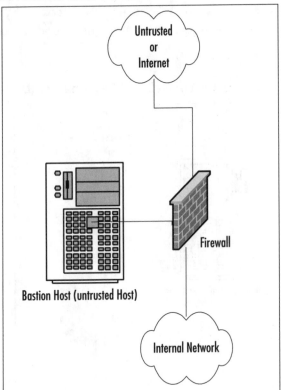

Figure 1.7 shows a generic dual-firewall DMZ configuration. In this arrangement, the bastion host can be protected from the outside and allowed to connect to or from the internal network. In this arrangement, like the conditions in Figure 1.6, flow can be controlled to and from both of the networks away from the DMZ. This configuration and method is more likely to be used if more than one bastion host is needed for the operations or services being provided.

Figure 1.7 A Dual Firewall With a DMZ

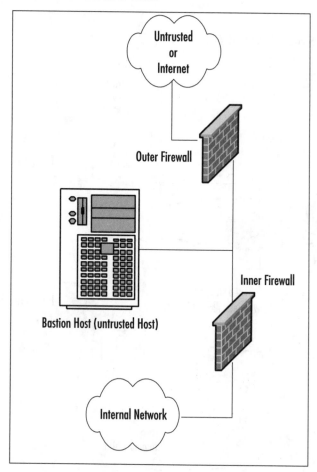

Untrusted
or
Internet

Outer Firewall

Bastion Host (untrusted Host)

Inner Firewall

Internal Network

Traffic Flow Concepts

Now that we've had a quick tour of some generic designs, let's take a look at the way network communications traffic typically flows through them. Be sure to note the differences between the levels and the flow of traffic and protections offered in each of them.

Figure 1.8 illustrates the flow pattern for information through a basic single-firewall setup. This type of traffic control can be achieved through hardware or software and is the basis for familiar products such as Internet Connection Sharing (ICS) and the NAT functionality provided by digital subscriber line (DSL) and cable modems used for connection to the Internet. Note that flow is unrestricted outbound, but the basic configuration will drop all inbound connections that did not originate from the internal network.

Figure 1.8 Basic Single-Firewall Flow

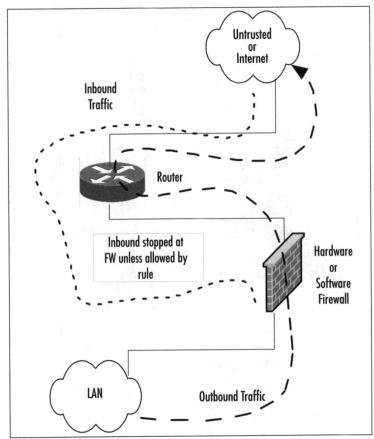

Figure 1.9 reviews the traffic flow in a network containing a bastion host and a single firewall. This network configuration does not produce a DMZ; the protection of the bastion host is configured individually on the host and requires extreme care in setup. Inbound traffic from the untrusted network or the bastion host is dropped at the firewall, providing protection to the internal network. Outbound traffic from the internal network is allowed.

Figure 1.9 A Basic Firewall With Bastion Host Flow

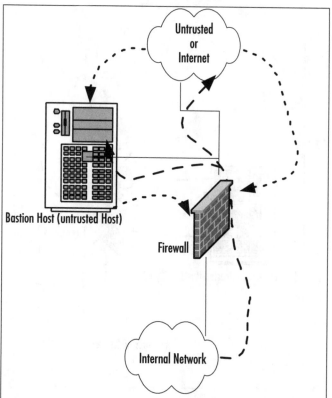

Figure 1.10 shows the patterns of traffic as we implement a DMZ design. In this form, inbound traffic flows through to the bastion host if allowed through the firewall and is dropped if destined for the internal network. Two-way traffic is permitted as specified between the internal network and the bastion host, and outbound traffic from the internal network flows through the firewall and out, generally without restriction.

Figure 1.10 A Basic Single Firewall With DMZ Flow

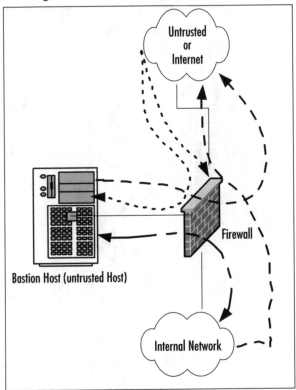

Figure 1.11 contains a more complex path of flow for information but provides the most capability in these basic designs to allow for configuration and provision of services to the outside. In this case, we have truly established a DMZ, separated and protected from both the internal and external networks. This type of configuration is used quite often when there is a need to provide more than one type of service to the public or outside world, such as e-mail, Web servers, DNS, and so forth. Traffic to the bastion host can be allowed or denied as necessary from both the external and internal networks, and incoming traffic to the internal network can be dropped at the external firewall. Outbound traffic from the internal network can be allowed or restricted either to the bastion host (DMZ network) or the external network.

Figure 1.11 A Dual Firewall With DMZ Flow

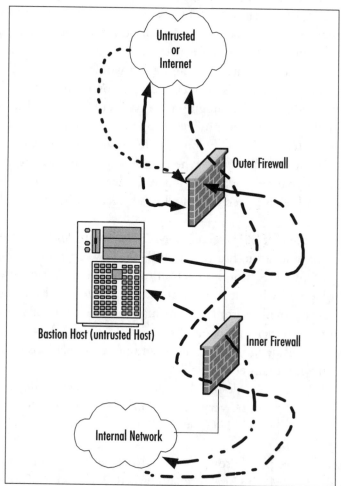

As you can see, there is a great amount of flexibility in the design and function of your protection mechanisms. In the sections that follow, we expand further on conditions for the use of different configurations and on the planning that it done to implement them.

Networks With and Without DMZs

As we pursue our discussions about the creation of DMZ structures, it is appropriate to also take a look at the reasoning behind the various structures of the DMZ and when and where we'd want to implement a DMZ or perhaps use some other alternative.

During our preview of the concepts of DMZs, we saw in Figures 1.4–1.7 some examples of potential design for network protection and access. Your design may incorporate any or all of these types of configuration, depending on your organization's needs. For instance, Figure 1.4 shows a configuration that may occur in the case of a home network installation or perhaps with a small business environment that is isolated from the Internet and does not share information or need to provide services or information to outside customers or partners. This design would be suitable under these conditions, provided configuration is correct and monitored for change.

Figure 1.5 illustrates a network design with a bastion host located outside the firewall. In this design, the bastion host must be stripped of all unnecessary functionality and services and protected locally with appropriate file permissions and access control mechanisms. This design would be used when an organization needs to provide minimal services to an external network, such as a Web server. Access to the internal network from the bastion host is generally not allowed, because this host is absolutely subject to compromise.

Figure 1.6 details the first of the actual DMZ designs and incorporates a screened subnet. In this type of design, the firewall controls the flow of information from network to network and provides more protection to the bastion host from external flows. This design might be used when it is necessary to be able to regularly update the content of a Web serve, or provide a front end for mail services or other services that need contact from both the internal and external networks. Although better for security purposes than Figure 1.5, this design still produces an untrusted relationship in the bastion host in relation to the internal network.

Finally, Figure 1.7 provides a design that allows for the placement of many types of service in the DMZ. Traffic can be very finely controlled through access at the two firewalls, and services can be provided at multiple levels to both internal and external networks.

In the next section, we profile some of the advantages and disadvantages of the common approaches to DMZ architecture and provide a checklist of sorts to help you to make a decision about the appropriate use (or not) of the DMZ for protection.

Pros and Cons of DMZ Basic Designs

Table 1.2 details the advantages and disadvantages of the various types of basic design discussed in the preceding section.

Table 1.2 Pros and Cons of Basic DMZ Designs

Basic Design	Advantages	Disadvantages	Appropriate Utilization
Single firewall	Inexpensive, fairly easy configuration, low maintenance	Much lower security capabilities, no growth or expansion	Home, small office/home office (SOHO), small business without

Continued

Table 1.2 Pros and Cons of Basic DMZ Designs

Basic Design	Advantages	Disadvantages	Appropriate Utilization
			need to provide services to others
Single firewall with bastion host	Lower cost than more robust alternatives	Bastion host extremely vulnerable to compromise, inconvenient to update content, loss of functionality other than for absolutely required services; not scalable	Small business without resources for more robust implementation or static content being provided that doesn't require frequent updates
Single firewall with screened subnet and bastion host	Firewall provides protection to both internal network and bastion host, limiting some of the potential breachpossibilities of anunprotected bastion host	Single point of failure; some products limit network addressing to DMZ in this configuration to public addresses, which might not be economic or possible in your network	Networks requiring access to the bastion host for updating of information
Dual firewall	Allows for establishment of multiple service-providing hosts in the DMZ; protects bastion hosts in DMZ from both networks, allows much more granular control of resources and access; removes single point of failure and attack	Requires more hardware and software for implementation of this design; more configuration work and monitoring required	Larger operations that require the capability to offer multiple types of Web access and services to both the internal and external networks involved

Configuring & Implementing...

Bastion Hosts

Bastion hosts must be individually secured and hardened because they are always in a position that could be attacked or probed. This means that before placement, a bastion host must be stripped of unnecessary services, fully updated with the latest service packs, hot fixes, and updates, and isolated from other trusted machines and networks to eliminate the possibility that its compromise would allow for connection to (and potential compromise of) the protected networks and resources. This also means that a machine being used for this purpose should have no user accounts relative to the protected network or directory services structure, which could lead to enumeration of your internal network.

DMZ Design Fundamentals

DMZ design, like security design, is always a work in progress. As in security planning and analysis, we find DMZ design carries great flexibility and change potential to keep the protection levels we put in place in an effective state. The ongoing work is required so that the system's security is always as high as we can make it within the constraints of time and budget while still allowing appropriate users and visitors to access the information and services we provide for their use. You will find that the time and funds spent in the design process and preparation for the implementation are very good investments if the process is focused and effective; this will lead to a high level of success and a good level of protection for the network you are protecting. In this section of the chapter, we explore the fundamentals of the design process. We incorporate the information we discussed in relation to security and traffic flow to make decisions about how our initial design should look. Additionally, we'll build on that information and review some other areas of concern that could affect the way we design our DMZ structure.

NOTE

In this section we look at design of a DMZ from a logical point of view. Physical design and configuration are covered in following chapters, based on the vendor-based solution you are interested in deploying.

Why Design Is So Important

Design of the DMZ is critically important to the overall protection of your internal network—and the success of your firewall and DMZ deployment. The DMZ design can incorporate sections that isolate incoming VPN traffic, Web traffic, partner connections, employee connections, and public access to information provided by your organization. Design of the DMZ structure throughout the organization can protect internal resources from internal attack. As we discussed in the security section, it has been well documented that much of the risk of data loss, corruption, and breach actually exists *inside* the network perimeter. Our tendency is to protect assets from external harm but to disregard the dangers that come from our own internal equipment, policies, and employees.

These attacks or disruptions do not arise solely from disgruntled employees, either. Many of the most damaging conditions that occur are because of inadvertent mistakes made by well-intentioned employees. Each and all of these entry points is a potential source of loss for your organization and ultimately can provide an attack point to defeat your other defenses. Additionally, the design of your DMZ will allow you to implement a multilayered approach to securing your resources that does not leave a single point of failure in your plan. This minimizes the problems and loss of protection that can occur because of misconfiguration of rule sets or ACL lists, as well as reducing the problems that can occur due to hardware configuration errors. In the last chapters of this book, we look at how to mitigate risk through testing of your network infrastructure to make sure your firewalls, routers, switches, and hosts are thoroughly hardened so that when you do deploy your DMZ segment, you can see for yourself that it is in fact secure from both internal as well as external threats.

Designing End-to-End Security for Data Transmission Between Hosts on the Network

Proper DMZ design, in conjunction with the security policy and plan developed previously, allows for end-to-end protection of the information being transmitted on the network. The importance of this capability is explored more fully later in the chapter, when we review some of the security problems inherent in the current implementation of TCP/IPv4 and the transmission of data. The use of one or more of the many firewall products or appliances currently available will most often afford the opportunity not only to block or filter specific protocols but also to protect the data as it is being transmitted. This protection may take the form of encryption and can utilize the available transports to protect data as well. Additionally, proper utilization of the technologies available within this design can provide for the necessary functions previously detailed in the concepts of AAA and CIA, utilizing the multilayer approach to protection that we have discussed in earlier sections. This need to provide end-to-end security requires that we are conversant with and remember basic network traffic patterns and protocols. The next few sections help remind us about these and further illustrate the need to design the DMZ with this capability in mind.

Traffic Flow and Protocol Fundamentals

Another of the benefits of using a DMZ design that includes one or more firewalls is the opportunity to control traffic flow into and out of the DMZ much more cohesively and with much more granularity and flexibility. When the firewall product in use (either hardware or software) is a product designed above the home-use level, the capability usually exists to not only control traffic that is flowing in and out of the network or DMZ through packet filtering based on port numbers but often to allow or deny the use of entire protocols. For instance, the rule set might include a statement that blocks communication via ICMP, which would block protocol 1. A statement that allowed IPSec traffic where it was desired to allow traffic utilizing ESP or AH would be written allowing protocol 50 for ESP or 51 for AH. (For a listing of the protocol IDs, visit www.iana.org/assignments/protocol-numbers.) Remember that like the rule of security that follows the principle of least privilege, we must include in our design the capability to allow only the absolutely necessary traffic into and out of the various portions of the DMZ structure.

DMZ Protocols

Protocol use within a DMZ environment is always problematic. We should be well aware of the potential risks that have been associated with protocol use in various implementations and those that are frequently and actively attacked because of the vulnerabilities that exist. Table 1.3 briefly overviews some of the known issues with various protocols. This table is not intended to be all-inclusive; rather, it is indicative of the fact that the DMZ designer must be aware of these limitations when designing a plan for DMZ structure and access both into and out of the DMZ.

Table 1.3 Protocols With Known Weaknesses

Protocol	Basic Weakness
Asynchronous Transfer Mode (ATM)	No authentication or encryption, subject to spoofing and interception
Internetwork Packet Exchange (IPX)	Designed for LAN use, doesn't scale well for wide area network (WAN) operations, high bandwidth usage with SAP broadcasts, aging protocol

Continued

Table 1.3 Protocols With Known Weaknesses

Protocol	Basic Weakness
Internet Protocol (IP)	No default data protection of packets, subject to many attacks, needed for connection to Internet
Kerberos	Vulnerable to buffer overflow attacks, replay, and spoofing to gain privilege and discover passwords, allowing potential for breach of service
Lightweight Directory Access Protocol (LDAP)	Some implementations are subject to buffer overflow and DoS attacks, with possibility of privilege elevation
Simple Network Management Protocol (SNMP)	DoS and buffer overflow attacks are possible, as are security risks posed by administrators who leave the community names and other information in default configurations; some conditions can result in privilege escalation and compromise
Secure Shell (SSH)	Privilege escalation, system compromise when code run under SSH credential, DoS attacks

Designing for Protection in Relation to the Inherent Flaws of TCP/IPv4

The current implementation of TCP/IPv4 contains a number of well-documented flaws that affect the design of both your security plan and your DMZ. Some of these problems were corrected in IPv6, but since implementation of this technology isn't on the immediate horizon, we must accommodate the weaknesses of the existing protocols when implementing the design of our DMZ. We must of necessity plan for certain known problems:

- Data, including passwords not protected by the operating system, are sent in clear text in TCP/IP packets

- SYN attacks, a DoS condition resulting from overflow of the wait buffer

- IP spoofing, allowing the attacker to pretend it is another host

- Sequence guessing, allowing reassembly or delivery of forged packets

- Connection hijacking, allowing man-in-the-middle attacks

- Lack of authentication capability in the protocol

You can find a good discussion of the problems with TCP/IPv4 and a more complete discussion of the flaws and improvements made in TCP/IPv6 at www.linuxsecurity.com/resource_files/documentation/tcpip-security.html. The design that we create for our DMZ structure will accommodate the weaknesses of the TCP/IP protocol and will provide the protection that is needed to stymie these types of attacks and their resulting potential for breach. To accomplish that goal, as we design we need to consider the various problems and design the working protections into the configuration of rules and ACL settings and consider the use of other protocols such as IPSec and L2TP to protect the data on the wire.

Public and Private IP Addressing

One of the primary reasons that the DMZ concepts have been so useful is that network administrators have a greatly expanded capability to utilize public and private addressing. As you will recall, the initial TCP/IPv4 implementations were based on class, with default subnet masks that limited to some degree the ability of network administrators to achieve true flexibility in their network designs. With the advent of classless addressing and improvements provided with the acceptance of that concept, much greater utilization has been made of functions such as NAT to provide addressing for the internal network without exposing that network to the dangers of the public network. The DMZ design must incorporate the methods and equipment being used for address translation and routing, and it becomes a method of hiding internal addresses from unwanted contact.

We also must plan for and use the ability to subnet within the private IP addressing ranges, which are shown in Table 1.4.

Table 1.4 Private IP Address Ranges

Private IP Range	CIDR Mask	Decimal Mask
10.0.0.0–10.255.255.255	/8	255.0.0.0
172.16.0.0–172.31.255.255	/16	255.255.255.0
192.168.0.0–192.168.255.255	/24	255.255.255.0

This allows us much greater flexibility in the segregation of the DMZ and assuring that the network addressing and contact between the protected network, the buffer (DMZ), and the outside world are more difficult for would-be attackers to penetrate.

Ports

Ports used in network communication become an extremely important tool in our ability to filter access levels and establish ACL functions on devices and in software implementations used to protect our assets. Recall that ports 0–1023 are reserved for specific uses and that all other ports are functionally available for use by applications. Registered ports include those from 1024 through 49151, and dynamic and/or private ports (used by applications for communication and session maintenance) are those from 49152 through 65535. The entire port list can be found at www.iana.org/port-numbers.

That means, of course, that the DMZ design must incorporate rules that block all traffic that is not necessary for the function of the DMZ or communications that must be carried through that area. Generally, this involves creating a rule set for the ACL that restricts or blocks all unused ports on a per-protocol basis to assure that the traffic is actually stopped. These rules that are created become an integral part of the DMZ defense. The design is often started from two "all or nothing" configurations: all ports open, closing as problems occur (bad), and all ports closed, opening as required (good, but requiring a great deal administration and learning in a new network that has not been fully documented). Either method can be considered in your design, although the latter provides much more security as you begin your quest to shut down intrusion.

The SANS Institute (www.sans.org) recommends the following port actions at a minimum as you design your DMZ and firewall blocking rules from external networks, as shown in Table 1.5. (The table is adapted from Appendix A of the SANS Top 20 list, which can be found at www.sans.org/top20.)

Table 1.5 Common Ports to Block

Service Type	TCP Port(s)	UDP Port(s)
Login Services	Telnet: 23, SSH: 22, FTP:21, NetBIOS: f139, rlogin: 512,513, 514	N/A
RPC and NFS	Portmap/rpcbind: 111, NFS: 2049, lockd: 4045	Portmap/rpcbind: 111, NFS: 2049, lockd: 4045
NetBIOS in Windows NT and W2K and XP	135, 139, 445(W2K and XP)	135, 137, 138, 445 (W2K and XP)
X Windows	6000 through 6255	N/A
Naming Services	DNS: Block zone transfers (TCP 53) except from external secondaries LDAP: 389	DNS: Block UDP 53 to all machines that are not DNS servers LDAP: 389

Continued

Table 1.5 Common Ports to Block

Service Type	TCP Port(s)	UDP Port(s)
Mail	SMTP: 25 to all machines that are not external mail relays POP: 109, 110 IMAP: 143	N/A
Web	HTTP: 80; SSL: 443, except to external Web servers. Also consider common high-order HTTP port choices, such as 8000, 8080, 8888	N/A
Small Services	Ports below 20, time: 37	Ports below 20, time: 37
Miscellaneous	Finger: 79; NNTP: 119; LPD: 515; SNMP: 161, 162; BGP: 179: SOCKS: 1080	TFTP: 69; NTP: 123; syslog: 514; SNMP: 161, 162
ICMP	Blocks incoming echo request (ping and traceroute), out-going echo replies, time exceeded, and destination unreachable messages, *except* "packet too big" messages (Type 3, Code 4)	*Note:* This setting will block known malicious uses, but it also will restrict your legitimate use of the ICMP echo request

The OSI Model

While we are reviewing the basics prior to designing our DMZ structure, we should also look briefly at the basis for traffic flow in our networks and how the data is transported and delivered from host to host. This review is not intended to be all inclusive but rather to point out that it is these traffic flow designs that strongly influence the consideration we must give to various technologies to properly defend our machines and data from attack or misuse. Recall that there exist two different but complementary designs of traffic flow and processing of data for network communication. The first is the *Open Systems Interconnection (OSI) model,* which formed the basis for all network communication as originally conceived. The OSI was followed, during the development of the TCP/IP protocol suite, by the *TCP/IP model,* which combines the functions of the OSI model layers. Figure 1.12 details the sections of the two models.

Figure 1.12 The OSI and TCP/IP Models

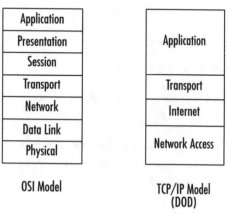

Recall that within both models, packets are assembled and headers from each layer are added as the packet is prepared for transport on the physical media. The header contains information about the processing that occurred to guide reassembly by the receiving machine. Through either process, when the packet is being sent from the sender to the receiver, a negotiated port is used to deliver the information to the receiving machine. While you're making design decisions for the DMZ access restrictions, it is important to keep in mind your communication needs for your existing or proposed services and applications. The launch point of the communication becomes important as we consider the design, because we must provide for communication that starts at the application level differently than the communication that is occurring at a level such as the transport layer or below. The various levels of the models provide the DMZ designer with a number of different places to institute the desired controls that can be utilized to restrict or allow traffic into and out of the DMZ.

Identifying Potential Risks from the Internet

Part of the identification process for identifying Internet-based risks is a thorough review of the original baseline analysis that you performed in relation to security. Risks identified from that analysis should be a part of your comprehensive DMZ design plan and should consider a number of potential problems, including:

- Virus and Trojan introduction to the network

- Possibility of enumeration of the network

- All entry points

- Unauthorized disclosure of information

- Remote control usage
  - VNC
  - Microsoft's Terminal Services
  - PCAnywhere and similar products
- Possible weak configurations allowing elevated access privileges

Evaluation and inclusion of these potential areas of entry and attack, along with others as may be defined in your plan, should be constantly reviewed during the design process and again prior to implementation to verify that the risks discovered and planned for are indeed taken care of.

Using Firewalls to Protect Network Resources

Firewalls have been and continue to be an integral part in the planning process for DMZ deployments. The design can include any or all of the basic designs we looked at earlier in the chapter and may very well incorporate multiple types of configuration, depending on your organization's needs to protect data and resources from different threat areas. Firewalls are not the only component of the design that is important, but they do play a major part in allowing the administrator to control traffic more completely, thus providing a higher level of protection.

Part of the design process includes evaluating and checking the performance of different hardware- and software-based firewall products. This book discusses some of the most-used technologies in later chapters, such as Check Point and Check Point NG, PIX, Nokia, and Microsoft's ISA Server. Additionally, firewall considerations are explored during discussions of protection of wireless networks and methods of protecting networks using Sun and Microsoft network operating system (NOS) software.

Using Screened Subnets to Protect Network Resources

As you proceed to a more advance design for your DMZ, conditions could drive a decision to employ screened subnets for protection or provision of services. The screened subnet, in some designs, actually becomes synonymous with DMZ in usage. However, the screened subnet is actually a security enhanced version of the multi-homed screened host configurations that were used in the past. It involves the use of more hardware but provides a more secure basis for configuration and blocking unauthorized access.

The screened subnet that we looked at earlier in the chapter can be configured in a number of different configurations dependent on need. The most simple of the constructions involves a multiple-interface firewall with the capability to filter traffic to more than one network. Although simpler, this design might not be appropriate to use in your environment if you plan to offer services such as Web, e-mail, FTP, or VPN connections from the public network to your private network. In these situations, a good case could be made for the dual-firewall approach, perhaps with multiple screened subnets that provide different services or access based on some criteria that you have identified during your planning process. Certainly, if offering services that involve e-commerce or access to confidential records (such as being HIPAA compliant in an enterprise involved with any type of patient records), your plan will most likely need to include multiple screened subnets, following the earlier suggestions that a multilayer approach be used to restrict access and retard attacks from outside.

Securing Public Access to a Screened Subnet

Public access to screened subnets is secured and restricted through a multilayer process, using a screening router to begin providing protection and a firewall in the next layer to protect the access point coming into the screened subnet. Figure 1.13 shows a possible configuration to begin this protection process.

Figure 1.13 A Basic Screened Subnet

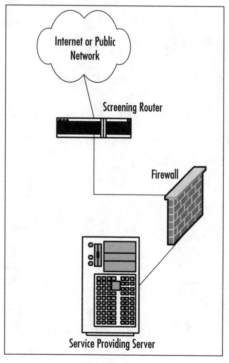

In this configuration, it is possible to limit the inbound traffic initially by configuring a rule set on the router; this piece might be provided by an Internet service provider (ISP), for example. Further levels of security can be developed as needed in your plan to protect assets on the screened subnet by firewall rule sets and hardening of the server providing services. Additionally, this design could be expanded or used for services or administration of screened subnets, providing greater security to the internal network as well.

Designing & Planning...

Know What You Want to Secure First

As you begin your DMZ design process, you must first be clear about what your design is intended for. A design that is only intended to superficially limit internal users' access to the Internet, for instance, requires much less planning and design work than a system protecting resources from multiple access points or providing multiple services to the public network or users from remote locations. An appropriate path to follow for your predesign path might look like this:

- Perform baseline security analysis of existing infrastructure, including OS and application analysis
- Perform baseline network mapping and performance monitoring
- Identify risk to resources and appropriate mitigation processes
- Identify potential security threats, both external and internal
- Identify needed access points from external sources
- Public networks
- VPN access
- Extranets
- Remote access services
- Identify critical services
- Plan your DMZ

Traffic and Security Risks

After beginning to research the necessary components for designing your protection plan, you will reach a point at which you are trying to assess the actual risks to security from which you are trying to protect your enterprise network. One of the first tools you might consider in this part of your evaluation is the SANS Top 20 list of the current most critical vulnerabilities to find out if there is something that you are not aware of. You can view this list at www.sans.org/top20/; it is updated frequently. This information can help you to at least begin to identify some of the risks involved and then to design a more effective plan to secure what you need to secure.

As we continue with our overview of DMZ design principles, we also need to discuss the management of resources and the challenges that occur in designing for administration and control of equipment and resources that may be located in the DMZ. The following sections detail a number of the areas that we must be aware of during our consideration of the design and its implementation.

Application Servers in the DMZ

Application server placement in the DMZ must be designed with tight control in mind. As in other screened subnet configurations, the basic security of the operating system must first be assured on the local machine, with all applicable patches and service packs applied and unused services disabled or removed if possible.

We spend a great deal of time in this book covering the hardening of your systems (Windows 2000, Sun Solaris, and the like) within the DMZ. Additionally, functionality of the application servers located in the DMZ should be limited to specific tasks that do not involve critical corporate data or information. Therefore, although it is acceptable to place a Web server in the DMZ with a supporting database server, neither of those servers may contain confidential or critical corporate information, because they are still located in an area in which they are considered to be untrusted. Critical or confidential information should not be accessible from or stored in the DMZ. For instance, as discussed in the following section, it is not acceptable to store any type of internal network authentication information on machines in the DMZ. Likewise, front-end servers or application proxy servers can be placed in the DMZ for other needs, such as an e-mail server front end or a DNS forwarder. In these instances, neither the e-mail front end nor the DNS server should store any information about the internal network or allow general communication to pass unchecked to or from the internal network. Traffic to these servers from the internal network should pass through a firewall restricting traffic to individual machines in both directions using specific port and address information.

Domain Controllers in the DMZ

Domain controllers for Windows networks or other directory services authentication servers should never have those services located within the DMZ if it's possible to keep them out. It is feasible in some configurations to provide a front end to these critical servers from within the DMZ, but it is not recommended, because compromise of the bastion host being allowed to communicate with the internal network through the firewall while requesting service could lead to compromise of the entire internal system. Access to your internal network that requires authentication should instead be handled in your design by the use of VPN solutions, including RADIUS and TACACS/TACACS+, discussed in the next section. It is possible, however, that domain controllers need to be placed within the DMZ depending on what services you plan to provide in the DMZ. For instance, if you were running a cluster that is highly available from the Internet on Windows 2000 servers, the cluster will not operate correctly without a domain controller present. For that reason, you have to accurately assess what you will need and analyze how to implement it and secure it.

RADIUS-Based Authentication Servers in the DMZ

Remote Authentication Dial-In User Service (RADIUS) servers, by definition and usage, are required to have full access to the authentication information provided by the Directory Services system in the enterprise, whether Windows, Novell, UNIX, Sun, or another OS. For this reason, the RADIUS server must be fully protected from attack and patched completely to avoid DoS conditions such as those detailed by CERT in advisories issued in 2002. The preferred option would have the RADIUS server located in the internal network, with proxied requests coming from a Routing and Remote Access Services (RRAS) server and restricted communication that would be allowed through the firewall to the RADIUS server only from the specified RRAS servers. Additionally, it would make sense to plan for the use of IPSec to further protect that traffic. Regardless, understand that you will need to analyze the need and deploy it based on a proper design that provides the service that is needed but still remains secure.

VPN DMZ Design Concepts

VPN usage has grown during the past few years. Many organizations embraced the possibility of VPN use as a method to communicate securely from remote offices. This led to a surge of connectivity that was requested in order to allow home "teleworkers" to perform their job functions without entering the secured environs of the actual workplace and its network.

A number of changes have been implemented in VPN technology in the recent past, and these have modified the thought process that we must undertake as we design our DMZ infrastructure. To begin with, VPN solutions should be created in a separate DMZ space, away from the other parts of the Internet-facing infrastructure, as well as your back-end private LAN. The VPN technologies now may incorporate the capability to enter your network space through public switched telephone network (PSTN) connections, Frame Relay connections, modem banks, and the public Internet as well as dedicated connections from customers and business partners that may utilize any of these access methods. Each of these connection types must be included in the plan, and entry points must be carefully controlled to allow the required access and protection of information while not allowing a back-door entry to our internal networks. A number of these plans are discussed in subsequent chapters of this book as different firewall configurations and designs are considered and discussed. When we're looking at the possibilities for VPN implementation and protection, it is extremely important to utilize all potential security tools available, including IPSec and its authentication and encryption possibilities. It is also important to evaluate the actual network design, in order to use RFC 1918 (private) addressing in the internal network and properly secure the addressing within the VPN, which should be registered addresses. Chapter 10 covers this topic more fully.

Advanced Risks

After your design has considered the basic issues for connectivity to your infrastructure, it is appropriate to begin to explore and plan for other areas that might need protection through your DMZ design. There are nearly infinite possibilities for incorporation into your overall design, including the ability to protect not only the internal network but e-commerce, business partner, and extranet connections. Additionally, your enterprise may be involved in the creation of hosted services, in which you are providing protection to Web, FTP, or other servers that require unique protections and the ability to provide management capabilities as well. This section visits a number of those potential areas that may be appropriate for coverage in the overall DMZ design.

Business Partner Connections

Business partner connections can provide a unique challenge to the DMZ designer. In the case of business partners, there is often a requirement to provide access to and from enterprise resource planning (ERP) packages such as those from Oracle, PeopleSoft, Microsoft's Great Plains software, and others that are currently in use to provide project management, packaging, and collaboration tools to members of multiple organizations. One of the challenges that can arise rather quickly is the question of how to appropriately allow connectivity between organizations with proper authentication and protection of information for all parties. Many of the basic designs that we've discussed previously, including the use of specifically screened subnets for VPN access, provide partial solutions to these issues, but each case also requires an in-depth evaluation and most certainly collaboration between the DMZ designers involved to appropriately channel the access entry points, remote access if needed, and authentication of the users from various entities to maintain the requirements of CIA. Chapter 10 covers this configuration more fully.

Extranets

Of the possibilities that can be explored in relation to business partner connections, extranets provide a great flexibility in their implementation and use by an enterprise. Extranets can be Web browser-based information stores, can allow contact by customers seeking catalog information, and can allow real-time or close to real-time tracking capabilities of shipments and the supply chain. Additionally, the extranet can be configured for collaborative efforts and used between business partners for the ultimate capability to share information and processes while working on joint projects. Extranets, much like the discussion earlier of VPN accesses, will usually be placed on isolated DMZ segments to segregate them from the hosting network's operations. These DMZ segments will house and host machines that will allow for the use of ERP software and the warehousing of information in common to the project. The use of extranet applications is most often Web browser based for the client that is seeking the information and not normally for storing highly sensitive data, although the data should still be protected.

Web and FTP Sites

Customer-based Web and FTP sites that are provided or hosted by your organization can again cause the DMZ design to change in some way. Hosting the information on customer-based sites requires the same processes that we've looked at in relation to hosting our own Web and FTP servers in the DMZ, with an additional requirement that some sort of remote management capability be provided for the customer to administer and monitor the sites. This hosting can lead to a plan that involves use of modems or other devices not protected by the DMZ design and must be carefully explored. Ensure that your DMZ design will not be compromised by the methods used to allow remote access to these servers and their administration by the client customer. It may be appropriate to host customer-based operations in a separate DMZ segment, away from your operation altogether.

E-Commerce Services

Among the possibilities that we may include in our overall DMZ design scheme is the possibility of hosting or supporting e-commerce services. As with other DMZ design considerations, the DMZ segment hosting e-commerce services must provide a level of isolation that protects such things as credit card information and transactions. It can include restrictions that block access from noncustomer address ranges, and it can also include restrictions on traffic to limit it to ports for Web services and Secure Sockets Layer (SSL) to protect the internal records being generated by the action of the services. E-commerce activities should also include restrictions that disable IP forwarding between servers and segregation of services such as noncritical database information among different servers for load balancing and to distribute security to a higher degree. No contact should be allowed between the e-commerce DMZ servers inbound to the internal network.

E-Mail Services

E-mail services are among the most used (and abused) services that are provided through a combination of access points, both external and internal. E-mail server front ends should be located in segregated DMZ subnets, and the firewalls allowing access into and out of the e-mail subnet should incorporate strong ACL rule sets that only allow communication on appropriate ports internally and externally. This construction should also include mail relay settings on the DMZ mail server that do not allow relaying of mail from any network other than the internal network, which limits the potential that your front-end server might be used for spamming. The external firewall that allows access to the e-mail front end should be configured to block outbound SMTP traffic that did not originate at the front-end server, and the front-end server should be configured to only relay mail to accepted internal addresses while rejecting all other communications. Great care must be used in the proper configuration of mail servers from all vendors when access is granted in any fashion from the external networks.

Advanced Design Strategies

Up to this point, the discussion of design has been directed at the access path design and the methods of securing access to the internal network from the external network. In most cases, the DMZ is used to block incoming traffic and control it more completely through the multiple layers that are placed in the design, thus offering tighter and tighter control that stops access to the internal network. Standard DMZ designs almost always default to a condition in which the internal network's access to the external public network is unrestricted.

Before we finish our discussion of basic designs, it is appropriate to explore briefly some of the ways we might consider blocking access from the internal network to the external network, either wholly or in part, if the security design we created earlier indicates a need to do so. In the next section, we visit some of the common conditions that your organization might wish to block or limit in your efforts to protect your assets and information.

Advanced DMZ Design Concepts

Intranet users have often been allowed full and unrestricted access to public network resources via the DMZ structure. Often the protection for the internal network involves using NAT or some proxied connectivity to allow outward flow while restricting inbound flow to requests originated within the internal network. You should think about some special considerations while you are working in this area. Let's list some of them and consider them in thought pattern as an addition to the overall design:

- General FTP use that is unrestricted may lead to security breach. Outbound FTP should not be allowed from the internal network.

- DMZ design lends itself to allowing control of unnecessary services that may be present on the external network. For instance, the DMZ design may incorporate outbound blocking of ports to services providing instant messaging, nonbusiness-related networks, and other restrictions as appropriate to your system.

- Known management ports for externally located devices and services should be blocked from the internal network.

Additionally, we must look at the applications that are in use from the internal network to determine the appropriate level of outbound access to accommodate those applications.

As we continue through the book, we'll find that a number of other considerations must be taken into account as we create the design plan. For instance, although many DMZ configurations are allowing access to a Web server that we are operating, there must be a method in place to advise us of the presence of potential hackers working within our borders. To this end, the DMZ design will also most often create a provision for some sort of IDS system placement in the various levels of the DMZ structure to evaluate and report on intrusion attempts. As with all services that we provide, the Web services servers must be continually evaluated and kept up to date in their levels of security and service packs.

Another conceptual area that must be visited is the difference between a DMZ that is established for the purpose of isolating or segregating the public network from your private network and a DMZ that is used for the purpose of isolating or segregating a portion of your internal network. The design you create should include the capability to establish internal DMZ structures to protect confidential information from the general LAN operation. This could include segregation of financials or provision for VPN access to the internal network that does not originate from the public network (such as Frame Relay PVC channels or PSTN modem access). Again, when dealing with these special cases, the designer must make absolutely sure that the design does not introduce a back-door situation that allows public network bypass of the DMZ structure through compromise of a host machine.

Remote Administration Concepts

Remote management and administration of the various pieces of hardware within the DMZ design you implement provide another challenge for the designer. Although it is extremely tempting to use the built-in capabilities of the various operating systems and the management software provided for many of our hardware devices, it is very important to give the alternatives a good long look. Use of these tools for normal management from within the internal network is almost certainly a quick recipe for breach and disaster.

It is certainly technologically possible to access the equipment in the DMZ through use of SSH, Telnet, or Microsoft's Terminal Services and to create firewall rules allowing traffic on the necessary ports to accomplish this task. So, what's the problem with using the built-in tools? *In-band* versus *out-of-band management* of your systems is the problem we need to work on. In-band management tools, including SNMP-based traps and management agents, rely on the integrity of the network they are mounted on to provide the reports and management capabilities we use to control the various hardware and configuration of hardware and servers. What happens when the underlying network capability is degraded, reduced, or overloaded through an equipment failure or a DoS attack? No management is possible, because we now can't reach the equipment. The other alternative is to provide some sort of out-of-band management capability. This can be accomplished in a number of ways, including serial connections to secured management ports on the devices to be managed or a separate management screened subnet, such as illustrated in Figure 1.14.

Figure 1.14 A Method to Provide Out-of-Band Management in the DMZ

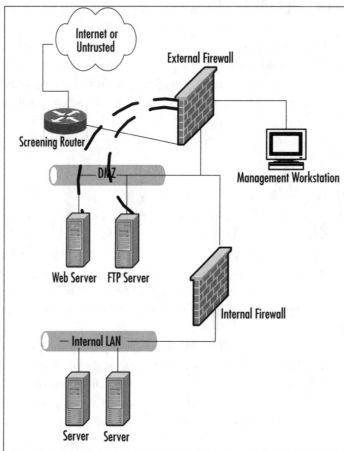

In this simplified design, the servers located in the DMZ are each configured as a multihomed machine, with the additional adapters (represented in the figure by dark dashed lines) configured to accept communications only from the designated management workstation(s), if your security policy allows multiple administrative units. The outside firewall is configured to allow specific port-based traffic to flow from the management workstation to the servers, and the management workstation is not accessible from either the untrusted network or the protected LAN. This eliminates much of the security vulnerability that is presented when management options only include in-band tools.

Authentication Design

Earlier in the chapter, we mentioned that it is generally inappropriate to locate a RADIUS server in a DMZ segment because it creates a condition in which the authentication information is potentially accessible to the public network, with a potential for breach of your DMZ. In some environments, it might be necessary to implement a plan to accommodate the authentication of users entering the DMZ from a public network. In this case, the DMZ design should include a separate authentication DMZ segment and the equipment in that segment should be hardened, as we previously detailed in our discussion of placement. At this point, it is possible to provide an RRAS server in the DMZ with no account information and utilize ACLs and packet filtering at the firewall to restrict and encrypt the traffic between the two machines to the authentication traffic. It is recommended that this process utilize IPSec, and it would require that Protocol ID 51 for IPSec and IKE traffic on port 500 (UDP) be allowed for the communication to occur. It is also possible that other third-party authentication products such as Cisco's CiscoSecure ACS could provide a gateway and controls to allow this functionality.

Summary

Chapter 1 gave us the opportunity to explore and review a number of important concepts in our preparation for designing an effective and secure DMZ structure. DMZ design includes a number of important steps that make the overall design process smoother and less subject to breach. These steps include the capability and duty to perform a complete physical and logical security analysis of the systems to be protected, followed by the adoption of an enterprise security policy to detail the path of management, monitoring, enforcement, and responsibility for various areas of the enterprise's security. Once we have completed a security analysis and have a security policy that has been supported and is in place, we have the opportunity to begin to think about the design of the DMZ structure. With the plan, it is possible to incorporate the principles of security, such as AAA and CIA, into the design to assure a higher level of security in the DMZ.

Generically, we create the basic DMZ structure after we have identified the assets and resources that need protection. This generic plan is followed by an evaluation of how the information currently flows in the organization and how it should be handled in a secure sense to isolate and protect the systems from compromise.

When the generic tasks have been completed, the design begins to take shape as we configure and define the various levels of the DMZ structure to provide necessary services to customers, employees, and partners. We're aware at this point that there are nearly infinite possibilities in the use of various equipment and configurations, and we're charged with creating a design that is functional and economically feasible in the reduction of risk. Here we begin to consider not only the best logical design but also the design that might be the most feasible to protect our data.

We find as we proceed that the level of service that we are providing and the connectivity needs of the various partners and operations greatly affect the level of configuration within the DMZ structure. We also find that it is possible to allow connectivity in multiple levels for various services while always striving to protect the internal network from harm.

Solutions Fast Track

Planning Network Security

☑ DMZ design requires that we first evaluate the physical and logical security and needs of the organization.

☑ The overall security plan and evaluation require input from all concerned parties in the organization at levels ranging from the mailroom to the boardroom to provide a valid analysis.

☑ Following the completion of the security plan, it is imperative that an overall enterprise security policy be written, approved, and implemented to assist in the evaluation of the need for DMZ protection. Without this document and definition of responsibility, DMZ design is fruitless.

DMZ Definitions and History

☑ DMZ use has been increasingly important as the enterprise architect designs for security while at the same time offering an ever-increasing array of services and connections to services in the network.

☑ The multilayer approach of using bastion hosts, screened subnets, and firewalls to provide finer and finer control of access when approaching the interior network has proven to be an effective means to securing the DMZ structure.

☑ DMZ design is never static. Like security plans and policies, DMZ designs are a work in progress at all times, and it should be understood that the design is a flowing work subject to constant upgrade and tweaking.

DMZ Design Fundamentals

☑ Multiple design possibilities exist, depending on the level of protection that is required in the particular enterprise configuration.

☑ DMZ designs generally consist of firewalls and segments that are protected from each other by firewall rules and routing as well as the use of RFC 1918 addressing on the internal network.

☑ DMZ design depends on the designer's ability to accurately assess the actual risks in order to design an adequate structure.

Advanced Risks

☑ Outside the normal DMZ structure, many other conditions may arise that require evaluation. These conditions include restriction of access to the public networks from the private networks, not only the protection of the public network access to the internal network.

☑ Business-to-business (B2B) and e-commerce activities require special consideration to provide protection of partner and customer data and information. They also demand a level of design separate from the basic needs.

☑ Provision of e-mail services and VPN connectivity to the private network via connection through the DMZ with a connection to the public network requires special considerations prior to design.

Advanced Design Strategies

☑ Consider the methods that might be used to provide VPN services to special connections such as Frame Relay and PVC circuits or modem-based dial-in access.

☑ Limit or restrict outbound traffic from the internal network to inappropriate services, such as FTP or messaging services.

☑ Provide for out-of-band management capabilities on all DMZ design segments as well as intrusion detection services where it is appropriate.

Frequently Asked Questions

The following Frequently Asked Questions, answered by the authors of this book, are designed to both measure your understanding of the concepts presented in this chapter and to assist you with real-life implementation of these concepts. To have your questions about this chapter answered by the author, browse to **www.syngress.com/solutions** and click on the **"Ask the Author"** form. You will also gain access to thousands of other FAQs at ITFAQnet.com.

Q: What is the difference between a DMZ and a screened subnet?

A: Although the terms are sometimes used interchangeably, the screened subnet is a variation of the screened host configurations that required dual or multihomed hosts to provide protection. In the case of the DMZ, the protection is most often provided through the use of screening routers and firewall appliances or software to more securely limit traffic and eliminate single points of failure.

Q: You mention that a security policy must be in place before designing a DMZ. Why should I go to all that trouble?

A: It is important that you as an administrator have a clear goal and vision about the levels of protection that you are responsible for and that you are expected to maintain. It is impossible to navigate the complexities of the DMZ design stage without first having a path to follow.

Q: Could you explain the difference between out-of-band and in-band management?

A: In-band management tools require that the network being managed and the devices connected to it utilize the same network. In the case of network problems or DoS attacks, the administrator would be unable to manage the equipment or rectify the problem. With out-of-band tools in place, management occurs on a different level, which may be a separate segment or serial port-based interaction with a console port on equipment. This capability is very important in the maintenance of your DMZ structure.

Q: A client has an outside office that needs to be able to authenticate to the internal network. The client would like to accomplish this task as inexpensively as possible while still maintaining security. What would you recommend?

A: In this case, the normal recommendation would be to use a modem-based RAS to allow access to the internal network, unless there was already a substantial DMZ structure in place to accommodate the traffic from the remote office.

Q: To provide the levels of security that are required in the large enterprise environment, what path would you recommend toward achieving the most complete design?

A: As we've discussed throughout the chapter, the most complete design requires security analysis, policy creation, and discussion with all stakeholders to appropriately implement the DMZ plan and structure.

Q: I thought that RADIUS was only for billing purposes?

A: Actually, RADIUS does have the capability to log access times and traffic, thus making auditing a simpler process. Its main use, however, is to screen the authentication process from outside networks and limit communication via the authentication mechanisms of our internal networks.

## Chapter 2

Windows 2000 DMZ Design

Solutions in this chapter:

- **Introducing Windows 2000 DMZ Security**
- **Building a Windows 2000 DMZ**
- **Windows 2000 DMZ Design Planning List**

- ☑ **Summary**
- ☑ **Solutions Fast Track**
- ☑ **Frequently Asked Questions**

Introduction

Microsoft has taken great strides in the past few years to enhance its security posture. Windows 2000 is only as secure as you can make it, so it's very important that you follow this chapter closely; everything you learn here will be used in the demilitarized zone (DMZ) of your network. In Chapter 1 we learned the fundamental security concepts revolving around the DMZ, what the DMZ is, and how to design a basic DMZ with traffic flows. In this chapter we now start to populate the DMZ with systems and the specifics of designing those systems to work within the DMZ. From Chapter 1, you'll recall what you learned about the basic DMZ and its overall reason for existence as well as its basic design. Here we cover how to design a Windows 2000-based network solution that will work within and around the DMZ segment. It's important to know this information as a security administrator or engineer because the DMZ (as you are now starting to see) can be very complex to work with and around. It will get even more complex as we move through this book. Building on the content of Chapter 1, this chapter shows you how to use your Windows systems within the DMZ design.

In this chapter you learn about Windows 2000 security but only as it relates to this subject matter. In other words, this chapter is not a general Windows 2000 security chapter, but rather is one customized to fit the needs of designing security within the DMZ. Of course, the chapter covers many security topics revolving around Windows 2000, but all the content will be tailored for the most part to security administrators working within a DMZ environment.

This chapter can serve as a rough design document to help you place your Windows 2000 systems and the services they run within the DMZ. Many administrators wonder how to place their systems within the DMZ, especially when those systems are Web or FTP servers facing the Internet and publicly accessible. It can be nerve shattering, especially with all the past publicity about Microsoft being an insecure system with many bugs, unchecked buffers, and a plethora of other problems, resulting in its products becoming the biggest target on the Internet today. This chapter (and following chapters) will remedy those fears by providing you with the answers and solutions you need to not only place the systems in and around the DMZ but also to protect them.

In this chapter we cover the basics of Windows 2000 DMZ security and introduce to you the proper placement of systems in and around it. (Chapter 13 and the bonus Appendix A, available online, focus entirely on how to lock down and harden Windows 2000 and other services such as IIS, so if you are only looking to harden systems, you might want to jump directly to those sections.)

> **NOTE**
>
> If you are looking for a book on how to harden and implement security with Windows 2000 in more granular detail without a focus on the DMZ segment, you can check out these other Syngress titles:
>
> - *Hack Proofing Windows 2000 Server* (ISBN: 1931836493)
> - *MCSE/MCSA Implementing and Administering Security in a Windows 2000 Network: Study Guide and DVD Training System (Exam 70-214)* (ISBN: 1931836841)

Introducing Windows 2000 DMZ Security

In this section we take a broad look at security concepts for Windows 2000 systems, tailoring all the content to DMZ-based hosts. This section of the chapter covers the following details:

- Fundamental Windows 2000 DMZ design

- Windows 2000 DMZ bastion hosts design

- Engineering Windows 2000 traffic in the DMZ

An introduction to Windows 2000 DMZ security must start with a general discussion of the concepts of applying a secure foundation to the core services running within the DMZ, all based on the Microsoft product line. When discussing Windows 2000-based security in the DMZ, we need to look at a few general concepts. What will be publicly accessible? Why do you need these services available? How will you control access to and from such resources? How will you maintain these services? Everything else is all about hardening the systems. Here we look at the general design. Remember, DMZs are the best place for you to place and secure your publicly used information and services such as an e-commerce site, a Web site, an FTP site, VPN-based services, and so on. In this chapter we look at proper placement of these needed services.

In this section of the chapter we also look at basic Windows 2000 DMZ bastion host design. This is really about placement of servers and why you would place them in specific spots on your network. Again, this is just placement; if you need to learn more granular details, turn to Chapter 13 to learn how to lock down the Windows 2000 OS to be placed on the DMZ.

The last section discusses basic traffic flows and the services and protocols Microsoft products use. With this information, you can design your systems so that all needed traffic will go through the firewalls, as well as preventing traffic that you do not want to go through the firewall. In later chapters, we show you how to configure those firewalls to allow the traffic to pass; you can come back to this chapter to get the data you need (such as port numbers for access control lists) to engineer your solution. As mentioned before, you need to read this book in its entirety to be able to complete your solution if you are not sure what to do at all, but if you have a Cisco PIX firewall that you need to implement with a Windows 2000 IIS 5.0 Server, you can probably just read this chapter, the PIX chapter (Chapter 5), and the chapter on how to secure Windows 2000 bastion hosts on the DMZ segment (Chapter 13).

Remember, you need to understand three very important concepts: why you are building a DMZ, where to place specific services, and how to engineer the traffic to and from those services. After that, you can worry about locking down those individual systems.

Fundamental Windows 2000 DMZ Design

Before we look at the fundamentals of securing the DMZ segment and its hosts, we need a general idea of what it's going to look like on a map. All good network designers plan the topology (hopefully with a topology map) and figure out in advance traffic flows, logical addressing, and any other factors that would affect the systems planned operation. If you choose not to follow this recommendation, you could find yourself very discouraged when the network does not function properly and systems cannot be accessed due to a simple (or complex) mistake you made in the design. A DMZ segment can be one of the most complicated segments on the network that you can design and implement. When you add Windows 2000 to the mix, you not only have to be an expert in security—you also must be an expert in network engineering, Windows 2000 system design, and the services to be made available. Look at it from this point of view: You want to set up a DMZ segment with a PIX firewall and a Windows 2000-based Web server. This should not be a complicated task in your mind, but think of all the areas you need to focus on:

- Network engineering
- Systems engineering
- Security analysis

Now take a look at Figure 2.1, which points out all three of these areas.

Figure 2.1 Fundamental DMZ Design

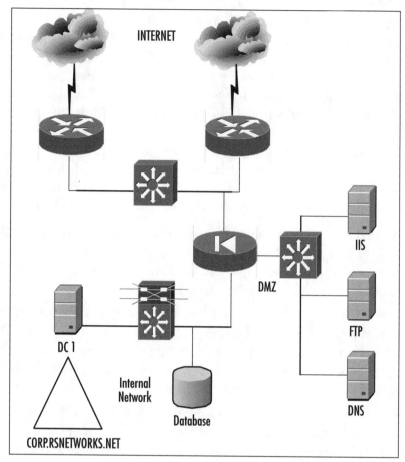

The reason we have segmented this figure into three sections is that it represents how you should design each section. Let's take a look at each section in more granular detail.

NOTE

In Figure 2.1, note also the use of high availability in your design. If your resources need to be in high demand, it is critical that you design high-availability features so that you can keep your services available in time of disaster. Here you can see the need for firewalls, redundant routers, and Internet connections to different points of presence (POPs), highly available Web services, and database services. Never rule out high availability for your solution if you can afford to implement it.

Network Engineering the DMZ

Your first step in designing a Windows 2000-based DMZ is to select all the networking hardware you will need. You must do an assessment of your needs to figure out what the hardware infrastructure will cost your company. You need to look at your *needs* first. When you are looking at the networking end of it, you should ask yourself, "What devices will I need, and how should I scale them?" Exploring these questions will bring answers based on networking gear and its cost. Since we've already mentioned Cisco, let's stick with that company's products for this example. In Figure 2.1 we looked at a very basic network infrastructure, but the needs are quite high for the future, so let's say that we decide to scale up the network hardware. We interviewed all departments that are part of the project to design and implement a DMZ infrastructure with an IIS Web server. After talking to everyone involved, we came up with a few important items:

1. We need to scale up the number of connections to the Internet, since the VPN services, external DNS, and other services will be added sooner than later. For this reason, we might need to have more port availability on our switch that is publicly accessible via the Internet.

2. We need to add more bandwidth and site-to-site VPN services off the external Internet routers. This need will become critical next year. This tells us that we had better not skimp on the Internet-facing routers and make sure that we purchase models that either have crypto cards (to use IPSec for VPNs) installed or that are upgradeable to them.

3. We need to eventually set up a load-balanced solution with multiple IIS servers and a possible backend database cluster. This tells us that we will need to scale the firewall, switches, and all other infrastructure to meet the needs for a possible e-commerce site, a load-balanced cluster, and so on.

Can you see why you must really plan this project out very well? There is nothing more frustrating than having to constantly replace equipment because you have not anticipated future needs and requirements. It always winds up costing more in the long run, so make sure that you do a solid needs assessment up front and scale your design to what you might need in the future.

> **NOTE**
>
> Even if your management team or project stakeholders decide it's not in the best interest of the project, organization, or the IT group to scale up or out resources (which adds immensely to the cost of the project), at least they'll know you brought it up—and when the need comes up in the future (as it usually will), it is on record that you at least tried!

Now you have done a complete needs analysis and have designed the infrastructure. (The initial design is shown in Figure 2.1.) You have noted that a redundant firewall should be used to ease the pain of failure as well as your scaling requirements. The management team responsible for purchasing and approving this design has stated that all is approved except the redundant firewall, which will be considered and purchased at a later date.

Now the network segment is designed, and after you run a test (maybe even a pilot or prototype), you are ready to implement it. Again, this chapter focuses on overall design. Since this book was written with all types of systems in mind, you can replace that firewall (currently PIX) with a Nokia firewall, a Check Point firewall of Microsoft ISA 2000. This book allows for that flexibility in design so that you can pretty much replace that firewall with whatever you are currently using or plan to use. We look at the specifics of adding rules and so on in later chapters.

Now that you have an idea of network design, let's continue with our plan to design it. Take a look at Figure 2.2.

Figure 2.2 Network Design of the DMZ

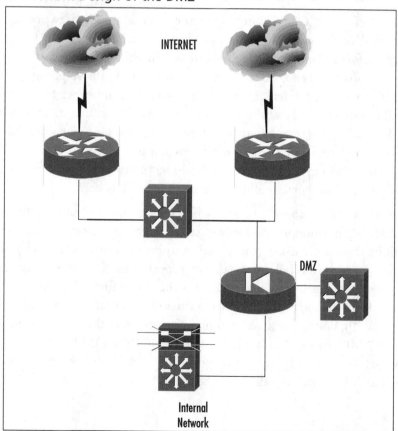

Since you have already selected your vendor's product line (Cisco) and have your needs analysis done, you can lay out your infrastructure. In Figure 2.2 you see that we have used Cisco routers, switches, and a firewall to build our DMZ segment. The Layer 3 switches in the internal network position were already in place. This is the LAN's default gateway and the switch responsible for segmenting the LAN into virtual LANs (VLANs). Chapter 9 of this book is all about building those VLANs; for now, we'll focus on design.

We've decided to use the following components for our DMZ:

- Two Cisco 3725 routers with T1 WAN interface cards (WICs) with which to connect to the Internet and Fast Ethernet ports to the external switch. We decided on two routers because we want to have a highly available solution to the Internet. If one link goes down, we have another to use, and we can offset the load in times of high demand. ISPs drop lines often. We chose this router model because we foresaw a future need to implement site-to-site VPNs, add more redundancy to the network, and leave room for a possible upgrade in not only bandwidth but also in the number of connections for backup lines later.

- We selected two Cisco switches for our external public network segment and for the DMZ. Now you have to do some research (or refer to Chapter 9 for more information), but basically your switch choice will be based on how many ports you need, the amount of traffic you will have going through it, the quality-of-service enhancements you would like, and other features such as dual power supply. Basically, your switch should be scaled to what you need and scaled up (or out) based on future needs. The best piece of advice we can offer you in terms of a decision on a switch is to research very heavily on the vendor's Web site to find what each model offers and how it can fit into your design based on current and future needs as well as cost.

- We selected a Cisco PIX firewall to be the "traffic cop" among the Internet, the DMZ, and the private LAN. Again, Chapter 5 focuses on this design (you will be shown the exact configuration to implement this solution), and that is where you can find all the details on a specific model. One design flaw we pointed out (but had to live with) was the single firewall design. Basically, we asked for a redundant solution (two firewalls with failover, as you will see in Chapter 9), but the cost was too high for now and the need was not as great. Again, this solution was implemented to make the DMZ and to control traffic to and from it, so the needed design was met with this requirement, but a second redundant firewall would be ideal.

NOTE

When planning your infrastructure, you always need to ensure that you plan the proper equipment list, no matter what vendor you pick. Basically, if you are purchasing this much equipment, presales support could be in order. Ask you vendor to show you user limits per device (how many users can use this device without affecting its performance simultaneously) as well as what type of traffic you will be pumping through it. Many times, the vendor can help you to design your network so that you don't fall short on what you need or you don't go into overkill where you might not need the extra power.

You can see that implementing a DMZ is not a cakewalk; it's all based on needs and analysis. It is something that you have to really plan out and design so that it comes out the way you want it and need it instead of becoming a costly disaster. In addition, note that we have only designed the actual infrastructure—we have not even plugged any intelligence into it. Future chapters point out how to add intelligence so that you can configure rules and other settings to make all the components work together. In the next section, we look at adding the systems into the segment.

Designing & Planning...

What Is a Site-to-Site VPN?

We have eluded to the need for a site-to-site VPN as a future requirement in our design. The purpose of this VPN is twofold. First, we want you to "think outside the box" and consider that there are such things as future requirements when designing a DMZ. Second, we want to ensure that this book is relevant to today's and tomorrow's future technology trends. Let's look at the Cisco router that we selected for this DMZ design as an example.

Key features for the Cisco 3725 and 3745 are:

- Two integrated 10/100 LAN ports
- Two integrated Advanced Integration Module (AIM) slots
- Three integrated WIC slots
- Two (Cisco 3725) or four (Cisco 3745) Network Module (NM) slots
- One (Cisco 3725) or two (Cisco 3745) High-Density Service Module (HDSM)-capable slots
- 32MB Compact Flash (default); 128MB maximum

Continued

- 128MB DRAM (default, single 128MB DIMM); 256MB DRAM maximum

- Optional in-line power for 16-port EtherSwitch NM and 36-port EtherSwitch HDSM

- Support for all major WAN protocols and media: LL, FR, ISDN, X.25, ATM, fractional T1/E1, T1/E1, xDSL, T3/E3, HSSI

- Support for selected NMs, WICs, and AIMs from the Cisco 1700, 2600 and 3600 Series 2 RU (Cisco 3725) or 3 RU (Cisco 3745) rack-mountable chassis

The VPN and encryption AIM are:

- AIM-VPN/HP DES/3DES VPN Advanced Integration Module for 3660 and 3745—High Performance

- AIM-VPN/EP DES/3DES VPN Advanced Integration Module for 2600 and 3725—Enhanced Performance

You are using this router because of the addition of the VPN and encryption AIM that are available with it. You need this added crypto card to be able to tunnel from one site to another over the Internet. You understand why we selected the router we did (for its scaling and functionality), so you need to know what a site-to-site VPN is now that you have the router hardware lined up. A site-to-site VPN (as shown in Figure 2.3) is a network solution that utilizes both public and private IP Internet connections to establish the WAN between all sites that you want to connect to like remote branch offices, business-to-business partner connections, and so on.

The benefits of using this solution are many. For one, VPN technology can run over public or private Internet-based solutions. In other words, you can utilize this design in just about any country in the world. Frame Relay (especially in international deployments) can be quite costly, so you might want to utilize a VPN connection to connect a remote branch more cheaply than with a costly Frame Relay connection. You can also augment your WAN with a backup solution based on VPN. VPN services are better in some ways because there is no Layer 2 breakdown, whereas VPN traffic is all Layer 3. Since there is no breakdown of data and rebuilding of data, it can be argued that a VPN solution is better when you're trying to utilize voice over IP (VOIP), QoS-based IP traffic, or the like. The difference we mentioned before (public vs. private

Continued

Figure 2.3 A VPN-Based Network

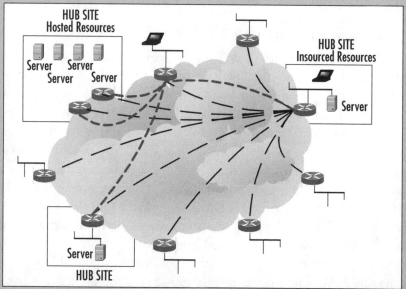

VPN technologies) is that a public VPN network setup will utilize any ISP's Internet service, whereas a private VPN network would be (for example) AT&T's private IP VPN network built only for use with private business and not publicly accessible via the Internet if you do not want it to be, basically using a Layer 3 private network. Both can be used at the same time with this solution, adding another degree of flexibility to your design.

The reason this information is so important is that in the future, you might only have an Internet connection to worry about for all your remote e-mail, Internet access, and WAN access. Therefore, the DMZ becomes even more critical at this point in the design phase. Each router you see in Figure 2.3 should be firewalled (with a DMZ, if the services are needed) especially if you are not using an ISP's private VPN solution. One last note: The design used in Figure 2.3 is called a *partial mesh*. This keeps the tunnel endpoint to a minimum, with no more than one to three hops to get to any site from any site. A full mesh keeps hop counts down, but tunnel maintenance is harder to maintain because you will have many more tunnels to maintain with a full mesh.

Now that you have designed your network, it is time to populate the segment with systems. In the next section we look at systems-engineering your DMZ.

Systems–Engineering the DMZ

You can now start to populate the DMZ and its surrounding areas. First, you need to think about access to and from the DMZ and the services that are needed. The reason behind this initial thought is that your end user, customers, potential customers, and outsiders will be able to utilize resources needed and only those needed resources— nothing more, nothing less. To start the engineering process, you will have to first make certain that you have these answers! What do you need? You should make sure that users can obtain the information that they need about your company without accessing the internal network and only accessing the DMZ, or accessing the Internal network safely if you chose not to implement a DMZ. Working with DMZs can be tricky (hence the need for this book), so if you can, it's always better to segment Internet-based resources via the DMZ for an added level of safety.

Now that you know your network layout, you have to think about other access to and from the DMZ. Your secret, protected, confidential, and proprietary information should be stored behind your firewall and DMZ on your internal network. Servers on the DMZ shouldn't contain sensitive trade secrets, source code, or proprietary information, or anything that can be used against you or your company—or that can be used to exploit or hack into your systems. (There's more on DMZ hacking techniques in Chapter 14.) A breach of your DMZ servers should at worst create an annoyance in the form of downtime while you recover from the security breach.

Here are examples of systems that could wind up on your DMZ:

- A Web server that holds public information. This can be IIS (since we are discussing Microsoft technologies in this chapter) or any other publicly accessible Web server. You can also think of FTP services, NNTP services, and other Web-based services to be accessed and utilized.

- Electronic commerce-based solutions always wind up on the DMZ. The front end of an e-commerce transaction server is the one through which orders are placed. Keep the back end, where you store client information, behind the firewall. You want to design this properly, because if you don't, you could compromise your entire client database (or personal and private data) if it's exploited.

- A mail server that relays outside mail to the inside will be a highly utilized solution, especially since spam and other e-mail exploits are common DMZ host-based targets for attacks.

- VPN solutions are prevalent in the DMZ. Other than the site-to-site VPN we already learned about, you also have VPN solutions in which you have a remote access solution so that clients can attach over the Internet to get to their files and other data needed on the corporate network. This data also has to be publicly accessible via the DMZ.

- Security devices such as intrusion detection solutions, honeypots, and other items you will learn about in Chapter 15.

These areas all need to be addressed when it comes to providing a solution for your systems and where to place them within the DMZ or around it. Take a look at Figure 2.4, which shows the placement of the systems within the DMZ.

Figure 2.4 Systems on the DMZ

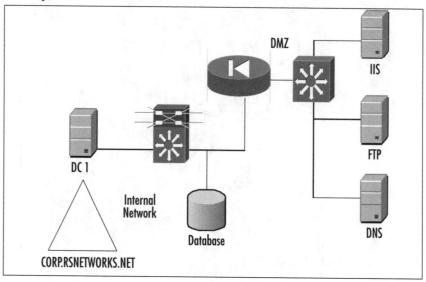

We have placed all the publicly accessible systems (such as Web, FTP, and DNS) on the DMZ so that Internet users can access them and not come into and through our internal network, which is to remain private. You can also see that we have placed our domain controller and all-important data (such as a SQL Server database) on the internal network. This keeps these resources secure and only accessed via proper channels and not exposed to the Internet for malicious exploits to take place.

Security Analysis for the DMZ

Once you have finalized the DMZ network segment design and placed your systems where they need to be (and you understand why they need to be there), you have to consider the security of such systems. Basically, to learn how to harden the systems themselves, you need to read through the chapters in this book that concern what security measures you need to take in the DMZ. If you want to implement an IDS for intrusion detection, for example, you can read Chapter 15 to learn how to do that, but to understand placement for your DMZ, take a look at Figure 2.5.

Figure 2.5 Implementing Security in the DMZ

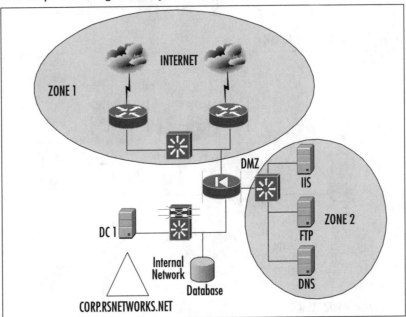

To keep the security analysis potion of your DMZ design to a minimum (the rest of the book is based on configuring security), you need to know the two biggest targets of attack and what you should be concerned about when considering your design.

Zone 1

Zone 1 of Figure 2.5 is where your public Internet connection is and where you are most vulnerable to exploitation. Zone 1 is where you need to consider your external router and switch security as well as the outside port of your firewall. You can read Chapter 9 to learn how to lock down this zone. Furthermore, Zone 1 is where you would consider placing your network-based intrusion detection system (although you can place it just about anywhere, depending on what you are trying to capture) as well as your honeypot. You can read Chapter 15 to learn about IDSs and their implementation around the DMZ.

Zone 2

Zone 2 is the actual DMZ. The DMZ is where we have placed our Windows 2000 servers and the services they offer, such as external DNS and Web services. To learn how to harden the systems on the DMZ (also called bastion hosts), you can read Chapter 13.

Building a Windows 2000 DMZ

Building a Windows 2000 DMZ is not very difficult; it's just that there are many moving parts that you need to be concerned with in the initial design and for consistent maintenance.

Consider this solution: You are the systems engineer responsible for designing, implementing, and maintaining a Windows 2000 DMZ segment that consists of an IIS Web server, an FTP site, an external DNS server, and an e-mail relay. That doesn't sound like a lot, but this is one tall order. Consider the following: You will have to know (or find the people who know) how to configure hardware such as routers, switches, and the firewall. You must have security applied to these items and others, such as an IDS if you need it or the design requires it. You have to place bastion hosts on the DMZ and configure security on them, including hardening the base OS (Windows 2000) and then applying the needed services and hardening them, too. Lastly, you need to know how to engineer the traffic to and from those services to other front-end or back-end systems, depending on what the design calls for. In this last example, consider having an internal DNS namespace and an external DNS namespace. How do you configure them to work together through the firewall? This is the point behind this chapter (and much of this book), which is to get you to think about these details so that your DMZ is a success, works properly, can be maintained, and is secure.

Now that we have taken a look at the fundamentals of laying out the hardware to create the DMZ, let's examine the details of populating it with a Windows 2000 solution.

Designing the DMZ Windows Style

Now that you have the fundamental placement, design, and understanding, let's get into more detail concerning the Windows 2000 platform, since there is much to think about and much to plan. In this section we cover domain models (how to configure your domain), devices that sit on your DMZ segment, the names and definitions of systems revolving around the DMZ, and much more. In this next section we look specifically at the domain model, which can confuse many architects who might not know the exact placement of the domain controllers (DCs) and where the logical boundaries of the domain sit with the DMZ segment.

Domain Considerations

Building a domain with a DMZ segment can be confusing. For one, you have probably heard many times that you should never expose a DC to the general public. If this advice is sound, how in the world do you set up domain-based logins if you need a domain-based account for a particular service to work? Consider the following: You need to implement a load-balanced cluster in your DMZ, and the cluster account must log into a domain for the service to work. If this were the case, where would you place the DC? Figure 2.6 offers a possible solution.

Figure 2.6 A Cluster in a DMZ

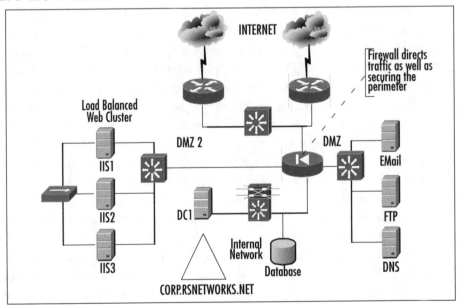

This solution is not impossible, but it can be tricky. Think of the traffic flow and other issues you need to consider with your design:

1. As you can see. with the Internet, your IIS load-balanced cluster will need to be accessible to the Internet users who will want to see your Web site.

2. If e-commerce solutions are available, the IIS servers need to know how to get to the back-end database, if that is what you need for your solution. You must have a way to get your IIS servers to communicate through the firewall to get to the SQL server.

3. You have two DMZ segments from your PIX firewall. You need to know how to set security levels on each and how to deny traffic coming from one segment to the other. If someone exploits your DNS server, it might only be a matter of time before they get to your second DMZ if you do not apply security so that it does not allow this type of activity.

4. Your cluster needs to access a DC if it is using the Cluster Service. Since this is a load-balanced solution, you can forgo that need, but if you place a cluster on the DMZ, you need a nearby DC to service your requests.

5. Your firewall should be configured to allow for external public Internet traffic to come to your Web sites, but your Web servers can only make requests to the database of the DC behind the firewall. The Web servers need to deliver what was requested of them to the Internet users.

6. Your firewall should also be configured so that your internal DNS server (not shown) can communicate with its forwarder on the DMZ. The internal e-mail server (also not shown) should be able to send e-mail back and forth to the relay on the DMZ. Users should be able to get to the FTP site.

As you can see, now that you have planned it, you only need to pay for it, implement it, and maintain it. That's easier said than done, which is why you have this book. Remember, this chapter is conceptual in nature; it's not until you get to some of the later chapters that you actually learn how to configure all this on the firewall.

NOTE

Depending on what model and type of firewall you use, you can in fact have different DMZ segments with different services on each to add even more security to your DMZ segments and hosts.

The Contained Domain Model

The type of domain model you need to deploy depends on your needs analysis. We cannot stress enough the importance of design when it comes to very detailed implementations that have many moving parts. With Windows 2000, you need to implement a *contained domain*, which is a Windows 2000 domain that will not cross or extend across any networks that are not controlled by the organization. In other words, you will have a domain isolated to your network, and nothing more. If you consider the DMZ, a contained domain is one that is isolated to the private LAN and does not extend past it, as shown in Figure 2.7.

Figure 2.7 A Contained Domain Model

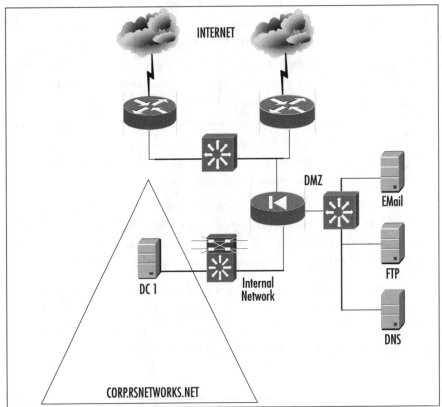

You can also view this model very simply as a single domain that incorporates all your needs and is only located at the hub site or the corporate office. If you extend a DMZ segment, the DC sites behind the firewall and the logical domain remains behind the firewall. You will not have remote sites with their own domains or DCs.

The Extended Domain Model

Now that you know what a contained domain is, let's look at the reverse—an *extended domain* model. The extended domain is a Microsoft Windows 2000 domain that extends past the protected network. The extended domain extends past the boundaries of the site and across WAN links. You can see an example in Figure 2.8. This type of network needs more functionality, including DCs from higher in the domain tree located at lower branches' sites. This can prove to be quite complicated, especially if you are using the partial mesh VPN layout that we looked at earlier in the chapter. Now that you have a firewall protecting your Internet connections, you must consider allowing ports needed by your DCs to open at each site that is firewalled. If you do not, you will not receive your synchronization and replication updates as well as other necessary services. This also needs to be considered when you're building and designing your DMZ, public Internet access, and so on with a Windows 2000 solution.

Figure 2.8 Examining the Extended Domain Model

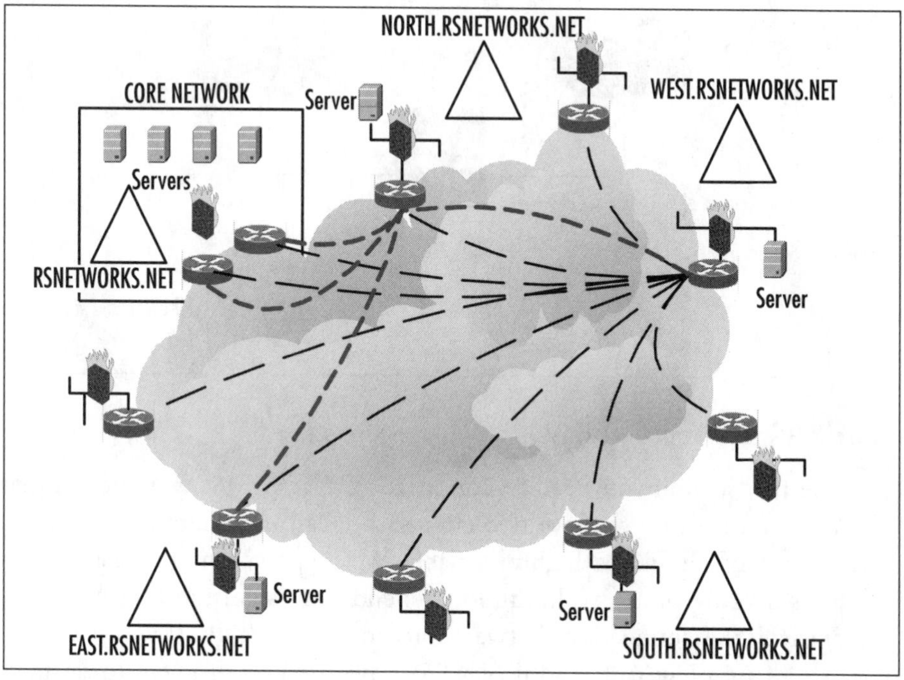

The Internet Connection

Your Windows 2000 solution revolving around the DMZ needs to allow for Internet access. What must be known about the Internet connection is that it should be able to handle the required bandwidth needs of the site. If you are using this Internet connection as your LANs Internet access for surfing and e-mail, and you decide to use it for a VPN as well, you need to analyze your requirements first. You can do a traffic flows analysis to ascertain the needed requirements quite quickly, but you need to know how to do the analysis and have the tools with which to do the analysis. If you do not, it is in your best interests to work with an outside vendor that does have the tools and experience to do so. Failing to do so will almost always result in bad performance and increased cost later when you need to reprovision the lines to a higher bandwidth. Everything you need to consider is shown in Figure 2.9.

Figure 2.9 Internet Connection Considerations

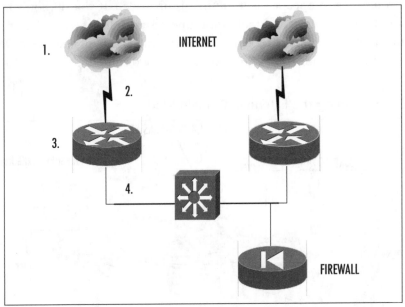

Figure 2.9 shows four sections:

1. The first section you need to consider is the actual ISP you are connecting to. You see here that we have two clouds; the reasoning here is that our Internet connection should be highly available. We suggest having at least two connections if your company's livelihood depends on use of the Internet. You can also diversify the connections between providers and POPs. If you have both POPs in, let's say, New York, and if New York has a major problem (or a single ISP goes down completely), you will still be available on the Internet.

2. Make sure you size your connections properly. Most vendors and ISPs have sizing tools that help you determine how much bandwidth you need to the

Internet. Basically, if we had two T1s here, we would have almost 3MB of traffic to and from the Internet, which is not too bad at all.

3. Make sure that you have the properly sized router. Make sure that the router can handle all the Internet-based traffic coming and going. Processing power, available memory, and other factors can hinder your response time, so do not make the router the bottleneck on the Internet.

4. Do not let the last leg of the segment (for the Internet connection), which is the connection into the firewall, be the bottleneck. Make certain that you have 100MB/full duplex or better here if possible. Most firewalls allow for Fast Ethernet connectivity.

Remember, anyone can connect to and use the Internet, so the number (and frequency) of your vulnerabilities will become much higher. Always make certain that all these areas are secured properly, and you can learn how to lock all this down in later chapters in the book.

Wide Area Network Link

A WAN link is really not much different from the Internet connection (they both use some form of leased lines), but in a traditional sense, a WAN link basically describes the connections from your company to others through the use of private lines. When we say *private*, we mean in the sense that it is not accessible via the Internet, which is a publicly accessible arena. The WAN link (T1, Frame Relay, ISDN) connects your remote sites up to the backbone located within the core site. Most traditional designs show a hub-and-spoke formation. Here, in Figure 2.10, a hub and spoke are shown connected to an Internet-based segment with a DMZ.

Figure 2.10 A WAN Connected to a Backbone with an Internet Connection

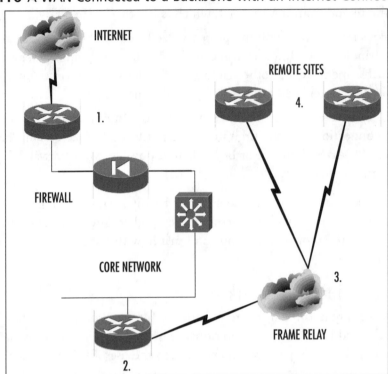

The reason that this concept is so important is that you will have to know how to get traffic from the LAN to either the WAN links or perhaps out to the Internet. How do you do this? Let's go through the process step by step while looking at Figure 2.10:

1. You need to consider the design. Look at Figure 2.10. We have a core network (where the major resources are located) connected to the Internet and also to a Frame Relay network with two remote sites. How do you direct the traffic? How do the remote sites access the Internet?

2. Look at Area 1; you can see that the Internet connection has been established correctly, as shown in the last section. Now you need to visualize how users will gain access the Internet. Basically, to the user, this process should be transparent: Click the Web browser and out you go! This is set via the proxy settings in the Web browser (as shown in Figure 2.11) or via the default gateway of the client (as shown in Figure 2.12). The proxy setting will be valuable to you if you use a proxy server to get to the Internet. (A proxy server DMZ-based system is described in Chapter 8, when we take a granular look at ISA 2000.) If you need to see what your default gateway is set at, you can do an

IPCONFIG /*all* to get all the IP settings for your Windows NT or 2000/2003 system. If you are using older 9x versions, WINIPCFG will do the same. You need to know what your default gateway is because this is how you will direct traffic in an enterprise DMZ. Remember, if you only have an Internet connection, the Internet connection-based router (or the firewall in front of it) can be your default gateway.

Figure 2.11 Proxy Settings for a Web Browser

Figure 2.12 Default Gateway Settings for a LAN Client

```
Microsoft Windows 2000 [Version 5.00.2195]
(C) Copyright 1985-2000 Microsoft Corp.


C:\>ipconfig /all


Windows 2000 IP Configuration


Host Name . . . . . . . . . . . . : SHIMONSKI-LAPTOP
Primary DNS Suffix  . . . . . . . :
Node Type . . . . . . . . . . . . : Hybrid
IP Routing Enabled. . . . . . . . : No
WINS Proxy Enabled. . . . . . . . : No
DNS Suffix Search List. . . . . . : rsnetworks.net


Ethernet adapter Local Area Connection 3:


Connection-specific DNS Suffix   . : rsnetworks.net
Description . . . . . . . . . . . : Wireless Network PC Card
Physical Address. . . . . . . . . : 00-23-15-26-1E-3D
DHCP Enabled. . . . . . . . . . . : Yes
```

Continued

Figure 2.12 Default Gateway Settings for a LAN Client

```
Autoconfiguration Enabled . . . . : Yes

IP Address. . . . . . . . . . . . : 192.168.2.100

Subnet Mask . . . . . . . . . . . : 255.255.255.0

Default Gateway . . . . . . . . . : 192.168.2.1

DHCP Server . . . . . . . . . . . : 192.168.2.101

DNS Servers . . . . . . . . . . . : 192.168.2.102

                                    192.168.2.103

Lease Obtained. . . . . . . . . . : Sunday, May 25, 2003 8:04:49 AM

Lease Expires . . . . . . . . . . : Monday, May 26, 2003 8:04:49 AM

C:\>
```

3. Now that you understand that portion, you need to understand Area 2, which is the default gateway for the LAN, as shown in Figure 2.10. Now you need to engineer the WAN link behind your default gateway, or it must be the default gateway if you have an Internet connection to get to. To get to the Internet or the Internet-based proxy/firewall, you need to know how to view the routes in your router. In Figure 2.13, we did a *show IP route* command on the Cisco router. This gave us a routing table, which we only show the beginning of. You can see here that the last line shows what's called the *gateway of last resort*. Your Windows systems will need to know what this is to get out to the Internet if they are connected anywhere on your internal LAN or if they are one of your remote sites. Figure 2.14 shows you the command to add this route.

Figure 2.13 The Routing Table on the WAN Router

```
WANROUTER#sh ip route

Codes: C - connected, S - static, I - IGRP, R - RIP, M - mobile, B - BGP
       D - EIGRP, EX - EIGRP external, O - OSPF, IA - OSPF inter area
       N1 - OSPF NSSA external type 1, N2 - OSPF NSSA external type 2
       E1 - OSPF external type 1, E2 - OSPF external type 2, E - EGP
       i - IS-IS, L1 - IS-IS level-1, L2 - IS-IS level-2, ia - IS-IS
       * - candidate default, U - per-user static route, o - ODR
       P - periodic downloaded static route


Gateway of last resort is 10.10.10.100 to network 0.0.0.0
```

Figure 2.14 Adding a Route to the Router

```
ip route 0.0.0.0 0.0.0.0 10.10.10.100
```

4. Area 3 is the frame cloud. The frame cloud needs to be engineered and provisioned properly, with the proper access port size and Committed Information Rate (CIR) based on your needs. Make sure you size the frame cloud properly and ask for a bandwidth and utilization report a few months after you use it to make sure you are not overpaying for what you don't need or undercutting your remote sites by not giving them the bandwidth they need to do their jobs. Remember, you need to allow your remote sites to access the Internet through your core, so you need to size the frame links (or any other WAN connection technology) properly.

5. Last but not least, take a look at the remote sites. Note that these sites need to travel up to the core router, and then the core router needs to send the Internet requests up the firewall, which directs the requests out to the Internet. Look at Figure 2.15. It clearly shows the traffic flow needs. And remember the gateway of last resort we saw in Figure 2.13? This same gateway will be used in the remote-side router, with one exception—the IP address of the gateway will be the core router, as shown in Figure 2.16.

Figure 2.15 Internet Traffic Out from a Remote Site

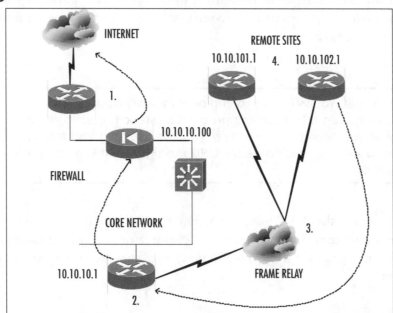

Figure 2.16 The Routing Table on the WAN Router

```
WANROUTER#sh ip route
Codes: C - connected, S - static, I - IGRP, R - RIP, M - mobile, B - BGP
       D - EIGRP, EX - EIGRP external, O - OSPF, IA - OSPF inter area
       N1 - OSPF NSSA external type 1, N2 - OSPF NSSA external type 2
       E1 - OSPF external type 1, E2 - OSPF external type 2, E - EGP
       i - IS-IS, L1 - IS-IS level-1, L2 - IS-IS level-2, ia - IS-IS
       * - candidate default, U - per-user static route, o - ODR
       P - periodic downloaded static route

Gateway of last resort is 10.10.10.1 to network 0.0.0.0
```

Take another look at Figure 2.15. It is imperative that you understand the flow here. A user at a remote site needs to access the Internet via the WAN link. The user is on the remote site LAN with an IP address of 10.10.102.5 /24 given via a DHCP server. The default gateway for the LAN is the 10.10.102.1 router. The user makes a request of the Internet, and because the IP address is not local to the LAN (10.10.10.100), the request must be forwarded to the default gateway on the LAN. Because of the route added (as shown in Figure 2.16), the router knows to forward the request up through the Frame Relay WAN to 10.10.10.1, which is the main core router through which the Internet is connected. You should start to see the picture here now. The core router now sends the request to the firewall (or proxy, or whatever you have configured), and it forwards the request once again to the Internet router on the perimeter of your network.

> **NOTE**
>
> Never forget: You will have to engineer the way back to the remote site router as well. You can add a routing protocol or static routes in reverse, depending on what you need to do. For help, you can use ping and tracing tools (*tracert* for Windows and *Traceroute* for UNIX) to figure out how to get to and from each site.

As you can see, the WAN link (in conjunction with the Internet connection) is very important to know how to design and engineer or you will be running around in circles trying to figure out why your Windows workstations cannot communicate over the Internet.

DMZ Perimeter Security

The DMZ is an isolated segment through which you simply allow services to Internet users while still maintaining some form of security on your network. To allow users to come into your corporate network unknown, unwatched, and consistently will surely lead to a hack attack down the line somewhere, if not instantly. In this section we look at all the areas you need to consider while building your Windows 200 DMZ. In the last section we took a good, hard look at where your internal resources need to be, how they need to be laid out, and some special considerations to take into account. Here we look at the reverse of your protected network (where your LAN meets your internal firewall port), which is the unprotected network. This is your DMZ and Internet connection, which make up your network perimeter. Although the claim is that they are "unprotected," we will make them "highly protected"—or as much as we can! Let's take a look.

External Router

The external router is the router that connects you to the Internet. Again, there can be more than one, and it's recommended (depending on your needs) that you have at least two connections the Internet. The external router connects the protected network and DMZ to the WAN Link. The router provides the first opportunity to actively permit or deny access for clients and servers and for network services. This means that you can apply ACLs, AAA, logging, and much more to the first line of defense of your network. Basically, you will want to read Chapter 9 in its entirety to learn how to lock down the Internet router, but for now, simply understand its importance in the design.

Firewall

As you already know, a firewall is the "traffic cop" in the middle of your DMZ, public Internet, and private LAN that handles incoming and outgoing traffic and places that traffic where it needs to be against the rules that you create for it—simple as that. Your firewall, if configured properly, will aid you in building and maintaining security on your perimeter network. A firewall is simply an enforcer of a security policy. (A security policy is explained in detail in the sidebar "Guidelines for Creating a Good Security Policy-Based DMZ.") A firewall should reside at the perimeter of your network and protect your data from malicious attackers and wrongdoers. As shown in Figure 2.17, your firewall can have many interfaces.

Figure 2.17 Firewall Interfaces

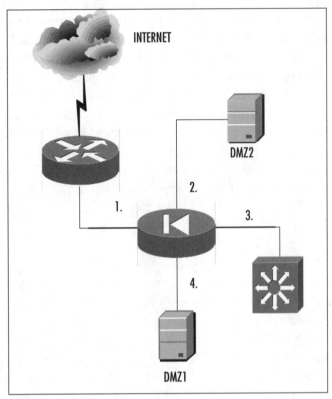

Let's look at each section to see what these interfaces can connect to. First off, Section 1 is the external WAN port on the firewall. This is the Ethernet connection that connects you to the external router. Section 2 is the first DMZ leg and has IIS Web services on it. Section 3 is the connection into the corporate network—the private network. Section 4 is the second DMZ leg with a DNS server on it. Basically, the point to show you that you could have multiple DMZs set by one single firewall! As you will see in Chapter 5, there are many ways you can deliver secure services though multiple DMZs with only one firewall. Three interfaces are recommended: one for incoming traffic, one for access to the demilitarized zone, and one that connects to the protected network. But remember, if you need more than one DMZ, you can create multiple ones.

NOTE

In Chapter 8, you will learn all about Microsoft's Windows-based proxy and firewall product, ISA Server 2000. ISA (which stands for *Internet Acceleration and Security*) allows you to build a DMZ firewall and create a protected solution with a Microsoft product.

Designing & Planning...

Guidelines for Creating a Good Security Policy-Based DMZ

We mentioned the importance of a firewall and alluded to the fact that a firewall is basically the enforcer of a security policy. This means that your firewall will be configured to mirror the needs and requests of the corporation. For instance, if you want to create a security policy that states, "no remote user can pass the DMZ. Only users needing to access our IIS Web server from the Internet can access that single server, and nowhere else can they go though or pass the DMZ." All you need to do is configure the rules on the firewall (PIX, Check Point, Nokia, ISA) to reflect that need, as shown in Figure 2.18.

Figure 2.18 Traffic Directed to an IIS System on the DMZ

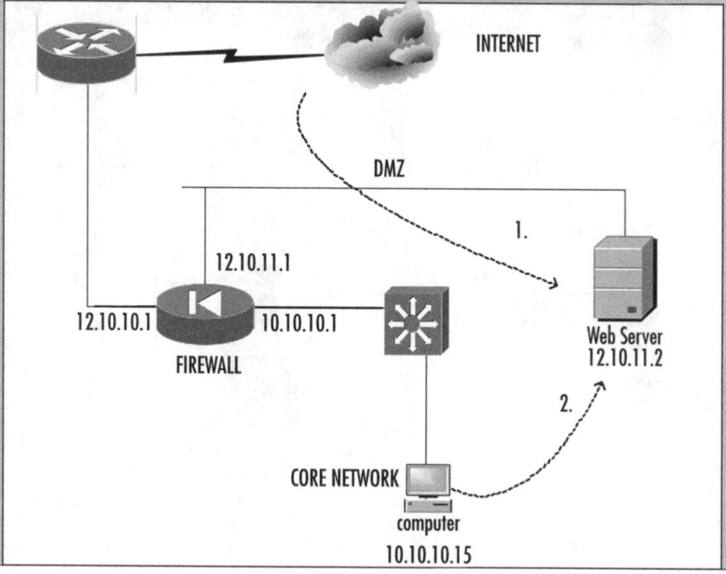

Let's dissect that need again against what we actually configure: The need was to have only Internet users access the IIS server at 12.10.11.2. This is done through the firewall and its ruleset. Basically, you add a rule to the firewall stating that any user needing to get to an IIS server should be sourced from the Internet. The firewall also knows that if the IIS server is compromised, no request from the 12.10.11 network needs to be going to the 10.10.10.0 subnet in the private network. As you see from Request 2 in the figure, you can't allow users to go through the firewall to attach to the Web server, because this capability is not in the security policy.

Extra DMZ Routers

Sometimes (if the size and complexity of the network dictate) you'll need to have a router on each leg of the firewall. This concept is illustrated in Figure 2.19. At times, you will get requests to either add security to the segment you are working on or add more and more devices to it, where you might need to either route or direct traffic. Many firewalls will not route like a router; in other words, a typical firewall will route the RIPv1 protocol where a router will route IS-IS, OSPF, EIGRP, RIP, and so on. A router does just that—it routes. A firewall can in fact route if it is configured to do so, but often, depending on how paranoid you are, you could decide to keep these services dependent on the device in which they sit.

Figure 2.19 Extra Routers Added into the DMZ Segment

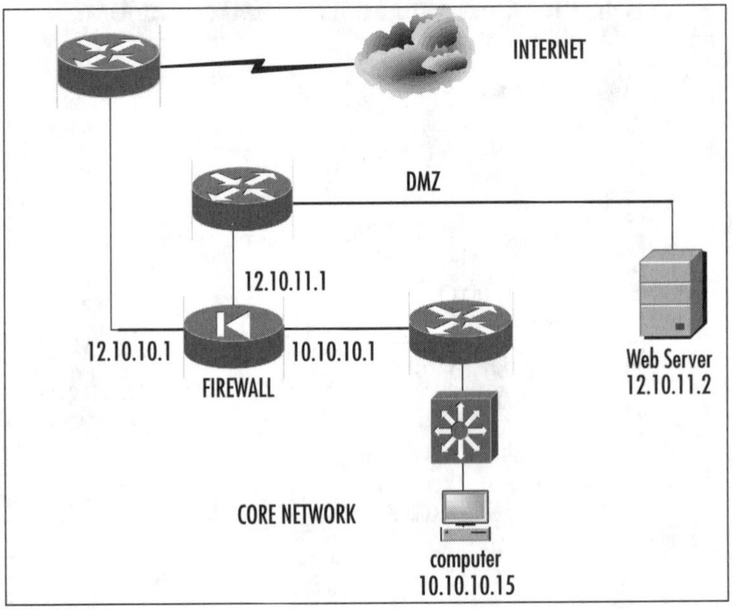

The added routers can increase security and flexibility, but they can also add complexity. The only real time you need to use this is when the firewall is not part of the protected network. The DMZ router filters on the services the DMZ provides and denies all other traffic. A good way to envision this is if you have a firewall that will do NAT. If the firewall provides NAT, the DMZ router will verify that all connections originate from the firewall, which will add to your safety. With the internal network router (shown in Figure 2.19), you can see another level of security against attack. The threat that lingers most on the internal network is the user. The end user can be the biggest threat on the internal network. If configured properly, the internal router can be used to protect your firewall and DMZ from internal attacks. The rules you set up on the router should mimic what is configured on the firewall. Remember when I mentioned that we only wanted external users to hit that IIS server? This is the way you can guarantee it with another level of security. (Router hardening and lockdown are covered in Chapter 9 of this book.)

> **NOTE**
>
> Although this solution might be deemed overkill, you never know what level of security a company and its security team are willing to use for the most protection. Never underestimate the client's needs; always bring up options in design meetings so that you can let the stakeholders in the project decide what they want to spend for the level of decreased risk.

Name Resolution for the DMZ

Too often, DNS and WINS servers are misplaced when people work with the DMZ. Is there a specific design you need to follow? In essence, yes, there is. The importance of name resolution in the DMZ only matters if you in fact need it. Let's look at a quick design map so you can follow along. Figure 2.20 shows you that it is very important to use static addressing on your DMZ and on your public Internet segments. This is because it minimizes the number of exposed hosts on your segment, it reduces the number of attackable hosts on those segments, and more important, it does not create a repository of information that can be used against you if exposed. If a hacker is able to tap into and exploit your DNS server, for example, they would have all IP and name information for your network. If your DMZ is not very large (which it normally is not), you should use static addressing. DNS, WINS, and even DHCP are more suitable for the internal network, where you are more likely to have more hosts and the like, so it is safer to put it there and only have to look for internal attacks.

Figure 2.20 Name Resolution in the DMZ

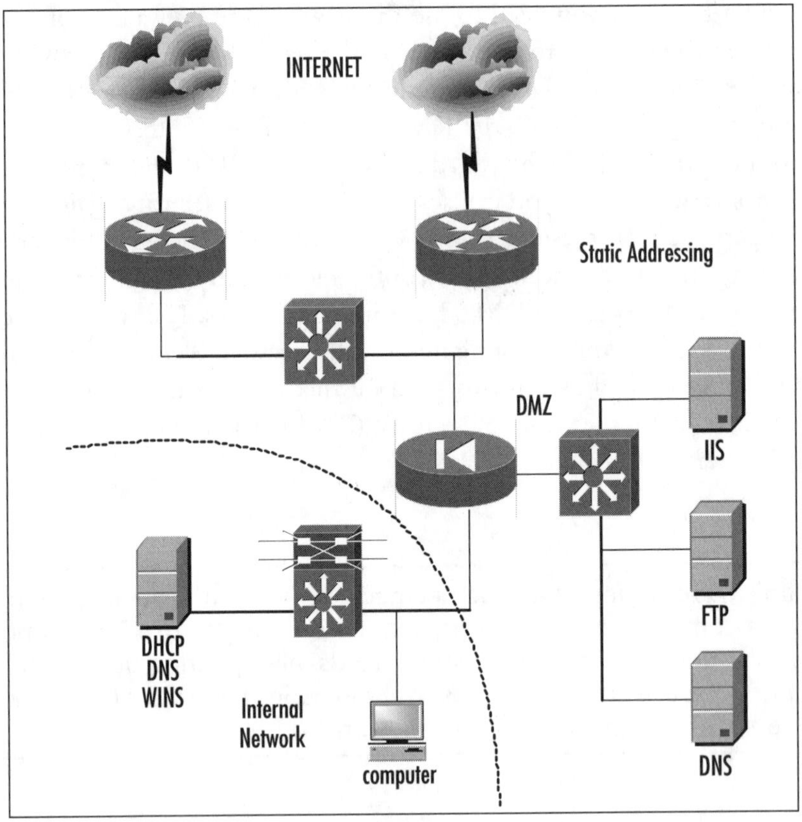

If you do decide to allow WINS (NetBIOS-based traffic), DNS, and DHCP through your firewall, you must allow for it by specifying the port number. Later in this chapter we cover traffic engineering, where you can find the details and port numbers for engineering this type of communication. Another item to mention with DHCP is that DHCP communication is done over User Datagram Protocol (UDP) ports 67 and 68, so this will allow the traffic through, but if you want the broadcasts from clients to pass through "looking" for a DHCP server, you need to add a relay address (called an IP Helper address by Cisco) to a routing device so that it will allow the broadcast through and you can specify the IP to deliver it to.

DMZ Mail Services

Too often, mistakes are made with e-mail service placement due to the administrator's lack of knowledge of how and where to place such services! There are really only two ways to place an e-mail server easily within a DMZ. For one, you can place the e-mail server (only one for this example) in the private network. The firewall in front of the e-mail server would be responsible for taking all requests in and out of the network and for securing the traffic to the e-mail server. Due to the server's design, it made the relaying of outbound Internet-based e-mail the responsibility of the e-mail server—only one single server. The question is then asked, however, "Why would we want to expose our e-mail server to the public Internet? What if somehow, someway, there was a way to attack the e-mail server directly through the firewall?" Figure 2.21 shows you the design we are talking about. You can see the e-mail server behind the firewall, allowing the public Internet access directly to your private corporate network.

Figure 2.21 E-Mail Server Behind the Firewall

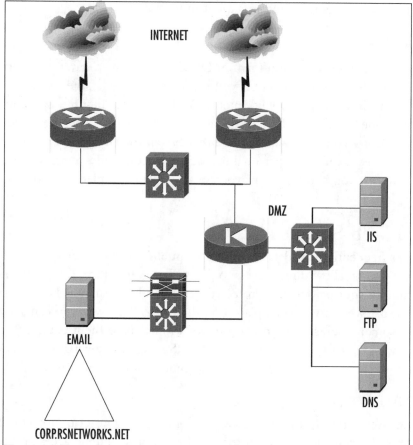

Mail Relay

There are several risks associated with the receipt of e-mail from potentially untrusted entities outside the site. Now that you can visualize this situation, let's consider an alternative. Would you want your Exchange 2000 server exposed in this manner? Would you want your Sendmail server attacked and penetrated so that the attacker has direct access into your network? Of course you wouldn't. Because of this vulnerability, it is common to simply add another e-mail server to the DMZ segment and use this server as a relay to and from the protected e-mail server in the private network. The server now becomes what's called an *e-mail relay,* and it will relay the mail to and from the Internet and to and from the mail server. If mail relays (IIS has an SMTP service that can be used as a relay) are compromised, you can simply reinstall the server from scratch and not lose a thing because all the server did was relay traffic. It is also common not to add any mail relay or forwarder to a Windows domain—again because it will most likely be attempted for an exploit in the future.

Web Servers

Web servers are the most common form of DMZ-based hosts today. Other services are needed, such as DNS and e-mail, but if you really think about it, the main reason DMZs even exist is due to the public Internet Web surfer feeding frenzy. Almost every company in business in the world now has a publicly accessible Web site, which means that just about every company worldwide either has an Internet presence or is looking to have one. Thanks to all these personal invitations to companies' corporate networks, it is imperative that you also think out your security plan completely or your network could be exploited.

External Web Server

Organizations frequently have data they want to publish to the external network via a Web server. Again, to allow direct access to the Web server via the Internet while the server is sitting in your private and protected LAN would be suicide. For that reason, allow an external Web server to be placed on the DMZ. This way you can allow all your visitors to come directly to your IIS server and not have them exploit that server only to find ways to get to other systems. If the IIS server is external on the DMZ, you can at least have some defense against it if it is compromised in any way.

Internal Web Server

Your internal Web server is nothing more than an intranet you set up for HTTP and other Web-based access for use within the LAN and not for public access. Your internal Web server will be secure from the Internet only if you never connect it to the Internet. Once you do, you move the server out to the DMZ and it becomes an external Web server.

Designing Windows 2000 DNS in the DMZ

The last (and most common) services to see on the DMZ both internally and externally are the DNS servers for your organization. If you are using DNS to resolve your company's IP address to easy-to-remember names, this section is for you. DNS services are now more than ever the most common service used for name resolution. Because of DNS's growing use, it is important that when you plan your Windows 2000 network, you are able to design the Internet namespace and the external namespace for the organization. You can also set up your own primary servers in the DMZ, or you can forward requests to others.

Figure 2.22 shows both solutions at work. For one, you can set up an internal namespace called PRIVATEDNS.NET. This is the company's Windows 2000 DNS solution that the entire Active Directory depends on. We do not want to expose that to the Internet if we don't have to. Now we can put a forwarder on the DNS server that resides in the DMZ. This is called the *external DNS server*, which will be explained shortly. The last scenario is to host your own public DNS servers. That means that even more traffic will come to your site, since others can use your DNS servers as well. If you opt to do this, make certain that you secure your solution perfectly.

Figure 2.22 Examining DNS in the DMZ

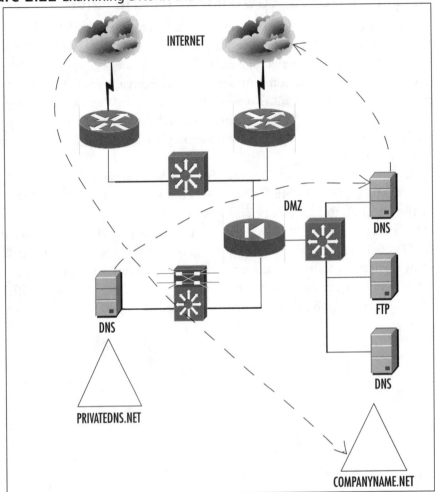

External DNS Server

The external DNS server resides in the DMZ and is for public use. The only information that should be on the external DNS server is the information that needs to be advertised to Internet clients—nothing more. You can use a Windows 2000 server, but it is not uncommon to see Linux on the DMZ doing DNS forwarding. Not one piece of internal DNS information should be kept on this system. The internal DNS server is unable to communicate directly with the external network, because it will be configured to send queries and receive the responses via the external DNS server. You have to ensure that DNS UDP connections are allowed through the firewall to the external DNS server or your solution might not work.

Engineering Windows 2000 Traffic in the DMZ

Once you have finalized the DMZ network segment design and placed your systems where they need to be (and understand why they need to be there), you have to consider traffic and applications flows, ACLs, and filtering. In this section of the chapter we review the concepts you need to allow for the proper traffic to flow where it is needed to and from the DMZ segment.

Traffic engineering can be tough. Think of it like this: You build your DMZ (using whatever firewall product you like—PIX, Nokia, Check Point, ISA 2000) and now you have to let services in and out. Other chapters in this book show you exactly how to do that (with these exact vendor products), but it is inherent that you at least understand the concept of it here and the fundamentals of design. Each chapter of the book grows more detailed as to how to configure each device, but the concepts of design and the initial layout are the most important by far.

First, you need to know what a port is. A port number is a number assigned to a service. You can think of an IP address and a port number as analogous to a street address and an apartment number. If you have ever lived in an apartment, you know that everyone in the apartment complex has the same street address. So what tells the mail carrier where to put everyone's mail? The apartment number does. If it weren't for the apartment number, all organization would end once the mail got to your street address. You would have to search through everyone's mail to find yours. This is the same concept behind IP addresses and port numbers. The port number is used by a particular service. When a request is made, the port number tells the computer which service it wants to talk to. You could say that the port number defines the endpoints of a connection. The format for using port numbers is the IP address followed by a colon and the port number. For example, let's say that we want to connect to the IP address 10.10.10.10 and we want to use the port for HTTP (port 80). The syntax would be 10.10.10.10:80.

There are three categories of port:

- Well-known ports
- Registered ports
- Dynamic/private ports

The Internet Corporation for Assigned Names and Numbers (ICANN) is responsible for managing port numbers. The well-known port numbers range from 0 to 1023. The registered port numbers range from 1024 to 49151. The dynamic and private ports range from 49152 to 65535. Most systems use the well-known port numbers to run system processes or privileged programs. The registered port numbers are not controlled by ICANN. Most of the time they are used with nonsystem processes or nonprivileged programs, such as an ordinary user running a program. Table 2.1 lists the well-known port numbers.

Table 2.1 Well-Known Port Numbers

Port Number	Transport Layer Protocol	Description
7	TCP, UDP	Echo
13	TCP, UDP	Daytime
19	TCP, UDP	Character generator
20	TCP, UDP	File Transfer Protocol (default data)
21	TCP, UDP	File Transfer Protocol (control)
22	TCP, UDP	SSH Remote Login Protocol
23	TCP, UDP	Telnet
25	TCP, UDP	Simple Mail Transfer Protocol (SMTP)
53	TCP, UDP	Domain Name Server (DNS)
67	TCP, UDP	Bootstrap Protocol Server
68	TCP, UDP	Bootstrap Protocol Client
69	TCP, UDP	Trivial File Transfer Protocol (TFTP)
79	TCP, UDP	Finger
80	TCP, UDP	World Wide Web HTTP
88	TCP, UDP	Kerberos
110	TCP, UDP	Post Office Protocol Version 3 (POP 3)
118	TCP, UDP	SQL Services
119	TCP, UDP	Network News Transfer Protocol (NNTP)
123	TCP, UDP	Network Time Protocol
137	TCP, UDP	NETBIOS Name Service
138	TCP, UDP	NETBIOS Datagram Service

Continued

Table 2.1 Well-Known Port Numbers

Port Number	Transport Layer Protocol	Description
139	TCP, UDP	NETBIOS Session Service
143	TCP, UDP	Internet Message Access Protocol (IMAP4)
156	TCP, UDP	SQL Service
161	TCP, UDP	SNMP
162	TCP, UDP	SNMPTRAP
179	TCP, UDP	Border Gateway Protocol
194	TCP, UDP	Internet Relay Chat Protocol
213	TCP, UDP	IPX
369	TCP, UDP	Rpc2portmap
389	TCP, UDP	Lightweight Directory Access Protocol (LDAP)
401	TCP, UDP	Uninterruptible Power Supply (UPS)
443	TCP, UDP	HTTP over TLS/SSL (HTTPS)
445	TCP, UDP	Microsoft-DS
464	TCP, UDP	Kpasswd
500	TCP, UDP	Isakmp
513	TCP	Remote login via Telnet (login)
514	UDP	Syslog
530	TCP, UDP	Rpc
563	TCP, UDP	NNTP over TLS/SSL (NNTPS)
568	TCP, UDP	Microsoft shuttle
569	TCP, UDP	Microsoft rome
593	TCP, UDP	HTTP RPC Ep map
631	TCP, UDP	Internet Printing Protocol (IPP)
636	TCP, UDP	LDAP over TLS/SSL (LDAPS)
637	TCP, UDP	Lanserver
689	TCP, UDP	NMAP

Continued

www.syngress.com

Table 2.1 Well-Known Port Numbers

Port Number	Transport Layer Protocol	Description
691	TCP, UDP	MS Exchange Routing
749	TCP, UDP	Kerberos administration
750	TCP, UDP	Kerberos version iv

What is so important about these ports is that when you get to later chapters of this book, you will have to come back here to get the numbers to plug into the ACLs and filters you create with your firewall of choice. Make sure that you understand the placement of DMZ hosts and then what traffic to let through before you attempt to configure your firewall, because the firewall configuration will solely depend on that information (port, service, placement) first! You can't direct traffic if you don't know where to send it and what numbers you need to plug in to get that movement in the first place. Use the following example for all the rest of the examples in future chapters. If you have the network design shown in Figure 2.23, what traffic map would you design?

Figure 2.23 Windows 2000 Traffic in the DMZ

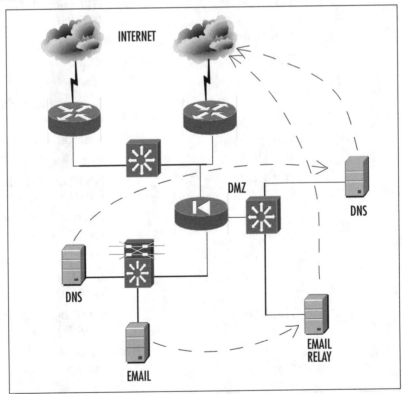

Let's look at this in more detail:

- You have an internal DNS server that needs to communicate with an external DNS server to forward requests.

- You have an external DNS server that needs to communicate with the Internet DNS.

- You have an e-mail server and its e-mail relay to the Internet to consider.

- You have an e-mail relay that needs to send mail to the Internet.

Now that you have looked at the traffic map, you need to configure the rules in the firewall. You will have to use DNS and e-mail ports from Table 2.1. For DNS, you can use port 53, and for e-mail services, you can use SMTP or POP3, which use ports 25 and 110, respectively. Again, there are many more services and many more ports, but if you lay out the map and think about the communication paths, you can easily plug in the numbers and then go to the appropriate chapter in the book to find out how to configure the necessary rules, filters, and ACLs.

Assessing Network Data Visibility Risks

Now that you have engineered the traffic to flow in and out of your network, what is really the risk of others seeing this traffic? Tools to eavesdrop on traffic (you can see them in Chapter 14, which is aptly named "Hacking the DMZ") are freely available on the Internet and can cause you much pain when you try to build a Windows 2000 DMZ. If you have NetBIOS traffic traversing your network, a network sniffer is all someone needs to learn, map, and disable your network. We won't spend too much time on this topic because it's really the concept you have to get down here. You need to think about the problems you could encounter while building your DMZ if you do let certain traffic traverse your network and over the Internet. For this reason, Microsoft always tells you to disable file and print sharing on your DMZ hosts, your home PC connected to the Internet—even your servers on your trusted network that are not needed as file or print servers. Yes, it's that serious, and reading through Chapter 14 will help you to realize that.

Configuring & Implementing…

Disable NetBIOS and SMB!

Disabling NetBIOS on servers in untrusted networks (or anywhere in general) is always a good idea. Just remember to test before you do, in case an application you are using is dependent on that service. Other than that, disable away. NetBIOS is by far the poorest form of secure name resolution you can find. Always use DNS if you can, but since your Windows networks are sure to have some legacy systems that are anything predating Windows 2000, you are sure to need NetBIOS. Always disable NetBIOS if it's not needed on your DMZ hosts or they will be exploited, without question. Servers in the perimeter network should have all unnecessary protocols disabled, including NetBIOS and server message block (SMB). These protocols should both be disabled to counter the threat of user enumeration. You can think of user enumeration as a form of information gathering so that the attacker can find other ways to attack from the information he or she has gathered. This information includes domain and trust details, shares, user information, groups and user rights, and even Registry information. You will want to disable NetBIOS whenever possible. To do this from a firewall, you can block all communication using the following ports:

- UDP/137 (NetBIOS name service)
- UDP/138 (NetBIOS datagram service)
- TCP/139 (NetBIOS session service)

SMB uses the following ports:

- TCP/139
- TCP/445

To disable these on a host, you can remove File and Printer Sharing for Microsoft Networks and Client for Microsoft Networks using the **Transmission Control Protocol/Internet Protocol (TCP/IP) Properties** dialog box in your **Local Area Connection** properties. Once you have done that, there is one more option. This is the easy way to disable SMB:

1. Open the **Device Manager** (you can get to it from the **Control Panel** of the Computer Management Console).

2. Once you open Device Manager (in Computer Management view, as shown in Figure 2.24), you can then show the hidden devices

(where the driver is) by right-clicking the **Device Manager** icon and selecting **View** and then **Show Hidden Devices**.

3. Expand the **Non-Plug and Play Drivers**.

4. Right-click **NetBIOS over Tcpip**, and then click **Disable**. Once this is done, you will disable the SMB direct host listener on TCP/445 and UDP 445.

5. Close the Computer Management console to finish.

Figure 2.24 Disabling NetBIOS over TCPIP

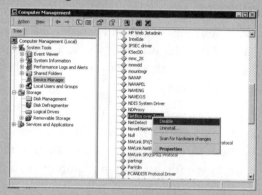

In sum, this shows you how to engineer traffic on a Windows 2000 network. You need to know how to direct traffic, as well as how to enable and disable it. A hacker can research just as easily as you can, and this is what they are looking for—the exploits you have forgotten about and left wide open.

Not all traffic engineering does good, so you need to test your efforts before going live into production. You could disable a service or driver only to find out an application that depended on it no longer functions properly. When you disable the NetBIOS over TCP/IP driver, for instance, you have effectively disabled the nbt.sys driver. This driver could be used by another application. Just be careful and test.

Until now we have looked at how to build a Windows 2000 DMZ. We have covered the network hardware needs and basic layout, the devices that will populate the DMZ, the types of systems you need to place on your DMZ, and lastly, the engineering of traffic through the DMZ. The last thing you need to know is the population of systems in the DMZ such as Windows 2000 hosts, DNS, and others. Again, this is covered in detail in Chapter 13.

Windows 2000 DMZ Design Planning List

In order for you to properly plan your Windows 2000 DMZ, follow these checklists to get yourself from start to finish. These are by no means all-inclusive lists, but they should serve you well in getting started, getting the foundation of what is needed up and running. Then, if necessary, you can populate the list with more items you need or want.

To successfully start your Windows 2000 DMZ implementation, begin with our initial discussion on planning: network engineering, systems engineering, and security analysis.

- **Network engineering**

  - First, start with your vision. You must have current network topology maps handy and a map of what it is you plan to do. There are many examples through this chapter and this book on how to make a proper topology map for your organization.

  - After the planning stage, you can either start to work on a prototype (or pilot) or go live. No matter what you decide, you should do some testing or visit a location (or another business) to analyze their Windows 2000 DMZ solution to see if your scaling requirements are right.

  - Don't undercut yourself. If you need to scale up or out, plan that in now, so you can get a jump on future requirements.

  - Get the devices you need, lay them out, test them, and then implement them into the design.

  - Make certain that you harden your network engineering devices. They will be exposed to the Internet and are just as vulnerable to attack as your Web or DNS servers.

- **Systems engineering**

  - Plan the placement (logically and physically) of your DMZ hosts. Since you are using Windows 2000, you can look at IIS for a Web and FTP server as well as an SMTP relay, Windows 2000 DNS services, Exchange 2000, ISA Server, and so on.

  - Once you plan your systems, you need to engineer the communications between devices in the DMZ and behind it.

  - Once you have the planned communications, you can start implementation.

- **Bastion hosts installation and lockdown**

    - As you populate the DMZ with hosts to provide services, you need to harden them.

    - Harden the base Windows 2000 Operating system first. (You'll find details in Chapter 13.)

    - Harden each individual service you implement. (You'll find details in Chapter 13 and the bonus Appendix A available online.)

- **Security analysis**

    - Run tests on your Windows DMZ to ensure that all devices are locked down, hardened, secure, and ready to provide services to the public Internet.

    - Test all connections and all devices, and use a plethora of tools to test different attacks.

    - Run service packs, hotfixes, and anything else to test, harden, secure, and tighten up the perimeter—or your network could be exploited. You can refer to Chapter 14 to learn how to hack the DMZ and test it.

Summary

Although this is only the second chapter in the book, you should start to see many concepts coming together. The demilitarized zone, or DMZ, is probably the smallest, most difficult to design and engineer segment on your network. In this chapter in particular, you should have acquired the foundation to lay out and build a Windows 2000-based DMZ. Again, it's not merely knowing Windows 2000, Cisco, or any other vendor's products that will get you through the design and implementation of a Windows 2000 DMZ, but all this knowledge put together underlies a simple set of concepts: Design the network, design the systems, and then test them all for security. We looked at that process in great detail in this chapter. You learned how to lay out all the hardware you need, set up a plan and a design with a topology map, plan where the systems will be placed—in front of, behind, and within the DMZ segment formed by the firewall you use. Other chapters focus on more granular aspects such as bastion hosts, hardening, testing, and so on, but this chapter should have laid out the groundwork for your design.

When considering Windows 2000 (or any other vendors OS), you need to consider system placement and traffic engineering. You need to know exactly what ports and services that OS needs to rely on to communicate and function properly. Although Windows 2000 is a secure operating system (Windows Server 2003 is even more secure), it is only as secure as you can make it. Therefore, it's very important that you followed this chapter closely since everything you learned here will be used in the DMZ of your network. The DMZ is the segment exposed to the Internet, so it is critical that you understand the concepts not only in this chapter but in this entire book. We can't stress it enough: If you place Windows 2000 on the DMZ, pay close attention to hardening techniques and proper traffic flows, or you could be exploited.

In this chapter we covered how you can design a Windows 2000-based network solution that will work within and around the DMZ segment. It's important to know this as a security administrator or engineer because the DMZ can be very complex to work with and around. In this chapter you learned how to use your Windows systems within the DMZ design.

Lastly, this chapter focused not on learning Windows 2000 security concepts but how to design the proper DMZ layout. In other chapters you will learn the granular details needed to implement security, harden systems, and test those systems to ensure that they were secured properly.

This chapter should have served as a rough design document to help you place your Windows 2000 systems and the services they run within the DMZ. It is common for many administrators to wonder how to place their systems within the DMZ, especially when they are Web or FTP servers facing the Internet and publicly accessible. As we mentioned in the chapter, it can be nerve shattering, especially with all the publicity Microsoft has gotten in the past as being an insecure system with many bugs, unchecked buffers, and a plethora of other problems resulting in becoming the biggest target seen on the Internet today. This chapter should help you to remedy those fears by providing you with the answers and solutions you need to not only place the systems in and around the DMZ but also to protect them.

Solutions Fast Track

Introducing Windows 2000 DMZ Security

☑ Before we look at the fundamentals of securing the DMZ segment and its hosts, we need a general idea of what it's going to look like on a map. All good network designers plan the topology (hopefully with a topology map) and figure out traffic flows, logical addressing, and any other factors that would affect the systems operating as advertised. If you choose not to follow this recommendation, you could find yourself very discouraged when the network does not function properly and systems cannot be accessed because of a simple (or complex) mistake you made in the design.

☑ The DMZ segment can be one of the most complicated segments on the network to design and implement. When you add Windows 2000 to the mix, you not only have to be an expert in security but also network engineering as well as Windows 2000 system design and the services to be made available. In sum, make sure you plan your implementation very closely.

☑ The three main sections you need to consider when building your Windows 2000 DMZ are network engineering, systems engineering, and security analysis.

☑ Your first step in designing a Windows 2000-based DMZ is to select all the networking hardware you will need. You must assess your needs, trying to figure out what the hardware infrastructure will cost your company. You need to look at needs first. When you are looking at the networking end of it, you should ask yourself, "What devices will I need, and how should I scale them?" Exploring these questions will bring about answers based on networking gear and costs.

☑ When planning your infrastructure, you always need to ensure that you plan the proper equipment list, no matter what vendor you pick. Basically, if you are purchasing this much equipment, presales support might be in order. Ask you vendor to show you user limits per device (how many users can use this device without affecting its performance simultaneously) as well as the type of traffic you will be pumping through it. Often, the vendor can help you design your network so that you don't fall short on what you need or do not go overkill where you might not need the extra power.

☑ When you want to populate the DMZ with Windows 2000 hosts, you need to think about access to and from the DMZ and the services that are needed. The reason behind this initial thought is that your end users, customers, potential customers, and outsiders will be able to utilize resources needed and only those needed resources—nothing more, nothing less. To start the engineering process, you have to first make certain that you have these answers! What do you need? You should make sure that users can obtain the information that they need about your company without accessing the internal network and only by accessing the DMZ or accessing the Internal network safely if you chose not to implement a DMZ. If you can, it's always better to segment Internet-based resources via the DMZ for an added level of safety. Now that you know your network layout, you have to think about other access to and from the DMZ.

☑ Your secret, protected, confidential, and proprietary information should be stored behind your firewall and DMZ on your internal network. Servers on the DMZ shouldn't contain sensitive trade secrets, source code, or proprietary information, or anything that can be used against you or your company—or be used to exploit or hack your systems. (There's more on DMZ hacking techniques in Chapter 14.) A breach of your DMZ servers should at worst create an annoyance in the form of downtime while you recover from the security breach.

☑ A Web server that holds public information is a common example of a DMZ host. This can be IIS (since we are discussing Microsoft technologies in this chapter) or any other publicly accessible Web server. You can also think of FTP services, NNTP services, and other Web-based services to be accessed and utilized.

☑ Electronic commerce-based solutions always wind up on the DMZ. This is the front end of an e-commerce transaction server through which orders are placed. Keep the back end, where you store client information, behind the firewall. You want to design this properly because if you don't, you could potentially compromise your entire client database (or personal and private data) if it's exploited.

☑ A mail server that relays outside mail to the inside will be a highly utilized solution in the DMZ, especially since spam and other e-mail exploits are common DMZ host-based targets for attacks.

☑ VPN solutions are prevalent in the DMZ. Other than the site-to-site VPNs we already learned about, you also have VPN solutions in which you will have a remote access solution so that clients can attach over the Internet to get to their files and other data needed on the corporate network. This also has to be publicly accessible via the DMZ.

Building a Windows 2000 DMZ

☑ Depending on the model and type of firewall you use, you can in fact have different DMZ segments with different services on each to add even more security to your DMZ segments and hosts. This might be necessary if you plan to segment your DMZ hosts even further. This would mean that you could place an IIS load-balanced cluster on one DMZ and an e-mail relay on another.

☑ Your Windows 2000 solution revolving around the DMZ needs to allow for Internet access. The Internet connection should be able to handle the bandwidth needs of the site. If you are using this Internet connection as your LANs Internet access for surfing and e-mail and you decide to use it for a VPN as well, you need to analyze your requirements first.

☑ A traffic flow analysis can be done to ascertain the needed requirements (for WAN links, Internet connections, and so on) quite quickly, but you need to know how to do the analysis and have the tools to do so. If you do not, it is in your best interests to work with an outside vendor that does have the tools and experience to do so. Not doing so will almost always result in bad performance and increased cost later when you need to reprovision the lines to a higher bandwidth.

☑ Sometimes (if the size and complexity of the network dictate) you'll need a router on each leg of the firewall. At times, you will get requests to either add security to the segment you are working on or add more and more devices to it, where you might need to either route or direct traffic. Many firewalls will not route like a router; in other words, a typical firewall will route the RIPv1 protocol whereas a router will route IS-IS, OSPF, EIGRP, RIP, and so on. A router does just that—it routes. A firewall can in fact route if it's configured to do so, but often, depending on how paranoid you are, you might decide to keep these services dependent on the device in which they sit. Keep your devices dedicated to what they do best when you can afford to do so and can use the added security.

☑ Too often, administrators mistake where to put DNS and WINS servers when working with the DMZ. Name resolution in the DMZ only matters if you in fact need it.

☑ Know how to place an e-mail server on the DMZ. There are really only two ways to place an e-mail server easily within a DMZ. For one, you can place the e-mail server (only one for this example) in the private network. The firewall in front of the e-mail server would be responsible for taking all requests in and out of the network and responsible for securing the traffic to the e-mail server. Due to the design of the server, it made the relaying of outbound Internet-based e-mail the responsibility of the e-mail server—only one single server. The question is then, however, "Why would we want to expose our e-mail server to the public Internet? What if there was a way to attack the e-mail server directly through the firewall?"

☑ It is common to simply add another e-mail server to the DMZ segment and use this as a relay to and from the protected e-mail server in the private network. The server now becomes an e-mail relay, and it will relay the mail to and from the Internet and to and from the mail server. If mail relays (IIS has an SMTP service that can be used as a relay) are compromised, you can simply reinstall the server from scratch and not lose a thing because all the server did was relay traffic. It is also common to not add any mail relay or forwarder to a Windows domain—again, because it will most likely be attempted for an exploit in the future.

☑ Web servers are the most common form of DMZ-based hosts today. Other services are needed, such as DNS and e-mail, but if you really think about it, the main reason DMZs even exist is because of the public Internet Web surfer feeding frenzy. Almost every company in the world now has a publicly accessible Web site, which means that just about every company worldwide either has an Internet presence or is looking to have one. Because of all these personal invitations to their corporate networks, it is imperative that you also think out your security completely or your network could be exploited.

☑ Organizations frequently have data they want to publish to the external network via a Web server. To allow direct access to the Web server via the Internet while the server is sitting in your private and protected LAN would be suicide. For that reason, we allow an external Web server to be placed on the DMZ. This way, you can allow all your visitors to come directly to your IIS server and not have them exploit that server only to find ways to get to other systems. If the IIS server is external on the DMZ, you can at least have some defense against it if it is compromised in any way.

☑ The last (and very common) services to see on the DMZ both internally and externally are the DNS servers for your organization. DNS services are now more than ever the most common service used for name resolution. Because of DNS's growing use, it is important that when you lay out your Windows 2000 network, you are able to design the Internet namespace and the external namespace for the organization.

☑ Once you have finalized the DMZ network segment design and placed your systems where they need to be (and understand why they need to be there), you have to consider traffic and applications flows, ACLs, and filtering.

Windows 2000 DMZ Design Planning List

☑ To successfully start your Windows 2000 DMZ implementation, you need to start with our initial discussion on planning: network engineering, systems engineering, and security analysis.

☑ To properly plan your Windows 2000 DMZ, follow the steps in our checklist to get yourself from start to finish. You can use the list incorporated in the end of this chapter to do the planning you need.

Frequently Asked Questions

The following Frequently Asked Questions, answered by the authors of this book, are designed to both measure your understanding of the concepts presented in this chapter and to assist you with real-life implementation of these concepts. To have your questions about this chapter answered by the author, browse to **www.syngress.com/solutions** and click on the **"Ask the Author"** form. You will also gain access to thousands of other FAQs at ITFAQnet.com.

Q: I would like to protect my Windows 2000 DMZ. What do hackers use to test, check, and penetrate my DMZ?

A: Tools that allow people to eavesdrop on traffic are freely available on the Internet and can cause you much pain when you're trying to build a Windows 2000 DMZ. If you have NetBIOS traffic traversing your network, a network sniffer is all someone needs to learn, map, and disable your network. You need to think about the problems you could encounter while building your DMZ if you do let certain traffic traverse your network and over the Internet.

Q: I need to look at allowing specific traffic through my firewall, and I am unsure who handles such assignments. Where should I look for this information?

A: The Internet Corporation for Assigned Names and Numbers (ICANN) is responsible for managing port numbers. The well-known port numbers range from 0 to 1023. The registered port numbers range from 1024 to 49151. The dynamic and private ports range from 49152 to 65535. Most systems use the well-known port numbers to run system processes or privileged programs. The registered port numbers are not controlled by ICANN. Most of the time they are used with nonsystem processes or nonprivileged programs, such as an ordinary user running a program. Visit www.iana.org for more information.

Q: What is the most common form of DMZ-based system in use today, and what is commonly seen on DMZs big or small?

A: Web servers are the most common form of DMZ-based hosts today. Other services are needed, such as DNS and e-mail, but if you really think about it, the main reason DMZs even exist is because of the public Internet Web surfer feeding frenzy. Because of all these personal invitations to companies' corporate networks, it is imperative that you also think out security completely or your network could be exploited.

Q: I am planning out a new DMZ infrastructure. I am unsure about the hardware I need or what vendor to select. What should I do to start my plan?

A: When planning your infrastructure, you always need to ensure that you plan for the proper equipment, no matter what vendor you pick. Basically, if you are purchasing that much equipment, presales support could be in order. Ask your vendor to show you user limits per device (how many users can use this device without affecting its performance simultaneously) as well as what type of traffic you will be pumping through it. Many times, the vendor can help you to design your network so that you don't fall short on what you need or do not go overkill where you may not need the extra power.

Q: I want to implement a DMZ, but I am hearing from management that there might be a future need for an e-commerce site. How does this affect my design now? Should I plan for this functionality, even though I do not know exactly when it might happen?

A: If there is a need to eventually set up a load-balanced solution with multiple IIS servers and a possible backend database cluster, you should plan for it in the design stages of the initial DMZ setup so that you don't have to repurchase new gear for it later. You should also see if this can be amended into the project plan by the stake-holders and the project manager so that if possible, the need can be finalized and you can scale your equipment for it before, not after the fact. Always get a needs analysis and a future needs analysis done early in the design phase of the project so that you know what you might want to incorporate in the design (such as load balancing). If e-commerce is the need, this tells you that you need to scale the firewall, switches, and all other infrastructure to meet the needs for a possible e-commerce site, a load-balanced cluster, and so on.

Q: Why would I need a site-to-site VPN, and how does it affect my Windows 2000 DMZ design?

A: If there is a need to add more bandwidth and site-to-site VPN services off the external Internet routers, you should at least be familiar with the design and why you are implementing it. For one, the VPN used in this manner replaces your current Frame Relay or other WAN technologies, or if this is a new installation, you can forego using these technologies in the first place. All the VPN does is encrypt your data over a public or private medium so that you can have the private-line feeling without the private-line price premium. These are popping up left and right as companies try to save money, so it is important that you know how to design them into your DMZ. You should also ensure that you purchase models either with crypto cards (to use IPSec for VPNs) installed or upgradeable to them

Q: When I plan my Internet connection, I am unsure as to what type of switch I need behind the external router, or if I even need a switch at all. Can't I just use a crossover cable to go from the router port to the firewall port?

A: If you need to scale up the number of connections to the Internet, such as the need for VPN services, intrusion detection systems, honey pots, other routers and so on, or you have other services that will be added sooner rather than later, you might need to put a switch in between the firewall and the external router. You might need more port availability on the switch so if you can get a switch, you have set yourself up to scale out in the future if needed. If this need is not there, you can skip this implementation and simply use a patch or crossover cable to connect your systems instead.

## Chapter 3

Sun Solaris
DMZ Design

Solutions in this chapter:

- **Placement of Servers**

- **The Firewall Ruleset**

- **System Design**

- **Implementation: The Quick, Dirty Details**

- **Hardening Checklist for DMZ Servers and Solaris**

- ☑ **Summary**
- ☑ **Solutions Fast Track**
- ☑ **Frequently Asked Questions**

Introduction

Solaris is a commercial UNIX operating system distributed by Sun Microsystems. The combination of Sun hardware and software makes systems using Solaris some of the best-performing servers in the world. However, Solaris can be used as more than just an ancillary of services such as database, Web, and mail. With roots in the Berkeley Software Distribution (BSD) UNIX world, Solaris is well equipped to perform as a DMZ server.

In this chapter, we discuss the use of Sun hardware and Solaris as a DMZ system. We begin with a discussion of the placement of servers in configurations to make the most of resources. We also discuss the use of firewall rules and how they may be implemented to provide security to the private and public network segments of a DMZ implementation.

After discussing the use of Solaris as a DMZ system, we focus on the Solaris system itself. The object of this discussion is examining the factors in creating a secure system to act as the DMZ server. Of the design, implementation, and maintenance phases common to every server, we focus on the design and implementation phases. In the discussion of these phases, we outline specific methods that can be applied to systems to create a secure design as well as maintain the integrity of the system during the implementation. Let's begin with a discussion of the placement of Solaris DMZ servers.

Placement of Servers

We can draw a parallel between the placement of a Solaris system that will provide DMZ services and the purchase of real estate with the mantra "location, location, location." Just as you do not want to purchase real estate that was previously a dump, you don't want to put the DMZ server in a location on the network that is a metaphoric trash heap, cluttered with the equivalent of network garbage. Placing the system that will function as the DMZ server at a position in the network that is both efficient and secure is of the utmost importance.

Placing the system on the DMZ usually depends on network requirements. Some network configurations, such as smaller networks, may place the DMZ server directly behind the router, as demonstrated in Figure 3.1.

Figure 3.1 Basic Implementation of a Solaris DMZ Server in a Small Network

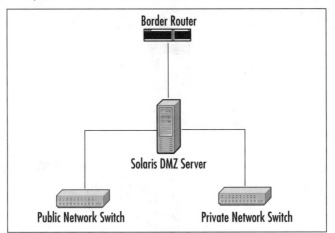

Although this is not the most ideal configuration because it does not permit easy scaling of network resources or easy integration high availability, this design should be sufficient for smaller networks. We can see from the diagram that network traffic first enters via the network router and next goes directly to the DMZ server.

From there, traffic proceeds to its next hop in the network infrastructure, which in this case is a switch on the public or on the private network. We can see that the router has a valid routable address on both interfaces. The DMZ server has a valid address on two interfaces, and on one interface it has a private network address. Traffic coming from and going to the private interface is translated using Network Address Translation (NAT).

In this type of configuration, the DMZ server is capable of handling a couple networks. However, when traffic grows to the point that the DMZ server can no longer handle the load, the network needs to be redesigned in order to scale outward to handle the additional traffic.

In addition, this configuration makes it difficult to monitor the network outside the DMZ server with network intrusion detection (IDS) tools. However, for small offices or businesses, this configuration is a workable solution.

In Figure 3.2, we see a configuration that is a little more advanced and scalable. When traffic enters the network, it crosses the border router. It then immediately goes to a switch, where it is passed to the DMZ server. From the DMZ server, it proceeds to the switch on the public network or the switch on the private network.

Figure 3.2 Advanced Implementation of a Solaris DMZ Server with External Switches and NIDS

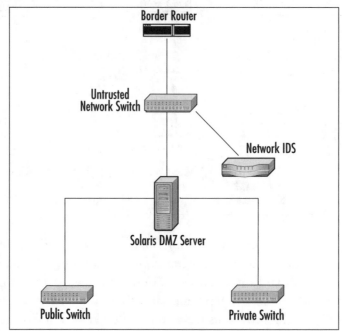

We should discuss a few noteworthy things in this configuration. First, we have a switch immediately behind the router. This is an important feature in the design because as the network grows, we may potentially add address space. In doing so, we could decide to add this network space to a different DMZ altogether due to business requirements. Placing a switch immediately behind the router gives us the ability to expand or contract the network as necessary. If a switch is not used, we could connect, via a patch or crossover cable, the border router directly to the Solaris system.

Also worth noting in this configuration is the IDS monitoring the network outside the DMZ. Note that it is connected only to the network outside the DMZ and has no other access. The host is connected to the outside network to provide monitoring of attempted attacks. Information gathered from this sensor could be crucial in identifying attacked and/or compromised hosts or, in most cases, a passive scan on the DMZ. Furthermore, this system has no other network access because it is in an unprotected location and could potentially be the victim of attack itself. This situation can be mitigated through access controls on the border router and DMZ systems, though the possibility will always exist due to the location of the system.

NOTE

Border router and switch security is covered in granular detail in Chapter 9.

We must also consider the need for high availability. In Figure 3.3, we have a configuration that differs slightly from the one shown in Figure 3.2.

Figure 3.3 Solaris DMZ Servers in a Conceptual Highly Available Configuration

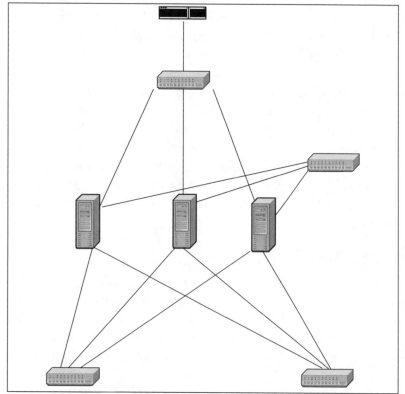

This figure contains many features similar to those in Figure 3.2. However, what is different is that rather than one DMZ system connected to the external network switch, three DMZs are connected to the external network switch. Additionally, there are several connections from these DMZ systems to the same public and private networks. We also see a connection between the DMZ systems.

This configuration shows a DMZ server cluster. All systems in the cluster maintain an active connection to other systems in the cluster via the hub. The only system in the cluster that maintains active connections outside the failover information hub is the active DMZ system. When the primary DMZ system fails, it deactivates (or is deactivated) via information over the failover communication network, and the next system in the cluster brings up its network interfaces to perform the job of the primary DMZ server.

These general network component configurations enhance network security. However, this is only part of the design. Equally important is the firewall ruleset, which we discuss in the next section.

The Firewall Ruleset

The firewall ruleset dictates the exact types of network activity permitted by the DMZ server. As the implementers of a DMZ system, we are responsible for the first line of security of both the public and private networks. This important task cannot be taken lightly.

In this section, we focus more on the firewall rulesets as they relate to the various requirements of the DMZ host. In each segment of the network handled by the DMZ server, we have a different set of requirements and expectations. We start with the private network rules, discussing the ideal private network firewall policy.

Following our discussion of the private network segment, we focus on the public network requirements and firewall ruleset. Some of the inherent risks of public network access are also outlined. We end our discussion of firewall rulesets with a brief examination of requirements for local host security.

The Private Network Rules

Because the security of both the public and private networks depends on a secure DMZ server, the firewall ruleset must be well conceived and sufficiently secure. However, although the firewall ruleset must be secure enough to prevent attack and compromise, it is equally important that the network at least be usable. Our quest to create a secure network should not necessitate jackboots as work footwear and an iron fist as a policy enforcement tool.

Therefore, we must evaluate the services a user needs to meet business requirements and balance our firewall policy against restricting the services a user does not need. It is often easier to inventory the services users need than the services they don't need. Though business networks are typically infinitely complex, let's keep it simple and say that our users need only Web, mail, and domain name service (DNS) access.

Configuring & Implementing...

DMZs and Internet Chat Clients

Internet chat clients have become a popular means of communication, and business is no exception to the trend. Often it is more productive and easier for coworkers to open an instant message (IM) to communicate rather than to perform a context switch by turning away from the computer and picking up the phone or physically leaving the workspace to consult with a colleague.

However, Internet chat clients are the bane of DMZ security. Many such clients piggyback communication on top of other protocols to circumvent filtering or even scan the firewall to determine how to reach the outside. Due to problems in these clients, it is possible for a remote user to exploit an issue that would result in a client-side attack. The attacker could gain access to the user's system with the privileges of the user and thus initiate a connection to the outside world that allows the attacker access.

It is difficult to prevent the use of these clients at the DMZ level, and it might be better to approach this issue with a security policy.

In Figure 3.4, we show a network design with a router at the top of the network. From the router, we go to a switch, then to the DMZ server. The DMZ server connects to switches on both the public and private networks as well. On the private network, we see a mail server. On the public network, we see a mail server, a DNS server, and a Web proxy server.

Figure 3.4 A Solaris DMZ Server with Hosts on the Public and Private Networks

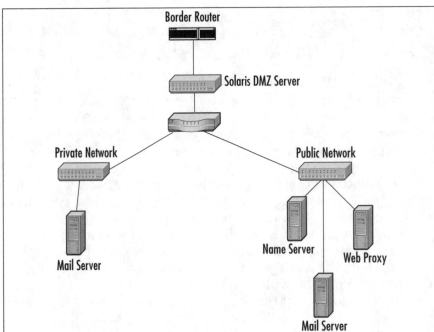

Even though users do not need access to the mail server outside the private network, the mail server on the private network needs the ability to access mail outside the network. The most secure way to do this is to allow the internal mail server to contact the mail server in the DMZ for mail, rather than allowing the mail server in the DMZ to indiscriminately send traffic through the firewall on port 25 to the internal mail server. This can be done using a tool such as rsync over SSH. We want the internal mail server to perform this task as a stateful action to prevent the piggybacking of traffic on the connection.

In terms of Web access, giving users unfettered access to the Web is, at the least, risky. Wise network design involves using a proxy server to filter potentially malicious Web content. However, we do not want to keep this proxy server in a location where it could pose a risk to the security of the private network. Therefore, we assume that the proxy server is in the DMZ.

To maintain the security of the private network, we want to place a firewall rule entry for the proxy server. This rule maintains the state of outgoing user connections to the proxy server, like that of the mail server, except this rule goes to the proxy server. Once these two rules are configured, we fall to our last rule in the ruleset, which expressly denies any other incoming or outgoing traffic.

Finally, we must take into consideration the domain name service. We use the domain name server on the public network to provide this service to users. The firewall rule set for the private network permits the query of the name server from the private network. We see an example of this configuration in Figure 3.5.

Figure 3.5 An Example of Rules Implemented on the Solaris DMZ Server for Private Network Traffic

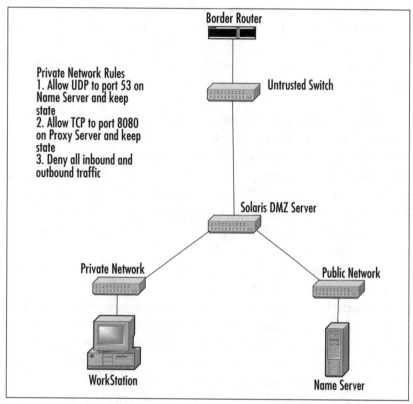

Now that we have a secure configuration for our private network, let's examine our public network configuration.

The Public Network Rules

Requirements for the public network often differ significantly from those for the private network. The public network usually provides a number of services available to the public Internet and some for private network users as well. The biggest consideration here is that the public network also requires accessibility by external users, which increases the exposure to potential attacks.

Public networks are conceptually much like private networks. They require giving users the ability to access services and should limit users' ability to deviate outside of accessing the allowed service set. In the previous section, the services we discussed were mail, Web, and name service. Let's assume that these services are also required on the public network.

In terms of Web service, we have already established that users of the private network will use a proxy server to access outside content. The proxy server needs access outside the public network, so we create a rule that maintains state, allowing access from the proxy server to networks outside the public network. The rule enforces the policy that the proxy server process may connect to any system on any port and must maintain state. No outside server is permitted to connect directly to the proxy server or the proxy server process.

The mail server on the public network requires different configuration. SMTP is a two-way protocol that requires the ability of the mail server to connect to outside mail servers as well as receive connections from outside mail servers. In the previously described private network configuration, the mail server on the private network will likely forward mail to the public mail server. From the public mail server, mail will then be sent to the appropriate receiving server. The public rule set should be configured to allow both incoming and outgoing connections that maintain state to the mail server process on the public mail server.

Finally, we must configure the public firewall ruleset for the domain name server. In the previous section, we stated that the name server would accept resolution requests from hosts on the private network. For the public network, we must alter this ability a bit. On the public network, the name server should only accept replies from other name servers. This name server should not be authoritative for the domain and should not otherwise accept resolution requests from users outside the public or private networks. Domain name service is inherently insecure. Although the only means to fix domain name service is a complete revision of the protocol itself, this configuration will at least insulate the service against many attacks. The public firewall rule should permit outbound requests from the domain name service process to any host on port 53 and should only permit responses to requests, if possible. In Figure 3.6, we see a manifest of firewall rules applied to the public network.

NOTE

Hardening tips, tricks, and techniques for bastion hosts located on the public network-based DMZ can be found throughout this book.

Figure 3.6 An Example of Rules Implemented on the DMZ Server
for the Public Network

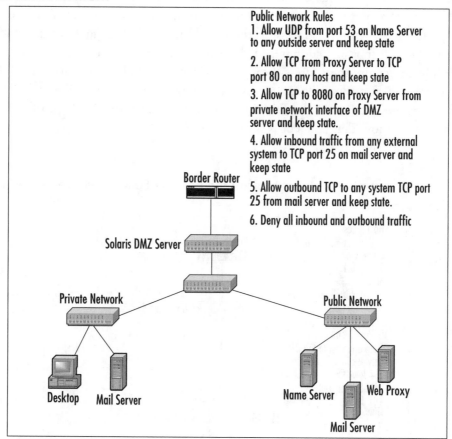

Public Network Rules
1. Allow UDP from port 53 on Name Server to any outside server and keep state

2. Allow TCP from Proxy Server to TCP port 80 on any host and keep state

3. Allow TCP to 8080 on Proxy Server from private network interface of DMZ server and keep state.

4. Allow inbound traffic from any external system to TCP port 25 on mail server and keep state

5. Allow outbound TCP to any system TCP port 25 from mail server and keep state.

6. Deny all inbound and outbound traffic

Now that we have discussed the use of the Solaris DMZ server, let's focus on the server's design and implementation details.

Server Rules

We have addressed the rules for both the public and private networks, but we have not discussed the rules for the host itself. Essentially, the DMZ host is the linchpin of the network, and accordingly, it must be resilient to remote attacks. The ideal implementation keeps the host unreachable, if not basically invisible, from all systems except the system from which remote administration may be performed.

As such, the firewall rule set implementation is pretty easy to conceptualize. Generally, the best policy is to deny all traffic to the host from all systems. Rules to permit traffic to the host for administration should be carefully implemented; we want to permit the administration host access to the administrative service on the DMZ server, but we do not want to give the host total access in the event that it is compromised.

In that same vein, it might be helpful to give hosts from which administrative access will be performed a static IP address on the private network. It is generally not the best idea to use DHCP to assign addresses to these hosts, since this could potentially allow another host to acquire the address through either legitimate or illegitimate means. Furthermore, it makes it possible in the firewall ruleset to specifically allocate access to the administrative interface of the DMZ server from the private IP address of the administration station. This concept is shown in Figure 3.7.

Figure 3.7 An Example of Rules Implemented on the Solaris DMZ Server to Protect the DMZ Server

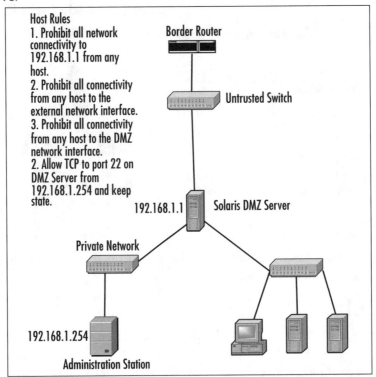

System Design

In the previous sections, we focused on the role of the DMZ server within the network. We discussed DMZ design, firewall rulesets for private networks, and firewall rulesets for public networks. These topics apply to the use of the DMZ server in the network environment; let's now focus our attention more closely to the design details of the server.

The process of deploying any type of server can be broken into three distinct phases:

1. The planning phase

2. The implementation phase

3. The maintenance phase

Let's look at a brief description of each of these phases. The *planning phase* typically involves designing the system. Details such as operating system selection, hardware selection, third-party software selection, operating system software installation details, and the like are decided during this phase. The planning phase is followed by the *implementation phase,* which entails assembling the hardware, securely installing the software according to specifications decided in the planning phase, configuring the host to meet design requirements, and testing the host to ensure stability and reliability. After the implementation phase has been completed, the system is placed into production, thus beginning the *maintenance phase.* During the maintenance phase, the system is continually monitored for signs of intrusion and performance issues. Additionally, the system is regularly patched with all critical and security-specific patches made available by the vendors of the software installed on the DMZ system over the course of its production life.

Our focus in this section is on the planning phase. We discuss two of the more popular firewall software packages available for Solaris. Selection of a firewall software package is important during the planning phase. However, we also want to fill in many of the other blanks that exist, such as the hardware on which the DMZ server will operate, the operating system revision that will be used for the implementation, and similar details.

When a building is built, blueprints specify the minute details, from the measurements and the plumbing to the storage closets. The foundation must first be designed before the structure design can begin. Once the foundation is designed, floor upon floor of the building climb into the sky until the structure design is completed. Then the details such as plumbing, drywall, and paint are applied to the building. Designing a DMZ server, or any server for that matter, is not much different in concept. We start by designing the foundation—selecting hardware. We then select software, which can be likened to designing the structure. Then we complete the details such as service offerings, security features, and configuration details—the proverbial plumbing, drywall, and paint.

Hardware Selection: The Foundation

It goes without saying that the hardware is the base of the entire system. The proper selection of hardware, to use another analogy, can be likened to buying a car. Sure, one can buy a Ferrari if it is affordable. But the problem is, once we marry and have kids, we are now stuck with a two-seat car and have to buy another car to fit our family and lifestyle. Arguably, if you can afford a Ferrari, you are likely to be able to afford a decent family car as well. However, if you are like everybody else working in technology these days, thoughts are not of a nice, new, shiny Volvo but instead a 1974 Pinto station wagon with minimal rust—paint optional.

Hardware selection is a process of picking a system with enough room to handle the current load yet scalable enough to add capacity for growth. This is a particularly important factor to consider in selecting hardware for a DMZ server. The two reasons are growth of network traffic and expansion of administered networks.

Growth of network traffic happens, plain and simple. A company could have an increase in network traffic thanks to increased popularity in the company Web site due to expanded offerings or other reasons, constituting an increased load through the public network segment. In addition, more staff could be hired, all requiring access to the Internet, which could constitute an increase in private network traffic and thus more load on the DMZ server.

A system that handles network traffic needs an abundance of two specific resources: processing power and memory (RAM). It is in RAM that the traffic is momentarily stored, evaluated against the configured firewall ruleset, processed, and either rejected or sent on its merry way to the destination.

Because of the resource needs as well as the likely possibility of growth, you should consider hardware that is capable of being expanded. Minimally, select hardware that is capable of adding RAM as well as faster processors. Even more ideal is a system that is capable of adding RAM as well as processors.

An older example of such as system is the Sun E420R. This rack-mountable system is designed to handle two disks internally, which is sufficient for our purposes. On the mainboard, the system is capable of handling 4GB of RAM and four Ultra-Sparc II processors. A newer example of a system capable of handling our needs is the rack-mountable Sun V480 Server. This system, like the E420R, has the ability to handle two disks internally. It is capable of handling up to four Ultra-Sparc III processors and up to 32GB of RAM.

Another factor to consider is the ability to add network interfaces. Select a system with space on the bus sufficient to add network interfaces. With Sun systems, two types of interface are available. We discuss these interfaces in more detail in the network hardware considerations section that follows.

From this discussion, we can draw a few conclusions about hardware selection. The first and more obvious is that we should select hardware capable of handling the load. Second, we should select hardware that is capable of being scaled to fit our current needs as well as our future needs. The difference between selecting hardware that cannot be expanded selecting and hardware that can be expanded equates to purchasing and building a new DMZ server once a year.

Let's focus in a little more detail on the common DMZ hardware requirements as well as network hardware considerations.

Common DMZ Hardware Requirements

Solaris is predominantly used on Sun or Sun-clone hardware. In some instances, it is also possible to use Intel-based Solaris to create a DMZ server and provide service to a network. However, due to variances in Intel-based hardware and the idiosyncrasies involved with making a working configuration on this platform, we omit Intel Solaris from our discussion. Instead, we focus this discussion entirely on Sun and Sun-clone hardware.

For the purpose of this discussion, Sun hardware is essentially the same across the board, whether you're using a 10BaseT (le) interface on a SparcStation20, a fast-Ethernet Interface on an Ultra80, or Gigabit interface on an Enterprise system. To create the standard three-legged DMZ system configuration, we require at least three network interfaces. These interfaces can be provided in one of two ways. We can use three separate interfaces, such as single Ethernet cards, each using a separate opening on the bus. This would provide us three separate cards, leaving the single point of failure on the system bus rather than in one network component.

Another configuration could be the use of a tool specifically designed for the job. This tool comes in the form of a Sun quad interface card. These are single cards containing, as their name implies, four network interfaces in one card. This gives us the benefit of consolidating all our network components into one slot on the system bus, leaving room for other components such as fiber channel cards or the like.

Of the card types available, the Ethernet cards, used in a set of three, would comprise the *le0, le1,* and *le2* interfaces on the system. The corresponding quad Ethernet card would give us interfaces *qe0* through *qe3*. The Fast Ethernet cards would give us *hme0* through *hme2*, with the quad Fast Ethernet card giving us interfaces *qfe0* through *qfe3*. Currently, quad gigabit Ethernet cards are not available. Therefore, for a gigabit configuration, we would be forced to use three separate cards.

Network Hardware Considerations

We must take a couple issues into consideration when we're planning to use a Solaris system as the DMZ server. The first of these issues is the speed of the cards the system will be using to service the network. The second issue is the hardware on the network to which the DMZ server will provide service.

Addressing the first issue, we must pay particularly close attention to this issue when we're using separate Ethernet interfaces. In this type of configuration, the primary interface on the host will most likely be used as one leg in the DMZ configuration. Therefore, the additional two cards purchased should have similar characteristics.

For example, most Sun SparcStation20 systems were distributed with a stock 10BaseT Ethernet interface. Therefore, wisdom would lead us to purchase additional 10BaseT Ethernet interfaces. This train of thought applies to other systems, such as the Ultra80, which, by default, includes a 10/100 fast Ethernet interface, and so forth.

In light of the first issue, we must also consider the second issue, which is the requirements of our network neighbors. Where possible, we want to use hardware that is at least of the same speed of the systems with which the DMZ server will be communicating. Typically, we want to place a DMZ server in a location between switches or between a router and a switch. In standard configurations, switches and routers have, at a minimum, Fast Ethernet interfaces.

Although it is possible to get by using interfaces of slower speeds than our neighbors, doing so creates a senseless bottleneck in the network. Minimal requirements should be using interfaces of the same speed as our network neighbors. A rule of thumb is to use interfaces that are at least as fast and capable of higher speeds than our network neighbors for future growth in network traffic and changes in network configuration.

Drawing on the previous section about DMZ hardware requirements, we must again consider the type of cards we will use to get the job done. Current ability to perform and future scalability are as important in this scenario as our budget. Getting the job done with separate Ethernet cards could be the cheaper solution, but when the network grows in the future, we will be forced to either replace the system with one that will provide additional slots on the bus for single Ethernet cards or, more realistically, convert the single Ethernet cards to quad Ethernet cards. Consider making this type of hardware a standard selection, because it provides multiple interfaces of the same speed and offers immediate scalability in a standard three-leg DMZ configuration, as one interface on the quad card is free, as well as the primary interface on the host.

Software Selection: The Structure

In the planning phase, the next most critical decisions concerning a DMZ server are the selections of various software packages. These software packages include the operating system that will run on the host as well as the firewall software package and any other third-party software packages that might be required. In using Sun hardware, it is a given that Solaris is the operating system of choice; it provides the best performance on the hardware, has the best symmetric multiprocessing code of operating systems, and provides the best support for Sun hardware.

Solaris is versatile enough to function well as a networking operating system, having its roots in the Berkeley UNIX implementations of UNIX. Like the Berkeley Operating Systems, Solaris, with the appropriate hardware, is capable of acting as a router in its default implementation. Unlike the BSD Operating Systems, Solaris requires additional software to provide advanced features such as packet filtering and stateful inspection.

One common theme across all networks is that no a single common software package is used to implement DMZ and firewall services. The fact of the matter is that although most available software packages offer a plethora of common features, the decision to use one particular type or brand of software often boils down to two factors: in-house expertise and money. The questions "Do we have the expertise to use this software?" and "Can we afford this software?" are the two influences on which selection is ultimately made.

This is not to say that there are not a number of other factors that come into play. One such factor is support. For example, some software might not offer the most cutting-edge features. However, when the price and accessibility of support are factored in, the return on investment significantly increases. Along that same vein, having an expert in-house that is capable of modifying the source code of a free software package to fulfill business requirements and resolve issues with the minimum amount of downtime can far outweigh the initial investment on software and support as well as the turnaround typically required with external support.

Popular Firewall Software Packages

There are many players in the firewall software market. Naming and describing them all could easily turn into a chapter in and of itself. Instead, here we mention two of the most commonly used firewall software packages available for Solaris.

Check Point FireWall-1

Though the statistics are a couple years old, at one point it was estimated that FireWall-1 was deployed on one of every four firewall implementations. FireWall-1's feature set as well as its complexity have made it quite popular with enterprises. The complexity of the software has also led to the creation of several levels of certifications for use of the product itself. This says little about the product but more about its wide use.

Check Point has roughly everything one would expect from a standard firewall package. It uses stateful packet filtering, works with multiple interfaces, and can perform NAT services. Some deployments can be configured to provide failover services in the event of loss of one firewall.

Prior to using FireWall-1 for a DMZ implementation, it is recommended that people using the software familiarize themselves with the package. Although the slick GUI for configuration could put some users at ease, inexperience with the software can minimally lead to a very frustrating experience. In addition to vendor documentation, another useful site from which you can obtain documentation is Phoneboy's homepage, located at www.phoneboy.com.

Darren Reed's IPFilter

IPFilter is a firewall software implementation developed and still maintained by Darren Reed. This personal project has turned into an industrial-strength firewall software implementation that rivals many commercial packages. It also plays on a field on which personal firewall software packages can't compete—it's free.

IPFilter provides stateful traffic inspection, much like any standard firewall software implementation. It additionally provides NAT functionality and can handle multiple network interfaces. These features are critical to the implementation of any DMZ.

The IPFilter software package can be downloaded from Darren Reed's site at http://coombs.anu.edu.au/~avalon/ip-filter.html. The package supports both 32- and 64-bit Sparc architectures. A 32-bit implementation can be easily compiled using the freely available GNU C Compiler and will essentially compile right out of the box. A 64-bit build requires a little more work, including obtaining a compiler capable of building binaries for the architecture. This particular situation is one in which the trial version of Sun Forte C Compiler comes handy.

High Availability of the DMZ Server

Another design issue that should be addressed in the planning phase is high availability. Designing, building, and deploying a DMZ server is a crucial step in securing a network. However, if the DMZ server fails, an outage of all network resources occurs until the system is either fixed or replaced. This includes a public network outage, which means public-facing systems in the DMZ cannot be reached by systems on outside networks. This also means network connectivity from the private network to external networks is affected.

Failure may occur for one of any number of reasons. Often, catastrophic failure such as the failure of a component in the system can result in the system becoming completely unavailable and requiring that the component is either repaired or replaced before normal network operations can resume. The goal of high availability is to minimize the amount of time lost when the DMZ server fails.

High availability is created by deploying two or more systems to perform the same job in what is called a *cluster*. One system in the cluster sits by idly while the other system serves client requests. The system serving continually monitors itself and sends information to its peers about its current state of operation. Should the system performing the job fail, the next system in the cluster identifies the failure and takes over the job performed by the failed system. Let's discuss some high-availability packages in a little more detail.

Check Point FireWall-1

As mentioned previously, FireWall-1 has a diverse set of features. One of these features is high availability, made possible through the ClusterXL module.

The ClusterXL module is diverse in its function. It can enable a cluster of FireWall-1 servers to act as failover systems. It can also be configured as a load-balancing system, which can aid in handling networks prone to large spikes of network activity.

Veritas Cluster Server

Cluster Server by Veritas is another high-availability software package. Cluster Server is a software package independent of other applications on the system and is not dependent on any one application. This independence offers the advantage of allowing a group of DMZ servers using firewall software packages that are not highly available to be configured into a cluster of failover hosts.

Cluster Server requires cluster configurations that have a means of communication between all nodes in the cluster via a network interface. This is a circumstance in which our previous discussion about the user of quad Ethernet cards applies. With an extra interface on the DMZ server, we can group together the DMZ server and backups into a cluster, making the network highly available.

Sun Cluster

Sun Cluster is another high-availability package. As the name implies, it is distributed and maintained by Sun. Sun Cluster is written specifically for Solaris and Sun hardware.

Like Veritas Cluster Server, Sun Cluster is independent of any particular application. Also like Veritas Cluster Server, the Sun Cluster software package can be used to make roughly any firewall software system highly available.

Host Security Software

Ensuring the reliability and integrity of the DMZ system means using host integrity-monitoring software to report activity that could indicate intrusion. Like many other security measures, integrity monitoring is a reactive measure that involves notifying staff responsible for the system in the event of noisy and messy compromise. However, knowing of a compromise after the fact is far better than never knowing about it at all.

For the most part, host integrity-monitoring software works in one of two ways. One method that host integrity software uses to monitor the system is by monitoring activity on the local system's ports to identify activity that could indicate a compromise. Any activity that is known by the software to represent a likely intrusion is reported.

The other method is the creation of a database of cryptographic hashes of binaries installed on the system. When the host integrity software is installed and configured, the software crawls the directories it is configured to monitor and creates the hash database. The host's integrity is maintained by checking the hashes of the monitored binaries and directories against the hashes contained in the database.

Although it might seem intuitive to use software that monitors both the ports on the DMZ server and the hashes of local binaries, it is best to use software that monitors only the local hashes. The reason for this is a matter of exposure. The addition of any network-aware services additionally exposes the system to attack.

Of the software available for host integrity monitoring, two packages are most commonly used. The first is the commercially available Tripwire package. The other widely used software package for this purpose is the Aide software package.

Other Software Considerations

To properly place a DMZ server in the network infrastructure, we typically put it in a location that is ideal for a number of other services. Often, it seems like a good idea to place services on the DMZ system that are used for the infrastructure of the network. These services can include things such as Web servers, domain name servers, mail servers, or other such services.

You must resist this temptation. As we discuss in the configuration section, the host that will be providing DMZ and firewall infrastructure to the network should run with the minimal number of services possible. There are many reasons for this approach; here we focus on two.

First, the DMZ server is dedicated to handling network traffic. As previously stated, this is extremely RAM- and processor-intensive activity. Running additional services consumes additional resources that can be dedicated to handling network traffic. Although the impact might not be readily apparent on a lightly loaded network, as the network traffic load handled by the DMZ server increases, the impact becomes much more apparent. Often, such a situation results in failure of systems to connect to hosts, because the system drops packets due to limited resources.

Second and more important, running network services on the system increases the system's exposure to potential vulnerabilities and thus potential attacks. The cornucopia of past vulnerabilities in the Berkeley Internet Name Daemon (BIND), in addition to the likely future continuation of the BIND vulnerability saga, is a prime example of the dangers of deploying services on the host. Sendmail and the numerous and frequent vulnerabilities in the software are other examples. Even intrusion detection software packages such as Snort are not immune to remote vulnerabilities, as displayed recently in the Snort TCP Stream Reassembly Buffer Overflow Vulnerability by the research team of Core Security Technologies.

Increasing the exposure to remote vulnerabilities with the DMZ server is, to put it bluntly, stupid. Should the system be compromised, an attacker is not only granted access to all hosts on the DMZ but full access to all hosts on the private network segment as well. Once the DMZ system is compromised, the network's integrity can no longer be trusted, and the attacker can direct traffic to wherever whim may lead.

The selection of hardware and software is important in the reliability, stability, and performance of the DMZ server. However, the next step in the planning phase has a far greater impact on the security and integrity of the system. Let's discuss the design of a secure system configuration.

Configuration: The Plumbing and Other Details

The configuration portion of system design is the stage in which we lay out the way the host will be implemented. We previously discussed the selection of hardware and software and the surrounding impact to performance; in this section we discuss the configuration details of hardware and software as they relate to security. Configuration can make the difference between a stable, reliable DMZ server that is resistant to remote attacks and one that is exposed and thus prone to attack and compromise when the next remote vulnerability is discovered.

Creating a secure DMZ server configuration requires the use of two distinct concepts: creating a secure configuration and using layers of security in our configuration. Because most security measures are reactive in nature, making security the basis of configuration at this stage is a fundamental change to the way security is typically handled, making it a proactive measure.

Our network will only be as secure as the design of the DMZ server itself. We must therefore create a configuration that exposes our DMZ server to no more risks than necessary. Let's look in depth at creating a secure configuration.

Disk Layout and Considerations

Before you can decide on a disk design, you must first gather some information. First, it is necessary to determine the size of the disks. This information can be gathered from the documentation or marketing literature for the selected system hardware. Or if the disks will be hosted on a storage system such as a RAID cabinet, get the size information for the allocated disks in the cabinet.

Now that you have the information about the disks, the next step is to decide on the type of file system the host will use. In some configurations, such as a cluster, the stock UFS file system might be sufficient. However, in other configurations, it might be wise to use a different file system, such as a journaling file system. One example of such a system is the Veritas File System.

Another consideration is disk failover. Using a RAID cabinet simplifies this issue, since many RAID cabinets handle the disk issues on the storage server side, allowing us to merely identify the device on which the data is located in the system PROM and configuring the disk cluster in the cabinet to worry about the failover for us. However, in configurations such as our previously mentioned hardware, we could be using local disks. In this case, we might have to use additional software to provide redundancy in the event of disk failure.

This task can be accomplished through other software packages, one of which is the Solstice DiskSuite. DiskSuite is a soft solution to creating RAID configurations. Using disks on the local system, DiskSuite can be used to create RAID 0, RAID 1, RAID 0+1 (also called *ten*), and RAID 5 configurations. Depending on business needs and availability of storage, the best solution is typically a RAID 0+1 configuration.

Once we've attended to these details, we can decide the layout of the disk. For our purposes, we assume the use of a 36GB disk. Although recommendations on disk layout vary, we can safely allocate space of the following minimums to the various file systems:

- For the root partition (/), a minimum for 500MB
- For the swap partition, at least twice the amount of physical memory (RAM)
- For the /usr partition, at least 1.5GB
- For the /opt partition, at least 500MB
- For the user home partition (typically /export/home), at least 1GB
- For the /var partition, as much of the remaining space as possible

Allocating as much space as possible to the /var partition gives us the benefits of plentiful log space. Even with this minimum recommended configuration, a system with 1GB of physical memory and a 36GB disk will have 31.5GB of space for log information. Although this might seem like a massive amount of space, a busy DMZ server with increased auditing and logging enabled will easily gobble up this space, as we see in the next section.

Increasing the Verbosity of Local Auditing

Local auditing is an important factor in preserving the integrity of a host. Audit data is the first line of information in which intrusion might be apparent. Audit trails also have a legal significance; whenever there is an intrusion, log data becomes evidence that may be admissible in court. It is for these reasons that audit configurations must be increased in verbosity.

Solaris includes a number of auditing choices with a stock installation of software. As with every UNIX implementation, Solaris provides the standard system-logging facility, syslog. Syslog is a good source of basic system information, but in addition to the standard audit trail provided by syslog, Solaris additionally implements other utilities, such as the Basic Security Module, or BSM, as it is commonly known.

BSM is a highly configurable, robust, low-level auditing tool. It is disabled in default implementations of Solaris but can easily be enabled. BSM logs data when system calls of an interest in regard to security are invoked. Data written to the BSM files is in binary format. The BSM configuration file is located at /etc/security/audit_control. More information about BSM is available through http://docs.sun.com.

Increased auditing directly translates to log files of increased size. Often, data generated by auditing falls into one of two categories: it is either too much and thus too cumbersome to review or is not understood and thus auditing is turned off. These problems are often a matter of proper BSM configuration. However, it goes without saying that large amounts of data can still be generated, even with proper configuration. This data is important and should be reviewed regularly. It should also be preserved for future reference, which we discuss in the next section.

Backup Considerations

DMZ servers, like all systems, have data that is irreplaceable. On other systems, this data could be customer information, credit card numbers, or other business information. On DMZ servers, business information equates to system logs, audit data, and firewall logs.

As mentioned in the previous section, this data is crucial, especially in the legal aspect. Therefore, this data must be backed up and saved for future reference and analysis. For this reason, we must take into consideration the backup of DMZ servers.

Since a Solaris DMZ server is, at its root, a Solaris server, backup differs little from other systems. Designing a backup solution is the same as any other host. However, we must take into consideration the sensitivity of the system.

Because a DMZ server is often the linchpin of networks and compromise of the system constitutes compromise of the network, we must make every effort to isolate it from attack, and backup is no exception. Although it is sufficient for other systems to initiate backups via storage networks and backup servers, it is important for the DMZ server to keep its data backed up in a location that is isolated from other systems. Additionally, media should be, if possible, in an append-only configuration.

Two other issues to consider are storage constraints and backup software. Will storage constraints permit nightly backup of the entire system? Or is a better solution to back up only the important files? These questions cannot be answered without evaluating the resources at your site.

Backup software, on the other hand, is a much easier issue to tackle. If you're using a configuration such as a master backup repository and NetBackup, the solution is pretty clear. On the other hand, if nothing as formal is in place, *ufsdump,* included with Solaris and a DLT drive, could be the best solution.

Remote Administration

Most servers are administered remotely through either a graphical tool or a tool that uses the command-line interface. Often, the servers are stored in a location that either is uncomfortable to work in, such as a cooled server room, or requires travel to the site to administer, which in most operations departments is out of the question, whether a remote c-location facility or the next room. DMZ servers are no different than any other server in this regard.

You must consider remote administration and the impact to DMZ servers. It is not recommended that you provide any remote services that may increase potential exposure to attack, but sometimes this simply is not an option. If you're using services for remote administration, you must provide access control for these services, such as firewall rules. Additionally, the use of cryptographically secure services such as secure shell (SSH) is recommended, because these services are less prone to the eavesdropping of potentially sensitive information, such as passwords, by peers and intermediaries on the network.

Putting the Puzzle Together

Before we can create a secure configuration, we must first know what to expect from a default configuration. After we have selected our operating system and third-party software, we need an idea of what to expect in terms of services, requirements, and default insecurities caused by the interactivity of all components. Having this information will better equip us to make informed decisions.

This is the phase in which we gather as much information as possible about the system in question. In many cases we can get most of the pertinent details online about default services started by the operating system and third-party software. Vendor sites as well as other third-party sites contain a wealth of information that can help us determine what hurdles we might face in creating a secure configuration.

Should this approach not yield sufficient information or should we decide to take a more hands-on approach for our specific configuration, we can always create a test implementation. This implementation is really no more than an experiment. The installation procedure is not meant to be secure, and the software installation is not meant to be kept for future production use. The idea is to put together all the components, hardware and software, to see how they all interact with one another.

Once we have created a test implementation, we must gather information from it. To gather local information about the default configuration, we can usually use local system tools. These tools include *ps(1)* and *netstat(1M)*. We use *ps* to gather information about the processes started by default on the system, as shown in Figure 3.8.

Figure 3.8 Getting a List of Executing Processes with the *ps* Command

```
modulus - PuTTY
# ps -ef |more
     UID   PID  PPID  C    STIME TTY      TIME CMD
    root     0     0  0 21:30:16 ?        0:00 sched
    root     1     0  0 21:30:16 ?        0:00 /etc/init -
    root     2     0  0 21:30:16 ?        0:00 pageout
    root     3     0  0 21:30:16 ?        0:01 fsflush
    root   312     1  0 21:30:41 ?        0:00 /usr/lib/saf/sac -t 300
    root   226     1  0 21:30:36 ?        0:00 /usr/lib/utmpd
    root    52     1  0 21:30:25 ?        0:00 /usr/lib/sysevent/syseventd
    root    62     1  0 21:30:27 ?        0:00 /usr/lib/picl/picld
    root   129     1  0 21:30:31 ?        0:00 /usr/sbin/rpcbind
    root   176     1  0 21:30:33 ?        0:00 /usr/lib/autofs/automountd
    root   152     1  0 21:30:32 ?        0:00 /usr/sbin/inetd -s
  daemon   166     1  0 21:30:32 ?        0:00 /usr/lib/nfs/statd
    root   750   749  0 22:24:49 pts/5    0:00 ps -ef
    root   186     1  0 21:30:33 ?        0:00 /usr/sbin/syslogd
    root   168     1  0 21:30:32 ?        0:00 /usr/lib/nfs/lockd
    root   215     1  0 21:30:36 ?        0:00 /usr/lib/power/powerd
    root   192     1  0 21:30:34 ?        0:00 /usr/sbin/cron
    root   211     1  0 21:30:35 ?        0:00 /usr/sbin/nscd
    root   315   312  0 21:30:41 ?        0:00 /usr/lib/saf/ttymon
    root   319   292  0 21:30:44 ?        0:00 /usr/dt/bin/dtlogin -daemon
    root   237   236  0 21:30:36 ?        0:00 /usr/sadm/lib/smc/bin/smcboot
    root   236     1  0 21:30:36 ?        0:00 /usr/sadm/lib/smc/bin/smcboot
    root   238   236  0 21:30:36 ?        0:00 /usr/sadm/lib/smc/bin/smcboot
    root   318     1  0 21:30:43 ?        0:00 /usr/lib/ssh/sshd
    root   305     1  0 21:30:41 ?        0:00 /usr/sbin/vold
    root   292     1  0 21:30:39 ?        0:00 /usr/dt/bin/dtlogin -daemon
    root   288     1  0 21:30:38 ?        0:00 /usr/lib/snmp/snmpdx -y -c /etc/snmp/conf
    root   313     1  0 21:30:41 console  0:00 /usr/lib/saf/ttymon -g -h -p modulus console login:
 -T sun -d /dev/console -l
    root   297     1  0 21:30:40 ?        0:00 /usr/lib/dmi/dmispd
    root   316   292  0 21:30:42 ?        0:02 /usr/openwin/bin/Xsun :0 -nobanner -auth /var/dt/A:
--More--
```

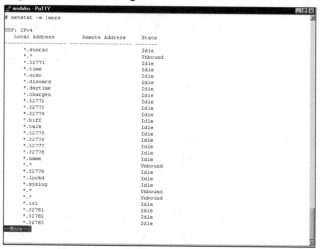

Once we have gathered process table information, we gather network socket table information with *netstat*, as shown in Figure 3.9.

Figure 3.9 Getting a List of Listening Services with the *netstat* Command

```
modulus - PuTTY
# netstat -a |more

UDP: IPv4
   Local Address         Remote Address     State
-------------------- -------------------- -------
      *.sunrpc                              Idle
      *.*                                   Unbound
      *.32771                               Idle
      *.time                                Idle
      *.echo                                Idle
      *.discard                             Idle
      *.daytime                             Idle
      *.chargen                             Idle
      *.32772                               Idle
      *.32773                               Idle
      *.32774                               Idle
      *.biff                                Idle
      *.talk                                Idle
      *.32775                               Idle
      *.32776                               Idle
      *.32777                               Idle
      *.32778                               Idle
      *.name                                Idle
      *.*                                   Unbound
      *.32779                               Idle
      *.lockd                               Idle
      *.syslog                              Idle
      *.*                                   Unbound
      *.*                                   Unbound
      *.161                                 Idle
      *.32781                               Idle
      *.32782                               Idle
      *.32783                               Idle
--More--
```

A great deal of information about default processes and services has already been written in two online articles by Hal Flynn: "Back to the Basics: Solaris and inetd.conf," Parts I and II, available at the following URLs:

- www.securityfocus.com/infocus/1490

- www.securityfocus.com/infocus/1491

Also see "Back to the Basics: Solaris Default Processes and init.d," Parts I, II, and III, at the following URLs:

- www.securityfocus.com/infocus/1358

- www.securityfocus.com/infocus/1359

- www.securityfocus.com/infocus/1360

Once we have gathered this information, we can create a model of our design.

Layering Local Security

The problem with most systems implemented on the Internet is that they are designed like candy: Many have a hard exterior that is crunchy and difficult to bite through, but once the hard shell has been breached, the center is soft and chewy.

This problem is not the fault of any one person in particular. Vendors design and create software this way. Administrators implement software this way. Security personnel run vulnerability scanners against the network and make the assumption that because there are no scanner events detailing remotely exploitable bugs, the systems are secure.

To Sun's credit, the company is making strides to combat this complacency. In Solaris versions through 7, we have file access control lists, an extension of the UNIX permission model designed to provide more granular access control. With Solaris 8, Sun implemented role-based access control (RBAC), which can be used to add power to or remove power from certain users.

Other third-party security software packages exist as well. Two additional features are restricted shells and restrictive environments. Let's briefly focus on each of these topics.

File Access Control Lists

As previously mentioned, file access control lists are an extension of the UNIX permission set. They are implemented at the file system level and designed to enforce security policy on a much more granular level. The tools *setfacl(1)* and *getfacl(1)* are used to manipulate these permissions.

The difference between standard permissions and file access control lists can be likened to allowing an entire group access to a specific file versus being able to select exactly which members of the group can access the file. Access control lists can also be used to limit which users in the world can read or execute a world-readable and/or world-executable file. A brief example of these programs appears in Figure 3.10.

Figure 3.10 Using *setfacl* and *getfacl* to Add and Restrict Access
Permissions for Individual Users

In implementations in which there is a small user base, file access control lists might be handy. By adding granular access control lists to programs that might be sensitive, such as *setuid* and *setgid* executables, you can effectively put these programs out of reach of the unprivileged attacker. Although this solution cannot mitigate every single potential risk and attack, it definitely raises the bar.

DMZ servers are not and should not be designed to handle local users outside of administrative staff, due to the sensitivity of the system. However, this solution provides an additional layer of security against unprivileged local users. It is not a useful countermeasure in attacks that result in remote administrative compromise.

Role-Based Access Control

Role-based access control, also known as RBAC, is another useful enhancement to the UNIX permission model. RBAC is designed to allow administrators to delegate certain permissions within the system to roles, giving power to role users. RBAC can also be used to remove power from users.

The removal of power from users consists of creating traditional UNIX user accounts as roles. This way, you are given the ability to granularly specify exactly what the user can and cannot do. Creating a role for these users can limit the impact of system compromise through a specific user account.

Restricted Shells

Restricted shells are an older solution to untrusted user access. Their name implies exactly what they are: a shell that is restricted. The restriction comes in the form of not permitting a user the ability to change certain profile information or escape his or her home directory.

Restricted shells can be useful in the event of a compromise of a user account on the DMZ system. If a user account is compromised through either a stolen password or a brute-force attack, the attacker gains access to an account in which the user can only execute programs contained in the home directory. Used in combination with RBAC, this can be a powerful configuration, because the user has the ability to only change to a role. However, if a program is made available within the directory that allows the user to execute shell commands, as is the case with most text editors, it is possible for the user to escape the restricted home directory by executing a standard shell.

Restrictive Environments

Restrictive environments are another useful means of mitigating risk locally. Like most other security measures, restrictive environments are, at best, a flaky solution if used as a sole means of maintaining host security. However, when coupled with other security measures, restrictive environments can significantly mitigate risk and increase the delta between a user gaining unauthorized access to a system and discovery of that breach.

Restrictive environments are often implemented in the form of a root directory change, also known as *chroot*. The principle is to create a pseudo-root directory from which a process executes. If the process is ever compromised due to vulnerability in execution, the attacker gaining access to the system with the privileges of the process is restricted to the pseudo-root directory. Known problems with *chroot* in some implementations can allow a user to escape the pseudo-root directory. However, as an additional layer of security, *chroot* is an excellent obstacle that can increase the precious amount of time leading to discovery from when a restricted account is compromised to when administrative privilege is compromised.

Auditing Local File Permissions

Local file permissions can be the boon or bane of DMZ system security model, and they have resulted in many heated arguments. In many modern UNIX systems, files installed on a system during a default implementation may put the system in a position of unnecessary risk. This is not necessarily the fault of the vendor; the program is written based on user request and often given privileged execution status due to the need to access information or perform operations that require privilege. However, unintentional programming errors within the program make it a risk to the integrity of the entire system.

It is possible to mitigate this risk through local file permission auditing. This is a process that requires research and attention to detail. It is possible to reduce the execution permissions of many programs. However, reckless removal of permissions can minimally result in breaking applications on the system but can have more severe consequences, such as making the system unusable.

Two methods can be used to enhance local file permissions and reduce privileges where possible: manual auditing and automated security tools. The selection of methods is a matter of both size of the job and personal preference. We discuss each method here.

Manual File Permission Auditing

Auditing file permissions manually can be tedious work, especially if the person doing the auditing is not intimately familiar with the idiosyncrasies of the operating system. Not knowing how to use tools supplied on the local system as well as where to locate documentation and information about various programs can cause the job to escalate from the level of an exercise in frustration to the level of an exercise in restraining oneself from beating the system with a sledgehammer, especially when the usual unrealistic deadlines loom.

For those more comfortable with the system or at least with the luxury of time, manual file system auditing can be beneficial in both allowing you to get even more familiar with the operating system and allowing you total control in local file permission security. This discussion assumes that the previous idea of building a test system that is used merely for information gathering in design is possible.

The two most useful system utilities for auditing local file permissions are *find(1)* and *man(1)*. Using *find* to locate files on the system installed with elevated privilege, as shown in Figure 3.11, makes the task significantly easier.

Figure 3.11 Using *find* to Get a List of Files with *setuid* Privileges on a Solaris System

Upon compiling a list of executables installed with elevated privileges, you must understand the purpose of the executable to determine whether or not permissions may be lowered. For example, the *su(1M)* program is installed with *setuid* root privileges Removing the *setuid* bit, however, usually has negative consequences, because users can no longer use the *su* program to log into a different account from the shell, including that of root. This is where the man program becomes handy. Understanding the purpose of the program, how it integrates into the environment, and whether or not it really needs elevated execution privileges in the configuration is essential and can only be understood through research and wisdom.

For programs not documented in manual pages, other resources exist. A good starting point is the Sun Documentation site, at http://docs.sun.com. If documentation of the program does not exist there, resorting to a search engine might be in order. If no documentation can be located on the program, the rule of thumb "If it ain't broke, don't fix it" applies.

Automated File Permission Auditing

For those with less time to perform file permission auditing or uncomfortable with it, it is likely a relief to know that others have already done much of the work of figuring out which programs really need elevated privileges. If digging into the system is not on your agenda for the day and you're apt to trust free tools, two widely used programs exist to perform much of this work for you.

The first of these programs is the Computer Oracle and Password System, or COPS. Originally written by legendary security professionals Dan Farmer and Gene Spafford, COPS audits the local system for insecure file permissions, executables with elevated privileges, and weak passwords. Although it is somewhat dated, it is well written and still extremely useful. It can be downloaded from the U.S. Department of Energy Computer Incident Advisory Capability at http://ciac.llnl.gov/ciac/ToolsUnixSysMon.html.

Another available tool is the Yet Another Solaris Security Package, or YASSP, as it is commonly called. YASSP is written specifically for Solaris and performs many of the same functions of COPS. This program is also a bit dated, but is an excellent utility for enhancing local file permission security.

One final tool we will mention is the FixModes script. Written by Casper Dik of Sun fame, FixModes is another utility designed specifically for Solaris. It audits the file system of the host for programs with insecure permissions and makes changes necessary to enhance local security.

Building the Model for Future Use

As a kid, I was astonished by models. My friends used to build incredibly detailed, scaled versions of things like planes, aircraft carriers, battleships, and helicopters. Lacking the manual dexterity and artistic gifts of many of my peers, my finished models often left much to be desired. An attempt at a model of the U.S.S. Enterprise once resulted in something that resembled a model train wreck.

So, if the thought of creating a model of a system brings out *your* anxiety of past childhood shortcomings, worry not; for this model, we need little more than a text editor or a pencil and paper if we want to use a low-tech solution. The process of creating a model can be approached by two methods: either listing what we need or listing what we don't need. In most configurations, it is easier to take the former route to creating a model than it is to take the latter.

In Table 3.1, we have created a model of a system using the method of listing what we need. As you can see, we have specifically listed our requirements on the left, and on the right we've made an inventory of items to fulfill our needs. We can be as minimal or as fancy as we want with our model; what counts is that we list everything we need and everything we are going to do to fulfill the requirements.

Table 3.1 A Model of a System Design Listing Only the Requirements of the Host

Network Service Requirements Description	Inventory
Access to services required from the private network	HTTP; SMTP; DNS
Access to services required from the public network for the private network	HTTP; SMTP
Access to services required from the public network for untrusted sources	HTTP; SMTP; DNS; FTP
Access required to DMZ host	SSH from private network

Host Requirements Description	Inventory
Speed of network connections	100BaseT
Number of network interfaces (minimum of three)	Five
Number of disks	Two
Disk size	36GB
Auditing utility	Basic Security Module
Backup method	Local DLT drive
Remote administration	SSH
High-availability software	Veritas Cluster Server

Continued

Table 3.1 A Model of a System Design Listing Only the Requirements of the Host

Host Requirements Description	Inventory
Local intrusion detection software	Tripwire
Firewall software	IPFilter
Software to harden system	Solaris Security Toolkit

Here are some things to keep in mind when you're building a model:

1. Ensure that hardware includes all the components necessary to create a DMZ server. This includes a minimum of three network interfaces.

2. Ensure that sufficient space is available for the configuration on the available drives, and allocate enough space for the file systems. Allocate as much space as possible to the file system that will be maintaining logs.

3. Plan to increase system audit verbosity.

4. Ensure that the backup solution is sufficiently secure, and take into account any limitations in storage that might exist.

5. Do not install any more software than absolutely required to perform the job. Third-party applications, such as firewall software, could have minimum software requirements. Consult vendor documentation for specific details.

6. Plan for high availability of the server.

7. Plan on implementing host integrity-checking software.

8. Plan to implement multiple layers of security.

9. Plan to audit local file permissions.

10. Disable all unnecessary processes. This is especially important of processes that are network-aware and may expose the system to potential attack.

11. Do not plan on providing network services from the DMZ server.

Once you've filled in as many of the blanks on these details as possible, you should proceed with design review. A peer review may also be helpful in this phase; a second set of eyes of a person with different ideas on design may be helpful in identifying any missed details or potential shortcomings in design. Upon successful review, implementation, which we discuss next, may proceed.

Implementation: The Quick, Dirty Details

The implementation phase of a DMZ server is pretty straightforward. As with all systems, the process consists of assembling the hardware, installing the software, installing the patches, then configuring the system. Whereas the process is the same across roughly all systems, we want to take particular precautions to ensure the integrity of the system through the entire evolution.

In this section, we look at the details necessary to ensure host integrity through this phase. Rather than giving a specific step-by-step outline of how you should install software on a server, we instead create a list of general guidelines that can be used to provide the maximum host security during the implementation process.

Media Integrity

A secure implementation cannot begin without first attaining valid media. Acquiring valid media usually is done in one of two ways: It is purchased from the vendor and delivered by a sales representative or mail, or it is downloaded via the Internet. Verifying the integrity of media delivered in hard form such as a CD is relatively easy; imply look at the shrink-wrap to see if it has been tampered with.

Verifying the integrity of media downloaded via the Internet, however, is a bit more difficult. To verify the integrity of such media, the vendor must give us some secure means of checking its validity. This is typically done through cryptography.

Often, the vendor makes available a file containing a one-way cryptographic hash value, usually on the same page as the media or within a link of the media. The file is then signed with a cryptographic key that can be verified as valid. This task is typically performed with a utility such as Pretty Good Privacy (PGP) or GNU Privacy Guard (GPG). Once the integrity of the media is verified, it is safe to proceed.

Physical Host Security

During the installation process, physical security of the host should be maintained. One way to ensure physical security is to not leave the host unattended during the installation process. However, if there is not adequate time to sit around and watch the installation bar slowly progress from the left to the right side of the screen, another method is to ensure that the system is stored in a secure location while unattended.

A secure location can be one of two things. One secure location is a locked office. The system can be placed in the office with the door locked while unattended. Another secure location is a rack. Both of these locations make the common assumption about locks, which are designed to keep the honest man out.

Host Network Security

As we've continuously emphasized in previous sections, the host should not be exposed to any unnecessary risk. With that in mind, the system should not be connected to any network resources at any point during the implementation phase. Keeping the system disconnected eliminates the possibility of any incoming remote attacks by entirely eliminating the vector.

Even though it is considered generally safe to implement systems with a connection to the network plugged into the host, this is making an assumption that could create a window of exposure. Although none is currently known in Solaris, past vulnerabilities have been discovered in operating systems that could permit a remote attacker to gain unauthorized access to the system. This would be an ideal time for the attacker to compromise the host, since it has little in terms of defense in place.

Additionally, just because no vulnerabilities are currently known in the installation process does not mean they do not exist. Furthermore, even after installation, a window exists in which vulnerable services executing on the host could be compromised. As we're seen recently, the time required by worms to propagate across the Internet has significantly decreased, making any window of exposure unacceptable. In short, do not permit network connectivity to the host at any point during the implementation phase.

Patch Application

Prior to attempting to apply the secure configuration details we have developed to the implementation, we should apply the recommended patch cluster to the host. This cluster, usually downloaded from SunSolve, comes in the form of a large, tarred, and compressed archive of updates to the system.

Configuring & Implementing...

Solaris Patch Management

Like every other operating system, Solaris patches are periodically released. The reasons for these patches vary, but they are often released for one of two reasons: system stability or system security.

The main clearinghouse for Solaris patches is the SunSolve site, located at http://sunsolve.sun.com. From this site, you can gain access to the latest patch cluster via either HTTP or FTP download. In addition, automated tools are available to manage patches on Solaris systems, such as the Sun PatchManager utility. More information is available at http://sunsolve.sun.com/patchpro.

Although it requires network access to attain, the archive should be transferred to the system in the most secure means possible. Often, this is by way of "sneakernet," which is to say archiving the patch cluster onto media and physically carrying it to the system.

Patches should be applied to the system before you attempt to implement configuration and hardening procedures. The reason for this is that when patches are applied to a system, the details of a configuration are often overwritten. Therefore, configuring and hardening the system, then applying the patches could result in the unexpected exposure of the system to potential attack due to configuration changes by the patches.

To summarize the creation of secure implementation leading up to hardening, we should minimally fulfill the following requirements:

1. Verify media integrity prior to system installation. This applies mainly to media obtained from the Internet.

2. Provide physical security to the host during the implementation phase. The system should never be left unattended during the implementation phase without being locked in a secure location such as an office or a rack.

3. Protect the system from attacks via the network during the implementation phase. This means not connecting the host to any network until the implementation phase has been completed.

4. Apply all patches to the system as a last step before conducting hardening and secure configuration procedures on the host. Patches will often change configurations, which could leave the host exposed to remote attack.

Solaris System Hardening

In some groups, system hardening is thought of as a separate phase in the system life cycle. However, system hardening is really just a subsection of system implementation. Hardening occurs before the system is connected to any network and should be periodically re-evaluated and performed again. This is because configuration is always apt to change, whether the changes come from administrative staff or other sources such as system patches.

The hardening of the system amounts to no more than the application of the design principles we developed during the planning phase. During the planning phase, we made several decisions about disabling this and that, changing the permission on files, and so forth. This phase of the implementation is where the rubber meets the road in terms of our original design.

Two methods can be used to harden a Solaris system, each with its benefits and drawbacks. One method, manual hardening, consists of making the changes by hand that are detailed in our system model during the planning phase. This method has the benefit of giving us complete control over the hardening process. The drawbacks of this method are the amount of time involved manually hardening the host, the esoteric knowledge required to create a hardened configuration, and human error. Manual hardening and configuration of Solaris DMZ servers is not for administrators who lack an intimate knowledge of UNIX systems and Solaris.

The other method of hardening hosts is the use of automated hardening tools. We have mentioned these tools before. Automated tools have the benefit of giving us a speedy, hardened configuration. Automated tools are also not prone to miss details due to human error. However, automated security tools have the distinct drawback of applying chainsaw methodology to system security. Additionally, you must trust another person's idea of a hardened system, relinquishing control of the configuration.

The decision of manual or automated hardening ultimately rests with the person implementing the system. The two important factors that influence the decision are time and expertise. In the next two sections, we discuss manual and automated hardening. In the manual hardening section, we discuss the steps that are generally considered the hardening best practices. In the automated hardening section, rather than discussing the functions of the tools themselves (they essentially all work the same), we discuss a few different available tools and highlight some of their features.

Manual System Hardening

We should preface this discussion with a short definition of system hardening. In the previous sections, we have emphasized the importance of limiting exposure so many times, it is almost painful to mention it again. However, we should be ready to feel the pain, because we are about to discuss it again.

System hardening is, for the most part, the limiting of exposure. The way hardening differs from other security precautions is that, although many other security precautions require the addition of software to enhance security, hardening typically involves the *removal* of software. In addition to the removal of software, it is also a procedural activity that typically involves the changing of permissions on files and directories as well as the removal or disabling of other components and features prone to abuse on the system.

Based on our initial design, we know which software and services we intend to keep. Our first step in hardening is to remove the software that we do not intend to keep. Afterward, we remove the services we do not intend to keep. We follow this step with some additional configuration variables that may enhance security.

Software Removal

No matter how much attention to detail we pay to the host during installation and how careful we are about the software we install, we inevitably end up with unintended software installed on the system. This is a fact that we must resign ourselves to and make plans to spend time combing through the installed software, removing that which we do not need.

Post-installation, we can get a list of installed software using tools distributed with the operating system. The two most important tools available for this job are the *pkginfo(1)* and *pkgrm(1M)* tools, installed with all Solaris installations by default. The *pkginfo* tool allows users to query the package database for installed packages in Sun package format, whereas *pkgrm* allows users to remove packages installed in Sun package format.

To get a listing of installed packages, one must first execute the *pkginfo* program. As shown in Figure 3.12, *pkginfo* displays the contents of the entire package database with the following information:

- The category into which the package falls

- The package instance

- A brief description of the package

Figure 3.12 Getting a List of Installed Packages with the *pkginfo* Command

We can redirect this information to a list for review, because often the output is quite long. Redirecting the output can be extremely helpful, since it can help us create a list of installed packages to evaluate for removal away from the console. We may also create a copy of this list and edit it to contain only the packages that we want to remove from the system. This type of list is useful if we want to write a script that invokes *pkgrm* to remove the packages.

Though the installation base of an end-user installation is relatively small, there is room for improvement. Obviously, a DMZ server is not going to require a plethora of language-compatibility packages to provide functionality. We can evaluate eliminating these to support only the language or languages used within our region. In addition, other compatibility packages, such as the packages for NFS, and the audio packages can also likely be removed.

Another suite of software packages to consider removing is the graphical desktop software itself. This comes in the form of Common Desktop Environment (CDE) and OpenWindows software on the Solaris platform. These software suites often contain numerous programs that execute with elevated privileges and have been notoriously "buggy" in the past. Unless required by other third-party applications that will be used on the system, such as firewall software, these suites should also be removed.

Upon removing all packages not required for the stable operation of the system, we should reboot the host and move on to disabling the unnecessary services and processes.

Disabling Services and Processes

The next most important part of hardening a system is the disabling of unnecessary services and processes. The majority of unneeded services and processes should have been eliminated in the software removal phase. We discussed this during the design phase; creating a model of the system and knowing what to expect in terms of default services and processes. However, in spite of our best efforts to eliminate the majority of unneeded software, some issues could still linger.

As we demonstrated in the section "Putting the Puzzle Together," we need to audit the system process table and network sockets table to identify any remaining pieces that might be disabled. The previously mentioned reference documentation, "Back to the Basics: Solaris and inetd.conf" and "Back to the Basics: Solaris and init.d," might also be of benefit during this stage as an aid in locating the origins of these services and processes.

Once the service or process is disabled, it might also be beneficial to modify the permissions of the program. Though this step might seem paranoid, we must consider that if a configuration error is ever made, whether out of innocence or malice, preventing the program itself from executing might be a failsafe that prevents a possible attack. It could seem rational to remove the program entirely, although this practice is not recommended due to the possibility of needing the program in some odd future circumstance. With the program in place, to enable it again, we merely change the permissions. If it is removed, we must reinstall the program, which could create additional work, requiring reinstall of the program, the application of any required patches, and the modification of the host intrusion detection system.

Once we've completed this step in the hardening process, we might consider implementing the host intrusion detection software, testing the host, and putting it in production, or we could consider additional configuration variables to further protect the host. This is as much a matter of preference as it is time constraints. Let's look in the next section at some miscellaneous configuration variables that could further enhance host security.

Miscellaneous Configuration Variables

A few additional configuration variables could also help enhance host security. Although not critical in nature to protecting the integrity of our DMZ server, they might be helpful in making the system more resistant to attack. These configuration variables might or might not be helpful in each particular configuration, depending on the system requirements. In some cases, these configuration variables may be possible, though in some configurations they could have a negative impact on performance or might not be possible due to software requirements.

The nonexecutable stack setting could be helpful in some configurations. The variable is designed to prevent the execution of code placed in stack memory on a system. In the stack-overflow problem that is commonly reported in various programs, this can prevent an attacker from exploiting the problem to execute arbitrary code, potentially resulting in privilege elevation. On the plus side, this is useful to some extent because it eliminates the ability to take advantage of a subsection of a class of vulnerabilities. On the negative side, it could break software depending upon executable stacks, and it does not insulate the system against other types of overflows such as those occurring on the heap or other vulnerabilities such as format string and input validation bugs. A nonexecutable stack can be enabled by placing the following entry in the /etc/system file:

```
set noexec_user_stack=1
```

Systems that have enabled this configuration send a segmentation violation signal (*SIGSEGV*) to programs that attempt to execute code on the stack. This activity is logged by the system log daemon, the log entry containing the name of the program the *SIGSEGV* occurred in, the process ID of the program this occurred in, and the user ID of the system user executing the program. This information could be useful debugging information if the variable is set on a system with software requiring an executable stack. The logging of attempts to execute code on the stack can also be disabled, if desired. It should also be noted that, in some circumstances, it might be possible to bypass this protection.

Another configuration variable that can make a host more resistant to attack is TCP connection request queue size. Solaris implements two queues for handling TCP traffic: the connection request queue and the established connection queue. The separation of the two queues is designed to make a system continuously available to systems that are already connected when a SYN flood occurs while independently handling the deluge of TCP SYN requests in another. In the event that the DMZ server is ever attacked via a SYN flood, the second queue may help the system continue to function, keeping established connections separated and functioning until they are terminated.

The default size of the TCP connection request queue is 1024 connections, although this can be modified from a minimum of one connection to a maximum of 4,294,967,296 connections. To modify the parameter, use the following configuration of the *ndd(1M)* command:

```
ndd -set /dev/tcp tcp_conn_req_max_q0 <number>
```

Here, *<number>* represents the maximum number of requests to keep in the connection request queue table. It is possible to insert this command into an initialization file to automatically set this variable in the later stages of system bootstrap.

Another configuration variable worthy of investigation is the *KEYBOARD_ABORT* parameter. This variable allows you to disable the keyboard abort key sequence (also known as *Stop-A*) from the operating system level. Setting this variable will not prevent a user from pressing Stop + A during a certain window of the system boot process. However, when the system has fully booted, this variable will prevent a user from pressing Stop + A to enter the EEPROM.

To set this variable, follow this procedure: In the /etc/default/kbd file, use a text editor to monitor the following parameter:

```
#KEYBOARD_ABORT=enable
```

This will reflect the following configuration:

```
KEYBOARD_ABORT=disable
```

One final area of configuration we discuss is that of the OpenBoot parameters. OpenBoot is the firmware used in EEPROM of Sun systems. For the most part, OpenBoot is used only to boot the operating system and to ensure the correct handling of some hardware during boot, but it also has features that can make the system more resistant to attack. These features are the security mode and the security password.

The *security-mode* parameter can be set to disable the modifying of OpenBoot parameters without a password. Additionally, *security-mode* can be set to prevent the system from being booted without knowledge of the OpenBoot password. The most ideal configuration is to use the latter type of configuration, although one must evaluate business requirements before instituting this change.

To configure the OpenBoot software to require a password to boot the system, make the following configuration changes. From the OpenBoot command line, execute the following command to enable password protection:

```
setenv security-mode full
```

This command should be followed with the setting of the OpenBoot password. This can be done with the following command, issued on the OpenBoot command line:

```
setenv security-password <newpassword>
```

Here *<newpassword>* is representative of the desired password for OpenBoot.

To enable only password protection on EEPROM configuration changes, use the word *command* in place of the word *full*. These parameters can also be manipulated from the command line using the *eeprom* command on a running Solaris system.

Now that we have discussed manual hardening techniques, let's discuss a few of the tools available to do the job for us.

Automated System Hardening

Essentially, automated system hardening involves using a prewritten tool to perform many if not most of the activities we have just discussed. In the section on auditing file permissions, we discussed a few of the more basic tools, including COPS, YASSP, and FixModes. In this section, we mention a couple more and discuss the use of such tools.

All system-hardening tools essentially work the same way. They are downloaded and placed on the system that is being hardened, they're unpacked, and if necessary, the source code written in whatever language is compiled into an executable. Most require some configuration information prior to execution, which may come in the form of a flat text file; others might prompt the user for this information when the program is executed.

Most of these tools are scripts and are interpreted by some shell such as Bourne Shell, Korn Shell, or Perl. Tools that require compilation are typically written in C; therefore, a C compiler such as the GNU C Compiler might be needed. It should be noted that a C compiler it not installed with Solaris, and any C compiler installed on Solaris systems should minimally be installed with restrictive permissions, such as root read-write-execute only.

Let's discuss two of the more advanced system-hardening tools available for Solaris: Titan and SST.

Titan

Titan is a tool authored by Brad Powell, Dan Farmer, and Matthew Archibald. It is not specific to the Solaris operating system; it might be used on several different implementations of UNIX. However, it does contain quite a bit of code, written in the form of modules, which are designed specifically for Solaris.

Titan is a modular program that audits the system at a low level and makes modifications to the operating system based on the predefined configuration. The most current release has features such as the MinimizeOS module, which can be used to *pkgrm* unneeded software packages. Titan also disables unneeded services, disables unnecessary processes, enables BSM, and changes system banners, to name a few other features.

Titan consists of both modules written in C and modules written in shell. It can be run against a system repeatedly. The designers recommend the use of the program with other tools, such as COPS, crack, Tiger, and SATAN.

SST

The SST is the Solaris Security Toolkit, also known as the Jumpstart Architecture Security Scripts (JASS). It is available from the Sun Blueprints portion of Sun Microsystems and owes much of its heritage to Alex Noordergraaf, Glenn Burnette, and Keith Watson. You can download it directly from the Sun Blueprints program.

SST is a highly configurable, extensive, flexible tool. It can be run as part of a Jumpstart configuration, where a Solaris system is installed via the network from another Solaris system, or it can be used in a standalone configuration. SST's features include many of the same features as Titan. It adds other security software to the system, such as OpenSSH, when used in the recommended configuration.

During the writing of this chapter, the author was also involved with the review of a forthcoming book from the Sun Blueprints program. The subject of the book is the Solaris Security Toolkit, and the authors are Alex Noordergraaf and Glenn Burnette. The book, *Securing Systems With the Solaris Security Toolkit,* is recommended for anybody interested in using SST. The book provides in-depth coverage of the toolkit.

When we have completed the hardening process, we still have two issues that should be addressed. After modifications to the system are complete, we must install, configure, and put into production the host-based intrusion detection system (HIDS). This step should be performed at the very end of the hardening process, since any changes to the system will cause the system to generate an alert. Once we've finished this step, we should conduct performance and stability testing. This can be done with the Sun Validation Test Suite (SunVTS), of which more information is available at http://docs.sun.com.

Designing & Planning…

Host-Based Intrusion Detection System Maintenance

HIDS require periodic maintenance. This is one of the burdens of monitoring the base of installed software on a system.

You might need to periodically regenerate the checksum database from which the IDS conducts its checks. This might be required when patches have been applied to the system, because the checksums of some monitored programs will likely change. This could also occur in the instance of software installation, removal, or configuration changes in some files.

Hardening Checklists for DMZ Servers and Solaris

Use this checklist as a starting point when hardening your Solaris DMZ servers:

- Has a model or diagram of the host been made?
- Is the host physically secured?
- Has the host been kept segregated from all networks?
- Have all the recommended patches been applied?
- Has increased logging of system activity been implemented?
- Are data backups secure from physical access?
- Are data backups secure from being overwritten?
- Have all remote administration utilities been sufficiently secured?
- Has all unnecessary software been removed?

- Has the system been hardened manually or by using an automated tool?

- Have all unnecessary services been disabled?

- Have all unnecessary processes been disabled?

- Has host security been layered using:

    - Role-based access control?

    - Granular file access control lists?

    - Restrictive environments?

- Have any additional security-enhancing system variables been set?

- Has the firewall rule policy been implemented for the host?

- Has the HIDS been installed?

Summary

In this chapter, we discussed the use of DMZ servers and Solaris. We began our discussion with details of the placement of DMZ servers. We examined a Solaris DMZ server implemented as a host directly behind the router, a host attached to a switch behind the router, and a cluster configuration attached to a switch behind the router. We came to the conclusion that configuration is only part of the equation.

In our discussion of firewall rules, we examined rulesets for both the public and private networks. We asserted that our private network should deny all traffic except for access to services required for business needs. Our public network configuration gave us enhanced security by allowing only traffic to the specified services required by both internal and external users.

We shifted our discussion from network use of Solaris as a DMZ system to building a Solaris DMZ system. We began with a discussion of selecting the right hardware to do the job and acquiring a minimum of three network interfaces to perform the job. We also discussed the benefits of using quad Ethernet cards.

Our hardware discussion was followed by an examination of software selection. We stated the fact that additional software would be required to provide DMZ services with a Solaris system, and we briefly mentioned the two popular software packages FireWall-1 and IPFilter. This discussion was followed with another about selecting high-availability software to keep a DMZ system available at all times. We examined the options of FireWall-1, Veritas Cluster Server, and Sun Cluster. Advisement against the dangerous tendency to place additional network services on the DMZ server and thus put the integrity of the server at risk was noted.

Configuration design was the subject of our next discussion, in which we examined several of the software configuration factors to consider in building a secure design. We examined disk layout, with an emphasis placed on creating a maximum amount of space for log files. We also looked at increasing log verbosity and the reasons to do so, such as acquiring legally admissible evidence. Considerations for backup and using media that is append-only were also noted as desirable.

Regarding configuration design, we also discussed putting the puzzle together by creating a test implementation of the software. This was done to give us an idea of what to expect in a default configuration, from which additional design decisions could be made. We also discussed the importance of using multiple layers of security, including file access control lists, RBAC, restricted shells, and restrictive environments. The necessity of auditing and checking the permissions of programs that execute with privileges and automated programs such as COPS, YASSP, and FixModes that do this job for us also was outlined.

The discussion of system design ended with building a system model. From our model, we were able to make decisions about what services we would require, what services and processes should be disabled, and what security precautions should be taken to protect the host. Our design created a culmination of all the secure system details we had previously discussed.

Implementation was the next topic we examined. Our implementation phase detailed general guidelines to use to preserve the integrity of a host. This included verifying the integrity of media using cryptography, ensuring physical security of the host so as not to allow unauthorized individuals access to the system, and securing the network side of the host by not connecting it to network resources until the implementation is complete. In addition, we noted that patch applications should be the final part of implementation that occurs prior to the hardening process.

We ended the chapter with an examination of the hardening process from both the manual and automated points of view. Of the manual hardening process, we discussed steps such as the removal of unnecessary software, disabling of unnecessary services and processes, and manipulation of miscellaneous configuration variables to enhance host security. We addressed the automated hardening process from the perspective of available tools to perform the job for us, including Titan and SST. We completed our implementation by installing host-based intrusion detection software and a performance-testing software package available for the host.

Solutions Fast Track

Placement of Servers

☑ DMZ servers should be placed behind network routers.

☑ An ideal DMZ server configuration is placing a switch between the network router and the DMZ server.

☑ High-availability configurations require the ability to connect multiple systems to the same network segments.

Firewall Ruleset

☑ The firewall ruleset is as important as the proper design and configuration of the networks serviced by the DMZ.

☑ Private networks should prohibit all network traffic by default and permit outbound access to systems that service business needs, such as Web proxy servers, mail servers, and domain name servers.

☑ Public networks should provide access to the required services while not allowing users to deviate connections to reaching unauthorized ports on systems in the DMZ.

System Design

☑ Hardware for the job should be evaluated for its expandability, and the proper hardware for the job such as quad Ethernet cards should be used.

☑ The proper software for the job, including firewall and high-availability packages, should be selected to provide stable, reliable performance with minimal impact in the case of a server failure.

☑ It is wise to create a test installation of a system to evaluate its default state prior to implementing the design.

☑ A model should be created of the system design that will serve as a reference during implementation.

Implementation: The Quick, Dirty Details

☑ The system should be implemented with the express concern of preserving host integrity. This involves checking media integrity, ensuring physical security of the host, ensuring network security of the host, and applying the recommended patch cluster.

☑ The system should be hardened to make it resistant to attacks. This involves either manually manipulating the operating system to create an attack-resistant configuration or using an automated tool to do the job.

☑ Host-based intrusion detection software should be installed on the system after hardening.

Hardening Checklist for DMZ Servers and Solaris

- ☑ All services not specifically required for operation of the DMZ server should be disabled. This involves auditing the inetd.conf file as well as the initialization script.

- ☑ All processes not specifically required for system operation should be disabled. This limits exposure to potential attack and lightens the load on system resources.

- ☑ Additional configuration variables that are not mandatory but might be helpful in providing a more secure configuration should be evaluated. These include nonexecutable stacks and EEPROM passwords.

Frequently Asked Questions

The following Frequently Asked Questions, answered by the authors of this book, are designed to both measure your understanding of the concepts presented in this chapter and to assist you with real-life implementation of these concepts. To have your questions about this chapter answered by the author, browse to **www.syngress.com/solutions** and click on the **"Ask the Author"** form. You will also gain access to thousands of other FAQs at ITFAQnet.com.

Q: Can multiple DMZ servers exist behind one router?

A: Absolutely. One of the best reasons for putting a switch behind a router is to allow for growth and distributing of DMZ services to other networks that might be implemented to distribute the load.

Q: Why should all incoming and outgoing network traffic be prohibited by default on the private network?

A: The private network typically contains desktop systems, which often have sensitive information stored on them. Prohibiting traffic into and out of the network prevents the propagation of some types of worms, such as those that use their own SMTP engines, and prevents remote access in the event that a desktop system is compromised via a back door.

Q: Why is host security focused on at the design stage rather than at the implementation stage?

A: Making security the basis of design makes the system implementer less apt to miss details such as increasing auditing, host-based intrusion detection, and fixing file permissions. Acknowledging these requirements early in design and reviewing them before implementing also gives the implementer a chance to plug any holes in design that he or she notices.

Q: Why is the name server for the private network on the public segment?

A: Some domain name service packages are a double-barrel shotgun of vulnerability. In one barrel, there is the ammunition of protocol problems in DNS that could lead to it being exploited to deny service or incorrectly resolve domains for users. In the other barrel, there are the consistent problems of remotely exploitable vulnerabilities that gain the attacker access to the host as the name service daemon user; typically root. It is better to place the server in a location in which, if it is compromised, it can only reach certain public systems, rather than it having free reign of the private network.

Q: I have securely implemented a test server during the design phase and would like to implement it into production. Should I do this?

A: If the integrity of the host can be trusted beyond the shadow of a doubt, why not?

Q: I was told never to install a C compiler on a sensitive system, especially one that services the network. Why is it mentioned in this chapter?

A: The belief that a system is more prone to compromise because a C compiler is installed on the host is a myth. First, an abundance of cheap Sparc hardware is floating around that an attacker could acquire to precompile nefarious tools. Second, sufficient access controls on the system will prevent an attacker with regular user privileges from executing the C compiler. Third and finally, it is possible to do many if not most of the same things done with a compiler with interpreters such as Perl.

Chapter 4

Wireless DMZs

Solutions in this chapter:

- **Why Do We Need Wireless DMZs?**
- **Designing the Wireless DMZ**
- **Wireless DMZ Examples**
- **Wireless LAN Security Best-Practices Checklist**

- ☑ **Summary**
- ☑ **Solutions Fast Track**
- ☑ **Frequently Asked Questions**

Introduction

The basic concept of the DMZ comes from the Korean conflict, which ended in 1953 with an armistice signed by North Korea, China, and the United States. The armistice terms included the establishment of what would be called the Demilitarized Zone, or DMZ for short, between North and South Korea to act as a separation—a wide strip of land where no weapons heavier than an infantry soldier's machine gun would be allowed. The intention was to prevent further conflict, since no formal peace resolution had been reached (and still has not been reached to this day, although North and South Korea signed a nonaggression treaty in 1991). In short, the DMZ was to keep the North Koreans in North Korea and out of South Korea. Over time, however, the DMZ was modified to allow traffic to pass between the two countries, albeit not exactly freely.

In today's computer networks, the concept of a DMZ has been borrowed from the Korean peninsula with the same basic idea: to keep people out of the protected network segment, typically referred to as the *private network* or the *intranet*. Typically, however, a DMZ presents certain network services *to the* public network while at the same time protecting the private network. If all you wanted to do was protect the internal network, you could easily (and with far less risk and effort) accomplish this task through the judicious use of routers and firewalls. The fact that you actually want to segregate network traffic into two groups is what necessitates the implementation and use of a DMZ solution. You need your public servers (Web, SMTP, and FTP servers and the like) to be accessible to the public network but still afforded some basic measure of protection. By the same token, you want to tightly control who and what type of access is allowed to enter the private protected network.

So the obvious question at this point might be something like, "How does this have anything to do with wireless LANs in the first place? I'd never put any servers on a wireless LAN segment, so I should not have any issues with wireless LANs and DMZs." Therein lies the problem: Too many people consider the wireless LAN (WLAN) to be just another *wired* network segment hanging off their core networks. Figure 4.1 offers some help understanding how the WLAN is integrated with the LAN in most cases.

Figure 4.1 Most WLAN Implementations Place the WLAN Inside the Firewall

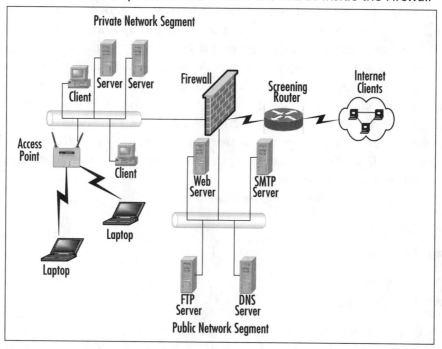

So far, so good. However, this still doesn't explain why WLANs inside the private network are bad. Moreover, it doesn't explain just what a WLAN DMZ is or how it works. That, therefore, is the purpose of this chapter. By the time you have finished reading this chapter you should have a good understanding of why WLANs are not be trusted and should never be considered part of the private internal network. You will also understand how the standard DMZ can be modified to integrate WLAN support and protection into its basic design. Lastly, you should gain some basic ideas as to how you might begin to be able to secure your network from the dangers presented by WLANs while providing your users with the benefits and advantages of wireless networking.

> **NOTE**
>
> You will learn how to configure and implement a wireless DMZ in Chapter 11.

Why Do We Need Wireless DMZs?

Why do we need wireless DMZs, or WDMZs, as they are known? That is a valid question and a tough one to answer for many people. To understand and believe in the absolute need for wireless network segments to be not only segmented from the wired network but protected as well is the foundation of this entire chapter. Perhaps you already know and accept that WLANs are inherently insecure. Perhaps you've accepted this fact outright but are unsure as to what makes them insecure or how they can be secured. Either way, the fact remains: 802.11b WLANs are insecure by their very nature and design. You can either accept this as fact and hope that no one decides to take advantage of it on your network, or you can take active steps toward securing your WLAN and your network as a whole.

In general, attacks on wireless networks fall into four basic categories:

- Passive attacks
- Active attacks
- Man-in-the-middle attacks
- Jamming attacks

In the next sections, we examine these four categories in some detail to help you get an idea of what can go wrong with a WLAN. The bottom line is this: WLANs should *never* be trusted and should never be placed inside the trusted, protected network. Thus, they must naturally be placed in a special form of DMZ: the wireless DMZ.

Passive Attacks on Wireless Networks

A *passive attack* occurs when someone listens to or eavesdrops on network traffic. Armed with a wireless network adaptor that supports promiscuous mode and the right software, an eavesdropper can capture network traffic for analysis. When the network interface card (NIC) is in promiscuous mode, every packet that goes past the interface is captured and displayed within the application window. Many tools are available that can sniff the wireless network, completely unbeknown to the administrator. One of the more common wireless sniffers is AiroPeek, from WildPackets (www.wildpackets.com).

A passive attack on a wireless network might not be malicious in nature. In fact, many in the war-driving community claim that their war-driving activities are benign or "educational" in nature.

Wireless communication takes place on unlicensed public frequencies—anyone can use these frequencies. This makes protecting a wireless network from passive attacks more difficult. However, by its very definition, a passive attack might not be an attack at all but merely a reconnaissance mission—information gathering for a future attack.

The supposed "passive attacker" is merely a bystander. The relative "passivity" of the interaction completely changes when there is criminal intent to either capture or change data on a network the user is not explicitly authorized to access.

Passive attacks are, by their very nature, difficult to detect. If an administrator is using Dynamic Host Configuration Protocol (DHCP) on the wireless network (a practice that is *not* recommended), he or she might notice that an unauthorized Media Access Control (MAC) address has acquired an IP address in the DHCP server logs. Then again, he or she might not. Perhaps the administrator notices a suspicious-looking car sporting an antenna out one of its windows.

NOTE

DHCP is not recommended on a WLAN because it makes it just that much easier for an attacker to gain access to your wired network. If the attacker can get past the rest of your configured security mechanisms, having a DHCP lease offered to him or her is just the icing on the cake. Like any guideline or rule, there are times when you cannot abide by these suggestions, because each network you support will have different restrictions and requirements.

If the car is parked on private property, the driver could be asked to move or possibly be charged with trespassing. However, the legal response may be severely limited, depending on the laws in your jurisdiction. In comparison, circumstances under which the war driver is susceptible to being charged with a data-related crime depends entirely on the country or state in which the activity takes place.

Passive attacks on wireless networks are extremely common, almost to the point of being ubiquitous. Detecting and reporting on wireless networks has become a popular hobby for many wireless war-driving enthusiasts. In fact, this activity is so popular that a new term, *war plugging*, has emerged to describe the behavior of people who actually want to advertise both the availability of an access point (AP) and the services they offer by configuring their Service Set Identifiers (SSIDs) with text such as "Get_food_here!"

War Driving

Most war-driving enthusiasts use a popular freeware program called NetStumbler, available from www.netstumbler.com. The NetStumbler program works primarily with wireless network adapters that use the Hermes chipset, because of its ability to detect multiple APs that are within range and Wired Equivalent Privacy (WEP), among other features. (A list of supported adapters is available at the NetStumbler Web site.) The most common card that uses the Hermes chipset for use with NetStumbler is the

ORiNOCO gold card. Another advantage of the ORiNOCO card is that it supports the addition of an external antenna, which can greatly extend the range at which the network adapter can detect and interact with a wireless network by many orders of magnitude, depending on the antenna used.

NOTE

War drivers often make their own Yagi-type (tubular or cylindrical) antenna. Instructions for doing so are easy to find on the Internet, and effective antennas have been made from such items as Pringles potato chip cans. Another type of antenna that can be easily homemade is the *dipole*, which is basically a piece of wire of a length that's a multiple of the wavelength, cut in the center and attached to a piece of cable that is connected to the wireless NIC.

A disadvantage of the Hermes chipset is that it doesn't support promiscuous mode, so it cannot be used to sniff network traffic. For that purpose, you need a wireless network adapter that supports the PRISM2 chipset. The majority of wireless network adapters targeted for the consumer market use this chipset (for example, the Linksys WPC network adapters). Sophisticated war drivers arm themselves with both types of cards, one for discovering wireless networks and another for capturing the traffic. In spite of the fact that NetStumbler is free, it is a sophisticated and feature-rich product that is excellent for aiding you in performing wireless site surveys, whether for legitimate purposes or not. Not only can it provide detailed information on the wireless networks it detects, it can be used in combination with a global positioning system (GPS) to provide exact details on the latitude and longitude of the detected wireless networks. NetStumbler displays information on the SSID, the channel, and the manufacturer of the wireless AP. There are a few things that are particularly noteworthy about this session. The first is that a couple of APs are still configured with the default SSID supplied by the manufacturer, which should always be changed to a nondefault value upon setup and configuration. Another is that at least one network uses a SSID that may provide a clue about the entity that has implemented it; again, this is not a good practice when you're configuring SSIDs. Finally, we can see which of these networks have implemented WEP.

> **NOTE**
>
> WEP is the basic security mechanism that was provided in the original 802.11b specification from the Institute of Electrical and Electronics Engineers (IEEE). It is based on the RC4 encryption algorithm, which is not such a bad thing. WEP, which is available in 64-bit and 128-bit implementations, is weakened by the use of a 24-bit initialization vector (IV) that increments in a predictable fashion, thus rendering WEP vulnerable to attack by several readily available cracking tools. WEP has been improved through the introduction of several newer technologies, such as LEAP, TKIP, and AES. The Wi-Fi alliance changed the requirements to become Wi-Fi certified in late 2002 to include Wireless Protected Access (WPA), which is a derivative of TKIP and provides for 802.1x port-based access controls and dynamic WEP keying. We examine LEAP, which also provides these solutions, in Chapter 11.

If the network administrator has been kind enough to provide a clue about the company in the SSID or is not encrypting traffic with WEP, the potential eavesdropper's job is made a lot easier. Using a tool such as NetStumbler is only a preliminary step for the attacker. After discovering the SSID and other information, the attacker can connect to the wireless network to sniff and capture network traffic. This network traffic can reveal a great deal of information about the network and the company that uses it.

For example, looking at the network traffic, the attacker can determine what Domain Network Service (DNS) servers are being used, the default home pages configured on browsers, network names, logon traffic, and so on. The attacker can use this information to determine if the network is of sufficient interest to proceed further with other attacks. Furthermore, if the network is using WEP, the attacker can, given enough time and the right tools, capture a sufficient amount of traffic to crack the encryption.

NetStumbler works on networks that are configured as *open systems*. This means that the wireless network indicates it exists and will respond with the value of its SSID to other wireless devices when they send out a radio beacon with an "empty set" SSID. This does not mean that the wireless network can be easily compromised, *if* other security measures have been implemented.

To defend against the use of NetStumbler and other programs to easily detect a wireless network, administrators should configure the wireless network as a *closed system*. This means that the AP will not respond to "empty set" SSID beacons and will consequently be "invisible" to programs such as NetStumbler, which rely on this technique to discover wireless networks. However, it is still possible to capture the "raw" 802.11b frames and decode them through the use of programs such as ethereal and WildPacket's AiroPeek to determine this information. RF spectrum analyzers can be used to discover the presence of wireless networks. Notwithstanding this weakness of *closed systems*, you should choose wireless APs that support this feature.

Sniffing

Originally conceived as a legitimate network and traffic analysis tool, sniffing remains one of the most effective techniques in attacking a wireless network, whether it's to map the network as part of a target reconnaissance, to grab passwords, or to capture unencrypted data.

Sniffing is the electronic form of eavesdropping on the communications that computers transmit across networks. In early networks, the equipment that connected machines together allowed every machine on the network to see the traffic of all others. These devices, repeaters and hubs, were very successful for getting machines connected, but they allowed an attacker easy access to all traffic on the network because the attacker only needed to connect to one point to see the entire network's traffic.

Wireless networks function very similarly to the original repeaters and hubs. Every communication across the wireless network is viewable to anyone who happens to be listening to the network. In fact, the person who is listening does not even need to be associated with the network in order to sniff!

The hacker has many tools available to attack and monitor a wireless network. A few of these tools are AiroPeek for Windows, Ethereal (www.ethereal.com) for Windows, UNIX or Linux and TCPDump or ngrep (http://ngrep.sourceforg.net) in a UNIX or Linux environment. These tools work well for sniffing both wired and wireless networks.

All these software packages function by putting your network card in what is called *promiscuous mode*. If the attacker is able to acquire a WEP key, he or she can then utilize features within AiroPeek and Ethereal to decrypt either live or post-capture data.

Active Attacks on Wireless Networks

Once an attacker has gained sufficient information from the passive attack, the hacker can then launch an active attack against the network. There is a potentially large number of active attacks that a hacker can launch against a wireless network. For the most part, these attacks are identical to the kinds of active attacks that are encountered on wired networks. These include, but are not limited to, unauthorized access, spoofing, DoS, and flooding attacks as well as the introduction of *malware* (malicious software) and the theft of devices.

With the rise in popularity of wireless networks, new variations of traditional attacks specific to wireless networks have emerged along with specific terms to describe them, such as *drive-by spamming.*, in which a spammer sends out tens or hundreds of thousands of spam messages using a compromised wireless network.

Because of the nature of wireless networks and the weaknesses of WEP, unauthorized access and spoofing are the most common threats to wireless networks. Spoofing occurs when an attacker is able to use an unauthorized station to impersonate an authorized station on a wireless network. A common way to protect a wireless network against unauthorized access is to use MAC filtering to allow only clients that possess valid MAC addresses access to the wireless network. The list of allowable MAC addresses can be configured on the AP, or it may be configured on a RADIUS server with which the AP communicates.

However, regardless of the technique used to implement MAC filtering, it is a relatively easy matter to change the MAC address of a wireless device through software, to impersonate a valid station. In Windows, this is accomplished with a simple edit of the Registry and in UNIX through a root shell command. (You can learn more on how this is done in Windows by reading the tutorial located at www.techrepublic.com/article.jhtml?id=t01820021125WCS01.htm.) MAC addresses are sent in the clear on wireless networks, so it is also a relatively easy matter to discover authorized addresses.

WEP can be implemented to provide more protection against authentication spoofing through the use of shared-key authentication. However, as we discussed earlier, shared-key authentication creates an additional vulnerability. Because shared-key authentication makes visible both a plaintext challenge and the resulting ciphertext version of it, it is possible to use this information to spoof authentication to a closed network.

Once the attacker has authenticated and associated with the wireless network, he or she can then run port scans, use special tools to dump user lists and passwords, impersonate users, connect to shares, and, in general, create havoc on the network through DoS and flooding attacks. These DoS attacks can be traditional in nature, such as a *ping flood, SYN, fragment,* or *DDoS* attacks, or they can be specific to wireless networks through the placement and use of *rogue access points* to prevent wireless traffic from being forwarded properly (similar to the practice of router spoofing on wired networks).

Spoofing (Interception) and Unauthorized Access

The combination of weaknesses in WEP and the nature of wireless transmission has highlighted the art of spoofing as a real threat to wireless network security. Some well-publicized weaknesses in user authentication using WEP have made authentication spoofing just one of an equally well-tested number of exploits by attackers.

One definition of spoofing is an attacker's ability to trick the network equipment into thinking that the address from which a connection is coming is one of the valid and allowed machines from its network. Attackers can accomplish this goal in several ways, the easiest of which is to simply redefine the MAC address of the attacker's wireless or network card to be a valid MAC address. This can be accomplished in Windows through a simple Registry edit. Several wireless providers also have an option to define the MAC address for each wireless connection from within the client manager application that is provided with the interface.

There are several reasons that an attacker would spoof. If the network allows only valid interfaces through MAC or IP address filtering, an attacker would need to determine a valid MAC or IP address to be able to communicate on the network. Once that is accomplished, the attacker could then reprogram his interface with that information, allowing him to connect to the network by impersonating a valid machine.

IEEE 802.11 networks introduce a new form of spoofing: authentication spoofing. As described in their paper, *Intercepting Mobile Communications: The Insecurities of 802.11*, authors Borisov, Goldberg, and Wagner identified a way to utilize weaknesses within WEP and the authentication process to spoof authentication into a closed network. The process of authentication, as defined by IEEE 802.11, is very simple. In a shared-key configuration, the AP sends out a 128-byte random string in a cleartext message to the workstation that is attempting to authenticate. The workstation then encrypts the message with the shared key and returns the encrypted message to the AP. If the message matches what the AP is expecting, the workstation is authenticated onto the network and access is allowed.

As described in the paper, if an attacker has knowledge of both the original plaintext and ciphertext messages, it is possible to create a forged encrypted message. By sniffing the wireless network, an attacker is able to accumulate many authentication requests, each of which includes the original plaintext message and the returned ciphertext-encrypted reply. From this, the attacker can easily identify the keystream used to encrypt the response message. The attacker could then use it to forge an authentication message that the AP will accept as a proper authentication.

The wireless hacker does not need many complex tools to succeed in spoofing a MAC address. In many cases, these changes are either features of the wireless manufacturers or can be easily changed through a Windows Registry modification or through Linux system utilities. Once a valid MAC address is identified, the attacker needs only to reconfigure his device to trick the AP into thinking he is a valid user.

The ability to forge authentication onto a wireless network is a complex process. No off-the-shelf packages that provide these services are available. Attackers need to either create their own tool or take the time to decrypt the secret key by using AirSnort or WEPCrack.

If the attacker is using Windows 2000 and his network card supports reconfiguring the MAC address, there is another way to reconfigure this information. A card supporting this feature can be changed through the System Control Panel.

Once the attacker is utilizing a valid MAC address, he is able to access any resource available from the wireless network. If WEP is enabled, the attacker will have to either identify the WEP secret key or capture the key through malware or by stealing the user's notebook.

Designing & Planning...

MAC Spoofing

For some time after it was introduced into production access points, administrators actually believed that MAC filtering was an effective solution on its own without using WEP or any other solutions. Taking that train of thought one step further, many administrators actually believed it was more secure to use only MAC filtering for security on their wireless networks. As they found out shortly thereafter, nothing could be further from the truth. To get an idea of its rightful place in the wireless security arena, let's look at two scenarios in which MAC filtering is being used.

The first scenario involves a small three-node wireless network that you have established in your house to allow your children's computers access to your cable modem connection as well as allowing you to work on your portable computer on the back deck—all without having to run CAT5 cable around the house to various locations. You have implemented MAC filtering but not WEP on your AP. Are you completely secure? Not at all. Are you secure enough? It depends on your interpretation of secure. Let's say now that you have implemented WEP as well on your small home network. Now are you secure? Yes. Why? It's unlikely that someone will park themselves in your driveway or otherwise close enough to your house for a long enough period of time (this could be several days in a small network, several hours in a large network) to capture enough traffic to crack your WEP key. In this case, you have put together a fairly effective protective mechanism to keep casual war drivers and most script kiddies off your wireless network, not to mention your next-door neighbor who simply wants to ride on your cable modem's bandwidth for a while.

Now consider the scenario in which you are building a large enterprise wireless network for a hospital. Not only do you need to provide wireless access in a large portion of the hospital building itself, but you also need to provide wireless network access to a small outpatient building 500 yards away from the main hospital building. Would you rely on only MAC filtering to ensure security in this case? Probably not. Just the same, you will probably be looking for a more robust and secure authentication and

Continued

authorization mechanism than WEP, such as LEAP with a RADIUS server, to protect the network transmissions themselves.

The moral of this discussion is, if you rely on simple protective measures to keep your wireless network secure, it will be just that much simpler for an attacker to break through your plan and gain access to your wired network. In short, use every possible means at your disposal to secure wireless networks without adding undue management traffic that causes the wireless network to be a nonviable solution. Also consider the use of wireless DMZs and VLANs to further segregate wireless traffic from your protected and trusted network backbone.

Denial of Service and Flooding Attacks

The nature of wireless transmission, and especially the use of spread-spectrum technology, makes a wireless network especially vulnerable to DoS attacks. The equipment needed to launch such an attack is freely available and very affordable. In fact, many homes and offices contain the equipment that is necessary to deny service to their wireless networks.

A DoS occurs when an attacker has engaged most of the resources a host or network has available, rendering that host or network unavailable to legitimate users. One of the original DoS attacks is known as a *ping flood*. A ping flood utilizes misconfigured equipment along with bad "features" within TCP/IP to cause a large number of hosts or devices to send an ICMP echo (ping) to a specified target. When the attack occurs, it tends to use a large portion of the resources of both the network connection and the host being attacked. This makes it very difficult for valid end users to access the host for normal business purposes.

In a wireless network, several events can cause a similar disruption of service. Probably the easiest way to do this is through a conflict within the wireless spectrum, caused by different devices attempting to use the same frequency. Many new wireless telephones use the same frequency as 802.11 networks. Through either intentional or unintentional uses of another device that uses the 2.4GHz frequency, a simple telephone call could prevent all wireless users from accessing the network.

Another possible attack would be through a massive number of invalid (or valid) authentication requests. If the AP is tied up with thousands of spoofed authentication attempts, authorized users attempting to authenticate themselves would have major difficulties in acquiring a valid session.

As demonstrated earlier, the attacker has many tools available to hijack network connections. If a hacker is able to spoof the machines of a wireless network into thinking that the attacker's machine is their default gateway, not only will the attacker be able to intercept all traffic destined for the wired network—he would also be able to prevent any of the wireless network machines from accessing the wired network. To do this, the hacker needs only to spoof the AP and not forward connections to the end destination, preventing all wireless users from performing valid wireless activities.

Not much effort is needed to create a wireless DoS. In fact, many users create these situations with the equipment found within their homes or offices. In a small apartment building, you could find several APs as well as many wireless telephones, all of which transmit on the same frequency. It would be easy for these users to inadvertently create DoS attacks on their own networks as well as on those of their neighbors.

A hacker who wants to launch a DoS attack against a network with a flood of authentication strings will in most cases not even need to be a highly skilled programmer. Many tools are available to create this type of attack, so even the most unskilled of black hats, the script kiddie, can launch one with little or no knowledge of how it works or why.

Many apartments and older office buildings do not come prewired for the high-tech networks in use today. To add to the problem, if many individuals are setting up their own wireless networks without coordinating the installations, many problems can occur that will be difficult to detect.

Only a limited number of frequencies are available to 802.11 networks. In fact, once the frequency is chosen, it does not change until it's manually reconfigured. Considering these problems, it is not hard to imagine the following situation occurring.

Let's say that a person purchases a wireless AP and several network cards for his home network. When he gets home to his apartment and configures his network, he is extremely happy with how well wireless networking actually works. Then, suddenly none of the machines on the wireless network are able to communicate. He phones the tech support line of the vendor that made the device. After waiting on hold for 45 minutes to get through, he finds that the network has magically started working again, so he hangs up.

Later that week, the same problem occurs, except that this time he decides to wait on hold when he phones the vendor. While waiting, he goes onto his porch and begins discussing his frustration with his neighbor. During the conversation, his neighbor's kids come out and say that their wireless network is not working.

So they begin to do a few tests (while still waiting on hold, of course). First, the man's neighbor turns off his AP (which is usually off unless the kids are online, to "protect" their network). When this is done, the original person's wireless network starts working again. Then they turn on the neighbor's AP again and the first man's network stops working again.

At this point, a tech support rep finally answers and the caller describes what has happened. The tech support representative has seen this situation several times and informs the user that he will need to change the frequency used in the device to another channel. He explains that the neighbor's network is utilizing the same channel, causing the two networks to conflict. Once the caller changes the frequency, everything starts working properly.

Man-in-the-Middle Attacks on Wireless Networks

Placing a rogue AP within range of wireless stations is a wireless-specific variation of a man-in-the-middle attack. If the attacker knows the SSID in use by the network (which, as we have seen, is easily discoverable) and the rogue AP has enough strength, wireless users will have no way of knowing that they are connecting to an unauthorized AP.

Using a rogue AP, an attacker can gain valuable information about the wireless network, such as authentication requests, the secret key that is in use, and so on. Often, the attacker will set up a laptop with two wireless adapters, in which one card is used by the rogue AP and the other is used to forward requests through a wireless bridge to the legitimate AP. With a sufficiently strong antenna, the rogue AP does not have to be located in close proximity to the legitimate AP.

For example, the attacker can run the rogue AP from a car or van parked some distance away from the building. However, it is also common to set up hidden rogue APs (under desks, in closets, etc.) close to and within the same physical area as the legitimate AP. Because of their virtually undetectable nature, the only defense against rogue APs is vigilance through frequent site surveys (using tools such as AirMagnet, NetStumbler, and AiroPeek,), visual site inspections, and physical security.

Frequent site surveys also have the advantage of uncovering the unauthorized APs that company staff members might have set up in their own work areas, thereby compromising the entire network and completely undoing the hard work that went into securing the network in the first place. This is usually done with no malicious intent but for the convenience of the user, who might want to be able to connect to the network via his or her laptop in meeting rooms, break rooms, or other areas that don't have wired outlets. Even if your company does not use or plan to use a wireless network, you should consider doing regular wireless site surveys to see if someone has violated your company security policy by placing an unauthorized AP on the network, regardless of their intent.

Network Hijacking and Modification

Numerous techniques are available for an attacker to "hijack" a wireless network or session. However, unlike some attacks, network and security administrators might be unable to tell the difference between the hijacker and a legitimate "passenger."

Many tools are available to the network hijacker. These tools are based on basic implementation issues within almost every network device available today. As TCP/IP traffic goes through switches, routers, and APs, each device looks at the destination IP address and compares it with the IP addresses it knows to be local. If the address is not in the table, the device hands the packet off to its default gateway.

This table is used to coordinate the IP address with the MAC addresses that are known to be local to the device. In many situations, this list is a dynamic one that is built up from traffic that is passing through the device and through Address Resolution Protocol (ARP) notifications from new devices joining the network. There is no authentication or verification that the request received by the device is valid. Thus a malicious user is able to send messages to routing devices and APs stating that his MAC address is associated with a known IP address. From then on, all traffic that goes through that router destined for the hijacked IP address will be handed off to the hacker's machine.

If the attacker spoofs as the default gateway or a specific host on the network, all machines trying to get to the network or the spoofed machine will connect to the attacker's machine instead of the gateway or host to which they intended to connect. If the attacker is clever, he will only use this machine to identify passwords and other necessary information, and he'll route the rest of the traffic to the intended recipients. If he does this, the end users will have no idea that this "man in the middle" has intercepted their communications and compromised their passwords and information.

Another clever attack can be accomplished through the use of rogue APs. If the attacker is able to put together an AP with enough strength, the end users might not be able to tell which AP is the authorized one that they should be using. In fact, most will not even know that another is available. Using this technique, the attacker is able to receive authentication requests and information from the end workstation regarding the secret key and where they are attempting to connect.

These rogue APs can also be used to attempt to break into more tightly configured wireless APs. Utilizing tools such as AirSnort and WEPCrack requires a large amount of data to decrypt the secret key. A hacker sitting in a car in front of your house or office is noticeable and thus will generally not have enough time to finish acquiring sufficient information to break the key. However, if the attacker installs a tiny, easily hidden machine in an inconspicuous location, this machine could sit there long enough to break the key and possibly act as an external AP into the wireless network it has hacked.

Attackers who want to spoof more than their MAC addresses have several tools available. Most of these tools are for use in a UNIX environment and can be found through a simple search for *ARP spoof* at http://packetstormsecurity.com. With these tools, the hacker can easily trick all machines on the wireless network into thinking that the hacker's machine is another machine on the network. Through simple sniffing on the network, an attacker can determine which machines are in high use by the workstations on the network. If the attacker then spoofs the address of one of these machines, the attacker might be able to intercept much of the legitimate traffic on the network.

AirSnort and WEPCrack are freely available. It would take additional resources to build a rogue AP, but these tools will run from any Linux machine. Once an attacker has identified a network for attack and spoofed his MAC address to become a valid member of the network, the attacker can gain further information that is not available through simple sniffing.

By just ARP spoofing the connection with the AP to be that of the host from which the attacker wants to steal the passwords, the attacker can cause all wireless users who are attempting to SSH into the host to connect to the rogue machine instead. When these users attempt to sign on with their passwords, the attacker is then able to, first, receive their passwords, and second, pass on the connection to the real end destination. If the attacker does not perform the second step, it will increase the likelihood that the attack will be noticed, because users will begin to complain that they are unable to connect to the host.

Jamming Attacks

The last type of attack is the jamming attack. This is a fairly simple attack to pull off and can be done using readily available, off-the-shelf radio frequency (RF) testing tools (although they were not necessarily designed to perform this function). Whereas hackers who want to get information from your network would use other passive and active types of attacks to accomplish their goals, attackers who just want to disrupt your network communications or even shut down a wireless network can jam you without ever being seen. The process of jamming a wireless LAN is similar in many ways to the way a DoS attack would target a network; the difference is that in the case of the wireless network, the attack can be carried out by one person with an overpowering RF signal. This attack can be carried out using any number of products, but the easiest way is with a high-powered RF signal generator, readily available from various vendors.

A jamming attack is sometimes the most difficult type of attack to prevent because the attacker does not need to gain access to your network. He or she can sit in your parking lot or even further away, depending on the power output of their jamming device. You might be able to readily determine the fact that you are being jammed, but you could find yourself hard-pressed to solve the problem. Indications of a jamming attack include clients' inability to connect to APs suddenly where there was previously no problem.

The problem will be evident across all or most of your clients (the ones within the range of the RF jamming device), even though your APs are operating properly.

Jamming attacks are sometimes used as the prelude to further attacks. One possible example includes jamming the wireless network, thereby forcing clients to lose their connections with authorized APs. In this time, one or rogue APs can be made available operating at a higher power than the authorized APs. When the jamming attack is stopped, the clients will tend to associate back to the AP that is presenting the strongest signal. Now the attacker owns all the network clients attached to his rogue APs. The attack continues from there.

In some cases RF jamming is not always intentional and could be the result of other, nonhostile sources such as a nearby communications tower or another WLAN that is operating in the same frequency range. Baby monitors, cordless telephones, microwave ovens, and many other consumer products may also be sources of interference.

You can take some comfort in knowing the fact that although a jamming attack is easy and inexpensive to pull off, it is not the preferred means of attack. For most hackers, the only real victory with a jamming attack is temporarily taking your wireless network offline.

Designing the Wireless DMZ

By now you should have an understanding of why the WLAN needs to be segregated from the wired segment. But you might not have an idea of how to create this separation. Enter the WLAN DMZ—a special breed of DMZ that can actually take on many forms, unlike the traditional DMZ implemented for all-wired segments of the network. When creating a DMZ for a traditional wired network, you typically have routers and firewalls that examine traffic for several items, including the following:

- **Destination port** Is the destination port an allowable port? For example, port 80 would typically be allowable because it is the default port for HTTP connections. On the other hand, you might be blocking connections to port 21 if you are not providing FTP services.

- **Source IP address** A common attack from the public side of the network involves spoofing the source IP address of inbound traffic. Most firewalls and routers today can be configured to drop these specially crafted packets at the borders of an organization. As well, you may configure internal routers and firewalls to disallow outbound traffic that does not have a valid source IP address matching that in use in your network. This can prevent the spread of attacks, specifically DoS attacks.

- **Destination IP address** In some cases, routers and firewalls may be configured to drop all packets that are not sent to valid internal IP addresses, especially in cases where the packet is being sent to a network broadcast address.

- **Packet data.** Many forms of attacks can be detected by certain routers and firewalls through analysis of the payload and the data contained within each packet. This not only prevents unauthorized users from gaining access to your protected network—it also adds another layer of security by keeping many forms of attacks from succeeding.

This short list is by no means all inclusive; it merely presents some of the more typical functions that are performed by the devices that make up the DMZ. But how does this apply to the unique problems presented by the WLAN? With the WLAN, you have an entirely different problem to cope with that you don't often have to worry about with wired segments: access. The ability to freely gain access to a wireless segment of a network and then subsequently gain access to the wired segment is the problem here. So the issue of creating a form of DMZ for the WLAN actually begins with controlling access to that WLAN. The reality is, however, that you can't easily do such a thing—at least not by the standards in place with wired segments.

In a wired network, you can take great strides toward preventing unauthorized clients from joining the network by performing actions such as placing switches in locked wiring closets, disabling unused ports on switches, and hiding away the bulk of the network infrastructure from prying eyes. True, these steps will not prevent a dedicated individual from finding a way to gain access, but they go a long way toward stopping them or making their job more difficult. With a wireless network, you can't really perform any of these actions—after all, someone need only be within range of your AP to begin the process of authenticating and subsequently associating with that AP. Once this has been accomplished, they can begin to run free on your *entire* network.

Designing & Planning…

"It Didn't Have WEP Enabled Because We Didn't Install It"

Earlier this year I heard a network administrator (whose name shall be withheld to protect the guilty) utter these very words about a Linksys AP that had been placed in one of his buildings. The organization in question certainly had enough funding to acquire an enterprise-quality AP, such as one

Continued

of the great models made by Cisco, ORiNOCO, or Symbol. The hole in the company's 5000+ node Class B network, however, was caused by a $100 Linksys AP that a user had placed in the building without authorization or knowledge as to how to secure the AP using either WEP or MAC filtering, which would have at least been a little better than placing it in operation with the factory-default settings in place, as I found it.

This problem is not confined to this particular organization. Users everywhere are seeing the power and flexibility that can be gained from WLANs. Unfortunately, users rarely stop to think about the problems their impromptu office improvements can bring about. What's even more troubling is that admins like the one I dealt with either don't understand the problems associated with WLANs or don't believe in them. After mapping out his network for this particular network admin, I think I was able to help him out along those lines.

So the reality that sets WLAN DMZs apart from every other DMZ configuration is that they not only have to provide all the traffic segmentation and protection that standard wired network DMZs provide, they also must control access. This calls for a different approach and different hardware than are typically used in DMZ implementations, as we see in the next section.

Wireless DMZ Components

With the challenges presented by WLANs, it comes as no surprise that the standard DMZ arrangement won't provide the required results. Figure 4.2 shows a simplified version of what was previously shown in Figure 4.1. This depicts one of two standard DMZ arrangements in which the firewall provides three interfaces: public, private, and DMZ.

Figure 4.2 One Example of a Typical DMZ Arrangement

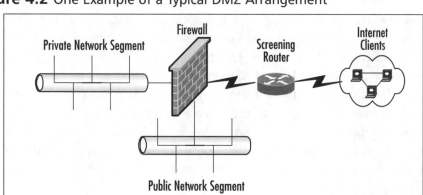

Unfortunately, this arrangement does not satisfy the requirement to limit traffic on the WLAN by controlling access to that WLAN itself. As previously discussed, another solution is needed—one that authenticates users and validates their privilege to access the WLAN (and thus the entire network) in the first place. Remember that no WLAN should ever be considered as secure as a wired LAN segment. With that knowledge, let's now examine some of the basic components that can be used to create the WLAN DMZ.

Access Points

Of course, it's no surprise that an AP is one of two items that forms the backbone of the WLAN. When it comes to choosing an AP, however, you have a multitude of choices, each presenting different benefits and costs. Do you pick the $100 AP that offers basic functionality, including MAC filtering and support for WEP, or do you pick the $600 AP that offers more advanced WLAN security functions, such as 802.1x port-based access control, RADIUS pass-through, and perhaps other features as well? This choice, like all network purchases, should be about more than just the monetary cost involved. Furthermore, the AP you choose should be complementary to the wireless network adapter you choose—meaning that if you opt for a more powerful and advanced AP, you should consider acquiring and using network adapters that can take advantage of the often vendor-specific features provided in the AP.

In simple terms, an AP is a Layer 2 device that serves as an interface between the wireless network and the wired network. APs are the wireless networking equivalent of a standard Ethernet hub in that they allow multiple clients using the same network technology to access the core network with a shared amount of bandwidth available to all clients. What sets the AP apart from its less advanced hub brethren is its ability to carry out many other additional functions—functions that will become important to creating your complete solution.

Network Adapters

The second piece of the puzzle is the network adapter. This, again, should be no big surprise, since you require the proper wireless network adapter to make the connection to begin with. As with the AP, the type of network adapter you choose will determine the types of security solution you can implement.

For example, let's suppose that you decided to use the Cisco Aironet AP 1100 with Cisco Aironet 352 network adapters and the Cisco Aironet Client Utility (ACU) software on the client computers. Using this arrangement, you could increase your security by taking advantage of Lightweight Extensible Authentication Protocol (LEAP), which provides strong authentication and traffic encryption without the problems associated with WEP. In Chapter 11, we examine how this combination of hardware and solutions can be used to provide increased security.

RADIUS Servers

RADIUS servers provide network users what's known as AAA: authentication, authorization, and accounting. In short, RADIUS servers are used on the back end of the network to provide a flexible and scalable system to authenticate users attempting to access network services. Originally developed for dial-in access using modems, RADIUS has proven flexible and powerful enough to handle authentication of users through various other connection means, including those attempting to make wireless connections to your network.

When RADIUS servers are combined with 802.1x port-based access control on APs, users are effectively prevented from accessing the network past the AP until they have been authorized against the RADIUS database. LEAP, discussed previously, takes advantage of 802.1x port-based access controls to further increase the security of the wireless and wired network. The RADIUS server performs the critical task of verifying that the user is authorized to gain access to the network through either an internal (native) database or by using the domain database (Active Directory).

NOTE

RADIUS is defined in RFC 2865. The behavior of RADIUS with EAP authentication is defined in RFC 2869. RFC can be searched and viewed online at www.rfc-editor.org. 802.1x is defined by the IEEE in the document located at http://standards.ieee.org/getieee802/download/802.1X-2001.pdf.

Enterprise Wireless Gateways and Wireless Gateways

The enterprise wireless gateway (EWG) is a relatively new piece of hardware that has only recently begun to appear on the market. Driven by the uniquely special needs presented by WLANs and their security, the EWG was created to provide enhanced security and management. An EWG is a specially designed and built hardware device that performs several key functions in one unit:

- **Router** EWGs have at least two Ethernet interfaces, one for the wireless segment and at least one for the wired segment. Many also offer additional failover interfaces for the wired segment. An EWG can also make certain that packets traversing the network destined for other subnets get to their intended source.

- **Firewall** Many of the EWGs currently on the market offer firewall-like services by providing stateful inspection of all traffic passing through them.

- **VPN server** Most EWGs typically provide VPN support, allowing clients to create VPN connections to the EWG (and thus the wired segment). They support IPSec, L2TP, and PPTP as well as RADIUS authentication for larger implementation.

The EWG is placed between the AP segment and the wired segment to control network access from the WLAN, as discussed in the next section.

Firewalls and Screening Routers

Firewalls and screening routers can still play a role in creating and implementing the WLAN DMZ. They provide the same protection and support that they would in a strictly wired network but are not enough by themselves to account for the various security concerns associated with the WLAN. This is due to the fact that firewalls and screening routers are devices primarily used for traffic filtering via user authentication. When used together with a well-crafted WLAN DMZ security solution, they still have a useful purpose.

Other Segmentation Devices

Although they will not be discussed here, there are several other segmentation devices that you should be aware of for use in controlling both traffic and access to your network. This list is presented here in the interests of making our discussion more complete. All these devices (and many more) can be used to segment portions of your network:

- SSH2 servers
- VPN servers
- Virtual LANs (VLANs)
- Layer 3 switches

Wireless DMZ Examples

Armed with a brief introduction to the pieces that make up the wireless DMZ, let's examine a few different scenarios that you could implement for your network.

Figure 4.3 shows an example arrangement that could be used to provide RADIUS authentication for wireless clients attempting to gain access to your network. In this example, both the wireless network adapter and the AP are Cisco products that support the use of LEAP. (We discuss LEAP in more detail in Chapter 11.) The process by which the client gains access to the network is outlined here briefly and explained in significantly more detail in Chapter 11.

1. The client computer requests to associate with the AP.

2. The AP, using 802.1x port access controls, blocks all access to the wired network segment.

3. The user performs LEAP authentication to the RADIUS server using the required credentials. This process involves the RADIUS server and the client performing mutual authentication. After this is done, the RADIUS server dynamically generates the Unicast session WEP key that will be used to secure the connection.

4. The RADIUS server then delivers this dynamic Unicast WEP key to the AP. The AP also encrypts the broadcast key with the Unicast key and sends it to the client.

5. The client and the AP use the dynamic WEP key to securely communicate, and the client is now associated with the AP. If required, a DHCP lease will be granted to the wireless client.

6. The client now securely accesses resources on the wired segment of the network.

Figure 4.3 Using RADIUS to Authenticate Users

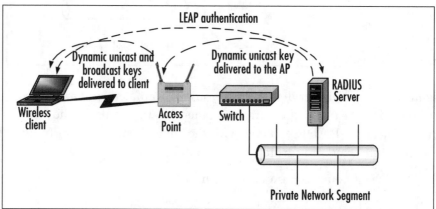

Figure 4.4 shows an example of how you might use a simple wireless gateway such as Reef Edge Dolphin to provide authentication and security through an IPSec VPN tunnel, if required. In this scenario, the wireless clients authenticate against the internal database of the Dolphin server, creating a VPN tunnel if desired.

1. The client computer associates with the AP.

2. The wireless gateway (Dolphin) blocks access to the wired network pending successful user authentication against its internal database.

3. The user authenticates to the Dolphin server.

4. If required, a DHCP lease will be granted to the wireless client.

5. If desired, a VPN tunnel is constructed to secure traffic.

6. The client now accesses resources on the wired segment of the network.

Figure 4.4 Using a Simple Wireless Gateway to Authenticate Users

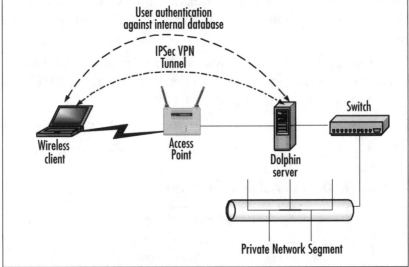

Figure 4.5 shows an overview of how you might implement an EWG on your network to provide security for the wireless segment. In this scenario, the wireless clients authenticate against a RADIUS server with the added benefit of a VPN tunnel being constructed by the EWG to further secure the traffic.

1. The client computer associates with the AP.

2. The client computer creates a VPN tunnel with the EWG.

3. The user performs authentication to the RADIUS server using the required credentials. The EWG acts as an authenticator (a go-between for the client and the RADIUS server).

4. The RADIUS server and the client authenticate per the VPN protocol being used.

5. If required, a DHCP lease will be granted to the wireless client.

6. A VPN tunnel is constructed between the client and the EWG in which to securely pass traffic.

7. The client now securely accesses resources on the wired segment of the network.

Figure 4.5 Using an Enterprise Wireless Gateway to Control Access

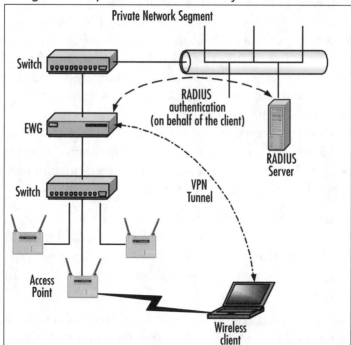

By now, you might be thinking that none of these solutions looks anything like a DMZ. That might be true, but appearances can be deceiving. Remember that the purpose of the DMZ is to keep unwanted (and potentially unsafe) traffic out of the protected internal network. All these solutions offer this capability by controlling access to your wireless network.

Wireless LAN Security Best-Practices Checklist

Although the primary focus here is the implementation of DMZ configurations, there are several other "best practices" that you can implement to further increase the security of your WLAN design. In recent months, the practice of implementing wireless networks has become somewhat routine to many administrators. Unfortunately, there is nothing routine about any network design and implementation. Administrators who want to implement wireless networks should exercise due care and diligence by becoming as familiar as possible with operation and vulnerabilities of wireless networks and *all* the available counter-measures for defending them.

Even though many currently implemented wireless networks support a wide range of features that can potentially be enabled, the sad fact is that most administrators do not use them. The media is full of reports of the informal results of site surveys conducted by war drivers. These reports provide worrisome information—for example, that most wireless networks are not using WEP and that many wireless networks are using default SSIDs, not to mention the advanced DMZ and VPN solutions we have outlined here briefly. Many of these networks are located in technology-rich areas, such as Silicon Valley, where you would think people would know better, making the information a potential source of serious concern.

There is really no excuse for failing to minimize the security threats created by wireless networks through the implementation of security features that are available on most wireless networks. The following checklist is a summary of common best practices that could be employed on many current or future wireless networks:

- Carefully review the available security features of wireless devices to see if they fulfill your security requirements. The 802.11 and Wi-Fi standards specify only a subset of features that are available on a wide range of devices. Over and above these standards, supported features vary widely; this is where the DMZ or the VPN comes into play.

- At a minimum, wireless access points and network adapters should support firmware updates, 128-bit WEP, MAC filtering, and the disabling of SSID broadcasts.

- Wireless vendors are continually addressing the security weaknesses of wireless networks. Check the wireless vendors' Web sites frequently for firmware updates and apply them to all wireless devices. You can leave your network exposed if you fail to update even one device with the most recent firmware.

- Always use WEP. Although it is true that WEP can be cracked, doing so requires knowledge and time. Even 40-bit WEP is better than no WEP.

- If static WEP keys must be used, always rotate them frequently.

- Always change the default administrative password used to manage the AP. The default passwords for wireless APs are well known. If possible, use a password generator to create a difficult and sufficiently complex password.

- Change the default SSID of the AP. The default SSIDs for APs from different vendors are well known, such as *tsunami* and *Linksys* for Cisco and Linksys APs, respectively. A fairly inclusive listing of default SSIDs can be found at www.area51partners.com/80211b.htm.

- Do not put any kind of identifying information in the SSID, such as the company name, address, products, divisions, and so on. By doing so, you provide too much information to potential hackers and are letting them know whether your network is of sufficient interest to warrant further effort.

- If possible, disable SSID broadcasts. This will make your network invisible to site survey tools, such as NetStumbler. However, this step will cause an administrative burden if you are heavily dependent on Windows XP clients being able to automatically discover and associate with the wireless network.

- If possible, avoid the use of DHCP for your wireless clients, especially if SSID broadcasts are not disabled. If DHCP is used, casual war drivers can potentially acquire IP address configurations automatically.

- Do not use shared-key authentication. Although it can protect your network against specific types of DoS attack, other kinds of DoS attacks are still possible. Shared-key authentication exposes your WEP keys to compromise.

- Enable MAC filtering where possible. It's true that MAC addresses can be easily spoofed, but your goal here is to slow down potential attackers.

- Learn how to use site survey tools such as NetStumbler and conduct frequent site surveys to detect the presence of rogue APs and to detect vulnerabilities in your own network.

- Don't place the AP near windows. Try to place it in the center of the building so that interference will hamper the efforts of war drivers and others trying to detect your traffic. Ideally, your wireless signal would radiate only to the outside walls of the building and not beyond. Try to come as close to that ideal as possible.

- If possible, purchase an AP that allows you to reduce the size of the wireless zone (cell sizing) by changing the power output.

- Educate yourself as to the operation and security of wireless networks.

- Educate your users about safe computing practices, in the context of the use of both wired and wireless networks.

- Perform a risk analysis of your network.

- Develop relevant and comprehensive security policies and implement them throughout your network.

Summary

Wireless LANs are attractive to many companies and home users because of the increased productivity that results from the convenience and flexibility of being able to connect to the network without the use of wires. WLANs are especially attractive when they can reduce costs by circumventing the need to install cabling to support users on the network. For these and other reasons, WLANs have become very popular in the past few years. However, WLAN technology has often been implemented poorly and without due consideration being given to network security. For the most part, these poor implementations result from a lack of understanding of the nature of wireless networks and the measures that can be taken to secure them.

WLANs are inherently insecure by their very nature—the fact that they radiate radio signals containing network traffic that can be viewed and potentially compromised by anyone within range of the signal. With the proper antennas, the range of WLANs is much greater than is commonly assumed. Many administrators wrongly believe that their networks are secure because the interference created by walls and other physical obstructions combined with the relative low power of wireless devices will contain the wireless signal sufficiently. Often, this is not the case.

As you've seen in this chapter, the standard notion of the typical DMZ does not apply very well to the WLAN. With a little bit of creativity, however, you can implement a WLAN DMZ. The goal of the DMZ is to control traffic crossing the network segment and to prevent unauthorized traffic from entering the protected private network; this result is offered by implementing the solutions that were outlined in this chapter. The most important thing that you, as the network administrator, can do is to fully understand your organization's security requirements and implement those requirements by making numerous solutions available. We examine the actual configuration and implementation of some of these solutions in Chapter 11.

Solutions Fast Track

Why Do We Need Wireless DMZs?

- ☑ WLANs are insecure by design and should *never* be trusted and should *never* be placed inside the trusted protected network.

- ☑ Attacks on wireless networks fall into four basic categories: passive attacks, active attacks, man-in-the-middle attacks, and jamming attacks.

- ☑ Examining the common threats to both wired and wireless networks provides a solid understanding in the basics of security principles and allows the network administrator to fully assess the risks associated with using wireless and other technologies.

☑ Threats can come from simple design issues, where multiple devices utilize the same setup, or intentional DoS attacks, which can result in the corruption or loss of data.

☑ Electronic eavesdropping, or sniffing, is passive and undetectable to intrusion detection devices.

☑ Tools that can be used to sniff networks are available for Windows (such as Ethereal and AiroPeek) and UNIX (such as TCPDump and ngrep).

☑ Sniffing traffic allows attackers to identify additional resources that can be compromised.

☑ Even encrypted networks have been shown to disclose vital information, such as the network name, in cleartext that can be received by attackers sniffing the WLAN.

Designing the Wireless DMZ

☑ The ability to freely gain access to a wireless segment of a network and then subsequently gain access to the wired segment is what makes implementing the wireless DMZ different from implementing the typical wired network DMZ. Therefore, the issue of creating a form of DMZ for the WLAN actually begins with controlling access to that WLAN.

☑ In a wired network, you can take great strides toward preventing unauthorized clients from joining the network by performing actions such as placing switches in locked wiring closets, disabling unused ports on switches, and hiding the bulk of the network infrastructure from prying eyes. This is not the case in the WLAN, where information is broadcast over radio waves.

☑ Where wired DMZs typically make use of firewalls and routers, WDMZs require other network hardware components, such as APs, RADIUS servers, network adapters, and EWGs.

Wireless DMZ Examples

☑   WDMZ designs can come in many forms. They all must, however, provide the same basic function: authenticating users and controlling access to the WLAN.

☑ You can opt to use a RADIUS-based solution to perform network authentication and authorization.

☑ You can use proprietary solutions such as Cisco's LEAP to provide additional protection. VPNs can be used to further secure communications of wireless clients.

Wireless LAN Security Best-Practices Checklist

☑ In addition to deploying a WLAN DMZ, there are several other things that you can do to add protection and increase security of your WLAN.

☑ Security begins with education. You should gain a full understanding of the security threats your WLAN is subject to. You should then gain a full understanding of how your wireless network hardware components can be used to put together a robust security solution.

☑ Perform a risk analysis and implement standardized security policies for your wireless and wired networks.

Frequently Asked Questions

The following Frequently Asked Questions, answered by the authors of this book, are designed to both measure your understanding of the concepts presented in this chapter and to assist you with real-life implementation of these concepts. To have your questions about this chapter answered by the author, browse to **www.syngress.com/solutions** and click on the **"Ask the Author"** form. You will also gain access to thousands of other FAQs at ITFAQnet.com.

Q: Do I really need to understand the fundamentals of security in order to protect my network?

A: Yes. You might be able to utilize the configuration options available to you from your equipment provider without a full understanding of security fundamentals. However, without a solid background in how security is accomplished, you will never be able to protect your assets from the unknown threats to your network through either misconfiguration, back doors provided by the vendor, or new exploits that have not been patched by your vendor.

Q: Given all the problems with wireless network security, wouldn't it be better to avoid using a wireless network in the first place?

A: Yes and no. How does the implementation of a properly secured wireless network impact your business model? Does this wireless network provide a useful function to your organization by allowing users to become more productive as they perform their assigned tasks? The decision to implement a wireless network is one that should not be taken lightly. Planning, just as with any network deployment, is the key to success. Don't simply put up a wireless network because it seems like a good idea; make sure that you have a clear-cut reason and plan of action before you get started. It's better to figure out how to secure your wireless network before you actually start installing it, thus preventing attackers from taking advantage of the easy pickings you have offered them.

Q: How can I protect my wireless network from eavesdropping by unauthorized individuals?

A: Because wireless devices are half-duplex devices, you cannot wholly prevent your wireless traffic from being listened to by unauthorized individuals. The only defense against eavesdropping is to encrypt Layer 2 and higher traffic whenever possible. This is where the VPN/DMZ combination solution comes into play.

Q: I've heard time and again that WEP is insecure. What makes WEP so insecure?

A: WEP is insecure for a number of reasons. The first is that the 24-bit initialization vector (IV) is too short. Because a new IV is generated for each frame and not for each session, the entire IV key space can be exhausted on a busy network in a matter of hours, resulting in the reuse of IVs. Second, the RC4 algorithm used by WEP has been shown to use a number of weak keys that can be exploited to crack the encryption. Third, because WEP is implemented at Layer 2, it encrypts TCP/IP traffic, which contains a high percentage of well-known and predictable information, making it vulnerable to plaintext attacks.

Q: How can I prevent unauthorized users from authenticating and associating with my AP?

A: There are a number of ways to accomplish this goal. You can configure your AP as a closed system by disabling SSID broadcasts and choosing a hard-to-guess SSID. You can configure MAC filtering to allow only those clients that use valid MAC addresses access to the AP. You can enable WEP and shared-key authentication. However, all these methods do not provide acceptable levels of assurance for corporate networks that have more restrictive security requirements than are usually found in SOHO environments. For corporate environments that require a higher degree of assurance, you should configure 802.1x port access control such as that offered by Cisco's LEAP combined with a back-end RADIUS server.

## Chapter 5

Firewall Design: Cisco PIX

Solutions in this chapter:

- Basics of the PIX

- Securing Your Network Perimeters

- Cisco PIX Versions and Features

- Making a DMZ and Controlling Traffic

- PIX Firewall Design and Configuration Checklist

☑ Summary

☑ Solutions Fast Track

☑ Frequently Asked Questions

Introduction

There are many ways to design and build your DMZ, and with so many products on the market, it might be difficult to decide which product is right for you. In the next few chapters we discuss several enterprise-level firewall solutions, including Cisco's PIX, Check Point's FireWall-1, and Microsoft's ISA 2000. We provide the information you need to decide which firewall meets the needs of your DMZ in terms of security, performance, functionality, manageability, stability, and reliability. Although all these products provide viable security solutions, they all have different requirements, features, and configuration methods that could lead you to choose one over the other. It is important to understand these products' capabilities and choose the product that meets the performance needs of your DMZ infrastructure and maintains a high level of security, one that you are comfortable supporting.

Reading this chapter, you will learn how to design and build a DMZ using Cisco's PIX firewall. We will advise you on the features of the PIX, guide you in the selection of the appropriate PIX hardware, and discuss different firewall arrangements as well as direct you on how to configure your firewall to securely pass traffic. By the end of this chapter you should be able to decide if the PIX is the right firewall for your DMZ infrastructure and, if you choose it, be able configure, manage, and support the PIX.

Basics of the PIX

Cisco's PIX firewall is one of the industry's best-selling firewalls, providing customers with high levels of security, performance and reliability. PIX, which stands for *Packet Internet Exchange,* was developed by Network Translation, Inc., in 1994 and purchased by Cisco in October 1995. The PIX firewall is a network appliance that does not use a general operating system like UNIX or Windows; therefore, inherent weaknesses found in these operating systems will not degrade the overall security of the firewall. The PIX utilizes the Adaptive Security Algorithm (ASA) to analyze every inbound packet, ensures that the network you are protecting is secure, and allows only legitimate traffic to pass through it. Some other features include Network or Port Address Translation (NAT or PAT), URL filtering, content filtering, IPSec VPN tunneling, and intrusion detection.

Cisco provides a complete line of PIX firewalls to meet your DMZ requirements, ranging from SOHO to carrier-class firewalls. The entire PIX line uses the same security algorithm but varies in performance, number of interfaces supported, and interface types. Depending on the chassis and license agreement, the PIX can support up to 10 interfaces, which allows the DMZ architect to design a large DMZ infrastructure. Cisco's PIX firewall line gives you the flexibility to support the needs of your DMZ infrastructure, no matter its size, complexity, or budget. As with all Cisco's products, hardware and software failures within the PIX are rare, but they can happen. The PIX offers high availability via its failover feature. A second PIX can provide stateful hot standby redundancy, which can maintain current open sessions so users won't notice that the primary unit has failed. The PIX's security features, purpose-built operating system, long mean time between failures (MTBF), resiliency, and low cost make it one of the most popular firewalls.

Securing Your Network Perimeters

The PIX is a powerful and versatile tool for securing your network. It can be used to secure your internal network from external parties—for example, Internet connections to third parties and business partners. The PIX can also be used on the internal network to protect sensitive data not only from outside parties but also from unauthorized employees or from employees who might have malicious intent. This book focuses on the network perimeter and the DMZ, but some of the same designs and security features can also be used internally.

The PIX provides the DMZ architect with a variety of design possibilities. In the next section, we go through several design possibilities, including a traditional "three-legged" firewall, a multi-DMZ infrastructure, and an internal/external firewall "sandwich." We also discuss adding firewall redundancy so that a single firewall failure would not bring down the entire infrastructure.

The Cisco Perimeter Security Solution

The most commonly implemented DMZ design in many small and medium-sized corporations is the traditional "three-legged" firewall. This design meets the needs of a site or sites in which internal users require the ability to access the Internet securely as well as send e-mails, access a locally hosted company Web site, or transfer files. Figure 5.1 shows how the traditional "three-legged" firewall fits into the network. The internal interface of the PIX firewall allows internal users to access both the DMZ and the Internet. The external interface connects the PIX to your local ISP router. The DMZ interface is where Web, FTP, e-mail relay servers, and any other services that need to be accessed by the Internet community are located. This design is very effective for low- to medium-traffic volume DMZ infrastructures that do not require high availability and can afford to have extended down time in the event of a firewall failure. Remember, if the firewall is down, internal users will not be able to access the Internet and DMZ services will not be accessible to the Internet community until the firewall is serviced.

Figure 5.1 Traditional "Three-Legged" Firewall

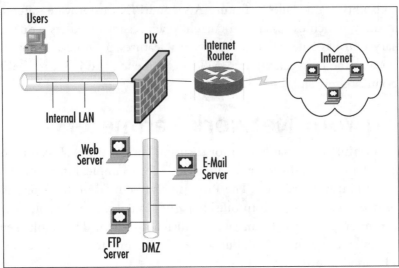

If high availability is required, the DMZ architect can consider adding a second PIX in conjunction with the PIX's failover feature, which allows the secondary PIX firewall to back up the primary PIX in the event of a failure. Figure 5.2 shows how redundancy can be added to the traditional "three-legged" firewall design. This design is ideal for corporations of all sizes, where the Internet/DMZ infrastructure is essential to the business and therefore they cannot afford downtime and require a resilient, highly available solution. Both the primary and secondary PIX firewalls need to be identical models and have the same interface options. Each PIX will have an interface on the internal, external, and DMZ LANs. When set up as a redundant pair, the PIX has the ability detect problems within the units or on any one of the interfaces and automatically failover to the backup unit. The PIX offers the option of *stateful failover*, which means that any open sessions on the primary will be automatically transferred to the secondary unit without client sessions disconnecting, so the failure is transparent to end users. In order for the PIX to support failover, some additional hardware is required, such as an additional interface to support the optional stateful failover feature and a Cisco proprietary cable for heartbeats between the primary and secondary units. We discuss the PIX failover feature and its requirements in detail later in this chapter.

Figure 5.2 Traditional "Three-Legged" Firewall with Redundancy

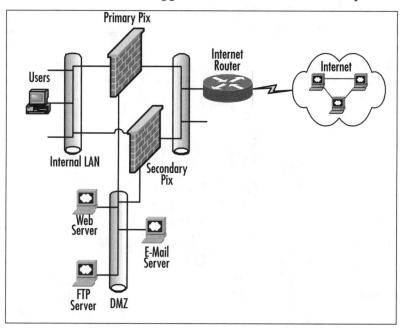

When you're given the task of building a DMZ in a large DMZ environment or when you need to support multiple service types, it might be desirable to separate them by adding additional "legs" to the DMZ. There are two reasons you might want to use a DMZ leg:

- An additional leg might be necessary if the number of servers has exceeded the number of available IP addresses for hosts on the DMZ subnet. By adding a DMZ interface, you can assign another IP range and add more servers.

- It's a good idea to separate service types. Service types are Web, FTP, e-mail, DNS, VPN, and remote access.

For example, Figure 5.3 shows a multiple DMZ environment with Web servers, e-mail relays, and FTP servers on the first DMZ leg (DMZ 1) and services such as VPN and dial-in user access on a second DMZ leg (DMZ 2). This setup separates the functions of the DMZs. DMZ 1 supports services that are publicly available over the Internet, such as the company's Web site. DMZ 2 supports remote users accessing resources on the internal LAN via a dial-in or VPN. By making remote users traverse the PIX, we make the internal LAN environment secure because rules can be set up to restrict remote user access. Adding DMZ legs helps keep the firewall rule sets manageable, especially when each DMZ has different access requirements. It also isolates any errors in configuration because a change on an access control list (ACL) for one DMZ will not affect the ACL of another DMZ interface. You can add redundancy by adding a secondary PIX, similar to the redundant traditional "three-legged" firewall design.

Figure 5.3 Multi-DMZ Infrastructure

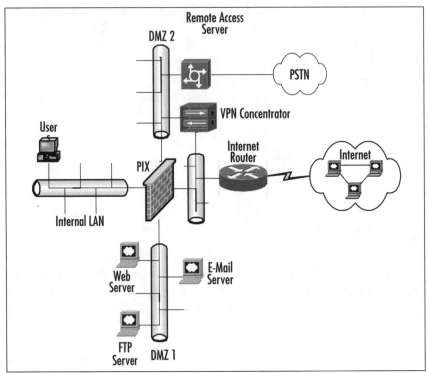

The previous designs are ideal for standard, multipurpose DMZ environments, but the internal/external firewall design (see Figure 5.4) is intended for the specific purpose of supporting an e-commerce site for which various levels of security are required. Large e-commerce sites separate the servers' functions into three components, consisting of a Web server cluster, an application server cluster, and a database cluster, which is most commonly known as a three-tier design. In this design, Internet users accessing an e-commerce site only interact with the Web servers on DMZ 1. The job of the Web server is to be the front-end GUI for the e-commerce site. The Web servers will in turn call upon the application servers on DMZ 2 to provide content. The application servers' job is to collect the information the user is requesting and provide content back to the Web server for the user to view.

The application server requests information by making SQL calls to the database servers on DMZ 3, which houses the site's data. Each component has different security requirements, which only allows necessary communication between DMZ 1, 2, and 3. The external PIX will only allow users to access the Web site on DMZ 1 via HTTP or HTTPS (SSL-enabled HTTP). The user community will not need to access any other part of the site, because the Web server will serve all the necessary content to the users; therefore, access is restricted to DMZ 1. The external PIX will allow the Web servers to make requests only to the application servers on DMZ 2 for content. DMZ 2 is located between the internal and external firewall sets with a Layer 3 switch acting as the default gateway for DMZ 2 as well as routing traffic though this environment. The internal firewall only allows the application servers to send SQL requests to the database servers located on DMZ 3. The internal firewall also allows administrators on the internal LAN to manage the e-commerce environment. For simplicity, Figure 5.4 does not show redundancy, but the internal and external PIX firewalls can be set up with failover. With the layered security approach, this solution provides a highly scalable and secure design that makes it difficult for hackers to compromise.

NOTE

To understand the traffic flows of the DMZ design just mentioned, you should look closely at Figure 5.4 and follow the traffic patterns from host to host. It is imperative that when you design a DMZ, you follow the notes listed here; always draw your scenario and plan it logically before you implement it physically. Because deploying a DMZ scenario is no easy task, your deployment will go more smoothly if you follow this advice.

Figure 5.4 An Internal/External Firewall Sandwich

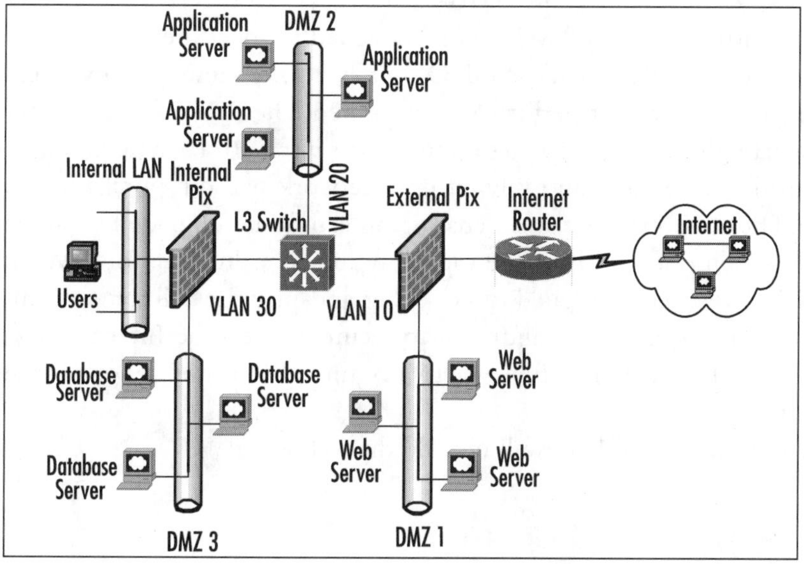

Cisco PIX Versions and Features

Cisco's PIX firewall solution provides several different chassis, software features, and licensing and interface options. In this section, we cover in detail the PIX hardware, features, and options that will help you decide if the PIX will provide functionality and performance to meet your DMZ requirements.

Cisco PIX Firewalls

The PIX firewall line consists of five models ranging from the SOHO model, PIX 501, to the high-performance service provider model, PIX 535. In order to determine the PIX to choose for your needs, you must first identify the requirements of your enterprise's Internet and DMZ infrastructure. To choose the proper firewall, you need to know some basic information: the number of DMZs (legs or interfaces) the firewall needs, approximate throughput required, number of users accessing resources through the firewall, and whether redundancy is required.

Once you have collected the requirements and have decided on a design, it's time to select the proper hardware that will serve to protect your DMZ infrastructure. The PIX firewall operating system is the same for all PIX models, so features such as NAT, URL filtering, content filtering, and VPN tunneling can be found across the entire line, depending on the software license purchased. Notice that the basic differences between the models mostly deal with the chassis interface options, performance, and cost. The next section details the five PIX model types and presents the information you need to choose the right chassis for your DMZ infrastructure.

The Cisco PIX 501 Firewall

The Cisco PIX 501 is an entry-level firewall designed to meet the needs of small or home offices. The PIX 501 provides SOHO users with the same security level and features as its bigger brothers, but performance is limited. The PIX 501 can support up to 50 users concurrently and incorporates a four-port switch 10/100Mb switch, so home users with broadband service can easily set up a network without purchasing an additional switch. The PIX 501 has a fixed chassis and cannot be upgraded to support additional interfaces so it does not have the capability to add a third leg (or DMZ leg).

The PIX 501 is strictly designed to be a plug-and-play firewall for very small networks that have broadband access and want to securely access the Internet as well as connect to a central or regional office via a VPN tunnel. It is not designed to support a DMZ infrastructure.

Key items of the PIX 501 firewall include the following:

- A 10-user license allows 10 internal IP addresses to access the Internet simultaneously, and the DHCP server feature supports up to 32 DHCP address assignments

- A 50-user license allows 50 internal IP addresses to access the Internet simultaneously, and the DHCP server feature supports up to 128 DHCP address assignments

- Fixed chassis, integrated four-port switch 10/100Mbps plus one Internet-facing 10/100Mbps port

- A 133MHz processor, 16MB RAM, and 8MB Flash

- 10Mbps clear-text throughput

- Optional encryption licenses are necessary if 168-bit 3DES or 56-bit DES VPN tunnels are needed

- Five VPN peers

- Small chassis (not rack mountable)

The Cisco PIX 506E Firewall

The Cisco PIX 506E is the next level up from the 501 and is designed to meet the needs of a remote or branch office. Unlike the 501, it has no license restriction that limits the number of users concurrently traversing the PIX. The 506E has a clear-text throughput of 20Mbps, which means you will probably max out the Internet connection at the remote site before the PIX becomes oversubscribed. This model supports no specific number of users because turning on features such as VPN tunneling or intrusion detection can reduce overall throughput.

As a guideline, you should not have more than 250 light to moderate Internet users, and if you need VPN tunneling, this number should be reduced further. The PIX 506E is also a fixed chassis and cannot be upgraded to support additional interfaces, so it does not have the capability to add a third leg (or DMZ leg). This model has two embedded 10BaseT Ethernet ports, which allow for an internal (protected interface) and an external interface (Internet-facing interface).

The PIX 506E is ideal for a small to medium-sized remote or branch office that requires secure Internet connectivity. It also has greater VPN performance, which allows for 25 VPN peers. Not only can a VPN tunnel connect the remote/branch site to a central site, but it can also accept remote users to VPN directly to office.

Key items of the PIX 506E firewall include the following:

- No user restriction license

- Fixed chassis, two embedded 10/100Mbps interfaces (internal/Internet facing)

- A 300MHz processor, 32MB SDRAM, and 8MB Flash

- 20Mbps clear-text throughput

- An optional encryption license is necessary if 168-bit 3DES or 56-bit DES VPN tunnels are needed

- 20Mbps DES VPN throughput

- 16Mbps 3DES VPN throughput

- Twenty-five VPN peers

- Small chassis (not rack mountable)

NOTE

It is important that you know the differences between the PIX firewall versions. This knowledge is imperative to solid DMZ design, because some models just can't be used to create a DMZ, and you don't want to waste your money or your time researching what do not need. It is clear, however, that if you want to deploy a DMZ segment, your efforts start with the PIX 515E.

The Cisco PIX 515E Firewall

Previously, we talked about the lower-end Cisco PIX firewalls, which are fixed models, support a small to intermediate number of users, and are *not capable* of supporting a traditional DMZ. Now let's discuss Cisco's enterprise-level firewall, which is modular, more powerful, and supports additional/multiple interfaces where a traditional DMZ can reside.

The Cisco PIX 515E, the first model in the modular line of PIX firewalls, is designed for small to medium-sized businesses but can also be used in larger organizations, if scaled properly. The PIX 515E has two embedded 10/100 Ethernet interfaces and can accommodate a variety of interface types, including one- or four-port Fast Ethernet interface cards (used to create the DMZ ports) and/or a VPN accelerator card (VAC) via two internal PCI slots. As we mentioned, optional modules inserted into the PIX 515E can be configured to support a DMZ by adding one or four-port Fast Ethernet interface cards used to create DMZ legs. The VAC can allow moderate-volume mobile users to remotely access corporate resources or connect remote sites to headquarters via site-to-site IPSec VPN tunnels. The PIX 515E provides the security, performance, versatility, and cost that make it very popular among network security and DMZ architects.

The PIX 515E is versatile enough to support a significant number of users as well as a DMZ environment that contains Web, e-mail, and FTP servers with volume that will not exceed its 188Mbps throughput. This is adequate for sites that have dual T3s (45Mbps each) or less to the Internet. You may ask, "Two T3s account for 90Mbps total, and it's only half the PIX's 188Mbps limitation?" However, it must be understood that dual T3s will push 90Mbps in each direction, accounting for 180Mbps of total throughput. However, if you are averaging 70 percent or more utilization or looking for scalability (if plans call for adding a T3 in the future), you should consider upgrading or choosing another chassis such as the PIX 525.

Key items of the PIX 515E firewall include the following:

- License choices are Restricted, Unrestricted, and Failover

- Modular chassis consists of two embedded 10/100 Ethernet ports and two PCI slots (32-bit/33MHz) for optional Fast Ethernet ports or VAC

- Maximum of six Fast Ethernet ports (including the two embedded 10/100 Ethernet ports)

- A 433MHz processor, 32MB (Restricted) or 64MB (Unrestricted) of SDRAM, and 16MB Flash

- 188Mbps clear-text throughput

- One hundred twenty-five thousand simultaneous sessions

- Optional encryption license is necessary if 168-bit 3DES or 56-bit DES VPN tunnels are needed

- 16Mbps (Restricted) or 63Mbps (Unrestricted w/VAC) 3DES VPN throughput

- Two thousand VPN tunnels

- Failover (Unrestricted and Failover)

- Rack-mountable chassis (one rack unit)

NOTE

As with all networking hardware, you need to have a good idea of the type and amount of traffic traversing your network as well as future growth before you can decide to purchase a particular type of hardware. This practice is known as doing a *traffic-flow analysis* on your network segments. Remember,

PIX throughput can be adversely affected by turning on features such as NAT, PAT, VPN, intrusion detection, and so on. Keep this in mind when you're sizing your firewall.

The Cisco PIX 525 Firewall

The Cisco PIX 525 firewall is designed to secure large enterprise locations and DMZs with high-volume Web traffic. In addition to the increased throughput, the PIX 525 also can accommodate a wider variety of interface types, including Fast Ethernet, Gigabit Ethernet, and/or a VAC. The PIX 525 has two embedded 10/100 Ethernet interfaces and is the first model in the PIX line that supports the optional Gigabit Ethernet interface. The ability for the PIX 525 to support up to eight Fast Ethernet interfaces also gives the DMZ architect the freedom to cost-effectively scale the DMZ.

The PIX 525 is ideal for enterprises with large user populations and moderate to heavy Internet access requirements and/or that have DMZ environments requiring significant throughput (not exceeding 370Mbps). With the optional VAC installed, it can also serve as the head end for a remote user VPN and/or a site-to-site VPN WAN, where some or all of your remote sites can be connected to the central enterprise location via IPSec VPN tunnels.

Key items of the PIX 525 firewall include the following:

- License choices are Restricted, Unrestricted, and Failover

- The modular chassis consists of two embedded 10/100 Ethernet ports and three PCI slots (32-bit/33MHz) for optional Fast Ethernet ports, Gigabit Ethernet, or VAC

- A maximum of eight interfaces (including the two embedded 10/100 Ethernet ports)

- A 600MHz Processor, 128MB (Restricted) or 256MB (Unrestricted) of SDRAM, and 16MB Flash

- 370Mbps clear-text throughput

- Two hundred eighty thousand simultaneous sessions

- Optional encryption license is necessary if 168-bit 3DES or 56-bit DES VPN tunnels are needed

- 30Mbps (Restricted) or 70Mbps (Unrestricted with VAC) 3DES VPN throughput

- Two thousand VPN tunnels (Unrestricted with VAC)

- Failover (Unrestricted and Failover)

- Rack-mountable chassis (two rack units)

The Cisco PIX 535 Firewall

The PIX 535 is Cisco's top-of-the-line firewall, providing the greatest performance and interface versatility designed for the service provider market. The PIX 535 has over two and a half times more throughput than its predecessor, with clear-text throughput reaching 1Gbps. Although it has no integrated Ethernet interfaces, the PIX 535 has nine PCI slots, which can support up to 10 Fast Ethernet interfaces, nine Gigabit Ethernet interfaces, a VAC, or a combination of the three. The PIX 535, with an unrestricted license, can support up to 10 interfaces, but you must consult the documentation before combining interfaces to determine the number of interface types that can work together. This process can be quite tricky and cause the firewall not to boot properly. You can find more information about installing a PCI card into the PIX 535 at the following site: www.cisco.com/univercd/cc/td/doc/product/iaabu/pix/pix_v53/inst-535/board.htm.

The PIX 535 is ideal for Internet service providers or enterprise locations that offer services to a very large user community, including support for a huge DMZ traffic load. As with the PIX 525, you can install an optional VAC in the PIX 535, and it can also serve as the head end for a remote user VPN and/or a site-to-site VPN WAN, where some or all your remote sites can be connected to the central enterprise location via IPSec VPN tunnels.

Key items of the PIX 535 firewall include the following:

- License choices are Restricted, Unrestricted, and Failover

- The modular chassis consists of nine PCI slots (four 64-bit/66MHz and five 32-bit/33MHz) for optional Fast Ethernet ports, Gigabit Ethernet, or VAC

- Offers a maximum of 10 interfaces

- A 1000MHz processor, 512MB (Restricted) or 1024MB (Unrestricted) of SDRAM, and 16MB Flash

- 1Gbps clear-text throughput

- Five hundred thousand simultaneous sessions

- An optional encryption license is necessary if 168-bit 3DES or 56-bit DES VPN tunnels are needed

- 45Mbps (Restricted) or 100Mbps (Unrestricted with VAC) 3DES VPN

- Two thousand VPN tunnels (Unrestricted with VAC)

- Failover (Unrestricted and Failover)
- Redundant power supplies
- Rack-mountable chassis (three rack units)

Cisco Firewall Software

The PIX Operating System (OS) is a feature-filled OS that provides a high level of security and performance. Because it is designed solely for the purpose of securing your network infrastructure and has an OS specifically built for it, it doesn't have the weaknesses inherent to general OSs such as Windows or UNIX. However, the PIX OS's lack of a general OS does not mean that the PIX has fewer features than its competitors. The PIX has a full set of security features and with its streamlined OS and specially designed hardware it has the ability to outperform many of its competitors.

Features include:

- **Purpose-built operating system** Eliminates the weaknesses found in most general OSs.

- **Adaptive security algorithm (ASA)** Method the PIX uses to provide stateful packet filtering, which analyzes each packet to ensure only legitimate traffic traverses the PIX.

- **URL filtering** Can limit URLs accessed by the user's base on a policy defined by the network administrator or a security policy. Requires an external Netpartner's WebSense server or N2H2 server.

- **Content filtering** Can block ActiveX or Java applets.

- **NAT and PAT** Hides internal addressing from the Internet and makes more efficient use of private address space.

- **Cut-through proxy** Authenticates users accessing resources through the PIX.

- **VPN** Capable of handling mobile user access and site-to-site VPNs utilizing DES, 3DES, and AES encryption methods.

- **Intrusion detection** Enables the PIX to protect against various forms of malicious attack with features such as DNSGuard, FloodGuard, MailGuard, and IPVerify as well as the ability to identify attacks via attack "signatures."

- **DHCP** Can act as a DHCP Client and/or Server.

- **Routing functionality** Can support static routes, RIP, and OSPF.

- **Support for RADIUS or TACACS+** Authenticating, authorizing, and accounting for users passing through the PIX or to enabled authentication for those connecting to the PIX's management interfaces.

- **Failover** Provides a resilient, high-availability solution in case of failure.

- **PPP over Ethernet (PPPoE) support** Compatible with xDSL and cable modems.

- **Common Criteria EAL4 Certification** Certain PIX OS versions have achieved the highest level of certification handed out by Common Criteria, an independent international security organization. You can find more information about Common Criteria at www.commoncriteria.org.

NOTE

In this chapter we have discussed how the PIX would provide stateful inspection. Let's take a closer look at this topic; it is very important to security because stateful inspection provides a deeper level of filtering than ACLs found in routers, which may only filter based on header information. Firewalls that perform stateful inspection analyze individual data packets as they traverse the firewall. In addition to the packet header, stateful inspection also assesses the packet's payload and looks at the application protocol. It can filter based on the source, destination, and service requested by the packet. The term stateful inspection refers to the firewall's ability to remember the status of a connection and thereby build a context for each data stream in its memory. With this information available to it, the firewall is able to make more informed policy decisions.

The Cisco PIX Device Manager

Cisco provides a few different options to configure and manage the PIX, including command-line (CLI) based serial console connection, Telnet, secure shell (SSH), and an application with a GUI called the PIX Device Manager (PDM). The PDM provides administrators with a browser-based GUI and gives people who might not be well versed in the PIX CLI the ability to easily configure and monitor the PIX via a Web browser. It is also very secure because the transmissions between the browser and the PIX are made secure by SSL. The PDM provides administrators with configuration wizards, performance graphs, and historical data to help with configuration and troubleshooting tasks. Even though the PDM covers most of the commands needed to configure, manage, and support the PIX, it does not support some commands that can only be configured via the CLI.

> **NOTE**
>
> The PDM software is separate from the PIX OS and is located in a separate file on the PIX Flash. Therefore, when you're upgrading software on the PIX, you might also need to upgrade the PDM software. The PDM is available for PIX OS version 6.0 and higher on all chassis types. The PDM does not require a license, but since it only supports encrypted communication to the browser (SSL), an encryption license is required in order to run the PDM. Cisco provides a no-cost DES license or a 3DES license for a fee.

The 501 and 506E are initially set up to work out of the box with PDM, but with the higher-end models, it is necessary to initially turn on PDM via the CLI prior to managing it via the PDM. The PDM works on a single device at a time and must be installed on the firewall separately from the PIX OS. To run the PDM, you need an activation key that enables Data Encryption Standard (DES) or Triple DES (3DES). You can find more information about installing the PDM via the following link: www.cisco.com/en/US/customer/products/sw/netmgtsw/ps2032/products_ installation_guides_books_list.html.

> **NOTE**
>
> The PDM is limited in that it can only manage one PIX at a time. If you have a large environment and manage a large number of PIX firewalls, you might consider using CiscoSecure Policy Manager (CSPM), which provides a Web-based GUI by which an administrator can manage many firewalls from one console. This tool makes managing firewalls easier by defining policies, standardizing configurations, and reducing human configuration errors.

Cisco PIX Firewall Licensing

Cisco's PIX firewall licensing requires some clarification. For the higher-end models (515E and greater), three main license options are available: Restricted, Unrestricted, and Failover. The Restricted license is just that—restricted. It limits the capabilities of the firewall; for instance, it does not allow for failover, it limits interface density, and it is shipped with reduced RAM, compared with the Unrestricted license. The Unrestricted license provides all the capabilities of the Restricted license but adds increased LAN interface density, more RAM, VPN acceleration, and failover. The Failover license is used in conjunction with the Unrestricted license. The backup or redundant PIX can be purchased with the Failover license at reduced cost, which makes the PIX one of the more cost-effective firewalls when configured as a redundant pair. In a scenario in which the primary firewall fails the secondary unit with the Failover license, the device will continue to perform all the capabilities the primary supported. (The secondary unit must have the same optional PCI cards as the primary.)

NOTE

PIX licenses can be upgraded. When you purchase an upgrade package, you will receive a new activation key unlocking the software enhancements of the new license as well as any additional hardware to bring the PIX to the correct hardware level to support the license's features. For example, if you upgrade a PIX 515E Restricted license to an Unrestricted license, you will receive an activation key and be able to benefit from another 32MB of RAM and a VAC.

When encryption is required to support IPSec VPNs or to enable the PDM, it is necessary to obtain either the 56-bit DES IPSec license or the 168-bit 3DES IPSec. The encryption licenses are available for all models. The only model that has a user restriction license is the PIX 501 model, which offers 10-user and 50-user license options.

NOTE

In order for the secondary or backup PIX with a Failover license to support a VPN client or the PCM as the primary, it will be necessary to obtain a separate 56-bit DES IPSec license or the 168-bit 3DES IPSec licenses for both the primary and the backup units.

Cisco PIX Firewall Version 6.3

PIX Firewall version 6.3 is the latest mainline release of the PIX operating system. PIX version 6.3 offers many new features as well as performance enhancements. Although many of the new features in this release of code pertain to VPN and support for voice over IP (VoIP), this release does provide several enhancements that could be useful in a DMZ environment, such as VLAN and OSPF support. PIX OS version 6.3 also fixes several bugs and vulnerabilities found in the previous release. This code does not yet meet the Common Criteria EAL4 certification, but it could have some additional functionality that might compel you to upgrade.

New features implemented in PIX version 6.3 include:

- **VLAN support** Enables the PIX to support multiple virtual interfaces via VLAN trunking.

- **OSPF** Supports Open Shortest Path First (OSPF) dynamic routing protocol.

- **Advanced Encryption Standard (AES)** Support for a new international encryption standard.

- **VPN Acceleration Card+ (VAC+)** The first release to offer support for the new VAC+ PCI Card option.

- **VPN NAT transparency** Circumvents issues arising from using a VPN when NAT/PAT is implemented by dynamically wrapping IPSec VPN packets in a UDP packet Cisco Secure PIX.

- **Access banner** The PIX will display a message to anyone who tries to connect to the PIX's CLI. It is important to configure a banner for legal purposes.

- **Management enhancements** Several enhancements have been made to the CLI, including ACL editing, syslog formats, access banners, and console inactivity timeouts.

For more information on PIX OS 6.3, visit www.cisco.com/warp/customer/cc/pd/fw/sqfw500/prodlit/pix63_ds.htm.

PIX Firewall PCI Card Options

In the previous section, we referred to several of the optional PCI cards that make the higher-end PIX chassis very versatile. These cards give the PIX the ability to handle multiple DMZ legs and increase VPN performance. In this section, we clarify the capabilities of these cards and their uses.

For 10/100Mbps Ethernet requirements, the PIX offers two types of PCI card: a single-port Fast Ethernet card and a four-port Fast Ethernet card. Even though the Fast Ethernet cards are 32-bit/33MHz PCI cards, they can fit in either the 32-bit/33MHz or the 64-bit/66MHz PCI slots on the PIX and can be configured for 10/100Mbps at either half or full duplex. The PIX 525 and 535 both support the Gigabit Ethernet 64-bit/66MHz PCI card. The Gigabit Ethernet multimode fiber PCI interface card can be inserted into either the 32-bit/33MHz or the 64-bit/66MHz PCI slots on the PIX. If you recall, the PIX 535 has both 32-bit/33MHz and 64-bit/66MHz PCI slots, but when inserted into 32-bit/33MHz, the cards will severely degrade device performance, so fill the 64-bit/66MHz PCI slots before inserting a card into the 32-bit/33MHz. The

PIX 525 only has 32-bit/33MHz PCI slots, so you have no choice but to install the card there and not receive the card's full throughput.

The PIX offers VACs, which offload all CPU-intensive encryption calculations, DES, 3DES, or AES, from the main processor and onto the VAC hardware. This improves not only VPN throughput but also overall firewall performance. Without the VAC installed, the encryption algorithm and its computations are performed by the PIX OS and the main CPU, which causes the PIX's overall performance to be severely impacted as the number of IPSec VPN tunnels and load are increased. If you need extensive use of IPSec VPN tunnels, consider installing the optional VAC, because it provides notable improvement in performance and security. At the time of this writing, there were two VAC options: the original VAC and the newer, improved VAC+. Besides increased performance, the VAC+ adds AES hardware acceleration, whereas the original VAC supports only DES and 3DES. It must be noted that VAC+ is only supported by PIX OS version 6.3(1) and later. At some point Cisco will "end of life" the original VAC and sell only the VAC+ as a separate option and include it in the Unrestricted license bundle.

Installing a New PCI Card

You have many items to think about when you're upgrading hardware on the PIX. You must take into account license restrictions, types of interfaces supported by each PIX model, available PCI slots, and cost.

For example, let's say that you are the administrator of an enterprise network and your boss tells you there is a project in the works whereby the company's new Web site will be hosted at your location. You need to build a DMZ environment to accommodate the Web servers. You take a look at your Internet infrastructure; it currently utilizes a PIX 515E, which only supports user access to the Internet. The PIX was originally shipped with the Restricted software license and the two embedded Fast Ethernet interfaces, which are both used by the inside and outside interfaces, and it has no optional PCI cards installed. In order to support a DMZ where the Web servers will reside, you need to add a third Fast Ethernet interface to the PIX. You look at Cisco's product catalog for the PIX and notice two options: a one-port Fast Ethernet PCI card and a four-port Fast Ethernet PCI card. Your first inclination might be to order the four-port Fast Ethernet PCI card for scalability reasons, but as we discussed earlier in the chapter, it is important to understand the limitations of the Restricted license. On the PIX 515E, the Restricted license only allows for a total of three Fast Ethernet interfaces, so if you purchased the four-port Fast Ethernet PCI card, you would also have to purchase the Unrestricted license upgrade in order to take advantage all the installed interfaces. This can be an expensive solution, since most of the PIX's cost is not in the hardware but in the licensing. Another solution is to order the one-port Fast

Ethernet PCI card, which will meet your current DMZ requirements, does not require a license upgrade, costs a fraction of the price of the previous option, but does not provide for scalability.

Adding a PCI card to the PIX 515E is a fairly simple process, similar to adding a PCI card to a regular PC. First, shut down and unplug the unit. Next, remove the PCI slot faceplate located at the rear of the PIX (fastened by two screws). This action exposes the PCI slots. You can now add the optional PCI card into an open slot (start at the top) and press the PCI card firmly into place. On the faceplate, remove one of the blank PCI slot covers to expose the newly inserted card, then reattach the faceplate and screws. Next, power on the firewall. In order to verify that installation of the PCI card was successful, you can use the *show version* command, which will display the number of interfaces installed. Refer to the Cisco Web site for further installation procedures, or once you order the extra PCI card, examine its accompanying manual.

Designing & Planning...

Putting It All Together

If a DMZ is correctly planned and designed, it will make simple the tasks of implementing, maintaining, and supporting the DMZ infrastructure. It is important to note that a DMZ cannot be properly designed without a clear vision of what the DMZ will support. Will the DMZ environment contain a handful of servers that provide the enterprise with basic services and therefore does not require much performance or resiliency? Or will the DMZ environment contain major services that the enterprise needs to be productive and profitable and therefore will need to be in operation at all times? Alternatively, will it be somewhere between these two scenarios? There is only one way to determine the category your DMZ infrastructure will fit into: You need to understand the business, the role the DMZ will play, the type of traffic the DMZ will support, the performance required, and plans for future growth.

Now let's say that you are the network architect for a company that sells wholesale auto parts, called Automania. Automania is a standard "bricks and mortar" company that normally does business by in-store sales, phone, fax, and catalog orders, but the company is looking to add the ability to sell auto parts on the Internet. The company sees Internet sales as a way to attract new customers and offer customers the ability to make purchases 24 hours a day, seven days a week, 365 days a year, which cannot be done without significant expense using conventional methods. The com-

Continued

pany hires a consulting firm to design and build the Automania.com Web site, where customers can shop over the Internet. The site's developers have designed an e-commerce site with a shopping cart feature so Internet users can browse for items, check prices, and finally, purchase auto parts. The company projects that the Internet business will show moderate sales at first as regular customers move from the conventional ordering system to the Web-based system, but the business could grow as the site attracts new customers.

Due to budgetary constraints, the developers have designed a small site that only requires two servers—a server that will contain the Web and application functions and a separate server for the database. The developers also had the forethought to design a scalable server environment where the number of servers supporting the site can expand as demand increases. The business expects about 10,000 hits and 1000 transactions a day at first, then steady growth.

As the network architect for the company, you are given the task of supplying the infrastructure to support the new Automania Web site. The company already has Internet connectivity via a broadband connection, and you are protecting your network using a low-end firewall that was easy to install and worked well but does not have the ability to support a DMZ. Now you realize that you must upgrade for entire Internet infrastructure in order to host the new Web site. It is now time to gather the information and requirements so you can design and build a DMZ infrastructure that will be able to support the new Web site for its launch and into the future.

You need to begin gathering information, starting with the facts and requirements:

- The facts are that the company is making a strategic move to offer its customers a new method to purchase auto parts as well as to attract new customers.

- The site is important to the growth of the business.

- The Web site will start out small but could grow as sales over the Internet increase.

- The site will be a scalable server environment with a single Web/application server and a database server.

- A DMZ will need to be built on site to support the new Automania.com Web site.

- The infrastructure currently in place is not capable of supporting the new Web site.

- The site is estimated to reach 10,000 hits and 1000 transactions a day at first, then grow steadily.

Continued

You next ask questions so you can be informed of data that was missing so you can move on to designing a solution:

- How much Internet bandwidth is required to support the site?
- What kind of security is needed? Will there be a need for both Web traffic and SSL traffic?
- Does the site require high availability?
- What are the connectivity requirements among the internal network, the Web/application server, and the database server?
- What is the budget for the DMZ infrastructure?

After you asked the questions, the developers and business managers come back to you with their answers. They tell you that since the site will only receive 10,000 hits and 1000 transactions a day, they initially need two T1s; as the site grows, they will add bandwidth. Since the site will be processing credit card transactions, both Web traffic (TCP port 80) and SSL (TCP port 443) need to be allowed to access the Web/application server from the Internet. The database should only be accessed by the internal LAN and should respond to Web/application server requests for information.

All Web servers and switches are 100Mbps full-duplex capable devices. Even though the servers can be a single point of failure, the DMZ infrastructure should be built with redundancy. The DMZ infrastructure should be built with scalability in mind, with close attention to the budget—in other words, do not over-engineer the infrastructure.

From this information, you can now start to develop your solution. Analyzing the requirements, you decide that the multileg DMZ with redundant firewalls offers you the most secure and scalable solution that fits your budget. The multileg DMZ allows you to separate the Web/application server into separate DMZs to allow for greater security. DMZ 1 will contain the Web/application server, and DMZ 2 will contain the database servers. Because users will only access the Web/application server, the firewall rules will be configured so it only accesses the server on DMZ 1 via the Web port (TCP port 80) and SSL port (TCP port 443). DMZ 2 will allow no connectivity from the Internet; it will only respond to requests made for data by the Web/application server or by the internal LAN for management. Separating the Web/application server and the database servers into different DMZs allows for greater security in the event the Web/application server is compromised by an intruder. Since the Web/application server is directly accessible by the Internet, it is always the most vulnerable. Furthermore, the design allows for the addition of a redundant firewall that will take over for the primary should the primary go offline.

Continued

The next step is to decide on a make and model of the firewall to use for this solution. You choose the Cisco PIX firewall line because it is a purpose-built firewall appliance, it has a Web-based and a CLI-based management interface, a modular design, strong security features, and performance. As you research the PIX model options, you immediately can cross off the 501 and 560E models because they do not support a third leg (interface) or failover. So you move onto higher-end models. The 515E, 525, and 535 can all meet the needs of your solution in terms of interfaces, failover, and performance, but since the requirements of our DMZ infrastructure are in the low to moderate level and due to our restrictions on cost, we can choose the PIX 515E. The PIX 515E comes with two embedded 10/100Mbps interfaces (one for the internal interface, one for the outside interface), but since the requirement is for two DMZs, you will need to order the four-port Fast Ethernet PCI card (two for interfaces DMZ 1 and DMZ 2, one interface for stateful failover, and one interface free). Since high availability is needed in this solution, you need to purchase two PIX 515E firewalls—one with the Unrestricted license and the second with the Failover license. For this example, let's skip the planning and designing of the Internet connectivity; it is discussed in detail in Chapter 9. Once you have gathered all the requirements, designed a solution, and purchased the equipment, you will be ready to configure, test, and launch the site.

Making a DMZ and Controlling Traffic

This section covers how to configure the PIX's basic and advanced security features to meet your solution's needs. We discuss in detail how to securely access the PIX and define security levels, NAT, access rules, routing, failover, and other security features.

Securely Managing the PIX

There are several ways to access the PIX in order to configure, troubleshoot, or monitor its status, including console access, Telnet, SSH, and the PDM. In this section, we discuss the advantages and disadvantages of each access method as well as how to configure some of the more secure methods. We also discus how to authenticate users and manage them via an external RADIUS or TACACS+ server.

The Console

Out of the box, the higher-end PIX chassis, including the PIX 515, must be initially set up via the console port. This task can be accomplished using the same method as you use to connect to a Cisco router or switch. You need a terminal program, such as

HyperTerminal, configured with the following parameters on the appropriate COM port:

- Bits per second to **9600**
- Data bits to **8**
- Parity to **None**
- Stop bits to **1**
- Flow control to **Hardware**

Connect your PC's COM port to the PIX's Console port using the adapter and the rolled ribbon cable that came with the PIX. You now have direct serial access to the PIX's CLI. Access to the console port can be protected by a password or authenticated via a TACACS or RADIUS server. This type of access can be used for general maintenance and monitoring or when access via other methods such as Telnet or SSH is useless due to configuration errors or malfunctions. Accessing the PIX via the console might be your last option to correct the problem before having to call Cisco's Technical Assistance Center (TAC) for assistance.

> **NOTE**
>
> Cisco TAC is responsible for providing Cisco's customers with assistance for technical and configuration issues for all Cisco's hardware and software products, including the PIX firewall. Cisco's TAC can be contacted by phone or via the following URL: www.cisco.com/en/US/support/index.html.

Telnet

The PIX provides the ability to Telnet to the command-line interface. The PIX allows for five simultaneous Telnet sessions from hosts or networks you specify via the *Telnet address* [*netmask*] [*interface_name*] command. This command allows you to identify the host(s) that can initiate a Telnet session as well as the interface in which to accept the connection.

Telnet access to the PIX firewall is allowed on all interfaces. However, for increased security on the most vulnerable interface, the outside of the interface with security level 0 (usually the interface facing the Internet), the PIX will only except Telnet sessions to the interface if it is IPSec protected. Therefore, Telnet access to the outside interface requires extra configuration to support IPSec. Some administrators may implement this for remote administration of PIX firewalls, but use this feature with great caution and only if absolutely necessary. As was the case with the console port, Telnet access can be protected by a password or authenticated via a TACACS or RADIUS server. Remember that Telnet traffic, when not used in conjunction with IPSec, is sent in clear text. If someone is sniffing your network, they can easily capture the PIX's Telnet password or enable password, or if you are using AAA, they will be able to obtain a user ID and password and use them later to open holes in the firewall or perform other malicious activity.

In sum, using Telnet is not recommended, because you could lose your credentials to a malicious attacker who is eavesdropping on your network. A more appropriate solution is to console in as mentioned previously. An even better in-band alternative is SSH.

SSH

One of the major weaknesses inherent to a Telnet session is that all data is sent in clear text. This can be a serious security vulnerability if someone is able to sniff your Telnet session to the firewall. The PIX can also support SSH version 1.*x*, which gives the administrator secure access to the PIX's CLI. All traffic between the administrator's workstation and the PIX is encrypted, which makes it difficult for a hacker to capture IDs and passwords or credentials in general. Unlike Telnet, which is available by default on almost every operating system, an SSH version 1.*x* client is required and usually needs to be installed on the workstation(s) that need to manage the PIX via SSH. As with Telnet, the PIX will allow five simultaneous SSH sessions from hosts or networks you specify via the *ssh* command. As with the other access methods, the PIX can be protected by a password or authenticated via a TACACS or RADIUS server. Unlike Telnet, the PIX allows SSH connectivity on all interfaces, including the outside interface. In order to configure SSH, the PIX firewall needs a DES or 3DES activation key to generate an RSA key pair and support encrypted communication between the client and the PIX.

The first task when setting up SSH is to create an RSA key pair and save it to the PIX's Flash. The configuration shown in Figure 5.5 identifies the code necessary to generate an RSA key pair, which consists of the PIX's hostname and domain name. The *ca generate rsa key 1024* command generates an RSA key pair with a key modulus of 1024 bits (the default is 768 bits). This code will not show in the PIX configuration, but the RSA key-pair configuration can be viewed by executing the *show ca mypubkey rsa* command. In order to save the generated RSA key pair so it will be available after a reboot, you need to save it into Flash by entering the *ca save all* command.

After the RSA key pair is generated, it is time to configure SSH. The example shows a workstation with the IP address 192.168.0.2 that is authorized to initiate an SSH session to the PIX's inside interface. Use the *ssh address* [*netmask*] [*interface_name*] command to define the IP host or IP address range that can access the PIX as well as on which interface to accept this connection. The *ssh timeout* command sets the amount of idle time, in minutes, before the session is disconnected.

Figure 5.5 SSH Configuration Example

```
pixfirewall(config)# hostname Pix515

Pix515(config)# domain-name syngress.com

Pix515(config)# ca generate rsa key 1024

Pix515(config)# ca save all

Pix515(config)# ssh 192.168.0.2 255.255.255.255 inside

Pix515(config)# ssh timeout 60
```

An authorized workstation—in this case, 192.168.0.2—with an SSH client can complete a session with the PIX. The SSH client will require a username and password, but if you are only using local passwords, you might ask, "What is my username?" In this case, the username is *pix,* but if AAA is configured, the username is your TACACS+ or RADIUS username and password.

The PIX Device Manager

The PDM provides administrators with a browser-based GUI that can be used to configure the PIX without having to know how to administer the CLI. The PDM provides administrators who are not well versed in the PIX CLI the ability to easily configure and monitor the PIX via a Java applet. All transmission between the browser and the PIX is securely transmitted via SSL. The PDM will provide you with configuration wizards, performance graphs, and historical data. In order to run the PDM, you need an activation key that enables DES or Triple DES 3DES on the PIX. It is important to remember that the PDM software is separate for the PIX OS and needs to be loaded into Flash separately (assuming it was not shipped with the PIX already loaded) before it can be used to manage the PIX. The PDM feature is not enabled on the higher-end PIX models (PIX 515E and greater) by default. In order for the PIX to accept and respond to HTTP requests, you need to enable the HTTP server within the PIX OS with the *http server enable* command. As with the other methods, you need to specify the interface and the IP address or IP range that can access PDM.

> **NOTE**
>
> Unlike the Web-based management interface on Cisco routers, PDM is a very useful tool for novice and even advanced firewall administrators. Besides the PDM providing a powerful GUI, all the traffic between the PIX and the browser is encrypted, which is lacking from the router's HTTP server implementation. As

with all unused services, if you are not planning to use PDM, make sure the HTTP server is disabled.

Figure 5.6 shows how to enable the HTTP server and specify that the host with the IP address 192.168.0.2 is the only device able to access the PDM. Once the PDM is enabled (and assuming you've already configured the interfaces on the PIX), you will be able to access the PIX via your Web browser using this URL: https://192.168.0.1. (In this example, the IP address of the PIX's inside interface is 192.168.0.1.)

You will be prompted to accept certificates and then prompted for a username and password. If you are using RADIUS or TACACS+ to authenticate access to the PIX, use the username and passwords assigned to you. If you are not using RADIUS or TACACS+, leave the username prompt empty and enter the enable password at the password prompt. In this chapter, we concentrate on the PIX CLI as the preferred method of configuring and managing the PIX, and as we mentioned earlier, there some advanced commands that the PDM does not support. If you do not need the PDM, make sure you disable the HTTP server on the PIX using the *no http server enable* command. Although the PDM can be very useful for managing and supporting the PIX, we recommend using SSH as the only form of remote administration of the PIX. Even though the PDM provides secure communication, it might be wise to disable it to reduce the entry points in the PIX's management interface, therefore limiting the PIX's exposure to attacks. SSH provides secure communication as well as access to all the PIX's CLI commands.

Figure 5.6 PDM Configuration Example

```
Pix515(config)# http server enable
Pix515(config)# http 192.168.0.2 255.255.255.255 inside
```

NOTE

Some corporate security managers only access the PIX's console port via a secure nonnetworked terminal in the data center or another form of secure out-of-band management. They will not permit access methods, such as Telnet, SSH, the PDM, or CSPM, in order to reduce the risk of a hacker breaking into the PIX using admin accounts and making unauthorized changes for other possible attacks. Although this access method is very secure, it makes PIX management and support very difficult.

Authenticating Management Access to the PIX

Suppose you have a large organization in which many administrators have access to the PIX for management, and the security policy calls for each admin to have a unique ID and password, so changes to the PIX can be tracked and administrators can be held accountable.

To accomplish this task, the PIX has a feature called *authentication, authorization, and accounting* (also known as *AAA*). AAA can authenticate users managing the PIX via CLI or the PDM tool. AAA can be applied to admins accessing the PIX via the following methods: console, Telnet, SSH, and HTTP. With AAA configured, the PIX will authenticate the username and password information with a local ID or an external RADIUS or TACACS+ server. If the PIX receives an "Accept" response from the RADIUS or TACACS+ server, the user will be allowed to gain access to the PIX. If a "Reject" message is received, the user will be denied access. The AAA feature can also limit the commands by authorizing each command an admin enters. This tool is useful if you have many administrators who have access to the PIX. You might want an administrator to have the ability to troubleshoot the PIX, which requires the use of *show* and *clear* commands, and provide other senior or advanced administrators the ability to make configuration changes to interfaces, access rules, routing, and so on. Unlike Cisco routers and switches, the PIX currently does not support accounting, which logs changes administrators make. However, the PIX can provide AAA services for traffic passing through the PIX, as we discus in detail later in this chapter.

Figure 5.7 details the configuration needed to implement authentication of administrative access to the PIX. The *aaa-server* command sets the server that will authenticate the admins IDs to either RADIUS or TACACS+. This command is also used to identify the interface on the PIX in which the RADIUS or TACACS+ resides, its IP address, and the encryption key used for encrypted communication between the PIX and the server and assigns it a group tag. In this example, we authenticate to a TACACS+ server. The IP address of the server is *192.168.1.50*, the shared encrypted key is *mykey*, and we assigned it the group tag of *AuthAdmin*. The *aaa authentication* command specifies the access method and matches it to a group tag. This example shows how to configure authentication for each of the methods discussed in this section. The last line in this example enables command authorization using the *aaa authorization* command.

> **NOTE**
>
> The Cisco Secure Access Control Server (ACS), which can act as either a TACACS+ or RADIUS server, also needs to be configured to complete the AAA implementation. You can find more information on ACS on Cisco's Web site at www.cisco.com/univercd/cc/td/doc/product/access/acs_soft/csacs4nt/acs31/acsuser/index.htm.

Figure 5.7 Configuring AAA

```
Pix515(config)# aaa-server AuthAdmin protocol tacacs+
Pix515(config)# aaa-server AuthAdmin (inside) host 192.168.1.50 mykey
     timeout 5
Pix515(config)# aaa authentication serial console AuthAdmin
Pix515(config)# aaa authentication Telnet console AuthAdmin
Pix515(config)# aaa authentication ssh console AuthAdmin
Pix515(config)# aaa authentication http console AuthAdmin
Pix515(config)# aaa authorization command AuthAdmin
```

PIX Configuration Basics

In this section, we cover the basic configuration steps needed to set up the PIX to provide internal user access to the Internet, support for a DMZ, and connectivity to the Internet. Here we discuss how to define interfaces, configure NAT, set access rules, and enable routing. By the end of this section, you will be familiar with the basic configuration steps for the PIX and be able to apply these steps to the configuration of your PIX firewall.

Defining Interfaces

Before configuring the interfaces on the PIX, you must have your design laid out and know the function of each PIX interface. This process includes:

- Naming the interface
- Assigning a security level
- Configuring an IP address
- Setting the speed and duplex of the interface

Figure 5.8 shows a design for a traditional "three-legged" firewall, which details the number of interfaces and their IP addresses required to implement this environment. The switches connecting the PIX to the inside, outside, and DMZ LANs are all capable of running at 100Mbps full duplex. Once the basic information has been compiled, we can begin to add the configuration needed to set up the interfaces on the PIX.

Figure 5.8 PIX Interface Configuration

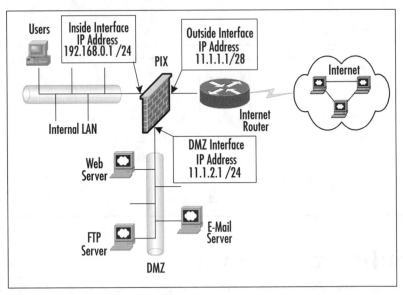

In configuring the interface, the first step is to name and define a security level for each active interface. When the PIX boots up, it assigns a hardware ID to each interface it detects and is licensed for. In this example, we have a PIX 515E with an optional one-port Fast Ethernet card inserted into one of the chassis' open PCI slots. The two embedded PIX 515E Fast Ethernet interfaces are assigned the hardware IDs *ethernet0* and *ethernet1*. The optional one-port Fast Ethernet card is assigned *ethernet2*. The PIX will allow you to logically name the PIX's interfaces except the inside interface, so you can rename them something more relevant. For example, the default interface name for the optional one-port Fast Ethernet is *intf2,* but we will rename it to better describe its usage and call it *DMZ,* since will house the DMZ LAN.

Once we choose the function and naming convention for the PIX's interfaces, we must now decide on a security level for each interface. You can assign security level between 0 and 100, where 0 is the least secure interface and 100 is the most secure interface. The most secure interface on the PIX is always the inside interface, which has a security level of 100, and the least secure is usually your Internet-facing interface, or the outside interface, which has a security level of 0. The security levels are designed to let the PIX know how to treat packets entering its interfaces. Sessions originating and entering the PIX on an interface with a high security level will be permitted to travel through PIX on any interface with a lower security level and allow packets associated with this session to return.

However, a session originating from a lower security interface will not be forwarded to an interface with a higher security level unless explicitly permitted by an ACL. Other interfaces, such as the DMZ interface in Figure 5.8, need to be assigned a value between 1 and 99, which signifies semitrusted networks and treats them as such, only allowing them access to the lower security interfaces, such as the outside interface or another DMZ interface with a lower security level.

For example, a user on the internal LAN can access a Web site on the Internet because the user's HTTP request will originate from the PIX's inside interface and be permitted to exit the outside interface and return due to the fact the inside interface has a greater security level than the outside interface. The same is true if the user wants to access a Web site located on the DMZ interface of the PIX, because the inside interface has a greater security level than the DMZ interface. If the user moved his or her workstation to the DMZ LAN, he or she would still be able to access a Web site on the Internet because the DMZ interface has a greater security level than the outside interface. However, if the user tried to access any resources on the PIX's inside interface, access would be denied because the DMZ interface has a lower security level than the inside interface unless access was explicitly allowed. Packets originating from the Internet and entering the PIX from the outside interface will not be forwarded on any of the PIX's other interfaces unless explicitly allowed via an ACL. Later in this chapter, we will discuss how to configure the PIX to allow access from an interface with a lower security level to an interface with a higher security level using ACLs.

NOTE

Prior to PIX OS version 5.3, it was necessary to define the outside interface as Ethernet0 and the inside interface as Ethernet1. Although this is not a requirement for PIX OS version 5.3 and greater, it is recommended that you continue to use this convention.

The naming and assignment of the security level of an interface is implemented using the *nameif* command. Figure 5.9 shows how to configure the DMZ infrastructure pictured in Figure 5.8. Within the *nameif* command, you need to associate the hardware ID to a logical name and a security level. In this case, Ethernet0 and Ethernet1 are left at their defaults, which are *outside* with a security level of 100 and *inside* with a security level of 0, respectively. The default configuration on Ethernet2 is overwritten and changed to *DMZ* with a security level of 50.

Figure 5.9 Configuring Interface Names and Security Levels

```
Pix515(config)# nameif ethernet0 outside security0
Pix515(config)# nameif ethernet1 inside security100
Pix515(config)# nameif ethernet2 DMZ security50
```

NOTE

The inside interface cannot be renamed or given a different security level. The outside interface can be renamed but not given a different security level. Security levels for DMZ interfaces can range from 1 to 99. When assigning security levels, keep expansion in mind and allow some space between security levels in case you have to add another interface with a security level that sits between two previously configured interfaces.

The next step is to configure the IP addresses for each of the active interfaces on the PIX. IP addresses should always be statically assigned to each active interface, except in the case where you are connecting to a broadband service provider that is assigning IP addresses dynamically to the PIX's outside IP address via DHCP. The *ip address if_name ip_address [netmask]* command is used to assign static IP addresses to each of the PIX's interfaces, as shown in Figure 5.10.

Figure 5.10 Configuring IP Addresses

```
Pix515(config)# ip address inside 192.168.0.1 255.255.255.0
Pix515(config)# ip address outside 11.1.1.1 255.255.255.240
Pix515(config)# ip address DMZ 11.1.2.1 255.255.255.0
```

The last step in the configuration of the PIX's interfaces is to set the speed and duplex and turn up the interface. By default, all the PIX's interfaces are disabled and set to autodetect speed and duplex settings. In the prior DMZ example, we said that all the segments were capable of running at 100Mb full duplex.

Figure 5.11 shows the use of the *interface hardware_id [hardware_speed] [shutdown]* command to configure each interface as 100Mbps full duplex as well as activating each interface by simply not adding the *shutdown* keyword to the *interface* command.

Figure 5.11 Setting Interface Speed and Duplex

```
Pix515(config)# interface ethernet0 100full
Pix515(config)# interface ethernet1 100full
Pix515(config)# interface ethernet2 100full
```

NOTE

It is always a good idea to hard-code the speed and duplex settings into both the PIX and the switch. It is common for the autodetect feature not to detect the correct settings, and you could end up with a speed or duplex mismatch, which will cause errors on the interfaces. In addition, if you have already configured your PIX but you do not think it is performing optimally, check these settings on the PIX and the switch to make sure they match. This is one of the major culprits in performance-related issues, especially in new installations.

Use the *show interface* command to display all interfaces on the PIX as well as its name, status, IP address, statistics, and settings. The display in Figure 5.12 shows a PIX with three interfaces. This command displays a good deal of useful information, but for the purpose of setting up the firewall's interface, let's focus on the first line of each interface, which displays the status of that particular interface, IP address, and the speed and duplex settings (highlighted in bold in the figures). The first line for each interface shows you the name of the interface as the availability of the interface would, shown as either "up" or "down." This line also shows the status of the line protocol. If line protocol is "up," the interface is operational and able to send and receive traffic; or it will show "down" when the cable is not plugged in or there is a problem with the cable. You can also use this command to view the automatically or statically discovered speed and duplex settings as well as the IP address assigned to each interface.

Figure 5.12 Show Interface DisplayPix515# show interface

```
interface ethernet0 "outside" is up, line protocol is up
   Hardware is i82559 ethernet, address is 0003.6bf6.b2db
   IP address 11.1.1.1, subnet mask 255.255.255.240
   MTU 1500 bytes, BW 100000 Kbit full duplex
        18621087 packets input, 1275940159 bytes, 0 no buffer
        Received 89741 broadcasts, 0 runts, 0 giants
        0 input errors, 0 CRC, 0 frame, 0 overrun, 0 ignored, 0 abort
        15491674 packets output, 1067317694 bytes, 0 underruns
```

Continued

Figure 5.12 Show Interface DisplayPix515# show interface

```
         0 output errors, 0 collisions, 0 interface resets
         0 babbles, 0 late collisions, 0 deferred
         0 lost carrier, 0 no carrier
interface ethernet1 "inside" is up, line protocol is up
   Hardware is i82559 ethernet, address is 0003.6bf6.b2dc
   IP address 192.168.0.1, subnet mask 255.255.255.0
   MTU 1500 bytes, BW 100000 Kbit full duplex
         20910291 packets input, 1556195344 bytes, 0 no buffer
         Received 35678752 broadcasts, 0 runts, 0 giants
         0 input errors, 0 CRC, 0 frame, 0 overrun, 0 ignored, 0 abort
         8330 packets output, 15696667 bytes, 0 underruns
         0 output errors, 0 collisions, 1105 interface resets
         0 babbles, 0 late collisions, 0 deferred
         35 lost carrier, 0 no carrier
interface ethernet2 "DMZ" is up, line protocol is up
   Hardware is i82559 ethernet, address is 0002.b322.404e
   IP address 11.1.2.1, subnet mask 255.255.255.0
   MTU 1500 bytes, BW 10000 Kbit full duplex
         0 packets input, 0 bytes, 0 no buffer
         Received 0 broadcasts, 0 runts, 0 giants
         0 input errors, 0 CRC, 0 frame, 0 overrun, 0 ignored, 0 abort
         0 packets output, 0 bytes, 0 underruns
         0 output errors, 0 collisions, 0 interface resets
         0 babbles, 0 late collisions, 0 deferred
         0 lost carrier, 0 no carrier
Pix515#
```

Configuring NAT

NAT is one of the basic features of the PIX firewall. NAT converts private, internal IP addresses into publicly routable addresses. You might want to translate or *to NAT* (using the term as a verb to describe this process) your internal addresses because they are nonroutable private addresses or to discourage attacks from the Internet. Request for Comment (RFC) 1918 lists the addresses that are available for private use on the internal network. The Internet Assigned Numbers Authority (IANA) has reserved the following three blocks of the IP address space for private networks:

- 10.0.0.0 through 10.255.255.255 (10 /8 prefix)

- 172.16.0.0 through 172.31.255.255 (172.16 /12 prefix)

- 192.168.0.0 through 192.168.255.255 (192.168 /16 prefix)

NOTE

You can learn more about RFC 1918 by visiting the RFC document online: www.cis.ohio-state.edu/cgi-bin/rfc/rfc1918.html

If you are using these addresses on your internal LAN and clients on the internal LAN need to communicate to Internet resources, you need to NAT these addresses to public addresses in order to be routed throughout the Internet. Public addresses are typically IP addresses assigned to your organization by the Network Information Center (NIC) or by your ISP. The problem facing IPv4 is that the public address pool has been depleted, so network administrators may no longer be able to assign public addresses to all clients on their internal LANs and have them access Internet resources without the use of NAT. So administrators are forced to assign private addresses to internal clients and use their allocated public addresses for NAT address pools and for services provided by the DMZ directly accessible by the Internet, such as Web and e-mail relays. NAT makes it possible for a small number of public IP addresses to provide Internet connectivity for a large range of hosts. PAT is sometimes used synonymously with NAT. However, NAT and PAT function slightly differently. NAT can provide a static one-to-one IP mapping between private and public addresses or dynamically map a large number of internal private addresses to a pool of public addresses. The problem with dynamic NAT is that once the pool of public addresses has been exhausted, the PIX will not be able to NAT additional internal address until an address in the public pool is free, whereas PAT can map very large numbers of private addresses to a single public IP address. PAT dynamically maps a connection requested from the private address range and assigns it a unique port number on a single public address as a connection is requested. As a result, a single public IP address can support up to 65,535 connections. Table 5.1 shows four addresses PAT'd to a single IP address. Notice that the only difference is the translated port. The PIX will hold a similar table in memory so it knows to which real address to send the reply traffic.

Table 5.1 Port Address Translation

Real Address	Real Port	Translated Address	Translated Port
192.168.1.2	1234	11.1.1.1	1024
192.168.1.3	1444	11.1.1.1	1025
192.168.1.4	1500	11.1.1.1	1026
192.168.1.5	1234	11.1.1.1	1027

NAT configuration statements are required for all connectivity through the PIX, even if NAT is not required. You need to configure the PIX not to NAT and let the real address flow through without being translated.

In this section, we break down the NAT configuration into two parts—outbound NAT and inbound NAT—because they require different commands to implement. Outbound NAT occurs when a device on a secure interface needs to communicate through a less secure interface to reach its destination. Inbound NAT occurs when a device on a less secure interface needs to communicate through a more secure interface to reach its destination.

NOTE

This book details how to set up a DMZ environment, but the PIX and all its features, including NAT, can be configured to accommodate many different requirements or designs. In this NAT section, we focus on how to set up NAT for some conventional DMZ designs. Keep in mind that the PIX's NAT and PAT features can be configured for a variety of scenarios, including connecting networks with conflicting IP addressing. You might have conflicting network addresses when your company acquires a company (or your company becomes acquired) with the same internal network numbering scheme. In today's world of mergers and acquisitions, this configuration will become a definite reality for most firewall administrators.

Outbound NAT

When a connection from a more secure interface to a less secure interface is necessary, a NAT or PAT statement needs to be configured, regardless of whether you need to NAT or PAT the address on the interface with the higher security interface. This tells the PIX whether or not to NAT or PAT the packet as they pass through the PIX. For example, if users on the inside interface, which are on private address space, need to access the Internet, they must be translated to a public address space that is routable on the Internet. There three options to configure outbound address translation are Static NAT, Dynamic NAT, and Dynamic PAT.

Outbound connections usually call for Dynamic NAT or Dynamic PAT. Configuring outbound NAT usually requires two steps. The first step is to identify whether NAT is required for a specified range of IP addresses and, if so, assign it a NAT ID. The second step is to assign the NAT ID to a public address pool for Dynamic NAT or a single public address to be used by PAT.

The *nat [(if_name)] nat_id ip_address [netmask [conn_limit [em_limit]]]* command is used complete Step 1. The *nat* command requires you to configure the interface to which the NAT should be applied, the NAT ID, the range of IP addresses to be translated, and connection limits. The *if_name* parameter tells the PIX to NAT connections initiated from the specified PIX interface that match the IP address range specified by the *ip_address netmask* parameters. The *nat_id* parameter is used to group the hosts to be translated and will be used later, in Step 2. If the *nat_id* parameter is set to 0, the PIX will not NAT the specified range.

The *conn_limit* and *em_limit* parameters specify the connection limit and the embryonic limit, respectively. The connection limit is the number of simultaneous connections allowed by the PIX initiated by the specified IP range, and the embryonic limit is the number of connections that have started but have not completed, meaning that they have not completed the three-way handshake. By default, both these parameters are set to 0, which means that the PIX will allow an unlimited amount of active connections and an unlimited number of embryonic connections or incomplete connections. Setting these parameters to numbers other than 0 allows the PIX to limit the number of connections made by the specified IP range and protect your network from propagating SYN or flood attacks.

These parameters are relevant in both internally and externally initiated connections settings. They will also protect your network from SYN or flood attacks initiated from the Internet. Since this type of protection is more relevant on connections initiated outside your network, we discuss the importance of setting these parameters later in the "Inbound NAT" section. Keep in mind that if you know the number of connections your internal users need and want to prevent internal clients from acting as a propagation point for flood attacks, it's a good idea to set the connection and embryonic limits to a value other than 0. Be careful not to set them too low, which would prevent valid connections to pass through the PIX. Once set, you need to monitor the number of connections from time to time to verify that increased usage from normal growth is not about to eclipse your limits, in which case you need to adjust your settings.

The *nat [(if_name)] 0 access-list acl_name* command tells the PIX not to NAT packets that match the criteria set by an access list. This gives the PIX the flexibility not only based on source IP addresses, as the standard *nat* command does, but also on destination IP address. In order for this command to function, it requires the creation of an ACL and the *nat* command with the *0 access-list* option. The ACL used with the *nat* command only matches on Layer 3 and must not contain any port specification. We explore ACLs in depth later in this chapter.

The second step assigns the NAT ID to a global address pool for Dynamic NAT or a single public address to be used by PAT. The *global [(if_name)] nat_id {global_ip [-global_ip] [netmask global_mask]}* command is used to tie the IP address range specified with the *nat* command to an IP address or a range of global IP addresses. In a outbound connection scenario where internal users need to access resources on the Internet, the global addresses need to be in the public address range so it can routed throughout the Internet. The *if_name* parameter is the outbound interface where the translated IP address will exit. The *nat_id* parameter ties the *global* command to the *nat* command, which identifies the IP addresses that need to be translated. The next parameter specifies if the PIX should perform Dynamic NAT or Dynamic PAT. If only one global IP address is specified in the *global_ip* parameter, the PIX will perform Dynamic PAT, but if a range of global IP addresses is specified, the PIX will perform Dynamic NAT. The *global_mask* parameter specifies the mask for the global IP addresses. If the *nat* command has a 0 specified as its *nat_id*, no *global* command is needed, since the 0 NAT ID means "do not NAT."

We use the diagram in Figure 5.13 as an example of how the *nat* and *global* commands work together to provide Dynamic NAT and PAT. We have a network with two internal LAN subnets, a PIX to provide secure access to the Internet for internal users and to support a DMZ with Web, e-mail, and FTP servers. Since the two-user subnet is on private address space, the IP addresses of internal PCs need to be translated to a public IP address in order to access Internet resource. The servers on the DMZ already have public addresses so they can initiate connections to resources on the Internet without the aid of NAT. The setup has several requirements, which are listed in Table 5.2. We need to configure PAT so all user PCs on internal LAN A can access the Internet via a single public address. Users on internal LAN B also need to access the Internet, but they have a special requirement that will enable the first seven addresses to be dynamically NAT'd and the rest can be translated via PAT. All access from the internal LAN to the DMZ should not be translated, nor should any access from the DMZ to the Internet.

Figure 5.13 NAT Example

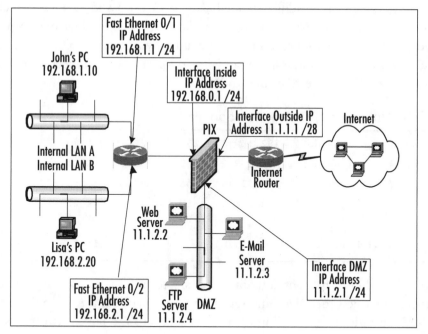

Table 5.2 Outbound NAT

Network/Device	Actual Address	Translated Address	Method
Internal LAN A	192.168.1.0 /24	11.1.1.2 /28	All PAT
Internal LAN B	192.168.2.0 /24	11.1.1.3–11.1.1.9 /28	Dynamic NAT (first seven addresses)
Internal LAN B	192.168.2.0 /24	11.1.1.10 /28	PAT (remaining addresses)
Web server	11.1.2.2 /24	11.1.2.2 /24	No NAT
E-mail server	11.1.2.3 /24	11.1.2.3 /24	No NAT
FTP server	11.1.2.4 /24	11.1.2.4 /24	No NAT

Figure 5.14 exhibits the configuration necessary to fulfill the PAT requirements of internal LAN A and the special NAT and PAT requirements of internal LAN B. The first step is to assign each internal LAN a separate NAT ID via the *nat* command. NAT ID 1 is assigned to internal LAN A, and NAT ID 2 is assigned to internal LAB B. Using the *global* command with a single global IP address and specifying NAT ID 1 will enable Dynamic PAT for all IP address on internal LAN A. All communication initiated from internal LAN A will exit the PIX with an IP address of 11.1.1.2. To meet

the special needs of internal LAN B, we first have to use the *global* command with a NAT ID of 2 and a global IP address range between 11.1.1.3 and 11.1.1.9, which allows for seven dynamic one-to-one NAT translations. Once the Dynamic NAT pool has been depleted, the remaining connections will be dynamically PAT'd to 11.1.1.10. If an IP address in the Dynamic NAT pool is freed up, the next connection request will be dynamically NAT'd before returning to PAT.

Figure 5.14 Outbound NAT Configuration, Part 1

```
Pix515(config)# nat (inside) 1 192.168.1.0 255.255.255.0 0 0
Pix515(config)# nat (inside) 2 192.168.2.0 255.255.255.0 0 0
Pix515(config)# global (outside) 1 11.1.1.2 netmask 255.255.255.240
Pix515(config)# global (outside) 2 11.1.1.3-11.1.1.9 netmask 255.255.
   255.240
Pix515(config)# global (outside) 2 11.1.1.10 netmask 255.255.255.240
```

Figure 5.15 exhibits the configuration necessary to fulfill requirements where internal users can access the DMZ and servers on the DMZ can access the Internet without NAT. In order to allow all internal users access to the DMZ without NAT requires the *nat* command with *0 access-list* option. This form of the *nat* command is necessary because, as you might recall, we already assigned the internal LAN A and LAN B NAT IDs that call for NAT. To override this behavior when internal users access the DMZ, we must specifically tell the PIX not to NAT internal LAN IP addresses when they access the DMZ.

The first step is to specify an ACL called *Inside2DMZ*, which specifies the source address as the internal address ranges (192.168.1.0 /24 and 192.168.2.0 /24) and the destination address of the DMZ address range (11.1.1.2.0 /24) to be excluded from the NAT translation. The next step is to apply the access list to the *nat* command, which lets the PIX know not to NAT internal IP addresses accessing the DMZ. To satisfy the last requirement, which lets the servers on the DMZ access the Internet with the aid of NAT, we specify the DMZ interface and the DMZ IP address range with the NAT ID of 0, which means to not NAT this range on this interface.

Figure 5.15 Outbound NAT Configuration, Part 2

```
Pix515(config)# access-list Inside2DMZ permit ip 192.168.1.0 255.255.255.
   0 11.1.2.0 255.255.255.0
Pix515(config)# access-list Inside2DMZ permit ip 192.168.2.0 255.255.255.
```

Continued

Figure 5.15 Outbound NAT Configuration, Part 2

```
     0 11.1.2.0 255.255.255.0
Pix515(config)# nat (inside) 0 access-list Inside2DMZ
Pix515(config)# nat (DMZ) 0 11.1.2.0 255.255.255.0 0 0
```

Inbound NAT

By default, the PIX will not allow access from an interface with a lower security level to access an interface with a higher security level. This type of inbound access has to been explicitly defined. The first step to allow this type of access is to define a NAT statement and the second step is to apply access rules. In this section, we discuss how to set up NAT to allow users on the Internet to access the PIX semisecure interfaces or DMZ interfaces. Access initiated directly from the Internet to the inside interface, or internal LAN, should be prohibited. Normal security policies prevent such access and only allow clients on the Internet to interact with devices on the DMZ.

As with outbound NAT, it is necessary to configure a NAT statement, regardless of whether network address translation needs to take place. Inbound NAT also has two options, to configure address translation including Static NAT and Static PAT. In setting up a DMZ, the most common option is the Static NAT option, where there is a one-to-one IP address mapping. Because there is a one-to-one mapping, this does not save public address space.

Another common configuration is Static PAT. Unlike Static NAT, Static PAT does save address space because it uses one public IP address and, depending on the port on which a request comes in, it translates to any number of private addresses. For example, you can have one IP address exposed to the Internet and have clients on the Internet make requests to this IP address for services such as Web content (TCP port 80) or SMTP (TCP port 25). Depending on the port the request is received on, the PIX will map and forward the request to the real IP of the Web or mail servers, respectively. This section focuses on the Static NAT and PAT commands needed to set up access to the DMZ. To configure Static NAT, the *static (if_name_high, if_name_low) ip_address_low ip_address_high [netmask mask] [conn_limit [em_limit]]* command is used. The syntax of this command can be confusing, so special attention is required because the command asks for the interface names in the reverse order than it asks for the IP addresses. In this form, the *static* command maps a virtual IP address on the less secure interface to the actual IP address on the more secure interface, creating a one-to-one IP mapping. The *if_name_high*, the interface with the higher security level, and *if_name_low*, the interface with lower security level, parameters specify the PIX's interfaces on which the address translation needs to occur. The *ip_address_low* parameter is the virtual IP on the PIX's

less secure interface that will be mapped to the real IP address specified by the
ip_address_high parameter on the PIX's more secure interface. The *mask* parameter in
one-to-one static mapping is set to 255.255.255.255 or host mask but can also be used
for a net static. A net static is useful in a situation in which you need to translate an
entire network but want to keep the host portion of the IP address the same. Figure
5.16 is an example of how to change the netmask so all hosts on network 11.1.1.0 /24
translate to a host on 10.1.2.0 /24. In other words, 11.1.1.1 will be translated into
10.1.2.1, 11.1.1.2 to 10.1.2.2, 11.1.1.3 to 10.1.2.3, and 11.1.1.254 to 10.1.2.254.

Figure 5.16 Inbound Net Static NAT Example

```
Pix515(config)# static (DMZ,outside) 11.1.1.0 10.1.2.0 netmask 255.255.
   255.0 0 0
```

Figure 5.17 is an example of a one-to-one NAT configuration. In this example,
there is a DMZ interface on the PIX with servers on the 10.1.2.0 /24 subnet. Since
the 10.1.2.0 /24 subnet is in the private range of addresses, it cannot be routed on the
Internet. The PIX's outside interface is on the 11.1.1.0 /28 subnet, which is with the
public address range. We have a Web server on the DMZ with an IP address of 10.1.2.2
that needs to accessed by the Internet, but since its on a private address, it cannot, so we
need to configure NAT using the *static* command. In this example, we create a one-to-
one IP mapping between 10.1.2.2 and 11.1.1.11. Users on the Internet will now be
able to access the Web server via the 11.1.1.11 address, and the PIX will then translate
the destination address to the real address, 10.1.2.2, and forward the packet to the Web
server. The Web server will then reply to the HTML request with the source address
10.1.2.2 and the destination address of the user. The PIX will receive the return packet
and this time change the source address from 10.1.2.2 to 11.1.1.11 and forward the
packet. The user on the Internet will receive the Web page and will never know that
NAT has taken place.

Figure 5.17 Inbound NAT Configuration with NAT

```
Pix515(config)# static (DMZ,outside) 11.1.1.11 10.1.2.2 netmask 255.255.
   255.255 0 0
```

As we mentioned earlier, a NAT statement is required for the inbound connectivity,
even if address translation is not required. In this case the *static* command has a slightly
different syntax, *static (if_name_high, if_name_low) ip_address ip_address [netmask][conn_limit
[em_limit]]*. You can see that the *ip_address_low* and *ip_address_high* parameters have been
replaced by duplicate *ip_address* parameters. This simply tells the PIX not to NAT the

specified the IP address or range and make the IP address visible to the less secure interface "as is." Figure 5.18 is an example of an inbound NAT configuration without NAT. The network 11.1.2.0 /24, located on the PIX's DMZ interface (refer back to Figure 5.13), is made visible to the outside interface so clients on the Internet can directly communicate with the servers on the DMZ without the use of NAT.

Figure 5.18 Inbound NAT Configuration Without NAT

```
Pix515(config)# static (DMZ,outside) 11.1.2.0 11.1.2.0 netmask 255.255.
    255.0 0 0
```

Configuring Static PAT, also known as *port redirection*, is slightly different from configuring Static NAT in that you do not specify a mapping based only on an IP address but also on the port. The *static (if_name_high, if_name_low) (tcp, udp) global_ip global_port local_ip local_port [netmask][conn_limit [em_limit]]* command is used to define Static PAT; as you might notice, it is very similar to Static NAT except that you are also defining ports. Static PAT only works with TCP and UDP packets. Figure 5.19 shows how to configure Static PAT for Web and SMTP traffic. In this example, if a request came to the IP address of the PIX's outside interface on TCP port 80 (WWW) or TCP port 25 (SMTP), it would be translated and forwarded to the real IP addresses of the Web server (10.1.2.2) and mail server (10.1.2.3), respectively. Notice that we supplemented the parameter *global_ip* with the keyword *interface,* which means to use the IP address of the outside interface as the *global_ip*.

Figure 5.19 Inbound Static PAT Configuration

```
Pix515(config)# static (DMZ,outside) tcp interface www 10.1.2.2 www
Pix515(config)# static (DMZ,outside) tcp interface smtp 10.1.2.3 smtp
```

In the previous section, we mentioned how setting the connection and embryonic limits could protect your internal network from propagating SYN attacks; in this section, we discuss how to protect the servers on your DMZ from SYN and flood attacks initiated from the Internet. If you recall, the connection limit is the number of simultaneous connections allowed by the PIX initiated by the specified IP range, and the embryonic limit is the number of connections that have started but have not completed, meaning the three-way handshake has not been completed. By setting the embryonic limit (*em_limit*) parameter in the *static* command to a value other than 0, 0 means unlimited, enabling SYN attack prevention via the PIX's TCP Intercept feature. Once the embryonic threshold is exceeded, the PIX will enter TCP Intercept mode, where the PIX will complete the three-way handshake on behalf of the server by intercepting all SYN packets and reply on behalf of the server with an empty SYN/ACK. The PIX will keep the state information, drop the packet, and wait for a reply from the client.

If the client replies with an ACK, the PIX will then complete the three-way handshake with the server, and the server will be able to communicate with the client. If the client fails to respond, the PIX sends exponential backoffs to the client. The PIX will operate in TCP Intercept mode until the number of embryonic connections falls below the threshold.

It is also a good idea to set the connection limit (*conn_limit*) to a value other than the default unlimited connection setting. Setting the connection limit can help mitigate the risk of flood attacks to servers that might be incapable of protecting themselves from this form of attack. For example, if you have an e-mail server that never exceeds a specific number of open sessions with other e-mail servers or clients and you would like to protect it from flood attacks, which can render the server useless, consider setting the connection and embryonic limit on the PIX's *static* command. Figure 5.20 shows a Static NAT configuration for an e-mail server located on the PIX's DMZ interface. The e-mail server's real IP address is 10.1.2.3 and is mapped to a publicly accessible address of 11.1.1.12. The connection and embryonic connection limits are set to 100 and 25, respectively, meaning the PIX will allow a no more than 100 simultaneous connections. If there are more than 25 embryonic connections, the PIX goes into TCP Intercept mode to protect the e-mail server from SYN or flood attacks. Be careful not set the limit too low, because that will prevent valid connections to pass through the PIX. Once the limit is set, you need to monitor the number of connections from time to time to verify that increased usage from normal growth is not about to eclipse your limits, in which case you will need to adjust your settings.

Figure 5.20 Preventing SYN and Flood Attacks

```
Pix515(config)# static (DMZ,outside) 11.1.1.12 10.1.2.3 netmask 255.255.
    255.255 100 25
```

NOTE

In PIX OS version 5.2 and later, the PIX will operate in TCP Intercept mode (also know as Flood Defender) once the embryonic limit has been reached. When in TCP Intercept mode, the PIX will complete the three-way handshake on behalf of the server by intercepting all SYN packets and reply on behalf of the server with an empty SYN/ACK. The PIX will keep the state information, drop the packet, and wait for a reply from the client. If the client replies with an ACK, the PIX will then complete the three-way handshake with the server, and the server will be able to communicate with the client. If the client fails to respond, the PIX sends exponential backoffs to the clients. The PIX will operate in TCP Intercept mode until the number of embryonic connections falls below the threshold. Prior to PIX OS version 5.2, if the PIX's embryonic limit was reached, it would allow no new connections to the server until the number embryonic connections fell below the threshold—in essence, accomplishing what a hacker wanted to do, which was to disrupt services provided by the server.

Verifying and Monitoring NAT

The PIX provides several commands in order to properly maintain, support, and troubleshoot the NAT feature. The *show xlate* and *clear xlate* commands provide the ability to show and clear NAT translations (also known as translation slots), respectively. The *show xlate* command shows active NAT and PAT translations. The *clear xlate* command clears active NAT or PAT translations and should be used when certain configuration changes are made to the PIX, including any changes related to the *aaa-server, access-list, alias, conduit, global, nat, route,* or *static* commands. It can also be useful for troubleshooting NAT or PAT problems. The *show conn* command is useful to identify all active connections and can be used to decide on values for the connection limit parameter in the *nat* and *static* commands. The *show static* command can be used to view all the static NAT translations.

Configuring Access Rules

One of the PIX's most important features is the ACL feature, which is used to create access rules that determine what connections can flow outbound from the PIX or inbound to protected resources. The ACLs allow the PIX to permit or deny access based on source IP address and/or port and destination IP address and/or port. Creating an ACL requires the use of the *access-list* command, where the firewall administrator can permit or deny access based on set criteria. It is important to remember that ACLs operate on a first-match basis, meaning that the PIX will work its way down the list and, when it finds a match, it will perform the specified action, whether it's a permit or deny. It will stop without proceeding to the next line. As you create an ACL, remember that order is important, especially with complex ACLs. Be careful to not permit access to an item higher in the list and then have an explicit deny for it later in the ACL, or vice versa. If ACLs are not carefully thought out, they might not have the desired effect of tight security, leaving security holes in your network. Furthermore, at the end of all ACLs is in implicit deny, meaning that if the PIX finished processing the access list lines and did not find a match, it will be denied.

The creation of an ACL requires the *access-list* command. This command is very similar to the *access-list* command found in Cisco's router IOS. The *access-list acl_id action protocol source_address operator src_port destination_address operator dest_port* command allows the firewall administrator to specify the actions, permit or deny, to packets that match a certain criteria and logically group them so they can be applied as a set of rules to a specific interface. The *acl_id* parameter is used to logically group and name a list of access rules that will later be used by the *access-group* command to assign the rules list to an interface. The *acl_id* can be a number or a name. The *action* parameter tells the PIX what to do with the packet if there is a match. The valid values are *permit*, which allows the packet to be forwarded, or *deny*, which drops the packet and does not allow connectivity. The *protocol* parameter is the name or number of the IP protocol, which includes but is not limited to IP, TCP, UDP, and ICMP. The *source_address*, *src_port*, *destination_address,* and *dest_port* parameters specify the elements on which the PIX will determine a match. To be considered a match, the packet in question must identically match all the configured parameters, which can include the IP address and/or port of the source and/or destination. If no source or destination port is specified, the PIX assumes you will permit or deny access regardless of the port, but if port specification is required, an operator is necessary. Valid operators include *lt* for less than, *gt* for greater than, *eq* for equal, *neq* for not equal, and *range* for an inclusive range.

To apply an ACL to an interface, use the *access-group* command. Unlike Cisco routers, which allow ACLs to be applied inbound or outbound, PIX ACLs can only be applied inbound to an interface. The *access-group acl_id in interface if_name* command is straightforward. There are only two parameters: the *acl_id*, the name or number of the ACL created with associated *access-list* command, and the *if_name* parameter, which sets the ACL to the specified interface. Only one ACL can be applied per interface.

NOTE

Like the Cisco router IOS ACLs, the PIX processes its ACLs on a first-match basis and has an implicit "deny all" at the end of the ACL. However, unlike Cisco router IOS, PIX ACLs do not use a wildcard; instead, they use a regular subnet mask in the ACL definition.

Creating an Outbound Access Control List

The PIX, by default, allows all connections initiated from a higher security-level interface to a lower-level interface. If you want to control access from the more secure interface, you can do so by creating an ACL and applying it to the interface with the higher security level. For example, if your security policy states that users from the internal network cannot initiate FTP sessions with servers on the Internet, you could prevent FTPs by implementing an outbound ACL. An outbound ACL allows the PIX to permit or deny access based on source IP address and/or port. Destination IP address and/or port or can be used with user authentication to assign an ACL to a specific user. In this section, we only discuss filtering up to Layer 4 (the transport layer), but we do discuss user authentication and content filtering, such as URL, ActiveX, and Java filtering, later in this chapter. To create and apply an outbound ACL is a two-step process. The first step is to create the ACL with the *access-list* command, and the second step is to apply the ACL to an interface with the *access-group* command.

If you recall the diagram in Figure 5.13, we had a PIX connecting two internal LANs, a DMZ, and the Internet. Figure 5.21 shows how to configure the PIX to allow only internal LAN A to connect to Internet sites via the standard Web port (WWW port 80), secure Web sites (SSL port 443), FTP sites (FTP port 21) on the Internet, and the local DMZ. Internal LAN B can only access the local DMZ. The first three lines of this ACL permit internal LAN A to access any resource on the Internet via TCP ports 80, 443, and 21. The next two lines allow both internal LAN A and LAN B to access the DMZ. Because access to the Internet was not explicitly permitted from internal LAN B, it will be denied. The last line in Figure 5.21 applies the ACL named *OutboundACL* inbound to the inside interface of the PIX.

Figure 5.21 Configuring and Applying Outbound ACLs

```
Pix515(config)# access-list OutboundACL permit tcp 192.168.1.0 255.255.
    255.0  any eq www
Pix515(config)# access-list OutboundACL permit tcp 192.168.1.0 255.255.
    255.0  any eq 443
Pix515(config)# access-list OutboundACL permit tcp 192.168.1.0 255.255.
    255.0  any eq ftp
Pix515(config)# access-list OutboundACL permit ip 192.168.1.0 255.255.
    255.0 11.1.2.0 255.255.255.0
Pix515(config)# access-list OutboundACL permit ip 192.168.2.0 255.255.
    255.0
11.1.2.0 255.255.255.0
Pix515(config)# access-group OutboundACL in interface inside
```

NOTE

Conduits, outbound, and *apply* commands have all been replaced by the *access-list* and the *access-group* commands. If you are still using these commands, consider converting them to the new commands. At some point Cisco will decide that the PIX will not support these commands in future PIX OS releases.

Creating an Inbound Access Control List

Unlike outbound connections, the PIX, by default, will not permit traffic initiated from a less secure interface to a more secure interface. For example, for a client on the Internet to be permitted to access the Web server on the local DMZ, an explicit ACL that permits port 80 traffic access must be created; otherwise, access will be denied. Inbound access lists are created and applied to interfaces using the same steps as outbound connections. Because the inbound ACL gives users on the Internet connectivity to your protected resources, it is very important to understand the importance of the inbound ACL. Any mistakes on this ACL can open security holes that hackers can exploit and use to enter your network for malicious purposes.

When creating inbound ACLs, be sure to be specific as possible. Figure 5.22 shows how to configure access from the Internet to specific TCP ports on the servers on the DMZ. The ACL allows any host of the Internet to access Web content (TCP port 80 or WWW) on the Web server, send mail to the mail relay server (TCP port 25 or SMTP), and send FTPs (TCP port 21 or FTP) to the FTP server. As with all ACLs, any access not explicitly permitted will be denied via an implicit *deny* statement at the end of the ACL. The ACL is applied to the outside interface using the *access-group* command.

Figure 5.22 Inbound Access List Configuration

```
Pix515(config)# access-list InboundACL permit tcp any host 11.1.2.2 eq www
Pix515(config)# access-list InboundACL permit tcp any host 11.1.2.3 eq smtp
Pix515(config)# access-list InboundACL permit tcp any host 11.1.2.4 eq ftp
Pix515(config)# access-group InboundACL in interface outside
```

Creating Turbo ACLs

The PIX OS version 6.2 adds a new feature called Turbo ACL, which decreases the time it takes to search long access lists. Turbo ACL does this by compiling the ACL so that searches are deterministic and take fewer CPU cycles. The problem with uncompiled ACLs is that as they get larger, it takes more time to find a match because the ACL is searched in a linear, top-down, fashion. A PIX with large, complex ACLs can cause a performance lag as well as increase latency for packets that pass through it. The PIX can decrease search times for ACLs with 19 lines or more by using the global *access-list compiled* command or the individual ACL *access-list acl_name compiled* command. Turbo ACLs should only be applied to ACLs that have 19 or more lines because compiled ACLs with fewer than 19 lines do not provide a performance upgrade compared with uncompiled ACLs. In order to configure a turbo ACL, you need configure the ACL as you normally would, then apply the global or individual ACL compile command. The global compile command compiles all configured ACLs that have 19 or more lines. The individual command allows you select a specific ACL to compile, but the ACL must have 19 or more lines. If a change is made to a compiled ACL, the PIX will automatically recompile the ACL so the change is reflected in the compiled ACL table.

NOTE

The PIX requires approximately 2.1MB of Flash to run Turbo ACL, which limits chassis that can support this feature. This feature might not work properly on the PIX 501 and the PIX 506E chassis because they come with only 8MB of Flash installed and cannot be upgraded.

Monitoring ACLs

The PIX has a couple of commands that can display and monitor ACLs as well as check to which interface they are bound. The *show access-list* command shows the contents of an access list, the number of hits (matches) per entry, and whether the ACL is a Turbo ACL or a standard uncompiled ACL. The *show access-group* command displays how the ACLs are bound the PIX's interfaces.

Configuring & Implementing...

Tips on Inbound ACLs

Understanding how to properly create an ACL is very important to the integrity of your network. A mistake on an ACL can open holes that hackers can easily exploit. It is very important to be very specific when you're defining an access list entry. The more specific the ACL, the fewer holes the hacker has to exploit. The order of the ACE in the access list is also important. Many people make the mistake of making broad permit statements, then later in the ACL using a specific deny, or vice versa. Always remember that the PIX will stop processing the ACL when the first match is made, and any lines below the match will not take effect. We have put together some tips on how to configure an ACL for some common services.

All access lists should start with an antispoofing ACL, which will prevent spoofing of the private address range (RFC 1918) from the Internet. A line for any public address space that your company has for internal use (not advertised to the Internet) should also be added here.

```
! To block spoofing of RFC 1918 Address ranges
Pix515(config)# access-list InboundACL deny ip 10.0.0.0
     255.0.0.0 any
Pix515(config)# access-list InboundACL deny ip 172.16.0.0
     255.240.0.0 any
Pix515(config)# access-list InboundACL deny ip 192.168.0.0
     255.255.0.0 any
```

This section of the ACL is quite simple. It allows users from the Internet to access the Web server via the standard Web port, TCP port 80, as well as SSL, TCP port 443.

```
! Allow WWW and SSL connections to the web server
Pix515(config)# access-list InboundACL permit tcp any host
     11.1.2.2 eq www
Pix515(config)# access-list InboundACL permit tcp any host
     11.1.2.2 eq 443
```

This section allows the use of Active or Passive FTPs to the FTP server. Because of the Application Inspection feature, you will not need to open any port besides TCP port 21. FTP usually requires ports 20, 21, and ports

Continued

greater than 1023 to be open to support Active or Passive FTPs, but not the PIX. Application Inspection is discussed later in this chapter.

```
! Allow Active or Passive FTPs to the FTP server
Pix515(config)# access-list InboundACL permit tcp any host
    11.1.2.4 eq ftp
```

Since ICMP is connectionless, you need to explicitly allow ICMP echo replies to be allowed to re-enter the PIX and forwarded back to the client on the internal LAN to initiate the echo via the ping utility. If you notice that the destination address is not the internal LAN IP address range but is the address of the outside interface IP range, this occurs because as an echo request from the internal LAN is sent through the PIX it is translated to an address on the outside interface IP range (as configured in the previous NAT section of this chapter). The echo reply will be sent to the translated address; therefore, the ACL should specify the translated address as the destination and not the real internal address range.

```
! Allow ICMP echo reply from a ping initiate from an
    internal interface Pix515(config)# access-list
        InboundACL permit icmp any 11.1.1.0 255.255.255.240
            echo-reply
```

Routing Through the PIX

The final step in the basic configuration of the PIX is to enable routing. By default, the PIX has no routes configured, so it does not know how to forward traffic. The PIX has three routing options: static routes, RIP, and OSPF. In this section we discuss how to configure static routing as well dynamic routing using the RIP and OSPF dynamic routing protocols.

Static Routing

Most PIX firewalls are configured using static routes because they are the simplest form of routing. Static routing hard-codes the next hop of a remote network so the PIX knows in which direction to send traffic when a network is not directly connected. Usually a PIX has a default route pointing to the Internet and static route(s) pointing to networks or subnets on the internal LAN. The *route if_name ip_address netmask next_hop [metric]* command is used to define a static route. The *if_name* parameter identifies the route's outgoing interface. The *ip_address* and *netmask* parameters make up the remote network that you want the PIX to route to, and the *next_hop* parameter is the IP address to which the PIX will forward traffic that matches the specified remote network. The *metric* parameter sets a weight to a route in case there are multiple paths to the remote network. The route with the smallest metric to the same remote network will be selected unless it becomes unavailable; then the next hop with second smallest weight will be selected to reach a remote network.

To illustrate how static routes are configured, let's use our familiar network setup shown in Figure 5.23. In the diagram, three networks are directly connected to the PIX: the inside interface (192.168.0.0 /24), the DMZ interface (11.1.2.0 /24), and the outside interface (11.1.1.0 /28). These networks do not require any type of routing, either static or dynamic, because they are directly connected, and the PIX will simply ARP for hosts located on these interfaces. However, the internal LANs are not directly connected; therefore, they require static routes so the PIX can forward traffic to the appropriate next hop. In this case, the next hop for both internal LANs (LAN A 192.168.1.0 /24 and LAN B 192.168.2.0 /24) is the Internal LAN router or 192.168.0.2.

The first two configuration lines in Figure 5.24 show how to configure the static routing for both internal LANs. Now that we accounted for routing the internal LANs, we must turn our attention to configuring routing so that devices on the internal LAN and the DMZ can access the Internet. This could a daunting task if we had to configure static routes for every network on the Internet, but the PIX has an option that lets you define a default route for traffic for which he PIX does not have a specific route. In this case, the default route is the Internet router or 11.1.1.14. The last configuration line in Figure 5.24 shows how to configure a default route to point the next hop, the Internet router. Notice that the syntax of the *route* command has been simplified by the use of double zeroes for the *ip_address* and *netmask* parameters. The expanded syntax of a default route is *route outside 0.0.0.0 0.0.0.0 11.1.1.14 1,* but the PIX allows you to abbreviate 0.0.0.0 for both the IP address and the mask to a simple double zero (0 0). Either the expanded or the abbreviated default route syntax will be accepted by the PIX. Assuming the internal router is configured with a default route to point to the PIX as the next hop, the PIX is now capable of routing between the internal LAN, the DMZ, and the Internet. We discuss routing on the Internal and Internet routers in detail in Chapter 9.

Figure 5.23 Configuring Static Routes

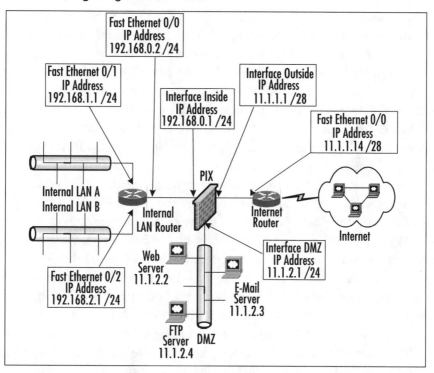

Figure 5.24 Static Route Configuration

```
Pix515(config)# route inside 192.168.1.0 255.255.255.0 192.168.0.2 1
Pix515(config)# route inside 192.168.1.0 255.255.255.0 192.168.0.2 1
Pix515(config)# route outside 0 0 11.1.1.14 1
```

Enabling RIP

In most PIX firewall implementations, the use of static routing meets the requirements for most DMZ designs. However, the PIX does offer dynamic routing capabilities that include support for Routing Information Protocol (RIP) versions 1 and 2 and OSPF. In this section, we discuss how to configure RIP, a distance-vector protocol , that uses hop count to determine a route's metric. A device running RIP periodically updates its neighbors of the routes it knows about. Since the scope of this book is directed toward building a DMZ infrastructure, we assume that if you are going to configure RIP, you are well versed in its capabilities, so we will not go into RIP's details any further.

RIP was a common interior dynamic routing protocol before the more robust routing protocols such as OSPF and EIGRP came into play. Nevertheless, RIP can be found on many networks today, and the PIX can "talk" to devices, like routers, that run RIP to eliminate the administrative burden of adding a new static route to the PIX each time a new LAN is added to the internal network.

The *rip* command is used to enable RIP on the PIX. Figure 5.25 shows how to configure RIP on the internal LAN or inside interface of the PIX. (Refer back to Figure 5.23 for the network setup.) In this case, the internal router is running RIP version 2 with MD5 authentication. The PIX needs to be able to communicate with the internal router so that the router can periodically update the PIX's RIP routing table. The PIX, in turn, needs to inform the internal router of the default route so that the internal router knows where to forward packets destined for the Internet. Once configured, if a new LAN is added to the Internal router, the router will send an update to the PIX notifying it of the new LAN without any extra configuration or static routes added to the PIX. The first configuration line in Figure 5.25 enables RIP version 2 with MD5 authentication on the inside interface of the PIX. Note that MD5 authentication must also be set on the internal router and the key (*mykey*) and key ID (*1*) must match for routing updates to take place between the router and the PIX. In this example, RIP is set to Passive mode, and the PIX will only listen to RIP version broadcast updates and update its RIP routing table accordingly. The second configuration line allows the PIX to advertise a default route back to the internal router so it will know where to send its traffic for which it does not have a specific route. The third line is the same as in the static route example where the PIX will forward Internet-bound traffic to the Internet router.

Figure 5.25 RIP Routing Configuration

```
Pix515(config)# rip inside passive version 2 authentication md5 mykey 1
Pix515(config)# rip inside default version 2 authentication md5 mykey 1
Pix515(config)# route outside 0 0 11.1.1.14 1
```

OSPF

Starting with PIX OS version 6.3, the PIX supports the OSPF link-state routing protocol. Many large networks implement OSPF as the dynamic routing protocol and with this new feature allow the PIX to communicate with routers on the network running OSPF to dynamically update the routing tables on both the PIX and routers on the network. Since OSPF is fairly complex, we will not go into its configuration on the PIX, but be aware that the PIX can support it if necessary. The PIX's implementation of OSPF is robust and can support almost all the OSPF functions and features found in

Cisco's router IOS. As with all routing protocols, if you decide to use this feature, be sure to use the OSPF authentication feature to ensure that you are sending and receiving routing information to trusted neighbors.

Configuring Advanced PIX Features

The PIX has many additional features that enable it to provide high availability, application layer security, and PIX management and support. The PIX supports features such as DHCP and VPNs that are out of the scope of this book. In this section, we cover topics such as failover, content filtering, cut-through proxy, application layer security, and securing some of PIX's management features.

The PIX Failover Services

When your DMZ design calls for a highly available firewall solution because downtime due to a problem with the firewall hardware will not be tolerated, consider using the PIX's failover feature. The failover feature allows you to set up a second PIX in Standby mode and if the primary, or active, PIX should go offline, the secondary PIX will switch to Active mode and take over for the failed PIX. If the optional stateful failover feature is configured, the secondary PIX can maintain operating state for active TCP connections during failover, so users will not lose their sessions as the PIX fails over to its backup unit. In order to enable failover, the primary and secondary PIX firewalls need to be identical in terms of chassis, OS version, and hardware options. We cover the requirements for failover later in this section.

The PIX offers two options that provide connectivity for the primary and secondary PIX firewalls to exchange heartbeats and configuration information. The first option is a Cisco proprietary high-speed serial cable connected to a special serial failover port on the PIX. The second option is to use one of the PIX LAN interfaces to carry heartbeat and configuration traffic. The advantage of using the Cisco proprietary high-speed serial cable to send heartbeat and configuration traffic is that it will not waste a LAN interface for a rather small amount of traffic. Instead, it uses a serial port specifically designed for failover. The disadvantage is that the high-speed serial cable is rather short (6 feet long), and if the PIX firewalls are not physically located close together, you cannot use the cable-based solution because the cable cannot be extended. If you have a situation in which the PIX firewalls are not physically located together, you can consider the second option, a LAN-based failover, which uses interfaces on each PIX to provide dedicated media for heartbeat and configuration traffic. The disadvantage of this option is that an interface on each PIX will be wasted just for heartbeat and configuration traffic. It is important to note that heartbeat and configuration traffic should not be confused with state traffic used for the stateful failover option, which the active PIX uses to send the standby PIX TCP state information. Although you can configure the PIX to carry heartbeat, configuration, and state traffic all on one interface on each PIX using the LAN-based failover option, doing so is not recommended.

When failover occurs, the standby PIX assumes all the IP addresses and MAC addresses on all interfaces of the failed PIX. Because there is no change to the IP address or MAC address information, other devices on the network will not be aware of a failure and that they are now communicating through a different device. Another feature of failover is that when a configuration change is made to the primary, it is automatically copied to the secondary PIX, and when a *write memory* command to save the configuration to Flash is issued on the primary, it also copies the configuration the to secondary's Flash.

What Causes Failover to Occur

To determine the health status of each PIX, the primary and secondary PIX poll each other. The poll interval is set using the *failover poll* command; the default is 15 seconds. Polls, also called *heartbeats*, are sent over all interfaces, including the failover cable. If either PIX misses two consecutive heartbeats, each PIX will go through a series of tests to determine which PIX is in trouble. Each unit goes through four tests to determine its health: a Link Up/Down test, a Network Activity test, an ARP test, and a Broadcast Ping test. Each PIX firewall performs one test at a time. If a unit passes a test and the other unit does not, the PIX that passed will take over. If both PIX units fail, they move on to the next test. At the default poll interval (15 seconds), the PIX units can take up to 45 seconds to run through all the tests and determine if failover should take place.

> **NOTE**
>
> When cable-based failover is implemented, the PIX will be able to immediately fail over to the secondary unit and skip the series of tests if the primary unit loses power due to a power failure or it is simply shut off. This is not possible with LAN-based failover, where a power failure of the primary unit must be detected via a series of tests.

Failover Requirements

In order to implement failover, you must make sure you have met all the following requirements before configuring failover:

- Both the primary and secondary PIX firewalls must be identical models. Only the PIX 515E, 525, and 535 support the failover feature.

- Run the same PIX OS version.

- Have the same amount of RAM and Flash.

- Have the same interface options.

- If encryption is required, the firewalls must run the same encryption type (DES or 3DES).

If you are configuring the stateful failover feature with the Cisco proprietary high-speed serial cable, the following items are required in addition to the standard requirements:

- Cisco proprietary high-speed serial to carry heartbeat and configuration traffic

- A dedicated interface on each PIX to carry TCP state traffic

- The interface used for stateful traffic must be, at minimum, set at 100Mb full duplex or at least as fast as the PIX's fastest interface

If you are configuring the stateful failover feature using the LAN-based failover option, the following items are required in addition to the standard requirements:

- A dedicated interface on each PIX to carry heartbeat and configuration traffic

- A separate dedicated interface on each PIX to carry TCP state traffic

- The interface used for stateful traffic must be, at minimum, set at 100Mb full duplex or at least as fast as the PIX's fastest interface

The last, but an important, requirement is to make sure you have the proper PIX license. The primary PIX must have the Unrestricted license, but the secondary unit can have either the Unrestricted license or the Failover license. In practice, when you're using the Unrestricted license and Failover license combination, it doesn't matter which PIX has the Unrestricted license or Failover license since it is possible for the secondary PIX to be promoted to primary or active state.

Configuring Stateful Failover with a Failover Cable

In this section, we cover how to configure stateful failover using the Cisco proprietary high-speed serial cable. In this setup, the serial cable is used to carry heartbeat and configuration traffic, and TCP state traffic is transferred to the secondary unit via a dedicated LAN interface. TCP state information needs to be passed from the active PIX to the standby PIX, so if a failure should occur, the secondary PIX can take over and the users will not lose their sessions.

As we mentioned earlier, cable-based failover uses a proprietary high-speed serial cable to carry heartbeat and configuration traffic between the primary and secondary PIX firewalls. The cable is labeled on each end with "Primary" and "Secondary" and should be connected to the each PIX's failover serial port. If you are using a combination of Unrestricted license and Failover license, you must plug the "Primary" end of the serial cable into the PIX with the Unrestricted license and the end labeled "Secondary" into the PIX with the Failover license. Figure 5.26 shows the rear of both the primary and secondary PIX units and where to plug in the serial cable. The diagram also shows the interfaces of the PIX. Notice that both PIX units have a total of four Fast Ethernet ports. Fast Ethernet interfaces 0, 1, and 2 are assigned to the outside, inside, and DMZ interfaces, respectively. The last remaining interface, Fast Ethernet interface 3, is dedicated to carrying state information from the primary unit to the secondary unit.

Figure 5.26 The Physical Layout of the Cable-Based Failover Setup

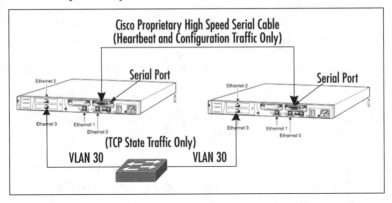

Before you start to configure cable-based stateful failover, you should first cable the units together, but make sure the secondary unit is shut down until the failover configuration has be entered into the primary PIX. First, start your failover configuration by configuring the interfaces. In Figure 5.27, we show the configuration for all the active interfaces on the PIX. The inside, outside, and DMZ interfaces you've seen before in our previous examples, but we added configuration statements for the interface that carries TCP state traffic called "stateful." Notice that the security level is set higher than the DMZ interface, the interface speed is set to 100Mb full duplex, and an IP address of 192.168.4.1 is assigned.

Figure 5.27 Failover Preconfiguration

```
Pix515(config)# nameif ethernet0 outside security0

Pix515(config)# nameif ethernet1 inside security100

Pix515(config)# nameif ethernet2 DMZ security50

Pix515(config)# nameif ethernet3 stateful security90

Pix515(config)# interface ethernet0 100full

Pix515(config)# interface ethernet1 100full

Pix515(config)# interface ethernet2 100full

Pix515(config)# interface ethernet3 100full

Pix515(config)# ip address inside 192.168.0.1 255.255.255.0

Pix515(config)# ip address outside 11.1.1.1 255.255.255.240

Pix515(config)# ip address DMZ 11.1.2.1 255.255.255.0

Pix515(config)# ip address stateful 192.168.4.1 255.255.255.0
```

Once the interfaces have been configured, we move on to the failover section of the PIX configuration. Figure 5.28 shows the command necessary to configure cable-based failover. The *failover* command enables the failover feature. The *failover poll* command sets the poll interval in which the PIX units send heartbeats to determine the health of the units. In this case, the poll interval is set to 5 seconds, and if two consecutive heartbeats are missed, both PIX units will run a series of tests to determine whether you should be active. We reduced the poll interval from the 15-second default, so the time it take to initiate failover tests and determine the active PIX is reduced. At the default settings, it could take up to 45 seconds to determine the healthy PIX, but at the new setting we reduced that number to about 25 seconds, and should a failure occur, it would be less noticeable.

The *failover ip address* command sets the IP address of the failover unit for each interface. When this configuration is copied to the secondary unit, it will use this address to communicate with the primary unit as well as allow you to Telnet or SSH into the secondary unit for management. The *failover link* command enables the optional stateful failover feature and tells the PIX on which interface to send the TCP state information. In this example we use the interface we named *stateful* to carry state information.

At this point you are ready to power on the secondary unit. The PIX will automatically detect that the secondary unit is online, and the primary unit will then copy the configuration to the Flash on the secondary PIX. Once the pair is synchronized, the PIX units will function as an Active/Standby pair. We discuss how to manage and maintain failover status later in this section.

Figure 5.28 Configuration of Stateful Failover with Failover Cable

```
Pix515(config)# failover
Pix515(config)# failover poll 5
Pix515(config)# failover ip address outside 11.1.1.13
Pix515(config)# failover ip address inside 192.168.0.3
Pix515(config)# failover ip address DMZ 11.1.2.5
Pix515(config)# failover ip address stateful 192.168.4.2
Pix515(config)# failover link stateful
```

Configuring Stateful LAN-Based Failover

In this section, we cover how to configure stateful failover using the LAN-based solution. Instead of using the proprietary high-speed serial cable, which limits the physical distance the PIX firewalls can be set apart from each other, the LAN-based solution uses one of the PIX's interfaces for heartbeat and configuration traffic. You can connect the interfaces via a switch or a crossover cable, which enables the PIX units to be set further apart.

There are a few drawbacks to this method. The first is that an interface on each PIX will be used solely for the purpose of heartbeat and configuration traffic. The second is that a power failure in either unit will take longer to detect. Finally, the configuration requires configuring both units before failover will function.

Figure 5.29 shows how the LAN-based stateful failover is physically laid out. The diagram shows a pair of PIX firewalls with six Fast Ethernet interfaces. Fast Ethernet interfaces 0, 1, and 2 are assigned to the outside, inside, and DMZ interfaces, respectively. The fourth interface, Fast Ethernet interface 3, is a dedicated interface assigned to carry state information from the primary unit to the secondary unit. The fifth interface, Fast Ethernet interface 4, is a dedicated interface assigned to carry heartbeat and configuration traffic from the primary unit to the secondary unit. Cisco recommends that the heartbeat and configuration traffic (shown on VLAN 40) and TCP state traffic (shown on VLAN 30) be located on separate switches or connected via a crossover cable.

Figure 5.29 Physical Layout of LAN-Based Failover Setup

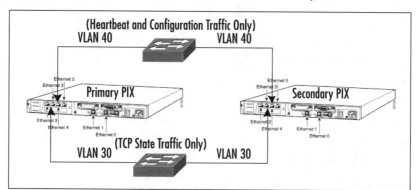

Unlike the cable-based solution, both PIX firewalls need to be configured before failover is fully operational. We begin with the primary unit, for which we need to define an interface for the heartbeat and configuration traffic, assign IP addresses to the failover unit, define the unit as a primary, and configure the stateful failover option. The configuration in Figure 5.30 should be combined with the configuration in Figure 5.27, which defines many of the interfaces, including the interface used for stateful failover.

In addition to the interfaces defined in Figure 5.30, we need to define another interface for heartbeat and configuration traffic. Figure 5.30 shows how to configure an interface named *heartbeat* with a security level of 95, an IP address of 192.168.5.1, and a speed defined as 100Mb full duplex. As with cable-based failover, we use the *failover* command to enable failover, set the poll interval to 5 seconds with the *failover poll* command, and set the IP addresses for all interfaces on the secondary unit using the *failover ip address* command.

The next group of commands is used to define the LAN-based failover. The *failover lan unit primary* command defines the PIX unit as the primary. The *failover lan interface* command tells the PIX on which interface to send and receive heartbeat and configuration traffic. In this example, we use the interface named *heartbeat*. For extra security, the PIX encrypts heartbeat and configuration traffic between the primary and secondary units by using shared keys. To specify the shared key, use the *failover lan key* command. We set the shared key in this example to *mykey*. The *failover lan enable* command lets the PIX know to disable cable-based failover and enable LAN-based failover. As with cable-based failover, the *failover link* command enables the optional stateful failover feature and tells the PIX on which interface to send the TCP state information. In this example, we use the interface we named *stateful* to carry state information.

Figure 5.30 Configuration of LAN-Based Failover (Primary)

```
Pix515(config)# nameif ethernet4 heartbeat security95
Pix515(config)# ip address stateful 192.168.5.1 255.255.255.0
Pix515(config)# interface ethernet4 100full
Pix515(config)# failover
Pix515(config)# failover poll 5
Pix515(config)# failover ip address outside 11.1.1.13
Pix515(config)# failover ip address inside 192.168.0.3
Pix515(config)# failover ip address DMZ 11.1.2.5
Pix515(config)# failover ip address stateful 192.168.4.2
Pix515(config)# failover ip address heartbeat 192.168.5.2
Pix515(config)# failover lan unit primary
Pix515(config)# failover lan interface heartbeat
Pix515(config)# failover lan key mykey
Pix515(config)# failover lan enable
Pix515(config)# failover link stateful
```

At this point, you need to configure the secondary PIX with the minimal number of statements shown in Figure 5.31 so it will be able to bring up the *heartbeat* interface. Once this process is completed, the primary PIX will be able to communicate to the secondary PIX via the LAN-based failover and copy its configuration to the secondary PIX's flash.

Figure 5.31 Configuration of LAN-Based Failover (Secondary)

```
Pix515(config)# nameif ethernet4 heartbeat security95
Pix515(config)# ip address stateful 192.168.5.1 255.255.255.0
Pix515(config)# interface ethernet4 100full
Pix515(config)# failover
Pix515(config)# failover poll 5
Pix515(config)# failover ip address heartbeat 192.168.5.2
Pix515(config)# failover lan unit secondary
Pix515(config)# failover lan interface heartbeat
Pix515(config)# failover lan key mykey
Pix515(config)# failover lan enable
```

Testing and Monitoring Failover

The status of the failover feature can be viewed using the *show failover* command. This *show* command details whether failover is active, the status of each interface on both the primary and secondary units, and several other statistics. You might be confronted with a situation in which you need to force failover to occur for maintenance reasons or to force the primary unit back into an active state after a fault has been fixed. Both these situations call for the use of the *failover active* command.

For example, to take the primary unit out of service for maintenance reasons, you can perform the *no failover active* command, which forces the primary unit to give up its active status and the standby or secondary unit to become active. When the maintenance on the primary unit is complete, you will use the *failover active* command to return the primary unit to active status. The *failover active* command is not limited to the primary unit; it can be used on either the primary or secondary, but if operational, all configurations changes should be performed on the primary unit.

> **NOTE**
>
> Should a fault occur and the PIX (configured for stateful failover) automatically fail over to the secondary unit, it will maintain state for TCP connections. However, once the fault on the primary unit is repaired and the primary PIX is forced to active status, all TCP will be disconnected because the secondary PIX does not send TCP state data to the primary unit. In other words, stateful failover occurs only from primary to secondary, not vice versa. You should consider returning the primary unit to active state after business hours or during times of low utilization to minimize the loss of connections.

Blocking ActiveX and Java

Many security managers consider ActiveX and Java applets a security risk and require the firewall to block hosts on the internal LAN from downloading them from Web sites. AcitveX controls (also known as *OCX controls*) and Java can be downloaded by users who access Web sites that call for and download ActiveX controls and Java applets. ActiveX and Java can add functionality to a Web site in the form of interactive forms, calendars, and calculators. However, they can also be used for malicious activities, including taking control of the desktop, causing PCs to crash, collecting sensitive information, and initiating attacks on other machines. The PIX is able to block ActiveX and Java applets by commenting out the *<APPLET>, </APPLET>, <OBJECT>,* and *</OBJECT>* tags in the HTML code so they cannot be executed. The PIX cannot discriminate between legitimate or malicious content, so the PIX will indiscriminately comment out this code. Therefore, all Web pages that rely on ActiveX and Java will not function properly. Configuring the PIX to block ActiveX controls and Java applets is simple. Figure 5.32 shows the *filter* commands necessary to block them on TCP port 80 (the standard Web port). You can also narrow the scope of the ActiveX and Java filtering by specifying the source and/or destination addresses with the *filter* command.

Figure 5.32 Configuring ActiveX and Java Blocking

```
Pix515(config)# filter activex 80 0 0 0 0
Pix515(config)# filter java 80 0 0 0 0
```

> **NOTE**
>
> The PIX will inspect each packet containing the specified port and look for and comment out the *<APPLET>*, *</APPLET>*, *<OBJECT CLASSID>*, *<OBJECT>*, and *</OBJECT>* tags in the HTML code, but if the tag is spread across multiple packets, the PIX might not be able to block the ActiveX control or Java applet.

URL Filtering

The PIX does support URL filtering, but it does so by utilizing a separate server running either the WebSense or N2H2 server. The WebSense or N2H2 server must be purchased separately from the PIX. The URL filtering feature is useful for limiting access to Web sites that could contain content that violates company policies, such as pornography and gambling. The PIX communicates with the WebSense or N2H2 server to determine if the Web content the user is requesting should be filtered or allowed.

Figure 5.33 shows how to configure the PIX to communicate with a WebSense server located on the PIX's inside interface with the IP address of 192.168.1.50 using the *url-server* command. The *filter url http* command specifies the range of source IP addresses that require HTTP filtering through the WebSense server. The *allow* keyword tells the PIX to allow all HTTP requests (even to filtered Web sites) to flow should connectivity be lost to the WebSense server. The *filter url except* command allows you the specify IP ranges that should be exempt from WebSense screening. In this case, users on the 192.168.2.0 /24 network are allowed to surf the Internet without URL filtering by the WebSense server.

Figure 5.33 Configuring URL Filtering

```
Pix515(config)# url-server (inside) vendor websense host 192.168.1.50
Pix515(config)# filter url http 0 0 0 0 allow
Pix515(config)# filter url except 192.168.2.0 255.255.255.0 0 0
```

Cut-Through Proxy

The cut-through proxy feature allows the PIX to authenticate users who access HTTP, FTP, and Telnet for inbound and outbound connections. Unlike standard proxy servers, the PIX authenticates users to an external RADIUS or TACACS+ database and, if allowed, the connection will be permitted directly between the client and the server. Access for HTTP, FTP, and Telnet services through the PIX can be applied on a per-user basis. When a user tries to access these services through the PIX, the PIX will prompt the user to enter a user ID and password. If the user has the required permission, the PIX will allow the requested connection to flow. If authorization is configured in conjunction with authentication, you can specifically restrict the Web, FTP, and Telnet hosts that a user can access.

The configuration in Figure 5.34 shows how to configure a cut-through proxy. The configuration is similar to the AAA for management access to the PIX. We start by using the *aaa-server* command to configure the type of authentication server (RADIUS or TACACS+), IP address, interface, encryption key, and group tag. The next three commands enable the PIX to authenticate, authorize, and track all requests for HTTP access through the PIX initiated from the inside interface using the *aaa authentication, aaa authorization,* and *aaa accounting* commands. To complete the cut-through proxy implementation, the RADIUS or TACACS+ server also needs to be configured; refer to your RADIUS or TACACS+ documentation for information on how to do so.

Figure 5.34 Configuring User Authentication and Cut-Through Proxy

```
Pix515(config)# aaa-server AuthOut protocol tacacs+
Pix515(config)# aaa-server AuthOut (inside) host 192.168.1.50 mykey
    timeout 5
Pix515(config)# aaa authentication include http inside 0.0.0.0 0.0.0.0
    .0.0.0.0 0.0.0.0 AuthOut
Pix515(config)# aaa authorization include http inside 0.0.0.0 0.0.0.0
    .0.0.0.0 0.0.0.0 AuthOut
Pix515(config)# aaa accounting include http inside 0.0.0.0 0.0.0.0 0.0
    .0.0 0.0.0.0 AuthOut
```

> **NOTE**
>
> If you require a cut-through proxy with user authorization, consider using TACACS+, because the PIX does not support authorization with RADIUS. In addition, if you require extensive HTTP authorization, consider using the URL filtering feature.

Application Inspection

Translating network addresses can cause problems if an application embeds an address or port information into the payload of a packet. If this situation occurs, it could cause the application to reject the packet or session if the address or port in the header does not match the information in the payload.

To overcome this problem, Cisco has developed the Application Inspection feature, also known as the *fixup*. As packets are translated and pass through the pix on known problematic application ports, the Application Inspection feature will check the payload of the packet for embedded addresses or ports, make the appropriate translations, and update the checksum. The packet is then forwarded to its destination, and the client or server on either end will be none the wiser that application inspection has taken place.

Application inspection also monitors applications that open secondary connections on separate ports to improve performance and allows dynamic ports to be opened for specific sessions. FTP is an application that requires application inspection because it starts a connection on the well-known TCP port 21 and then dynamically opens another port to transmit data. By default, application inspection is enabled for several well-known applications, including FTP, SMTP, HTTP, SQLNET, SIP, H323, and RSH. The configuration example in Figure 5.35 shows how to configure application inspection for HTTP on port 8080 using the *fixup protocol* command. Application inspection can also protect mail servers by only allowing certain SMTP commands to be executed on the mail server. This feature, also called MailGuard, allows only the following commands to be executed on the mail servers: *HELO, MAIL, RCPT, DATA, RSET, NOOP,* and *QUIT.*

Figure 5.35 Configuring Application Inspection

```
Pix515(config)# fixup protocol http 8080
Pix515(config)# fixup protocol smtp 25
```

Intrusion Detection

The PIX's Intrusion Detection System (IDS) analyzes packets that enter a specified interface(s) on a PIX and compares them to 55 predefined attack signatures. The types of attack signature the PIX inspects for are related to the most common DoS attacks and information-gathering scans. Should the PIX detect a match, it can instantly drop or reset the session or send an alert. Figure 5.36 shows how to configure the PIX to inspect all packets coming in on the outside interface of the PIX. Should a match to an attack signature occur, all packets related to the malicious session will be dropped and the attack will be thwarted.

Figure 5.36 Configuring IDS

```
Pix515(config)# ip audit name DropAttacks attack action drop
Pix515(config)# ip audit interface outside DropAttacks
```

FloodGuard, FragGuard, and DNSGuard

The PIX has many features that protect itself and resources it is protecting from DoS attacks. The FloodGuard feature protects the PIX from a form of DoS attack in which an attacker tries to overload the PIX with user authentication requests. To protect itself, the PIX actively closes certain half-open or idle connections to reclaim resources. This feature is enabled by the use of the *floodguard enable* command, a feature that is enabled by default.

The FragGuard feature can stop IP fragment packet attacks, such as teardrop and land, from traversing the PIX. FragGuard analyzes fragmented packets and prevents IP fragment attacks by matching a secondary fragmented packet to a valid initial fragmented packet as well as other checks specified by RFC 1858 (an RFC that details security considerations for IP fragment filtering). The FragGuard feature can be enable using the *sysopt security fragguard* command. This feature is disabled by default, but when enabled, it is active on all interfaces.

DNSGuard identifies an outbound DNS query request and allows only a single DNS response back. A host may query several DNS servers for a response, and the PIX allows only the first answer to the query back in; additional responses from other servers are dropped. DNSGuard is enabled by default and cannot be configured or disabled.

Securing SNMP and NTP

Network management systems can manage the PIX's status via Simple Network Management Protocol (SNMP). For security reasons, the PIX allows only read–only SNMP access. To securely configure SNMP on the PIX, a shared key, or community string, is required to authenticate requests to and from the management system. The key must match on both the management system and the PIX firewall. As shown in Figure 5.37, the SNMP key is set to *mySNMPstring* using the *snmp-server community* command. The *snmp-server host* command specifies the management station that will communicate with the PIX and the interface in which the management station resides. In this example, the management station is 192.168.1.50 and it is located on the PIX's inside interface. Only devices specified with this command and the proper community string will be able to communicate with the PIX via SNMP. The *snmp-server host* command also allows you to specify whether the PIX will be polled by the management system (with the *poll* keyword) or whether the PIX will send traps to the management system (with the *trap* keyword).

Figure 5.37 Configuring SNMP

```
Pix515(config)# snmp-server community mySNMPstring
Pix515(config)# snmp-server host inside 192.168.1.50 poll
```

Network Time Protocol (NTP) allows the PIX to synchronize its clock with a time source. It is a good idea to have the clock set on all network devices, especially security devices, so if an attack occurs, it will be easier to identify the sequence of events of an attack. Figure 5.38 shows how to configure NTP with authentication to ensure that the PIX is receiving its time from a trusted time source. In the example, the key is set to *myNTPkey* and the NTP server is located on the PIX's inside interface and has the IP address of 192.168.1.50.

Figure 5.38 Configuring NTP

```
Pix515(config)# ntp authenticate
Pix515(config)# ntp trusted-key 1
Pix515(config)# ntp authentication-key 1 md5 myNTPkey
Pix515(config)# ntp server 192.168.1.50 key 1 source inside
```

PIX Firewall Design and Configuration Checklist

Use this checklist in designing and configuring your PIX firewall:

1. Gather DMZ requirements.

2. Design the DMZ environment to the specification of the requirements.

3. Select one of the five PIX firewall chassis.

4. Select the optional components of the PIX firewall.

5. Select the correct PIX OS license (Restricted, Unrestricted, and Failover).

6. Optionally, select an encryption license (DES and 3DES).

7. Configure the PIX's console and terminal interfaces.

8. Set security levels on the PIX interfaces.

9. Set IP addresses and speed/duplex settings on the active interfaces.

10. Configure outbound NAT statements.

11. Configure inbound NAT statements.

12. Configure outbound access rules controlling access from internal resources to specific resources on the Internet or other less secure interfaces.

13. Configure inbound access rules controlling access to resources on the DMZ. Remember to be as specific as possible.

14. Configure static or dynamic routing.

15. Should high availability be required, configure the failover or stateful failover feature.

16. If required, configure URL filtering, cut-through proxy, application inspection, and intrusion detection.

17. Lock down SNMP and NTP.

Summary

The PIX firewall is a powerful tool for protecting the enterprise's internal network and its DMZ. Built on a purpose-built operating system, the PIX firewall appliance can provide the security, performance, resiliency, and flexibility to meet all your DMZ infrastructure needs. Five PIX firewall models can provide network architects with several different options to meet their needs—from a small DMZ environment to service provider-class environments. This chapter discussed a couple popular DMZ designs that will meet the needs of many DMZ planners. Use these designs to create the DMZ that best fits your requirements. Remember to choose your design based on your technical requirements and financial constraints. The PIX operating system is purpose-built and packed with features, which makes the PIX highly secure but at the same time provides many of the features found in firewalls based on general operating systems.

The PIX can be configured via a Web-based configuration and management tool called PIX Device Manager (PDM) or via a command-line interface. Always use a secure form of communication when managing the PIX, such as SSH, which encrypts traffic between the client and the PIX, instead of Telnet, which communicates in clear text. This makes the PIX easy to configure and manage for both the novice and the advanced PIX administrator.

We covered how to configure many of the PIX's basic functions, including defining interfaces, NAT/PAT, access rules, and routing, which are essential to the PIX's secure operation. The PIX gives the DMZ planner the flexibility to individually set security levels to each DMZ interface, which can be used to control traffic and maintain the network's integrity. NAT and PAT can be used to hide network internal address or convert private IP addresses into publicly routable addresses. Access rules allow the DMZ planner to limit access to resources on the DMZ via predefined ACLs. The PIX can support a variety of routing protocols, including RIP and OSPF, but most DMZ infrastructures utilize static routing for its security, simplicity, and effectiveness. To provide additional functionality, we also covered how to configure failover for high availability, content filtering, and application layer security.

At this point, you have all the information you need to decide if the PIX firewall is the right device for your DMZ infrastructure in terms or features, functions, and performance. Perhaps more important, this chapter gave you a good idea of how the PIX is configured and managed.

Solutions Fast Track

Basics of the PIX

☑ The PIX is a network security appliance with a purpose-built operating system, which reduces the risk of security flaws inherent in firewalls built on general-purpose operating systems.

☑ There are five PIX models that can provide a high level of security and performance for any size network, from SOHO to a large enterprise or service provider.

☑ The Adaptive Security Algorithm (ASA) allows the PIX to provide stateful inspection firewall services, track the state of all communications, and prevent unauthorized network access.

Cisco PIX Versions and Features

☑ The fact the PIX has a purpose-built operating system does not mean it does not have the features of firewall built on a general OS. In fact, the PIX has a strong security algorithm along with features that include but are not limited to URL filtering, content filtering, DHCP, and intrusion detection.

☑ In addition to securing the network, the PIX can support mobile user and site-to-site VPNs.

☑ The latest main release of the PIX operating system is PIX OS version 6.3, which includes enhancements to VPN features, support for VLANs, and support for new, optional hardware.

Securing Your Network Perimeters

☑ The PIX provides several design possibilities to secure your network and the DMZ, including the traditional "three-legged" firewall, multi-DMZ, and internal/external firewall sandwich configurations.

☑ The PIX can support DMZs of all sizes and capabilities, including high-volume e-commerce sites.

☑ All the designs can also support high availability with the use of a second PIX as a hot standby firewall in the event of failure of the primary PIX.

Making a DMZ and Controlling Traffic

☑ Apply security levels to active interfaces so that the PIX knows how to protect and restrict access networks and devices on each interface.

☑ NAT or PAT enables the PIX to hide addresses and translate private addressing to public addresses that are routable throughout the Internet. For the PIX to pass traffic between interfaces, a NAT and/or PAT statement is required, regardless whether network address translation is needed.

☑ Access control lists enable the PIX to restrict access to devices on all interfaces, including the DMZ.

☑ Routing allows the PIX to forward traffic out the correct interface and on to the receiving device or next hop. The PIX supports static and dynamic routing in the from of RIP and OSPF.

Advanced PIX Features

☑ Failover enables the PIX to provide high availability in case of a failure. In addition, the PIX supports stateful failover, so user connections through the PIX should remain active as failover occurs.

☑ URL, Java, and ActiveX filtering prevents access to restricted sites and protects users from downloading dangerous content and applications.

☑ IDS and application inspection delve into the packets to make sure there is no malicious activity flowing through the PIX.

PIX Firewall Design and Configuration Checklist

☑ Use the checklist at the end of the chapter when you are designing and configuring your PIX firewall.

Frequently Asked Questions

The following Frequently Asked Questions, answered by the authors of this book, are designed to both measure your understanding of the concepts presented in this chapter and to assist you with real-life implementation of these concepts. To have your questions about this chapter answered by the author, browse to **www.syngress.com/solutions** and click on the **"Ask the Author"** form. You will also gain access to thousands of other FAQs at ITFAQnet.com.

Q: Does the PIX support other desktop protocols, such as AppleTalk and IPX?

A: The PIX supports only IP. If you need to pass AppleTalk or IPX protocols through the PIX, you must encapsulate them within an IP tunnel. Tunneling of protocols through the PIX can be dangerous and should only be done in a controlled environment.

Q: What routing protocols does the PIX support?

A: The PIX can support static routing, RIP (versions 1 and 2), and OSPF. The PIX does not support EIGRP and IGRP, Cisco's proprietary routing protocols.

Q: Can the PIX protect the internal LAN from viruses or worms?

A: By default, the PIX does provide some application-level protection for popular applications such as FTP and mail. In addition, the PIX does have IDS feature that can protect against 55 predefined attack signatures, providing protection against some popular DoS attacks. However, in order to protect against viruses and/or worms, you should consider a standalone IDS unit, antivirus applications on workstations and servers, and patching flawed or susceptible software.

Q: Can a PIX 515 and PIX 515E used together for failover?

A: No. Both PIX units must be exactly the same model and must have the same amount of memory, Flash, and interface cards. Even though the PIX 515E is an enhanced version of the PIX 515, the models cannot be used together as a failover pair.

Q: Does the PIX have packet-capture capabilities, similar to a sniffer?

A: Yes. PIX version 6.2 supports packet-capture capabilities that allow the administrator to capture packets on specific interfaces and to filter captured packets via ACLs. The capture buffer can be viewed via the CLI or downloaded via a TFTP server.

Q: Does the PIX cut-through proxy work the same as a proxy server?

A: No. The PIX's cut-though proxy feature does not work like a standard proxy server, because the PIX will authenticate the user, and if permitted, the PIX will allow the client to communicate directly with the remote server. A standard proxy server will act as intermediate device where the client will request a connection to a remote device; it intercepts all requests to the real server to see if it can fulfill the requests itself. If it cannot, it forwards the request to the real server on behalf of the client, so the client never directly communicates to the remote server.

## Chapter 6

Firewall and DMZ Design: Check Point NG

Solutions in this chapter:

- **Basics of Check Point NG**

- **Securing Your Network Perimeters**

- **Making a DMZ and Controlling Traffic**

- **Check Point NG Secure DMZ Checklist**

- ☑ **Summary**

- ☑ **Solutions Fast Track**

- ☑ **Frequently Asked Questions**

Introduction

A key component of any security policy is a well-designed DMZ. Because hosts in the DMZ are externally accessible over the Internet, your DMZ's design can make or break the overall security of your network because the DMZ can be the entry point for malicious-minded individuals into your network.

There are two types of traffic to keep in mind when you're considering controlling traffic flowing to and from a DMZ: traffic originating from or destined for your internal network, and traffic originating from or destined for the Internet. Although you might think that the connection point to the Internet is the most vital one, it is equally important to consider the access point to your internal network. Not only does this consideration provide a second layer of inspection for traffic traversing the DMZ to reach internal hosts, it also allows you to protect your network from malicious activity originating from within—an occurrence that's growing more and more common.

In this chapter, we review the basics of Check Point NG FireWall-1/VPN-1 to give you a solid understanding of how the firewall operates and the features it makes available to you. We then go into detail about several Check Point features that are key to developing a well-secured DMZ, including how to best configure these features to secure your network perimeters. Finally, we document the steps to set up the DMZ from scratch in FireWall-1/VPN-1, from setup of the physical interface to rule base configuration.

Basics of Check Point NG

Check Point NG FireWall-1/VPN-1 is a full-featured firewall that runs on a variety of platforms, including Sun Solaris, Microsoft Windows NT/2000, and dedicated appliances manufactured by Nokia and Check Point.

Designing & Planning...

Operating System Selection

Choosing the operating system to use for your Check Point FireWall-1/VPN-1 firewall is important to the overall effectiveness of the product in securing your network. A well-configured firewall installed on an operating system with security flaws that make the network easy to compromise serves little purpose in securing a network. Malicious users may gain access to the operating system and then use that access to disable the firewall's security policies.

Among Check Point's supported operating systems, there is not necessarily one that is the most secure. Each can be configured more or less securely. However, in general, Windows and Sun should be hardened before they are used as firewalls, because they do have inherent security issues as a result of their wide range of possible use. The dedicated appliances manufactured by Nokia and Check Point have pre-hardened operating systems that can generally be used as is, provided they are up to date in terms of security patches.

Key features of Check Point NG FireWall-1/VPN-1 are stateful inspection, network address translation, content security on various levels, multiple types of authentication mechanisms, and SmartDefense, which provides DoS and other malicious activity detection.

FireWall-1/VPN-1 also has significant VPN capability, for both site-to-site and user-to-site configurations. Site-to-site VPN is interoperable with products from all other major firewall vendors. For user VPN access, two varieties of VPN client—SecuRemote and SecureClient— are available, with the latter providing personal firewall functionality in addition to the standard VPN features of SecuRemote.

Stateful Inspection

The underlying technology behind Check Point NG FireWall-1/VPN-1 is a proprietary inspection system known as *stateful inspection*. The premise behind stateful inspection is that it is ineffective for a firewall to determine whether to allow or deny each packet based solely on that packet's individual characteristics.

FireWall-1 takes numerous other factors into account in examining packets, including data from all layers within the packet, data from previous related packets, and information received from related applications. Combine this with the capability to manipulate data within each packet as it flows through the firewall, and FireWall-1 moves from the realm of simple packet filter to a much more robust solution.

Network Address Translation

As is standard on most firewalls, FireWall-1 supports NAT with a variety of options. NAT is available in Hide mode, where many hosts are hidden behind one routable IP address, and Static mode, where there is a one-to-one mapping between internal and external IP addresses. FireWall-1 also allows you to manipulate the service of translated packets.

In addition to the ability to manually configure NAT rules, FireWall-1 provides automatic NAT configuration based on easy-to-configure menu options per network object. Not only does this feature increase ease of use, it also allows for a more organized, central method of NAT configuration.

Management Architecture

FireWall-1/VPN-1 uses a distributed architecture, where the management and enforcement points can run on separate servers. As a result, it is possible to manage multiple enforcement points with a single management server.

Check Point provides a comprehensive graphical user interface (GUI), which runs on a variety of platforms, to be used as a single configuration point for all firewall functionality. The GUI, called SmartDashboard, provides separate views for object lists; standard, translation, and desktop rule sets; and VPN, in addition to a graphical view of your network.

Because of the two separate communication points—GUI to management server and management server to enforcement point—there is an inherent increase in security in terms of management functionality, compared with a more open model that has configuration access directly to the enforcement point.

Securing Your Network Perimeters

Before getting down to configuration of your DMZ, it is important that you have a general security policy that will maintain your network's overall security. It does no good to have a perfectly secure DMZ if other aspects of your firewall's security configuration are flawed and allow unintended access into your network.

The network perimeter is the interface on your firewall that faces a source that is not trusted. The most common example of this perimeter is an interface out to the Internet, but it is possible to have additional network perimeters—such as a connection to another organization's network—and the configuration for these would be the same, except for differences in specific access requirements.

The Check Point Perimeter Security Solution

Check Point NG FireWall-1/VPN-1 can be used in any conceivable DMZ configuration, including the traditional "three-legged" design, a multi-DMZ setup, and the dual-firewall "sandwich" configuration, where separate firewalls protect the external and internal networks from each other.

Because Check Point's management architecture, as we discussed, can involve separation of the management console from the enforcement points as well as separation of the management GUI from the management console, it is important to plan the location of each of these when you are designing your network. Figure 6.1 illustrates a typical "three-legged" firewall design, with management console and GUI separate from the enforcement point.

Figure 6.1 "Three-Legged" Firewall with Distributed Check Point Architecture

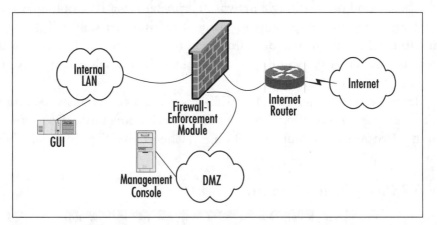

In this case, the management console is in the DMZ, whereas the GUI is on the internal LAN. Having the management console in the DMZ allows you to use that console to manage firewalls that are located on external networks, either on the Internet or on third-party networks (none of which are shown on this diagram). If the management console is to be used only to manage firewalls on the local network, it could be located on the internal LAN, which would provide some additional security.

Note that the management console could be located on the internal LAN and still be able to manage external firewalls through NAT. However, this setup does add complexity to the management architecture.

Configuring Check Point to Secure Network Perimeters

Check Point NG FireWall-1/VPN-1 provides you with a number of tools to allow you to effectively secure your network perimeter.

First we discuss antispoofing, which is an important feature to ensure that your security policy is not bypassed. We then go into the configuration of SmartDefense, an effective way of preventing malicious attacks that could be directed at your network perimeters. Here you can verify your antispoofing configuration, DoS protection, IP-related security settings, and protection against service-based attacks to such services as DNS, FTP, HTTP, and SMTP.

In addition, we cover how you can customize Check Point's stateful inspection architecture, allowing for more granular control over what packets are dropped as a result of these checks. Finally, we examine the use of Check Point's security servers to provide an extra layer of authentication and screening at the network perimeter.

Antispoofing

One popular method of breaching a network perimeter is via IP spoofing. A malicious user could attempt to use IP spoofing to manipulate his or her source IP address, appearing to originate from an address from within your network. The goal of this attack is to bypass deny rules you have in place, since the firewall may perceive the user as being part of your internal network.

In order to prevent IP spoofing, FireWall-1 contains a comprehensive antispoofing feature. To configure antispoofing, first open the Check Point **SmartDashboard** and bring up the **Properties** of your firewall object. Choose the **Topology** tab, shown in Figure 6.2.

Figure 6.2 Firewall Object Topology

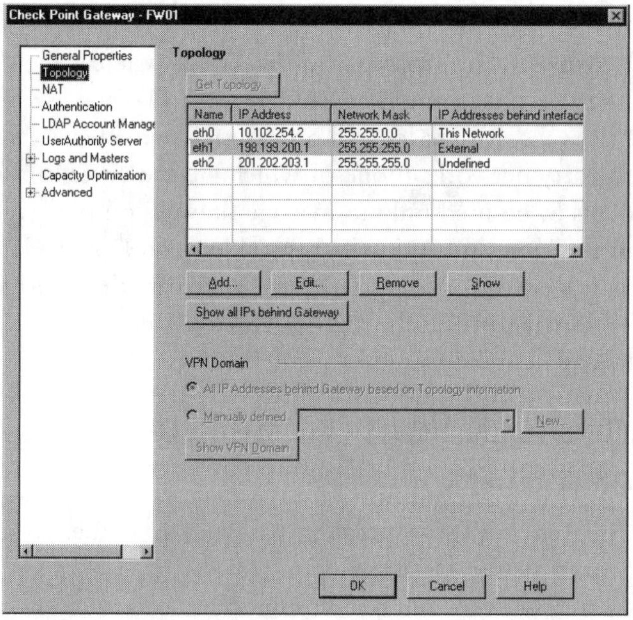

Each interface of the firewall is listed here. You will notice the field "IP Addresses behind interface," which relates to the antispoofing configuration and specifies the type of host residing on that interface. Here there are three interfaces listed: eth0, the internal network; eth1, the external, Internet-facing network; and eth2, the DMZ. Let's look at the antispoofing configuration for each interface.

Highlight **eth0**, choose **Edit**, and then the **Topology** tab (see Figure 6.3).

Figure 6.3 Interface Topology

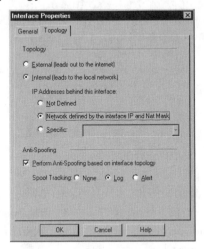

Here you specify whether this interface is *external*, which means it is Internet-facing, or *internal*, which applies to all other interfaces. Next, you need to specify the IP addresses hosted by this interface. Although there is a Not Defined setting, this choice is not recommended, because it removes the antispoofing capability for this interface.

Choose **Network defined by the interface IP and Net Mask** if the only network behind this interface matches the network defined in the General tab. Alternatively, choose **Specific** and specify a previously defined network object if there are additional networks hosted behind this interface.

By choosing either of the latter two options, you provide the firewall with the information it needs to perform antispoofing on this interface. More specifically, because the firewall is aware of the IP addresses behind each interface, it is able to check that traffic originating from each address is actually sourced at the matching interface.

To enable antispoofing, turn on **Perform Anti-spoofing based on interface topology**. You can also specify the tracking method the firewall should take when spoofing is detected. It is important to track spoofing so that you can take additional preventative action against the malicious user and his or her network.

Repeat the above procedure for each interface on the firewall, and be sure to install the policy to have these changes take effect.

Configuring & Implementing...

Antispoofing Dropping Valid Packets

It is important to remember that when antispoofing is configured, you must ensure that all IP networks behind an interface are specified in the topology configuration. If a network is left out, the firewall will assume traffic from that network is spoofed, and it will drop those packets. Therefore, when adding a new network to your firewall, it is important to remember the extra step of updating the topology information for the interface that will host that network.

SmartDefense

New to Check Point NG, SmartDefense is an amalgamation of various attack detection and notification systems present in previous Check Point versions. With all these options configurable from one location, the task of configuring your firewall to detect all these attacks is greatly simplified.

To access the SmartDefense configuration, open the Check Point **SmartDashboard**, go to **Policy**, and then choose **SmartDefense** (see Figure 6.4).

Figure 6.4 SmartDefense General Settings

In the General tab, you have the option Update SmartDefense. This option checks to see if there are any new versions of SmartDefense available, and if there are, allows you to install these updates. There is also a link here to open the SmartView Tracker, which is where all tracking information about detected attacks is stored Select **Anti Spoofing Configuration Status** (see Figure 6.5).

Figure 6.5 SmartDefense Antispoofing

Here, SmartDefense checks to see whether antispoofing is fully configured. This check looks for any interface on your firewall that does not have IP addresses specified. Because antispoofing works only if IP information is set for each interface, any time this information is missing you are at risk of a spoofing attack. Select **Denial of Service** (see Figure 6.6).

Figure 6.6 SmartDefense Denial of Service

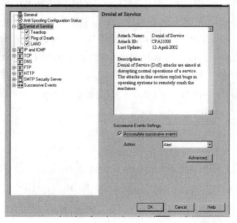

A DoS attack involves sending a large number of requests for particular services. Because your network is so busy dealing with all the excessive requests, it is not able to respond to valid requests, or at least not at its usual pace.

SmartDefense provides protection against three types of DoS attack: teardrop attacks, which can crash servers by sending overlapping IP fragments; ping-of-death attacks, which can crash servers by sending ICMP packets that exceed the normal maximum size of a packet; and LAND attacks, which can affect network devices by sending packets with specified properties.

In the main DoS window, select **Accumulate successive events** to have the firewall keep track of attacks over time and consider them part of the same occurrence rather than tracking each one individually. Choose **Advanced** (see Figure 6.7).

Figure 6.7 Advanced Configuration

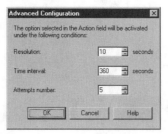

Here, you can set **Resolution**, which specifies the number of seconds over which an attack must occur for action to be taken. This relates to the **Attempts Number** option, which is the number of times that attack must occur within the number of seconds specified. The **Time Interval** option sets how long information about an attack should be stored before it is removed from the firewall.

To enable each of the three types of DoS attack protection, expand the drop-down list of attack types under the main **Denial of Service** option, and check each type of attack to enable. By default, all three are enabled, and it is probably wise to leave them enabled unless you have a specific reason to do otherwise. The single option available for each attack is the tracking setting, which specifies how the firewall should track detected attacks of that type.

Next is the IP and ICMP section. There are three types of verification in this category: fragment sanity check, packet sanity, and max ping size. Note that the first two checks cannot be disabled. The fragment sanity check attempts to determine whether fragmented packets are fragmented for a valid reason—the packet is too big to be transmitted as a whole—or not. The packet sanity verification looks at a number of aspects of each packet, such as headers and flags, and looks for anything out of the ordinary. The max ping size setting allows you to specify how large ICMP packets may be.

In the **TCP** section, choose **SYN Attack** (see Figure 6.8).

Figure 6.8 SYN Attack

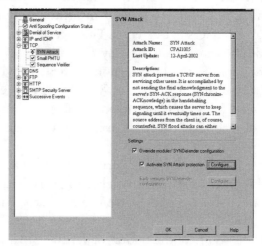

A SYN attack can slow down or stop a server by sending multiple incomplete handshake sequences. The acknowledgment step of the sequence is left out, so the server continually attempts to signal for this response, tying up its resources.

By choosing **Override modules' SYNDefender configuration**, you can enable SYN attack protection on enforcement modules even if they have SYNDefender, a component of previous versions of Check Point FireWall-1/VPN-1, enabled. Disabling this option enables the **Early version SYNDefender configuration** option, which contains the traditional SYNDefender settings.

To enable SYN attack protection, choose **Activate SYN Attack protection** and then **Configure** (see Figure 6.9).

Figure 6.9 SYN Attack Configuration

Here, you can set the tracking option for SYN attacks detected and whether you would like to track activity that is actually identified as an attack, rather than individual occurrences. The **timeout** value specifies the number of seconds the firewall should wait for the acknowledgment part of the handshake before marking the session as possibly being part of an attack. The **Attack Threshold** sets the number of sessions without acknowledgments that must occur before the firewall concludes that a SYN attack is in progress. Finally, set **Protect external interface only** to ignore unusual SYN activity on all other interfaces but external. This option is normally selected, since SYN attacks originate on the Internet and usually from forged IP addresses.

The remaining two options in the TCP section are **Small PMTU** and **Sequence Verifier**. The small PMTU section allows you to specify the smallest packet size allowed. This capability is useful because of the potential for an attack that involves sending a high number of very small packets, causing the network to slow down or stop because it is busy processing all these packets.

The sequence verifier function allows for verification that packets are being sent in the correct sequence. This prevents attacks that relate to packet sequence number manipulation. You have the option to track out-of-state packets that are anomalous or suspicious, or all such packets.

Next, click **DNS**. Here, you have the option of verifying that all traffic flowing to the UDP port normally used for DNS queries is actually DNS traffic. This prevents other types of potentially malicious traffic being sent to the DNS server.

In the **FTP** section, the first option, which cannot be disabled, is to prevent FTP bounce attacks. The next section relates to the FTP security server, which we discuss in further detail in the following section. In short, the FTP security server allows authentication and content checking for FTP connections passing through the firewall. Choose **Allowed FTP Commands** (see Figure 6.10).

Figure 6.10 Allowed FTP Commands

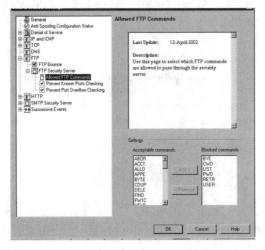

Here, there are two sections: acceptable commands and blocked commands. These options allow you to specify what FTP commands are permitted on FTP connections that use the FTP security server. This is useful to prevent the use of commands that could be used maliciously, or even to provide a more limited FTP service—for example, users may only be allowed to send files but not retrieve them.

The HTTP section provides protection against HTTP worms as well as configuration for the HTTP security server. Choose **General HTTP Worm Catcher** (see Figure 6.11).

Figure 6.11 General HTTP Worm Catcher

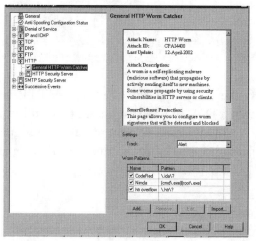

Here you can select from three built-in worm patterns—CodeRed, Nimda, and htr overlow—and can define or import additional worm patterns. This option is especially useful given the fact that new HTTP worms are continually discovered. By being able to manually add a worm pattern, you have the ability to protect yourself from newly discovered worms even before a vendor releases a preventative patch.

Just as with the FTP security server configuration described earlier, an HTTP security server provides protection against the malicious use of an HTTP server within your network. Choose **HTTP Format Sizes** (see Figure 6.12).

Figure 6.12 HTTP Format Sizes

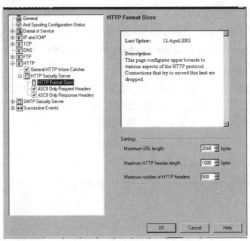

Here, you can specify the maximum size of a URL, HTTP header, and number of HTTP headers. This prevents DoS attacks that attempt to exploit these limits.

Similarly, the SMTP Security Server section provides configuration options to screen the content of mail transmitted through the firewall to mail servers. Choose **SMTP Content** (see Figure 6.13).

Figure 6.13 SMTP Content

Select **Add "received" header when forwarding** to have the SMTP security server append this header to forwarded messages. Choose **Watch for bad SMTP commands** to allow the firewall to detect invalid SMTP commands sent by a remote server that might be intended for malicious purposes. You can also specify the number of no-effect and unknown commands permitted before the firewall will drop the connection.

Choose **Mail and Recipient Content** (see Figure 6.14).

Figure 6.14 Mail and Recipient Content

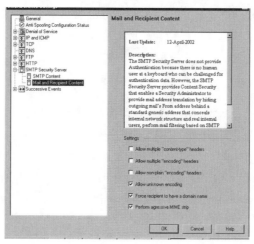

These settings allow for additional content security around SMTP connections. For example, **Force recipient to have a domain name** means mail cannot be send through the security server with no domain name—a technique that could be used to cause external mail to appear as coming from the internal domain.

The final settings under Successive Events relate to how often events must occur before they are of significance and how much memory the firewall should allocate to this type of detection.

Stateful Inspection Customization

Another important aspect to securing your network perimeters is the ability to customize FireWall-1's stateful inspection mechanism. By adjusting these values as circumstances change around your network, you can ensure that you are taking full advantage of this powerful feature.

To access the stateful inspection properties, open the Check Point **SmartDashboard** and go to **Policy**, and then choose **Global Properties**. Select **Stateful Inspection** (see Figure 6.15).

Figure 6.15 Stateful Inspection

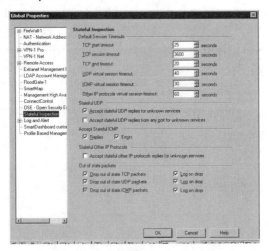

The first set of definable values is for session timeouts. All these values relate to the number of seconds that must elapse for various aspects of a TCP, UDP, and ICMP session. By shortening these values, you reduce the risk of DoS attacks penetrating your network perimeter. However, if the timeout values are too low, you could end up dropping valid connections to your network that are slow for other reasons, such as poor network or server performance. The default values are a good starting point, and you can adjust these as required based on the performance of valid network traffic and the characteristics of malicious traffic.

Next are settings for stateful UDP. Selecting **Accept stateful UDP replies for unknown services** instructs the firewall to allow UDP connection replies, even if it is unaware of the service type. Enabling this option also allows you to select **Accept stateful UDP replies from any port for unknown services**, which allows UDP connection replies on any port, as opposed to only the port on which the connection originated.

Similarly, you can configure the way the firewall deals with ICMP requests in the next section: Accept Stateful ICMP. These settings relate to ICMP packets that are allowed based on stateful information about TCP or UDP connections. Selecting **Replies** allows ICMP reply packets, whereas selecting **Errors** permits ICMP error packets.

Selecting **Accept Stateful other IP protocols replies for unknown services** relates to packets that are not TCP, UDP, or ICMP. This choice instructs the firewall to accept these packets, provided they meet the usual state criteria.

Finally, the Out of State Packets section defines what the firewall should do with packets that are determined to be out of state—whether they should be dropped, logged, or both.

Making a DMZ and Controlling Traffic

Now that we have covered the various aspects of securing your network perimeters, let's move on to the actual setup and configuration of the DMZ. This section includes configuring the physical interface that will be used for the DMZ, adding network objects, and configuring access rules to allow access to and from the DMZ.

Configuring the DMZ Interface

Setting up a DMZ requires a physical interface on the firewall to be used for DMZ traffic. First you need to have an interface available on the server or appliance on which your firewall runs. Ensure that the interface is configured and recognized in the operating system. Both these tasks are outside the scope of this guide; consult your hardware and operating system documentation for more information.

Once the interface is available and ready to use, the next step is to add it to the list of interfaces of your firewall object. Open the Check Point **SmartDashboard**, edit the **Properties** of your firewall object, and choose **Topology**. Click **Add** to be brought to the screen shown in Figure 6.16.

Figure 6.16 Add Interface

When entering a name for the interface, be sure the name matches the name of the interface used by the operating system. Before setting the IP address, you need to obtain a routable IP subnet from your Internet provider, to be used on the DMZ. You or your Internet provider will need to route this subnet to your firewall. Set **IP Address** to the first usable IP address in the DMZ subnet—in this example, 201.202.203.1, with a net mask of 255.255.255.0. Go to the **Topology** tab (see Figure 6.17).

Figure 6.17 New Interface Topology

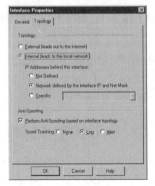

Designing & Planning…

DMZ with Network Address Translation

Instead of using routable IP addresses for your DMZ, it is also possible to configure a DMZ with private addresses. In this case, you would have to use NAT to allow traffic from the Internet through the external interface to reach DMZ hosts. Although this solution does provide an additional layer of security, it is also important to keep in mind the extra load it places on your firewall; translating large amounts of packets consumes its resources. Therefore, if you have a DMZ host that will have very high throughput levels, such as a busy Web server, it might not be practical to use private addressing.

Since this is not an Internet facing network, choose **Internal**. To specify the IP addresses behind this interface, choose **Network defined by the interface IP and Net Mask**, since we will not have any additional networks behind this interface. This means that 201.202.203.0 through 201.202.203.254 are permitted to transmit and receive data to and from this interface.

Enable **Perform Anti-Spoofing based on interface topology** to have the firewall detect all spoofing attempts, and choose the tracking level that suits your needs.

Configuring Access Rules

Now that the DMZ interface is configured and ready for use, the next step is to install and connect the servers that are to reside in the DMZ to this interface. In general, you would connect the firewall DMZ interface to a switch and then connect the DMZ-residing servers to that switch. In our example, we have one Web server and one mail server sitting behind the DMZ, with IP addresses 201.202.203.2 and 201.202.203.3, respectively.

Define each server to sit in the DMZ as a network object by choosing **Manage | Network Objects | New | Node | Host**. See Figure 6.18.

Figure 6.18 New DMZ Host

Set the name, IP address, and an option comment and color for the Web server. Follow the identical procedure to define the mail server. Next, we will define rules for HTTP and HTTPS access to the Web server and SMTP access to the mail server (see Figure 6.19).

Figure 6.19 Rule Base for DMZ Access

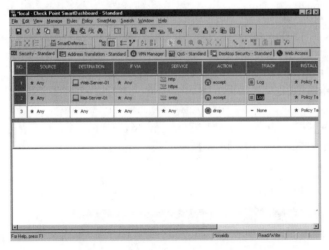

The first rule permits any source to access the HTTP (80) and HTTPS (443) TCP ports of the Web server; the second rule permits any source to access the SMTP (25) port of the mail server. It is important to note, though, that because there are no other rules present besides the cleanup rule, hosts on the internal network will not be able to access either of these servers. Therefore, it is important to remember to add specific rules to permit traffic from the internal network to the DMZ (see Figure 6.20).

Figure 6.20 Rule Base for DMZ Access from Internal

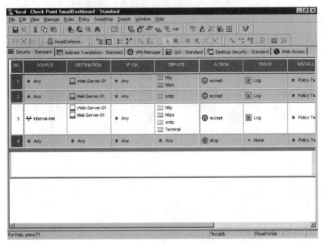

Rule 3 permits traffic from the Internet network, 10.102.254.0 as defined in the firewall object's topology, to access both the Web and mail servers. The services allowed are the same as from the Internet, plus the Terminal service, which can be used for remote administration of these devices.

Combine a rule base such as this with all the previously mentioned perimeter security procedures, and you can be sure your DMZ hosts remain secure.

Configuring Network Address Translation

You can use NAT in any number of scenarios when private IP addresses are used and need to access, or be accessed from, external networks. One of the most common instances where NAT is used is for access from workstations on the internal network to the Internet, for activities such as Web browsing or file transfers.

To configure NAT in Check Point FireWall-1/VPN-1, open the **SmartDashboard** and go to the **Address Translation** tab. See Figure 6.21.

Figure 6.21 Address Translation Tab

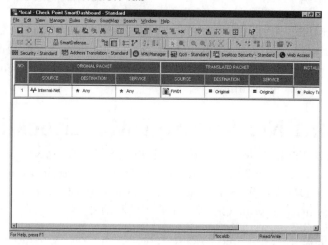

Here, Rule 1 allows access from the internal network, 10.102.254.0, to the Internet. This access is allowed by translating all packets originating from the internal network to the external IP address of the firewall, 198.199.200.1. Conversely, returning traffic from the Internet to the internal network is translated from 198.199.200.1 back to the IP address of the originating node.

Note that for Rule 1, we used Hide mode NAT because we want to hide all the internal IP addresses behind one external address. This is also referred to as many-to-one NAT.

Static mode NAT, in contrast, is used in a one-to-one NAT situation—for example, when an internal host needs to be accessed from the Internet. In this case, a Static NAT rule would be set up to translate packets to and from the internal and external IP addresses.

In our case, we will not add a rule to allow access to the internal hosts, since we assume all access to nodes within our network will be via the DMZ. Generally, this is a more secure architecture, since you limit external access to just one area of your network, protecting hosts in other areas in case of a security compromise.

Note that it is not necessary to add NAT rules for access to the DMZ from the internal network. Since both segments use the firewall as their gateway, it is not necessary to use translation to allow access between the two; the firewall is able to provide direct access to and from both networks.

Routing Through Check Point FireWall-1/VPN-1

It is important to keep IP routing in mind when configuring the firewall. All routing functionality is handled by the operating system; FireWall-1 assumes proper routing is in place to allow access to defined networks.

Due to the fact that routing functionality is not part of the firewall's configuration, a discussion of that topic is out of scope here. Consult the documentation of your operating system or firewall appliance for information on how to configure static or dynamic routing in each environment.

Check Point NG Secure DMZ Checklist

Here is a checklist of the key elements to take into account when you're building a secure DMZ in a Check Point NG environment. Keeping these in mind as you prepare and implement your DMZ will greatly aid in both the ease of setup and the overall functionality and security of your Check Point NG DMZ:

- SmartDefense is configured to detect, block, and log DoS and other attacks
- All firewall interfaces have IP addresses specified in their topology configuration
- All firewall interfaces have antispoofing enabled
- Stateful inspection is tuned to catch as many out-of-state packets as possible
- Network interface added and configured in operating system
- Network interface added to FireWall-1 configuration, antispoofing enabled
- Routable network assigned by ISP and routed to firewall

- Network objects for DMZ hosts defined
- NAT configured for outbound access from internal network
- Rules added to rule base to allow access to DMZ hosts from Internet
- Rules added to rule base to allow access to DMZ hosts from internal network
- Static or dynamic routing configured in the operating system

Summary

Because the nature of a DMZ is to allow access from the Internet to hosts on your network, it is important to maintain a complete security policy surrounding access to these hosts. Building a secure DMZ with Check Point NG FireWall-1/VPN-1 involves many aspects of the firewall's feature set. It is important to use all these features to ensure that there are no weak links in your security policy.

FireWall-1/VPN-1's stateful inspection architecture provides a good fundamental inspection layer for all traffic traversing the firewall to reach DMZ hosts. More effective than a simple packet filter, the ability to make filtering decisions based on packet state and context is a powerful mechanism from which your DMZ security will benefit.

Add to this the attack-prevention systems that are part of SmartDefense, as well as a complete antispoofing configuration, and the full picture of what it takes to build a secure DMZ comes into focus. Defining rules to allow specific access to hosts within the DMZ is a final step that must be done, keeping in mind only the access that is actually required to these hosts.

Solutions Fast Track

Basics of Check Point NG

☑ Stateful inspection provides enhanced filtering based on state, context, and other information about each packet.

☑ NAT, configurable manually or automatically, allows for translation of source, destination, and service for each packet.

☑ A distributed management architecture provides additional security by eliminating a direct connection between configuration client and enforcement point.

Securing Your Network Perimeters

☑ Enable antispoofing for all interfaces on the firewall to prevent spoof attacks.

☑ Use SmartDefense to protect your network from multiple types of attacks, including DoS attacks.

☑ Customize stateful inspection to catch the maximum number of out-of-state packets.

Making a DMZ and Controlling Traffic

☑ Install DMZ hosts on a separate interface on the firewall.

☑ Add rules to the rule base to allow access from the Internet and from the internal network to the DMZ.

☑ Configure static or dynamic routing in the operating system to allow access to and from the DMZ.

Check Point NG Secure DMZ Checklist

☑ Follow the Check Point NG Secure DMZ Checklist when you're planning and running a Check Point NG DMZ.

Frequently Asked Questions

The following Frequently Asked Questions, answered by the authors of this book, are designed to both measure your understanding of the concepts presented in this chapter and to assist you with real-life implementation of these concepts. To have your questions about this chapter answered by the author, browse to **www.syngress.com/solutions** and click on the **"Ask the Author"** form. You will also gain access to thousands of other FAQs at ITFAQnet.com.

Q: Do I need a separate physical interface on the firewall for the DMZ, or can I share another interface?

A: For the maximum level of security, you should have a separate interface for the DMZ. Using VLANs or other techniques, you could share another interface for the DMZ, but the firewall will not be able to protect the DMZ from traffic on the shared interface.

Q: The firewall is dropping legitimate packets because it reports they are out of state. How do I correct this?

A: One common cause of this problem is a configuration in which traffic is delivered to a node on one firewall interface and the node transmits the response on a different firewall interface. The stateful inspection engine will not recognize this traffic as legitimate. The solution is to ensure that all traffic moving to and from each node is using the same interface.

Q: Is it necessary to restrict traffic to or from the internal network to or from the DMZ? Can't I just open all access between them?

A: It is important to keep in mind that not all malicious activity comes from the Internet. You need to protect your network from internal attacks as well, and so it is good security practice to only allow access that is actually required, even between the internal and DMZ segments.

Q: What is the best way to deal with alerts generated by SmartDefense?

A: In general, if SmartDefense has detected a security violation, it is a good idea to block all access from the offending host to your network, if possible. You can then notify the network administrator of that network so that he or she can deal appropriately with the offending user.

Q: Is it necessary to have separate hosts for the enforcement point, management console, and GUI?

A: No. Your firewall will operate normally if two or all three of these components are installed on the same host. However, by dividing them into separate hosts, you have the advantage of additional flexibility in terms of being able to manage multiple enforcement points. There is also an increased level of security if the management console is not on a host accessible to the Internet, such as the enforcement point.

## Chapter 7

Firewall and DMZ Design: Nokia Firewall

Solutions in this chapter:

- Basics of the Nokia Firewall

- Securing Your Network Perimeters

- Nokia Firewall and DMZ Design Checklist

☑ Summary

☑ Solutions Fast Track

☑ Frequently Asked Questions

Introduction

The Nokia IP Series appliance is a router that provides critical security services through the use of ACLs and/or third-party applications. Nokia's partnership with Check Point provides firewall services using FireWall-1/VPN-1. Check Point FireWall-1 uses its patented Stateful Inspection technology to inspect packets flowing through the Nokia appliance. Stateful Inspection keeps a record of each connection request and dynamically opens up the ports for allowed connections. Once a connection is terminated, the ports are dynamically closed until the next request. This system is more secure than packet filtering, which leaves ports opened or closed. In addition, Nokia's partnership with ISS provides intrusion detection services with RealSecure.

Nokia's underlying OS, IPSO, is based on the FreeBSD operating system. The IPSO OS has been presecured and does not require a license for its use. In addition, the IPSO OS is highly optimized for traffic forwarding. IPSO also provides a wide range of routing services and protocols. All Nokia IP Series appliances use IPSO except for the Small Office Security Product Line, a separate product line that utilizes different technology and is not discussed in this chapter. For more information on the Small Office Security Product Line, refer to Nokia's Security Products page at www.nokia.com/security.

This chapter will guide you in designing a DMZ using the Nokia platform. We discuss and show you how to formulate a design plan. We also discuss the two different types of DMZ, a "three-legged" DMZ and a traditional DMZ. and the advantages and disadvantages of each. Finally, we show you how to implement your solution.

Basics of the Nokia Firewall

Nokia offers multiple platforms ranging from the IP100 series for the SOHO environment to the IP700 series for the enterprise environment. One of the Nokia platform's key strengths is the use of a platform-independent OS and third-party applications. Current versions of IPSO can be used across most platforms. The exception is the (IP350/IP380) Trooper Platform, which uses a separate IPSO, IPSO 3.5.1. Future IPSO releases will support all Nokia platforms using the same technology. Nokia uses Check Point FireWall-1/VPN-1 to provide firewall services across all platforms. Check Point does not provide different software packages for each platform. Rather, it relies on the license applied to enable desired functionality.

The idea of platform-independent OSs and software reduces the need for extra storage overhead for multiple software packages. It also provides ease of administration and deployment.

Choosing the Right Platform

Since the smallest Nokia IP appliance offers at least three 10/100 Ethernet interfaces, it is possible to design a DMZ solution with each appliance. In addition, Check Point FireWall-1/VPN-1 functionality is enabled by the features of the license, not by the software package. Since Check Point FireWall-1/VPN-1 is only limited by its license, it is important to choose the correct platform for the intended environment. In the next section, we discuss the current Nokia Platforms available and the environments in which they should be deployed.

Nokia IP120 Appliance

The IP120 appliance is a desk or wall-mountable appliance intended for the small satellite office environment. It has three embedded 10/100 Ethernet ports, standard IPSO IP routing functionality, and full Check Point FireWall-1/VPN-1 functionality (depending on the license feature). The IP120 appliance has no hardware upgrade options.

The IP120 has the following key features:

- Three embedded 10/100 Ethernet interfaces
- 128MB RAM (nonupgradeable)
- Two serial ports—one for local console connectivity and an auxiliary port for external modem connections for remote administration.
- High-availability support using VRRP

Nokia IP350/IP380 Platforms

The IP350/IP380 platforms are rack-mountable 1RU platforms intended for the medium-sized enterprise environment. They contain four embedded 10/100 Ethernet interfaces, on-board hardware encryption acceleration, full IPSO IP routing functionality, and full Check Point FireWall-1/VPN-1 functionality (depending on the license interface). The IP350 and IP380 also contain two Type II PCMCIA slots that support the use of a PCMCIA modem for dial-in remote administration.

The IP350 and IP380 share the following key features:

- Four embedded 10/100 Ethernet interfaces
- On-board Hardware Encryption Acceleration
- Two Type II PCMCIA slots

- Two PMC expansion ports for optional modules. Each PMC expansion port supports the following modules:

  - Dual-port 10/100 Ethernet interface module

  - V.35/X.21 module

  - ISDN-BRI module

- Two serial ports—one for local console connectivity and an auxiliary port for external modem connections for remote administration

- High-availability support using VRRP or IP clustering

Table 7.1 outlines the key differences between the IP350 and IP380 platforms.

Table 7.1 Differences Between the IP350 and IP380 Platforms

Features	IP350	IP380
Secured firewall throughput	350Mbps	600Mbps
VPN throughput encryption acceleration upgrade	60Mbps	90Mbps or 130Mbps with
Maximum memory supported	512Mb	1GB
Upgrade encryption acceleration module	No	Yes

Nokia IP530 Platform

The IP530 platform is a rack-mountable 2RU intended for the medium-sized to large enterprise environment. It contains four embedded 10/100 Ethernet interfaces, full IPSO IP routing functionality, and full Check Point FireWall-1/VPN-1 functionality (depending on the Check Point license). The IP530 platform also has three CPCI slots for expandability, an internal PMC slot for hardware encryption acceleration, and two Type II PCMCIA slots for PCMCIA modem support.

The IP530 platform has the following key features:

- Four embedded 10/100 Ethernet interfaces

- One internal PMC slot for optional hardware encryption acceleration

- Hard drive mirroring option

- Three CPCI expansion slots; each CPCI expansion slot supports one of the following modules:

  - Single- or dual-port Gigabit Ethernet interface module

  - Quad Port 10/100 Ethernet interface module

- Single- or dual-port V.35/X.21 module

- T1/E1 with CSU/DSU module

- HSSI module

- ISDN-BRI

- Two Type II PCMCIA slots

- Two serial ports—one for local console connectivity and an auxiliary port for external modem connections for remote administration

- High-availability support using VRRP or IP clustering

Nokia IP710/IP740 Platform

The IP710/IP740 platform is a rack-mountable 3RU appliance intended for the large enterprise environment. It is currently the top-of-the-line security appliance that offers support for redundant power supplies and warm swapability for mirrored hard drives. It contains four embedded 10/100 Ethernet interfaces, full IPSO IP routing functionality, and full Check Point FireWall-1/VPN-1 functionality (depending on the Check Point license). The IP710/IP740 platform also has four CPCI slots for expandability, an internal PMC slot for hardware encryption acceleration, and two Type II PCMCIA slots for PCMCIA modem support.

The IP710/IP740 platform has the following key features:

- Four embedded 10/100 Ethernet interfaces

- One Internal PMC slot for optional hardware encryption acceleration

- A hard drive mirroring option

- Four CPCI expansion slots; each CPCI expansion slot supports one of the following modules:

    - Single- or dual-port Gigabit Ethernet interface module

    - Quad Port 10/100 Ethernet interface module

    - Single- or dual-port V.35/X.21 module

    - T1/E1 with CSU/DSU module

    - HSSI module

    - ISDN-BRI

- Two Type II PCMCIA slots

- Two serial ports—one for local console connectivity and an auxiliary port for external modem connections for remote administration.

- High-availability support using VRRP or IP clustering

NOTE

The key difference between the IP710 and the IP740 is the bus speed. The IP740 operates at a 66MHz bus speed, and the IP710 operates at a 33MHz bus speed.

Configuring the Nokia Appliance

The Nokia appliance arrives from the factory without configuration. The initial configuration must be done through the local console. All Nokia appliances have a console port to connect to for configuration. The console cable is provided with the Nokia appliance. Using a terminal emulator program, you may connect to the Nokia via a serial connection to begin the configuration.

Once the basic configuration has been entered and saved, you may configure the Nokia appliance for remote administration via SSH, Telnet, or Voyager. SSH, Telnet, and Voyager settings are configurable in Voyager under the **CONFIG | Security and Access Configuration** section. In addition, Nokia introduced the Command Line Interface Shell (CLISH) in IPSO 3.6 for IPSO configuration. CLISH may be accessed via an SSH, Telnet, or console session.

Serial Console Access

The Nokia appliance arrives from the factory without configuration. All Nokia appliances have a console port to connect to for configuration. The cable is provided with the Nokia appliance. Using a terminal emulator program, you may connect to the Nokia via a serial connection to begin the configuration. The terminal connection should be configured to use 9600 bits per second, 8 data bits, no parity, 1 stop bit, and no flow control. Figure 7.1 shows the appropriate settings using the HyperTerminal program.

Figure 7.1 HyperTerminal COM1 Settings

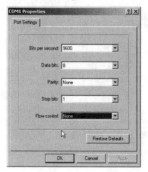

Configuring IPSO Settings

Once you have properly configured your terminal emulator and connected to the Nokia appliance, you will see the initial startup screen. You will be prompted to enter a hostname for the appliance. You will be prompted to choose a password for the user **admin**, as shown in Figure 7.2.

Figure 7.2 Initial Setup Screen

Once you've chosen a password, you will be prompted to choose between using a remote Web browser Voyager or Lynx to configure the Nokia appliance. Choose option **1** to use a remote Web browser. You will be prompted to configure an interface for IP connectivity. Figure 7.3 shows the configuration prompts.

Figure 7.3 Configuration Screen to Set Up Remote Voyager Connectivity

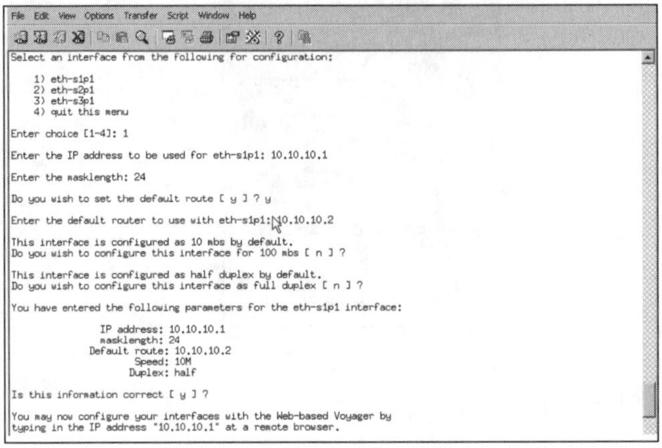

Choose option **2** if you do not have IP connectivity to configure the Nokia appliance. You may use Lynx or CLISH to configure the Nokia appliance. Lynx is an ASCII-based Web browser built into IPSO. CLISH is the CLI shell for IPSO.

Designing & Planning…

Using Voyager

Voyager is a Web-based configuration tool used to configure the Nokia appliance. Voyager is intuitive and easy to use. We could go into each Voyager section to show you how to configure the Nokia appliance, but doing so would occupy too many pages for the purpose of this chapter. Instead, download the *Voyager Guide* from Nokia's support site at https://support.nokia.com for a full guide to Voyager configuration. For complex configurations, you can use CLISH to set up the Nokia appliance.

Using CLISH

Nokia introduced CLISH in IPSO 3.6 for IPSO configuration. CLISH is invoked at the command prompt by typing in the command:

```
Nokia[admin]#clish.
```

CLISH is a robust CLI that allows the administrator to define IPSO settings step by step or automatically through the use of a text file. CLISH is extremely useful when you have multiple appliances to configure. The syntax for the commands is the same whether they are input manually of through the use of a text file. To manually input the settings one by one, invoke CLISH by typing **clish**. To have CLISH read the input automatically from a text file, invoke the following command. In this case, the –s flag saves the configuration:

```
Nokia[admin]#clish -f <filename> -s.
```

Here are some other common commands and their uses. To configure the default gateway, use this command:

```
Nokia>set static-route default nexthop gateway address 205.226.27.2
    priority 1 on
```

To configure a static route, use the following command:

```
Nokia>set static-route 10.254.253.0/24 nexthop gateway address 10.254.254.2
    priority 1 on
```

To configure an interface's physical settings, use this command:

```
Nokia>set interface eth-s2p1 auto-advertise on duplex full speed 10M
    active on link-recog-delay 6
```

To configure an interface's logical settings, use these commands:

```
Nokia>add interface eth-s2p1c0 address 10.254.254.1/24
Nokia>set interface eth-s2p1c0 enable
```

To configure a proxy ARP entry, use the following command:

```
Nokia>add arpproxy address 10.254.254.152 interface eth-s2p1c0
```

Developing a standard template is very useful if you want to plan ahead and configure the Nokia appliances. A standard template is also very helpful if you configure Nokia appliances on a consistent basis. You will save configuration time by having the settings read into IPSO. You may use the pound sign (#) to insert comments. CLISH will not read the text preceding the # as configuration lines. Figure 7.4 shows the configuration file Clishconfig.txt read into memory and saved.

Figure 7.4 Using CLISH to Read Settings from a Text File

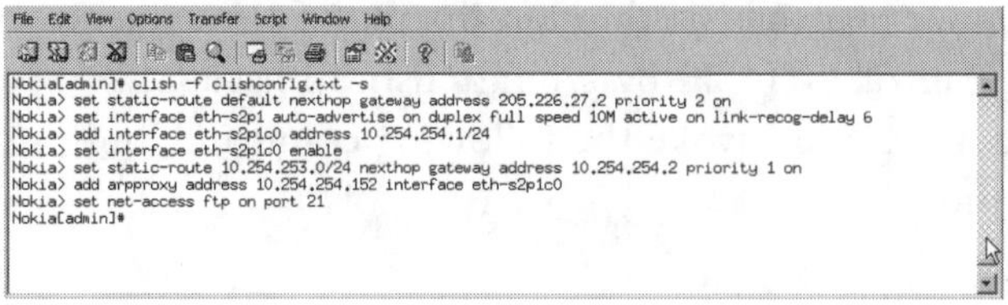

Here is a sample template file:

```
#Set Default gateway
```

set static-route default nexthop gateway address *a.b.c.d* priority *X* on

```
#Set Physcial Interface
```

set interface *eth-sXpX* auto-advertise on duplex full speed *XM* active on link-recog-delay *X*

```
#Set Logical interface
```

add interface *eth-sXpXcX* address *a.b.c.d/x*

set interface *eth-sXpXcX* enable

```
#Set Static route
```

set static-route *a.b.c.d/x* nexthop gateway address *a.b.c.d* priority *X* on

```
#Set Proxy ARP
```

add arpproxy address *a.b.c.d* interface *eth-sXpXcX*

For more information, consult the *Command Line Reference Guide* for IPSO 3.6, available for download at https://support.nokia.com, for additional command syntax.

Software Installation

The Nokia appliance comes preinstalled with IPSO and all the partner applications, including Check Point FireWall-1/VPN-1. However. it is not guaranteed that the latest software binaries are installed. The latest IPSO versions are available at http://support.nokia.com. All Check Point binaries must be obtained from Check Point's Web site at www.checkpoint.com/services/index.html. Keep in mind that you must have a separate valid logon for each site.

NOTE

CLISH does not currently support the installation or upgrade of third-party packages and IPSO packages.

Using Nokia Horizon Manager

Nokia Horizon Manager (NHM) is Nokia's enterprise platform management tool. You may install and/or upgrade third-party applications or IPSO packages simultaneously for multiple platforms through the use of the NHM GUI. NHM checks the validity of an upgrade or installation before proceeding. This is a very powerful tool for dealing with multiple appliances. NHM comes with a free five-node license and is available for the Windows and Solaris platforms.

Using Voyager

Choose **Config | System Configuration Section | Install New IPSO Image** to upgrade the IPSO operating system. Choose **Config | System Configuration Section | Manage Installed Packages | FTP and Install Packages** to upgrade or install third-party applications. Refer to Figure 7.5 to see a sample screen from Voyager.

Figure 7.5 IPSO Installation/Upgrade

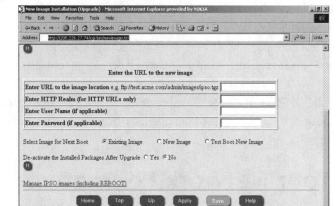

Installing IPSO

Use the *newimage* command to upgrade to a newer version of IPSO. Type the following command to begin the interactive IPSO installation process:

```
Nokia[admin]#newimage -i
```

You will be prompted for the location of the new IPSO binary. The current *newimage* script allows you to load images from a CD-ROM, anonymous FTP server, FTP server with authentication, or the local file system. The CD-ROM option is currently valid only for the IP400 series platform. Refer to Figure 7.6.

Figure 7.6 IPSO Upgrade Screen

The *newimage* command carries over the settings from the previous IPSO installation. To return a Nokia appliance to factory default settings, remove the /config/active link using the command *rm /config/active* at the command prompt and reboot the appliance. Use this command with caution because you will lose your settings on reboot.

Installing the Check Point Software

Use the *newpkg* command to install a third-party partner application. In this case you will have a Check Point FireWall-1/VPN-1 package ready. The choices are the same as for the *newimage* command. The installation will prompt you to choose between an upgrade or a fresh install if it detects the presence of a previous Check Point installation. Installing the Check Point package as an upgrade will carry over previous Check Point settings. Installing the Check Point package as a fresh install will not carry over previous Check Point settings.

Securing Your Network Perimeters

The Nokia appliance's ease of configuration minimizes the complications of implementing a DMZ. However, there are still some basic steps you must take to ensure success. Let's look at those steps now.

Plan Ahead

Gather the information and develop a plan before you begin configuring your Nokia appliance. Have a backout plan in place in case you cannot continue with the new configuration. Whether you are designing a DMZ for a new network or integrating the DMZ into an existent network, proper planning will minimize headaches and unexpected downtime. This section details some steps to take before you being your configuration.

Know the Purpose of Your DMZ

Before you begin, gather all the necessary information about the DMZ. You should know what services the DMZ will provide and to whom. Know if the DMZ will be a new setup or if it will be integrated into an existing network. Typically, building a new DMZ will not affect a production environment, since production traffic does not flow through this setup yet. If you plan to integrate a DMZ into an existing network, there is the potential for downtime. Internet services could be interrupted as you bring up a DMZ. Sometimes you will be required to apply firewall hotfixes and/or patches that require a reboot. Remember to have a backout plan in place in case you are unsuccessful in your implementation for reasons beyond your control. Having a detailed network diagram will help you organize and build your DMZ.

DMZ Type

Decide on the type of DMZ to use. A three-legged DMZ setup is the most common DMZ. It is administratively easier to set up and manage since there is only one firewall to manage. A traditional DMZ firewall setup is more secure but requires longer setup time and requires more management overhead. You now have at least two firewalls to manage. Choosing the right DMZ depends on the amount of security required. For example, internal networks that involve sensitive information should always be separated by another firewall. The best practice is to follow the security policies defined by the site into which the DMZ will be integrated.

New or Existing Network

Know if this is a new or existing network you are integrating the DMZ into. Configuring a new network and DMZ allows you to design every aspect of the configuration. Consider the IP addressing scheme while taking into account scalability. Integrating a DMZ into an existing network requires more planning. You have to consider how to integrate the DMZ into the network without drastically affecting the existing network topology.

Network Plan

Create an accurate network diagram for a new setup or have an accurate copy of the existing network's diagram available. You must understand the network before you create or modify it. Having an accurate network diagram will be effective in troubleshooting if network problems are encountered during the setup.

Time Constraints

Know how much time you have to implement the solution. You should have a pretty good idea of how much time is needed to implement your solution. Unfortunately, sometimes things do not go smoothly, and you will need to allocate time for troubleshooting. Estimate your time window to complete the project, and add some time for troubleshooting if something goes wrong.

You should also have an emergency backout plan in case the solution cannot be implemented in the time frame allocated. This is especially important when you're integrating a DMZ into an existing production environment. It is very easy to back out from changes in IPSO. Before you begin configuring an existing environment, back up the current configuration using Voyager. You may switch to the original configuration at any time. Switching between configurations is done in Voyager under **Config | Manage Configuration Sets**. The configuration files are stored in the /config/db directory. Figure 7.7 shows the Configuration Set Management page.

Figure 7.7 Configuration Set Management

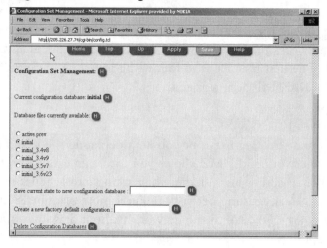

Remember to create a separate Check Point FireWall-1 rule base for the DMZ configuration. When you have to back out of the new configuration, all you have to do is reload the original rule base.

Available Support Assistance

Know if and when you have access to key support personnel. Should you encounter any difficulty during the implementation, you might need technical assistance. Verify whether or not you have support for the time period that you are implementing your solution.

The Nokia Perimeter Security Solution

At this point you are familiar with the basics of configuring the Nokia appliance for administration. You have been introduced to the various methods to administer and configure the Nokia appliance using SSH, Telnet, Voyager, and CLISH. You have been shown how to upgrade IPSO images and load or upgrade the Check Point FireWall-1/VPN-1 software package. We are now ready to discuss Check Point address translation rules. The next sections describe the various forms of network address translation and how to apply them.

Configuring Check Point FireWall-1 Address Translation Rules

There are three ranges of private, nonpublicly routable IP ranges. They are the 10.0.0.0/8 networks, the 172.16.0.0/12 networks, and the 192.168.0.0/24 networks. They are also known as RFC 1918 addresses. RFC 1918 addresses the lack of publicly routable IP addresses for every host wanting to connect to the Internet. By assigning their internal networks with these private IP addresses, administrators allow for IP connectivity for their internal environments. When these hosts need to access the Internet, they must use some form of address translation to conceal their real IP addresses, since ISPs will not route RFC 1918 address ranges.

This is where Check Point FireWall-1 comes into the picture. Because IPSO does not have an address translation functionality, it relies on Check Point FireWall-1 to do Static, Port, and Hide network address translation. In the following section, we discuss the three methods of address translation, their purposes, and how to properly configure each type using Check Point FireWall-1.

Configuring Static Network Address Translation (Static NAT)

Static NAT is a one-to-one translation. You configure a Static NAT when you want to provide an external service to the public Internet, such as Web services or FTP services. Let's look at the example in Figure 7.6. The internal IP address of the Web server is 10.10.10.2/24, listening on Port 80. The public IP address is 205.226.27.2. A host on the Internet sends a request to 205.226.27.2 on port 80. When the packet reaches IPSO, it passes it to Check Point FireWall-1, which looks at its address translation table and translates the destination to 10.10.10.2 on port 80. The Web server 10.10.10.2 receives the request and sends a response. The response is received by the Check Point FireWall-1, which properly translates the source IP address to 205.226.27.2. This process is illustrated in Figure 7.8. It is important to note that by default, the host's source port is not changed when the RFC 1918 address is translated. To configure a host for Static NAT, create a Host object in Check Point SmartDashboard. Enter the RFC 1918 address in the General tab, and under the NAT tab choose **Static** for the type of NAT and enter the publicly routable IP address. Figure 7.8 shows the Host's NAT tab; Figure 7.9 shows the NAT rules that are automatically created.

> **NOTE**
>
> When you use the automatic NAT feature in Check Point FireWall-1, inbound and outbound rules are automatically created.

Figure 7.8 Automatic Static NAT

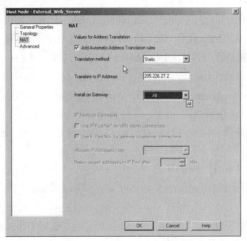

Figure 7.9 Automatic Inbound and Outbound Rules Are Created

Check Point FireWall-1 NG gives the option of automatic ARP configuration. The Automatic ARP configuration setting is configured in the SmartDashboard under

Policy | Global Properties | NAT—Network Address Translation. Occasionally, the Automatic ARP configuration functionality will fail in IPSO. It is better to disable Automatic ARP configuration in NG and set a Proxy ARP entry in IPSO.

It also is recommended that you configure NAT to **Translate on destination client side**. When this option is enabled, FireWall-1 applies the translation on the inbound interface or the first interface on which the packet is received. Consider the following scenario, outlined in Figure 7.6. The Web server's Static NAT IP address is 205.226.27.2. The real IP address is 10.10.10.2. A client on the Internet sends a connection request to 205.226.27.2 on port 80. Using translation on the destination client side, FireWall-1 accepts the connection and applies any NAT rules on the inbound (external) interface. Since the NAT rule is applied on the inbound interface, the packet will now have a destination IP address of 10.10.10.2. IPSO will do a route lookup and forward the connection request through the correct interface. This is a great feature because you will not need to configure a static host route for Static NAT.

> **NOTE**
>
> These settings only affect Static NAT configurations.

Figure 7.10 shows where both the **Translate destination on client side** and the **Automatic ARP** options are configured.

Figure 7.10 Global Network Address Translation Settings

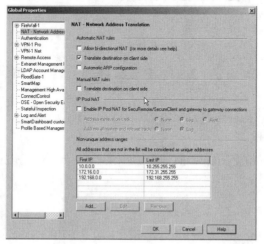

Configuring Static Port Address Translation (Static PAT)

Static PAT is used when you have more services to provide than the available number of routable public IP addresses. Static PAT is an advanced form of Static NAT. Whereas Static NAT is a one-to-one relationship for all destination ports for a particular host, Static PAT is a one-to-one relationship for a specific destination port. For example, you have two services you want to provide on separate servers, FTP and HTTP, but you only have one public routable IP address available. If you were to use Static NAT, you would only be able to Static NAT one server. Using Static PAT, you may Static NAT multiple servers for specific ports only.

> **NOTE**
>
> When you're configuring Static PAT, Check Point FireWall-1 address translation rules must be manually configured. Remember to enable **Translate destination on client side** for Manual NAT rules. Refer to Figure 7.8 to see where it is enabled.

Let's look at the following example:

- You have one free public IP address, 205.226.27.2.
- You have a Web server for which the internal IP address is 10.10.10.2/24.
- You have an FTP server for which the internal IP address is 10.10.10.3/24.
- You need the public to access the 10.10.10.2 for Web services and 10.10.10.3 for FTP services.

Create the following Host objects in Check Point FireWall-1:

- A Host object **External_PAT_IP** is configured with the IP address 205.226.27.2.
- A Host object **Internal_DMZ_Web_Server** is configured with the IP address 10.10.10.2
- A Host object **Internal_DMZ_FTP_Server** is configured with the IP address 10.10.10.3

Now follow these steps:

1. Create a security rule that allows HTTP and FTP services to the External_PAT_IP host.
2. Create two address translation rules.

3. For the Web server, create a rule that sets the **Destination** under **Original Packet** to the **External_PAT_IP** Host object.

4. Set the **Service** under **Original Packet** to **HTTP**.

5. Set the **Destination** under **Translated Packet** to the **Internal_DMZ_Web_Server**.

6. For the FTP server, create a rule that sets the **Destination** under **Original Packet** to the **External_PAT_IP** host object.

7. Set the **Service** under **Original Packet** to **FTP**.

8. Set the **Destination** under **Translated Packet** to the Internal_DMZ_FTP_Server.

Figures 7.11 and 7.12 illustrate the security and address translation rules.

Figure 7.11 Static PAT Security Rules

Figure 7.12 Static PAT Address Translation Rules

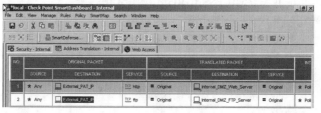

Configuring HIDE Network Address Translation (Hide NAT)

Hide NAT is a many-to-one translation. When a large number of hosts need to access the Internet, but these hosts do not need to be accessed from the Internet, Hide NAT should be used. This choice protects the internal network or networks from the Internet by concealing the real IP addresses. In a situation in which the internal networks use RFC 1918 addressing and they need to access the Internet, Hide NAT must be used (since ISPs will not route RFC 1918 addresses). In cases in which the internal networks are publicly addressed but do not need to be accessed from the Internet, implementing Hide NAT adds an extra layer of protection by concealing the true IP addresses of the hosts. Hosts on the Internet will see the source IP address of the hosts as the Hide NAT IP address. The external IP address of the firewall is commonly used as the Hide NAT address. Figure 7.13 illustrates the NAT tab of the network object Internal_172.16; Figure 7.14 illustrates the address translation rules created when Hide NAT is automatically configured.

In the example, a network object Internal_172.16 will Hide NAT behind 205.226.27.1, the external IP address of the firewall.

Figure 7.13 The Network Objects NAT Tab

Figure 7.14 The Hide NAT Address Translation Rules

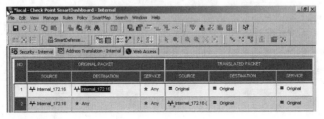

Building the DMZ

Now that you are familiar with configuring the Nokia platform, let's consider some practical DMZ designs.

Three-Legged DMZs

Our first design is a new setup and uses the three legged DMZ method. This type of design utilizes the Nokia to provide firewall services for the DMZ and the internal networks on the same appliance. The advantage of this design is its ease of implementation, since you are configuring one appliance to control all your networks. In addition, this design provides ease of manageability and troubleshooting. There is only one Check Point rule base and one set of IPSO settings to deal with. However, this design is less secure than a dual-firewall system. General best practice in the industry is to implement multiple layers of security. It is up to you to consider the risk factors when choosing a DMZ. Consider the scenario shown in Figure 7.15.

Figure 7.15 The Three-Legged DMZ

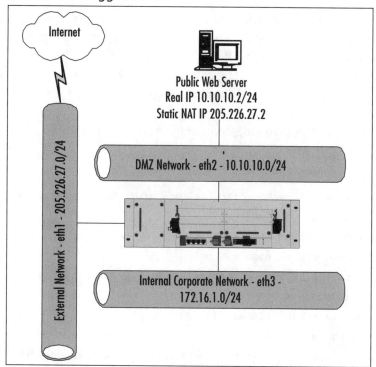

You want to set up a Web farm to establish an Internet presence. The requirements are as follows:

- The Web server should only be accessed by external clients for Web services.
- The Web server in the DMZ should be statically NAT'd.
- The external clients should not have access to the internal corporate network.
- The internal corporate network should only have necessary access to the outside Internet, including the DMZ using Hide NAT.

The network specifications for the three-legged DMZ are as follows:

- The default gateway is 205.226.27.3.

- The external interface is 205.226.27.1/24.

- The DMZ interface is 10.10.10.1/24.

- The internal interface is 172.16.1.1/24.

- The Static NAT IP of the Web server is 205.226.27.2.

- The real IP of the Web server is 10.10.10.2.

You now need to configure IPSO. Whether you choose to use Voyager or CLISH to configure the settings, you will set up all the interfaces with the appropriate IP addresses. You will set up a Proxy ARP for the Static NAT.

As mentioned in the previous section, Voyager is a Web-based configuration tool for IPSO. You might access the Nokia appliance using the format http:// *ip_address of the appliance*.

Using CLISH, run the following commands to configure the Nokia appliance:

```
Nokia[admin]#clish
```

```
Nokia>set interface eth1 auto-advertise on duplex full speed 100M active
    on link-recog-delay 6
Nokia>add interface eth1c0 address 205.226.27.1/24
Nokia>set interface eth1c0 enable
Nokia>set interface eth2 auto-advertise on duplex full speed 100M active
    on link-recog-delay 6
Nokia>add interface eth2c0 address 10.10.10.1/24
Nokia>set interface eth2c0 enable
Nokia>set interface eth3 auto-advertise on duplex full speed 100M active
    on link-recog-delay 6
Nokia>add interface eth3c0 address 172.16.1.1/24
Nokia>set interface eth3c0 enable
Nokia>set static-route default nexthop gateway address 205.226.27.3
    priority 1 on
Nokia>set static-route 205.226.27.2/32 nexthop gateway address 10.10.10.2
    priority 1 on
Nokia>add arpproxy address 205.226.27.2 interface eth1c0
Nokia>save config
```

NOTE

Static host route is set if Check Point **Translate Destination on Client side** is not enabled.

Now we want to configure the proper Check Point FireWall-1 security and address translation rules. Configure a stealth rule for the gateway. Here we also opted to configure a separate rule that drops and logs any connection attempts from the DMZ Web server to the internal corporate network. This rule was created to ease log auditing. The cleanup rule would have done the same job. It is a best practice not to allow hosts in the DMZ to connect to the internal corporate networks. Hosts in the DMZ are open to various vendor-specific exploitations; should they be compromised, the amount of damage done to the internal network will be minimal. Configure the Web server to accept HTTP traffic only. This leaves less opportunity for hacker exploitation. Configure the internal corporate network to access the Internet. Figures 7.16 and 7.17 show a sample security and address translation rule base.

Figure 7.16 A Security Rule Base for a Three-Legged DMZ

Figure 7.17 An Address Translation Rule Base for a Three-Legged DMZ

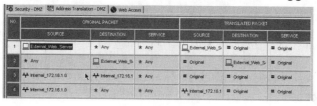

A Traditional DMZ

A traditional DMZ adds an extra layer of protection for the internal corporate network by using an additional firewall to secure the corporate network. Consider the setup shown in Figure 7.18.

Figure 7.18 Traditional DMZ Design

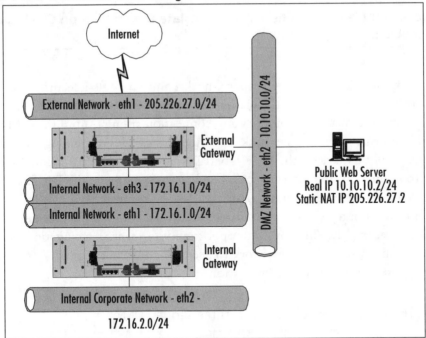

You want to set up a Web farm to establish an Internet presence. The requirements are as follows:

- The Web server should only be accessed by external clients for Web services.

- The Web server in the DMZ should be statically NAT'd.

- The external clients should not have access to the internal corporate network.

- The internal corporate network should only have necessary access to the outside Internet, including the DMZ using Hide NAT behind the internal gateway.

- The external gateway will Hide NAT all connections originating from the internal gateway.

The network specifications for a traditional DMZ are as follows:

- The external gateway's default gateway is 205.226.27.3.

- The external gateway's external interface is 205.226.27.1/24.

- The external gateway's DMZ interface is 10.10.10.1/24.

- The external gateway's internal interface is 172.16.1.1/24.

- The internal gateway's default gateway is 172.16.1.1.

- The internal gateway's external interface is 172.16.1.2/24.

- The internal gateway's internal interface is 172.16.2.1/24.

- The Static NAT IP of the Web server is 205.226.27.2.

- The real IP of the Web server is 10.10.10.2.

IPSO Configuration

Using CLISH, load the following commands from the text file externalconfig.txt to configure the external gateway:

```
Nokia{admin}#clish -f <externalconfig.txt> -s


set interface eth1 auto-advertise on duplex full speed 100M active on
    link-recog-delay 6
add interface eth1c0 address 205.226.27.1/24
set interface eth1c0 enable
set interface eth2 auto-advertise on duplex full speed 100M active on
    link-recog-delay 6
add interface eth2c0 address 10.10.10.1/24
set interface eth2c0 enable
set interface eth3 auto-advertise on duplex full speed 100M active on
    link-recog-delay 6
add interface eth3c0 address 172.16.1.1/24
set interface eth3c0 enable
set static-route default nexthop gateway address 205.226.27.3 priority
    1 on
set static-route 205.226.27.2/32 nexthop gateway address 10.10.10.2
    priority 1 on
add arpproxy address 205.226.27.2 interface eth1c0
```

NOTE

Static host route is set if Check Point **Translate Destination on Client side** is not enabled.

Using CLISH, load the following commands from the text file internalconfig.txt to configure the external gateway:

```
Nokia{admin}#clish -f <internalconfig.txt> -s
```

```
set interface eth1 auto-advertise on duplex full speed 100M active on
    link-recog-delay 6
add interface eth1c0 address 205.226.27.1/24
set interface eth1c0 enable
set interface eth2 auto-advertise on duplex full speed 100M active on
    link-recog-delay 6
add interface eth2c0 address 172.16.2.1/24
set interface eth2c0 enable
set static-route default nexthop gateway address 172.16.1.1 priority 1 on
```

Configuring Check Point FireWall-1 Security and Address Translation Rules

In our traditional DMZ design, you have two sets of security and address translation rules to configure: the external gateway and the internal gateway. The external gateway configuration does not change. However, the internal gateway will need a new set of rules. Let's take a look at the security and address translation rules.

External Gateway

The rules for the external gateway will be the same as in a three-legged DMZ configuration. The internal gateway will Hide NAT behind the external gateway's IP address 205.226.27.1. The difference is the configuration on the internal gateway. Refer to Figures 7.9 and 7.10.

Internal Gateway

The internal gateway protects the internal corporate network. Here is an additional network scheme; 172.16.2.0/24 was used to configure the internal corporate network. The internal corporate network will Hide NAT behind the internal gateway's external IP address, 172.16.1.2, to access the Internet. In turn, the external gateway will provide Hide NAT services for the 172.16.1.0/24 network. Configure a stealth rule for the gateway. Configure a rule to not allow the internal network 172.16.1.0 network to connect to the internal corporate network. Again this is done for log manageability purposes. Configure a rule to allow the internal corporate network to connect to the Internet and finally configure a cleanup rule. Refer to Figures 7.19 and 7.20.

Figure 7.19 Internal Gateway Security Rule Base

NO.	SOURCE	DESTINATION	SERVICE	ACTION	TRACK	
1	✴ Any	🖥 Internal_Gateway	✴ Any	⊘ drop	📋 Log	✴
2	┿ External_172.16.1.0	┿ Internal_172.16.2.0	✴ Any	⊘ drop	📋 Log	✴
3	┿ Internal_172.16.2.0	✴ Any	✴ Any	⊕ accept	📋 Log	✴
4	✴ Any	✴ Any	✴ Any	⊘ drop	📋 Log	✴

Figure 7.20 Internal Gateway Address Translation Rule Base

NO.	ORIGINAL PACKET			TRANSLATED PACKET		
	SOURCE	DESTINATION	SERVICE	SOURCE	DESTINATION	SERVICE
1	┿ Internal_172.16.2.0	┿ Internal_172.16.2	✴ Any	≡ Original	≡ Original	≡ Original
2	┿ Internal_172.16.2.0	✴ Any	✴ Any	┿ Internal_172.16.2	≡ Original	≡ Original

Additional Considerations for Designing a DMZ

Security is a major concern whenever you are providing services to the public Internet. Vendor exploits are being discovered and exploited every day. Sometimes when a vendor patch is available, it might be too late. Hackers could already have compromised the security of your DMZ. This section outlines some additional steps to take to secure your environment.

Network Address Configuration

It is generally good practice to conceal the internal corporate network when accessing the DMZ. If a host in the DMZ is compromised, the hacker might have the ability to detect what IP addresses are accessing the compromised host through the use of packet-sniffing utilities such as *snoop* and *tcpdump*. This is significant because the hacker will have the ability to construct a network topology based on the IP addresses detected. The presence of RFC 1918 IP addresses will make it easier for hackers to construct a topology. Internal corporate networks using registered IP addressing schemes are vulnerable as well. The hacker can use a simple *traceroute* tool to figure out if the address scheme is part of the Internal topology. You will note in Figures 7.12 and 7.9, in both FireWall-1 rule bases, the DMZ is not allowed to originate outbound connections. This prevents the compromised host from acting as a jump point for an attack.

Certain scenarios require additional hosts to be present on the internal network that connects the internal and external gateways and NAT not be applied when a host on the internal corporate network accesses a host on the internal network. In addition, the internal network Hide NATs behind the external gateway for Internet access. In this scenario, the external gateway needs to have a route for the internal corporate network (172.16.2.0/24) that uses 172.16.1.2 as the gateway. This presents a security issue in the form of an ICMP redirect.

Let's consider Figure 7.12. Host A 172.16.2.25 on the internal corporate network accesses Host B 172.16.1.25 on the internal network, and no NAT is configured between the two networks. Host A sends a connection request to Host B. Since Host B's default gateway is 172.16.1.1 (external gateway), it will forward its reply to the external gateway. The external gateway will look in its routing table and forward the reply to 172.16.1.2 (internal gateway). At the same time, the external gateway will send an ICMP redirect telling Host B (172.16.1.25) to send all further replies to Host A (172.16.2.25) using 172.16.1.2 (internal gateway) as the gateway. A hacker will see this and deduce the location of the secondary gateway.

ICMP redirection is on by default in IPSO configurations not using VRRP or clustering. It can be shut off on a per-interface basis. To disable ICMP redirection, you need to modify the *icmp_no_rdir* variable in IPSCTL. At the command prompt, type the command:

```
ipsctl -w interface:<logical interface name>:family:inet:flags:icmp_no_
    rdir 1.
```

To enable ICMP redirects, use the value 0 instead of 1. Figure 7.21 shows ICMP redirect successfully shut off for interface.

Figure 7.21 Disabling IPSO ICMP Redirects

Modifications to IPSCTL variables do not survive a reboot. Insert the *ipsctl* command at the end of /etc/rc file above the line **exit 0** so that ICMP redirect is disabled at startup.

First mount the file system before you edit the /etc/rc file using the command:

```
Nokia[admin]#mount -uw/
```

Configuring a Second DMZ

In many scenarios, multiple types of service are provided to the public. Many companies provide a variety of services, such as Web and FTP services. In such a scenario, you could place the FTP server and the Web server on the same DMZ network segment. However, if a host on that segment is compromised, the entire segment could be compromised. Hackers will exploit different vulnerabilities on a host to gain access to and exploit vulnerabilities on another host. The best solution is to configure separate DMZ segments for each type of service. In the configuration shown in Figure 7.22, the public FTP server and the public Web server are on separate segments. In addition, configure a Check Point rule to *drop* connection attempts between the two DMZ networks. This solution applies to both types of DMZ designs.

Figure 7.22 Using Multiple DMZs

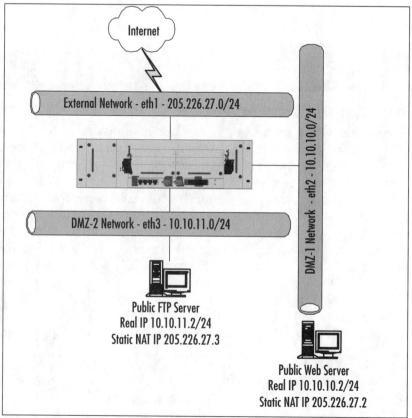

Adding Another Layer of Security Using Access Control Lists

Introduce an extra layer of security by configuring ACLs in IPSO. ACLs take precedence before Check Point FireWall-1. When a packet is forwarded to the interface, IPSO processes the packet before handing it off to Check Point. Keep in mind that if the packet is not allowed by IPSO, the packet will be dropped and Check Point will not see the packet.

NOTE

Currently, IPSO does not contain a logging mechanism for its ACL. Consider the type traffic you want Check Point to log when configuring ACLs in IPSO. You might want to be alerted to suspicious activity by reviewing your Check Point logs on a regular basis.

Configuring & Implementing...

Access Control Lists in IPSO

IPSO contains ACL functionality. ACLs are configured under **Voyager | Config | Traffic Management Configuration Subsection | Access List**. Let's briefly look at some of the basic functionality. Some of the basic actions the ACL can take are DROP, REJECT, SKIP, and ACCEPT. The DROP action quietly drops a packet. The REJECT action sends an ICMP control message back to the host. Generally it is a good idea to silently drop connection attempts rather than reject the connection and send an ICMP control message. This would alert the hacker to the presence of a gateway. The SKIP action negates the effects of the rule, and ACCEPT accepts the connection request. IPSO ACLs process rules from the top down. If the packet matches no defined rules, it is processed by the default rule. The default rule accepts all connections by default and is always the last rule. All rules added to the ACL go above the default rule. The default rule may be configured for DROP or ACCEPT actions only and may not be deleted.

You may only configure one ACL at a time to associate with a logical interface in the inbound or outbound direction. You may specify multiple interfaces and direction set to apply to an ACL.

Here is a sample CLISH configuration to create an ACL for logical interface eth-s2p4c0 to drop all IMCP traffic:

- To create an ACL called *dropallicmp*:

```
Nokia>add acl dropallicmp
```

- To associate ACL *dropallicmp* with logical interface *eth-s2p4c0* in the inbound direction:

```
Nokia>set acl dropallicmp ininterface eth-s2p4c0
```

- To create a rule above the default rule:

```
Nokia>add aclrule position 1
```

- To add the newly created rule to drop all ICMP traffic:

```
Nokia>set aclrule dropallcimp position 1 action drop srcaddr
     0.0.0.0/0 destaddr 0.0.0.0/0 srcport 0-65535 destport 0-
         65535 protocol 1 tcp_estab yes tos any dsfield none
             qspec none
Nokia>save config
```

Refer to the *Command Line Interface Guide* for more information on ACL configuration using CLISH. As you can see from this example, ACL configuration in CLISH can be tedious. Utilize Voyager to input your ACL rules, since that makes it much easier to edit and view.

Nokia Firewall and DMZ Design Checklist

Here is a sample checklist for planning your Nokia DMZ:

- Know what the DMZ will be used for.
- Read your corporate security policy dealing with DMZs.
- Have an accurate network diagram.
- Know how sensitive the internal network is.
- Select the proper DMZ to implement based on your corporate security policy.
- Develop a proper backout procedure.
- Set a reasonable time frame to implement the solution and include time to troubleshoot.
- Know when you have access to Nokia Support when technical difficulties are encountered.
- Select the proper Nokia platform.
- Configure IPSO settings.
- Configure Check Point FireWall-1 security and address translation rules.

Summary

The Nokia platform is a secure and easy platform to use in implementing a DMZ solution. The Nokia operating system IPSO is a highly secured OS optimized to forward traffic. In addition, Nokia's wide range of configuration tools makes it a very strong solution.

The first step in planning a DMZ design is to develop and document a plan. Create a checklist of requirements. Know what the DMZ is going to be used for, understand the type of DMZ that is best suited for your environment, have an accurate network diagram or design, understand your time constraints for implementation, and know who you can ask for help if you encounter any trouble. Remember to have a proper backout procedure if the solution is not working.

The two types of DMZ employed in networks today are the three-legged DMZ and the traditional DMZ. The three-legged DMZ is more commonly deployed in today's DMZ. The three-legged DMZ is less secure in design, but its ease of configuration and manageability make it very desirable. The traditional DMZ segregates the internal private networks from the DMZ through the use of an additional firewall. This type of design is secure but harder to configure and manage. In addition, the cost of additional equipment could be a prohibitive factor. Some aspects to consider when deciding on your DMZ implementation are security requirements, ease of configuration, ease of manageability, and cost.

Finally, it is important to remember that integrating DMZs and firewalls into your networks is only part of the whole security solution. Active log auditing, integrating intrusion detection devices, authentication, and security awareness training are some of the other integral components to corporate information management security.

Solutions Fast Track

Basics of the Nokia Firewall

- ☑ The Nokia platform comes from the factory without configuration. The initial configuration must be done via local console access only.

- ☑ IPSO does not provide NAT functionality. IPSO uses Check Point FireWall-1 to provide NAT functionality.

- ☑ Check Point FireWall-1 uses its patented Stateful Inspection to protect the hosts behind the Nokia firewall.

☑ The Nokia platform can be managed via a console using a console cable provided by Nokia or by remote dial-in using an external modem or a PCMCIA modem.

☑ The Nokia platform can be remotely managed via SSH, Telnet, HTTP, or HTTPS. These settings are configured in Voyager. Refer to the *Voyager Reference Guide* for details on configuration.

☑ CLISH is the command-line interface shell for IPSO configuration.

☑ For complex configurations, configure CLISH to read from a text file for faster results.

☑ The *newimage −i* command is used to upgrade your IPSO operating system.

☑ The *newpkg* command upgrades or installs third-party applications.

☑ The Nokia appliance might not arrive with the latest software installed. Always check the Nokia and Check Point Web sites for the latest available software.

☑ Voyager can be used to install and upgrade both IPSO and Check Point Firewall-1/VPN-1 software.

☑ Currently CLISH cannot be used to install or upgrade IPSO or Check Point FireWall-1/VPN-1 software.

Securing Your Network Perimeters

☑ A three-legged DMZ design uses the same appliance to secure the internal private networks and to provide public services.

☑ A traditional DMZ design segregates the internal private networks through the use of additional firewalls.

☑ Configure ACLs on the Nokia platform to drop traffic before it is passed through to Check Point. However, use ACLs with caution, since IPSO does not have logging functionality for its ACL mechanism.

☑ When securing networks always use the layered approach. Configure upstream routers with ACL as the first line of defense against hackers.

☑ Implementing a DMZ is only one step in providing security for your networks. Active monitoring of logs and implementing intrusion detection sensors are required to provide a more secure environment.

Nokia Firewall DMZ Design Checklist

☑ Follow the Nokia firewall and DMZ design checklist when planning and setting up your Nokia firewall and DMZ. This checklist provides a good starting point for deploying your DMZ infrastructure.

☑ Select the proper Nokia appliance to implement your solution. Check Point FireWall-1 packages are limited by the license, not by the software package. Although this eases software package management, it allows for improper placement of a Nokia appliance. Consult www.nokia.com/securitysolutions for more information on choosing the right platform.

☑ Choose the DMZ design based on your security requirements and your corporate security policy. A multiple-layer approach provides more security but increases management overhead. Lock down the DMZ hosts to the service ports provided. Do not leave DMZ hosts open on all service ports. This exposes your DMZ to hackers taking advantage of vendor-specific exploits.

☑ Always apply the latest vendor security patches. Remember the "recommended patch" usually means you should apply this patch immediately.

☑ Set aside enough time to implement your solution, and include time to troubleshoot if the solution is not functioning as intended. Make sure you have a backout plan. Nokia allows for real-time loading of saved IPSO configurations. Use a new Check Point FireWall-1 security and address translation policy. You may easily revert to the original policy if needed.

☑ Have a proper network diagram. This will aid you in designing the DMZ. Know the type of NAT needed for your configuration. Static NAT is a one-to-one relationship. Static PAT is a one-to-one relationship on a per service port level. Hide NAT is a one-to-many relationship.

Frequently Asked Questions

The following Frequently Asked Questions, answered by the authors of this book, are designed to both measure your understanding of the concepts presented in this chapter and to assist you with real-life implementation of these concepts. To have your questions about this chapter answered by the author, browse to **www.syngress.com/solutions** and click on the **"Ask the Author"** form. You will also gain access to thousands of other FAQs at ITFAQnet.com.

Q: How do I prevent Nokia from accepting ICMP redirects?

A: Nokia appliances are native routers. Routers in general do not accept ICMP redirects because routers use static and dynamic routing to determine a route.

Q: Where should I place an intrusion detection appliance?

A: Generally, it is a good idea to place an IDS wherever security is critical.

Q: Does Nokia support the use of 802.1q VLANs?

A: Yes, Nokia supports 802.1q VLAN configurations. As a matter of fact, it is recommended over multihoming an interface, since FireWall-1 sees each logical interface as a separate interface. This creates a cleaner interaction with FireWall-1 when dealing with antispoofing issues.

Q: I want to use one of Nokia's high-availability solutions, VRRP or IP clustering. Will I have to configure anything differently?

A: The basic principles and configuration still apply. If you are using high availability, you must create a gateway cluster in your Check Point FireWall-1 configuration. If you are using Check Point Sync to synchronize the state tables, you will lose one interface per Nokia as the dedicated sync interface. If you are using Nokia IP Clustering, you will lose another dedicated interface to IP Clustering Sync in addition to the Check Point sync interface. Plan ahead for your hardware requirements and choose the right platform.

Q: Does Check Point FireWall-1 support port forwarding with its external IP address?

A: Check Point FireWall-1 does not support this functionality. Some vendors support port forwarding with the firewall's external IP address. This is another configuration of Static Port NAT where it takes advantage of the fact that the firewall is not listening on some ports such as Port 80 for Web services. Since it is not used, some vendors allow the listening port to be used by an internal host on the DMZ.

Q: Does IPSO support other desktop protocols, such as IPX or AppleTalk?

A: No, IPSO supports only IP.

Q: What routing protocols does IPSO support?

A: IPSO supports static routing, RIP (versions 1 and 2), OSPF, IGRP, and BGP. You must configure Check Point FireWall-1 security rules to accept this traffic. Please note that the IP120 does not support the use of BGP.

Firewall and DMZ Design: ISA Server 2000

Solutions in this Chapter:

- Configuring a Trihomed DMZ

- Publishing DMZ SMTP Servers

- Publishing a Web Server

- Publishing an FTP Server on a Trihomed DMZ Segment

- External Network Clients Cannot Use the DMZ Interface to Connect to the Internal Network

☑ Summary

☑ Solutions Fast Track

☑ Frequently Asked Questions

Introduction

As we've seen, a demilitarized zone (DMZ) is a network segment that lies between the internal network and the Internet. Consider a DMZ segment as a type of "no man's land" where anyone or anything unfortunate enough to find its way to that segment is considered free game for attack. You must assume that any network host placed on a DMZ segment will be attacked and compromised. Maybe not today, maybe not tomorrow, but some day.

A DMZ segment can have public or private addresses. If you have two ISA Server computers, or an ISA server and another firewall, you can create a "back-to-back DMZ." The back-to-back DMZ can have public or private network addresses. When you use public addresses, your DMZ segment becomes a direct extension of the Internet. The major difference between the Internet and your public address DMZ segment is that the hosts on the DMZ segment are under your administrative control.

The private address DMZ segment isn't considered a direct extension of the Internet, the reason being that a network address translator or proxy has to be interposed between the private address DMZ hosts and the Internet. The private address DMZ segment is more secure because there is no way to directly route packets to and from the Internet; the packets must traverse the NAT or proxy.

Configuring a Trihomed DMZ

ISA Server supports the *trihomed DMZ* configuration. It is this configuration that we recommend and will therefore look at in this chapter. The trihomed DMZ has the following interfaces:

- A public interface with a public network address
- A DMZ interface with a public network address
- An internal network interface with a private network address

The trihomed DMZ setup is less flexible than the back-to-back DMZ configuration because you don't have the choice between public or private network addresses. The trihomed DMZ demands the use of public IP addresses. You cannot use private addresses on the DMZ segment of a trihomed ISA Server computer.

The public addresses on the DMZ segment must consist of a subnet of the pubic address block assigned to you by your ISP. One of the most common errors we see when looking at problematic trihomed DMZ configurations is when the ISA Server administrator has configured the DMZ segment network ID to be on the same network ID as the external interface of the ISA server. The public interface and the DMZ interface must be on two different network IDs.

The reason for having the public and DMZ segments on different network IDs is that packets moving from the external network to the DMZ segment are routed. Routers can only route packets between different network IDs. Routers will not route packets between two interfaces on the same network (moving packets between two interfaces on the same network ID would be considered "bridging"). When you configure the ISA server as a trihomed DMZ, you are creating a routed connection between the external interface and the DMZ segment.

The fact that the ISA server acts as a mere packet filtering router between the external interface and the DMZ segment is something you should consider before implementing the trihomed DMZ. While a packet filtering router certainly has its place, you might want a bit more access control over what moves into and out of your DMZ than what a packet filtering router has to offer.

The packets moving between the external interface of the ISA server and the DMZ segment are not subject to the Firewall or Web Proxy services' access policies. You cannot control inbound or outbound access to and from the DMZ segment using user/group identification and destination sets. In addition, you can't take advantage of the protection you would receive by NATing between the external interface and the DMZ segment.

Access control into and out of the DMZ segment is based solely on:

- Source IP address

- Destination IP address

- Source TCP or UDP port

- Destination TCP or UDP port

- ICMP type and code

- IP Protocol number

> **WARNING**
>
> The trihomed DMZ configuration introduces a single point of failure. If a network intruder is able to compromise the ISA Server computer configured for a trihomed DMZ, that attacker will have access to the DMZ segment *and* the internal network.

There are several "gotcha's" to the trihomed DMZ configuration. Pay close attention and you'll get it done right the first time!

The Network Layout

In our trihomed DMZ lab, we'll configure the trihomed DMZ according the layout shown in Figure 8.1. There are three network segments:

- The public network: 192.168.1.0/24
- The DMZ segment: 192.168.1.0/26 (subnet ID 64)
- The internal network: 10.0.0.0/24

Note that the DMZ segment hosts will be on a network ID different from the external interface of the ISA server. In this example, we are using a private network ID on the external interface and the DMZ interface. In a production environment, both the external and DMZ interfaces would be connected to public networks. Note that we've subnetted the external network ID so that we can represent the situation you'll run into when subnetting your public address block.

Figure 8.1 ISA Server with a Trihomed DMZ Configuration

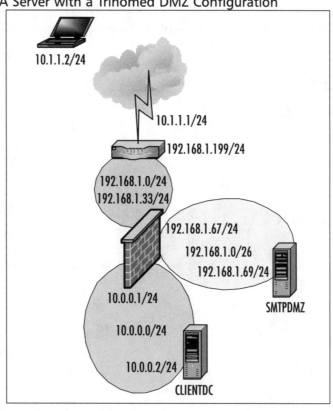

Let's look at the server configuration more closely so that you can use these to configure your own trihomed DMZ test setup.

CLIENTDC

Here is the server configuration for the CLIENTDC computer on the internal network.

```
IP Address: 10.0.0.2/24
DG: 10.0.0.1 (the internal interface of the ISA Server)
DNS: 10.0.0.2
WINS: 10.0.0.2
DNS Service installed and configured to resolve public host names
WINS Service installed
Active Directory installed
Microsoft Exchange 2000 installed
NetBIOS Name: CLIENTDC
FQDN: CLIENTDC.internal.net
```

ISA

Here is the configuration for the internal, external and DMZ interfaces on the ISA server.

Internal Interface

```
IP Address: 10.0.0.1/24
Default Gateway: None
DNS: 10.0.0.2
WINS: 10.0.0.2
```

External Interface

```
IP Address: 192.168.1.33/24
Default Gateway: 192.168.1.199 (the internal interface [LAN interface] of the
router)
DNS: NONE
WINS: NONE
```

DMZ Interface

```
IP Address: 192.168.1.67/26
Default Gateway: None
DNS: NONE
WINS: NONE
DNS Service NOT installed
WINS Service NOT installed
Active Directory NOT installed
NetBIOS Name: TRIHOMEISA
FQDN: TRIHOMEISA.internal.net
Member of the internal network domain.
```

DMZSMTPRELAY

```
IP Address: 192.168.1.69/26
DG: 192.168.1.67 (the ISA Server's DMZ interface)
DNS: NONE
WINS: NONE
```

```
No services installed except Internet Information Services
NetBIOS Name: SMTPDMZ
FQDN: SMTPDMZ.external.net
```

Router

The router in this lab is a dual-homed Windows 2000 computer configured as a router using the Routing and Remote Access Service (RRAS).

Interface #1 (the DMZ Interface)

```
IP Address: 192.168.1.199/24
Default Gateway: NONE
DNS: NONE
WINS: NONE
```

Interface #2 (the Public Interface)

```
IP Address: 10.1.1.1
Default Gateway: NONE
DNS: NONE
WINS: NONE
NetBIOS name: ROUTER
FQDN: N/A
No services installed other than RRAS
```

Laptop (External Network Client)

```
IP Address: 10.1.1.2/24
DG: 10.1.1.1 (the public interface of the router)
DNS: 10.0.0.2
WINS: 10.0.0.2
No services installed
NetBIOS name: EXTERNALCLNT
FQDN: N/A
```

Exchange 2000 is installed on a domain controller on the internal network. We did this so we could test the SMTP relay server on the DMZ segment's ability to forward SMTP messages to Exchange 2000 Server's SMTP service on the internal network.

Note the default gateway configuration on the DMZ host machine. The default gateway for all hosts on the DMZ segment is the IP address of the ISA Server interface connected to the DMZ segment. One of the more common errors we see is that ISA Server administrators configure the DMZ hosts to use the external interface (or even the internal interface) of the ISA server as the default gateway.

Configuring the ISA Server

You should plan your ISA Server configuration in advance, and then configure the server accordingly. The reason for this is the ISA server doesn't like you to add and remove interfaces after the ISA Server software is installed. This is not to say that you can't add and remove interfaces, it's just that you might run into unexpected and difficult to troubleshoot problems if you do. It's a far superior decision to install and configure the interfaces on the ISA Server computer *before* you actually install the ISA Server software.

There will be times when you will need to add or remove an interface after installing the ISA Server software. One way to make sure that nothing expected happens is to uninstall ISA Server and then reinstall it after adding or removing the interface. The drawback of this approach is that you need to reconfigure the ISA server. You can use one of the available import/export scripts to do this, but these scripts don't store the entire server configuration (such as the SMTP filter settings).

WARNING

You can't use the ISA Server integrated backup file together with an ntbackup of ISA Server folder hierarchy and the system state because the system state is no longer valid after adding or removing an interface. The ISA Server integrated backup file is only useful for restoring a previous configuration on the same ISA Server installation. If you uninstall and reinstall, the integrated backup file will be of no use.

Use the following procedure to add or remove an interface:

1. Go into the **Services** applet in the **Administrative Tools** menu and set the startup type of the following services to **disabled**:

    - Microsoft Web Proxy

    - Microsoft Firewall

    - Microsoft ISA Server Control

    - Microsoft Schedule Content Download

    - Microsoft H.323 Gatekeeper

2. Shut down the ISA server and add the interface.

3. Start the ISA server and log in as an administrator.

4. After adding the new interface, configure the TCP/IP settings for that interface. If you removed an interface, there's nothing more you need to do.

5. Go back into the **Services** applet in the **Administrative Tools** menu and set the startup type for each of the ISA Server services to **automatic**.

6. Restart the ISA server. All the services should start up normally. Confirm that the ISA Services started normally by checking the **Application** log in the **Event Viewer**.

ISA Server also doesn't appreciate it if you change the IP address on any of its interfaces while the ISA Server services are running. You might want to change IP addressing information on the interfaces while working with your trihomed ISA Server setup, as it's common to test out different subnetting configurations. If you want to change IP addressing information on the ISA Server computer's interfaces after ISA Server is installed, perform the following procedure:

1. At the command prompt, type **net stop mspfltex** and press **Enter** to stop the services listed.

2. Next, type **net stop gksvc** and press **Enter** to stop the Gatekeeper service.

3. Now, type **net stop IPNAT** and press **Enter** to stop the NAT driver.

4. Change the IP addressing information on the interface of your choice.

5. After changing the IP addressing information, type **net start mspfltex** at the command prompt and press **Enter**.

6. Type **net start IPNAT** and press **Enter** to start the ISA Server NAT driver.

7. After starting the packet filter extensions and the NAT driver, type **net start isactrl** to start the ISA Server Control Service.

8. Start the Web Proxy and Firewall services by using **net start "Microsoft Web Proxy"** and **net start "Microsoft Firewall"** (the quotation marks are required).

The ISA Server services should start up without problems and you won't need to restart the ISA Server computer.

Ping Testing the Connections

We agree that ping is one of the most useful tools in our network diagnostics arma-mentarium. This is especially true when testing connectivity between the computer interfaces participating in your trihomed DMZ configuration. This brings us our first challenge: the default settings on the ISA server do not allow us to ping any of the interfaces we need to test in our trihomed DMZ.

> **WARNING**
>
> Perform this testing only when the ISA server is not connected to the Internet. Although ISA Server is able to handle denial of service (DoS) exploits based on ping, allowing ping requests to the external interface is considered a security risk. Enable the ping filters during your testing while not connected to the Internet, and then disable the ping filters when testing is done and before you connect the server to the Internet.

There are several packet filters included in the default ISA Server configuration:

- ICMP unreachable in
- ICMP timeout in
- ICMP source quench
- ICMP ping response (in)
- ICMP outbound
- DNS filter
- DHCP client

The *ICMP unreachable in* packet filter allows the ISA server to receive ICMP unreachable messages from routers on the Internet. The *ICMP timeout in* packet filter allows the ISA server to receive ICMP timeout messages from Internet routers. These ICMP timeout messages are critical to the functioning of *tracert*, so if you want to use *tracert* to test external network hosts, don't delete that filter!

The *ICMP source quench* filter allows the ISA server to receive ICMP source quench messages from upstream routers. The source quench message allows routers to tell the ISA server to slow down sending data because the router sending the message is too busy. The *ICMP ping response (in)* filter allows the ISA server to receive ICMP query responses to an outbound ping request. If the ISA server did not have this filter, it would be able to send outbound pings (ICMP query requests), but wouldn't be able to accept the ping responses (ICMP query responses).

The *ICMP outbound* filter allows all ICMP message types and codes outbound from the ISA server and from the internal network. The ISA Server computer will always be able to use this filter, but on the internal network, only SecureNAT clients will be able to use this filter. If an internal network client is configured as *only* a Firewall and/or Web Proxy client, it won't be able to use the ICMP outbound filter. Only the SecureNAT client configuration can use non–TCP/UDP protocols.

The *DNS* filter allows the ISA server to send and receive DNS queries and perform its duties as proxy DNS server for Web Proxy and Firewall clients. The *DHCP client* filter allows the ISA server to use DHCP on the external interface. While this isn't an optimal situation, the ISA server can support DHCP on its external interface.

NOTE

Many cable companies employ DHCP technologies that prevent the ISA server from rebinding the same IP address. When the ISA server tries to use a DHCP request message to rebind its IP address, it receives a NACK from the DHCP server and must go through the DHCP discover process. This keeps the ISA server acting as a DHCP client from keeping the same IP address across lease periods. The cable companies believe this will discourage users from setting up Internet servers (such as Web, FTP, and SMTP) on their connections. You can use Jim Harrison's *ISA_IP_Refresh.vbs* tool to get around this problem. Just schedule this tool to run before 50 percent of your lease period runs out. Make sure to make this a recurring schedule. Download this tool at http://isatools.org.

Creating an Inbound ICMP Ping Query Packet Filter on the ISA Server External Interface

We need packet filters to allow ping testing. The first interface we should test is the ISA server's external interface. A packet filter to allow inbound ICMP Ping Query must be created in order to ping the external interface of the ISA server. Perform the following steps to create the inbound ICMP Ping Query packet filter:

1. In the **ISA Management** console, expand your server name and then expand the **Access Policies** node. Right-click on the **IP Packet Filters** node, point to **New**, and then click **Filter**.

2. Type the name of the filter on the first page of the **IP Packet Filter Wizard** (Figure 8.2). In this example, we'll call it **ICMP Ping Query (in)** and click **Next**.

Figure 8.2 The New IP Packet Filter Welcome Page

3. On the **Filter Mode** page (Figure 8.3), select **Allow packet transmission** and click **Next**.

Figure 8.3 The Filter Mode Page

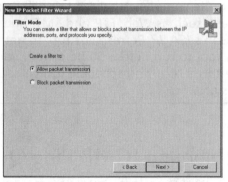

4. On the **Filter Type** page (Figure 8.4), select the **Predefined** option button and click the Down arrow in the drop-down list box. Select the **ICMP ping query** filter and click **Next**.

Figure 8.4 The Filter Type Page

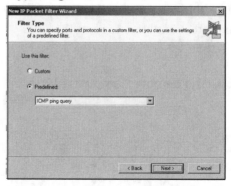

5. On the **Local Computer** page (Figure 8.5) select the IP address on which you want to receive the ICMP ping query messages. In this example, we have a single IP address bound to the external interface of the ISA server. Because there is a single IP address on the external interface, we can select the **Default IP addresses for each external interface on the ISA Server computer**. This allows 192.168.1.33 to accept ICMP ping query messages. What if we had multiple IP addresses bound to the external interface of the ISA server *and* we wanted to allow inbound ICMP ping query requests on each address? In that case, we need to create several inbound ICMP ping query packet filters; one for each IP address bound to the external interface of the ISA server. *There is no way to create a single "global" inbound ICMP ping query packet filter.* Select the default option and click **Next**.

Figure 8.5 The Local Computer Page

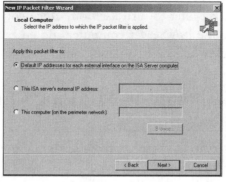

6. On the **Remote Computers** page (Figure 8.6), select which remote computer will be able to send ICMP ping query messages. In this case, we want to allow all remote computers to send the query. Select **All remote computers** and click **Next**.

Figure 8.6 The Remote Computers Page

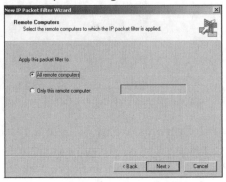

7. Review the settings on the last page of the wizard and click **Finish**.

8. From the external client computer **(Laptop)**, open a command prompt and type **ping 192.168.1.33**. You will see replies to your ICMP ping queries. The reason for this is the ISA server has a packet filter allowing it to receive your ping query messages. The ISA server already had a pre-built packet filter that allowed it to respond, the **ICMP outbound** packet filter.

9. Go back to the client computer and type **ping –t 192.168.1.33**. Return to the ISA server and right-click on the ICMP ping query packet filter you just created and click the **Disable** command.. Notice that it takes a few seconds for the packet filter to turn itself off. Once you see the ping queries time out, go back to the ISA Server computer and enable the inbound **ICMP ping query** packet filter. Watch how long it takes for the packets to be allowed.

Creating an Inbound ICMP Ping Query Packet Filter to the DMZ Host's Interface

Creating packet filters to allow access to the external interface of the ISA server is easy. You can use the built-in packet filter types when you run the wizard and get it right every time. Things aren't quite so straightforward when you create packet filters to allow access to the hosts on the DMZ segment.

Let's create a packet filter that allows inbound ICMP query messages to the DMZ host at 192.168.1.69 (refer to Figure 8.1 to refresh your memory on the setup). The packet filter looks like what you see in Figures 8.7 and 8.8. This packet filter allows inbound ICMP query requests to the DMZ host computer. Notice in Figure 8.8 that we included the IP address of the specific DMZ host's IP address. If you want to allow pings to all the hosts on the DMZ segment, you could select the **These computers (on the perimeter network)** option and enter the **network ID** and **subnet mask** for the DMZ segment.

NOTE

You don't need a packet filter to allow ICMP queries to the external interface of the ISA server in order to allow the ISA server to pass through the ICMP query to the DMZ host. This means you can deny ICMP Query messages to the external interface of the ISA server and allow ICMP Query messages to a host on the DMZ segment.

Figure 8.7 The Filter Type Tab on the DMZ Ping Query Packet Filter

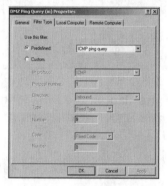

Figure 8.8 The Local Computer Tab on the DMZ Ping Query Packet Filter

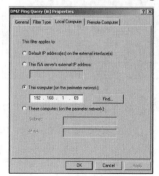

Go to the external network client computer (**Laptop**) and ping **192.168.1.69** after you create the **DMZ Ping Query (in)** packet filter. What happened? It didn't work! Why?

The reason the ping request from the external network client didn't work is that there wasn't a packet filter allowing an outbound response to the incoming ICMP ping query packet. You might think that if you created a packet filter allowing incoming ICMP ping query packets that the ISA server would create a "dynamic packet filter" that would automatically open a filter for a response—it doesn't.

The packet filter allowing the DMZ host to reply to the incoming ICMP ping query looks like what you see in Figures 8.9 and 8.10.

Figure 8.9 The Filter Type Tab for the DMZ ICMP Response Packet Filter

Figure 8.10 The Local Computer Tab on the DMZ Ping Response Packet Filter

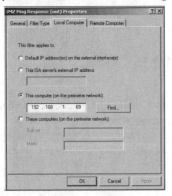

ICMP Echo Reply (ping response) messages have a *Type* value of 0 and a *Code* value of 0. ICMP Echo Request (ping query) messages have a *Type* value of 8 and a *Code* value of 0.

NOTE

The Internet Message Control Protocol (ICMP) is used for more than just ping and tracert diagnostic testing. For a good overview of ICMP, check out Microsoft's KB article Q170292 "Internet Control Message Protocol (ICMP) Basics."

Now with the two filters DMZ Ping Query (in) and DMZ Ping Response (out) the DMZ host computer will be able to accept the ping queries and send out ping responses. Go to the external client computer (**Laptop**) and ping the DMZ host at **192.168.1.69**. Bingo! It works.

Pinging the ISA Server Interfaces from the DMZ Hosts

The DMZ host needs to be able to communicate with its default gateway, which is the IP address of the ISA Server interface on the DMZ segment. It's important to test connectivity with the DMZ interface, and ping is a good tool to test connectivity.

There's just one problem: you can't ever ping the ISA Server interfaces from a DMZ host! It seems somewhat strange that a DMZ host can't ping a local interface, especially when that interface is the DMZ host's default gateway.

It appears that it's the responsibility of the ISA Server Control Service (isactrl) for blocking the ICMP echo requests from the DMZ host to the ISA Server's DMZ interface. If you go to the command prompt and type **net stop isactrl**, it will stop a number of services. You'll also notice that you can now ping the ISA Server DMZ interface from the DMZ host computer. If you type **net start isactrl** at the ISA Server computer, only the ISA Server Control Service will start; the Firewall service will not automatically start with it. Try pinging the ISA Server's DMZ interface now. It doesn't work!

Since we can't create any packet filter or set of packet filters to allow pinging any of the ISA Server interfaces from a DMZ host, we'll have to find another method to test connectivity between the ISA server and the DMZ host. The best way to do this is to configure packet filters that allow external network clients to ping DMZ hosts.

Creating a Global ICMP Packet Filter for DMZ Hosts

In the previous examples, we tried to be selective and created packet filters for very specific traffic. In actual practice you might find it better to create an "all purpose" ICMP packet filter that will allow all hosts on the DMZ segment to use ICMP to ping external hosts and to be pinged by external hosts.

Figures 8.11 and 8.12 describe this custom packet filter. Notice in this DMZ ICMP All (both) packet filter that traffic is allowed in both directions for *all ICMP types* and *all ICMP codes*. For the Local Computer, we include the entire IP subnet rather than a particular host on the subject. This makes it simple to ping any host on the DMZ segment from an external host, and to ping an external host from any DMZ host.

Figure 8.11 The Filter Type Tab on the DMZ ICMP All Packet Filter

Figure 8.12 The Local Computer Tab on the DMZ ICMP All Packet Filter

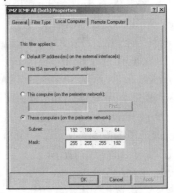

Publishing DMZ SMTP Servers

SMTP servers often find themselves on DMZ segments. The SMTP server is a good candidate for the DMZ segment because it must accept incoming SMTP messages from Internet-based SMTP servers. This direct contact with Internet servers makes the SMTP server computer vulnerable to attack, and thus a candidate for a DMZ segment.

You can create a packet filter to allow incoming SMTP messages to the SMTP server on the DMZ. Your first thought might be that you can use the predefined SMTP server packet filter—wrong! The reason for this is the SMTP server needs to negotiate a series of instructions with the SMTP client machine. If you use the predefined SMTP server packet filter (when you run the Packet Filter Wizard), you won't be able to receive SMTP mail on the DMZ SMTP server.

Try this: Run the Packet Filter Wizard on the ISA server. On the **Filter Type** page, select the **SMTP** filter. Configure the filter to allow SMTP traffic to the DMZ host computer and allow all remote computers to use the filter. Figure 8.13 shows the predefined SMTP selected on the Filter Type page of the Packet Filter Wizard. This SMTP packet filter allows inbound access to TCP port 25.

Figure 8.13 The Filter Type Page

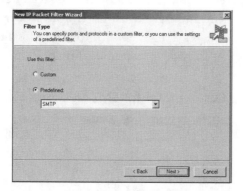

After creating the SMTP filter, go to the external network client, open a command prompt, and try to telnet to the SMTP service on the DMZ host. Using our network diagram, you would go to the **Laptop** computer, open a command prompt, type **telnet 192.168.1.69 25**, and press **Enter** (Figure 8.14).

Figure 8.14 The Telnet Attempt Fails

As we discussed earlier, these default packet filters work just fine when the service you want to make available is listening on the *external interface of the ISA server*. For example, if you were running Exchange 2000 on the ISA server itself, you could create an SMTP packet filter using the predefined SMTP packet filter settings found in the Packet Filter Wizard and the packet filter would work great! However, as you've seen, the predefined packet filters don't work very well for DMZ hosts.

Since the predefined packet filter doesn't work, you'll need to create a custom SMTP packet filter. Use the **Custom** option in the Packet Filter Wizard. On the **Filter Settings** page, configure the options as shown in Figure 8.15. This is a bidirectional filter. This custom filter allows all TCP source ports to send messages to TCP port 25 on the DMZ host computer. Moreover, because the packet filter is bidirectional, the DMZ host computer can send messages to all ports from its own TCP port 25. This allows the SMTP client on the external network to send messages, and the SMTP server on the DMZ segment to receive responses (Figure 8.16).

Figure 8.15 Creating a Custom Filter for SMTP Messages

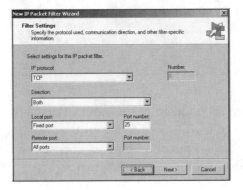

Figure 8.16 Inbound and Outbound Packets Allowed by the Custom SMTP Packet Filter

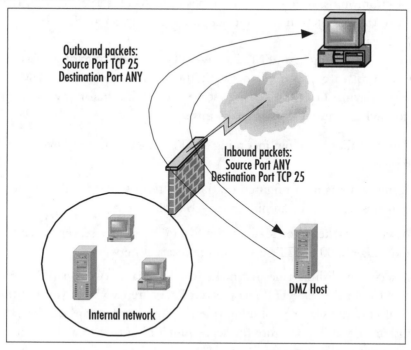

After creating your bidirectional SMTP server packet filter, go back to the external network client and try to telnet to the DMZ SMTP Server host computer again. You should see something like what appears in Figure 8.17. The successful telnet session indicates that the channel between the external client and the SMTP server on the DMZ segment is intact.

Figure 8.17 Custom SMTP Packet Filter Allows a Successful Telnet Session

Publishing a DMZ SMTP Mail Relay Server

In the last section, you saw how you can publish an SMTP server on a DMZ segment. Let's now take this one step further and see how you publish an SMTP *mail relay* server on the DMZ segment.

The DMZ host acting as an SMTP relay will relay mail to another SMTP server under your control. In our example network, the SMTP server on the DMZ segment is configured to relay mail to the Exchange server on the internal network. We need to fulfill the following requirements to make this scenario work:

- A packet filter to allow incoming SMTP messages to the DMZ mail relay server.

- Remote domains configured on the mail relay server to allow relay for mail domains under your administrative control.

- A second packet filter to allow the SMTP mail relay server to send mail to the Exchange 2000 SMTP server on the internal network.

- A server publishing rule that makes the internal network SMTP server available to the DMZ SMTP relay server. There are two ways you can do this: 1) configure the server publishing rule to allow connections on the external interface, and 2) configure the server publishing rule to allow connections from the DMZ interface.

Figure 8.18 shows our goals in terms of network traffic flow for the first scenario:

1. A packet filter allowing inbound TCP 25 from any port. This packet filter allows any Internet host to send SMTP messages to the mail relay server on the DMZ segment.

2. A second packet filter allows the DMZ SMTP relay server to send packets to the IP address on the external interface of the ISA server that is used to publish the internal network Exchange 2000 SMTP service. We need to create this packet filter to allow the DMZ SMTP server to have access to the server publishing rule.

3. A server publishing rule that allows the DMZ mail relay server to send packets to the internal network Exchange 2000 SMTP service.

Figure 8.18 Publishing a DMZ Mail Relay Server

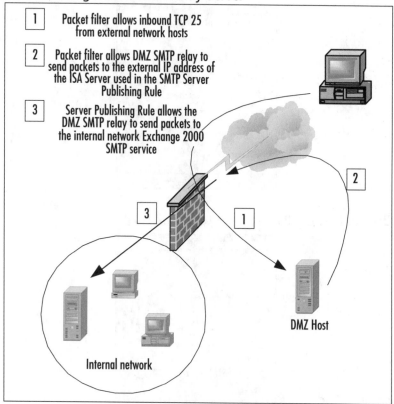

The packet filter you created to allow incoming SMTP messages to the DMZ mail relay server is the same as the one you created in the previous section (Figure 8.15). However, in the first scenario, you need a second packet filter to allow the SMTP mail relay to *send* mail to the internal network Exchange 2000 SMTP service (the DMZ mail relay server acts as an SMTP client in this circumstance). Figures 8.19 through 8.21 demonstrate the packet filter you need to create to allow the SMTP relay server to send SMTP messages to the published Exchange 2000 SMTP server when the Exchange 2000 SMTP service is published on the external interface.

Note this packet filter's level of selectivity. On the Local Computer tab (Figure 8.20), you see that it applies *only* to the SMTP mail relay server. Only the SMTP mail relay server will be able to use this filter to send out messages to TCP port 25. You can see on the Remote Computer tab (Figure 8.21) that this filter will only allow outgoing messages to TCP port 25 to be sent to 192.168.1.33. This is the IP address on the external interface of the ISA server on which we will publish the internal network Exchange server's SMTP service.

Figure 8.19 Packet Filter Allows Outbound TCP 25

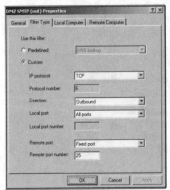

Figure 8.20 Limiting the Packet Filter to a DMZ Host

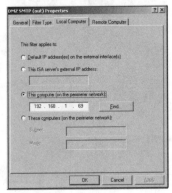

Figure 8.21 Setting the Remote Computer Limitation for the Packet Filter

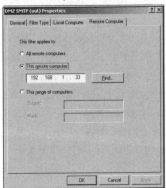

NOTE

Remember that the DMZ segment and the external interface of the ISA server are on different network IDs. In Figures 8.19 through 8.21, notice that the DMZ host is IP address 192.168.1.69 and the external interface of the ISA server is at 192.168.1.33. These might appear to be on the same network ID if you're used to working with classfull addressing. However, the DMZ segment uses 26 bits for its network ID and is on subnet ID 64, which puts the DMZ segment on a different network ID from the external interface.

You need to create remote domains on the SMTP mail relay server to prevent your DMZ SMTP server from becoming an open relay. The remote domains allow the SMTP mail relay server to receive mail for mail domains under your administrative control and *reject incoming mail for all other mail domains.* This prevents spammers from using your DMZ mail relay server as a gateway for their evil spamming deeds!

Perform the following steps to create the remote domain, and configure the remote domain to relay to the published SMTP server:

1. Open the **Internet Information Services** console from the **Administrative Tools** menu.

2. Expand the **server name** and then expand the **Default SMTP Virtual Server** node.

3. Right-click the **Domains** node, point to **New**, and click **Domain**.

4. On the first page of the **New SMTP Domain Wizard** (Figure 8.22), select the **Remote** option and click **Next**.

Figure 8.22 Specifying a Remote Domain

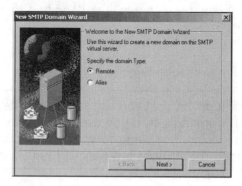

5. On the **Select Domain Name** page of the **New SMTP Domain Wizard** (Figure 8.23), type in the name of your mail domain. For example, if your Exchange server will be accepting mail for your users at external.net, type in **external.net** in the **Name** text box. Click **Finish**.

Figure 8.23 The Select Domain Name Page

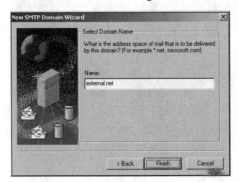

6. Double-click on the remote domain you created. Place a check mark in the **Allow incoming mail to be relayed to this domain** check box (Figure 8.24). This allows the SMTP service to forward mail sent to this mail domain. Select the **Forward all mail to smart host** option, and then type in the **IP address** of the external interface of the ISA server used in the server publishing rule to publish the internal network SMTP server. The reason why you put the external address of the ISA server is that the external interface is listening on behalf of the internal network's SMTP server. It is important that you put the IP address in brackets. If you don't, the SMTP server will treat it as an FQDN and try to resolve the IP address to an IP address! Click **Apply**, and then click **OK**.

NOTE

It's extremely important that you use square brackets when you configure the IP address of the smart host. If you use parentheses, it will not work! If you find that messages are not being forwarded to your smart host, double check that you included the straight brackets ([ ]) in your smart host configuration.

Figure 8.24 Configuring the Relay

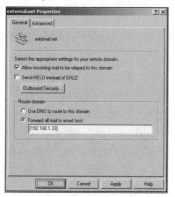

The final step is to create the server publishing rule for the internal network SMTP server. The publishing rule includes a client address set that we'll use to prevent any server except the one on the DMZ from sending mail to it.

1. Expand the **Publishing** node in the left pane of the **ISA Management** console, and right-click the **Server Publishing Rules** node. Point to **New** and click **Rule**.

2. Give the rule a name on the first page of the **New Server Publishing Rule Wizard**. In this example, we'll name the rule **Exchange SMTP Service**. Click **Next**.

3. On the **Address Mapping** page (Figure 8.25), put in the internal IP address of the Exchange server and the IP address on the external interface of the ISA server on which you want to listen for incoming SMTP messages. Click **Next**.

Figure 8.25 Creating the Address Mapping

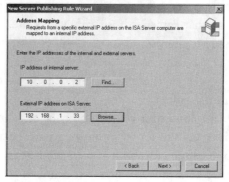

4. On the **Protocol Settings** page, select the **SMTP Server** protocol. Click **Next**.

5. On the **Client Type** page, select the **Specific computers (client address sets)** option.

6. On the **Client Sets** page (Figure 8.26), click **Add** to add the client address set. In this example, we've already created a client address set named 69. The IP address 192.168.1.69 is included in this client address set. When we limit access using this client address set, only the computer with the source IP address 192.168.1.69 will be able to use this rule to send incoming SMTP messages to the internal network Exchange server. Click **Next** after adding the client address set.

Figure 8.26 Creating a Client Address Set

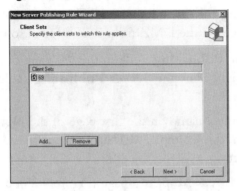

7. Review the settings on the last page of the wizard. If they are correct, click **Finish**. If you made a mistake, click **Back** to get to the place where you can fix it.

That's it! The only thing left is to add the address of your SMTP relay server to a public DNS server so that Internet hosts can access the MX records for your mail domain. External SMTP clients and servers will be able to send mail to the SMTP mail relay server on the DMZ. The SMTP mail relay server forwards the mail to the internal network Exchange server via the external IP address on the ISA server used in the SMTP server publishing rule.

With this setup, no computer on the Internet can send mail directly to the internal network SMTP server via the server publishing rule, because the client address set in the SMTP server publishing rule limits access to the rule so that only the SMTP mail relay server on the DMZ segment can use it. You can test this yourself by trying to telnet into the internal network Exchange server from a host other than the one included in the client address set. It won't work!

The first scenario shows how you can use packet filters to allow the DMZ host to send traffic to the external interface of the ISA server to access the published Exchange 2000 server. Another way to allow only the SMTP mail relay server on the DMZ segment to access the Exchange 2000 SMTP service on the internal network is to use the DMZ interface IP address in the server publishing rule. In this case, the ISA server will only listen for SMTP messages on the DMZ interface; it will not listen for SMTP messages on the external interface. In this case, you need to configure the following (Figure 8.27):

- A packet filter allowing external network hosts to send SMTP messages to the DMZ mail relay server

- Remote domains on the DMZ mail relay server

- A server publishing rule that publishes the internal network Exchange 2000 SMTP service to the IP address on the DMZ interface of the ISA server

Figure 8.27 SMTP Server Publishing Rule on the DMZ Interface

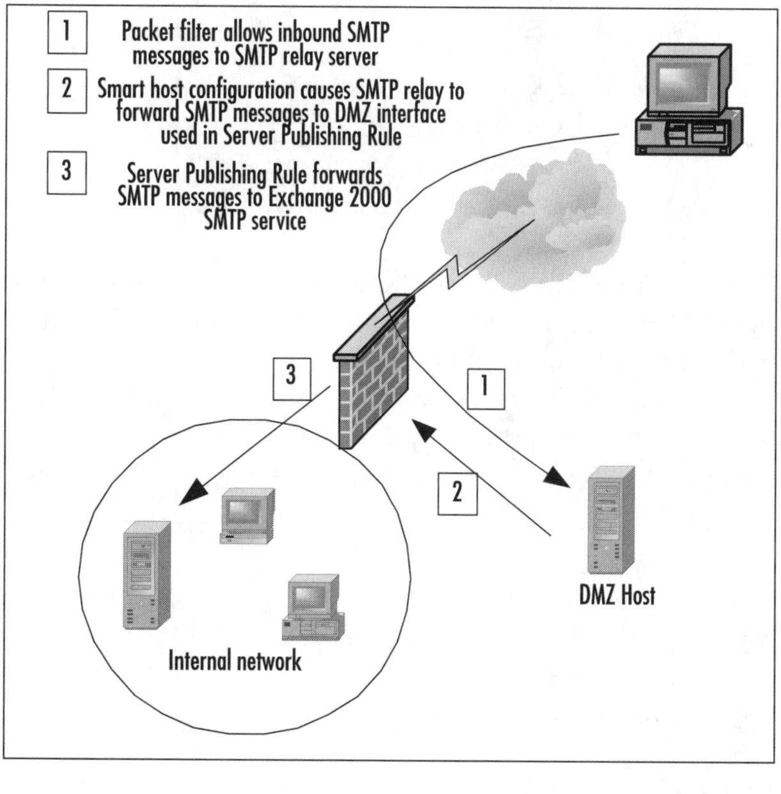

This configuration limits connections to the Exchange 2000 SMTP server publishing rule to the IP address of the ISA server's DMZ interface. In this case, you do not need to create a packet filter to allow the DMZ host access to the IP address of the ISA server's DMZ interface because the DMZ interface is local to the SMTP relay server. The server publishing rule should be configured to allow only the DMZ mail relay server access to the server publishing rule.

Publishing a Web Server

Publishing a Web server on the DMZ segment is easy. Create a packet filter that allows bidirectional traffic with the destination being TCP port 80, from any source port. Select the **Custom** option in the **New Packet Filter Wizard**, and then use the settings shown in Figure 8.28.

Figure 8.28 HTTP Packet Filter

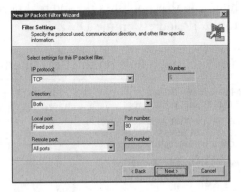

Although you don't get all the frills, bells, and whistles you get when you publish a Web site using a Web publishing rule, publishing a site on a DMZ segment using a packet filter has one big advantage: you get the actual source IP address of the host making the request in the Web server's log files (Figure 8.29). This is a limitation of Web publishing; you could also get the source IP address of the Internet host in the Web server's log files by putting the Web server on the internal network and using a server publishing rule.

Figure 8.29 Log File Showing the IP Address of the Internet Host Computer

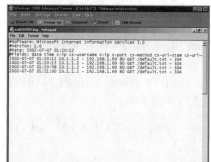

Publishing an FTP Server on a Trihomed DMZ Segment

The File Transfer Protocol (FTP) is one of the most popular, but also the most misunderstood protocol. We get questions every day from router and firewall administrators asking why a particular FTP client or server configuration isn't working. If these administrators understood how FTP works, they could easily solve their FTP problems.

Once you understand FTP and how it affects your firewall or router configuration, you'll be in much better shape to fix your FTP-related problems.

How FTP Works

FTP is a messy protocol in that it requires multiple connections, sometimes in both directions. In the ISA Server world, we call protocols that require multiple connections "complex protocols." How connections are made depend on the FTP protocol mode. There are two FTP modes:

- Normal or PORT or Active
- Passive or PASV

Normal or PORT or Active Mode FTP

When an Active mode FTP client sends a request to an FTP server, the client opens *two* response ports. The first is used to send a request to the FTP server on the server's TCP port 21. This creates the FTP command channel. FTP commands and responses are sent to and from the FTP server and client through the command channel. The second response port is used to accept data from the FTP server.

When the FTP client establishes the command channel link, the FTP client sends over the command channel a request for data. Included in this request is a response port (the second port opened by the FTP client) to which the FTP server can send the data. The FTP server sends the data from the FTP server's TCP port 20 to the response port indicated by the FTP client in the PORT command.

For example, a PORT mode FTP client wants to obtain a file from an FTP server. The sequence of events would go like this:

1. FTP client opens response ports TCP 6000 and TCP 6001 (random ports in the high number range).

2. FTP client sends a request to open a command channel from its TCP port 6000 to the FTP server's TCP port 21.

3. FTP server sends an "OK" from its TCP port 21 to the FTP client's TCP port 6000 (the command channel link). The command channel is established at this point.

4. FTP client sends a data request (PORT command) to the FTP server over the command channel. The FTP client includes in the PORT command the data port number it opened to receive data. In this example, the FTP client opened TCP port 6001 to receive the data.

5. FTP server opens a *new inbound connection* to the FTP client on the port indicated by the FTP client in the PORT command. The FTP server's source port is TCP port 20. In this example, the FTP server sends data from its own TCP port 20 to the FTP client's TCP port 6001.

Note in this conversation that two connections were established: an outbound connection initiated by the FTP client, and an inbound connection established by the FTP server. It's also important to realize that the information contained in the PORT command (sent over the command channel) is stored in the data portion of the packet.

Passive or PASV Mode FTP

Passive or PASV mode is the most popular implementation of FTP, the reason being that PASV mode is a bit more secure because it does not require you to allow new inbound connections. Most popular browsers default to PASV mode FTP when the browser is used to access FTP sites. One of the major advantages of PASV mode is that the FTP server does not need to create a new inbound connection when responding to the FTP client's request for data. All new connections are outbound connections. As we'll see later, this can make PASV FTP more firewall friendly.

The PASV mode FTP client opens two response ports when it initiates a connection with the FTP server. This is similar to how the PORT mode FTP client behaves.

The initial connection establishes the command channel. The FTP server accepts the command channel request on its own TCP port 21.

After establishing the command channel, the FTP client sends to the FTP server a *PASV* command through the command channel. The *PASV* command tells the FTP server to open a port for the data channel. The FTP server opens a TCP port in the ephemeral port range (>1023) and tells the FTP client the port number opened via the command channel. Once the FTP client obtains the TCP port number for the data channel, the FTP client initiates a new connection to the FTP server to establish the data channel.

For example, a PASV mode FTP client wants to obtain data from an FTP server. The sequence of events would go like this:

1. FTP client opens response ports TCP 6000 and TCP 6001 (random ports in the ephemeral port range).

2. FTP client sends a request to open a command channel from its TCP port 6000 to the FTP server's TCP port 21.

3. FTP server sends an "OK" from its TCP port 21 to the FTP client's TCP port 6000. The command channel is now established.

4. FTP client sends a *PASV* command requesting that the FTP server open a port number that the FTP client can connect to establish the data channel.

5. FTP server sends over the command channel the TCP port number with which the FTP client can initiate a connection to establish the data channel. In this example, the FTP server opens port 7000.

6. FTP client opens a new connection from its own port TCP 6001 to the FTP server's data channel 7000. Data transfer takes place through this channel. This represents a new outbound request made by the FTP client.

Note that the PASV mode FTP client initiates all connections; the FTP server never needs to create a new connection back to the FTP client. This eliminates the need for the FTP server to create a "backchannel" or a new inbound secondary connection.

Challenges Created by the FTP Protocol

Challenges the FTP protocol creates are different depending on whether you're the client side or the server side firewall administrator. Let's look at the FTP protocol from the following perspectives:

- The PORT mode FTP client-side firewall

- The PORT mode FTP server-side firewall

- The PASV mode FTP client-side firewall

- The PASV mode FTP server-side firewall

PORT Mode FTP Client-Side Firewall

How do you handle PORT mode requests from your FTP clients? These are the ports you need to allow inbound and outbound to support PORT mode FTP client requests made from behind your firewall:

- **Outbound** TCP port 21 (to support the control channel)

- **Inbound** TCP ports 1024 and above (to support the data channel)

The packet filters required to support PORT mode FTP clients don't lead to a very secure firewall/router configuration. Another significant problem is that you must allow new inbound connections (non-ACK packets) access to the internal network. Allowing new, unsolicited inbound connections to such as wide range of ports represents a definite security concern.

One way of dealing with this problem is to allow inbound connections to the ephemeral ports from source port TCP 20. In this way, you limit access to what is assumed to be the FTP server data port. The problem is that there are a number of tools available allowing you to set your source port manually. You cannot be sure that incoming connections from TCP port 20 are actually sourcing from an FTP server. The reason for this is that packet filters do not examine the data portion of the request.

You can improve on the situation somewhat by limiting inbound access to the high-number ports only from TCP port 20 and from a limited number of IP addresses of trusted FTP servers. The major drawback here is that you must be able to identify (in advance) the trusted FTP server addresses. You still have to be concerned with someone spoofing a source port and IP address.

PORT Mode FTP Server-Side Firewall

What if you're the firewall/router administrator who has to deal with an FTP server behind your firewall? In this case, you need to open the following ports:

- **Outbound** TCP ports 1024 and above (to allow the FTP server to connect to the FTP client's source port)

- **Inbound** TCP port 21 (to allow the FTP client to establish the control channel)

This is less hazardous than the situation the FTP client-side firewall administrator has to handle. However, it's still considered poor security practice to allow such a wide range of ports outbound access just to support a single server application. Any client on the internal network will have access to network services on the Internet that use the high-number TCP ports for a primary connection.

One way to improve the situation is to allow outbound access to the high-number ports only when the source port is TCP port 20. In this way, you can assume that only the FTP servers behind the firewall are able to connect to these high-number ports on the Internet. You could strengthen this even more by limiting access from TCP port 20 to the high-number ports to the IP addresses of the FTP servers on your internal network. You still have to deal with problems of spoofed IP addresses and manipulated port numbers.

PASV Mode FTP Client-Side Firewall

If you're the firewall administrator on the PASV mode FTP client side, you'll need to open the following ports:

- **Outbound** TCP port 21 and TCP ports 1025 and above (to allow the FTP client outbound access to the FTP server's control channel and data ports)

- **Inbound** TCP ports 1025 and above (to allow the FTP server to send data to the FTP client)

The port requirements aren't that different from those required by the PORT mode FTP client, with the exception that the PASV mode FTP client requires outbound access to TCP ports 1025 and above. While this doesn't seem like a big difference, it is in fact a tremendous difference.

In order to allow the PASV mode FTP client outbound access to the FTP server, you must let these clients have outbound access to all high-number ports. Since you have no way of determining in advance what high-number port the FTP server will assign to the data channel, all the high-numbered ports must all be opened outbound.

This might be okay if you had a way to ensure that only the FTP clients access FTP servers on these ports. The problem is you cannot easily control what applications access what ports. Even if you did limit just FTP clients to these ports, you would be blocking other applications access to the high-number ports—a less than ideal situation!

To add insult to injury, you must also allow inbound access to all high-number ports (assuming that your firewall is not stateful). The result is that you must allow inbound and outbound access to all high-number ports—an untenable security configuration.

> **NOTE**
>
> Note in this discussion that we're talking about nonstateful packet filters. In this case, you need to open ports to allow the FTP server to send packets to the high-number ports the FTP client software opens to send and receive data. With a stateful firewall, you will not need to open these ports for PASV connections, because the response sent by the FTP server is over a connection already established by the FTP client. ISA Server is a stateful firewall when using protocol rules and publishing rules, but it is not stateful when passing packets to hosts on a public address trihomed DMZ segment.

One way you can improve the packet-filtering situation is to limit access to outbound TCP 21 from certain clients. However, you still run into the spoofing problem. ISA Server solves this problem by using protocol rules, which can be applied to client address sets and/or users/groups.

PASV Mode FTP Client-Side Firewall

These are the ports you need to open on the server side of the PASV mode connection:

- **Outbound** TCP ports 1025 and above (so the FTP server behind the firewall can send responses to the FTP client)

- **Inbound** TCP port 21 and TCP ports 1025 and above (so the FTP client can establish the command channel and the data channel)

This is the converse of the packet filter configuration required to support the FTP client. TCP ports 1024 and above must be opened for inbound and outbound access. You could get a modicum of control by limiting what IP addresses have access, but you run into the same problems as you do with the PASV clients.

Using Packet Filters to Publish the PORT Mode FTP Server

Now that you understand FTP better, let's get to the business of creating packet filters to support FTP servers in the DMZ.

Let's create packet filters to support the PORT mode FTP server. PORT mode requires that we allow inbound requests to TCP port 21 from any port, and outbound requests from TCP 20 to any port. Figure 8.30 shows the configuration for each of the packet filters.

Figure 8.30 Creating Packet Filters to Support a PORT Mode FTP Server

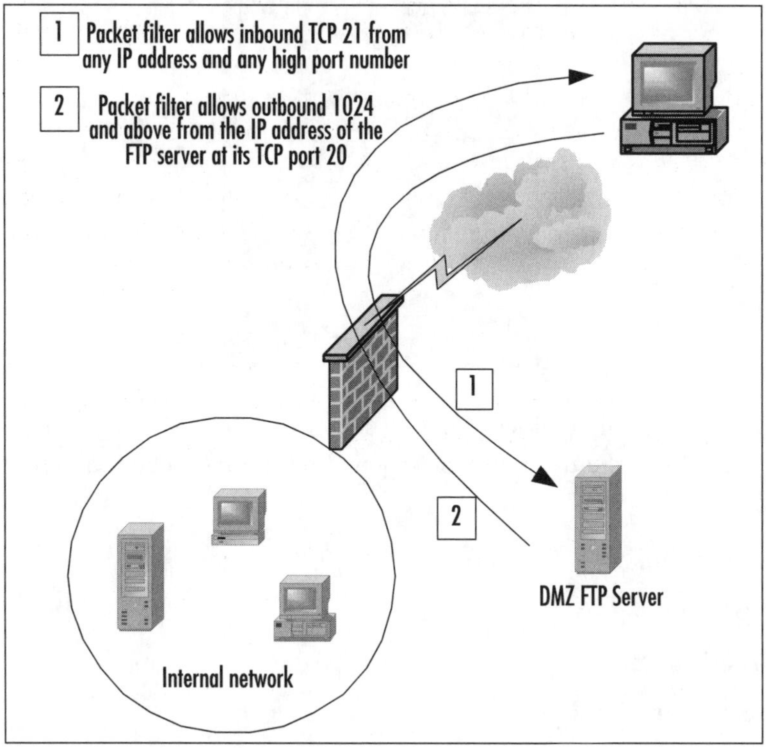

The first packet filter allows the inbound connection to TCP port 21 and establishes the control channel (Figure 8.31). It is set with the following parameters:

- **Filter name** FTP 21 (in)
- **IP protocol** TCP
- **Direction** Both
- **Local port** Fixed port
- **Local port number** 21
- **Remote port** All ports

Figure 8.31 Packet Filter to Allow Inbound TCP Port 21

The second packet filter allows the FTP server on the DMZ segment to send data out its TCP port 20 to the dynamic port opened by the FTP client computer (Figure 8.32).

- **Filter name** FTP 20 (out)
- **IP protocol** TCP
- **Direction** Both
- **Local port** Fixed port
- **Local port number** 20
- **Remote port** All ports

Figure 8.32 Packet Filter to Allow the FTP Server to Respond from TCP Port 20

Using Packet Filters to Publish the PASV Mode FTP Server

You can use packet filters to allow access to PASV mode FTP servers on your DMZ segment. The first packet filter allowing creation of the FTP control channel is the same as the one you created to allow PORT mode FTP connections. The second packet filter allows the FTP client on the external network to make the inbound connection request to the FTP server on a high port (Figure 8.33).

Figure 8.33 Packet Filter to Allow Access to PASV Mode FTP Server

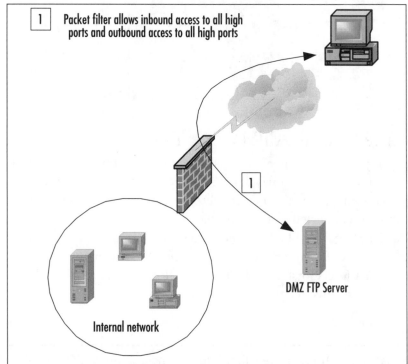

These are the parameters for the packet filter to support the PASV mode FTP in the DMZ:

- **Filter name** FTP PASV (in)
- **IP protocol** TCP
- **Direction** Both
- **Local port** Dynamic
- **Remote port** All ports

Notice that this isn't the most secure packet filter. This filter allows all high source port connections to all dynamic port (ports 1024 through 5000) connections on the FTP server (Figure 8.34).

Figure 8.34 Packet Filter for the PASV Mode FTP Server

Beware the "Allow All" Packet Filter

Sometimes you just want to open all ports inbound and outbound to and from the DMZ segment for testing purposes. This "All Open" packet filter configuration is useful for "proof of concept" testing. You definitely don't want to allow this filter to be active when the server is connected to the Internet.

The "All Open" packet filter does not allow all traffic to move into and out of the DMZ segment. For traffic moving to and from the DMZ segment, you need to create "All Open" packet filters for ICMP, TCP, and UDP individually. The "All Open" packet filter requires at least three separate packet filters.

NOTE

Note that these three packet filters do not include an "All Open" IP protocol filter. If you need to allow access to particular IP protocols (such as IP protocol 47 for GRE), then you should create those packet filters separately.

For example, suppose you want to allow all TCP traffic inbound and outbound to and from the DMZ segment. Figure 8.35 shows the Filter Settings page in the New IP Packet Filter Wizard. If you wanted to create an "All Open" packet filter for UDP packets, just change the **IP protocol** to **UDP**.

Figure 8.35 An "All Open" TCP Packet Filter

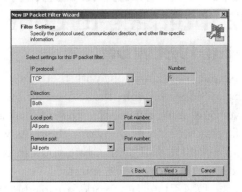

An ICMP "All Open" packet filter is shown in Figure 8.36. The *IP protocol* is set for ICMP. The *direction* is Both. The *Type* is All types, and the *Code* is All Codes.

Figure 8.36 An "All Open" ICMP Packet Filter

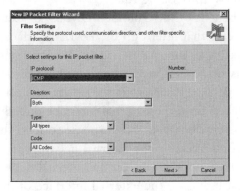

NOTE

Placing FTP servers in the DMZ segment requires that you open many ports to allow inbound and outbound access. You can get around this problem by placing your FTP servers on the internal network. You can take advantage of the FTP Access application filter when you use server publishing rules to publish FTP servers on the internal network. The FTP Access application filter will manage the ports for you. The FTP application filter will dynamically open the required ports, and then close them when the FTP session is complete. You can even place the FTP server in an internal network, LAT-based DMZ to improve security.

External Network Clients Cannot Use the DMZ Interface to Connect to the Internal Network

People have tried some unusual configurations with the trihomed DMZ setup. One of the most popular is trying to "loop through" the ISA server by publishing an internal network server via a server publishing rule so that the internal server is accessed through the DMZ interface by an external network client. As we covered earlier in our discussion on publishing the SMTP mail relay server, you can create a server publishing rule that listens only on the ISA server's DMZ interface.

Publishing servers to the DMZ interface works great when the client is a DMZ host. However, publishing servers to the DMZ interface does not work at all if the client is on the external network. The ISA server will not allow external network clients to access the DMZ interface. If you create a server publishing rule that listens on the DMZ interface, only hosts on the DMZ segment will be able to access the internal network server via this server publishing rule.

This a nice security benefit of the trihomed DMZ. For example, if you create an SMTP server publishing rule that listens on the DMZ interface, an SMTP mail relay server can forward packets to an internal network SMTP server via the server publishing rule. External network clients, no matter how hard they try, will *not* be able to access the internal network SMTP server via the server publishing rule because the ISA server will never pass packets from the external interface directly to the DMZ interface.

ISA Server likes to be efficient. It makes no sense to loop through the DMZ if you need to communicate with servers on the internal network. If you want external network clients to communicate with servers on the internal network, create a Web or server publishing rule that listens on the external interface of the ISA server. Sure, you can get to the internal network *indirectly* by using an intermediary computer such as an SMTP mail relay server, but you cannot loop through the DMZ interface to access an internal network server (Figure 8.37). It's impossible so don't even try.

Figure 8.37 External Network Client Attempting to Loop through the External

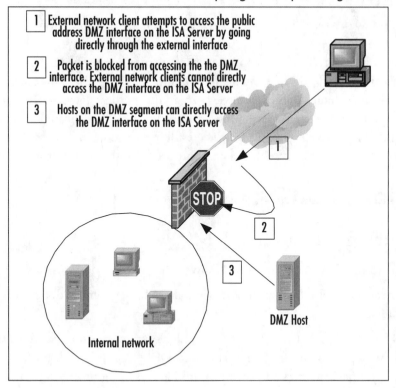

Summary

In this chapter, we covered principles of trihomed DMZ configuration. Packets moving from the external network to the trihomed DMZ segment are always routed. Network Address Translation (NAT) never applies to packets moving between the external network and the trihomed DMZ segment. The reason for this is the trihomed DMZ segment must always contain public addresses. In addition, these packets are not subject to same access policies that control inbound and outbound access through publishing and protocol rules. The ISA server acts as a packet-filtering router instead of providing full-featured firewall capabilities available when you use publishing and protocol rules.

Solutions Fast Track

Configuring a Trihomed DMZ

- ☑ Trihomed DMZ segments must always use public addresses.

- ☑ Access control to and from a trihomed DMZ segment is done with packet filters.

- ☑ "Dynamic" packet filtering is not available when creating packet filters to allow access to and from the trihomed DMZ segment. You must create explicit packet filters for both inbound access and outbound responses.

- ☑ The trihomed DMZ configuration provides a single point of failure. If possible, you should consider implementing a back-to-back DMZ if you require a non–LAT-based DMZ segment.

- ☑ The external interface and the DMZ interface must be on different network IDs. If you put the external and DMZ interfaces on the same network IDs, you create a bridge. You need to route packets, not bridge them.

- ☑ You can install multiple DMZ segments. The "trihomed" DMZ is an example of a single public-address DMZ segment. You can add more DMZ adapters and have multiple public-address DMZ segments. However, you will need to subnet your block appropriately.

- ☑ The predefined packet filters apply to packets arriving at the external interface of the ISA server. You need to create custom packet filters to allow packets to and from DMZ hosts.

Publishing DMZ SMTP Servers

☑ SMTP relay servers work well on DMZ segments.

☑ SMTP relay servers can directly communicate with the DMZ interface.

☑ External network servers can never directly communicate with the DMZ interface.

☑ The SMTP relay on the DMZ needs to be configured with remote domains. The remote domains are those mail domains over which you have administrative control.

☑ The SMTP relay can forward packets to the external interface of the ISA server or to the DMZ interface.

☑ The preferred security solution is to publish the internal network SMTP to the DMZ interface, and then configure the SMTP relay on the DMZ to use the IP address of the DMZ interface as its smart host.

☑ You must configure custom packet filters to allow inbound access to the SMTP relay; the predefined packet filters won't do the job.

☑ Access controls should be placed on the server publishing rule that publishes the internal network SMTP server so that only the DMZ mail relay can use the server publishing rule.

Publishing a Web Server

☑ Publishing a Web server on the DMZ segment requires a custom packet filter.

☑ You can configure a SQL server publishing rule to allow a Web server access to an internal network SQL server. Like the SMTP relay, its best to use the DMZ interface IP address in the SQL server publishing rule.

Publishing an FTP Server on a Trihomed DMZ Segment

☑ The FTP protocol creates special challenges to firewall security; it definitely was not designed with security in mind.

☑ PASV mode FTP provides more security on the client side because all connection requests are outbound. This is in contrast to PORT mode, where the FTP server needs to be allowed to make a new inbound connection to send data to the FTP client.

☑ Running FTP servers in the trihomed, public-address DMZ creates security issues because a large number of ports must be opened to support the protocol. You can temper some of the security issues by restricting access to the packet filters to special IP addresses and source ports.

☑ You will have a higher level of security for your FTP servers if you place them on the internal network. The FTP application filter will manage connections for published FTP servers. This removes the requirement of opening a large number of ports into the DMZ.

External Network Clients Cannot Use the DMZ Interface to Connect to the Internal Network

☑ External network clients can never directly communicate with the DMZ interface.

☑ DMZ hosts can directly communicate with the DMZ interface.

☑ External network clients can access internal network resources with the help of an intermediary on the DMZ segment. For example, an external network SMTP server can send messages to an internal network SMTP server by going through the DMZ SMTP mail relay server.

Frequently Asked Questions

The following Frequently Asked Questions, answered by the authors of this book, are designed to both measure your understanding of the concepts presented in this chapter and to assist you with real-life implementation of these concepts. To have your questions about this chapter answered by the author, browse to **www.syngress.com/solutions** and click on the **"Ask the Author"** form. You will also gain access to thousands of other FAQs at ITFAQnet.com.

Q: Why would I create a trihomed DMZ? There seems to be many disadvantages to this configuration.

A: The trihomed DMZ configuration does have its share of disadvantages. First, you introduce a single point of failure. If someone compromises the ISA server, he has direct access to both the DMZ segment and the internal network. Second, you must use static packet filters to allow inbound and outbound to and from the DMZ segment. The trihomed DMZ configuration should be considered an "economy" solution.

Q: We use Exchange 5.5 on our internal network. I would like to put an IIS server on the DMZ segment and allow users to access the internal network Exchange server from an OWA server on the DMZ. Can I do this? If so, how?

A: You can do this, but there's a major problem with this type of configuration. In order for the OWA server to allow users to log in to OWA, you must make the server a member of the internal network domain. This creates a major security problem, as you've extended your private network's security zone into the DMZ segment. This is especially problematic because the trihomed DMZ segment is a direct extension of the Internet and is protected only by static packet filters. However, the configuration is possible. You'll need to allow intradomain communications through the ISA server. This is accomplished by creating a number of server publishing rules.

Q: I can't connect to my DMZ! I've run Network Monitor on my servers on the DMZ segment, and no packets from external network clients are arriving to the servers on the DMZ. What could the problem be?

A: The most common reason for this is that you've put the external interface and the DMZ segment on the same network ID. Remember that the ISA server must be able to route packets between the external network and the DMZ segment. In order to route packets, the ISA server external and DMZ interfaces must be on different network IDs.

Q: I can't ping the external interface from a DMZ host. Why not?

A: Don't worry, this is normal. There is no combination of packet filters that will allow you to ping the external interface of the ISA server. If you need to test connectivity, you should use telnet. If the services aren't yet in place, you can use Jim Harrison's very cool *WinSock Tool*. You can find the WinSock Tool at http://isatools.org.

Q: I have an ISA server with three NICs: LAN—192.168.1.0/24, DMZ—192.168.2.0/24 and WAN—xxx.xxx.xxx.xxx. I want to create a trihomed DMZ. Will this work?

A: You can create a private address LAT-based DMZ, but the ISA server will not recognize it as a DMZ segment. The ISA server only recognizes DMZ segments that are not in the LAT. You could take the DMZ NIC out of the LAT, but then external network clients would not be able to reach it, because the ISA server routes packets from the external network to the DMZ. Routing won't work when you use private addresses; you need a Network Address Translator (NAT) to do this. The problem is that ISA Server will never NAT between the external network and the DMZ segment.

Q: I want to put multiple Web servers on the DMZ segment. How should I configure my DNS to support these multiple Web servers?

A: You can put as many Web servers on the DMZ segment as you have IP addresses available. You will need to enter the addresses for these Web servers in your public DNS. Put the actual IP addresses of these servers in the DNS; do not put the IP address of the external interface of the ISA server into the DNS. The reason for this is that external network client connect directly to the servers on the DMZ. In contrast, when you publish internal network servers via a Web or server publishing rule, you enter the IP address on the external interface of the ISA server (used in the publishing rule) into the public DNS.

Q: I want to ping my internal network clients from the DMZ, but I can't seem to get the right combination of packet filters. What do I need to do to allow DMZ hosts to ping internal network computers?

A: You can't ping internal network clients from the DMZ. The reason for this is that DMZ hosts are considered part of the external network. The only way in which external network hosts can communicate with internal network hosts is through publishing rules. ISA Server supports publishing only TCP- and UDP-based protocols. Since ping uses ICMP instead of TCP/UDP, you cannot publish "ping servers."

DMZ Router and Switch Security

Introduction

When people think about securing their DMZs, they mostly think about firewalls, intrusion detection systems, VPNs, and hardening of servers within the DMZ. These are all parts of the process, but there is more to securing a DMZ than considering just these items. Some DMZ planners overlook hardening the routers or switches supporting the DMZ so that they cannot be exploited and used as tools to penetrate the network. Routers and switches connect all the devices on the DMZ to the enterprise network as well as the rest of the world; they are the devices that connect the bastion hosts, firewalls, VPNs, and intrusion detection systems to build the infrastructure. This makes routers and switches prime targets for hackers to exploit and glean information about the network they support or to use simply as springboards to other devices. Routers and switches on the DMZ, and anywhere else on the network, can also be used to protect resources that they connect via security features, including ACLs, VLANs, and private VLANs, to name a few. In this chapter, we present information on how to design and configure some important security features of routers and switches that enable them to run securely and protect the devices that they connect.

Securing the Router

In this section, we cover how routers are implemented within a DMZ environment. We discuss topics such as the placement of routers in traditional DMZ environments, routing traffic in and out of the DMZ, applying access restrictions, and how to lock down the router's many features and services. The configuration of the Cisco router Internetwork Operating System (IOS) is consistent across the entire Cisco router product line, especially as it relates to security. This makes it very easy to standardize security measures and policies across the network. This standardization allows the network administrator to create security templates that are applied to new router implementations. The following sections provide valuable recommendations, techniques, and configuration information that will increase the integrity and security of your DMZ so hackers will find it difficult, if not impossible, to hack into the network via the DMZ by exploiting your Internet-facing routers.

Router Placement in a DMZ Environment

Routers are essential to routing traffic in and out of the enterprise network. Routers connect the enterprise to the Internet and route traffic internally within the enterprise network. In this section, we focus our attention on the routers involved in connecting the DMZ environment to the internal network as well as the Internet. Figure 9.1 illustrates an enterprise location with two internal LANs, a DMZ, and connectivity to the

Internet. The diagram shows the use of two routers, one a multilayer switch with routing capabilities (for simplicity we call it a *router* from now on) directing traffic on the internal LAN and an Internet router providing connectivity to the Internet via a link to an ISP. Between the routers is a firewall to protect the internal LAN and provide secure connectivity to the DMZ's resources. In this example, we assume that static routes are configured correctly on the firewall, but if you need further details on how to configure the firewall to route traffic, refer back to the firewall configuration chapters earlier in this book. At this point we need to set up routing so that internal users can access resources on the Internet and that a user on the Internet can access resources on the DMZ.

Figure 9.1 Router Placement in a Traditional DMZ Environment

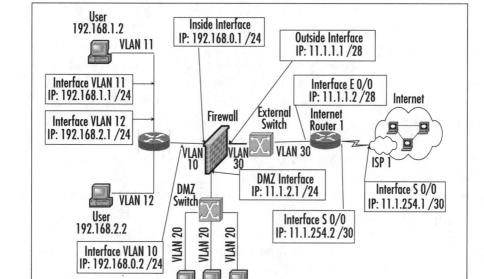

First, let's work on routing traffic from the internal LAN destined for the Internet. In this example, we assume that there is no proxy server and that users will access the Internet via a default route. Should a proxy server be used, make sure that the internal users can access the proxy server and in turn the proxy server can access the Internet. Proxy servers are usually located on the DMZ, which allows internal users to connect to it and has the ability to communicate to resources on the Internet. This prevents any direct communication from clients on the protected internal network to Internet resources; all communication must flow through the proxy server on the DMZ.

All routers on the internal LAN need to know where to send traffic destined for a resource on the Internet via a static route or dynamic routing update. This could be a daunting task if you had to add static routes or dynamically route each network on the Internet on the internal routers—not to mention it would take a lot of memory and CPU cycles.

To reduce the amount of administration and computing power needed on internal routers, a default route or gateway of last resort is used to route traffic to the Internet. This means that if a router does not have a specific route to a destination, it will forward it to its configured default route until it reaches a device that can intelligently route the traffic, usually as the packet reaches the ISP's network. In the example in Figure 9.1, the internal multilayer switch provides connectivity for the internal LAN. For users on the internal LANs who require access to the Internet, the internal router must have a default route or gateway of last resort pointed to the firewall's inside IP address. In this case, the router's default route would be 192.168.0.1. In turn, the firewall should NAT the internal address to a publicly routable address and forward the packet to the Internet router. The Internet router will then forward the packet to the ISP, where it will be intelligently routed to its destination. The internal router requires two commands to implement a static route, as shown in Figure 9.2. The *ip route* command sets the default to 192.168.0.1 (the inside interface of the firewall), and the *ip classless* command lets the router route to unknown subnets.

Figure 9.2 Configuring a Default Route

```
InternalRouter(config)# ip route 0.0.0.0 0.0.0.0 192.168.0.1
InternalRouter(config)# ip classless
```

NOTE

If there are other routers behind the internal multilayer switch or router (but still within the internal network) and you are using a dynamic routing protocol, you need to redistribute the default route into the routing protocol so it can announce to other routers on the network the existence of a default route. The redistribution procedure may differ depending on the dynamic routing protocol in use. Refer to the following URL for more information on advertising a default route and select the routing protocol(s) used on your network: www.cisco.com/univercd/cc/td/doc/product/software/ios122/122cgcr/fipr_c/ipcpr t2/index.htm

At this point we have discussed how requests from the internal LAN are routed to the Internet. Now we must look at how the replies are routed back and how requests initiated from the Internet are routed to resources on the DMZ. The routing protocol of choice on the Internet is Border Gateway Protocol (BGP), which enables the dynamic routing of networks across the Internet. BGP is an Exterior Gateway Protocol (EGP) used to connect autonomous systems. In Figure 9.1, we showed the Internet router connecting to ISP 1 for connectivity to the Internet. In some cases, this router is provided by and managed by the ISP, so the enterprise administrators do not have to worry about its configuration; they just point their default route on the firewall to the Internet router's local Ethernet interface (11.1.1.2). The ISP will worry about routing the enterprise's public addressing (11.1.1.0 /28 and 11.1.2.0 /24) across the Internet so that users on the internal LAN can browse the Internet and users on the Internet can reach the DMZ. However, if you (meaning the enterprise) manage the Internet router on your premises and the ISP manages the connection on its end, there usually will be two options. The first option is to point a default route to the ISP's border router on the serial connection and the ISP will statically route your public address space (11.1.1.0 /28 and 11.1.2.0 /24) to your end as well advertise it across the Internet. Figure 9.3 shows the routes needed to configure the Internet router for a default route to the Internet via the ISP as well as routes to reach the DMZ located on the DMZ leg of the firewall.

The second option is to use BGP to send and receive routing updates to and from the ISP. Though not usually implemented with a site that has only one Internet link and one ISP, this method does provide the ability to dynamically send and receive routes to and from the ISP. This option is usually used for enterprises with multiple links to the Internet and multiple ISPs. We discuss BGP in more detail in the next section.

NOTE

Generally, your ISP will handle BGP and routing to the Internet. Many times, however, it will not. Either way, this information is important for you to know because when you want to secure your DMZ, it's better to know how everything works, and every detail needs to be clear, so you at least know where your vulnerabilities might lie. Nothing could be worse than to have an exploit performed via BGP on your Internet-facing router(s) when you don't even know how they connect or how BGP works with your DMZ.

Figure 9.3 Configuring a Default Route

```
InternetRouter(config)# ip classless
InternetRouter(config)# ip route 0.0.0.0 0.0.0.0 11.1.254.1
InternetRouter(config)# ip route 11.1.2.0 255.255.255.0 11.1.1.1
```

Table 9.1 shows the routing tables for all enterprise-managed devices involved when static routes are used to configure the network shown in Figure 9.1. Notice how the Internet router has no knowledge of the internal LAN routes (192.168.0.0 /24, 192.168.1.0 /24 and 192.168.2.0 /24). This is because the private address space is not routable through the Internet; furthermore, the internal source addresses are NAT'd to public addresses on the 11.1.1.0 /28 subnet by the firewall.

Table 9.1 Routing Table

Device	Route	Next Hop
InternalRouter	192.168.0.0 /24	Local—VLAN10
	192.168.1.0 /24	Local—VLAN11
	192.168.2.0 /24	Local—VLAN12
	Default	192.168.0.1
Firewall	192.168.0.0 /24	Local—inside interface
	11.1.2.0 /24	Local—DMZ interface
	11.1.1.0 /28	Local—outside interface
	192.168.1.0 /24	192.168.0.2

Continued

Table 9.1 Routing Table

Device	Route	Next Hop
	192.168.2.0 /24	192.168.0.2
	Default	11.1.1.2
InternetRouter	11.1.1.0 /28	Local—interface E 0/0
	11.1.254.0 /30	Local—interface S 0/0
	11.1.2.0 /24	11.1.1.1
	Default	11.1.252.1

Border Gateway Protocol

As we mentioned in the previous section, BGP is the routing protocol used to dynamically route packets across the Internet. BGP routes traffic between networks that are under different administrative controls. These networks are known as *autonomous systems (AS)*. BGP allows government, education, and enterprise networks across the world to communicate with each other seamlessly. BGP is highly scalable, flexible, and very robust—and it needs to be because there are well over 100,000 BGP routes on the Internet.

Some of the key features of BGP are:

- Is a path-vector protocol
- Uses TCP port 179 to communicate with neighbors
- Supports classless interdomain routing (CIDR) to reduce the size of the Internet's routing tables by classless summarization
- Currently in version 4
- When BGP runs between AS, it is considered an *external BGP (EBGP);* BGP running inside an AS is referred to as an *internal BGP (IBGP)*
- Uses the following attributes to determine route selection:
  - **Next Hop** The next-hop address that is used to reach the destination.
  - **Weight** Cisco proprietary parameter to assign weights to routes. The path with higher weight is preferred.
  - **Local Preference** Preferred path used to exit an AS. The path with the higher local preference ID is preferred.
  - **Origin** Defines how a network was originated. Values are *IGP* for routes originated in the same AS, *EGP* for routes learned outside the AS, and

incomplete for routes injected into BGP through another protocol, or *redistribute*.

- **AS-PATH** This value indicates the different AS paths that need to be traversed.

- **Multi Exit Discriminator (MED)** Used to suggest to an external AS preferred route into an AS.

- **Community Attribute** Provides a way of grouping destinations, to which routing decisions can be applied.

- Determines the best path for a route by applying the following 10 routing decisions, in order:

  - If the path specifies a next hop that is inaccessible, do not consider it.

  - Prefer the path with the largest administrative weight.

  - If the weights are the same, consider the path with the higher local preference.

  - If the local preferences are the same, prefer the path from which the local router originated.

  - If no route was originated, prefer the route with the shortest AS path.

  - If all routes have the same AS-path length, prefer the path with the lowest origin code.

  - If the origin codes are the same, prefer the path with the lowest MED metric.

  - If the paths have the same MED, prefer external paths over internal paths.

  - If the paths are still the same, prefer the path through the closest IGP neighbor.

  - Lastly, prefer the path with the lowest IP address for the unique BGP router ID.

BGP is a very complex routing protocol. Trying to explain all its nuances in this brief section would not be possible. However, we do cover some basic features as well as how to secure BGP updates, because that is what you will be concerned about while securing your DMZ infrastructure.

The design and configuration of BGP has been the topic of many books and articles, including the *BGP Case Studies* document located on Cisco's Web site at www.cisco.com/warp/public/459/bgp-toc.html. We assume that if you are considering administering a BGP connection to your ISP, you have extensive knowledge of the protocol and you are comfortable supporting it.

As we mentioned in the previous section, all ISPs offer a managed service that provides the customer with the equipment, configuration, and support needed for the links connecting the site to the Internet. This means that the ISP will take care of managing all aspects of running the Internet router pictured in Figure 9.4. All the customer has to do is connect the Internet router's Ethernet interface to the external switch and configure a default on the firewall route to point to the Internet router. Easy, right? Well, if you ever dealt with some ISPs, you know it can be difficult to get them to make changes or even have them provide performance reports and statistics for the router and the Internet link. However, in many cases this is still the best option if you have limited technical resources and only one ISP.

Should you have multiple links to different ISPs and the technical resources required, it could be advantageous to control the Internet-facing router(s) yourself. This solution will allow you more control of how Internet traffic enters and exits you network via the different ISPs. BGP has many "knobs and switches" that allow you to shape the flow of traffic so that the best path is taken. Controlling the Internet-facing router(s) also gives you complete access into the router for detailed reports and statistics of router and Internet link performance as well as more visibility for applying and managing security and for troubleshooting problems.

NOTE

AS numbers are assigned by the American Registry for Internet Numbers (ARIN). In order for the enterprise to receive its own AS, it must meet some requirements, including that the site must be multihomed, meaning that it has connectivity to more than one ISP. For more information on AS number registration, visit ARIN's Web site at www.arin.net/registration/asn/index.html.

In Figure 9.4, we show connectivity to the Internet via a link to ISP 1. For simplicity, we break ARIN's multihomed requirement for this example. The enterprise has a registered public address space (11.1.1.0 /28 and 11.1.2.0 /24) and an AS number (AS 200) that it wants advertised to the Internet so that internal users can access the Internet and users on the Internet can access resources on the DMZ. To accomplish this task, we need to configure BGP on the Internet router to advertise the enterprise's public addresses to its BGP neighbor at ISP 1 (which is fully managed by the ISP) as well as receive routing updates from ISP 1.

Figure 9.4 A Single BGP Neighbor to an ISP

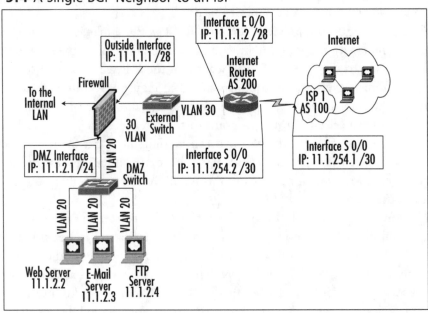

In global configuration mode, we enable BGP and set the AS number to 200 on the Internet router using the *router bgp* command, as shown in Figure 9.5. The *no synchronization* command disables BGP from checking its interior gateway protocol (IGP) before it advertises the route to its neighbor.

We use the *network* statement to tell BGP what local networks to advertise. In this case, we need to advertise both the 11.1.1.0 /28 and 11.1.2.0 /24 subnets to the Internet. The subnet 11.1.1.0 /28 is directly connected to the router, so it knows how to reach the subnet. However, subnet 11.1.2.0 /24 is not directly connected but is located on the firewall's DMZ interface. In order to advertise this route, we must add a static route to 11.1.2.0 /24 (the last line in the example) to point to the firewall so that the Internet router can effectively advertise this route to its neighbor and the route to its destination. Once we have established the AS and the networks we need to advertise, we can move on to establishing a neighbor to the ISP router.

To configure a neighbor, we use the *neighbor remote-as* command to specify the neighbor IP address and its AS number. In this example, the IP address of the neighbor is 11.1.254.1, and the AS for ISP 1 is 100. The *neighbor password* command enables MD5 authentication of routing updates to and from the ISP. Not all ISPs require this option to be set, but it is a good idea to implement it so that hackers spoofing the ISP can't inject bad routes into the Internet router.

It is also a good idea to add a route map, distribution list, filter list, or prefix list to limit the routes being advertised or received by your AS. This can also stop your connection to the Internet from mistakenly becoming a transit AS, where traffic from one AS will transverse your AS to reach the destination, which can inundate your Internet link with unwanted traffic. In the example, we use a *route-map* to allow the router to only advertise the enterprise's registered public address space (11.1.1.0 /28 and 11.1.2.0 /24) to the ISP using the *neighbor route-map* command and a route map that calls on access list 5. The *no auto-summary* command disables the autosummarization of advertised routes. Assuming that the ISP has configured its end, at this point you should be able to establish a neighbor peering with the ISP and be able to share BGP routing information. To view the status of BGP neighbors, use the *show ip bgp neighbors* command or the *show ip bgp summary*; to view BGP routes, use the *show ip bgp* command.

Figure 9.5 BGP Example

```
InternetRouter(config)# router bgp 200

InternetRouter(config-router)# no synchronization

InternetRouter(config-router)# network 11.1.1.0 mask 255.255.255.240

InternetRouter(config-router)# network 11.1.2.0 mask 255.255.255.0

InternetRouter(config-router)# neighbor 11.1.254.1 remote-as 100

InternetRouter(config-router)# neighbor 11.1.254.1 password myBGPpassword

InternetRouter(config-router)# neighbor 11.1.254.1 route-map RoutesOut out

InternetRouter(config-router)# no auto-summary

InternetRouter(config)# route-map RoutesOut permit 10

InternetRouter(config-route-map)#  match ip address 5

InternetRouter(config)# access-list 5 permit 11.1.1.0 0.0.0.15

InternetRouter(config)# access-list 5 permit 11.1.2.0 0.0.0.255

InternetRouter(config)# ip route 11.1.2.0 255.255.255.0 11.1.1.1
```

NOTE

If you are taking in full BGP routes from your ISP, make sure you have enough memory in the routers supporting BGP. Because the Internet has over 100,000 routes, you need a minimum of 128MB of RAM.

Access Control Lists

ACLs allow a router to filter traffic that passes through it based on a certain set of criteria. A router can filter a number of protocols, but since DMZs mainly use IP, we concentrate here on IP ACLs. ACLs can be applied inbound or outbound on any interface on the router and filter on source and/or destination IP address. If more refined filtering is necessary, an ACL can also filter source and/or destination ports such as Telnet at port 23 or SMTP at port 25. ACLs can be placed anywhere on your network, but in this section, we concentrate on creating and applying ACLs in key areas within your Internet/DMZ infrastructure. Depending on your design, you might need to place ACLs in other strategic areas in order to protect your network resources.

ACLs are processed top down, and when a match is found, the router executes the action (*permit* or *deny*) and stops checking for further matches. Therefore, the order of the lines that make up the ACLs is very important. Many people make the mistake of making broad *permit* statements, then later in the ACL configure a specific *deny* statement, or vice versa. This might not provide the desired effect, so be careful when creating ACLs, because a simple ACL error can open holes in your network that hackers can exploit. All ACLs have an implicit *deny all* statement appended at the end, so if a packet is not explicitly permitted it will be denied.

There two types of IP ACL: standard and extended. A *standard ACL* can only filter based on the source IP address and mask. The command to create a standard ACL is *access-list access-list-number action source-IP [source-wildcard] [log]* in global configuration mode. As you can see, the command has many parameters, which we have broken down here:

- **Access-list-number** Groups the ACL entries together. For standard ACLs, the number must be between 1 and 99 or between 1300 and 1999.

- **Action** Defines the action the router will take if the entry is matched. The values are *permit* or *deny*. The *permit* action allows the packet to continue; the *deny* action drops the packet.

- **Source IP** The source IP address of the packet. This can be any valid IP address or the keyword *any* to signify all IP addresses.

- **Source-wildcard** The wildcard mask or bits to applied to source IP to determine a range of addresses. If no wildcard mask is specified (it is optional), the router assumes you are specifying a single host.

- **Log** *Log* matches to the access to the console or syslog if configured (it is optional).

The example in Figure 9.6 illustrates a standard ACL. The ACL number is 1 and only permits to a host with the IP address of 192.168.1.50 and any device within the subnet 10.10.0.0 /16. All other traffic is dropped and logged.

NOTE

ACLs can be used in many devices, not just routers. Today almost any device you purchase that offers some form of security is able to create an ACL.

Figure 9.6 Standard ACL Example

```
DMZRouter(config)# access-list 1 permit 192.168.1.50
DMZRouter(config)# access-list 1 permit 10.10.0.0 0.0.255.255
DMZRouter(config)# access-list 1 deny any log
```

An extended ACL can filter on the source and/or destination IP address as well as filter on source and/or destination port. Extended ACLs can also filter on other characteristics of each specific protocol—for instance, the established bit for TCP and the many different functions of ICMP, to name a few. The command to create an extended ACL is *access-list access-list-number action protocol???????????????????????????????????wild-card [operator [port]] [log]]* in global configuration mode.

- ***Access-list-number*** Groups the access list entries together. For extended ACLs, the number must be between 100 and 199 or 2000 and 2699.
- ***Action*** Defines the action the router will take if the entry is matched. The values are *permit* or *deny*. The *permit* action allows the packet to continue; the *deny* action drops the packet.
- ***Protocol*** The name or number of an Internet protocol. The most common values are TCP, UDP, IP, and ICMP. If IP is defined, it means all the Internet protocols, including but not limited to TCP, UDP, and ICMP.
- ***Source-IP*** The source IP address of the packet. This can be any valid IP address or the keyword *any* to signify all source IP addresses.
- ***Source-wildcard*** The wildcard mask or bits to apply to the source IP to determine a range of addresses.
- ***Destination-IP*** The destination IP address of the packet. This can be any valid IP address or the keyword *any* to signify all destination IP addresses.
- ***Destination-wildcard*** The wildcard mask or bits to apply to the destination IP to determine a range of addresses.

- ■ *Operator* This is optional; operands used to compare source or destination ports. Possible operands are *lt* (less than), *gt* (greater than), *eq* (equal), *neq* (not equal), and *range*.

- ■ *Port* The number or name of a TCP or UDP port (optional).

- ■ *Log* *Log* matches to the access to the console or syslog if configured (optional).

NOTE

We listed only some of the most common parameters used in an extended ACL. There are several other parameters for each specific Internet protocol. Cisco routers also support named ACLs, where names can be given to the standard and extended ACLs instead of assigning a number. For further details on ACLs, refer to Cisco router IOS documentation or the following URL: www.cisco.com/univercd/cc/td/doc/product/software/ios122/122cgcr/fipr_c/ipcprt1/1cfip.htm#1109098.

Figure 9.7 shows an example of an extended ACL. The ACL number is 102 and allows ICMP connectivity to and from any host, allows only SNMP access to devices on the 192.168.1.0 /24 subnet from all hosts, and lastly, permits UDP access from the 192.168.2.0 /24 subnet to the 192.168.1.0 /24 subnet. As with all ACLs, any access not explicitly permitted will be denied.

Figure 9.7 Extended ACL Example

```
DMZRouter(config)# access-list 102 permit icmp any any
DMZRouter(config)# access-list 102 permit tcp any 192.168.1.0 0.0.0.255
    eq snmp
DMZRouter(config)# access-list 102 permit udp 192.168.2.0 0.0.0.255
    192.168.1.0 0.0.0.255
```

To apply an ACL to an interface, use the *ip access-group access-list-number {in | out}* command in interface configuration mode. Access lists can be applied inbound or outbound on an interface. The example in Figure 9.8 applies ACL 102 inbound to Fast Ethernet interface 0/0.

Figure 9.8 Extended ACL Example

```
DMZRouter(config)# interface fastethernet 0/0
DMZRouter(config-if)# ip access-group 102 in
```

Configuring & Implementing...

Tips on Configuring ACLs for the Ingress Interface of Internet-Facing Routers

In the example in Figure 9.9, we show a typical enterprise branch office with an internal LAN, a DMZ, and connectivity to the Internet. The firewall will protect the internal LAN and the DMZ, but the LAN segment in front of the firewall is left unprotected, as is the Internet router. Assuming that you control the Internet router, meaning that it is not part of a managed service by your ISP, you can apply an ACL to provide some protection for devices connected to the outside LAN, including the Internet router, switches, and any other device that might be outside the firewall. ACLs can be applied to the ingress or egress interfaces on the router to filter access. In this configuration template, we cover how to configure ACLs to protect against unauthorized access and prevent common hacking techniques. We then finish by discussing how to apply the ACL to the Internet-facing router's inbound interface, as shown in Figure 9.9.

All ingress Internet router ACLs should start with an antispoofing ACL, which will prevent spoofing of the private address range (RFC 1918) from the Internet. This would be your internal numbering scheme, which would use the 10.0.0.0, 172.16.0.0-172.31.255.255, and 192.168.0.0 address ranges. A line for any public address space that your company might have for internal use (not advertised to the Internet) should also be added here as well. The exclamation point was added for visual and explanation purposes only and is not needed, nor will it be shown in the configuration.

```
! To block spoofing of RFC 1918 Address ranges

IntRouter(config)# access-list 110 deny ip 10.0.0.0
    0.255.255.255 any

IntRouter(config)# access-list 110 deny ip 172.16.0.0
    0.15.255.255 any

IntRouter(config)# access-list 110 deny ip 192.168.0.0
    0.0.255.255 any
```

Continued

Figure 9.9 Ingress Internet-Facing Router ACL

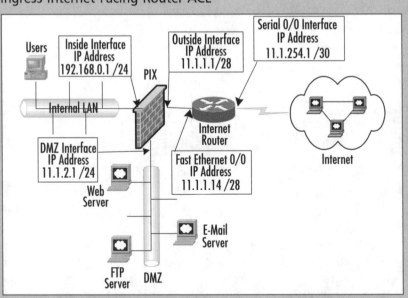

To only allow ICMP echo replies to enter the network from pings originated from the internal network, you must first permit the echo replies, then deny all other ICMP traffic so that pings initiated from the Internet will not be able to enter the network. This is an optional step but can be useful to prevent some DoS attacks.

```
! Allow ICMP echo reply from a ping initiated from the
    internal LAN
IntRouter(config)# access-list 110 permit icmp any any echo-
    reply
IntRouter(config)# access-list 110 deny icmp any any
```

Since the Internet router is the first line of defense against DoS attacks or worms, this ACL can be a point where known attacks or worms can be thwarted or isolated. For example, to mitigate the exposure of the SQL Slammer worm, Cisco recommended the following ACL at ingress and egress points of the network. This step is optional but can be an effective option in trying to prevent a fast-moving attack or worm from spreading any further.

```
! Stop the SQL Slammer worm from spreading
```

Continued

```
IntRouter(config)# access-list 110 deny udp any any eq 1434
```

After you have all the specific entries defined, you must add the *permit all* statement so that legitimate traffic can flow through the router.

```
! Permit all other access
IntRouter(config)# access-list 110 permit ip any any
```

The last step is to apply the ACL the Internet ingress points. In this case, we apply ACL 110 to Serial 0/0 on the Internet router.

```
IntRouter(config)# interface serial 0/0
IntRouter(config-if)# ip access-group 110 in
```

Security Banner

All network devices should present the legitimate end user, unauthorized user, or administrator logging into the system with a legal message prior to the login screen. The message should contain the following four items, at a minimum:

- Unauthorized access is prohibited.

- Unauthorized access is unlawful, and violators may face civil and/or criminal prosecution.

- Access or attempted access to the system may be recorded and used as evidence in court.

- Any applicable federal, state, or local laws should be cited.

These notices help in the prosecution of any unauthorized person who attempts and possibly succeeds in entering the system. Unfortunately, even criminals have rights, and in order to protect your network, these legal notices are necessary in order to pursue conviction of intruders, should the need arise. The security banner should be a legal notice and not contain any information about the device users are accessing, including the name of the device, make, model, or function. This information could be useful to intruders trying to break into the system. You should always check with your legal and security departments prior to configuring the security banner on your devices to make sure it is worded correctly, meets corporate policies, and will hold up in court.

The Cisco router can display your legal message prior to the login screen with the use of the *banner login* command. Figure 9.10 shows an example of a security banner.

Figure 9.10 Configuring a Security Banner

```
DMZRouter(config)# banner login ^
                Warning!!!  You have accessed a private network.
                UNAUTHORIZED ACCESS IS PROHIBITED BY LAW
        Violators may be prosecuted to the fullest extent of the law.
    Your access to this network may be monitored and recorded for quality
        assurance, security, performance, and maintenance purposes.

    ^
```

NOTE

There are also different levels of logging in to a Cisco device, and other banners can be constructed at different levels of login. For example, let's say that you have Banner MOTD, which stands for *message of the day*. If you configure banners, make sure you test them out to ensure that you have configured the proper one. If your device is compromised, you will not want to provide the attacker with any information whatsoever. When using tools such as a Vulnerability Scanner or Analyzer, hackers can do entire scans (sweeps) of large IP address ranges, and the tools they use will provide the banner information to them. They can then go through the logs searching for any useful information. If you use banners, ensure that they provide *no* useful information at all.

Securely Administering the Router

In this section, we cover how to configure the router so that management interfaces and services are protected and locked down. We secure all the entries into the CLI or via Web management. To secure this access, we need to secure all in-band and out-of-band connectivity options to include the console, auxiliary, Telnet, SSH, and HTML. This is done to prevent hackers from making changes to the router's configuration, gathering important network information, or using the compromised router as a launching point for other attacks. You will learn how to use TACACS+ or RADIUS servers to authenticate, authorize, and log access to the router. Lastly, we discuss using and securing managements services such as SNMP, NTP, and syslog.

Console and Auxiliary Ports

Routers have console and auxiliary ports to allow direct serial access to the routers' CLI. By default, there is no security on these interfaces, so it is very important to secure these entry points into the router's CLI; if they are left unconfigured, a hacker with physical access to the router can literally connect a laptop to the router's console or auxiliary port and access the network without any interference. If you purchase a new router and basically configure it to pass traffic without locking it down with the methods described in this chapter, it is highly likely that you will suffer an attack. Access to the console and auxiliary port can be protected by a password or authenticated via a TACACS or RADIUS server. This type of access can be used for general maintenance and monitoring or when access via other methods such as Telnet or SSH are rendered useless due to configuration error or malfunction, where accessing the router via the console may be your last option to correct the problem before having to call Cisco's TAC for assistance.

NOTE

Cisco TAC is responsible for providing Cisco's customers with assistance for technical and configuration issues for all Cisco's hardware and software products, including the PIX firewall. Cisco's TAC can be contacted by phone or via the following URL: www.cisco.com/en/US/support/index.html.

By default, no password is set on the console and auxiliary ports. It is very important to apply a password via the *password* command to the console or auxiliary interface to protect and discourage unauthorized personnel from attaching to the console or auxiliary ports and obtaining unabated access to exec mode. As always, the password should be a nondictionary word, difficult to guess, and it should contain a combination of letters, numbers, and special characters. Any time you use an easily guessed password, it will definitely be cracked via a dictionary or brute-force attack. (This topic is covered in Chapter 15, "Hacking the DMZ.") Passwords can contain up to 80 characters, are case sensitive, and cannot begin with a number. When possible, use TACACS or RADIUS to authenticate access to the console port, especially when you are configuring this router for the DMZ, since it will be accessible via the Internet for scans and attacks. It is very easy for an attacker to fake an address, scan your router, and apply a tool to try to crack its password. When using a tool like RADIUS, you have the benefit of using AAA to a directory to verify identity. We discuss how to configure TACACS or RADIUS support later in this section. Always apply an *exec-timeout* timeout so a session will time out after an idle period—in this case, 15 minutes. The example in Figure 9.11 illustrates how to use these commands to secure the console and auxiliary ports.

NOTE

If you want the most secure router (or switch) with virtually no way to penetrate it, consider using only out-of-band management via the console. If you lock your router in a closet or cabinet and only use console access, there is very little in the way of penetration that can be done. This situation becomes a nightmare to administer, but then again, it is only an option for you to choose, depending on your need for high security or what your security policy dictates.

Figure 9.11 Configuring Console and Auxiliary Ports

```
DMZRouter(config)# line con 0

DMZRouter(config-line)# password H@rd2Cr@ck

DMZRouter(config-line)# exec-timeout 15 0

DMZRouter(config)# line aux 0

DMZRouter(config-line)# password H@rd2Cr@ck

DMZRouter(config-line)# exec-timeout 15 0
```

Telnet

The Cisco router provides the ability for you to Telnet to the CLI so you can manage and administer the device. The router usually allows for five simultaneous Telnet sessions from hosts or networks you specify via an ACL. As is the case with the console port, Telnet access can be protected by a password or authenticated via a TACACS or RADIUS server. Remember that Telnet traffic is sent in clear text, and if someone is sniffing your network they can easily capture the router's Telnet password or the enable password, or if you are using AAA, they will be able to obtain a user ID and password and use them later for other malicious activity.

Figure 9.12 shows how to configure the five Telnet sessions on the router under the *line vty 0 4* virtual terminal line configuration section. You can apply a password to the virtual interface via the *password* command. Remember to use a password that is hard to guess and is a combination of characters and numerals.

Follow the same rules of selecting a password as in the console section. For further protection, apply an access list that limits the host(s) that can (are allowed by you to) Telnet to the router. In this example, we used the *access-class* command to apply access list 10, which allows only the host with IP address of 192.168.1.50 to Telnet to the router. As with the console port, apply an *exec-timeout* timeout so a session will time out after an idle period—in this case, 15 minutes. The *transport input* command specifies the type of protocol to allow on this line. In the example, we allow only Telnet sessions on this line.

Figure 9.12 Telnet Configuration Example

```
DMZRouter(config)# access-list 10 permit host 192.168.1.50
DMZRouter(config)# line vty 0 4
DMZRouter(config-line)# password H@rd2Cr@ck
DMZRouter(config-line)# access-class 10 in
DMZRouter(config-line)# exec-timeout 15 0
DMZRouter(config-line)# transport input Telnet
```

SSH

One of the major weaknesses inherent to a Telnet session is that all data is sent in clear text. This can be a serious security vulnerability if someone is able to sniff your Telnet session to the router. This eavesdropping and snooping of your connection, either promiscuously or via a man-in-the-middle (MITM) attack, can provide just about any attacker with your full set of credentials because they will not be secured via encryption. The router can also support SSH version 1.*x*, which gives the administrator secure access to the router's CLI. All traffic between the administrator's workstation and the router is encrypted, which will make it difficult for a hacker to capture IDs and passwords. Unlike Telnet, which is available by default on almost every operating system, an SSH version 1.*x* client is required and usually needs to be installed on the workstation(s) that need to manage the router via SSH. As with the other access methods, the router can be protected by a password or authenticated via a TACACS+ or RADIUS server.

NOTE

To use SSH, you need SSH configured on the device you are going to connect to, and you must run an SSH client on your workstation. Most UNIX/Linux distributions provide SSH, or you can download SSH to use on other OSs such as Windows from vendors that provide it. Two providers that are most common are www.ssh.com and www.openssh.org.

In order to configure SSH, an IOS loaded image must support DES or 3DES encryption in order to generate a RSA key. If the IOS meets this requirement, we can configure SSH as shown in Figure 9.13. The router must be assigned a hostname and a domain name prior to generating a RSA key. In this case, the hostname is *DMZRouter* and the domain name is *syngress.com*. To generate a RSA key, use the *crypto key generate rsa* command, which will prompt you to enter a modulus; at this prompt you need to enter 1024.

Depending on the router, this process could take some time to complete because the RSA key generation is processor intensive. Some of the lower-end router models can take several minutes to generate a key.

Once the prompt is returned to you, set the SSH timeout, which specifies how long the router should wait for the client to respond during the negotiation phase, using the *ip ssh time-out* command. In this example, it is set at 60 seconds, which is a good timeout, but you can set it however you see fit. You can also specify a limit for authentication retries, after which the connection is reset and the client will lose connectivity. In this case, the *ip ssh authentication-retries* command is used to set the authentication retry limit to 3.

When you're implementing SSH, it is necessary to create a local user database or authenticate users via a TACACS+ or RADIUS server because SSH requires a username and password. In this example, we created a local username using the *username* command to create the user *robadmin* with the password *letmein* for simplicity. But again, we recommend using a TACACS+ or RADIUS server to authenticate SSH users. If you cannot afford to set up a RADIUS server, you can set the local credentials. Like Telnet, SSH can support five SSH simultaneous sessions by default. To configure the five SSH sessions on the router under the *line vty 0 4* virtual terminal line configuration section, we need to specify the user's local ID and passwords to authenticate SSH users using the *login local* command.

As with the Telnet example, we used the *access-class* command to apply access list 10, which only allows the host with an IP address of 192.168.1.50 to SSH to the router, applied an *exec-timeout* timeout so sessions will time out after 15 minutes of idle time, and used the *transport input* command to only allow SSH sessions on this line. When we say *SSH to a router*, it's the same idea as if you were to Telnet to a router. For more information on SSH, visit this URL: www.cisco.com/warp/public/707/ssh.shtml.

Figure 9.13 SSH Configuration Example

```
DMZRouter(config)# ip domain-name syngress.com
DMZRouter(config)# crypto key generate rsa
The name for the keys will be: syngress.com
Choose the size of the key modulus in the range of 360 to 2048 for your
    General Purpose Keys. Choosing a key modulus greater than 512 may
        take a few minutes.
How many bits in the modulus[512]? 1024
Generating RSA keys.... [OK].
```

Continued

Figure 9.13 SSH Configuration Example

```
DMZRouter(config)# ip ssh time-out 60

DMZRouter(config)# ip ssh authentication-retries 3

DMZRouter(config)# username robadmin password letmein

DMZRouter(config)# access-list 10 permit host 192.168.1.50

DMZRouter(config)# access-list 10 deny any log

DMZRouter(config)# line vty 0 4

DMZRouter(config-line)# login local

DMZRouter(config-line)# transport input ssh

DMZRouter(config-line)# access-class 10 in

DMZRouter(config-line)# exec-timeout 15 0
```

NOTE

Of course, you would want to use a stronger password, but for our example, this is fine. Remember, the easier the password is to crack, the more likely it is that you will be exploited, no matter what kind of security posture you implement. Always use strong passwords whenever possible.

HTTP

Some newer versions of the Cisco IOS support Web-based management and configuration of routers using HTML through a Web browser. This feature is not very effective for the support and day-to-day maintenance of the router, so it should *always* be disabled, especially on routers on the DMZ or outside the firewall. To make things worse, communication between the browser and the router happens in clear text, including usernames and passwords. This feature is disabled by default, but if it's active, you might want to disable it using the *no ip http server* command.

WARNING

Sometimes you will not know that the HTTP server is running because it does not show up in the router configuration. Always try to disable the HTTP server, even if you do not see it in the configuration.

Enable Passwords

To keep an unauthorized user from making configuration changes, an enable password should be configured so that only authorized users can access the privileged mode. The enable password is separate from line passwords that allow a user access to exec mode, which only allows a user to show statistics and view interfaces, not to make configuration changes.

There are two methods to apply an enable password. The first is via the *enable password* command, which should not be used because it is possible to reverse its encryption algorithm using several tools readily available on the Internet. The second method is via the *enable secret* command (as shown in Figure 9.14), which is the preferred method because it uses a nonreversible encryption method. The *service password-encryption* command encrypts all passwords on the router, so they are not shown in clear text when the configuration is shown or written. Remember to use difficult-to-guess passwords that contain characters and numerals. A password can contain up to 25 alphanumeric characters. By default, this feature is disabled, but you should enable it on all routers. This is critical because if your router is penetrated, an attacker can easily show the router configuration and get the passwords. If you enable this feature, the router passwords will be tough to get even if the router is taken over by an attacker.

Figure 9.14 Configuring Enable Password

```
DMZRouter(config)# service password-encryption
DMZRouter(config)# enable secret H@rd2Cr@ck
```

AAA

AAA stands for *authentication, authorization, and accounting,* which enables the router to verify, control, and track users who access the router for administrative purposes.

- **Authentication** The process of validating the claimed identity of an end user or a device, such as a host, server, switch, router, or firewall.

- **Authorization** Granting access rights to a user or groups of users.

- **Accounting** The methods to establish who performed a certain action, such as tracking user connections and logging system users.

The AAA feature can authenticate a user who logs into the router to an external RADIUS or TACACS+ server. RADIUS or TACACS+ servers contain the IDs, passwords, and privileges for each user defined to their databases. They can also log information from the time a user logged to a system to the command a user entered. If the router receives a "Success" response from the RADIUS or TACACS+ server, the user will be allowed to gain access to the device. If a "Fail" message is received, the user will be denied access; it's as simple as that.

The AAA feature can also limit the commands by authorizing each command an administrator enters. This feature is useful if you have many administrators who have access to the router. You might also want some administrators to have the ability to troubleshoot the router, which requires the use of *show, clear,* and *debug* commands, as well as to provide other senior or advanced administrators the ability to make configuration changes to interfaces, access lists, routing protocols, and so on. The accounting feature tracks and logs all the logins and changes an administer makes. AAA is very useful for large organizations in which many administrators have access to the company's routers for management purposes and the security policy calls for each admin to have a unique ID and password, so changes to the router can be tracked and administrators can be held accountable. AAA can be applied to administrators accessing the router via the following access methods: console, Telnet, SSH, and HTTP.

AAA is a very useful feature that works very well for administrative access as well as for authenticating and authorizing traffic that flows through the router. A discussion of this topic is out of the scope of this book; if you need more in-depth information about AAA, check out the following site: www.cisco.com/univercd/cc/td/doc/product/software/ios122/122cgcr/fsecur_c/fsaaa/index.htm.

In Figure 9.15 you can see the commands necessary to enable AAA to authenticate users accessing the router for administrative purposes, authorization of commands an administrator can enter, and logging of administrative logins to a TACACS+ server. Prior to configuring AAA, keep in mind that you also need to configure the TACACS+ server itself for this example to work correctly, but we only show the router portion of the configuration. To enable AAA on a router, use the *aaa new-model* command in global configuration mode. To authenticate users who want to access the router to the TACACS+ server, use the *aaa authentication login* command. In this example, we use the keyword *default* to signify that it will be the default method for all sessions including the console, Telnet, SSH, and HTTP.

With this set as the default, from now on when you console, Telnet, SSH, or HTTP into the router, you will be prompted for a username and password instead of just for a password. This prompt will ask the user to supply a full set of credentials that will not only be verified but logged as well. We also set a fallback option, should the router not be able to reach the TACACS+ server, to the enable password. If the TACACS server is down or if the router is off the network for any reason, you will still be able to log into the router using the enable password. The *aaa authorization commands* statements authorize all commands, whether in exec mode (level 0) or privileged mode (level 15), to the

TACACS+ server, which verifies whether the administrator is authorized to execute a specific command. In the example, should the TACACS+ server be unreachable, the router will authorize all commands. To log all the administrative sessions (logins and logouts) to the TACACS+ server, use the *aaa accounting exec* command. To specify the IP address of the TACACS+ server(s), use the *tacacs-server host* command. To specify the encryption key, which encrypts communication between the TACACS+ server and the router, use the *tacacs-server key* command. In the example, the TACACS+ server is 192.168.1.50 and the key is *MyTACACS-KEY*.

We have only brushed on some of the capabilities of AAA; again, refer to the URL mention earlier for more details on how to configure other aspects of the AAA feature.

Figure 9.15 Configuring AAA

```
DMZRouter(config)# aaa new-model

DMZRouter(config)# aaa authentication login default group tacacs+ enable

DMZRouter(config)# aaa authorization commands 0 default group tacacs+ none

DMZRouter(config)# aaa authorization commands 15 default group tacacs+ none

DMZRouter(config)# aaa accounting exec default start-stop group tacacs+

DMZRouter(config)# tacacs-server host 192.169.1.50

DMZRouter(config)# tacacs-server key MyTACACS-KEY
```

SNMP

Simple Network Management Protocol (SNMP) allows network management systems to monitor, collect statistics, and even make configuration changes to the Cisco router. SNMP version 1 is the most commonly used version of the protocol, but unfortunately, it is the least secure, because it uses a community string, which is like a password, that is passed over the network unencrypted, in clear text, just like Telnet. SNMP version 2 is considered more secure because it uses message digest authentication (MD5), so if your management system permits, use SNMP version 2 to manage your routers.

Cisco routers support SNMP versions 1, 2, and 3. If your management system does not yet support version 2 or greater, take a look at the example in Figure 9.16, which takes you through the steps to increase security for SNMP version 1. Since we know that the SNMP requests should only come from a management system, you should be able to create an access list that only permits the specific management system(s) to send SNMP messages to the router.

In the example, we created access list 10, which only permits the management system with the IP address 192.168.1.50, denies all other source addresses, and logs the failed attempts. The *snmp-server community* command is used to set the community string, define the rights (*RO* for Read Only or *RW* for Read/Write) and to apply an access list all in one line. In this case we created two community strings—one for read-only access (*mySNMPReadKey*) and one for read/write access (*mySNMPWriteKey*). Both community strings have access list 10 applied to them, so only the specified management server can send the router SNMP messages. It is important to not use the well-known community strings *public* for read-only access or *private* for read/write access because they are commonly used and easily guessed. Not only that, but most vulnerability scanners have a preset to scan all devices using common string names such as *public* and *private*. Try to use community strings that are a little more challenging (even the strings in the example are too simple), and try not to use the same community strings for all devices on the network. Furthermore, try to avoid SNMP on devices accessible by the Internet if possible because of its inherent weakness and vulnerabilities. If you need to run SNMP on devices accessible to the Internet, do not configure community strings enabling read/write, because if they are hacked, the intruder can possibly reconfigure the router, causing major problems.

> ## WARNING
>
> Using *public* and *private* (the default community string names) for any device on your network is not only unadvisable—it's a practice known to every hacker. Never use these, no matter what. Always change them or disable SNMP from the device.

Figure 9.16 Configuring SNMP

```
DMZRouter(config)# access-list 10 permit 192.168.1.50
DMZRouter(config)# access-list 10 deny any log
DMZRouter(config)# snmp-server community mySNMPReadKey RO 10
DMZRouter(config)# snmp-server community mySNMPWriteKey RW 10
```

Syslog

System logging (syslog) can record several events, from system status to security violations. These events can be sent directly to a console or terminal session, buffered in RAM, and/or sent to a syslog server. The information in the syslog can assist you in troubleshooting a system or network problem and recording matches or violations in an access list. This information can be time-stamped in order to determine the time and sequence of a problem or an attack. Syslog messages are tagged with one of seven severity levels: emergencies, alerts, critical errors, warnings, notifications, informational, and debugging. It is recommended to log syslog messages to both RAM and a syslog server, because once the buffer in RAM is full, the oldest entry is overwritten, and when the router is reloaded, the entries in RAM are lost.

In Figure 9.17 you are shown how to set up syslog to log events to RAM and a syslog server. The *service timestamps log datetime msecs* command time-stamps log entries with the date and time (to the millisecond) for each recorded event. The *logging trap level* command sets the severity level to be forwarded to the syslog server to *informational*, which means it will record all events from emergencies to informational ones and send them to the syslog server. The *logging syslog_ip* command sets the IP address of the syslog server to 192.168.1.50. The *logging buffered level* command sets the severity level to debugging, which enables the router to log messages to RAM for all severity levels.

Figure 9.17 Configuring Syslog

```
DMZRouter(config)# service timestamps log datetime msecs
DMZRouter(config)# logging trap informational
DMZRouter(config)# logging 192.168.1.50
DMZRouter(config)# logging buffered debugging
```

Configuring & Implementing…

The Importance of Logging Events

Logging events can be very useful for troubleshooting your network device, whether a router, switch, or server. However, log files are essential to determining how an attacked compromised your network and what parts of the network were attacked. Furthermore, log files are important to help prove in a court of law that an attack or an unauthorized event occurred.

On routers, logs can be saved to the router's memory buffer or sent to a syslog server. Log events sent to a buffer file in the router's memory are erased once the router is rebooted. This means that if the router is rebooted, it will lose all historical information, including very important data that could prove an attacker is guilty of penetrating the network. If you are not logging to a syslog server, an attacker can cover his trail by clearing syslog files of the devices he penetrated or force the router to reboot. It is a good practice to send log information to a syslog file so that all log events are stored in a central place. Then if an attack occurs, the files can be quickly

Continued

assembled and sent or shown to the proper authorities. It is also important for the logged events to have accurate timestamps (down to the second or even millisecond, if possible). To guarantee accurate timestamps, all devices on the network must have their clocks synchronized, which will make it easier to determine the sequence of events of an attack. Synchronization of the clocks on all devices on your network can be implemented using Network Time Protocol (NTP), discussed in the next section.

Network Time Protocol

NTP synchronizes a router's clock with a time source, which helps keep time accurate on all network devices. When an attack occurs, it might be necessary to keep the time consistent on all network devices in order to determine a sequence of events by checking the timestamps in the logs. To enable NTP only requires the *ntp server* command to specify the IP address of the time source. Figure 9.18 shows how to further protect the NTP service by also configuring optional message digest algorithm 5 (MD5) NTP authentication. In the example, the router will synchronize its time with the NTP server (192.168.50.1) and authenticate using the key *NTPkey*.

Figure 9.18 Configuring NTP

```
DMZRouter(config)# ntp authenticate
DMZRouter(config)# ntp authentication-key 1 md5 NTPkey
DMZRouter(config)# ntp trusted-key 1
DMZRouter(config)# ntp server 192.168.1.50 key 1
```

Disabling Unneeded IOS features

As with many operating systems, some functions and features may be turned on by default on a router's IOS to make configuration and management easier. Unfortunately, these functions and features can also give away vital information or expose the router to malicious attacks. In this section, we discuss some of the functions and features that can safely be disabled to mitigate the risk of an intruder obtaining network topology information or exploiting a weakness in the router's code. We strongly suggest that you read all this information very carefully because most routers are exploited due to unneeded, or more likely unknown, services that are running. This holds especially true for older routers with older versions of code. Newer routers come with current IOS that will normally not make some of these exploits available (such as directed broadcasts, for example, that could be used in a Smurf attack), but you can never be too sure, especially with your Internet-facing routers or routers within your DMZ. Remember, all it takes is a script kiddie with a tool like NMAP to check out what you have and possibly exploit it.

Before we begin, make certain that anything you disable is not really needed, because by disabling services, you could "break" applications such as CDP, which we discuss next, that might have been dependent on those services.

Cisco Discovery Protocol

Cisco Discovery Protocol (CDP) is a Cisco proprietary network management protocol that operates on Layer 2. CDP allows a router to discover several characteristics of a directly connected neighbor, including the type of Cisco device, model, IOS, and IP addresses of the device. An attacker can use this feature to map out a network and determine other devices on the network and thus formulate an attack plan. This feature can be very useful for troubleshooting or managing a network, but it should never be used on an unsecured network such as the external or DMZ LANs. If possible, CDP should also be disabled on routers on the internal network. By default, CDP is enabled on all interfaces. To disable CDP on the entire router, use the *no cdp run* command in global configuration mode; to disable CDP on specific interfaces, use the *no cdp enable* command in interface configuration mode.

> **NOTE**
>
> As mentioned, make certain that none of your network management devices rely on CDP. Hopefully they do not, but in some cases they do. A general rule of thumb is, *never* use CDP on any device within the DMZ, because this protocol will be exploited to help map out what is located within your DMZ. If you have four Cisco devices in the DMZ using CDP, all it takes is one hacker to crack one of them to learn about the others.

Redirects

Cisco routers can tell a device on a subnet whether there is a better router or other network device on the same subnet that can direct the packet to its destination in a more direct fashion. This prevents a packet from being received and sent out the same interface to another router on the same subnet. To accomplish this, when the router receives a packet and the next hop is on the same subnet as the sending device, the router sends an ICMP redirect message to the sending device so it will forward all future packets directly to the next-hop router without involving the original router. This makes the path to the destination more efficient and direct, as well as eliminating the unneeded processing of packets by other routers. Unfortunately, hackers can use ICMP redirects to shape and point traffic to other destinations and disrupt traffic flow. To stop a router from sending ICMP redirects, use the *no ip redirects* command in inter-face configuration mode. ICMP redirects are enabled by default. It is also a good idea to deny ICMP redirects using ACLs to prevent devices sending ICMP redirects to other devices on your network and thus protect path integrity.

> **NOTE**
>
> As you can see (and will see even more as we continue), ICMP can be used to wreak havoc on a network. ICMP was meant to be used as an informational troubleshooting tool, but it can be manipulated to cause more bad than good at times. If you disable ICMP altogether, you will remove the options to use troubleshooting tools such as *ping* and *traceroute*. Make sure you enable and disable ICMP wisely to disrupt hackers looking to take advantage, but to also give you a way to still troubleshoot your network. A word of advice is, if pos-sible, remove the ability for ICMP to be used for attacks (as you are learning in this section) as well as to disable the ability to ping your Internet-facing router from the Internet.

Unreachables

When a router receives a packet and it has no route for the destination, it will reply with an ICMP unreachable packet to the original packet's sender. A hacker can use this information to figure out the subnets used on the network, which could be useful information to a hacker as he maps out the network and launches an attack. To stop a router from sending ICMP unreachable messages, use the *no ip unreachables* command in interface configuration mode. ICMP unreachable messages are enabled by default.

Directed Broadcasts

When a directed broadcast packet traverses a network, it behaves like a unicast packet and is forwarded throughout the network as a unicast packet would be. The difference is that when it reaches the router that is directly connected the destination subnet, the router will rewrite the direct broadcast packet as a link layer broadcast packet and flood the subnet. All replies are sent to the originator of the direct broadcast. Directed broad-casts are used in "smurf" attacks in which a device continuously sends ICMP echo messages with a false source address to a directed broadcast address so that all devices on the destination subnet have to send echo reply messages to the false source address. Either that, or the flood of ICMP traffic goes directly to a single host, paralyzing it by denying it service from any other request. The device with the real source address will be flooded with echo reply messages, which can cause the device's performance to be severely degraded. To prevent this type of DoS attack, use the *no ip directed-broadcast* command. This command stops the router from converting a direct broadcast packet to a link layer broadcast packet. In most cases, directed broadcasts are enabled by default.

> **NOTE**
>
> Newer versions of IOS have this command already configured on the interface, but you should check it anyway just in case.

Proxy ARP

Proxy ARP enables hosts on the LAN with no default gateway configured to determine how to get to other networks or subnets. A host sends an ARP request message to determine where to send traffic for a remote network or subnet to all devices on the subnet. If a router on the same subnet as the host has a route to the network or subnet in question, it will send a proxy ARP reply message to the host with its own MAC address, so the host can send all traffic destined to the remote network or subnet to the router. The router will then forward the packet to the destination. Even though proxy ARP has many legitimate uses, it can also be used by a hacker to determine which networks or subnets are connected to the network. Proxy ARP is enabled by default, but it can be disabled using the *no ip proxy-arp* command in interface configuration mode. With the use of DHCP servers or statically configured default gateways, it is should not be necessary for the proxy ARP feature to be enabled.

Small Services

Several services, known *as small services*, perform functions that are rarely used but if left turned on can be exploited to launch DoS attacks. Before we continue, let's quickly explain what a *service* is, as the term is used in this context. If you were to look at www.iana.org, you could easily find the port numbers for many known services such as Telnet (23), SMTP (25), and so on. Small services are the same, but they are very low on the numbered port. For example, where well-known ports operate from ports 0–1023, small services operate in the first 20 ports within this range, both on TCP and UDP. These services include *chargen, echo, daytime,* and *discard*. Most of these services have legitimate functions, but they also leave the router vulnerable to certain types of DoS attack. For example, character generation (*chargen*) can generate a string of ASCII data to a user who Telnets to TCP port 19 on the router, as shown here:

```
Telnet 10.0.0.1 19
```

Although this is simple, an attacker can use the chargen service to tie up the CPU, which can severely degrade router performance. You can see the attack using the *show processes cpu* command. You will see a rise in CPU usage, which, if underpowered, could crash the router. That's pretty bad for a service you will never use legitimately. Since these services are so rarely needed (can you see a need to have a *chargen* attack performed on your router?), it is recommended that you shut down these services by using both the *no service tcp-small-servers* and *no service udp-small-servers* commands in global configuration mode on all routers, including routers on the internal, external, and DMZ networks.

NOTE

Prior to IOS version 12.0, both TCP and UDP small services were enabled by default, but IOS 12.0 and greater TCP and UDP small services are disabled by default. Check the version of your routers and ensure that these two commands are not enabled since there really is no need for them, especially on your Internet-facing routers.

Finger

The finger service is a carryover command from the UNIX world; it allows attackers to learn which users are logged in to the router without actually logging into it. This feature is not needed. If you need to know who is logged in to your routers, consider using a TACACS+ or RADIUS server, which can produce reports on who is logged in. By default, this service is enabled. Use the *no ip finger* command in global configuration mode to disable the finger service on all routers on your network. Although it's rarely used, it is recommended that you disable this service even if you don't see it disabled in your configuration. Finger is very informative, and many hackers boast about how much they can learn from devices unknowingly running finger. Many hackers find it because it often won't show up disabled in the configuration. Run the *no ip finger* command on your devices, or run a vulnerability scanner on your router externally to see if finger is in fact running.

IP Source Routing

The Cisco router can support source IP routing where the information in the IP packet specifies the path the packet will take to the destination instead of routing based on the destination address. This capability can be dangerous because the packet sender can control the packet's path. If this feature is enabled, an intruder can manipulate the packet's path and possibly circumvent security points within the network. This feature should never be enabled, since source routing is rarely used. IP source routing is enabled by default and can be disabled with the *no ip source-route* command in global configuration mode.

> **NOTE**
>
> It should be noted here that packets could easily be created or forged. Most people think that it takes a college degree in programming to create a packet, but that only means that they haven't scoured enough of the Internet to find the tools they need. You can create falsified data with most protocol analyzers. When we talk about hackers causing most of these attacks against your routers (or any other devices), be aware that they are in fact creating or replaying data against you.

Bootp Server

If bootp services are not needed on the router to assign dynamic IP addressing to clients, it is recommended that this service be disabled. To disable this feature, use the *no ip bootp server* command in global configuration mode. Although vulnerabilities are not common, they can still be exploited by inundating the router with bootp requests, which can cause high CPU utilization and possibly cause the router to crash. The Bootp protocol is used by workstations and other devices to obtain IP addresses and other information about the network configuration. There should be no need to offer the service outside your internal LAN, which is usually provided by a separate server and not the router, and it could offer useful information to intruders.

Other Security Features

The security tips, services, and features discussed in the previous sections referred to standard features of the router IOS, which means that they are found in all IOS releases. However, Cisco does offer more security functionality through the many different feature sets the Cisco router offers, including an IOS firewall and IOS intrusion detection services (IDS) as well as VPN capabilities. These features allow the router to perform stateful packet inspection and detect attacks via signatures, just as their dedicated firewall or IDS appliance counterparts would, in addition to normal router functionality. This makes the router more than a device that directs traffic throughout the network; it becomes a legitimate security device.

Since the focus of this book is to secure the DMZ, we won't cover every little security feature you can enable with Cisco-based devices, but if you need extra functionality, you can research it very easily on Cisco TAC. It should be noted as well that this extra functionality does come at a cost, because these services require more memory and CPU power. Unlike dedicated firewall or IDS devices, where the hardware is optimized for these functions, the router relies on the software to provide firewall and IDS functionality. This means that the router may be bogged down performing all the extra services such as stateful packet inspection or intrusion detection, so latency may increase as traffic passes through it and routing updates are missed, which can cause serious network stability problems. A common rule of thumb is either scale up or scale out. In other words, don't be cheap when ordering a device to do it all, or simply use dedicated devices for dedicated services. In a large DMZ environment, use a dedicated firewall or IDS unit instead of the router IOS versions for these features. However, these features are useful for securing small to medium-sized locations requiring Internet access or for securing connections to business partners or third parties, so analyze your requirements and plan accordingly.

NOTE

In an enterprise DMZ environment, a router running the IOS firewall or IDS feature set should never replace a dedicated firewall device. Even though the router can perform many of the functions a dedicated firewall such as the PIX or an IDS unit, like the 4200 series sensor, can perform, it is not optimized for this purpose and is not recommended.

Securing the Switch

Switches have evolved over the last few years from simple Layer 2 devices to very intelligent network devices that are able to cover all seven layers of the OSI model. Examples are the Cisco Content Smart Switch (CSS) or the Content Switching Module (CSM) on the Catalyst 6500, which can load-balance up to the application level.

These innovations enable the switch to become a powerful tool for implementing a network infrastructure. Some of the functions and features added to the switch over the switch's lifetime include VLANs, trunking, and Etherchannel as well as features to help secure the network, such as port security and private VLANs. The advances in switch hardware and software have also made the switch more than just a Layer 2 device and have bridged the gap between the switch and the router. Many of the new switches can now perform many of the upper-layer functions performed by the router, such as routing and ACLs, and some switches can even perform application layer load balancing. As you can see, the switch is in a state of flux, with new enhancements evident in each release of switch software.

This part of the chapter mainly deals with the securing of the switch itself and some Layer 2 security-related features. Although there are many switches on the market, we recommend the Cisco Catalyst switch model line because these models are feature rich, highly secure, and have a CLI similar to the Cisco router line, which makes administration easier.

Cisco Switches

Unlike the Cisco router IOS, which is uniform across all the models, the Cisco Catalyst switch has two different operating systems. One has a set-based CLI, known as the CAT OS, and the second uses a CLI very similar to the Cisco router IOS. As we just mentioned, it is very clear that Cisco is phasing out the set-based CAT OS in favor the IOS version of the command line. This will make the support for router and switches easier for administrators because they will have the same "look and feel" and share many of the same commands in terms of the CLI. Although some Cisco switches support both operating systems, many of the new switches only support the IOS version, including the Catalyst 2950 and 3550 as well as the new supervisor cards for the Catalyst 4500 series switch.

For this reason, the examples in this section only pertain to the IOS version of the Catalyst operating system. However, if you are running a CAT OS version of the switch's operating system, the concepts and commands can be ported over to the CAT OS. To complicate things further, the features of the Catalyst switch are not always consistent across the model line. To help clarify some features supported by each switch, we list some of the details of the most popular switches, as they pertain to the DMZ.

NOTE

For more information on how to secure Catalyst switches running the CAT OS version of the operating system, refer to this URL: www.cisco.com/warp/customer/473/103.html.

Catalyst 2950

The Cisco Catalyst 2950 series switch is designed to be an access layer switch that provides end stations access to the network. The Catalyst 2950 has a fixed-chassis configuration and offers wire-speed Fast Ethernet and Gigabit Ethernet performance. Cisco offers several different chassis options that can fulfill many of the Layer 2 needs of a small to medium-sized network. This switch can work as a standalone switch or part of stackable solution. The Catalyst 2950 can run two software types or images: Standard and Enhanced Images.

Both images are Cisco IOS based, which means the CLI is very similar to that of the Cisco router. The Standard Image offers basic switch functionality, including Fast Ethernet, VLAN, basic quality of service (QoS), and cluster management support. The Enhanced Image offers all the features of the Standard Image plus advanced QoS, security, spanning tree, and Gigabit Ethernet support. In a DMZ environment, this switch is mainly used in small DMZ implementations or as a utility switch in larger environments where certain parts of the DMZ need to be isolated or to interconnect a small number of hosts.

Catalyst 3550

The Cisco Catalyst 3550 series switch is designed as an enterprise-class access switch that offers multilayer capabilities. Like the Catalyst 2950, the 3550 has a fixed-chassis configuration that offers wire-speed Fast Ethernet and Gigabit Ethernet performance. Cisco offers several different chassis options that can fulfill many of the Layer 2 needs of a medium-sized network as a standalone switch or part of a stackable solution. This switch can also have Layer 3 and 4 functionality, including IP routing, which allows it to be implemented in the core, distribution, or access layer of a small enterprise network. Also like the Catalyst 2950, the 3550 has two software images, the Standard Multilayer Image and the Enhanced Multilayer Image, which you have to order as either SMI or EMI. The Standard Multilayer Image provides basic static routing capabilities. The Enhanced Multilayer Image provides more advanced IP routing, including EIGRP, OSPF, and BGP, as well as multicast routing, enhanced security rate limiting, and HSRP. This switch has the performance and functionality to interconnect the servers and firewalls in a small to medium-sized DMZ environment.

Catalyst 4500

The Cisco Catalyst 4500 series switch is a chassis-based solution designed to provide converged network (data, voice, and video) connectivity. The chassis-based design gives the Catalyst 4500 the flexibility to provide multiple combinations of Fast Ethernet and Gigabit Ethernet line cards to fit three different chassis types to meet the requirements of medium-sized to large networks. The brain of the Catalyst 4500 is contained within the supervisor engine. The supervisor engine controls all the functions of the switch and the newer versions, including Supervisor Engines III and IV, which today only support the Cisco IOS. Some of the older versions support the Catalyst OS. Like the other models, the Catalyst 4500 Cisco IOS software can support Layers 2, 3, and 4, including all the features of IP routing, QoS, security, and multicast routing. This switch can perform the Layer 2 switching functions within the wiring closest as well as in the distribution or core layer in a medium-sized network. This switch has the performance and functionality to perform well in a medium-sized DMZ environment.

> **NOTE**
>
> It is recommended that if you can stomach the price, go with the 4500 because you also get options for having multiple power supplies for disaster recovery, backplane speed switching, and the flexibility of having a modular design. If you wanted to change all your devices in your DMZ to Gigabit port speed, you would only need to replace a blade, not the whole switch.

Catalyst 6500

The Cisco Catalyst 6500 series switch is a feature-rich, very flexible and versatile switch that can provide high performance in all parts of the network, including your wiring closets, network core, server farm, and the DMZ. The Catalyst 6500 can operate between Layers 2 through 7, which allows it to provide simple Layer 2 connectivity to complex Layer 7 content load balancing. The Catalyst 6500 is a chassis-based switch with four different chassis type and line cards that can be inserted to accommodate any possible service requirement, from Fast Ethernet to 10 Gigabit Ethernet. (10 Gigabit Ethernet is the newest standard of Ethernet to be standardized by the IEEE) The Catalyst 6500 can also accommodate WAN interfaces, including T1 to OC-48, which makes this a very powerful, modular, and versatile chassis. As with the Catalyst 4500, the brain of the Catalyst 6500 is located on the supervisor card, which provides multilayer switching capabilities. Other modules are also available to grow your investment in the 6500 to include the following optional components:

- Multilayer Switch Feature Card (MSFC)
- Content Switching Module (CSM)
- Intrusion Detection System Module (IDSM)
- Firewall Services Module (FWSM)
- Network Analysis Module (NAM)
- Policy Feature Card (PFC)

All of these cards can provide this switch with the greatest features and functionality of any switch on the market. In other words, this switch can do it all, and it is like having a switch, router, firewall, and IDS all in one chassis. This switch can run on the Catalyst OS as well as the Cisco IOS, but new features and enhancements lag a few months on the CAT OS version, so it would be in your best interest to ensure that you run IOS. The versatility, functionality, reliability, and performance this switch brings make it a favorite among DMZ architects. If you have a large DMZ infrastructure, consider using this switch—you will not be disappointed.

Securely Managing Switches

As with Cisco routers, Cisco switches offer many of the same management interface options to configure and support the switch, including the console, Telnet, SSH, and HTML. In this section, we concentrate on the management interfaces of the Cisco Catalyst 2950, 3550, 4500, and 6500 series switches. Because they have similar CLIs, these interface options are configured using the same commands as the router. Since all these switches have the ability to run Cisco IOS, which is the CLI similar to Cisco routers, we focus on the differences among the interface types as well as differences in configuration in an effort to avoid duplicating the management interface configuration described earlier, in the router section of this chapter.

One major difference you might notice is that switches do not have an auxiliary port the way the router does, so this topic is, of course, not covered here. We do cover how to configure the switch so that management interfaces and services (such as SSH, Telnet, console, and HTTP) are protected and locked down. We secure all the entries into the CLI to prevent hackers from making changes to the switch's configuration, gathering important network information, or using the compromised switch as a launching point for other attacks. You will learn how to use TACACS+ or RADIUS servers to authenticate, authorize, and log access to the switch. We also go over using and securing managements services such as SNMP, NTP, and syslog.

NOTE

Technically, you would apply many of the same lockdown procedures you learned while reading about routers in the beginning of this chapter. It is important, however, that you read through this section to learn all the differences, especially with VLANs, as well as how to apply port-based security where needed. It's a sure thing that you will have a switch in your DMZ, so read on and learn where you might be vulnerable and what to do about it.

Before we continue, we need to cover one very important point. Do not use a hub in your DMZ. For one, with today's technical advancements, using hub-based technology is simply ridiculous. If you invest the money in your infrastructure to build a DMZ in the first place, make certain that you at least "switch" this segment. For one, you get many technical advancements out of the code running on the switch, as you will see in the following sections. You can also build virtual LANs, which is a very important security advancement, as you will learn shortly. Lastly, using a hub is dangerous if it is compromised. If someone is able to attach a Sniffer to your hub, the attacker will be able to eavesdrop promiscuously on every transmission that traverses that device.

Console

Out of the box, the switch will act like a dumb switch with ports all set to autosense speed and duplex as well as placing all ports in VLAN 1. In ordered to initially configure the switch's features as well as other management interface options, you need to access the switch's console port, which provides direct serial access into the switch CLI. By default, there is no security on the console interfaces; therefore, it is very important to secure this entry point into the switch's CLI. If it is left unconfigured, a hacker with physical access to the switch can literally connect a laptop to the switch's console port and access the network without any interference. Access to the console port can be protected by a password or authenticated via a TACACS or RADIUS server. This type of access can be used for general maintenance or monitoring or when accessing the switch via other methods such as Telnet or SSH are rendered useless due to configuration error or malfunction. In this case, accessing the switch via the console could be your last option to correct the problem before you have to call Cisco's TAC for assistance.

By default, no password is set on the console port. It is very important to apply a password to this interface via the *password* command to protect and discourage unauthorized personnel from attaching to the console port and obtaining unabated access to exec mode. As always, the password should be a nondictionary word, difficult to guess, and contain a combination of letters, numerals, and special characters. Line passwords can contain up to 25 characters, are case sensitive, and cannot begin with a number. When possible, use TACACS or RADIUS to authenticate access to the console port. We discuss how to configure TACACS or RADIUS support later in this section. Always apply an *exec-timeout* timeout so a session will time out after an idle period. The example in Figure 9.19 illustrates how to use these commands to secure the console ports.

Figure 9.19 Configuring a Console Password

```
DMZSwitch(config)# line con 0
DMZSwitch(config-line)# password H@rd2Cr@ck
DMZSwitch(config-line)# exec-timeout 15 0
```

Telnet

The Catalyst switch provides the ability to Telnet to the CLI. The switch allows up to 16 simultaneous Telnet sessions from hosts or networks you specify via an ACL. As was the case with the console port, Telnet access can be protected by a password or authenticated via a TACACS+ or RADIUS server. Remember that Telnet traffic is sent in clear text, so if someone is sniffing your network, they can easily capture the switch's

Telnet password or enable password, or if you are using AAA, they will be able to obtain a user ID and password and use them later for other malicious activity.

In order to configure Telnet, you will first need to configure the management VLAN, which is VLAN 1 by default, with an IP address, and if the switch will be accessed for outside the local subnet, you will need to configure a default gateway. Figure 9.20 shows how to configure the 16 Telnet sessions on the switch under the *line vty 0 15* virtual terminal line configuration section. Apply the password via the *password* command. Follow the same rules of selecting a password as in the console section. For further protection, apply an access list that limits the host(s) that can Telnet to the switch. In this example, we used the *access-class* command to apply access list 10, which only allows the host with IP address of 192.168.1.10 to Telnet to the switch. As with the console port, apply an *exec-timeout* timeout so a session will time out after an idle period. In this case, it is 15 minutes.

Figure 9.20 Telnet Configuration Example

```
DMZSwitch(config)# interface Vlan10

DMZSwitch(config-vlan)# ip address 192.168.1.50 255.255.255.0

DMZSwitch(config)# ip default-gateway 192.168.1.1

DMZSwitch(config)# access-list 10 permit host 192.168.1.10

DMZSwitch(config)# line vty 0 15

DMZSwitch(config-line)# password H@rd2Cr@ck

DMZSwitch(config-line)# access-class 10 in

DMZSwitch(config-line)# exec-timeout 15 0
```

NOTE

You should never use VLAN 1 as anything other than your management VLAN. As you might have noticed in the example in Figure 9.20, the management VLAN is set to 10 because all unassigned and inactive ports belong to VLAN 1 by default. To reduce the risk of unauthorized access, the management VLAN should be set to something other than VLAN 1. In addition, if you explicitly use VLAN 1 for your entire network, one compromised switch gives them all away—in other words, all management information is compromised. Do not assign ports to VLAN 1, especially in your DMZ.

SSH

One of the major weaknesses inherent in a Telnet session is that all data is sent in clear text. This can be a serious security vulnerability if someone is able to sniff your Telnet session to the switch. Most recent versions of the Catalyst switch IOS can now support SSH version 1.*x*, which gives the administrator secure access to the switch's CLI. All traffic between the administrator's workstation and the switch is encrypted, making it difficult for a hacker to capture IDs and passwords. Unlike Telnet, which is available by default on almost every operating system, an SSH version 1.*x* client is required and usually needs to be installed on the workstation(s) that need to manage the switch via SSH. As with the other access methods, the switch can be protected by a password or authenticated via a TACACS or RADIUS server. In order to run SSH on a switch, you need to obtain a special crypto version of the switch IOS software image, which enables you to switch to encrypt SSH sessions. To configure SSH, refer to the router section of this chapter, since the implementation of SSH on both the router and the switch are the same.

> **NOTE**
>
> In today's enterprise infrastructures, not using SSH is a crime. With all we know about how vulnerable the TCP/IP version 4 stack is, why would we continue to use SSH? Most times, we use it because it is extremely easy. You learn how to configure SSH in this chapter, and we recommend that you use it; to not use it is simply being lazy. As a configuration note, to allow SSH to pass your firewall, you need to open TCP port 22.

HTTP

Some newer versions of the Cisco IOS support Web-based management and configuration of switches using HTML through a Web browser. Unlike a router, some switches offer a more advanced HTTP interface that allows administrators to configure, manage, and support standalone switches as well as a cluster of switches. However, in a DMZ environment, it is recommend that this feature be disabled for security reasons because the communication between the switch and the Web browser is unencrypted. This feature is disabled by default, but if it is active, you can disable it using the *no ip http server* command. For best security results, do not activate this feature, especially in the DMZ.

Enable Passwords

To protect an unauthorized user from making configuration changes, you should configure an enable password so that only authorized users can access privileged mode. The enable password is separate from line passwords that allow a user access to exec mode, allowing a user to show statistics and view interfaces but not make configuration changes. As with the router, there are two methods to apply an enable password on a switch. The first is via the *enable password* command, which should not be used because it is possible to reverse it using several algorithms readily available on the Internet. The second method is the *enable secret* command, which is the preferred method because it uses a nonreversible encryption method. The *service password-encryption* command encrypts all passwords on the switch so they are not shown in clear text when the configuration is displayed.

AAA

As with many features of the switch, the functionality and configuration of AAA is the same as the router's implementation of AAA. This makes configuring AAA consistent for all routers and switches across the network, improving the security integrity of the devices that support the network. With AAA you are able to validate the identity of an administrator, grant separate access rights to users or groups, and log changes made to the switch so that administrators are held accountable for their actions. Whenever possible, use AAA to secure the switches on the network.

Since the configuration of AAA is similar to the router's implementation, we only show you an example of how AAA is used to secure the DMZSwitch in Figure 9.21. In this example, we used AAA to authenticate administrative sessions, authorize all commands executed, and log all sessions on the switch to a TACACS+ server. Once AAA authentication is enabled, by default AAA will be used to authenticate, authorize, and log on all management interfaces, including the console, Telnet, and SSH. Therefore, all users accessing the switch will need to have a username and password to enter the switch.

Figure 9.21 Configuring AAA

```
DMZSwitch(config)# aaa new-model
DMZSwitch(config)# aaa authentication login default group tacacs+
    local-case
DMZSwitch(config)# aaa authorization commands 0 default group tacacs+ none
DMZSwitch(config)# aaa authorization commands 15 default group tacacs+
    none
DMZSwitch(config)# aaa accounting exec default start-stop group tacacs+
DMZSwitch(config)# tacacs-server host 192.168.1.50
DMZSwitch(config)# tacacs-server key MyTACACS-KEY
```

Syslogs, SNMP, and NTP

As we have seen, the advantage of having similar CLIs for both the switch and the router is that they share many of the same commands that make device configuration and support easier and consistent across devices. These similarities enable you to consistently configure and secure services such as syslog, SNMP, and NTP on routers and switches across the network. Be sure to follow all the same security precautions presented in the router portion of this chapter when you're configuring these services on the switch. Figure 9.22 shows a sample configuration for these services.

Figure 9.22 Configuring Syslog, SNMP, and NTP

```
DMZSwitch(config)# access-list 10 permit 192.168.1.50
DMZSwitch(config)# access-list 10 deny any log
DMZSwitch(config)# snmp-server community mySNMPReadKey RO 10
DMZSwitch(config)# snmp-server community mySNMPWriteKey RW 10
DMZSwitch(config)# service timestamps log datetime msecs
DMZSwitch(config)# logging trap informational
DMZSwitch(config)# logging 192.168.1.50
DMZSwitch(config)# logging buffered debugging
DMZSwitch(config)# ntp authenticate
DMZSwitch(config)# ntp authentication-key 1 md5 NTPkey
DMZSwitch(config)# ntp trusted-key 1
DMZSwitch(config)# ntp server 192.168.1.50 key 1
```

Security Banner

As we mentioned earlier in this chapter, security banners should be configured on all network devices on the network, including the switch. This banner is a legal statement that any unauthorized access to the device is prohibited and if violated could lead to criminal or civil prosecution. It is very important to configure this banner in order to legally pursue a hacker who might attempt and possibly succeed at breaking into the network and disrupting business. As with many of the switch commands, the configuration of the login banner is the same as on the router, using the *banner login* command.

Disabling Unneeded IOS features

Like the router, the switch has services, functions, and features that can be turned on by default on a switch's IOS to make configuration and management easier. Unfortunately, these functions and features can also give away vital information or expose the switch to malicious attacks. The switch might not have the extensive list of unneeded services that the router has, but it does have some of the potentially hazardous services enabled by default.

As with the router, TCP and UDP small servers and finger should *always* be disabled, since they provide no useful function, especially in your DMZ. It is also recommended that CDP be disabled to prevent hackers from obtaining important information about directly connected devices on the DMZ or outside the firewall. However, on the internal LAN, it might be necessary to run CDP because it is used for some plug-and-play functionality built into the Cisco IP telephony (AVVID) solution. As we mentioned earlier in the chapter, disabling unneeded services is good a good idea; disabling needed services is not. Do an analysis of your network for the applications used and what they depend, remembering that turning services off at times will paralyze an application you might depend on. The rule of thumb for DMZ-based services is, less is better. Do not run what you do not need, analyze what you do need for vulnerabilities, and remove or replace as necessary. The configuration in Figure 9.23 shows how to disable some of the common unneeded service on the switch.

Figure 9.23 Disabling Unneeded Services

```
DMZSwitch(config)# no service tcp-small-servers
DMZSwitch(config)# no service udp-small-servers
DMZSwitch(config)# no ip finger
DMZSwitch(config)# no cdp run
```

VLAN Trunking Protocol

VLAN Trunking Protocol (VTP) is an automated method of distributing VLAN configuration information throughout a management domain. This process eases some of the pain of having to configure VLAN information on every single device you add to your network. VTP is a Layer 2 messaging protocol that maintains VLAN configuration consistency by managing the addition, deletion, and renaming of VLANs within a VTP domain. VTP minimizes misconfigurations and configuration inconsistencies that can result in a number of problems, such as duplicate VLAN names and incorrect VLAN specifications. The switch has three VTP modes:

- **Server** In server mode, an administrator can create, modify, and delete VLANs and specify other configuration parameters for the entire VTP domain. VTP servers advertise their VLAN configurations to other network devices in the same VTP domain and synchronize their VLAN configurations with other network devices based on advertisements received over trunk links. VTP server is the default mode.

- **Client** In client mode, the switch behaves the same way as a VTP server, but switches configured as clients will not allow you to create, change, or delete VLANs.

- **Transparent** In transparent mode, the switch will not participate in VTP, which means it will not advertise its VLAN configuration and does not synchronize its VLAN configuration based on received advertisements. However, transparent network devices do forward VTP advertisements that they receive out their trunking LAN ports.

This can be a very useful feature on the internal network, but on the DMZ switches or switches outside the firewall, it can be dangerous. You should avoid using server and client modes to manage VLANs on the DMZ because there are inherent risks with this feature. If your network is not properly protected, a hacker can inject faulty VLAN information, corrupting the VLAN databases on all switches in the VTP domain. Because there are usually fewer switches and VLANs on a DMZ, it might not be necessary to use this feature, since VLANs can be configured just as easily and securely on each switch without the aid of VTP. To change the switch from server mode, the default, to transparent mode, use the *vtp mode transparent* command in global configuration mode for all switches on the DMZ and outside the firewall. Should VTP be necessary on any part of the network, always secure it with MD5 authentication using the *vtp password* command.

VLANs

A VLAN is a feature that enables a switch or a group of switches to logically segment a network so that the network architect can group hosts across the LAN by department, application, or function instead of by the users' physical location. Each VLAN creates a separate broadcast domain, and broadcasts will not cross VLANs. VLANs operate in Layer 2, the data link layer. In order for communication of devices between VLANs to occur, Layer 3, network layer, routing will need to take place. Figure 9.24 illustrates a switch with three VLANs configured showing three different broadcast domains. Basically, the diagram shows how a switch can be configured to logically act like three different switches. VLANs are useful to cost effectively partition your network into logical parts.

Figure 9.24 A VLAN

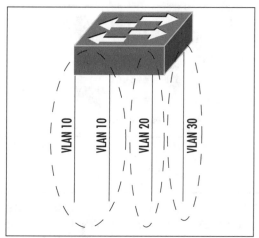

In recent versions of IOS code for Cisco switches, there are two ways to configure VLANs: VLAN database mode and config-vlan mode. In database mode, the switch allows you to configure VLANs in the normal range, which includes 1 to 1005, and save them to the VLAN database. In config-vlan mode, the switch allows you to configure in the normal as well as the extended range, which includes 1006 to 4094. In config-vlan mode, VLANs in the normal range are saved in the VLAN database, and VLANs in the extended range are stored in the switch's configuration file. To configure extended VLANs, the switch needs to be in transparent mode. Figure 9.25 shows how to set up a VLAN and select individual ports to the defined VLAN using config-vlan mode.

VLANs can be statically defined, as our example shows, or dynamically defined by a MAC address. In a DMZ environment, the ports used within the DMZ are usually statically defined to a specific VLAN. As shown in Figure 9.25, the configuration of VLAN 20 is started with the *vlan* command in global configuration mode. This command puts you in config-vlan mode, where the VLAN can be named and the maximum transmission unit (MTU) can be configured. In this example, VLAN 20 is given the name *DMZ2,* and the MTU is set to the default value of 1500 bytes. To statically define an interface to participate in VLAN 20, use the *switchport mode access* command to set the interface as a nontrunking single VLAN port, and use the *switchport access vlan* command to associate the port to a VLAN—VLAN 20, in this case. To show the status of the VLANs, use the *show vlan* command.

Figure 9.25 Configuring and Applying VLANs

```
DMZSwitch(config)# vlan 20

DMZSwitch(config-vlan)# name DMZ2

DMZSwitch(config-vlan)# mtu 1500

DMZSwitch(config)# interface fastethernet 0/1

DMZSwitch(config-if)# switchport mode access

DMZSwitch(config-if)# switchport access vlan 20
```

NOTE

Avoid using VLAN 1, the default VLAN for all ports on the switch. If trunking is necessary, a dedicated VLAN other than VLAN 1 should be used to avoid the possibility of VLAN hopping and double-tagged 802.1q attacks. Avoiding the use of VLAN 1 altogether will keep it from being used in access mode on any nontrunked ports. For additional security, any unassigned ports should be disabled, but some switch administrators place them in an unused VLAN, which, in essence, has a similar effect.

Designing & Planning...

Tips for Designing VLANs in a DMZ

VLANs are a cost-effective way to segment a network because a single switch can be used to support many segmented LANs. This can be very useful on the internal network, where users are grouped by department, application, or function.

In a DMZ environment, incorrect use of VLANs can cause a security flaw or weakness in your network's defenses. Figure 9.26 shows *incorrect* use of VLANs. The diagram shows a small branch office or small enterprise office with an internal LAN, a DMZ, and connectivity to the Internet. A single switch is used to support the entire infrastructure and has three VLANs configured—VLANs 10, 20, and 30. VLAN 10 houses all the internal users, VLAN 20 supports the DMZ, and VLAN 30 connects the firewall to the ISP's Internet router at the site.

The problem with this implementation of VLANs is that a single switch logically partitions the different security zones on the network. The switch

Continued

is not a security device and should not be counted on to securely partition the network, even with the use of VLANs. Each zone, the trusted internal LAN, the semitrusted DMZ, and connectivity to the untrusted Internet should have its own set of switches, and the switches should never have VLANs that cross zone boundaries. In the scenario pictured in Figure 9.26, the entire network could be in jeopardy should a hacker attack the switch, penetrate it, and exploit it. Since the switch has ports outside the firewall, this makes it easy to attack. Should the switch be compromised, a hacker can bypass the firewall because the switch has a presence on all parts of the network—a hacker's dream. At this point, the hacker can shut down ports, reconfigure VLANs, and so on to cause a major disruption and security issue on the network. Furthermore, with a presence on the outside of the firewall, the switch is susceptible to DoS attacks and other forms of attack that focus on other features such as trunking.

Figure 9.26 Improper VLAN Use

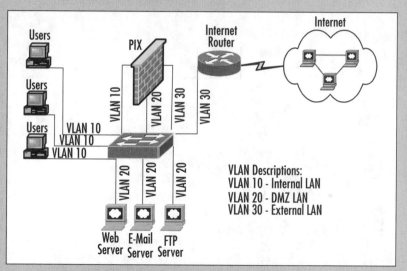

To mitigate these risks, use separate switches for each security zone. This solution prevents an attack on a switch from disrupting the entire network and compromising security. Figure 9.27 shows a proper VLAN implementation in which separate switches are used for each security zone, all separated by the firewall. The diagram shows an internal switch configured with VLAN 10 connecting all the internal users to the inside or protected interface of the firewall. VLAN 30 only connects the outside or Internet-facing interface of the firewall to the ISP Internet router located at the site. Notice that there are two DMZ LANs supported by this firewall:

Continued

one DMZ on VLAN 20 and the second on VLAN 25. These VLANs are located on the same switch, known as the *DMZ switch*. The use of VLANs to separate DMZs is a common and accepted practice in designing and building DMZs because both DMZs reside in the same security zone, the semitrusted DMZ zone.

For further security, consider using a separate switch for VLAN 20 and a separate switch for VLAN 25. The use of multiple separate switches servicing each DMZ VLAN is usually complicated by the cost of the switches and the common use of large, chassis-based switches that can accommodate a large number of servers, so some DMZ architects take the security risk in return for performance and manageability. In any event, an attack on a switch or switches on the DMZ will only affect the DMZ; the rest of the network will operate normally. This is because the switches in each zone are physically isolated, and connectivity between the zones is protected by the firewall. Therefore, if one switch is compromised, the attacker will need to penetrate the firewall's defenses before moving to or attacking another zone.

Figure 9.27 Proper VLAN Use

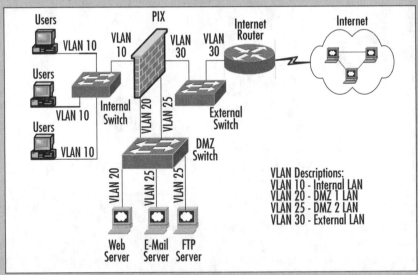

Private VLANS

Hackers often look to exploit a server or other end station that has not been hardened or patched to gain entrance to a network and launch further attacks from the compromised device. (You learned how to harden hosts on the DMZ in earlier chapters.) From the compromised device, the hackers have free access to any device on the local LAN segment because there are no firewalls or ACLs in the way to prevent them from attacking local devices. To reduce the risk of attackers using a compromised box to attack other devices on the same LAN segment, Cisco has introduced a feature called private VLANs (PVLANs).

On a DMZ, many devices do not need to communicate with other devices on the same DMZ LAN to function normally. For instance, a company's e-mail relay server might not need to communicate with the company's Web server, located on the same DMZ LAN, to operate normally, but they are on the same LAN segment so they are free to talk to each other. This can be a problem if a hacker compromises one of the boxes. Let's use the Web server as an example in which a hacker can exploit the server, then use the Web server to launch DoS or other attacks on the e-mail server or any other server on the DMZ. A PVLAN can isolate or group devices on a VLAN, so these devices can only communicate with other devices on LAN segments that they would need to communicate with to provide normal operation. With PVLANs, a port on a switch can be configured as an isolated, community, or promiscuous port. An *isolated port* on a switch can only communicate with the promiscuous port. A *community port* allows communication between other devices within the same community and the promiscuous port. The *promiscuous port* can communicate with all devices with the PVLAN, including the isolated and community ports. This port designation is usually used for the default gateway device.

> **NOTE**
>
> Although you might think that this is overkill on security for a DMZ, you would be surprised at how many engineers wish they knew how to add layers of security like this with PVLANs. If you need added security, this is one way to go. In your organization, you should assess the amount of security you need and apply it with tips and tricks such as the one described here.

Figure 9.28 shows how PVLANs are used to isolate and group servers so that devices can only communicate with other devices on the same LAN that provide normal communication and functionality. In this example, we isolated the e-mail relay server and grouped the Web and application servers. The switch's connection to the firewall is in promiscuous mode to allow communication to flow in and out of the DMZ LAN. The switch will only allow the e-mail server to communicate to the firewall to get to the internal LAN or the Internet. The Web and application servers are grouped into a community, meaning that they can communicate between any device within their community as well as the firewall so they can get to the internal LAN or the Internet. IP addressing and masking should be assigned as you would normally, through DHCP of static addressing. If you are using static addressing, be vigilant as to how you track your assignment, because when PVLANs are in use it is possible for a ping to fail but the address you are pinging to be in use.

Figure 9.28 A Private VLAN

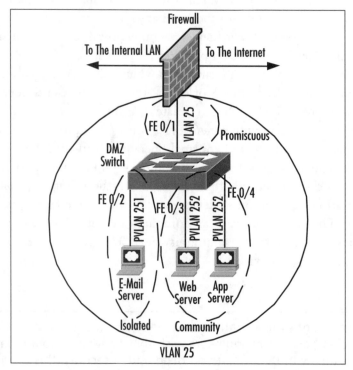

NOTE

Not all Cisco Catalyst switches and Cisco IOS or Catalyst OS versions support PVLANs. As for the switches that do support PVLANs, not all support the community port functionality. If you are interested in using this feature, be sure to check the Catalyst switch documentation prior to implementation or purchasing of hardware, or visit the following URL: www.cisco.com/warp/customer/473/63.html.

To configure PVLANs the switch must be set to transparent mode. In this example, we configure PVLANs as per the diagram in Figure 9.28. Let's start with the configuration of primary and secondary PVLANs. PVLANs are configured similarly to a standard VLAN with the exception of establishing the role the PVLAN will play using the *private-vlan* command in config-vlan mode. The options include *primary*, which signifies the primary VLAN; *isolate*, which signifies all devices on this PVLAN are set to isolated; and *community*, which groups devices that can communicate between one another. In Figure 9.29, we configured three PVLANs, which include the primary PVLAN (VLAN 25), isolated PVLANS (VLAN251), and a community PVLAN (VLAN 252). Once the roles of the PVLANs have been established, we need to associate the secondary PVLANs to the primary using the *private-vlan association* command in config-vlan mode of the primary PVLAN. In this case, we are associating secondary PVLANs, VLANs 251 and 252, to primary VLAN 25.

Figure 9.29 Configuring Private VLANs

```
DMZSwitch(config)# vlan 25
DMZSwitch(config-vlan)# private-vlan primary
DMZSwitch(config)# vlan 251
DMZSwitch(config-vlan)# private-vlan isolate
DMZSwitch(config)# vlan 252
DMZSwitch(config-vlan)# private-vlan community
DMZSwitch(config)# vlan 25
DMZSwitch(config-vlan)# private-vlan association 251,252
```

The next step is to configure the switch's interfaces (ports) and apply the PVLAN associations. We start with the promiscuous connection that supports connectivity to the firewall on Fast Ethernet interface 0/1, as shown in Figure 9.30. We use the *switchport mode private-vlan promiscuous* command to set the interface to promiscuous mode. Then we must map the primary and secondary PVLANs to this promiscuous interface using the *switchport private-vlan mapping* command. In this example, the port will be promiscuous for primary VLAN 25 and secondary VLANs 251 and 252. Next, the e-mail server on Fast Ethernet interface 0/2 needs to be associated to the isolated PVLAN using the *switchport mode private-vlan host* command to set the port to host mode and the *switchport private-vlan host-association* command to associate the port to isolated PVLAN 251. The same commands are used to set the Web and application servers, on Fast Ethernet interface 0/3 and 0/4, respectively, to community PVLAN 252. At this point the e-mail server will only be able to communicate through the firewall and the Web and application servers can communicate between themselves and through to the firewall. To display PVLAN information, use the *show vlan private-vlan* command.

Figure 9.30 Applying Private VLANs to Ports

```
DMZSwitch(config)# interface fastethernet 0/1
DMZSwitch(config-if)# description Connection to the Firewall
DMZSwitch(config-if)# switchport mode private-vlan promiscuous
DMZSwitch(config-if)# switchport private-vlan mapping 25 251,252
DMZSwitch(config)# interface fastethernet 0/2
DMZSwitch(config-if)# description Connection to the E-mail Server
DMZSwitch(config-if)# switchport mode private-vlan host
DMZSwitch(config-if)# switchport private-vlan host-association 25 251
DMZSwitch(config)# interface fastethernet 0/3
DMZSwitch(config-if)# description Connection to the Web Server
DMZSwitch(config-if)# switchport mode private-vlan host
DMZSwitch(config-if)# switchport private-vlan host-association 25 252
DMZSwitch(config)# interface fastethernet 0/4
DMZSwitch(config-if)# description Connection to the App Server
DMZSwitch(config-if)# switchport mode private-vlan host
DMZSwitch(config-if)# switchport private-vlan host-association 25 252
```

Securing Switch Ports

The port security function is a Layer 2 security feature that allows the switch to block packets that enter a port that does not match a dynamically or statically configured source MAC address. This feature allows you to specify and limit the number of MAC addresses that access a port on the switch. This feature can prevent users from adding unauthorized devices to the network and discourage the unauthorized addition of hubs or other switches to the network.

In a DMZ environment, port security allows only specified MAC addresses to communicate on the DMZ LAN, therefore preventing the insertion of unauthorized devices for malicious activity. There three ways to define secure MAC addresses on most switches: static, dynamic, and sticky. *Static-secure* MAC addresses are manually configured on the switch port. *Dynamic-secure* MAC addresses are learned dynamically by the switch but need to be relearned when the switch is restarted. *Sticky-secure* MAC addresses can be dynamically learned or statically configured. When they're dynamically learned, the switch converts and enters them into the switch's configuration. Because sticky-secure MAC addresses can be written and saved to the switch's configuration file, there is no need to relearn any dynamic addresses after a reload. The switch will detect a port security violation when a MAC address that is not statically or dynamically defined tries to access a switch port, a MAC address that is statically or dynamically defined to a switch port attempts to access another switch port on the same VLAN, or the maximum number of allowed MAC addresses has been exceeded. The switch can be configured to react in protect, restrict, or shutdown mode when a violation occurs. In protect mode, the switch drops unknown source MAC addresses but will not log the violation. In restrict mode, the switch drops unknown source MAC addresses but records the violation. Shutdown mode is the switch's default setting; in this mode the switch will disable the port and record the violation.

The *switchport port-security* command is used to enable port security on an interface. This is the only mandatory command needed to configure port security. At this point, the switch will allow only one dynamically defined source MAC address to access the port, and if a violation occurs, the port will be disabled. At this point, you can add optional commands that define static or sticky MAC address entries, change the number of MAC addresses that have access to the port, and change the switch's reaction to a violation. To specify a static MAC address, use the *switchport port-security mac-address* command. To specify multiple static entries, this command can be entered up to 128 times per interface on most switches. The *switchport port-security mac-address* command enables sticky MAC addresses. To specify the maximum number of MAC addresses an interface can accept, use the *switchport port-security maximum* command. The maximum will vary from switch to switch; the default is one. Use the *switchport port-security violation* command to change the method by which the switch handles a violation. The valid values are *protect, restrict,* and *shutdown,* the default value. Use the *show port-security* command to verify your port security configuration. To clear dynamic or sticky MAC addresses, use the *clear port-security* command.

The example in Figure 9.31 shows port security enabled on two interfaces on the switch. On the first interface, the statically defined MAC address of *0001.0002.0003* will be only address allowed to access the port. If a violation occurs, the switch will disable the port. On the second interface, the switch allows for 10 dynamically defined MAC addresses to access the port. The sticky command allows the switch to convert the dynamic MAC address and copy it to the switch's configuration so that when the switch is restarted, the MAC addresses will not have to be relearned. On this port the switch drops packets from invalid MAC addresses and records violations.

Figure 9.31 Configuring Port Security

```
DMZSwitch(config)# interface fastethernet0/1
DMZSwitch(config-if)# switchport mode access vlan 20
```

Continued

Figure 9.31 Configuring Port Security

```
DMZSwitch(config-if)# switchport port-security
DMZSwitch(config-if)# switchport port-security mac-address 0001.0002.0003
DMZSwitch(config-if)# switchport port-security maximum 1
DMZSwitch(config-if)# switchport port-security violation shutdown
DMZSwitch(config)# interface fastethernet0/2
DMZSwitch(config-if)# switchport mode access vlan 20
DMZSwitch(config-if)# switchport port-security
DMZSwitch(config-if)# switchport port-security maximum 10
DMZSwitch(config-if)# switchport port-security mac-address sticky
DMZSwitch(config-if)# switchport port-security violation restrict
```

IOS Bugs and Security Advisories

As you know, from time to time bugs or security vulnerabilities are found in software after it is released to the public. The software loaded in Cisco routers and switches is no different. Just like Windows or UNIX operating system software, Cisco constantly releases new versions that contain new or enhanced functionality but also releases fixes for any bugs or vulnerabilities discovered in previous releases. It is very important to keep up to date on any potential security issues on your network, including making sure that the devices supporting your network infrastructure do not have any weaknesses. Cisco has set up a page on its Web site that announces security advisories and notices for its entire product line, including Cisco routers and switches. The page is constantly updated with new advisories and fixes to known problems related to Cisco hardware and software as well as mitigation techniques for new attacks to prevent them from spreading. This page also contains links on how to report an attack as well as how to report a vulnerability to Cisco about one of its products. You can find the Cisco Product Security Advisories and Notices page at the following URL using a valid CCO login ID: www.cisco.com/warp/customer/707/advisory.html.

> **NOTE**
>
> Cisco also provides several white papers called SAFE Blueprints that break down the different parts of a network into separate modules and details how to protect and secure each module. Many of the tips and items listed in this chapter can be found in these documents. Be sure to read these documents before designing and configuring your DMZ; they will provide you with sound network design and security strategies. The SAFE documents can be found at

the following URL: www.cisco.com/en/US/netsol/ns110/ns170/ns171/ns128/net-working_solutions_package.html.

Cisco also provides an *IOS Essentials* document the that details many of the features of the IOS and how to configure it securely. The *IOS Essentials* document can be downloaded from the following URL: www.cisco.com/public/cons/isp/documents/IOSEssentialsPDF.zip.

DMZ Router and Switch Security Best-Practice Checklists

When designing and configuring routers and switches on your DMZ, make sure that you follow the checklists presented in this section to make sure you have covered some of the important tasks that can increase the security and integrity of your network. If you have already set up your DMZ, go through the list to determine whether you can improve the security on the devices you already have in place.

Router Security Checklist

Here is a checklist to follow to ensure router security:

- Authenticate routing updates on dynamic routing protocols.
- Use ACLs to protect network resources and prevent address spoofing.
- Secure the management interfaces:
  1. Secure all management interfaces, including the console, auxiliary, and virtual terminal ports using hard-to-guess passwords or a TACACS+ or RADIUS server.
  2. Use SSH instead of Telnet.
  3. If possible, use AAA to authenticate, authorize, and log administrative access to the router using a TACACS+ or RADIUS server.
  4. Disable the HTTP server, which disables configuration and management of the router through a Web browser.
- Lock down the router services:
  1. If possible, use SNMP version 2. Use ACLs to restrict access to SNMP.
  2. Disable CDP.
  3. Use authentication and ACLs to secure NTP.

- Disable interface-related services:
    1. Disable redirects.
    2. Disable ICMP unreachables.
    3. Disable directed broadcast.
    4. Disable proxy ARP.
- Disable unneeded services:
    1. Disable TCP and UDP small services.
    2. Disable CDP.
    3. Disable finger.
    4. Disable IP source route.
    5. Disable the bootp server.
- Keep up to date on IOS bug fixes and vulnerabilities and upgrade (sometimes downgrade) if necessary.

Switch Security Checklist

Here is a checklist to follow to ensure switch security:

- Secure the management interfaces:
    1. Secure all management interfaces, including the console, and virtual terminal ports using hard to guess passwords or use a TACACS+ or RADIUS server.
    2. Use SSH instead of Telnet.
    3. If possible, use AAA to authenticate, authorize, and log administrative access to the switch using a TACACS+ or RADIUS server.
    4. Disable the HTTP server, which disables configuration and management of the switch through a Web browser.
- Lock down the router services:
    1. If possible, use SNMP version 2. Use ACLs to restrict access to SNMP.
    2. Use authentication and ACLs to secure NTP.
- Disable unneeded services:
    1. Disable TCP and UDP small services.

2. Disable CDP.

3. Disable finger.

- Use VLANs to logically segment a switch.

- Use PVLANs to isolate hosts on a VLAN.

- Use port security to secure the input to an interface by limiting and identifying MAC addresses of the hosts that are allowed to access the port.

- Do not use VTP on the DMZ switches. Configure DMZ switches for transport mode.

- Keep up to date on IOS bug fixes and vulnerabilities and upgrade (sometimes
downgrade) if necessary.

Summary

As we have seen in this chapter, routers and switches do more than simply provide connectivity between hosts on a network. They can also provide a higher level of security for the network if they are implemented and configured correctly. Routers direct traffic in and out of the enterprise network and are usually the first line of defense when the network is connecting to the Internet. Access control lists, or ACLs, on the ingress ports on the Internet-facing routers can provide the first point of defense on the network before traffic is forwarded to the firewall. Access lists can be used to prevent address spoofing, certain DoS attacks, and other known attacks from entering the network. Since routers are key parts of an interconnecting network, they are prime targets of hackers. Hackers will try to infiltrate routers to glean information or use them as launching pads for further attacks. This is why it is important to lock down routers' management interfaces and services—to make them difficult for an intruder to hack.

As with routers, switches have an increasing role in the security of a network. The switch provides many features, including port security. VLANs and PVLANs provide the tools to keep the devices on the DMZ secure. It is also important to lock down the switch's management interfaces and services so that hackers cannot break into the switch to change VLAN configurations, change port settings, or use the switch to connect to other parts of the network.

New attacks and new vulnerabilities are uncovered every day. It is very important to keep up to date on security notices and advisories posted on the various security Web sites as well as Cisco's site. When a flaw in the hardware or software of your network devices is exposed, it is very important to patch, upgrade, or find a workaround to the issue at the earliest possible time to prevent an intruder from taking advantage of the vulnerability to break into or disrupt the enterprise network.

Solutions Fast Track

Securing the Router

☑ Router placement and routing in a DMZ environment are essential to connect the enterprise location to the Internet. Proper routing, whether statically or dynamically, is important to directing traffic to the Internet so that internal users are able to access the Internet and users on the Internet can access the DMZ.

☑ Often the Internet-facing router is the first line of defense in a DMZ infrastructure. Placing ACLs on the Internet-facing router's inbound interface can help protect the network from several types of DoS attack.

☑ Securing router management interfaces and services is important to prevent intruders from taking over the router and making configuration changes or using it as a launching pad for other attacks.

☑ It is also important to disable any unneeded services on the router to prevent security holes that could be exposed when these services are activated.

Securing the Switch

☑ Proper use of VLANs is essential to protecting the integrity of the network. Use physically separate switches and different VLANs in each security zone.

☑ Take advantage of the switch's security features, such as port security and private VLANs, to enhance security on the DMZ.

☑ Securing the switch's management interfaces and services is important to prevent intruders from taking over the switch and making configuration changes or using it as a launching pad for other attacks.

☑ It is also important to disable any unneeded services on the switch to prevent security holes that may be exposed when these services are activated.

IOS Bugs and Security Advisories

☑ Make sure the router and switch software is free of any relevant bugs and any known vulnerabilities.

☑ Any security notices and advisories should be checked on a regular basis for the latest attacks and mitigation techniques. Make changes or upgrades where appropriate.

☑ Take advantage of security white papers to identify security "best practices" and learn how to secure routers and switches on your network.

DMZ Router and Switch Security Best-Practice Checklists

☑ Follow the Security Best-Practice Checklist and make sure you have covered all the tasks that can help improve security for routers and switches on your DMZ.

Frequently Asked Questions

The following Frequently Asked Questions, answered by the authors of this book, are designed to both measure your understanding of the concepts presented in this chapter and to assist you with real-life implementation of these concepts. To have your questions about this chapter answered by the author, browse to **www.syngress.com/solutions** and click on the **"Ask the Author"** form. You will also gain access to thousands of other FAQs at ITFAQnet.com.

Q: How much memory should my router have to receive the complete BGP routing table from my ISP?

A: We recommend a minimum of 128MB of RAM in the router to store a complete global BGP routing table from one BGP peer. If you store complete BGP routes from multiple peers, you must add more memory.

Q: How can I reset a BGP session?

A: When changes are made in the configuration of BGP, you usually have to reset the session to the neighbors for the changes to take effect using the *clear ip bgp* command.

Q: What is the difference between the *ip default-gateway, ip default-network*, and *ip route 0.0.0.0/0* commands?

A: The *ip default-network* and *ip route 0.0.0.0/0* commands are used to route any packets for which the router does not have an exact route match in its routing table. The *ip default-gateway* command is used only when IP routing is disabled on the router.

Q: Should I authenticate routing protocols? Which routing protocols support authentication?

A: Yes, you should always use authentication for routing updates so hackers can't tamper with routing tables. RIP v2, EIGRP, OSPF, and BGP all support authentication of routing updates.

Q: How do you route traffic between VLANs?

A: In order to route between VLANs, you need to have a switch with Layer 3 routing capabilities—for example, the 3550, 4500, and 6500 with MSFC—or connect the individual VLANs to a router.

Q: How many MAC addresses can you define using port security?

A: This number varies from switch to switch:

- 128 MAC addresses per interface on the Catalyst 2950/3550 series switches
- 1024 MAC addresses per interface on the Catalyst 4500/6500 series switches

## Chapter 10

DMZ-Based VPN Services

Solutions in this chapter:

- **VPN Services in the DMZ**

- **Designing an IPSec Solution**

- **Connecting B2B Sites**

☑ **Summary**

☑ **Solutions Fast Track**

☑ **Frequently Asked Questions**

Introduction

Virtual private networks (VPNs) are quickly supplanting leased lines as a cost-effective and practical way of providing WAN communication between a central network and various remote networks or extranet partner networks. However, implementing VPN services in the DMZ has its share of difficulties. For one, you must determine the placement of the VPN tunnel termination point. In order to identify the location for this device, you must conduct an evaluation as to the security of the device itself. Can it withstand an attack? Are there known vulnerabilities in the software?

Additional points to consider are the type of VPN to use. Most people equate VPNs with IPSec, but other technologies, such as Layer 2 Tunneling Protocol (L2TP), Point-to-Point Tunneling Protocol (PPTP), Multiprotocol Label Switching (MPLS), and Generic Routing Encapsulation (GRE), have their uses as well as their drawbacks in constructing VPNs. Still other proprietary solutions lie ahead in the planning phase, especially with Cisco and its Tunnel Endpoint Detection (TED) and still others to consider.

Another factor that affects VPN device placement and VPN design is the function of the VPN. More and more companies are turning from dialup services to VPNs for remote access connectivity for telecommuters as well as mobile workers. The prime motivating factor in this move appears to be an overall lower cost of ownership with VPNs compared with dialup phone lines.

VPN Services in the DMZ

VPN services in the DMZ are designed to provide connectivity to two primary groups of users:

- Business partners
- Remote users

Remote users can be broken further into three general categories:

- Branch offices
- Telecommuters
- Mobile workers

This section focuses on the various uses of VPN services as well as how these services can be leveraged to reduce the total cost of WAN connectivity for an enterprise.

A traditional corporate WAN is shown in Figure 10.1. Branch office networks are connected through either a circuit-switched data path such as ISDN, providing low-end, broadband connection, or through packet-switched technologies such as Frame

Relay or leased lines (T1, DS3, etc.). The cost of such a WAN topology increases significantly as the number of sites increases and the number of interconnections between the sites increases. For a fully meshed topology with four endpoints, six Frame Relay or serial connections are required. In general, a full meshed network with n nodes requires $(n(n-1))/2$ links. This system quickly becomes quite expensive as the number of nodes increases. VPNs provide dramatic flexibility in network design as well as a reduced total cost of ownership in the WAN.

Figure 10.1 Fully Meshed Enterprise WAN Connectivity

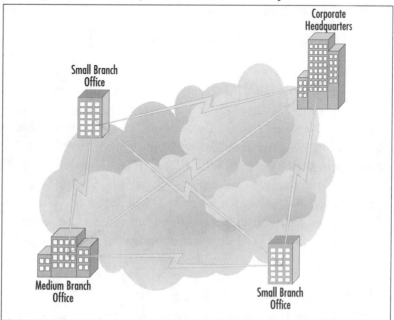

There are a variety of ways to implement VPN services, including at the enterprise-edge router, the firewall, or a dedicated VPN appliance. Additionally, MPLS can be provided by the ISP for site-to-site VPN traffic. Another possibility is the virtual private dialup network (VPDN). Primarily used for remote-access connection to an enterprise campus network, this type of VPN combines the traditional dialup network through the PSTN with either Layer 2 Forwarding (L2F) or L2TP. All of these various technologies are available in today's marketplace, but the most popular VPN technology, by far, is the IPSec VPN. This type of VPN is the focus of this chapter.

VPN Deployment Models

One of the first decisions you must make when you're deploying a VPN is choosing a device to serve as the termination point for the VPN tunnel. This decision is primarily driven by the placement of the VPN tunnel endpoint but also the capabilities of the device that will serve as the tunnel endpoint. IPSec VPNs require devices capable of handling both the traffic traversing outside the VPN as well as the VPN traffic and the encryption of the data across the VPN. Insufficient computing power results in a slow connection over the VPN and poor performance overall. Many vendors address this problem by offering VPN accelerator modules (VAMs) onboard processors designed to provide encryption services for the VPNs.

Deployment of VPNs in the enterprise DMZ is primarily done through the three models listed here and shown in Figures 10.2–10.4:

- VPN termination at the edge router
- VPN termination at the corporate firewall
- VPN termination at a dedicated appliance

Each of these deployment models presents its own difficulties that must be addressed in order for the VPN topology to be successful. One concern that must be addressed is the use of Network Address Translation (NAT). Due to its design, IPSec is not capable of traversing NAT devices. The problem comes when the NAT device changes information in the IP header of the IPSec packet. The changes will result in an incorrect IPSec checksum that is calculated over parts of the IP header. There are vendor workarounds for this problem, where the IPSec packet is encapsulated in a UDP or TCP packet and then transmitted to the other side. At the present time this solution is an Internet draft and has not reached request for comment (RFC) status. The ports to use for such communication are negotiated during tunnel setup.

VPN Termination at the Edge Router

Termination of the VPN at the edge router has the benefit of ensuring that all VPN traffic must conform to external firewall policy in order to reach the internal network. This topology (shown Figure 10.2) is best deployed for extranet connections where the business partners do not require access to the internal network but do require access to servers in the DMZ itself that might not necessarily be exposed to normal Internet traffic. Tunnel termination on the router eliminates the need to configure IPSec through NAT. As the number of business partners connecting through VPNs increases, the load on the routers due to the encryption and decryption of packets entering and exiting the VPN tunnels also increases. This situation requires the use of VAMs in order to offload the encryption/decryption process from the router CPU.

Figure 10.2 VPN Termination at Edge Routers

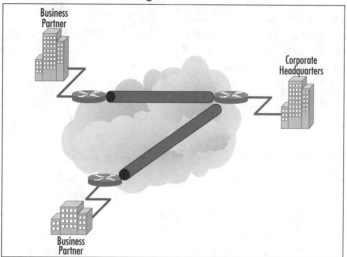

The VPN Dilemma

When you're planning the type of network that you see in Figure 10.2, it is imperative that you understand what the cloud represents in the middle of all the sites, tunnels, and routers. This is the most confusing aspect of VPN design, and more so, this explanation should help you to understand why this chapter is included in this book and how it relates to a DMZ.

First, WAN links such as Frame Relay were traditionally used to get corporate data from one place to another over telecommunication circuits. A technology like Frame Relay had been utilized in many, many deployments around the globe. Now, as more services are leaning toward IP (layer 3 services such as voice and video), a faster, more flexible solution is needed. Now, with the pervasiveness of the Internet, you can pretty much get an Internet connection anywhere, but this is not true with a technology like Frame Relay or ISDN.

Basically, with VPN technology, the ability to encrypt data over "any" connection has raised the bar. You can basically have a WAN connection with a user, business partner, or another site using a simple Internet connection instead of having to build a port and PVC, for example. The flexibility is great, and even more important, the time to get up and running is shorter in some cases, too, when you're ordering and provisioning circuits. The dilemma with the cloud in the figure is this: Basically, with VPNs, the cloud can be anything,

Continued

but you will lean more toward the public Internet when using VPNs because that's where your encryption investment will pay off. You "need" the encryption on the Internet. This is also why it is so important that you understand DMZ technology; now your WAN links will go out your traditional Internet connection, and most likely, you will be hosting some form of services on the DMZ to utilize that public Internet connection.

VPN Termination at the Corporate Firewall

Termination of the VPN at the corporate firewall allows for direct access from branch networks to the internal corporate core network. Remote users can then access all internal services without having to authenticate a second time. This particular topology (shown in Figure 10.3) is best reserved for LAN-to-LAN connections such as branch-office-to-corporate-enterprise networks, but it can also be used for WAN connections if there is a router in front of the firewall to direct traffic over the Internet. The drawback to this topology is that as more branch offices are connected to the corporate office, the load on the firewall increases due to the increased amount of encryption each VPN requires. When the load on the firewall reaches a point at which there an overall impact on network connectivity, it is best to either add a VAM to the firewall or offload the VPN services to a dedicated device.

Figure 10.3 VPN Termination at the DMZ Firewall

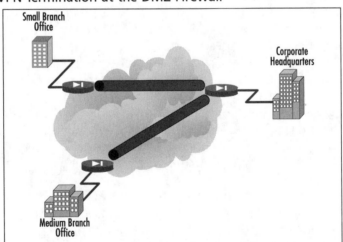

> **NOTE**
>
> Although they're not shown in Figure 10,3, there are routers in front of the firewalls, providing routing functionality while the VPN tunnel terminates on the firewall directly behind it when attached to the Internet, which is depicted. If there are no routers in front of the firewalls, you can also connect and route with firewalls that perform this service, but most commonly, you will see a router on the edge.

VPN Termination at a Dedicated VPN Appliance

Dedicated VPN appliances are designed to provide VPN tunnel services for LAN-to-LAN connections. Termination of the VPN at the corporate firewall allows for direct access from branch networks to the internal corporate core network. Remote users can then access all the internal services provided without having to authenticate a second time. This particular topology (shown in Figure 10.4) is best reserved for LAN-to-LAN connections such as branch-office-to-corporate-enterprise networks. The drawback to this topology is that as more branch offices are connected to the corporate office, the load on the firewall increases due to the increased amount of encryption each VPN requires. When the load on the firewall reaches a point at which there is an overall impact to network connectivity, it is best to either add a VAM to the firewall or offload the VPN services to a dedicated device.

Figure 10.4 VPN Termination at a Dedicated VPN Appliance

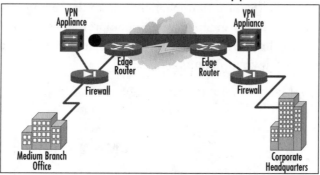

A further benefit to this deployment model is the ability to utilize the VPN appliances in conjunction with wireless networks. The original IEEE 802.11 wireless network specification had significant weaknesses that left wireless network open to easy attack, and subsequently left the internal LAN open to attack as well. Isolating wireless networks "outside" the internal LAN in a DMZ and requiring users to utilize a VPN to access the corporate network helps address some of the weaknesses in wireless LANs (WLANs). You can read about WLAN VPN planning and deployment plans in Chapters 4 and 11.

Topology Models

The deployment models we've discussed represent how VPNs can be implemented in order to provide access to either the DMZ or to the internal corporate network. This section focuses on the various topologies in which these models can be deployed. There are four general topologies to consider:

- Meshed (both fully and partially meshed)
- Star
- Hub and spoke
- Remote access

Each of these topologies is considered in greater detail in this section.

Meshed Topology

Like their traditional WAN counterparts, meshed VPN topologies can be implemented in a fully or partially meshed configuration. Fully meshed configurations have a large number of alternate paths to any given destination. In addition, fully meshed configurations have exceptional redundancy because every VPN device provides connections to every other VPN device. This topology was illustrated in Figure 10.1. Even with the replacement of traditional WAN services such as Frame Relay or leased lines, fully meshed topologies can be expensive to implement due to the requirement to purchase a VPN device for every link in the mesh. A simpler compromise is the partial-mesh topology, in which all the links are connected in a more limited fashion to other links. A partial-mesh topology is shown in Figure 10.5.

Figure 10.5 Partial-Mesh VPN Topology

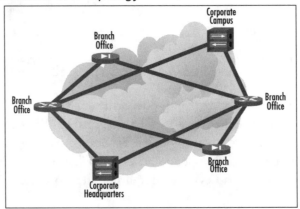

NOTE

Another issue you should be aware of with full versus partial-mesh topology is the number of tunnels you need to configure and manage. If you have 100 sites and add one router, think of all the connections you must make to rebuild a full mesh! In essence, the partial mesh is the way you want to go, but you might see an extra hop in the route from place to place because you will no longer have a single hop to any single destination. There is always give and take. Think about what method suits your design needs, and implement that method accordingly.

Star Topology

In a star topology configuration, the remote branches can communicate securely with the corporate headquarters or central site. However, intercommunication between the branches is not permitted. Such a configuration could be deployed in a bank network so that compromise of one branch will not immediately lead to the compromise of a second branch without being detected. In order to gain access to a second branch, the attacker would have to first compromise the central network that would hopefully be able to detect such an attack. A star topology configuration is shown in Figure 10.6.

Figure 10.6 Star VPN Deployment Topology

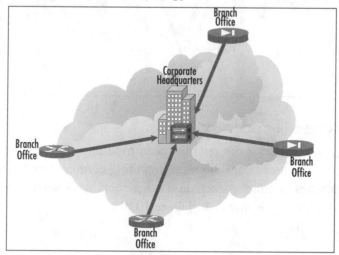

Hub-and-Spoke Topology

A hub-and-spoke topology by design looks very similar to the star topology. However, there is one significant difference: Unlike the star topology, all branch or stub networks in a hub-and-spoke topology are able to access other branch or stub networks. The central, corporate network works as a simple transit point for all traffic from one end of the network to another. As traffic transits through the central corporate network, the data is decrypted, inspected, and re-encrypted for transmission to the final destination. This topology has more risk inherent in the design than the star topology because an attacker who is able to compromise one branch network might then be able to attack another branch network through the VPN without being required to attack the central, corporate network. This topology is shown in Figure 10.7.

Figure 10.7 Hub-and-Spoke VPN Topology

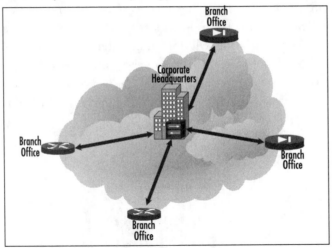

Remote Access Topology

A final topology to consider is the remote access topology. Built on the hub-and-spoke VPN topology, this design focuses more on providing connectivity for remote users such as telecommuters, mobile workers, and other users who need access from nonstatic IP addresses. This topology is shown in Figure 10.8.

Figure 10.8 Remote Access VPN Topology

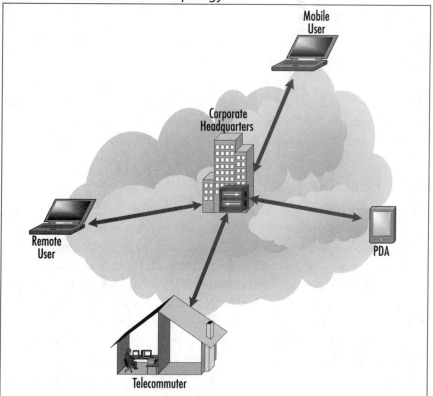

The next topic we examine is deciding whether to place the systems within the DMZ or in front of the DMZ.

Placement of Devices

Now that we have looked at some of the more common designs of the VPN, we need to know where to place the systems in or around the DMZ. Consider the following design points:

- If you are using a topology in which the VPN tunnel is established on the edge router, you do not have to really worry about the DMZ. The DMZ will site off the firewall behind the edge router.

- If you are using a topology in which the VPN tunnel is established on the firewall, you need not worry about anything except for the edge/perimeter router and what it lets or does not let through it.

- If you are using a topology in which the VPN tunnel is established on a separate device, you will have to consider where to place that VPN tunnel. Placing the VPN in the DMZ or around it is fine, depending on how much security you want to implement.

- Make sure that you open the proper ports (www.iana.org) if you are using IPSec or any other encryption protocol that you might have blocked via ACL or filter.

- Be careful of placement and the use of NAT and IPSec, which are used with VPNs. Basically, NAT gives IPSec problems and is known to "break VPNs." Make sure you anticipate this placement in your plan and design.

Business Partner Connections

In addition to branch offices and other remote connections such as data centers, many enterprises have business partners who require secure communications to servers (such as database servers or servers running middleware applications) within the corporate DMZ. There are several ways to ensure such communication: traditional WAN connectivity, SSL, and VPNs. Traditional WAN connectivity includes such technologies as Frame Relay, leased lines, or dialup connectivity. Each has significant costs associated with it. SSL is an alternative, but it is currently utilized with TCP and it is predominantly designed for secure Web transactions and for relatively low-bandwidth connections. VPNs provide the ideal solution for business partner connections due to their flexibility in the level of security they can provide, relative ease of management, and the ability to provide a greater degree of variance in the type of traffic that passes through the tunnel. VPNs offer an excellent alternative to traditional WAN technologies.

Remote Access Services

Remote access services can benefit greatly from VPNs, and IPSec-based VPNs in particular. Companies can move away from central dialup servers and 1-800 numbers and toward a decentralized model. In this model, shown in Figure 10.9, companies contract with local service providers for dialup service to the Internet for remote users. To access the corporate network, users must dial into the local service provider (Step 1) and authenticate to the service provider's access server. Once service provider access is granted, the user must use a VPN in order to access the corporate network (Step 2). In order to allow users to authenticate against corporate resources when they dial into the service provider's access server, a VPN can be used to connect the access server with an authentication server in the corporate DMZ. This enables the service provider to authenticate users in accordance with the corporate security policy. In this model, the easiest VPN technology to deploy is IPSec-based VPNs. The need to invest in access server hardware is eliminated, along with the extra phone lines and their cost, and replaced with a new business expense: the cost of the dialup service from the provider.

Figure 10.9 Decentralized Access Using VPN

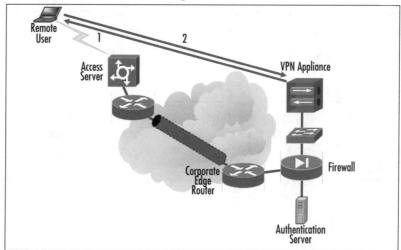

Nokia

Nokia VPN services are offered in two platforms: a dedicated VPN appliance, the VPN-1 Net, and an integrated firewall/VPN appliance. The VPN-1 Net appliance integrates Check Point's VPN-1 Net software with Nokia's purpose-built platforms running IPSO, Nokia's operating system. VPN-1 Net contains basic predefined security policies and integrates the Check Point Stateful Inspection engine to provide access control without full firewalling functionality. Nokia's firewall/VPN appliance integrates Check Point's VPN-1/FW-1 software on a hardened platform running Nokia's operating system IPSO. Nokia's VPN offerings provide a variety of features, some of which are listed here:

- IP clustering Nokia VPN appliances can be grouped together in to a "virtual" appliance gateway.

- Active Session Failover This feature enables the use of active session failover for uninterrupted service. It allows the individual gateways to share security associations in order to provide a seamless transition from one gateway to another in the event of failure.

- Centralized management As more VPN nodes are added to corporations that look to VPNs as a low-cost alternative to traditional WANs, the need for a simplified, centralized management structure is critical.

- Firewall integration The firewall/VPN appliance provides for a tight coupling of a secure proprietary networking OS integrated with third-party applications designed for security solutions.

For greater ease of management and quick configuration of VPNs, the Check Point software includes One Click VPN, which condenses the normal multistep VPN setup and management processes into a single step. This makes it quick and easy to deploy VPNs, whether they are remote access, intranet, or extranet VPNs.

> **NOTE**
>
> It is important that you understand how to set up multiple VPN systems to see which one is cost-effective and a good fit for your organization. You can learn more about the Nokia VPN at this link: www.nokia.com/nokia/ 0,8764,152,00.html.

NetScreen VPNs

NetScreen VPNs are integrated with the NetScreen firewall product. They allow for access control as well as authentication and network segmentation. NetScreen firewalls utilize a "security zone-based" model in which the network is separated into areas, or zones, that are distinct and separate from one another. The zones can be one or more physical or logical interfaces. This structure allows the device to cover VPN tunnel interfaces as well.

Each zone is governed by its own security policy, and the NetScreen firewall applies the policies between pairs of security zones in order to control the type of traffic allowed between the zones. NetScreen products offer a variety of VPN features:

- **Redundancy** Although path redundancy at the physical layer is critical in order to recover from a connection failure, redundancy at the logical VPN layer is also important to minimize downtime. NetScreen VPNs support full redundancy in their VPNs by utilizing "standby" tunnels that mirror the VPN's security associations. In the event of failure in the live tunnel, the standby tunnel takes over in less than 1 second.

- **Dynamic VPNs** Dynamic VPNs help minimize the time required to manage VPNs. This is achieved through the use of dynamic routing through the VPN tunnels in order to communicate network topology as well as link state information.

- **Security zones** As mentioned, security zones allow the network administrator to divide the physical network into a series of virtual sections with various levels of trust. Security zones can be implemented with their own individual security polices. The policies can offer firewall, VPN, and DoS mitigation capabilities. This structure provides several benefits, including an increased interface density, containment of unauthorized users and attacks, simplified management, and lower policy creation costs.

Cisco VPNs

Cisco has integrated VPN technology into most of its networking products. These products include routers, PIX firewalls, and the VPN 3000 series concentrator. Most if not all of Cisco's IOS images for its routers have a version that includes VPN and firewall services as a feature set. Each of these devices provides approximately the same level of VPN services, as described in the sections that follow.

Cisco IOS VPN

IOS VPN services allow the network administrator to terminate the VPN tunnels at an external or internal interface of the router. This allows considerable flexibility in the design of the VPN. Some of the more important site-to-site VPN features available in Cisco IOS are:

- **Diverse networking environment support** IPSec is a Unicast, IP-only protocol, but Cisco's IOS VPN software features accommodate multicast and multiproctocol traffic. In addition, routing protocols are supported across the VPN. Scaled mesh VPN topologies are supported through Cisco's Dynamic Multipoint VPN (DMVPN) feature. DMVPN allows network administrators and users to better scale large and small IPSec-based VPNs by combining GRE tunnels, IPSec encryption, and Next-Hop Resolution Protocol (NHRP). This allows for an easier deployment of meshed VPN topologies by automating the provisioning of connections between spoke sites as well as dynamically setting up connections based on network traffic.

- **Timely, reliable delivery of latency-sensitive traffic** Cisco's IOS VPN feature set enables traffic to be prioritized up to the application layer. This facilitates differentiated QoS policies by application type rather than just TCP port number. This system results in increased transmission reliability and better response time of business-critical applications traversing the VPNs.

- **V3PN solution** By combining advanced QoS, telephony, networking, and VPN features with purpose-built hardware platforms, Cisco's VPN offerings are able to deliver a VPN infrastructure capable of transporting converged data, voice, and video traffic across a secure IPSec network. This is known as Voice- and Video-Enabled IPSec VPN, or V3PN.

- **VPN scalability and feature sets** Cisco's IOS VPN supports a wide variety of features that are essential to VPNs. These features include data encryption, tunneling, broad certificate authority support for public key infrastructure (PKI), stateful VPN failover, certificate auto-enrollment, stateful firewall, intrusion detection, and service-level validation.

- **VPN management framework** Managing multiple VPN devices over multiple sites requires not only robust VPN configuration management and monitoring capabilities but also device inventory and software version management features. Cisco's CiscoWorks VPN/Security Management Solution (VMS) combines Web-based tools for configuring, monitoring, and troubleshooting enterprise VPNs as well as other devices such as firewalls and network- and host-based IDS.

PIX Firewall VPN

The PIX firewall line of products also provides VPN capabilities. These capabilities are designed to allow businesses to securely extend their networks across low-cost Internet connections to mobile users, business partners, and remote offices. The PIX firewall VPN provides several key features:

- **Standards-based IPSec VPN** The PIX solution provides for a standards-based site-to-site VPN utilizing the Internet Key Exchange (IKE) and IPSec protocols.

- **Multiplatform, multiclient support** The PIX firewall VPN supports a wide range of remote access VPN clients, including Cisco's own software VPN client on various platforms (Microsoft Windows, Linux, Solaris, and Mac OS X) and Cisco hardware-based VPN clients (PIX 501, 506E, VPN 3002 client, and the Cisco 800 and 1700 series routers). In addition to supporting IPSec-based VPNs, the PIX also supports PPTP and L2TP clients that are found in Microsoft Windows operating systems.

- **Encryption** The PIX utilizes one of three cryptographic algorithms for data confidentiality and integrity protection. These algorithms are the 56-bit Data Encryption Standard (DES), the 168-bit Triple DES (3DES), and the Advanced Encryption Standard (AES) algorithm. The AES implementation in the PIX supports up to 256-bit encryption.

3000 Series VPN Concentrator

The third major product in Cisco's VPN lineup is the 3000 series concentrator. The concentrator provides dedicated VPN services for remote access as well as LAN-to-LAN connectivity. The 3000 series provides for a wide range of models, from the 3005 for small enterprise networks to the 3080, designed for large enterprise networks. The 3000 series concentrator includes a software client that allows for easy configuration of IPSec tunnels by remote users. Additionally, a hardware version of the client, the 3002 concentrator, provides remote IPSec connectivity for telecommuters.

Cisco EasyVPN

A recent software enhancement that simplifies VPN deployment in Cisco devices is Cisco Easy VPN. This feature centralizes VPN management and provides for the single deployment of consistent VPN policies and key management methods, thereby simplifying remote-site VPN management. The software consists of two components: the Easy VPN Remote and the Easy VPN Server.

The Cisco Easy VPN Remote feature allows Cisco IOS routers, Cisco PIX firewalls, and Cisco VPN 3002 hardware clients or software clients to act as remote VPN clients. These devices can receive security policies from a Cisco Easy VPN Server, thus minimizing VPN configuration requirements at the remote location. This cost-effective solution is ideal for remote offices with little IT support or large customer premises equipment (CPE) deployments in which it is impractical to individually configure multiple remote devices. This feature makes VPN configuration as easy as entering a password, increasing productivity and lowering costs as the need for local IT support is minimized.

The Cisco Easy VPN Server allows Cisco IOS routers, Cisco PIX firewalls, and Cisco VPN 3000 concentrators to act as VPN headend devices in site-to-site or remote access VPNs, where the remote office devices are using the Cisco Easy VPN Remote feature. Using this feature, security policies defined at the head end are pushed to the remote VPN device, ensuring that those connections have up-to-date policies in place before the connection is established. In addition, a Cisco Easy VPN Server-enabled device can terminate VPN tunnels initiated by mobile remote workers running Cisco VPN client software on PCs. This flexibility makes it possible for mobile and remote workers, such as salespeople on the road or telecommuters, to access their headquarters' intranet on which critical data and applications exist.

Windows VPN

Microsoft has integrated VPN solutions into its Windows 2000, Windows XP Home Edition, Windows XP Professional, and Windows 2003 products. Additionally, a downloadable application, the Microsoft L2TP/IPSec VPN client, is available and allows users of older versions of Microsoft Windows (such as NT 4.0, ME, and 98) to create VPN connections. Additional information as well as a download link for this client are available from Microsoft: www.microsoft.com/windows2000/server/evaluation/news/bulletins/l2tpclient.asp.

The implementation of VPNs in Windows is based on a combination of IPSec and L2TP, as described in RFC 3193. For every L2TP connection, the IPSec Encapsulating Security Payload (ESP) Transport Mode is negotiated utilizing 3DES as an encryption algorithm. L2TP encapsulates PPP frames to be sent over a variety of network protocols, including IP, X.25, Frame Relay, or asynchronous transfer mode (ATM) networks. L2TP is documented in RFC 2661.

L2TP over IP uses UDP to send the tunneled data. The packet payloads are L2TP-encapsulated PPP frames that can be encrypted and/or compressed. In this case, IPSec provides the encryption of the payload data. Figure 10.10 shows the structure of an IP packet containing an L2TP packet.

Figure 10.10 IP Packet Transporting an L2TP Frame

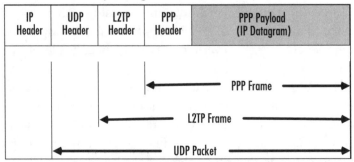

In addition to the L2TP/IPSec VPN solution from Microsoft, there is also support for PPTP as a VPN technology in the Windows operating system. PPTP functions are divided between a PPTP Access Controller (PAC) running on a dial-access platform and a PPTP Network Server (PNS) that operates on a general-purpose operating system. Windows allows for the PAC and the PNS to exist on a single platform by utilizing Windows Remote Access Service (RAS) for the PAC dialup capabilities as well as the VPN service for the PNS. PPTP uses an enhanced GRE mechanism to provide a flow- and congestion-controlled encapsulated datagram service for carrying PPP packets. Some service providers do not allow GRE packets to traverse their networks, so that could be an obstacle to deploying PPTP as a VPN solution.

Designing an IPSec Solution

This section focuses on the design of an IPSec solution for a given scenario. The focus here is on the identification of the various needs that drive the choices within an IPSec design.

Designing & Planning…

Tuning VPN Traffic

As noted earlier in the chapter, placing the VPN in the network depends on whether the tunnel endpoint should terminate at the edge router, on a dedicated VPN appliance in a DMZ leg of the firewall, or on the internal interface of the firewall itself. However, we failed to cover one aspect of this question: the amount of VPN traffic and its effect on the firewall or edge router. Due to the nature of IPSec, which encapsulates the data it is carrying, the IPSec packet sizes are larger than what can normally be handled by a router. Therefore, IPSec traffic tends to get fragmented by an edge device such as a router, resulting in poorer VPN performance. In order to accommodate this situation, it is generally recommended that the Maximum Segment Size (i.e., the maximum packet size) be reduced in order to accommodate the additional IPSec headers. This can mean that it is best to reduce the packet size to approximately 1400 bytes (from the standard 1500 bytes in an Ethernet packet).

Designing an IPSec Encryption Scheme

Most vendors support one of three encryption schemes in their VPN solutions: the Digital Encryption Standard (DES), Triple-DES (3DES), and the Advanced Encryption Standard (AES). AES is the chosen replacement for the aging DES algorithm. DES provides for the use of a 56-bit encryption key that has been proven to be inadequate for long-term security needs. 3DES uses a 168-bit encryption key, is based on the DES algorithm used in a threefold manner, and is considered a stop-gap measure until AES can be fully deployed. AES provides for key sizes ranging from 128 bits (the minimum required by NIST, according to the competition) to 256 bits and provides for the use of 192-bit keys.

The real choice of an encryption scheme comes down to the level of security needed in the VPN as well as the encryption speed desired. As noted earlier, DES has long been proven insecure against an attacker with sufficient computing means at his or her disposal. 3DES has yet to be compromised; however, it is significantly slower than DES and AES. AES has significant performance and security improvements over DES and 3DES, but it is still the proverbial "new kid on the block" as far as encryption algorithms go. Until now, no known attacks or weaknesses exist in AES that could result in the compromise of encrypted data. Given these factors, the choice comes down to 3DES or AES.

In addition to choosing an encryption algorithm, the administrator must decide to use either the IPSec Authentication Header (AH) or Encapsulating Security Payload (ESP) protocol. Similarly, the administrator must choose between transport and tunnel mode.

Designing an IPSec Management Strategy

Another thorn in the side of IPSec is management. In order for a VPN tunnel to be established between two peers, the peers must be able to negotiate a security association (SA). An IPSec SA is a one-way, cryptographically protected connection between a sender and a receiver that affords security services to traffic. The SA is defined for one direction only, and therefore a bidirectional connection (such as a VPN tunnel) requires two SAs—one for each direction. An SA is defined by three values:

- **Security Parameters Index (SPI)** This identifies the security association under which a received packet will be processed.

- **Destination Address** This is the address of the destination endpoint for the SA.

- **Security Protocol Identifier** This identifies whether the association is an AH-based or an ESP-based SA.

In order to establish an SA, the two VPN endpoint devices must have a way of authenticating each other. This can be accomplished through either a preshared key or digital certificates. Preshared keys require that the network administrator configure the secret key on all VPN devices that are going to establish tunnels with each other. This could require that the key be communicated to a party (such as an extranet partner) at the other tunnel endpoint through an out-of-band method. Additionally, since keys should be changed frequently, the administrator must coordinate changing keys at periodic intervals. Preshared keys are sufficient for a small deployment, but they quickly become unmanageable in a large, enterprise deployment of VPNs.

Another method of authentication between IPSec peers utilizes a PKI in order to provide the necessary information for a VPN endpoint device to authenticate to another. In this scheme, the signed X.509 certificates for both devices in the VPN are available from a certificate server at a certificate authority (CA). Each device retrieves the public key for the IPSec peer from the CA and uses it to encrypt its authentication challenge to the other side. If the peer is able to respond with the proper reply to the challenge, it is determined that authentication has succeeded. This allows both sides to prove their identity before negotiating the SA. For small deployments, PKI requires more administrative overhead than preshared keys and should not be used. For larger, enterprise-size deployments of VPNs, PKI provides significant benefits and is desired over preshared keys.

Designing Negotiation Policies

IPSec-based VPN tunnel parameters must be negotiated between the endpoint devices. This negotiation involves the announcements of encryption schemes the devices support (DES, 3DES, AES) as well as the message authentication code (MAC) hash algorithm that will be used to verify the integrity of the IPSec packets. Typical supported MAC hash algorithms include MD5, SHA-1, and HMAC. These parameters are included as part of the tunnel SA and are negotiated using the Internet Key Exchange (IKE) protocol (formerly known as the Internet Security Association and Key Management Protocol).

Designing Security Policies

IPSec security policies are defined as a set of conditions that define an action. The conditions typically determine whether traffic passing through the device is to be encrypted and sent through the VPN tunnel or allowed to pass through unencrypted to a device outside the tunnel. For example, a simple policy would be:

If <condition> then <action>

Here, <condition> can be the source IP address, the destination IP address, the source or destination port, or the IP protocol being used. The <action> can be to deny the traffic, allow it, or pass it through the VPN tunnel. Figure 10.11 shows an example of a security policy being used to segregate IPSec traffic from non-IPSec traffic.

Figure 10.11 An IPSec VPN Security Policy

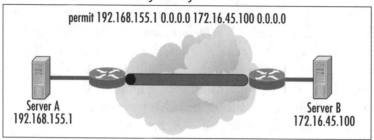

In this example, the security policy is shown at the very top. Any traffic with a source IP address of 192.168.155.1 whose destination is 172.16.45.100 is permitted into the tunnel. Once traffic has been identified as valid for the tunnel, the traffic is encrypted according to the tunnel encryption scheme. All traffic that does not match this security policy is allowed to pass through the router interfaces unencrypted and outside the VPN tunnel.

Designing IP Filters

IP filters can be used to restrict traffic coming from an external network through the VPN tunnel. These filters can limit access only to certain servers on port 80 or allow a broader level of access to the DMZ as a whole. VPN tunnel filters act like ACLs on firewalls and edge routers by giving administrators the ability to define traffic that is permissible. Unlike ACLs on routers and firewalls, IP filters tend not to be stateful and therefore may require more explicit rules in order to provide for proper two-way communication through the tunnel.

Defining Security Levels

Security levels are used to determine which security policies to implement and where. A network with a high security level may restrict traffic significantly, such that only encrypted traffic is allowed to access the network. Typically, networks with higher security levels contain more sensitive information and have a more restrictive access policy as well as a more restrictive security policy. Medium security levels allow a broader range of traffic in and out of the network but may still require strong authentication or encryption to protect the data in the communication. A low security-level network may allow for plain-text communication protocols such as Telnet, FTP, or HTTP to access information on servers in the network. Furthermore, the amount of restriction on the traffic might be minimal.

Connecting B2B Sites

Business-to-business (B2B) connectivity has been made immensely easier with the emergence of the Internet and even easier still with the maturation and availability of VPN technologies. In the past, B2B connectivity utilized leased lines or dialup connections for the exchange of information and technology between two companies. VPNs have eliminated that need. However, trust is still of great concern. As with any business relationship, the trust between two companies can deteriorate at a rapid pace. Consider the relationship of Cisco Systems Inc. and Dell Computer Corporation. In early 2003, the longtime business relationship between the two was terminated, with Cisco Systems citing Dell's entry into the switch marketplace as a factor.

Extranets

Extranets are B2B networks that are based on Internet network technology. An extranet can be viewed as part of a company's intranet that is made accessible to other companies, to the public, or that comprises components that enable the collaboration with other companies. Excellent examples of extranets include the Federal Express Tracking System (www.fedex.com/us/tracking/) and the UPS Tracking System (www.ups.com/WebTracking/track). These systems allow users to access both FedEx and UPS public sites, enter their tracking numbers, and locate any package still in the system. Additionally, a user with either a FedEx or a UPS account can enter all the information needed to prepare a shipment form, obtain a tracking number, print the form, and schedule a pick-up—all from the convenience of the user's computer and a Web browser. Other uses of extranets include:

- Private newsgroups between companies to share valuable experiences and ideas between business partners
- The sharing of educational material or training programs
- Shared product catalogs accessible only to a select group within the industry
- Project management for intercorporate projects

As with any other connection, the main point to consider in terms of VPN extranet implementation is the termination point for the VPN tunnel. For extranets, there are two possibilities: at the edge router or at a dedicated VPN device in a DMZ leg of the firewall. It is not recommended that the VPN be terminated at the firewall because of the need to ensure that the extranet business partner is controlled. Terminating the VPN at the inside interface of the firewall may provide the partner with significant access to corporate information as well as complete access to the corporate network. Although the extranet partner may be trusted today, tomorrow that partner might well be a competitor.

VPN Security

VPN security is perhaps a more critical function of overall network security due to the fact that extranet VPNs rely on the security of business partners. Unlike remote office or branch networks that fall under the jurisdiction of the corporate security umbrella, extranet partners that connect into a corporate DMZ through a VPN might not follow the same methods or implement the same security policies. It is not unheard of for a secure network to be exploited by an attacker taking advantage of an extranet partner's VPN. This leads to the need to apply differing levels of trust to each VPN tunnel termination point. Many VPN appliances allow for the application of IP filters in the tunnel, much like a firewall. To ensure the highest level of security in the case of an extranet partner whose network security status is unknown, it is best to terminate the VPN tunnel at the edge router or at a VPN appliance in a designated DMZ off the firewall. These two cases are illustrated in this section.

In Figure 10.12, the termination point for the VPN tunnel allows the extranet partner's traffic to access the DMZ between the firewall and the edge router. This allows the tunnel to bypass the ACL on the edge router's external interface but still requires the traffic to comply with the firewall's security policy. In Figure 10.13, the tunnel is terminated at a VPN appliance in a second DMZ leg of the firewall. This tunnel also bypasses the ACL on the edge router as well as the security policy on the *external* interface of the firewall, but—in order for the traffic to access devices within the corporate headquarters network—the traffic must comply with a defined security policy on the firewall's DMZ interface. The traffic permitted by policy defined on this interface could be considerably different from the traffic permitted by the policy on the firewall's external interface. This provides the flexibility to provide a higher level of trust between the extranet partner's network and the corporate network. As an added level of security, you can deploy IDS at the extranet tunnel termination point to monitor traffic arriving from the external partner network.

Figure 10.12 Extranet VPN Termination on an Edge Router

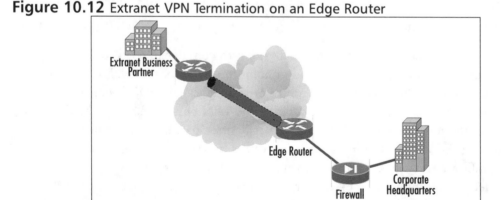

Figure 10.13 Extranet VPN Termination at a VPN Appliance

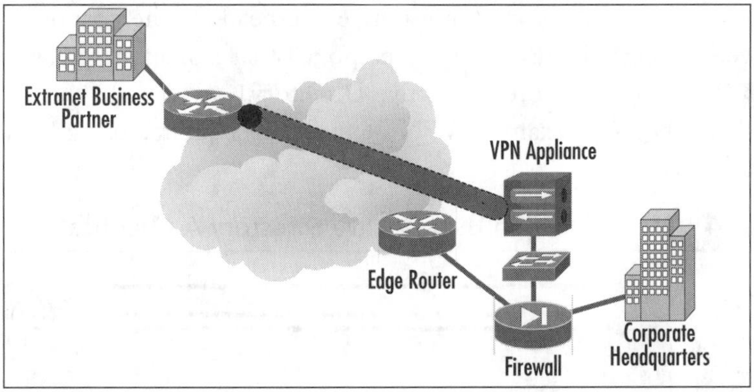

Configuring & Implementing...

Vendor IPSec Enhancements

One of the key issues that must be addressed when you're designing an IPSec VPN solution for extranets is the equipment to be used. IPSec itself is an IETF standard based on a whole range of RFCs, but there has been enough leeway and confusion in the development of IPSec that vendors have implemented proprietary enhancements to the protocols. At best, these enhancements can result in no impact in the configuration and implementation of the VPN. At worst, they can, in some cases, result in significant difficulties in getting a VPN tunnel to work, if at all. The IETF is working on resolving the issues with vendor enhancements to the IPSec protocol, but this solution is not currently available and might not be for another 12 to 18 months. The simple workaround is to ensure that either both parties are using the same vendor's VPN product or that the products being used are tested and certified as compatible with other vendor VPN equipment.

Active Directory Security

It might be that a business partner requires more access to your corporate network than just data on a group of servers. Other methods, such as data mirroring or utilizing dual–homed servers, can accommodate such a case, the practical and more secure solution is to implement such a design using an IPSec VPN. Microsoft provides integrated software on the Windows server that allows for the deployment of a quick and easy VPN solution to address this scenario. This solution provides for greater ease on the part of the remote user as well as lower administrative overhead for the corporate administrator and is achieved through the use of an IPSec policy that is maintained and managed using Group Policy objects stored in Active Directory.

Figure 10.14 shows an example VPN connection sequence using Windows Active Directory authentication.

Figure 10.14 VPN Connection Using Active Directory Authentication

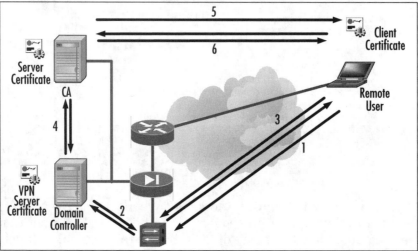

Here is the sequence of steps used in the authentication of the user:

1. The remote user initiates a request to access the network via VPN connection. The user logs in using her username and password for the domain.

2. The VPN server requests authentication from the domain controller. If the VPN server is able to authenticate to the domain controller, the VPN server checks the authorization of the requesting user for VPN access.

3. If the domain controller authorizes the requesting user for VPN access, the VPN server and the remote client start an IKE exchange.

4. The domain controller authenticates the CA server and authorizes the CA server to issue a certificate to the remote user.

5. The remote user is issued a certificate from the CA. This certificate allows the encryption process to finish.

6. The IPSec VPN is now established and the remote user is able to access the corporate network with all the permissions she normally would have as if she were physically present at the corporate network and connected to it.

Summary

VPNs have quickly come to supplant traditional WAN technologies such as Frame Relay, leased lines, and dialup networks. They reduce the total cost of ownership of the WAN by eliminating recurring costs associated with those technologies and utilizing the underlying and nascent IP technology a company has deployed. The key to VPN utilization in a DMZ focuses on the deployment of the VPN in the DMZ itself. There are three primary methods of terminating VPN tunnels in a DMZ: at the edge router, at the firewall, and at a dedicated appliance in a DMZ leg of the firewall. Each method has its advantages and disadvantages. Terminating the VPN at the edge router allows traffic to reach servers outside the firewall or in the same leg of the firewall as the VPN appliance. Terminating a VPN tunnel at the inside interface of a firewall, however, allows direct access to the internal network, which could actually lower the security posture of the internal network.

In addition to these deployment models, there are four deployment topologies to consider: mesh (both fully and partially), star, hub and spoke, and remote access. Each topology has advantages and disadvantages that should be carefully considered before implementation.

Once the deployment method and topology for the VPN have been chosen, the next step is to identify and design an IPSec security solution. This step includes identifying the encryption algorithm to use as well as the type of IPSec protocol and transport method. Tunnel negotiation characteristics must be decided as well in order to ensure that both sides of the tunnel are configured properly. Determining the IPSec security policy will identify the traffic characteristics used to distinguish traffic destined for the IPSec VPN tunnel and traffic that will bypass the tunnel.

VPNs have advanced a long way since the days of leased lines and Frame Relay. The development of IPSec and other technologies has vastly changed the landscape with regard to WAN deployment, extranet partner connections, and B2B interaction and communication. As VPNs continue to mature, they will become the dominant force in these areas by helping drive down the total cost of ownership of the WAN.

Solutions Fast Track

VPN Services in the DMZ

☑ There are three general deployment models of VPN services in the DMZ: at the edge router, at the internal interface of the firewall, and at a dedicated VPN device in a DMZ leg of a firewall.

☑ The four topologies for VPNs are mesh (both fully and partially), star topology, hub–and–spoke topology, and remote access.

☑ The difference between a star topology and a hub–and–spoke topology lies in the fact that in a star topology, the branch or stub networks are not able to communicate with one another. They can only communicate with the central corporate network.

☑ IPSec is not capable of traversing NAT devices without some modification. The problem comes when the NAT device changes information in the IP header of the IPSec packet. The changes will result in an incorrect IPSec checksum that is calculated over parts of the IP header. There are workarounds for this problem., however.

☑ When the number of VPNs connecting to the router, firewall, or VPN appliance becomes sufficiently large, it might be necessary to install a VPN accelerator module (VAM) into the device to offload many of the cryptographic functions used in the VPN.

Designing an IPSec Solution

☑ There are three main choices for encryption schemes in IPSec: DES, 3DES, and AES. AES deployment is not as wide at present, so it might not be possible to use that encryption algorithm. DES has been proven insecure against an attack with sufficient resources. 3DES is the only current algorithm that is widely available and provably secure.

☑ Message integrity is provided through the use of the MD5, SHA-1, or HMAC hash algorithms.

☑ Before an IPSec VPN tunnel can be established, the session parameters must be negotiated through the use of Internet Key Exchange.

☑ IPSec security policies define the traffic permitted to enter the VPN tunnel.

Connecting B2B Sites

☑ Extranets are B2B networks based on Internet network technology. An extranet can be viewed as part of a company's intranet that is made accessible to other companies, to the public, or that comprises components that enable collaboration with other companies.

☑ For partner extranets, there are two possible VPN deployment models: VPN tunnel termination at the edge router or VPN tunnel termination at a dedicated device on a DMZ leg of the firewall.

☑ VPN security is a critical function of overall network security due to the fact that extranet VPNs rely on the security of the business partners.

Frequently Asked Questions

The following Frequently Asked Questions, answered by the authors of this book, are designed to both measure your understanding of the concepts presented in this chapter and to assist you with real-life implementation of these concepts. To have your questions about this chapter answered by the author, browse to **www.syngress.com/solutions** and click on the **"Ask the Author"** form. You will also gain access to thousands of other FAQs at ITFAQnet.com.

Q: Why does IPSec have difficulty traversing a NAT firewall unmodified?

A: Incompatibilities between NAT and IPSec can be caused by myriad issues, some of which are described here:

- The AH incorporates the IP source and destination addresses in the keyed message integrity check. NAT devices make changes to address fields and therefore invalidate the message integrity check.

- TCP and UDP checksums have a dependency on the IP source and destination addresses through inclusion of the "pseudo-header" in the calculation IPSec. ESP only passes unimpeded through a NAT device if TCP/UDP are not involved. This can be accomplished through the use of IPSec tunnel mode or IPSec/GRE. It is also possible for ESP to pass unimpeded through a NAT device if checksums are not calculated (as is done with IPv4 UDP).

For a more complete overview of problems between NAT and IPSec, see the IETF Security working group's Internet draft, "IPSec-NAT Compatibility Requirements," at www.ietf.org/internet-drafts/draft-ietf-ipsec-nat-reqts-04.txt.

Q: How does IKE work?

A: The Internet Key Exchange (IKE) protocol is designed to provide mutual authentication of systems as well as the establishment of a shared secret key to create in IPSec SA. IKE operates in two phases. Phase 1 provides mutual authentication of the systems as well as the establishment of session keys and is known as the ISAKMP SA. Phase 2 provides for setting up the IPSec SA.

Q: What is the significance of terminating a VPN tunnel on a firewall's internal interface?

A: Terminating a VPN tunnel on a firewall's internal interface allows all VPN traffic to access the internal directory in one hop. This might not be desirable, and if IP filters cannot be applied to VPN tunnel traffic, other methods, such as having the VPN tunnel terminate within an isolated VLAN, must be employed to restrict the traffic.

Q: What is the benefit of placing the VPN appliance in a DMZ leg of the firewall, as was shown in Figure 10.11?

A: Placing the VPN appliance in a DMZ leg of the firewall allows for the application of a unique firewall policy that is specific for the VPN traffic. The public interface of the VPN appliance sits outside the firewall while the private interface is in the DMZ leg of the firewall.

Q: What other types of VPNs are available besides IPSec?

A: Other VPN technologies do exist. They include Point-to-Point Transport Protocol (PPTP), which was originally developed by Microsoft, and Layer 2 Tunneling Protocol (L2TP), which was a merger of Microsoft's PPTP and Cisco Systems' Layer 2 Forwarding (L2F) protocol. PPTP is defined in RFC 2637, and L2TP is defined in RFC 2661.

## Chapter 11

Implementing Wireless DMZs

Solutions in this chapter:

- **Implementing a Wireless Gateway with Reef Edge Dolphin**

- **Implementing RADIUS with Cisco LEAP**

- ☑ **Summary**

- ☑ **Solutions Fast Track**

- ☑ **Frequently Asked Questions**

Introduction

As they say, talk is cheap. In Chapter 4, we examined the various reasons that your wireless network segment is not to be trusted in the same way that you would normally trust a wired network segment and the reasons that a WDMZ is needed. In Chapter 4, we also looked at some basic wireless DMZ designs; we implement those designs in this chapter. (If you need a refresher on WDMZ fundamentals, please revisit Chapter 4.) With a wired DMZ, you are attempting to (for the most part) control the type of traffic going into and out of your network. This is not completely the case with WDMZ implementations, however. As you saw previously, the number-one concern with WLANs is controlling access—who can get on your wireless network and how you control that access.

The ways you can implement security on your wireless network are varied and limited only by your imagination. As outlined in Chapter 4, the measures you can take to increase security are not limited only to implementing DMZs or VPNs but also include many items that could be characterized as good administrative practices. In the following sections, we examine some potential solutions that you might implement to provide the net effect of a DMZ for your WLAN.

These solutions are certainly not all inclusive—you can add to them as you see fit or even create your own solutions. Many fine products are on the market that you can leverage to increase your network's security by controlling access to your wireless network. This chapter looks at a couple of them in depth so that you can utilize them immediately within your WLAN infrastructure.

Implementing a Wireless Gateway with Reef Edge Dolphin

The first solution we examine is freeware. Free is always a good thing, especially in the IT industry! Reef Edge (www.reefedge.com) produces several commercial products for use in securing wireless networks, including Connect Manager. Dolphin is a somewhat scaled-down version of Connect Manager that still provides the same basic features as well as being free.

Dolphin runs a hardened version of Linux and, once installed, acts almost the same as any other network appliance. The chief difference is that console and Telnet logins are not supported; all access is via the SSL-secured Web interface. An aging piece of Intel 586 hardware can be quickly and easily transformed into a secure wireless gateway, proving access control from the wireless network to the wired network, which we demonstrate in this chapter. Dolphin is a noncommercial product and not to be used in large implementations, but it does provide an ideal (and affordable) solution for SOHO applications and serves as an excellent test bed for administrators who want to get their feet wet with wireless without opening their networks to nefarious individuals. If you find that Dolphin is to your liking, you might want to consider contacting Reef Edge to purchase Connect Manager or an edge controller. You will be able to easily move up to these solutions with the knowledge you gain by configuring and using Dolphin.

NOTE

SSL was developed in 1996 by Netscape Communications to enable secure transmission of information over the Internet between the client end (Web browsers) and Web servers. SSL operates between the application and transport layers and requires no actions on the part of the user. SSL is not a transparent protocol that can be used with any application layer protocol; instead, it works only with those application layer protocols for which it has been explicitly implemented. Common transport layer protocols that make use of SSL include HTTP, SMTP, and NNTP.

SSL provides the three tenants of PKI security to users:

- **Authentication** Ensures that the message being received is from the individual claiming to send it.
- **Confidentiality** Ensures that the message cannot be read by anyone other than the intended recipient.
- **Integrity** Ensures that the message is authentic and has not been altered in any way since leaving the sender.

Dolphin provides some robust features that are typically found in very expensive hardware-based solutions, including secure authentication, IPSec security, and session roaming across subnets. Users authenticate to the Dolphin server over the WLAN using SSL-secured communications and then are granted access to the wired network. Dolphin supports two groups of users, users and guests, and you can control the access and quality of service of each group as follows:

- **Users** Trusted users who can use IPSec to secure their connection and access all resources.

- **Guests** Unknown users who are not allowed to use IPSec to secure their communications and have access control restrictions in place.

Lastly, Dolphin supports encrypted wireless network usage through IPSec tunnels. Through the creation of IPSec VPN tunnels, users can pass data with a higher level of security (encryption) than WEP provides.

To begin working with Dolphin, you need to register for the Reef Edge TechZone at http://techzone.reefedge.com. Once this is done, you will be able to download the

CD-ROM ISO image and bootable diskette image files from the Reef Edge download page. The server that you are using for Dolphin must meet the following minimum specifications:

- Pentium CPU (586) or higher

- 64MB RAM

- 64MB IDE hard drive as the first boot IDE device

- IDE CD-ROM

- Diskette drive if the CD-ROM drive being used is not El Torrito compliant (see www.area51partners.com/files/eltorito.pdf for more information on this specification)

- Two PCI network adapters from the following list of compatible network adapters:

  - 3Com 3c59x family (not 3c905x)

  - National Semiconductor 8390 family

  - Intel EtherExpress 100

  - NE2000/pci

  - PCNet32

  - Tulip family

The Dolphin implementation is depicted in Figure 11.1.

Figure 11.1 Dolphin Provides Gateway Services for the Wireless Network

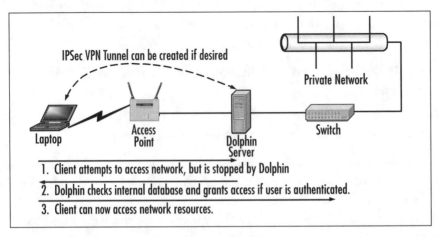

Installing Dolphin

Once you've gathered all the required items, you can begin installing Dolphin on your server. To do so, perform these steps:

1. Create the CD-ROM from the ISO image. If required, create the bootable diskette from the floppy disk image.

2. Connect a keyboard, mouse, and monitor to the Dolphin server.

3. Power on the Dolphin server and place the Dolphin CD-ROM in the CD-ROM drive. If your computer is not capable of booting directly from the CD, you will also need to use the boot diskette.

4. When prompted to start the installation, select **OK**.

5. When prompted, accept the **EULA**.

6. When prompted, acknowledge that installing Dolphin will erase the contents of the first physical disk.

7. After the installation has been completed, restart the Dolphin server as prompted.

8. After the restart, you will see a long series of dots followed by this message:

    ```
    System Ready.  IP address:   192.168.0.1/255.255.255.0.
    ```

    This value represents the wired side of the Dolphin server and can be changed later if you desire by completing the steps in the "Configuring Dolphin" section of this chapter.

9. You will need to determine which network adapter is which on the Dolphin server. Configure the network adapter on your management station with the IP address of 10.10.10.10 and a subnet mask of 255.255.255.0, as shown in Figure 11.2.

Figure 11.2 Configuring the Network Adapter

10. Using a crossover cable connected directly between your management station and one of the network adapters on the Dolphin server, ping the Dolphin server with an IP address of 10.10.10.1. If you get an echo reply, as shown in Figure 11.3, you have located the wireless side of the Dolphin server. If you don't get an echo reply, make the connection to the other network adapter on the Dolphin server. Attempt to ping the other network adapter on the Dolphin server with the IP address of 10.10.10.1 to verify connectivity.

Figure 11.3 Finding the Wireless Side of the Dolphin Server

11. The wired side of the Dolphin server initially has the IP address of 192.168.0.1 with a subnet mask of 255.255.255.0, as mentioned in Step 8. You can, however, change the IP addresses and subnet masks of both the wireless and wired side of the Dolphin server if you so desire, as discussed in the next section, "Configuring Dolphin."

12. Configure your management station with an IP address in the 192.168.0.x range, such as 192.168.0.180, and connect it to the wired side (192.168.0.1) of the Dolphin server, preferably through a switch, but you can use a crossover cable to make a direct connection.

13. Configure your wireless client for DHCP so that it can receive an IP address and DNS server information from the Dolphin server. (You can change the DHCP values passed out later in this procedure.)

14. Connect the AP to the wireless side of the Dolphin server (10.10.10.1). Ensure that the AP and the wireless side of the Dolphin server are configured correctly, with IP addresses on the same subnet. You should now have an arrangement like the one shown in Figure 11.4.

Figure 11.4 Making the Dolphin Connections

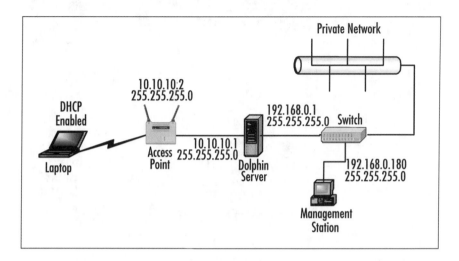

15. Force the wireless client to renew its DHCP lease and check to see that that it looks something like the one shown in Figure 11.5.

Figure 11.5 Verifying the DHCP Lease

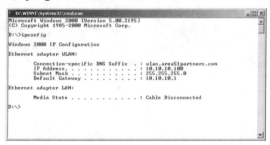

16. From the wireless client, ping the Dolphin server wireless side at 10.10.10.1 to verify connectivity.

17. From the wireless client, ping the Dolphin server wireless side again, using the DNS name mobile.domain.

18. From the wireless client, attempt to access resources on the wired network. Acknowledge the SSL connection if prompted to do so (although you won't actually see any SSL-secured pages until you attempt to log in in the next step). If you see the Web page in Figure 11.6, congratulate yourself—your Dolphin installation is operating properly!

Figure 11.6 Connecting to the Dolphin Server

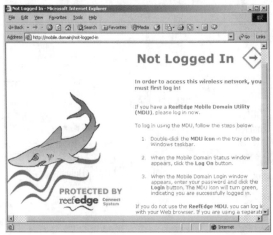

19.   Log in from the page shown in Figure 11.7 using the username **temp** and the password **temp**.

> **NOTE**
>
> Although these are the default credentials to enter your Dolphin system, it is critical that you change them once you are done with the initial configuration. Once you have created your first user account, Dolphin will delete the temp account for you automatically to ensure that no one compromises the server or gains unauthorized network access.

Figure 11.7 Logging into the Dolphin Web Page

20. If login is successful, you will see the page shown in Figure 11.8. Notice that the IPSec key shown at the bottom of the page is actually your shared key that you would use to create IPSec connections.

Figure 11.8 Login Is Successful

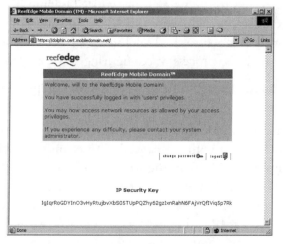

21. You can now log in to the Dolphin Web management interface by entering **https://mobile.domain/admin** into your browser. You will be prompted to log in as shown in Figure 11.9.

Figure 11.9 Logging into the Administrative Interface

NOTE

If you don't have a crossover cable, you can use a switch or hub and two standard straight-through cables. Simply connect the Dolphin server to the management station through the switch or hub. Ensure that you are using the uplink port on the switch or hub and, if required by your hardware, ensure that the uplink port is selected for uplink via regular use. Also make sure that you are on the right network segment with correct IP addressing configured.

Configuring Dolphin

Your Dolphin server is now installed and operable on your wireless network. You now need to perform some configuration and management tasks before your server is ready to be placed into production. You need to add users to the Dolphin database who will be allowed to gain access to the wireless network. (Dolphin does not support RADIUS and thus must use a local user database.) In addition, you might want to change the IP addresses and subnets assigned to the Dolphin server network adapters. The following steps walk you through the process of configuring some of these options:

1. Log in to the Dolphin server by completing Steps 18–21 of the previous procedure.

2. From the menu on the left side of the window, click the **Wired LAN** link. This provides you with the capability to change the wired-side properties, as shown in Figure 11.10. In most cases, you'll need to change the wired-side IP address from the default configuration of 192.168.0.1 because this is typically reserved for use by the default gateway. Be sure to enter the default gateway and DNS server IP addresses as well to enable wireless network clients to access network resources. After making your changes, click the **Save** button. (Note that you will have to restart the Dolphin server to commit the changes to the running configuration. You can, however, make all your changes and then restart the server.)

Figure 11.10 Changing the Wired-Side Network Properties

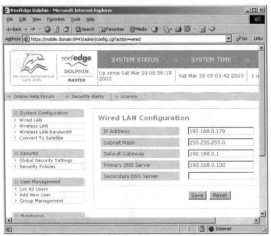

3. Click the **Wireless LAN** link to configure the wireless-side properties, as shown in Figure 11.11. You can change all these properties as you see fit. By

default, the Dolphin server is configured with the domain name reefedge.com and DHCP address range of 10.10.10.10–10.10.10.253. After making your changes, click the **Save** button.

Figure 11.11 Changing the Wireless-Side Network Properties

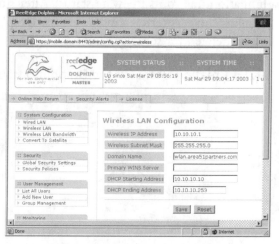

4. If you want to configure the quality of service that wireless clients receive, click the **Wireless LAN Bandwidth** link to configure your values, as shown in Figure 11.12. After making your changes, click the **Save** button.

Figure 11.12 Dolphin Provides Quality of Service Controls for Wireless Clients

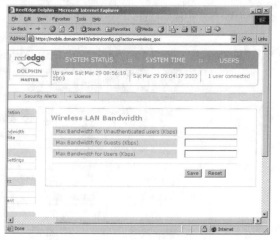

5. You need to create a list of authorized users for Dolphin—that is, a listing of users who can authenticate to Dolphin and then be granted wireless network access. Click the **Add New User** link to open the User Management page shown in Figure 11.13. Note that you can only choose between the users group and the guests group—Dolphin does not support creating custom groups (a limitation due to its freeware status). After supplying the required information, click **Save**. After creating your first Dolphin user, the "temp" account will be deleted for security reasons.

Figure 11.13 Creating Users for the Dolphin Database

6. If you want to configure additional security policies, click the **Security Policies** link to open the Security Policies for User Groups page shown in Figure 11.14. This page allows you to configure the equivalent of a firewall rule set for your Dolphin server.

Figure 11.14 Creating or Modifying Security Policies

7. The last thing you need to do before restarting your Dolphin server is to change the administrative password. To do this, scroll the page all the way to the bottom and click the **Admin Password** link. Click **Save** after making your change (see Figure 11.5).

Figure 11.15 Changing the Administrative Password

8. Restart your Dolphin server. After Dolphin has completed loading, you will see the familiar series of dots, this time followed by the new wired-side IP address that you have configured.

Improving the User Experience

Should you not want authorized users to need to use the Web interface to Dolphin to authenticate, you can equip them with a small utility that Reef Edge also makes available that can be used to perform regular and IPSec secured logins/logouts. The process to install and use this utility is outlined here:

1. Download the **Active TCL** package from Active State at www.activestate.com/Products/Download/Download.plex?id=ActiveTCL and install it onto your wireless client computer.

2. Download the **TCL TLS 1.4** package from Reef Edge's download page. Create a folder called **tls1.4** in the lib directory of the Active TCL installation path and extract the contents of the TLS 1.4 archive into this folder.

3. Download the **dolphin_status.tcl** file, also located at the Reef Edge download page.

4. Once Active TCL has been installed, the dolphin_status.tcl file will act as executable and can be double-clicked to open. Place the dolphin_status.tcl file in a convenient location on the client computer.

5. Execute the **dolphin_status.tcl** file to get the login prompt shown in Figure 11.16. You have the option of creating an IPSec tunnel at this time as well.

Figure 11.16 Using the dolphin_status.tcl File to Log In

6. The tcl file will create a configuration file named *dolphin* in the same directory it is located in.

Configuring & Implementing...

Using Enterprise Wireless Gateways

Don't think of Dolphin as a full-featured EWG. However, you should consider it a wireless gateway. For a full-featured EWG, you might want to consider one of the more capable and robust (and more expensive) solutions that are offered from one of the following vendors:

- **Bluesocket** www.bluesocket.com
- **Columbitech** www.columbitech.com
- **Reef Edge** www.reefedge.com
- **Sputnik** www.sputnik.com
- **Vernier Networks** www.verniernetworks.com
- **Viator Networks** www.viatornetworks.com

These more robust solutions offer the same features as Dolphin—authentication and VPN support—but they also provide many other options, such as RADIUS server support, hot failover support, and multiple protocol support (such as WAP, 3G, and 802.11). The EWG market is still in

Continued

a great deal of flux as vendors try to refine their products. That does not mean, however, that you cannot create very secure solutions using today's technology. A word of caution, though: You should expect to find bugs and other errors with most of these solutions because the technology is still so new. Caveat emptor.

Dolphin Review

As you've seen in this chapter, the Dolphin product provides a very inexpensive solution for small wireless environments. It is very lightweight and has minimal hardware requirements; you most likely have an old PC stuffed in a storage room that could be turned into a dedicated wireless gateway by installing the Dolphin application on it.

On the up side, Dolphin is easy to use and configure, is inexpensive, and provides a relatively good amount of security for smaller organizations. In addition, Dolphin supports the creation of IPSec-secured VPN tunnels between the wireless clients and the Dolphin server. On the down side, Dolphin is limited in the number of users it can support as well as the number of groups you can create to classify users. Dolphin also does not provide for the use of an external RADIUS server. These limitations, however, are clearly stated by Reef Edge because Dolphin is not intended for commercial usage. If you have a small home or office wireless network that needs to be secured by an access-granting device, Dolphin might be an ideal choice for you.

Now that we've spent some time looking at the freeware Dolphin product, let's step up the discussion and examine some more robust (and therefore more costly) solutions that you might implement to secure a larger wireless network and control user access in a larger enterprise environment.

Implementing RADIUS with Cisco LEAP

The use of RADIUS servers to authenticate network users is a longstanding practice. Using a RADIUS server dynamic per-user, per-session WEP keys combined with IV randomization is a fairly new practice. Enter Cisco's proprietary offering (now being used by many third-party vendors), LEAP.

LEAP is one of approximately 30 different variations of the Extensible Authentication Protocol (EAP). Other variants include EAP-MD5, EAP-TLS, EAP-TTLS, and PEAP. EAP allows other security products (such as LEAP) to be used to provide additional security to Point-to-Point Protocol (PPP) links through the use of special Application Programming Interfaces (APIs) that are built into operating systems and, in the case of the Cisco Aironet hardware, hardware device firmware.

LEAP (also known as EAP-Cisco Wireless) uses dynamically generated WEP keys, 802.1x port access controls, and mutual authentication to overcome the problems inherent n WEP. 802.1x is an access control protocol that operates at the port level and sites between any authentication method (LEAP in this case) and the rest of the network. 802.1x does not provide authentication to users; rather, it translates messages from the selected authentication method into the correct frame format being used on the network. In the case of our example, the correct frame format is 802.11, but 802.1x can also be used on 802.3 (Ethernet) and 802.5 (Token Ring) networks, to name a few. When you use 802.1x, the choice of the authentication method and key management method are controlled by the specific EAP authentication being used (LEAP in this case). The basic process by which a user gains access to the network when LEAP and 802.1x are in use was explained in Chapter 4.

NOTE

RADIUS is defined by RFC 2865. The behavior of RADIUS with EAP authentication is defined in RFC 2869. RFC can be searched and viewed online at www.rfc-editor.org. 802.1x is defined by the IEEE in the document located at http://standards.ieee.org/getieee802/download/802.1X-2001.pdf.

LEAP creates a per-user, per-session dynamic WEP key that are tied to the network logon, thereby addressing the limitations of static WEP keys. Since authentication is performed against a back-end RADIUS database, administrative overhead is minimal after initial installation and configuration.

LEAP Features

Through the use of dynamically generated WEP keys, LEAP enhances the basic security WEP provides by significantly decreasing the predictability to the user hoping to determine the WEP key through the use of the WEP key-cracking utility. In addition, the WEP keys that are generated can be tied to the specific user session and, if desired, to the network login as well. Through the usage of Cisco (or other third-party components that support LEAP) hardware from end to end, you can provide a robust and scalable security solution that silently increases network security not only by authenticating users but also by encrypting wireless network traffic without the use of a VPN tunnel. (You can, however, opt to add the additional network overhead and implement a VPN tunnel as well to further secure the communications.)

Cisco LEAP provides the following security enhancements:

- **Mutual authentication** Mutual authentication is performed between the client and the RADIUS server. In addition, the AP and the RADIUS server perform mutual authentication. By using mutual authentication between the components involved, you prevent the introduction of both rogue APs and RADIUS servers. Furthermore, you provide a solid authentication method to control who can and cannot gain access to the wireless network segment (and thus the wired network behind it). All communications carried out between the AP and the RADIUS server are done using a secure channel, further reducing any possibility of eavesdropping or spoofing.

- **Secure-key derivation** A preconfigured shared-secret secure key is used to construct responses to mutual authentication challenges. It is put through an irreversible one-way hash that makes recovery or replay impossible and is useful for one time only at the start of the authentication process.

- **Dynamic WEP keys** Dynamic per-user, per-session WEP keys are created to easily allow administrators to quickly move away from statically configured WEP keys, thus significantly increasing security. The single largest security vul-nerability of a properly secured wireless network (using standard 802.11b security measures) is the usage of static WEP keys that are subject to discovery through special software. In addition, maintaining static WEP keys in an enter-prise environment is an extremely time-consuming and error-prone process. Using LEAP, the session-specific WEP keys that are created are unique to that specific user and are not used by any other user. In addition, the broadcast WEP key (which is statically configured in the AP) is encrypted using the ses-sion key before being delivered to the client. Since each session key is unique to the user and can be tied to a network login, LEAP also completely elimi-nates common vulnerabilities due to lost or stolen network adapters and devices.

- **Reauthentication policies** Policies can be set that force users to reauthenti-cate more often to the RADIUS server and thus receive fresh session keys. This can further reduce the window for network attacks as the WEP keys are rotated even more frequently.

- **Initialization vector changes** The IV is incremented on a per-packet basis, so hackers cannot find a predetermined, predictable sequence to exploit. The capability to change the IV with every packet, combined with the dynamic keying and reauthentication, greatly increases security and makes it that much more difficult for an attacker to gain access to your wireless network.

NOTE

WEP is a shared-key authentication process that uses a pseudo-random number generator and the RC4 stream cipher. The RC4 stream cipher is adequate; however, the weakness in WEP lies in the IV. In most implementations, the IV starts at 0 and is incremented by 1 for each packet transmitted on the network. Given the relatively small number of IVs available (2^{24}), the IV will roll over, given enough time, which can be as little as one to five hours in a busy network. The IV is transmitted in cleartext with each encrypted packet, thus allowing an attacker to easily create a table of packets and compare known packet information to determine the WEP key. Several freeware utilities are available for just this task.

To learn more about the problems associated with the IV, see Chapter 7 of *MCSE/MCSA Implementing and Administering Security in a Windows 2000 Network: Study Guide and DVD Training System (Exam 70-214)* by Will Schmied (Syngress Publishing 2003, ISBN 1931836841).

Building a LEAP Solution

To put together a LEAP with RADIUS solution, you need the following components:

- A Cisco Aironet AP that supports LEAP. Currently, this includes the 350, 1100, and 1200 models. The 350 is the oldest of the bunch and offers the least amount of configurability. The 1100 is the newest and runs IOS, offering both CLI- and GUI-based management and configuration.

- A Cisco Aironet 350 network adapter.

- The most up-to-date network adapter driver, firmware, and Aironet Client Utility (ACU). You can download this driver using the Aironet Wireless Software Selector on the Cisco Web site at www.cisco.com/pcgi-bin/Software/WLAN/wlplanner.cgi.

- A RADIUS server application that supports LEAP. For our purposes, we use Funk Software's (www.funk.com) Steel Belted Radius/Enterprise Edition.

As shown in Chapter 4, our LEAP solution will look (basically) like the diagram shown in Figure 11.17.

Figure 11.17 The Cisco LEAP and RADIUS Solution

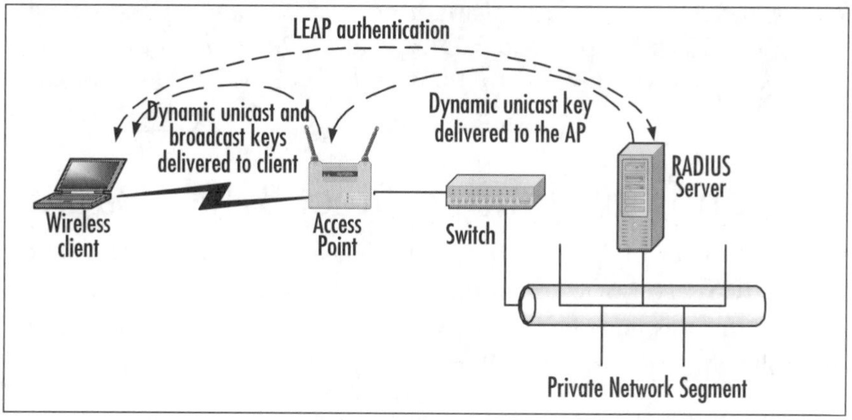

Designing & Planning

Nothing in Life Is Perfect...

LEAP has two potential weaknesses that you need to be aware of.

The first weakness is that the EAP RADIUS packet transmitted between the AP and the RADIUS server is sent in cleartext. This packet contains the shared secret used to perform mutual authentication between these two devices. The reality of this weakness, however, is that you can mitigate its potential effects by having good physical security and network authentication policies for your wired network. An attacker would have to plug directly into a switch sitting between the AP and the RADIUS server and use a special network sniffer capable of sniffing over a switched network, such as dsniff.

The second weakness of LEAP is that the username is transmitted in cleartext between the wireless client and the AP. This opens the door to the possibility of a dictionary attack. Note that the password is encrypted using MS-CHAPv1. Your defense against a dictionary attack on your LEAP user's passwords is to implement a solid login policy for your network. For example, if you are using Active Directory and performing network authentication against it using domain user accounts, you could require strong passwords through the Password Policy options and account lockout through the Account Lockout Policy options.

Continued

> For more information on configuring Active Directory for enhanced security, see *MCSE/MCSA Implementing and Administering Security in a Windows 2000 Network: Study Guide and DVD Training System (Exam 70-214)* by Will Schmied (Syngress Publishing 2003, ISBN 1931836841).

Installing and Configuring Steel Belted Radius

To get started with your LEAP/RADIUS solution, you first need to install and configure the RADIUS server of your choosing. As stated previously, we'll use Steel Belted RADIUS (SBR) for this purpose because it integrates tightly with Cisco LEAP. Perform the following steps to get SBR installed and configured for LEAP:

1. Download the SBR installation package from the Funk Web site (www.funk.com). You can download it for a 30-day trial if you are not ready to purchase.

2. Provide your name and organization's name as well your product key, as shown in Figure 11.18. Note that you can opt to exercise the 30-day trial if you desire. Click **Next** to continue.

Figure 11.18 SBR Has a "Try It Before You Buy It" Feature

3. On the next page, select the **SBR Enterprise Edition** option and click **Next** to continue.

4. Click **Yes** to accept the EULA.

5. Click **Next** to start the setup routine.

6. Select your installation location, as shown in Figure 11.19. Note that you will want to install both the Radius Admin Program and the Radius Server shown in Figure 11.19. Click **Next** to continue.

Figure 11.19 Choosing the Installation Options and Location

7. Continue with the installation routine to complete the installation process.

8. When the installation has completed, ensure that the **Yes, launch Radius Administrator** option is selected, and click **Finish**. The Admin application opens. Select the **Local** option and click the **Connect** button. If the display you see is something like that shown in Figure 11.20, you've successfully installed SBR.

9. Close the **SBR Admin** application to begin the configuration of SBR for LEAP.

Figure 11.20 Launching the Admin Application

10. Navigate to the SBR installation directory and open the **Service** folder. Locate and open the **eap.ini** file for editing. For this example, we use native RADIUS authentication, meaning that users will be authenticating directly against the SBR RADIUS database. (You can, optionally, configure SBR for Windows domain authentication as discussed later in this chapter.) Under the **[Native-User]** heading, remove the semicolon from the first three items to enable LEAP. Save and close the **eap.ini** file (see Figure 11.21).

Figure 11.21 Configuring SBR for LEAP

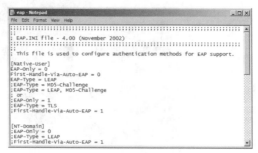

11. From the **Services** console located in the **Administrative Tools** folder, restart the Steel Belted Radius service to force it to reload the eap.ini file. Launch the **SBR Admin** application and connect to the local server.

12. Click the **RAS Clients** option to configure SBR for the Cisco Access Point, as shown in Figure 11.22. Note that the AP is the RAS client since it is performing authentication on behalf of the wireless network client. Click the **Add** button to create a new client, and click **OK** to confirm it. Next, specify the client IP address (the IP address assigned to the AP) and the type of client (Cisco Aironet Access Point).

Figure 11.22 Configuring the RAS Client Properties

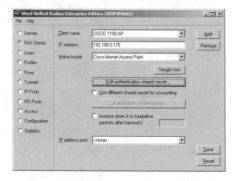

13. Click the **Edit** authentication shared secret button to enter the shared secret to be used for the AP and SBR server to authenticate each other, as shown in Figure 11.23. After entering your shared secret, click the **Set** button to confirm it. (Remember your shared secret; you will need it again when you configure the AP later.) Click the **Save** button on the RAS Clients page to confirm the client details.

Figure 11.23 Entering the Shared Secret

14. Click the **Users** option to create native users (users internal to the SBR server), as shown in Figure 11.24. Click the **Add** button to add a new username. After entering the username, click **OK** to confirm it.

Figure 11.24 Creating Native Users

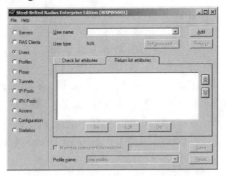

15. Next, click the **Set password** button to open the Enter User Password dialog box shown in Figure 11.25. You need to leave the **Allow PAP or CHAP** option selected because LEAP actually makes use of an MS-CHAPv1 derivative. After setting the password, click the **Set** button to confirm it. Click the **Save** button on the Users page to confirm the user.

Figure 11.25 Entering the User Password

16. Click the **Configuration** option to set the authentication methods (and their order) to be used, as shown in Figure 11.26. Since we are using native users, ensure that the **Native User** option is placed first in the list. Click **Save** to confirm the change if required.

Figure 11.26 Selecting the Authentication Methods

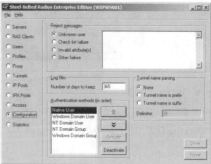

Configuring LEAP

Once you've gotten your RADIUS server installed and configured, the hard work is behind you. All that is left now is to configure LEAP on the AP and client network adapter. To configure LEAP on the AP, perform the following steps. (Note that the exact screen will vary among the 350, 1100, and 1200 APs—the end configuration is the same, however. For this discussion, a Cisco Aironet 1100 AP is used with all configurations performed via the Web interface instead of the CLI.)

1. Log in to your AP via the Web interface.

2. Configure your network SSID and enable EAP authentication, as shown in Figure 11.27. Save your settings to the AP after configuring them.

Figure 11.27 Enabling EAP Authentication

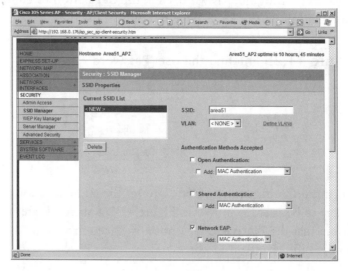

3. Enter a 128-bit broadcast WEP key, as shown in Figure 11.28. Save your set-
    tings to the AP after configuring them.

Figure 11.28 Entering the Broadcast WEP Key

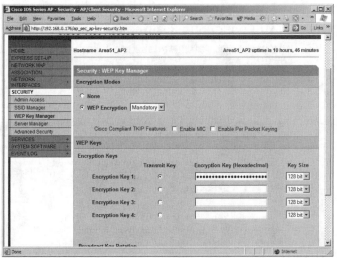

4. Configure your RADIUS server IP address and shared-secret key information,
    as shown in Figure 11.29. In addition, you need to ensure that the **EAP
    Authentication** option is selected. Save your settings to the AP after
    configuring them.

Figure 11.29 Configuring the RADIUS Server Information

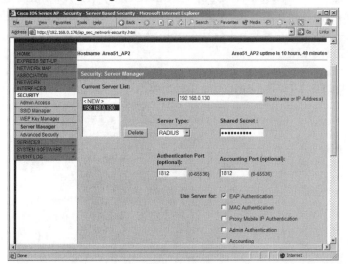

5. If you want to enable a reauthentication policy, you can do so from the Advanced Security, EAP AUTHENTICATION page shown in Figure 11.30. The default option is Disable Reauthentication. Save your settings to the AP after configuring them.

Figure 11.30 Configuring Reauthentication

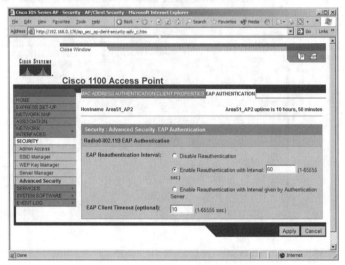

To enable the wireless client for LEAP, first ensure that it is using the most recent firmware and drivers, as discussed previously. Once you've got the most up-to-date files, proceed as follows to get the client configured and authenticated using LEAP:

1. Launch the **Cisco Aironet Client Utility (ACU)**, shown in Figure 11.31. Notice that the ACU reports that the network adapter is not associated with the AP. This is normal at this point because the AP is configured to require LEAP authentication.

Figure 11.31 Using the Cisco ACU

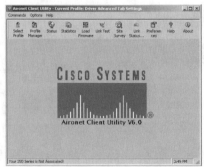

2. Click the **Profile Manager** button to create a new profile, as shown in Figure 11.32. Click the **Add** button to enter the new profile name, and then click the **OK** button to begin configuring the profile.

Figure 11.32 Creating a New Profile

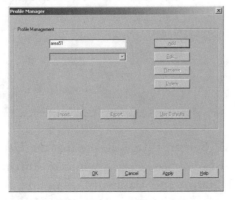

3. On the **System Parameters** tab, shown in Figure 11.33, be sure to enter the correct SSID for your network (as configured previously for the AP).

Figure 11.33 Configuring the SSID for the Profile

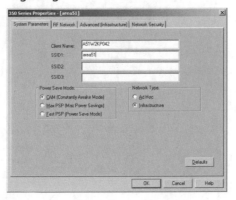

4. Switch to the **Network Security** tab and select **LEAP** from the drop-down list, as shown in Figure 11.34. After selecting LEAP, click the **Configure** button.

Figure 11.34 Configuring the Authentication Method

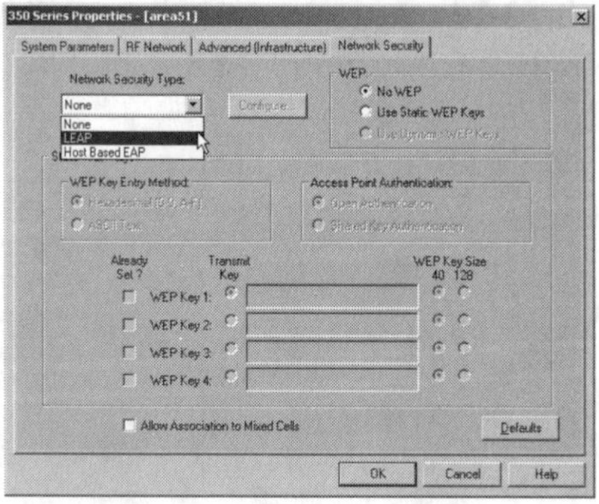

5. On the **LEAP Settings** page, ensure that the **Use Temporary User Name and Password** option is selected with the **Automatically Prompt for LEAP User Name and Password** suboption. Remove the check mark from the **Include Windows Logon Domain with User Name** option because we are using Native mode authentication in this example. Click **OK** after making your configuration (see Figure 11.35).

Figure 11.35 Configuring LEAP Options

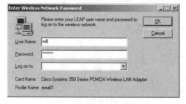

6. Click **OK** twice more and you will be prompted with the LEAP login dialog box shown in Figure 11.36. Enter your details and click **OK**.

Figure 11.36 Logging into the Wireless Network Using LEAP

7. If you look at the SBR Admin application on the Statistics page, you can see successful and failed authentications. Notice that the statistics shown in Figure 11.37 represent clients that are being forced to reauthenticate to the RADIUS server fairly often.

Figure 11.37 Monitoring the RADIUS Server Statistics

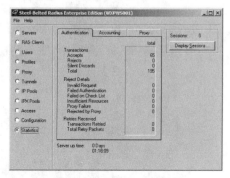

Windows Active Directory Domain Authentication with LEAP and RADIUS

In the preceding sections, we only looked at creating native users in Steel Belted Radius. As mentioned, however, you can create AD domain users and authenticate directly against Active Directory. This offers many advantages, such as preventing dictionary attacks by enforcing account lockout policies. If you want to use domain user accounts for LEAP authentication, you need only perform the following additions and modifications to the procedures we outlined earlier in this chapter:

1. You first need to make modifications to the eap.ini file as shown in Figure 11.38. Under the **[NT-Domain]** heading, remove the semicolon from the first three items to enable LEAP. Save and close the eap.ini file.

Figure 11.38 Modifying the eap.ini File for Domain Authentication

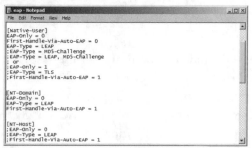

2. From the **Services** console located in the **Administrative Tools** folder, restart the Steel Belted Radius service to force it to reload the eap.ini file. Launch the **SBR Admin** application and connect to the local server. On the **Configuration** page, shown in Figure 11.39, ensure that the **NT Domain User** and **NT Domain Group** options are enabled and are at or near the top of the list. Click **Save** to confirm the change if required.

Figure 11.39 Checking Authentication Methods

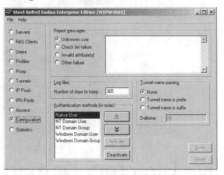

3. Go to the **Users** page and add a new user, as described previously. This time, however, you will have the option to select a domain user, as shown in Figure 11.40. Select your domain user and click **OK**. Click **Save** to confirm the addition of the domain user.

Figure 11.40 Adding a Domain User

4. Open the **ACU** and edit the profile in use (the one you created previously). Switch to the **Network Security** tab and click the **Configure** button next to the Network Security Type drop down (where **LEAP** is selected). Ensure that the **Use Windows User Name and Password** option is selected as shown in Figure 11.41. In addition ensure that a check is placed next to the **Include Windows Login Domain with User Name** option.

Figure 11.41 Configuring LEAP Options for Domain Authentication

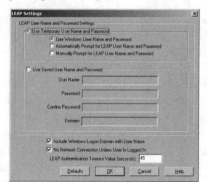

5. Click **OK** three times to save and exit the profile configuration.

6. Login to the network using LEAP and your domain user credentials.

LEAP Review

Now that you've had a chance to examine the workings of Cisco's LEAP, you should see quite a few benefits to be gained through its use. LEAP, implemented with Funk Software's Steel Belted Radius, is an ideal and very robust security solution for any size wireless network. By forcing users to authenticate to a back-end RADIUS server and creating per-user, per-session dynamic WEP keys, LEAP provides greatly enhanced authentication and security for your wireless network.

LEAP addresses all WEP's vulnerabilities and is being implemented into the 802.11b standard by the Wi-Fi Alliance (www.wi-fialliance.org), which has implemented LEAP into its standards under the name of Wi-Fi Protected Access (WPA). You can read more about WPA at the Wi-Fi Alliance Web site. In addition, Cisco has licensed the LEAP technology to several third-party vendors, so you can expect to see many more LEAP-compatible devices in the near future. For example, Apple's AirPort network adapter already supports LEAP with version 2 or better firmware.

Designing & Planning...

Securing Your WLAN

If you feel like you're the one-legged man in the kicking contest when it comes to securing your WLAN, you're not alone. Many solutions exist today, but putting one together for your network can be a complicated and frustrating experience. You can find several local and national consulting organizations, including our own (www.area51partners.com), that can help you figure out what type of security you need and how you can implement it. The problem with all of this, however, is that it does little good to pay someone to come in and implement a solution if you don't plan to have them support it for you in the long run. Furthermore, you might have a hard time selling the expense of many of these solutions to management.

Sometimes it's very hard to find the answers you need unless you know what you are looking for. As with any other IT area, you might consider training for and certifying in wireless networking. Although CompTIA at one time promised a Wireless+ exam and Cisco offers some specialty wireless network certifications, the most obvious choice at the present time is to look into the training and certification offered by Planet3 Wireless. Although not for everyone, the challenging four-level certification program Planet3 offers will get you trained and certified in all aspects of wireless network theory, design, implementation, operation, and security. Check out the training and certification offered by visiting the Planet3 site at www.cwne.com.

Summary

In this chapter we examined two different solutions that can be implemented fairly quickly and easily in your network to create the effect of a DMZ. Recall that in most cases the standard DMZ mentality does not apply to wireless networks. You can, however, still create the net effect of limiting traffic and controlling access by using these (and many other) types of solutions.

The wireless gateway represented by the Dolphin server is a scaled-down version of what you might expect to find in a typical EWG. It provides for network access control by preventing wireless users from going any further than the Dolphin server until the user has authenticated successfully. In addition, Dolphin provides you with the capability to create IPSec VPN tunnels for your wireless clients, thus adding data protection to the user authentication. Many vendors are now proving EWG solutions, each with its own caveats and special features. The solution you choose will be decided in part by your needs and in part by what you can acquire in your price range.

Cisco's LEAP is a variation of the standard EAP protocol that provided superior 802.1x port-based access control between LEAP-compliant network adapters and APs. Using a back-end RADIUS server designed to work specifically with LEAP, you can achieve a superb level of security through the use of mutual authentication.

Solutions Fast Track

Implementing a Wireless Gateway with Reef Edge Dolphin

- ☑ Wireless gateways are implemented to control access to the network by authenticating users against an internal or external database.

- ☑ Wireless gateways can also perform other tasks, including enforcing security by group, implementing quality of service bandwidth controls, and many other advanced security functions such as VPN tunnels and mobile IP roaming between APs.

- ☑ Dolphin is a freeware wireless gateway that provides authentication of users against a local database and optional support for IPSec VPN tunnels for data protection. In a small, noncommercial environment, Dolphin can be quickly and economically put into use to increase network security by controlling wireless network access.

Implementing RADIUS with Cisco LEAP

☑ LEAP addresses all the problems inherent in the use of WEP in a wireless network. The largest vulnerabilities come from static WEP keys and the predictability of IVs.

☑ LEAP creates a per-user, per-session dynamic WEP key that are tied to the network logon, thereby addressing the limitations of static WEP keys. Since authentication is performed against a back-end RADIUS database, administrative overhead is minimal after initial installation and configuration.

☑ Policies can be set to force users to reauthenticate more often to the RADIUS server and thus receive fresh session keys. This can further reduce the window for network attacks because the WEP keys are rotated even more frequently.

☑ The IV is changed on a per-packet basis, so hackers cannot find a predetermined, predictable sequence to exploit. The capability to change the IV with every packet, combined with the dynamic keying and reauthentication, greatly increases security and makes it that much more difficult for an attacker to gain access to your wireless network.

Frequently Asked Questions

The following Frequently Asked Questions, answered by the authors of this book, are designed to both measure your understanding of the concepts presented in this chapter and to assist you with real-life implementation of these concepts. To have your questions about this chapter answered by the author, browse to **www.syngress.com/solutions** and click on the **"Ask the Author"** form. You will also gain access to thousands of other FAQs at ITFAQnet.com.

Q: Do I really need to understand the fundamentals of security in order to protect my network?

A: Yes. You might be able to utilize the configuration options available to you from your equipment provider without a full understanding of security fundamentals. However, without a solid background in how security is accomplished, you will never be able to protect your assets from the unknown threats to your network through misconfiguration, back doors provided by the vendor, or new exploits that have not been patched by your vendor.

Q: Isn't just using WEP enough protection from both an authentication and an encryption standpoint?

A: No. Certain tools can break all WEP keys by simply monitoring the network traffic (generally requiring less than 24 hours to do so).

Q: Why is WEP (by the IEEE 802.11b standard) insecure?

A: WEP is insecure for a number of reasons. The first is that the 24-bit IV is too short. Because a new IV is generated for each frame and not for each session, the entire IV key space can be exhausted on a busy network in a matter of hours, resulting in the reuse of IVs. Second, the RC4 algorithm used by WEP has been shown to use a number of weak keys that can be exploited to crack the encryption. Third, because WEP is implemented at Layer 2, it encrypts TCP/IP traffic, which contains a high percentage of well-known and predictable information, making it vulnerable to plaintext attacks.

Q: Where can I find more information on WEP vulnerabilities?

A: Besides being one of the sources that brought WEP vulnerabilities to light, www.isaac.cs.berkeley.edu has links to other Web sites that cover WEP insecurities.

Q: How can I protect my wireless network from eavesdropping by unauthorized individuals?

A: Because wireless devices are half-duplex devices, you cannot wholly prevent your wireless traffic from being listened to by unauthorized individuals. The only defense against eavesdropping is to encrypt Layer 2 and higher traffic whenever possible.

Q: Is LEAP the end-all security solution for wireless networks?

A: No. As we've seen, as good a solution as LEAP is, it still has its weaknesses and vulnerabilities—however small and controllable they might be. The wireless security field is one of the most rapidly changing ones in the area of IT and information security. Newer alternatives, such as EAP-TTLS, are available, and many more will be available in the next few years. The bottom line is that you must find the security solution that offers you the ideal balance—one that gives you the required level of security while still maintaining the desired level of usability.

## Chapter 12

Sun Solaris Bastion Hosts

Solutions in this chapter:

- **Configuring the Fundamentals**
- **Controlling Access to Resources**
- **Auditing Access to Resources**
- **Authentication**
- **Bastion Host Configuration**
- **Sun Solaris Bastion Host Checklists**

- ☑ **Summary**
- ☑ **Solutions Fast Track**
- ☑ **Frequently Asked Questions**

Introduction

Complexity breeds problems. Nowhere is this axiom truer than in the realm of information security. Your DMZ is a complex enough segment as it is; our goal is to keep it as easy to manage as possible. Deciding what servers to place in your DMZ, where to place them, and how they will interact is probably the hardest aspect of the design phase. Each servers populates the DMZ needs special attention with regard to security, and that is the focus of this chapter.

What do we mean when we say that we need to pay special attention to the DMZ-based servers? Imagine your internal network lay bare to the world. That, in essence, is your DMZ segment and the hosts contained within it. Although you could opt to deploy firewalls at your network edge and possibly even internally between logical segments, strict security on the edge of your DMZ is not going to do much to protect the resident servers.

The servers in the DMZ must be able to stand on their own. This chapter shows you, through the concept of minimization, how to secure a computer running the Solaris Operating Environment to the point that it can reliably operate in your DMZ. What the chapter does not show you, however, is a cookie–cutter approach to system security. There is no magic pill you can take to make your system secure. The tasks a Solaris server can be used to accomplish are so numerous, and the specific needs of each type of deployment are so varied, that the most we can hope to accomplish is to lead you toward a methodology and provide some sound baseline examples.

> **NOTE**
>
> In Chapter 3, we looked at the logical design of the Solaris systems within a DMZ segment. In this chapter, we look at the "how to" involved in providing physical resources for these logical tasks. Our goal is to guide you through the decision-making process and provide a framework for the methodology you will employ in configuring a system to reside in the DMZ.

Configuring the Fundamentals

Generally, when deploying a Solaris computer, we install the operating system and then go through the hardening process. Often, however, this hardening process is limited to disabling some unneeded services and removing some default usernames. With a DMZ-resident system, this is not enough. Every component must be scrutinized, starting from the installation onward. Fortunately, the Solaris Operating Environment is ultimately configurable and was created and has been maintained based on the highest level of security concerns. In order to properly secure your DMZ server, you must start this configuration as early as possible, and that means before the installation.

System Installation

Each system in the DMZ should do only one thing; there is no need for general-purpose computing in this environment. Since this is the case, you have a lot more flexibility when it comes to the way that you build the machine. You should only include the absolute minimal elements of the operating environment to support the function for which you are building the system. The reason for this minimalism should be obvious: Vulnerabilities can't hurt you if you don't use the software that opens your network to vulnerabilities.

You might think that simply selecting the Core installation cluster would do the trick. This isn't true, however. Figure 12.1 shows an example of some of the extraneous software that will be included. This screen, which allows you to select additional support you need, is available by selecting **Customize** when you're selecting the software distribution you will install.

Figure 12.1 Core Software Extras

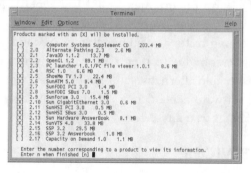

We can remove all the software listed here without any adverse impact on our server. After the entire installation is complete, you'll also want to make sure to remove the extra packages included in the default installation. On my test system, a SparcStation 5, with the Core OS installation, a *pkginfo* command revealed the following packages:

system	SUNWatfsr	AutoFS, (Root)
system	SUNWatfsu	AutoFS, (Usr)
system	SUNWauda	Audio Applications
system	SUNWaudd	Audio Drivers
system	SUNWftpr	FTP Server, (Root)
system	SUNWftpu	FTP Server, (Usr)

system	SUNWil15cs	X11 ISO8859-15 Codeset Support
system	SUNWilcs	X11 ISO8859-1 Codeset Support
system	SUNWnisr	Network Information System, (Root)
system	SUNWnisu	Network Information System, (Usr)
system	SUNWpcelx	3COM EtherLink III PCMCIA Ethernet Driver
system	SUNWpcmci	PCMCIA Card Services, (Root)
system	SUNWpcmcu	PCMCIA Card Services, (Usr)
system	SUNWpcmem	PCMCIA memory card driver
system	SUNWpcser	PCMCIA serial card driver
system	SUNWpsdpr	PCMCIA ATA card driver
system	SUNWsndmr	Sendmail root
system	SUNWsndmu	Sendmail user
system	SUNWxwdv	X Windows System Window Drivers

It is a generally accepted best practice to remove these packages on a DMZ-resident server. For example, if you plan on running a server in the DMZ, you most likely won't need a display attached. Unless you have a compelling reason, you should avoid starting the Common Desktop Environment (CDE) or OpenWindows. These require RPC services, which present several problems for security. First, they rely on the portmapper, which has a long history of vulnerabilities. Second, they are real trouble spots for firewall administration, due to their very nature. Managing your servers via a console connection is a suitable alternative and generally isn't much harder to do. Unfortunately, charting software dependencies is one of the more difficult tasks and boils down to a good deal of trial and error.

Minimizing Services

In addition to superfluous drivers, you get many services you might not need. As an example, even after selecting the Core bundle, you'll have an NFS client and server and an LDAP client. If you aren't planning on using these services, their presence makes little sense. You'll also have Sendmail running, but it won't be the most current version, and the configuration won't be one of your choosing.

The next step we need to accomplish is closing down some of these default services. Like many other operating systems, a default Solaris installation is intended to be easy to use, not necessarily secure. There are many additional services included in even the most minimal installation, but it is a simple task to remove them.

There are two ways that the Solaris Operating Environment can start a daemon: via the *init* process or via *inetd*. The *init* process, PID 1, is the "mother of all processes" and is responsible for running the run control scripts for each run level. These scripts are located in the /etc/rc#.d directories, where # corresponds to the selected run level. Note that Solaris reads each rc directory as it progresses to the final run level; it does not merely read that final level's directory.

You need to examine each rc directory in turn and look for daemons that are being started that you might not want or need. Some of the more obvious examples are:

- /etc/rcS.d:
  - **S65pcmcia** Allows support for pcmcia.
  - **S35cacheos.sh**
  - **S41cachefs.root** Support for the cache file system.
- /etc/rc2.d:
  - **S71rpc** RPC listener
  - **S73nfs.client** NFS client routines
  - **S47asppp** Sun's PPP daemon
  - **S92volmgt** Volume management
  - **S88sendmail** Starts Sendmail
- /etc/rc3.d:
  - **S15nfs.server** NFS server routines.
  - **S73nfs.client**
  - **S76snmpdx**

You also need to examine the /etc/inetd.conf file and comment out some of the silly daemons that are started here. Among these are *sprayd*, a utility intended to test the RPC subsystem. There exists a possibility that a malicious attacker could flood your system with bogus RPC requests and create a DoS condition. Table 12.1 lists the default services started by the *inet* daemon and describes why they should be disabled. Usually we can totally do away with any *inetd* started daemons. There is generally no need for them on your DMZ system.

Table 12.1 Default Services Started by the *inet* Daemon

Service	Description
File Transfer Protocol	Used to allow your computer to act as an FTP server; should be replaced by a secure alternative, such as SSH.
Telnet	Allows users to remotely access your machine, but the authentication information is passed in clear text, as are all the commands and responses. This service should be replaced by SSH.
Trivial Nameservice	An obsolete naming service, maintained for compatibility.
Shell	One of the infamous r* services. Any needed functionality should be replaced by SSH.
Login	One of the infamous r* services. Any needed functionality should be replaced by SSH.
Exec	One of the infamous r* services. Any needed functionality should be replaced by SSH.
Comstat	Used by an archaic mail program; usually not needed.
Talk	Allows users to send each other messages. Since you won't have users on a DMZ system, this functionality is wasted.
UUCP	Another obsolete service that is maintained for compatibility.
Finger	Used to find out information about the users on a system. Since you don't have users (even if you did, you don't want to reveal info about them!), this service is useless.
Time	Connections to this service are greeted with the system time. Not terribly risky, but it is an information leak that you should probably avoid. NTP is a better way of synchronizing clocks, anyway.
Echo	Does just as the name implies. Any input sent to the system is returned to the sender. This service, used in conjunction with the *Chargen* service, can initiate a simple DoS.
Discard	The proverbial bit-bucket.
Chargen	Generates data and can be used to generate a simple DoS attack. www.cert.org/advisories/CA-1996-01.html gives more information.

Continued

Table 12.1 Default Services Started by the *inet* Daemon

Service	Description
Rquotad	Used by the NFS server when quotas are enabled. Since you won't be using NFS, and since you don't have users, you surely don't need this service.
Rusersd	Provides similar information to the finger service and should be disabled for similar reasons.
Sprayd	Intended for testing the RPC subsystem; can also be used to DoS that subsystem.
Walld	Used to send messages to users. Disabled for the reasons we've already covered.
Rstatd	This RPC service can divulge sensitive performance information about your system. You probably don't want that, so it is best to disable.
Printer	Causes your server to accept and process print jobs. Disable this service because *lpd* (the print service software) has a long and troubled history. You don't need it to print.

Additional Steps

After you have installed the operating environment, you'll need to install application software. A key rule at this stage is to do your utmost to use packages. Although many people prefer to compile from source, this practice leads to several problems. Primarily, it requires that a compiler be installed on the system. This is an unnecessary risk and should be avoided as much as possible. You might be wondering why having a compiler on a system is a particularly bothersome risk. You might even be weighing the "risk versus reward."

Although it is true that an attacker with access to your system could download and install a compiler all on his or her own, it is still strongly advised that you not have a compiler resident. Imagine a scenario in which an attacker is on your system and has no compiler available. This malcontent is forced to either download a fairly large compiler installation bundle or download precompiled exploit software. There is a good chance that the attacker will be pressed for time and might not want to spend the extra 10 minutes to download the compiler. Using precompiled binaries would be slightly less likely to succeed, depending on the attacker's skill level. Additionally, your IDS might detect the FTP transfers and alert on them. FTP transfer logs might record the activity. These reasons, and others, all help make the decision to ban compilers. Now consider the scenario in which an attacker has a compiler available on your system. A user with simple access can transfer source code via some covert channel, perhaps as the data in a DNS query, and compile a custom attack program built especially for your machine. This simplifies the attacker's task and minimizes your ability to discover and recover from this attack.

Second, manually building the machines introduces keystrokes. In other words, the probability of human error is increased with each interaction between machine and administrator. For this reason, we want to ensure that all DMZ-resident systems are built using an automated process.

Solaris makes this requirement simple by offering the included Jumpstart software. Taking the time to build your own custom package is well worth the eventual return of time that an automated install gives you.

Configuring & Implementing…

Jumpstart Your Server!

The Jumpstart functionality, included on the Solaris installation media, is used to automate the installation process for a server or groups of servers. There are immediately obvious security benefits of an automated installation and some not so obvious ones as well. Among the latter are:

- The installation via Jumpstart is faster than that done via CD-ROM.
- Configurations can be tightly controlled when all systems are built from the same image.
- Multiple systems can be built simultaneously and without administrative intervention.

However, there are also some risks. The primary caution is to build your systems on a separate network. The Jumpstart software is made available to the system being installed via NFS, and as such the NFS server requires a relaxed security posture. However, the risks can be properly mitigated and provide a sound solution. Another caveat is that since the Jumpstart clients use bootp, which is broadcast, normally configured routers won't forward the request from client to server. Although this problem can be corrected, it is best to simply create an isolated segment for the purpose of Jumpstarting.

Continued

Another very nice feature of Jumpstart is that system configuration, including security settings, can be automated via the use of *finish scripts*. The Jumpstart server runs these scripts after the installation phase has been completed. You can also automate your application installations, leaving you with a production-ready server with minimal fuss!

System Patching

Once you have installed all the applications you plan to use and you have tested and verified functionality, you must apply the latest patches. You should make this practice a way of life. Nothing in the DMZ should remain unpatched for any length of time. There are just too many people out there who feed off well-known vulnerabilities. You have to do your best to remove the proverbial "low-hanging fruit" from their reach.

Patching is relatively simple. Sun publishes the necessary patches for the Operating Environment on its SunSolve Patch Portal, located at http://sunsolve.sun.com/pub-cgi/show.pl?target=patchpage. Once you download the most current patches and uncompress the file, you need do nothing more than run the installation shell script. Again, be aware that patches often change system settings, including security-related settings. Be careful and ensure that security is maintained.

Removing SUID Programs

Another step that you must perform regularly is checking for programs needlessly configured with the SUID or SGID bit. This bit (really a file permission setting) allows any user to execute a program with the same privilege assigned to the owner. Usually, we are concerned with SUID files that allow the executing user to assume the privileges of the root user. A common method to detect these files is via a *find* command such as:

```
find / -type f  \( -perm -u+s -o -perm g+s \) -ls
```

You can redirect the output to a file for later perusal and as a historical record. As we mentioned, you'd be surprised how many times these sneaky files seem to "reset" themselves after some patch or another. The tricky part comes in digesting all the output, and it becomes especially tough when you aren't really familiar with the function of a particular *suid* or *sgid* command. For example, our install of Solaris 8 came with 59 binaries with either *suid* or *sgid* set. Although we know the purpose of many of them, we can't say that for all. This *awk* command is useful:

```
awk '/ f none [246]/ {print}' /var/sadm/install/contents
```

Not only does this command list *suid/sgid* files, but it also includes the package from which those files were installed. Using this command, we can get a little more information about a new or unknown command. Unfortunately, there is no magic bullet that tells you specifically which files can and can't be left *suid/sgid*. Just as with package selection, this is something you need to determine based on your system's needs. Some applications require unusual things. There is help, however. Sun distributes a wonderful tool called FixModes, written by Casper Dik and available at www.sun.com/blueprints/tools/. As the name implies, the tool automatically runs through your file system and corrects some of the permissions on the default installation. It is highly recommended that you test this tool because it saves a lot of headaches and keystrokes.

TCP/IP Stack Hardening

Another setting change you need to make involves the default TCP/IP stack settings. This is done using the *ndd* command, but unfortunately, the changes do not persist on reboot. You'll need to create a custom startup script, say *S99nddconfig*. To do this, create an empty file called *nddconfig* in the /etc/init.d directory and set its owner to root:root and its permissions to 744. The next step is to create symbolic links to this file as both */etc/rc2.d/S99nddconfig* and */etc/rc3.d/S99nddconfig*. This enables the changes to remain in place even after the system restarts.

Now you have a file, but what do you put in it? You need to fill this file with *ndd* commands. Some recognized best-practice settings are:

- *ndd -set /dev/ip ip_forward_src_routed 0*
- *ndd -set /dev/ip ip_forwarding 0*
- *ndd -set /dev/ip ip_forward_directed_broadcasts 0*
- *ndd -set /dev/ip ip_ignore_redirect 1*
- *ndd -set /dev/ip ip_strict_dst_multihoming 1*
- *ndd -set /dev/ip ip_ire_arp_interval 6000*
- *ndd -set /dev/arp arp_cleanup_interval 6000*
- *ndd -set /dev/tcp tcp_strong_iss 2*

You might need to add more to mitigate a SYN flood attack, for example, but these are a good start.

At this point, you have a system that is much more secure than it was "out of the box," but it isn't perfect. We highly recommend that you test and use one of the better open-source and freely available hardening scripts. If you don't think that these canned programs suit your needs, you should opt to create your own. Either way, automating system security is critical to repeatable, predictable settings and is a boon to overall security.

Controlling Access to Resources

Now that we have built our Solaris server, have minimized the installed software, have removed default services, and are communicating on the network, we have a pretty clean and lean machine. Our single-purpose server is listening for connections on only the essential ports, and we are feeling fairly secure. We aren't done yet, however. We have a few additional tasks to complete: We need to restrict *who* can connect to us!

Many people are certain that the only way to secure a DMZ, or any network for that matter, is by the use of a firewall. Certainly, a firewall is a very nice way to easily protect systems, but it is not the only way. Proper host security is often sufficient to make a network firewall redundant. Consider the need for additional security to satisfy "defense in depth." We can defend at the boundary with a firewall, at the host with proper security, and over the network by defining and enforcing trusted communication paths. Figure 12.2 displays a high-level representation of these three areas.

Figure 12.2 Access Control Defense in Depth

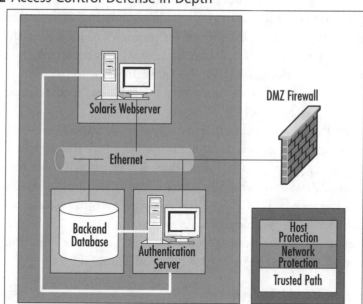

In this section, we examine two methods of protecting who can access the services being offered by a DMZ-based server:

- **Method 1** Access control based on IP address.
- **Method 2** Access control based on cryptographic communications.

Address-Based Access Control

Address-based access control focuses on authenticating the initiator based on its IP address. Although this seems like a weak means of identifying traffic (specifically because IP addresses can be "spoofed," or forged), it is becoming increasingly difficult to spoof IP traffic on the Internet, and with good host security (strong TCP sequence number generation) ,this is a fairly reliable "lightweight" access control method.

One of the most trusted and widely implemented methods of protecting access to a host is the TCP Wrappers program. This program provides:

- Access control based on source or destination address

- Logging of successful connections

- Logging of failed connections

- The ability to respond to suspected malicious activity

The TCP Wrappers program, interestingly enough, was developed in 1990 as a response to a hacker attack on a university computer system. Hackers launched destructive attacks against Eindhoven University of Technology in Eindhoven, the Netherlands. Entire systems were being erased, and there was no way to backtrack the connections or to protect the systems. Fortunately for the university and for the Internet at large, Wietse Venema was employed at the university. His response to the attacks was to develop what we know today as TCP Wrappers.

Unfortunately, this program is not a panacea. TCP Wrappers cannot easily protect heavyweight daemons, such as Sendmail, because of the way they operate. Additionally, TCP Wrappers cannot protect RPC-based services. This shouldn't be too much of a concern for our DMZ system. We really won't be using any RPC-based software on our customer-facing servers. RPC-based servers are, due to the nature of RPC, difficult to secure and provide many problems for firewall administrators. Furthermore, many RPC servers have a history of security vulnerabilities. The more common functions requiring RPC that we won't be using are NFS, NIS, and CDE.

Configuring TCP Wrappers

The TCP Wrappers are configured in the inetd.conf file. The following example displays a common configuration, wrapping the *ftp* and *telnet* daemons:

```
ftp       stream     tcp     nowait   root   /usr/sbin/tcpd    in.ftpd
telnet    stream     tcp     nowait   root   /usr/sbin/tcpd    in.telnetd
```

Notice here that the sixth column has been modified to call *tcpd*, the TCP Wrappers binary. This is as simple as can be, which explains the popularity of this utility. Also note that the third column contains *tcp'* not *tcp6*. Some older versions of TCP Wrappers contained a condition by which all source addresses were shown as 0.0.0.0 and hence denied. This is because those versions of the TCP Wrappers program aren't aware of IP version 6. There are two solutions to this problem. The first is simply to "fall back" to IPv4. This is done by changing the protocol field in the inetd.conf file to *tcp* instead of *tcp6*. The second, more preferred method is to update to a current version of TCP Wrappers and to compile in support for IPv6. You can find an IPv6-aware version of TCP Wrappers at ftp://ftp.porcupine.org/pub/ipv6/. The current version there is 7.6. Be sure to check the Makefile and look for the following:

```
###############################################################
# System dependencies: whether or not your system has IPV6
#
# If your system has IPv6 and supports getipnode* and inet_pton/inet_ntop
# uncomment the following (Solaris 8)


# IPV6 = -DHAVE_IPV6
```

As instructed, uncomment out this line and you'll be back in the game. As usual, the *inetd* daemon must be restarted after the changes. Simply send a *SIGHUP (kill –HUP <PID_of_inetd>)* to the PID of the *inetd* process.

Access to the services we have just modified is controlled via two configuration files, hosts.allow and hosts.deny. Their contents are nearly self-explanatory. Each file is made up of stanzas containing at least three directives, separated by a colon.:

- Field 1 denotes the service that is being described in this stanza and is as found in the inetd.conf file. For example, the entry for *ftp* must start with *in.ftpd*. The entry also supports a wildcard directive, *ALL*. As a rule, use this only in the deny file.

- Field 2 specifies the source address to which this rule is being applied. Multiple addresses can be supplied by separating each with a space. It is essential *not* to use DNS names here. Although they are supported, they introduce the chance of an identity attack via DNS poisoning. You can also use *ALL* here, but the same caveat applies. Additionally, the keyword *LOCAL* is allowed. This keyword uses the netmask and IP of the host to determine if the system is in the same subnet and applies the rule if it is.

- Field 3 is used to supply optional arguments and is itself separated into a colon-separated list. These arguments are where you can get quite clever. The options are:

- **RFC931** Send an *ident* request to the source. We don't find this very useful anymore, but based on the massive volume of *ident* requests blocked by the edge router where we work, someone must!

- **BANNERS /path/to/file** Specifies a file containing a warning banner to be displayed.

- **SPAWN /path/to/command** This allows you to launch a command to react to the connection attempt. This is often used to send an administrative e-mail or to create a log entry of some sort. You can be very creative here. Use this feature to your best ability!

A sample hosts.allow might look like this:

```
In.ftpd: 10.0.0.0/255.255.255.0 192.168.0.101: BANNERS /etc/
    security.banner
In.telnetd: 10.0.0.1 : BANNERS /etc/security.banner
```

A sample hosts.deny file might resemble:

```
ALL: ALL
```

After you have created a configuration sufficient to support your needs, it is vital that you check it for any errors. This is, after all, a security program. We wouldn't want to introduce any vulnerabilities. To this end, TCP Wrappers comes with two utility programs to validate the configuration: *tcpdchck* and *tcpdmatch*. The first of these examines your new inetd.conf file for any errors in syntax; the second allows you to specify a source IP address and learn if it would be blocked. This is actually very handy for those of us not as practiced in calculating subnet membership quickly based on an address and a mask.

Designing & Planning…

Sound the Alarm!

TCP Wrappers (*tcpd*) is in and of itself a handy utility for both logging and controlling access to resources, but it isn't a catchall solution. One of the handier features of *tcpd* is its ability to log information about connections. This ability, however, extends only to the services that are being wrapped. In the case of your DMZ, only a very few services will be offered by each server, and these services will generally be available to the public. The question is, how will we

Continued

detect connection attempts to unauthorized services without opening those services? With *tcpd*, we can't.

Fortunately, there is a solution. For many years, a program called Klaxon has been available. Klaxon listens on a port for connections and logs the information about the connecting system. This allows us to gather statistics about connections without actually having a "heavyweight" daemon active on the port. Deploying Klaxon on some ports used by commonly vulnerable daemons allows you to detect primitive port-scanning attempts.

Notice, however, that we said *connections*. Klaxon can't detect some of the more subtle scanning methods that use crafted packets to elucidate some sort of predictable response. For this, we have another handy tool, called *Tocsin*. This program logs port-scanning attempts that do not actually create a connection and is specifically designed to catch SYN probes. Another benefit is that you only need one system running Tocsin per subnet, because it monitors the entire segment. Both Klaxon and Tocsin are available at www.eng.auburn.edu/~doug/second.html.

Cryptographic Access Control

If you think TCP Wrappers is handy, wait until you use the functionality of IPSec! TCP Wrappers relies on the relatively weak condition of source IP address, but IPSec allows you to use powerful cryptographic mechanisms to define a systemwide policy. This policy also applies to outgoing data, something that TCP Wrappers can't accommodate. There are some drawbacks, but all in all, an IPSec policy is, in and of itself, a tremendous security tool. Combining IPSec with other sensible security measures makes for very good host security.

As we alluded to, an IPSec configuration is called a *policy*. This policy resides in a configuration file, named according to your own standard. The policy file is read and applied to the system using the /usr/sbin/ipsecconf command. The policy file is rather like a firewall configuration file, but you must keep in mind that each stanza only pertains to a traffic flow in one direction. This policy is not stateful, so you must ensure that each outgoing entry has a corresponding inbound entry, if necessary, and vice versa. It is also necessary to realize that since your policy files don't reside in any standard system file, they don't persist after reboot. If you want them to do so, you can configure the policies in the /etc/inet/ipsecinit.conf file. Now that we have the standard caveats out of the way, let's get on to business.

As we mentioned, using a simple policy file and the *ipsecconf* command configures the policy. The *ipsecconf* command has several options, the two most interesting of which are detailed in Table 12.2.

Table 12.2 Options for the *ipsecconf* Command

Option	Description
-d index	Deletes the policy directive specified by the associated index. You can discover the indexes associated with each entry using the *ipsecconf* command without any arguments.
-f	Used to flush (remove) all existing policies configured on the system.
-a filename	Specifies the file to be used to configure the IPSec policy on the system, and puts that configuration into effect.

Creating an IPSec Policy File

The policy file isn't all that complicated. It is composed of configuration stanzas in the form:

```
{pattern} action {properties}
```

The pattern and properties can be composites, but only one action is permitted per stanza. There is pretty good flexibility in creating the elements of the policy entry, and Table 12.3 details the allowable data. Note that the criteria are very broad and allow good flexibility with regard to possible configurations.

Table 12.3 Pattern Configuration Options

Pattern Type	Description
Source address/prefix length	The source address that should be matched. An optional prefix length can be used to specify how many bits of the address are significant. The prefix length should not be specified in the case where you include the source netmask.
Destination address/prefix length	The destination address that should be matched. An optional prefix length can be used to specify how many bits of the address are significant. The prefix length should not be specified in the case where you include the destination netmask.
Source netmask	The source netmask to be matched. This is only significant when the source address has been specified.
Destination netmask	The destination netmask to be matched. This is only significant when the destination address has been specified.

Continued

Table 12.3 Pattern Configuration Options

Pattern Type	Description
Source port	The source port to be matched.
Destination port	The destination port to be matched.
Upper-level protocol	This is the protocol—TCP, for example—to which this policy should apply.

The action field can be any of the following:

- *Apply*
- *Permit*
- *Bypass*

Apply is useful for outgoing packets and is used to apply some defined property to that datastream. *Permit* is specified to allow acceptance of an inbound datagram pursuant to its passage of the policy constraints. These two actions will probably be used on 90 percent of your entries. *Bypass*, which is the highest-priority action, specifies packets (and their direction, such as inbound) that will be allowed to bypass the policy checks. Because *Bypass* is the highest priority action, it will be checked and applied before the other checks. You have been warned. Also be aware that the remaining policy entries will be checked in order, so be careful with that as well.

The third portion of a policy entry is made up of the properties that will be modified on the data packet. This is where we specify the encryption or authentication that will be used. In many cases, encryption here is needless overhead. Generally, it's a good idea to use IPSec as a way to created a trusted communication path for data, not necessarily to protect confidential data. In this case, IPSec's Authentication Header (AH) is sufficient. Table 12.4 describes the authentication and encryption algorithms that can be selected here.

Table 12.4 Encryption and Authentication Configuration Options

Pattern Type	Acceptable Values
Authentication algorithm	This setting, if present, defines the algorithm used for the AH on the packet. It can be any of the following: MD5 HMAC-MD5 SHA1 SHA HMAC-SHA1 HMAC-SHA

Continued

Table 12.4 Encryption and Authentication Configuration Options

Pattern Type	Acceptable Values
	The first two options both describe the MD5 algorithm; the remaining entries all would configure the HMAC-SHA algorithm.
Encryption algorithm	This setting, if present, defines the encryption algorithm to be used for outbound packets and checked for on inbound packets. It can be either of the following: DES or DES-CBC 3DES or 3DES-CBC

Now that you have an idea of what options to use, let's look at how to use them. Figure 12.3 is a sample IPSec policy. The comments, denoted by a line beginning with a hash mark (#), define what each step is doing. We have used sample hostnames for the source and destination addresses. As usual, these must be resolvable. In a DMZ, you are probably best served by using IP addresses. This avoids the potential of an attacker succeeding with a DNS poisoning attack.

Figure 12.3 Simple IPSec Policy

```
# Begin IPSec policy.
# DMZ Private Webserver
#
# Authenticate all traffic to port 80, inbound.
#
{ dport 80 } permit { auth_algs HMAC-SHA1 dir in }
#
# Authenticate traffic between our webserver and a database server.
#
{saddr Webserver daddr Databse } apply { auth_algs HMAC-SHA1 }
#
# Encrypt traffic between our webserver and our loghost
#
{saddr Webserver daddr Logger } apply { encr_algs 3DES }
#
```

Many more advanced configurations are possible with the use of IPSec. For example, you can have defined security associations or use dynamic security associations. You can protect specific ports or protocols or networks. We highly encourage you to be creative and experiment with the IPSec policy in your environment.

At this point, we would be derelict if we didn't mention the emerging *de facto* standard in secure system access: SSH. SSH is a drop-in replacement for the insecure *r*★ services—*rsh, rlogin,* and *rcp.* Although these are simple to use and easy to configure, they are remarkably bad as far as security is concerned. SSH (really *ssh, slogin,* and *scp*) mitigate the weaknesses of the *r*★ commands with cryptographically sound authentication and transport. They can also use TCP Wrapper-like access control, assuming the binaries were built with *libwrap* support. There should be no other method of system access in a DMZ, aside from direct console connections. You'll find the necessary software (free of charge) and lots of documentation at www.openssh.org/. There are also numerous commercial distributions of SSH, if you need to go that route.

Auditing Access to Resources

Knowing what your server is doing is crucial to preserving a secure computing environment. Sun has provided a very robust kernel-level logging program known as the Basic Security Module, or BSM. Also included is the old standard, syslog. The problem is, syslog is as bad as BSM is good. In a DMZ environment, you should do your utmost to avoid the use of syslog. If you must use syslog, be sure to stop it from listening for new messages on all but the central logging machine (if you are using one). In addition, make sure that the central logging system only accepts messages from trusted systems, perhaps using a mechanism like TCP Wrappers, a host or network-based firewall, or as we discuss later, IPSec.

You might wonder why we advise against the use of syslog. After all, it is the standard logging method in the UNIX environment. If it has lasted this long, it must be pretty good, you might suppose. Unfortunately, you would be wrong. In a DMZ environment, centralized logging is critical. Accuracy is also of supreme importance. Syslog struggles in both these requirements:

- Syslog's facility.level configuration method causes the loss of some information that might be interesting.

- The use of UDP as a transport method lacks reliability.

- There is no application-layer integrity checking, thus amplifying the preceding issue.

- Redundant logging is not easily implemented.

- Syslog does not support message authentication.

With these issues in mind, we highly advise the use of a syslog replacement, such as syslog-ng. These replacements usually use TCP as opposed to UDP. They also usually support some sort of authentication mechanism. Syslog-NG has some very nice features, such as the use of regular expressions to filter messages. The specific application-logging method you use is really site specific. WE can't tell you which is best. We merely emphasize that logging must be done—and the more of it, the better.

The SunScreen Basic Security Module

Although syslog, or one of its substitutes, is handy for logging application information, it doesn't provide all the granularity we want in the DMZ environment. To afford such granularity of logging, we opt for the SunScreen BSM. When BSM auditing is enabled, all security-sensitive kernel events produce an audit log. BSM isn't only a kernel-level logging utility, however. The following user programs can also generate an audit entry:

- bin/login
- /usr/bin/su
- /usr/bin/newgrp
- /usr/bin/in.ftpd
- /usr/sbin/rexd
- /usr/sbin/in.uucpd
- /usr/bin/passwd
- /usr/sbin/mountd
- /usr/sbin/crond
- /usr/sbin/init
- /usr/sbin/halt
- /usr/sbin/uadmin

BSM Configuration

As with many things, everything that can be done won't be done. You need to decide which of the available events will be recorded in your audit trail. To begin this selection, you first must understand what exactly an audit event is and the way that the available data is organized. There are a couple of key configuration files used in enabling BSM. The first of these is the audit_class file. This file defines our *classes*. These classes are containers for events and are the selectable, auditable element. The format of the audit_class file is:

```
mask:name:description
```

This file really won't any editing, but it is good to give it a look to see what classes you have available. Example classes are *lo* (login/logout), *ad* (administrative), and *na* (nonattributable). A complete listing of all available audit events can be found in the audit_control(4) manpage. The real importance of this file comes when we map events to a class. The events are more granular, and you might want to do some editing with them. They are configured in the audit_event file. An example from this file is shown in Figure 12.4.

Figure 12.4 An /etc/security/audit_event Sample

```
6165:AUE_ftpd:ftp access:lo,na

6166:AUE_init_solaris:init(1m):ad,na

6167:AUE_uadmin_solaris:uadmin(1m):ad,na

6168:AUE_shutdown_solaris:shutdown(1b):ad,na

6169:AUE_poweroff_solaris:poweroff(1m):ad,na
```

Note that many events make up the class. Since the class is the selectable element, the granularity out of the box might be a bit coarse for some installations. Editing the audit_event file and changing the class assignment is a good way to alter the behavior of BSM. Also note that you can easily define a new class or combine existing classes into larger-scoped single classes.

At this point you have familiarized yourself with the available classes (or maybe created one or two of your own) and you have assigned events to these classes. Now you need to define which of these classes will be logged. The events that will actually generate an audit event are configured in the /etc/security/audit_control file. This file contains entries like the following:

```
dir:/var/audit

flags:lo

minfree:20

naflags:lo
```

The first line directs the *auditd* subsystem to store the audit information in the /var/audit directory. The second line directs that audit events of the *lo* (login) class be recorded. The third line, *minfree:20,* directs the *auditd* subsystem to execute the *audit_warn* shell script when free space falls below 20 percent. The *audit_warn* script generates a warning to the administrator informing him or her of the space problem. The last line, *naflags,* defines the nonattributable events that are to be audited. These define events that cannot be linked with a particular user.

Another file used to configure BSM is the /etc/security/audit_user file. This file contains per-user directives and allows a finer grain of auditing. Perhaps you have some temporary accounts that you offer to consultants, or there is a user who is suspected of malicious operation within the enterprise. You can specify that these accounts be monitored more closely. Conversely, you can also specify flags that will not be audited. To is a very handy tool for creating an investigative or auditor user. If you don't necessarily want their activities messing up the datastream, you can exclude their activity from auditing. The format of the audit_user file is as follows:

```
username:flags_to_audit:flags_to_not_audit
```

The flags are the same as those found in the audit_control file. When you enable BSM auditing of user commands (the *ex* class), it's a good idea to also turn on auditing of the arguments to those commands. By default, BSM only logs the command, which might not be very useful and certainly isn't complete. Entering the *auditconfig* command with the *-setpolicy* option allows you to tighten the scope a little.

```
auditconfig -setpolicy +argv
```

Viewing Audit Data

To process the audit data, you need to use the *auditreduce* and *praduit* commands. The *auditreduce* command is used to select and optionally delete records from the audit file; this command is often used to generate data that will be piped to the *praudit* command. We recommend reading the man pages for each of these commands to familiarize yourself with the many options. Let's take a brief look at some of the more useful ones, presented in Table 12.5.

Table 12.5 Options for the *auditreduce* Command

Option	Description
-r /path	Specifies an alternate audit_root directory. Use this option to view files archived to an alternate directory.
-s server	Specifies a server directory. Use this option if you log to a central server.
-a dste-time	Finds records on or after the specified date and time; can be grouped with the *–b* option to form a range.
-b date-time	Finds records on or before the specified date and time; can be grouped with the *–a* option to form a range.
-d date-time	Selects records from the specified date and time.
-c classes	Allows you to specify a particular audit class.
-u user	Selects the entries for a specific user.

Another very nice way to examine audit logs is by using a GUI. Sun doesn't ship one, but several are available via third parties. One, called bsm.jar, and is a simple Java-based program that you can run on a secondary system, one not connected to the Internet. Figure 12.5 shows you the friendly interface window.

Figure 12.5 BSM GUI

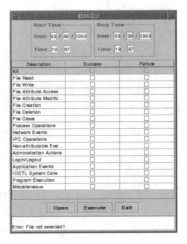

This program, written by Jay Danielsen and available at http://home.twmi.rr.com/jayd/bsm.html, allows you to select an audit log such as those located in the */var/audit* directory and query based on a time range of any of the available event types, as shown in the figure. There is a bit of a performance issue (the author of the code describes it as an alpha release), but the program can come in very handy when you need to look for a specific type of information with minimal fuss. Finally, remember (as always), if you have detected a root-level compromise, *no* log file can be trusted. Although BSM records its data in a binary format, there is nothing to prevent a root-privileged attacker from inserting, deleting, or otherwise altering that data.

Authentication

Mandating that users authenticate themselves to your system is a very good way of adding another layer of security. Unfortunately, it is also a good way of adding a lot of administration. The decision to use authentication in a DMZ environment should be based on several factors. Among these are:

- **The sensitivity of the data being accessed** Obviously, if you are using your DMZ to host an FTP server, which is perhaps used to distribute software fixes, you will likely opt for anonymous access. If, however, that data being distributed consists of sensitive quarterly reports being shared with select business partners, you want to ensure that you know just who is getting what.

■ **The constituency expected to access the data** The people who are going to be using the server is a major factor on the decision to authenticate. You can't expect credentials from a universal constituency, but you surely would from a set of registered customers.

■ **The availability of existing authentication infrastructure** The ability to leverage existing authentication infrastructure will add greatly to the possibilities regarding user authentication. It is unlikely that a new authentication infrastructure would be created for a special-purpose server, but it is not unlikely that the existing client database could be made available.

This list cannot be considered inclusive of all possible factors; many will be determined by your business needs, but the three listed here are a good idea of the dominant considerations.

This section assumes that you are opting to use authentication. It shows you how, using the concept of an *n-tier* design, to securely authenticate to a DMZ–resident authentication server. We don't presume to suggest what authentication method you should use. You have many options.—LDAP, Kerberos, and NIS+, just to name a few. It's even possible to mingle with Microsoft's Active Directory. We also don't presume to suggest configurations for the specific method you have selected. Configuring any of the example authentication methods would fill (and has filled!) an entire book.

Figure 12.6 shows us a very simplified *n-tier* design. In this image, the public server is available for connections from the outside. It is a multihomed system but is not able to pass traffic between those interfaces. The secondary interface on this server is connected to a service network, where reside supporting systems. In this case, we have a database server and an authentication server on this network. We prefer to use obviously different addressing on this service network. For example, if your public server were addressed as 192.168.0.101, you would set the service network to use something from, say, the 10.0.0.0 reserved address space. In this way, it is clear to everyone that this network is "out of band."

Figure 12.6 Conceptual *n-tier* Design

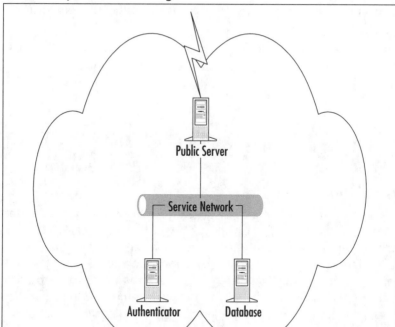

Although some administrators might opt for a firewall to separate the public servers from the private servers, doing so could be overkill. Since we are using a network that is both logically and physically separated, strong host security, including authenticated data communication paths (using IPSec, for example), is sufficient. Additionally, we can avoid the overhead and complexity of introducing a firewall.

Bastion Host Configuration

Now that you have a hardened server running the Solaris Operating Environment, you need to put it into play. In this section, we discuss some of the more commonly deployed server configurations. We start, however, with one thing that should be common among all the configuration types: *chroot*, a UNIX system call that, as you might have guessed, changes the processes view of the file system, causing it to believe that the working directory at the time of the *chroot()* call is actually the root directory. This tool is a boon for security inasmuch as the running process doesn't actually have access to the true file system. This is similar to allowing a user to log on, but setting the user's shell to the restricted shell. It is not, however, a cure-all. There are several ways for a wily user to escape a *chroot()* environment, but the fact that these ways exist doesn't make the *chroot()* functionality less useful. It's a good idea to run any DMZ-resident service within a *chroot()* environment. It's also a good idea to run as a nonprivileged user. This lessens the chance that, if your system is exploited, the exploit can be used to gain additional accesses.

How, exactly, you implement a *chroot()* environment is pretty straightforward, and many good solutions made up of prewritten shell scripts are available.

Configuring & Implementing…

Chroot(): Jail or Playpen?

Although a *chroot()* environment is indeed good for security, please don't consider it a cure for all ills. It is, in the right situation, a trivial matter to escape the restrictions it imposes. On a Web server, where the attacker can expect a Perl interpreter to be available, the execution of a simple script will cause the *chroot* environment to fail. We don't detail here the exact steps to take for the breakout, but rest assured there are numerous exploits, both in traditional languages such as C and in scripted languages such as Perl, available on the Internet.

The moral of this short story is simple: Don't present an attacker the ability to compile programs. In other words, in a security-sensitive environment such as the DMZ, do your best to do without Perl, a C compiler, or any other tools that an attacker might find handy. Don't have FTP or TFTP client software loaded, and limit connections from the inside out to trusted locations. This way, even if an attacker does get into the jail, you are making it as hard as possible for them to escape.

SMTP Relays

Probably one of the most commonly deployed DMZ systems is the mail relay. Furthermore, one of the most common mail relay systems is the ubiquitous Sendmail. Unfortunately, Sendmail also has one of the worst reputations regarding security of any common Internet application. Recent versions of Sendmail have done a lot to diminish that reputation, but we still see exploitable errors in these current versions. Its upside is versatility: Sendmail is so fully featured that most folks won't do without it. Here you'll see how placing a Sendmail server in the DMZ, acting as a mail relay, is the perfect solution for this dilemma.

Initially, let's look at a simplified diagram of a pretty standard DMZ placed SMTP relay. Figure 12.7 shows this diagram, which features internal mail users sending mail to their internal mail system. Mail bound for parts unknown would be forwarded through the firewall and to the Sendmail server within the DMZ. Configuration of the internal mail server is beyond the scope of this section, since it would vary based on the product you have selected (Domino, Exchange, or the like).

Figure 12.7 Simplified Mail Relay Implementation

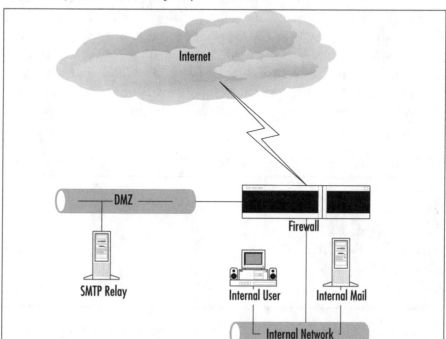

The main goals of having an SMTP relay server external to the network are simple. By separating internal and external mail, we:

- **Protect our internal mail servers from external attack** This is done by limiting communication from the outside to the internal mail server to only those packets coming from the relay system.

- **Provide a security "choke point"** Since all messages, both inbound and outbound, must come through this relay, we can easily check for viruses, screen message content, or check for unwanted attachments.

- **Conceal internal information** Again, since we have a choke point, we can use this system to rewrite message information, such as the domain information. With proper configuration, *joe@hr.east.mycompany.com* can become *joe@mycompany.com*.

Additionally, since the Sendmail server in the DMZ is running only as a mail gateway, we can take advantage its ability to run the Sendmail process as an alternate user, as opposed to the root user. Figure 12.8 demonstrates an example Sendmail configuration that would support these goals. This configuration would be stored in a *sendmail.mc* file and should be saved in */usr/lib/mail/cf*. You need to modify the included Makefile to point to your configuration file or manually execute the *M4* macro processing program. The new sendmail.mc will be relatively simple, merely specifying some system information. The key is the *DOMAIN* directive, which tells the configuration creation processor where to look for more detailed settings. In the case of the default configuration, shown in Figure 12.8, we see that we are telling the M4 program to look for the *solaris-generic* file. The domain files on Solaris are located in */usr/lib/mail/domain*. Modify this line to point to your own domain file. You also need to manually create that domain file.

Figure 12.8 Generic Solaris Sendmail Macro File

```
divert(0)dnl
VERSIONID(`@(#)main-v7sun.mc        1.2  (Sun)  01/27/98')
OSTYPE(solaris2.ml)dnl
DOMAIN(solaris-generic)dnl
MAILER(local)dnl
MAILER(smtp)dnl
```

The domain file is where the heart of the configuration is located. This is where we add unique features, and we keep even those to a minimum. As with every step, minimization is the key. Figure 12.9 shows us a sample domain file, and Table 12.6 explains some of the more interesting settings. Note that we have recommended setting *RUN_AS_USER*. Be very cautions about this *userid*. It should own the Sendmail queue directory, and that's it. No privileges beside that one should be associated with this user.

Figure 12.9 Generic Solaris Domain Macro File

```
FEATURE('masquerade_entire_domain')dnl
FEATURE('masquerade_envelope')dnl
MASQUERADE_AS('mycompany.com')dnl
MASQUERADE_DOMAIN('mycompany.com')dnl
FEATURE('mailertable')dnl
FEATURE('access_db')dnl
MAILER('smtp')dnl
define('confRUN_AS_USER', 'mail:mail')dnl
```

Table 12.6 Generic Solaris Domain Macro File Explanations

Directive	Description
FEATURE('masquerade_entire_domain')dnl	Causes all subdomains of the domain specified in the MASQUERADE_DOMAIN to be masqueraded.
FEATURE('masquerade_envelope')dnl	Rewrites the entire header.
MASQUERADE_AS('mycompany.com')dnl	Defines the domain behind which outgoing messages will be "hidden."
MASQUERADE_DOMAIN ('mycompany.com')dnl	The domain that will be rewritten in the masquerade process.
FEATURE('mailertable')dnl	Defines a file that contains mail-routing information for specific domains.
FEATURE('access_db')dnl	Specifies an access control database file. This file is used to control what domains you will or will not accept mail from.
define('confRUN_AS_USER', 'mail:mail')dnl	The defined user will become the owner of the Sendmail process, all files written by Sendmail, all processes invoked by Sendmail, and so on.

Let's also look at examples for the *mailertable* and access files. These are very simple in format. The *mailertable*, as mentioned, defines where to route mail. The second entry, with a leading dot, indicates that all subdomains will be handled as well as the full domain indicated in the first line.

```
/etc/mail/mailertable:
```

```
mycompany.com              smtp:[internal_mail.mycompany.com]
.mycompany.com             smtp:[internal_mail.mycompany.com]
```

The access file specifies for what domains we will relay mail:
```
/etc/mail/access:
```

```
Connect:internal_mail.mycompany.com    RELAY
To:mycompany.com                            RELAY
```

Note the brackets around the *destinationmail* addresses in the *mailertable* example. These tell Sendmail not to query for MX records but instead to send the mail directly.

Since we know where that mail will be routed, this is the preferable method. Now that you have configured the files in question, you need to format them. You can accomplish this task simply by the *makemap* command. The format to create the /etc/mail/access file, for example, is:

```
makemap hash /etc/mail/access < /etc/mail/access
```

FTP and Web Servers

In my opinion, the single most exposed server types are Web and FTP servers. The best thing to do to ensure the security of your network is to place these servers in a DMZ type network. This does not, however, do much for the overall security of the server itself. Furthermore, due to the way that users interact with these server types, we see a greater potential for vulnerabilities. For example, a custom application may be deployed on a Web server that does insufficient input checking and causes an exposure of the information it is meant to collect. How can you protect against this situation? Additionally, many folks still don't use encryption to protect their data, so data interception is a problem, as is the potential of a replay attack.

You have already taken the first step toward security by buying and reading this book; awareness is critical. By following the examples in these chapters, such as minimizing the installed software base, limiting access to the system by some sort of filtering mechanism, and actively patching your servers, you will go a long way toward protecting the unprotectable. Another key step, running in a *chroot()* environment, will minimize exposure should your security be breached. We often see use of the production Web server for developmental purposes. This should never be done! If software is available, some hacker will find it.

With all this said, we assume that you will be running Apache on this Solaris system. After you've done all the right things, system-wise, be sure to check the following Apache-specific security settings.

- Ensure that the server root directory, all its subdirectories, and its parent branch are all owned by the root user and only writable by the root user.

- Ensure that the httpd executable binary is owned by the root user and not executable by other users.

- If users need to create their own files, create a special "content" directory for them.

- Unless absolutely necessary, disable Server Side Includes (SSI). If necessary, only enable SSI for files with a special extension—for example, .shtml.

- Do not allow script execution in general directories; instead limit execution to defined directories.

- Don't name your executable directory commonly, such as *cgi-bin* or *scripts*. Attackers look here first, and you can key off failed access to these directories as an attack attempt.

- Create a nonprivileged user for Apache to switch to.

- Do not allow content publishers to override security settings on directories. In the server configuration, set the *AllowOverride* to *None*.

- By default, deny access to all files on the system, then open the configuration to allow only specific directories.

With these changes, you will go a good way toward securing the Apache software. As we alluded to, however, the real danger is in the applications running on that server. Vigilance and security awareness are the only fixes there.

Sun Solaris Bastion Hosts Checklists

This section is a quick reference checklist. You shouldn't think that following a checklist is better than using an automated configuration solution. The purpose of this checklist is simply to guide you toward what needs to be done with regard to system hardening.

- Install the Core software bundle.

- Remove any extraneous software packages.

- Install any additional software packages required for your applications.

- Apply the latest patch cluster.

- Remove vulnerable files that cannot be removed as part of a larger package removal.

- Remove or lock out useless user accounts.

- Remove *r** binaries.

- Disable services that are not required both via *inetd* and in the *rc** process.

- Create a *nddconfig* script and add it to the startup process.

- Modify /etc/system to create strong sequence number generation and to protect against buffer overflow attacks.

- Ensure that logging is correctly configured.

- Fix file and directory permissions (FixModes).

- Ensure that the ftpusers file exists and contains the appropriate usernames.

- Check mount options on all file systems.

- Restrict *cron* and *at job* creation.

- Configure appropriate login banners.

- Configure *su* attempts to be logged to syslog by setting SYSLOG=YES in /etc/default/su.

- Set the following values in /etc/default/login. These settings help foil brute-force login attacks:

  - SYSLOG=YES

  - SLEEPTIME=5

  - RETRIES=3

  - SYSLOG_FAILED_LOGINS=0

Summary

This chapter touched on many issues. We started with a default Solaris Operating Environment installation, and through some widely accepted best practices, we turned that system into a battle-ready machine. Although we didn't go into excruciating detail on all the steps, you should now have a good idea of the process. Remember, as always, security is a moving target. The specific steps change from release to release, from vulnerability to vulnerability. The methodology, however, is likely to remain stable for some time to come.

We also covered some of the finer points regarding the configuration of specific system types. The same caveats apply here. You must be sure that you have the most current, secure version of the software. This also implies that you have to be aware of the security features of that software, and you cannot be overly loyal to any one version or software. If Sendmail isn't the solution you need, other solutions are available. If you don't like the default Solaris FTP server, consider *proftp*, or *WU-ftpd*. Both of these are widely supported and available. Just be sure that you do your best and that you remain vigilant and aware.

Solutions Fast Track

Configuring the Fundamentals

☑ Don't rely on the Core software bundle to represent the core functionality of the Operating Environment. Take the extra care necessary to truly minimize the installation.

☑ Follow all the established best practices. If possible in your environment, try some of the automated hardening programs such as YASSP, JASS, or Titan.

☑ Remember, configurations tend to drift. You must actively monitor the settings and ensure that security is kept at a maximum.

Controlling Access to Resources

☑ TCP Wrappers is a nice, easy method to restrict who can connect to services and allows some added functionality for unwanted connections.

☑ IPSec should not be overlooked as a method of access restriction and to protect the links between servers within the DMZ.

☑ If you have a critical system, consider the use of SunScreen as a host-based firewall. You may also use alternatives, such as IPFilter.

Auditing Access to Resources

☑ Do consider alternatives to Solaris' native syslog utility. If you must use syslog, remember to control access to the central server.

☑ Don't be afraid to try a third party logging enhancement, such as syslog-ng.

☑ BSM produces a great deal of data and isn't easy to churn through, but do consider using it. Also try some of the open-source BSM log viewers.

Authentication

☑ Try to take advantage of the flexible authentication options provided by Solaris, including Kerberos or LDAP.

☑ Protect the data channel between the public server and the authentication server. Do not allow any external hosts to connect directly to the authentication server.

☑ Consider using sound authentication mechanisms, thus avoiding the issue of sending a password over the network. S/Key is an example of one such mechanism.

Bastion Host Configuration

☑ Consider using a *chroot()* environment at all times. The *chroot()* function attempts to ensure confinement of your application in the event that it is compromised.

☑ Run applications in the context of a nonprivileged user whenever possible. This minimizes the potential that an exploited application could lead to systemwide exploit.

☑ Be alert and vigilant, and monitor these systems as closely as possible!

Sun Solaris Bastion Hosts Checklists

- ☑ The purpose of the checklist is simply to guide you toward what needs to be done with regard to system hardening.

- ☑ Following a checklist is never preferable to using an automated configuration solution.

Frequently Asked Questions

The following Frequently Asked Questions, answered by the authors of this book, are designed to both measure your understanding of the concepts presented in this chapter and to assist you with real-life implementation of these concepts. To have your questions about this chapter answered by the author, browse to **www.syngress.com/solutions** and click on the **"Ask the Author"** form. You will also gain access to thousands of other FAQs at ITFAQnet.com.

Q: I have heard that there is some uncertainty associated with prosecuting hackers if you don't have a login banner warning them away. You mention that I should configure banners, but what files should contain them?

A: You should configure banners in the following files:

- /etc/default/telnetd
- /etc/default/ftpd
- /etc/issue
- /etc/motd

Q: You mention that I should use a canned hardening script. What are some good choices?

A: There are several, including Titan and YASSP. Sun also distributes a very good hardening process called JASS, which is designed to be run as part of the Jumpstart process, but it can also be run standalone.

Q: You mention creating a *chroot()* environment, but you don't provide much information as to how to do it. Can you shed a little light on this?

A: As the Perl slogan goes, There Is More Than One Way to Do It. Each instance has its peculiarities, so a general approach is not possible. There are a couple of handy references, however. The first is found in the manual page for in.ftpd on your Solaris 8 system. This man page includes a sample shell script to *chroot()* the standard FTPD on Solaris. Another reference is the very well-written article from Sunworld's archives, available at www.theadamsfamily.net/~erek/snort/cell/. It is well worth the read.

Q: Now that I have hardened my Solaris system, how do I monitor for changes to the configuration?

A: Many software programs track this sort of activity. Two popular commercial applications are ESM, from Symantec, and Tripwire. These can both monitor file system changes; ESM features the ability to monitor many more settings (and consequently has a larger footprint). There are also open-sourced software packages, like AIDE. This program is very similar to Tripwire and is freely available.

Q: Do you consider host-based IDS systems beneficial?

A: I am a strong proponent of host-based IDS, but beware the attack of killer data. These systems tend to produce such a bounty of information that an operator can be overwhelmed. With proper tuning and automation, however, these applications can be very beneficial for your security.

Q: Should I consider using a host-based firewall in the DMZ?

A: Many people might consider it overkill, but a host-based firewall could be the right addition in the right circumstances. Most of the security measures we have recommended, such as IPSec, make a host firewall redundant in many situations. When you don't know who will be connecting to you, however, there are few better alternatives. You should consider reading Sun's excellent article on using SunScreen Lite as a host-based firewall. Check out www.sun.com/blueprints.

Q: This chapter focuses on Solaris, but are the solutions proposed applicable to other UNIX and UNIX-like operating systems?

A: Yes and no. Each UNIX system is unique in many ways. The commands, files, and other specifics certainly differ, and sometimes extremely. The methodologies, however, can be applied generally.

## Chapter 13

Windows 2000 Bastion Hosts

Solutions in this chapter:

- Configuring the Fundamentals

- Remote Administration of DMZ Hosts

- Vulnerability-Scan Your Host

- Bastion Host Configuration

- Checklists

☑ Summary

☑ Solutions Fast Track

☑ Frequently Asked Questions

Introduction

In March 2003, Internet trend analysis company Netcraft put the count of Microsoft-based Web servers at over 1 million IP addresses and ranked Internet Information Services (IIS) as the second most popular Web server running on the Internet today (after Apache). Yet Microsoft platforms take a bad rap when it comes to security in a DMZ context. After all, the most noticeable and talked-about Internet worms—Nimda, Code Red, and SQL Sapphire—all live and breed on Windows. However, this does not speak to Windows 2000's built-in security mechanisms so much as it highlights the poor planning that all to often accompanies a new Windows 2000 DMZ server build. This chapter will help you, the systems engineer, avoid the most common pitfalls in deploying Windows 2000 to a hostile Internet-facing environment using mostly on-board, built-in tools.

NOTE

A natural companion to this chapter is Syngress Publishing's *Hack-Proofing Windows 2000*, which goes into more detail on a number of topics not covered in depth here due to space considerations. One chapter alone cannot possibly explore all topics that the 716-page *Hack-Proofing* covers in detail, such as Microsoft's implementation of the IPSec protocol suite, certificate and Kerberos authentication infrastructures, and NT 4.0 to Windows 2000 upgrading mechanisms and strategies.

Furthermore, Microsoft is well aware of its less-than-stellar reputation in the security space—after all, its products are primarily designed for ease of use, with an eye toward serving all possible roles in the enterprise. To address this issue, Redmond launched the Trusted Computing Initiative in 2002, and one result is the excellent reference guide, *Microsoft Windows Security Resource Kit*. Published in March 2003 by Microsoft Press, this 720-page volume and accompanying CD-ROM prove (some would say, finally) that Microsoft has "got religion" about security.

Configuring the Fundamentals

Environmental, network-based security devices such as firewalls and router ACLs generally protect for the services you *do not* intend to offer to the general Internet population (internal e-mail, database manipulation, or server and domain maintenance). Host-based, OS- and application-level security, thus, is necessary to "harden" the services you *do* intend to provide against misuse and unintended exploitation (World Wide Web, file transfer, and e-mail services being the most common).

Furthermore, the DMZ-hardening procedures discussed here are designed to make it difficult for an attacker to use one exploited service in the DMZ to gain further access or control of the entire system, other systems in the environment, or internal systems.

Domain Members or Standalone Servers?

One of the main selling points of Windows 2000 is the ease of remote administration through Active Directory domains and the associated Global Policy Object (GPO) and Organizational Unit (OU) models. The basic premise of these mechanisms is that the changes applied at the domain or OU level will be reflected on all servers in the domain, without the need for visiting each individual device with host-specific credentials. Unfortunately, this same ease of centralized administration can empower an attacker with domain credentials to cause domainwide compromises and outages. With this in mind, you should isolate servers in the DMZ not only from your organization's internal network but from one another as much as possible. Adhering to this configuration philosophy helps ensure that an attacker who manages to totally compromise (or "own," in the hacker parlance) one host in your DMZ cannot easily "island hop" between servers, or worse, gain a direct, logical path to your internal network.

Thus, for the purposes of maximum security, this chapter focuses primarily on standalone servers. This is not to say we abandon the concept of remote administration entirely; after all, most system engineers are loath to visit each of dozens of machines across many data centers simply to install a new, critical patch.

Instead, the configuration guidelines in this chapter will enable an administrator to perform administrative functions on DMZ servers from a central management station in a secure fashion without the need for domain authentication.

If an Active Directory domain structure is absolutely required in your environment, Microsoft does have a white paper available that discusses the network and host configuration steps required in order for AD to function properly. You can find the paper at www.microsoft.com/windows2000/techinfo/planning/activedirectory/adsegment.asp. This paper discusses which ports are required to be open between the DMZ hosts and the domain controller, suggestions for IPSec configuration, and Registry edits to further limit the number of TCP ports needed for authentication and replication.

Finally, most of the techniques outlined in this chapter are applicable to both standalone servers and domain members, so no matter what your situation and security requirements, you should be able to apply the material presented here to your DMZ environment.

Installing from Scratch

To begin, let's start with a clean installation of Windows 2000. It might be a popular topic on Microsoft Certified System Engineer tests, but upgrading an existing installation of NT 4.0 to Windows 2000 is simply too risky when you're building DMZ hosts; too many (and often less than obvious) older, less secure defaults are retained in the name of backward compatibility. You will save yourself a lot of heartache and guesswork down the road by simply backing up your site-specific data (such as a Web or FTP site) and migrating that data over to a brand-new, fresh installation of Windows 2000.

Disk Partitions

Before installation begins, you first partition your available drives into at least two volumes: one for the system partition, where the operating system will live, and one for data, where your Web site (or FTP site) will live. Optionally, you should consider a third partition for logs. If you have the hardware, you should also consider hosting these volumes on separate physical drives and drive arrays. This partitioning strategy is common in UNIX-based environments (with different mount points for /var, /usr, and /home, for example), but it's surprisingly less so in Windows. Partitioning not only increases the separation between the data and system functions of the server; it also simplifies backup and restoration procedures in the case of a failed system partition. Additional disks and disk arrays also allow for easier recovery from physical failures.

Unlike UNIX OSs, Windows does not, by default, require a separate logical "swap" disk. Windows' memory paging is handled by the pagefile.sys file. Some performance increases can be gained by hosting this file on its own physical partition, and separating this IO-intensive file from the main system and data disks can help reduce disk fragmentation on these drives. As a practical example of this configuration's inherent security value, consider Nimda. Most Nimda attacks rely on breaking out of the Web site root directory, traversing the file system, and running the Windows command interpreter by issuing GET requests like this one:

```
GET /scripts/..%5c../winnt/system32/cmd.exe.
```

Because we've separated the operating system from the Web site through disk partitions, this specific attack becomes impossible, even when no security hotfixes are applied.

Of course, during installation, you will choose NTFS as your file system. FAT and FAT32 lack the file-level security required for any reasonably secure host. FAT and FAT32 partitions lack the ability to set the file-level discretionary access control lists (DACLs, or more commonly, ACLs) needed to restrict user access to files and commands, or security access control lists (SACLs) required for auditing access, discussed later in this chapter.

The end result should look something like Figure 13.1, which is a view of the Storage | Disk Management panel in the Computer Management MMC.

Figure 13.1 Separate Disk Volumes

Removing Optional Components

In this chapter, we build a hardened Web server, so all the optional Windows components should be deselected during installation. Either they do not play a direct role in serving Web pages or performing system maintenance (as is the case for Solitaire and Paint) or they require additional, post-installation configuration (such as IIS and Terminal Services) for enhanced security. Note that Figure 13.2 shows all Windows components are deselected during installation.

Figure 13.2 Windows Components

Notice that by default, IIS is selected for installation, but as you can see in the figure, it is deselected here. IIS in Windows 2000 is installed, by default, with virtually all services started, so as soon as a new system is started for the first time, it is immediately susceptible to IIS-based attacks. Rather than taking time out in the initial installation to configure IIS, it's almost always better to hold off on that step until we're ready to concentrate fully on that task.

Service Packs and Hotfixes

After the base Windows 2000 installation is complete, apply the latest service pack. As of this writing in mid-2003, the latest is SP 3, but check Microsoft's site at www.microsoft.com/windows2000/downloads/servicepacks to ensure you have the latest available.

Windows 2000 has the feature of "remembering" service pack installed files, and so newly installed components install using the most current service pack version by referencing the source files listed in %windir%\inf\LAYOUT.inf and %windir\inf\DRVINDEX.inf.. This somewhat underdocumented feature enhancement of Windows 2000, introduced in Service Pack 1, saves a significant amount of time and eliminates the human error that used to be associated with making minor system state changes to a running Windows server.

Finally, install the latest appropriate hotfixes. The most current list can be found at www.microsoft.com/technet/security/current.asp, which includes detailed descriptions of the issues addressed and download locations for the hotfixes. The minimum required hotfixes for a post–SP3 Windows 2000 server install as of this writing are outlined in Table 13.1.

Table 13.1 Required Server Hotfixes (Post SP 3)

Microsoft Bulletin	KB Article	Title
MS02-042	Q326886	Flaw in Network Connection Manager Could Enable Privilege Elevation
MS02-045	Q326830	Unchecked Buffer in Network Share Provider Can Lead to Denial of Service
MS02-051	Q324380	Cryptographic Flaw in RDP Protocol Can Lead to Information Disclosure
MS02-062	Q327696	Cumulative Patch for Internet Information Service
MS02-065	Q329414	Buffer Overrun in Microsoft Data Access Components Could Lead to Code Execution
MS02-070	Q329170	Flaw in SMB Signing Could Enable Group Policy to Be Modified
MS02-071	Q328310	Flaw in Windows WM_TIMER Message Handling Could Enable Privilege Elevation
MS03-007	Q815021	Unchecked Buffer in Windows Component Could Cause Web Server Compromise
MS03-010	Q331953	Flaw in RPC Endpoint Mapper Could Allow Denial of Service Attacks

Unfortunately, most hotfixes do not use the same updating mechanisms as the service packs. Microsoft has indicated it will incorporate this functionality in hotfix installations in the future, but in the meantime, reinstallation of hotfixes after a state change (such as a new service installation) is still required.

Finally, notice that client-side components are not included on this list, such as the latest Internet Explorer and Outlook Express rollup patches (MS03-015 and MS03-014, respectively). The reason for this is that we do not, under any circumstances, expect server administrators to surf the Web, read e-mail, or otherwise treat our hardened, DMZ-based servers as clients, so these components should never be used (and this restriction should be enforced by appropriate egress firewall rules). Applying and maintaining patch levels on Windows servers is one of the most painful aspects of maintaining server health, so we want to keep the number of hotfixes installed to a minimum.

Note that as part of Service Pack 3, Microsoft introduced the Automatic Updates service to enable servers with direct (or proxied) Internet access to pull hotfixes from Microsoft as they're published. Unfortunately, this is not particularly appropriate for many sites where change control procedures are followed and new patches are tested first in a lab setting before being rolled out to production. Furthermore, while it's becoming exceedingly rare, Microsoft has been known to release hotfixes that break core operating system functionality. Running Automatic Updates can trigger a doomsday scenario of automatically breaking your entire DMZ without warning. Controls are available to configure Automatic Updates to require administrator confirmation before installation, but it's easier and safer to simply disable it. The other side of the coin, of course, is that you will have to manage your own patch scheduling and deployment.

Designing & Planning…

Disk Imaging

Many larger enterprises employ automated installation procedures through products such as Symantec's Norton Ghost or PowerQuest Drive Image. Not only do these solutions save time, they also ensure that all new systems are configured securely out of the box. Automation and security go hand in hand, so if these are available to you, by all means, use them. Human error through skipping a step or clicking the wrong check box is a common cause of inadvertent system insecurity and can lead to disaster, for both your server and your career.

Creating a New Local Administrator

After installation, one of the first tasks to complete is to create administrator user accounts for any engineer responsible for the ongoing maintenance of this server. Windows 2000 does ship with a built-in Administrator account; however, it should not be used for normal administration.

Engineers assigned to keep up with the maintenance of DMZ servers should do so with credentials tied to them, personally, in order to maintain reasonable audit trails in case of mistakes or misuse.

Creating a new account is a straightforward process using the NET commands. Log on to the server as Administrator, click **Start**, then click **Run**, then type **cmd** to start the CLI. Next type the following commands (substituting your name where appropriate, of course):

```
net user joe_blow J0eBl0w$ /add
net localgroup Administrators joe_blow /add
```

This command creates a user *joe_blow* with the elite password of *J0eBl0w$*. (A better password would be wholly random, since common dictionary-attack tools would easily crack this example password.) To ensure that the account was created and joined to administrators, use these *net* commands by themselves with no options:

```
net user
net localgroup
```

Of course, one of the advantages of having DMZ servers act as members of a Windows domain is the ability to add domain accounts to local groups. If this is the case for your enterprise, do not use local Administrator-level accounts at all.

Log out, and log back in with your new administrator rights. Repeat this process for any other engineers assigned to this server.

Security Configuration Through the Microsoft Management Console

Now that we have a new Windows 2000 server installation, it's time to explore the details of applying an enhanced security-conscious configuration. This will serve to establish the necessary foundation of a highly secure server to host your DMZ applications.

What used to be a fairly lengthy process involving many different tools (the Registry Editor, the Services control panel, the User Manager) is now centered around only two snap-ins to the Microsoft Management Console (MMC).

To begin, start the MMC with **Start | Run | mmc**, and load the two snap-ins for **Security Configuration and Analysis** and **Security Templates** with **Console | Add-Remove Snap-in | Add**. You're quite likely to be using this MMC set (shown in Figure 13.3) more than once, so save it by clicking **Console | Save As** and naming it something descriptive, like **SECEDIT.msc**.

Figure 13.3 Starting the Security Template Editor

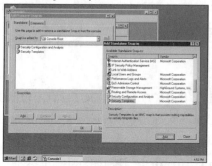

Next, create a new security template by copying an existing baseline. Presuming this is a fresh installation, hisecdc is a good starting point, since this is one of the more restrictive default security policies. This policy is Microsoft's recommended baseline for domain controllers (often the most valuable Windows devices in an enterprise), so it incorporates enhanced security controls such as restricted access to event logs and stronger minimum authentication requirements, and it empties the Power Users group. Right-click it, select **Save As**, and in keeping with Microsoft's naming convention, rename it **hisecdmz**, as shown in Figure 13.4.

Figure 13.4 Saving the HiSecDMZ Security Template

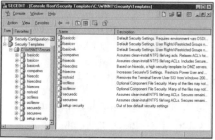

You'll want to spend some time getting to know this security policy, since it will be the foundation for your hardened DMZ host. Keep in mind that you are merely editing a policy template, not the actual policy that's enforced on the server. Any changes you make here will not be applied until the next section, "Applying the High-Security

DMZ Template." In addition, remember to save this policy routinely after making changes; no auto-save feature is in effect here.

The other important policy template to note is *setup security*. Hisecdmz is an incremental policy definition and builds on the default security configuration with which Windows 2000 is shipped. Thus, when applying your new hisecdmz policy, it assumes your overall system security is identical to a fresh installation of Windows 2000. If this is not the case (for example, if you have manually changed some user and group rights, changed some default ACLs, or the like), you will want to apply the setup security policy *before* applying hisecdmz.

To customize hisecdmz, you need to edit several template items. Let's take a look at each of them.

Account Lockout Policy (Under Account Policies)

There is really only one setting you need to worry about in the Account Lockout Policy template item:

■ **Account lockout duration** By default, this is set to 0, or infinite. However, setting this to 5 minutes will still buy you near-total protection against live, online brute-force password guessing against local accounts while ensuring that logon service remains available to legitimate users. Given the Account lockout threshold setting of five attempts before an account lockout, you've slowed your attacker to an average of one guess per minute. That gives him or her about 60,000 attempts in 42 days, before the password must be changed according to the Maximum Password Age item. The default password policies of Passwords must meet complexity requirements, and minimum password length of eight characters ensures that your users' passwords will be one of approximately 8^{62} possible passwords (that's many, many billions of combinations). Thus, an online password attack is virtually impossible to carry out successfully. (Offline attacks, using a stolen copy of the server's SAM database, do not respect the lockout threshold.)

Audit Policy (Under Local Policies)

Customize these auditing categories for your DMZ server to lay the groundwork for your auditing strategy. Suggested settings are:

■ **Audit account logon events** Set to **No Auditing**. This audit setting is useful only for tracking when a local account is used to log on to another computer, so it is primarily useful for domain controllers.

- **Audit account management** Keep this setting **Success, Failure**, which tracks when passwords are changed, accounts are created and deleted, and group membership changes. Unexpected activity here, especially the creation of new users in the Administrator group, can indicate a system compromise.

- **Audit directory service access** Set to **No Auditing**, since it only tracks changes to Active Directory objects.

- **Audit logon events** Set to **Success, Failure**. This is the most critical audit item, since audit category will let you know who is trying to log on and who is succeeding. This is the place to look for those live brute-force password crackers or logons (hopefully, failed!) from accounts you've never seen before. Activity such as this could indicate a failure in your network or physical security controls, and for some reason, unknown users are being presented with the opportunity to log on to the server.

- **Audit object access** Keep at **Success, Failure**. Object access auditing is the core of a monitored system; it tracks accesses to all objects with a SACL defined. This is explained in more detail later, in the "Registry and File System ACLs" section.

- **Audit policy change** Keep at **Success, Failure**. You will want to know when someone changes your meticulously crafted policy, either by accident or on purpose. An attacker who has successfully compromised a system may attempt to alter the system policy, for example, to disable IPSec rules to allow himself to extend his control over the system.

- **Audit privilege use** At first glance, this looks to be an important auditing category. However, in practice, it tends to generate far more data about a user's actions than you will be able to digest. Set this to **No auditing** for day-to-day production use, since virtually all the actions you will care about will be covered under other categories, such as system events or group membership changes.

- **Audit process tracking** Like privilege use, this is another category that is most useful for troubleshooting a particular process. Set it to **No auditing** unless you're diagnosing specific problems.

- **Audit system events** Keep at **Success, Failure** to be notified via the Security log whenever the system shuts down and is restarted. These events are also recorded by the System log, but keeping them here can help alert you when unexpected startups and shutdowns occur. This becomes especially important in the face of an Internet-borne, successful DoS attack.

When complete, your auditing strategy should reflect the selections shown in Figure 13.5.

Figure 13.5 Completed Auditing Policy

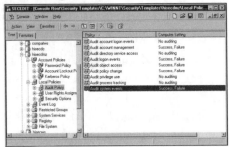

User Rights Assignment (Under Local Policies)

For each of these items, check the **Define this policy** box and make the following modifications.

- **Access this computer from the network** Set this to only **Authenticated Users**. This overrides the default setting of Everyone. although it sounds like you're limiting access to only people with accounts on this server, users who are viewing Web pages or transferring files via FTP are, in fact, authenticated as IUSR_*computername,* and this account is explicitly granted logon rights when IIS starts. This setting goes toward preventing "island hopping" from another, compromised DMZ server (which could have a configuration error, an unintended firewall exception, or some other less secure setting) to this one. In order to access this machine at all, an attacker would need more than mere access to the physical wire and would have to compromise at least one account locally.

- **Bypass traverse checking** Set this to **Administrators**. Traverse checking ensures that a user has the file system rights to a particular object and rights to its immediate parent object (such as a parent directory). Thus, if a particular subdirectory were unintentionally made vulnerable to, say, Everyone: Write under an otherwise secure directory that had an explicit "IUSER_*servername*" deny ACL, the anonymous Internet user account would still not be able to exploit the Everyone: Write object.

- **Debug programs** Check the **Define this Policy** box, but leave the list blank. This right allows a user to attach a debugger to a running process. Generally, this is not part of normal day-to-day troubleshooting. This level of troubleshooting indicates that there are some serious issues with the server, and it's generally not wise to perform this sort of in-depth analysis on a running server in the DMZ. A lab network is a much more appropriate venue for debugging.

- **Deny access to this computer from the network** Set this to the **Administrator user** (not the Administators group!). Note that if you wanted to deny anonymous Web access, you could add IUSR_*servername* to this list as well, since this takes precedence over the preceding Access policy.

- **Deny logon as a batch job** Set to **Administrator**.

- **Deny logon as a service** Set to **Administrator**. Both of these should be set for the same reasons given previously: We don't want an unidentified Administrator performing automated tasks on our servers. These three settings can block an attacker who has somehow managed to both compromise the built-in Administrator account and created an unforeseen method of logging in as this user from the network, or run services or batch jobs as this user. To restate our original build philosophy with hardened DMZ servers, the goal here is to make it difficult or impossible for a successful compromise of one element (in this case, the local Administrator account) to be used to inflict further damage or extend the attacker's control over the compromised system.

When complete, your User Rights strategy should reflect the selections shown in Figure 13.6.

Figure 13.6 User Rights Assignment

Security Options (Under Local Policies)

This is where many of the more restrictive security settings come into play. Note that enabling many of these options will break communication with "down-level" Windows clients and servers—namely, anything older than Windows 2000. If NT 4.0 servers still persist in your environment, you need to test these setting carefully in a lab setting or investigate your upgrade options to Windows 2000. The same goes for non-Microsoft but SMB-aware servers, such as Samba machines.

- **Message text for users attempting to log on** This setting gives some legal protection against unauthorized access. Fill this in with a "keep out" message, such as **Authorized users only, violators will be prosecuted.** This message will be seen by anyone attempting to log on at the console. Your organization's legal department may provide some more descriptive text to scare hackers away. Of course, any criminal hacker will ignore this warning, but there are anecdotal legal stories of otherwise criminal acts against systems being excused by judges because the defendant had been presented with a logon banner reading, "Welcome to server.navy.mil!" Keep in mind that this message is shown only to those people who have access to the console (either physically or via a Terminal Services session), so its legal use is likely restricted to people who could logically see it. Again, check with your legal department.

- **Message title for users attempting to log on** This is the title for the preceding message. Something simple like **Warning** or **Authorized Access Only** should suffice.

- **Number of previous logons to cache (in case domain controller is not available)** Hopefully, this is a standalone server, but if domain credentials are being used to log in, this should be set to **0**.

- **Rename administrator account** As mentioned earlier, the local Administrator account is the most popular user account for attack. Changing this account name to something nondefault can help prevent the success of automated attacks originating from another network, such as an automated password-cracking attack against the local Administrator account. Again, this becomes especially important in the unfortunate case of one server in the DMZ becoming compromised and brought into service as an attack platform against this DMZ server. Try not to pick something too obvious, like Admin or root. A good option is **dmzadmin**—but since criminal hackers could be reading this book, we suggest you pick something different.

- **Rename guest account** For the reasons already cited, this option should be selected as well. The Guest account is very low privileged, but it still can be used as part of an attack. Code Red, for example, adds Guest to the local Administrators group. Since this account name is mentioned specifically in Code Red's payload, merely renaming this account would prevent such a group membership modification from succeeding.

Figure 13.7 gives an idea of what these Security Options settings should look like.

Figure 13.7 Security Options

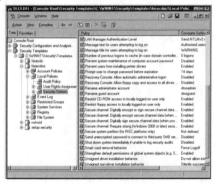

Event Log

The first part of setting up proper logging was under **Local Policies | Audit Policies**. Here's where event logging, as a service, is set up:

- **Settings for Event Logs** The names of the items are all very self-explanatory. Figure 13.8 is the suggested configuration. One item to note is the policy for **Shut down the computer when the security audit log is full**. The intent behind this policy is that an attacker could fill up the security event log quickly by generating thousands of bogus events, and then perform his crime, knowing it would not be logged. Of course, by enabling this option, you allow the attacker to fill your log with thousands of events and force a blue-screen crash. Essentially, you need to choose (in the form of an organizational policy) which is worse: a guaranteed successful DoS attack or a possibly successful total compromise of the server. (By the way, this same logic applies to account lockouts after bad password guesses.)

Figure 13.8 Settings for Event Logs

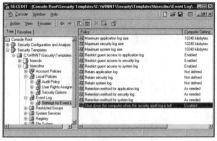

Restricted Groups

The Restricted Groups item defines who is allowed in certain groups. Its most obvious use is to maintain a static and exclusive list of administrators. To do so, right-click

Restricted Groups and click **Add Group**. Next, enter **Administrators**. The Administrators group will appear in the right pane. Next, double-click **Administrators**, and add the user accounts you created previously. Note that the built-in Administrator account will always be a member of Administrators, no matter what you define here.

System Services

Windows 2000 ships with a number of services installed, started, and running as LocalSystem. Most of these services won't be needed in the normal operation of a DMZ-based server, so here is where we define what services are allowed to run. *Note:* Because IIS isn't installed yet, you will not see it on this list. (Remember, during our initial installation, we deselected *all* Windows components until we are ready to concentrate on installing and configuring specific services.) The process for editing the security policy for services is:

1. Double-click the service to configure (for example, **Alerter**).

2. Check the box for **Define this policy setting in the template**.

3. Immediately, a group access list box is presented. For services you will be disabling, click **Remove** (which removes everyone's rights to stop and start the service), and grant the following access rights:

   - Administrators **Full Control**

   - Authenticated Users: **Read** and **Start, Stop, and Pause**

   - System: **Read** and **Start, Stop, and Pause**

   Then click **OK**.

4. Next, click the radio button for **Disabled**. (*Note:* If you're not sure if a service is actually needed or not, set this to **Manual** to allow the operating system to automatically start in case it's needed.).

5. Press **OK**.

Repeat this process for each service you want to disable, which will be most of them. The only services we'll require for the server function as a manageable Web server are the following:

   - Event Log

   - IPSEC Policy Agent

   - NT LM Security Support Provider

   - Plug and Play (required by Windows 2000)

- Protected Storage

- Remote Procedure Call (RPC)

- Security Accounts Manager

- Task Scheduler

- Telnet (we'll harden this with IPSec policies)

- Terminal Services Windows Management Instrumentation (required for the Security Editor to apply changes)

- Windows Management Instrumentation Driver Extensions

For engineers familiar with default Windows 2000 installations, this list might seem surprisingly, even radically, short. It is. Remember, when Windows 2000 was released, security wasn't exactly at the forefront of Microsoft's marketing strategy, so a number of not-strictly-required services are enabled by default to ensure that new servers are able to "just work" out of the box. By planning for a minimal Windows installation, we reduce the "attack surface" of our servers by not offering the services we don't use. Incidentally, by disabling these services, you'll notice your server boots faster, has more available memory, and keeps CPU utilization down. Who says security and usability are mutually exclusive?

This all said, keep in mind that specific applications could require other services. Specifically, the COM+ Event System and Indexing Service are sometimes needed by certain Web applications. Normal troubleshooting activities will also likely require the Performance Logs and Alert and the Logical Disk Manager services. It should go without saying that engineers should *thoroughly* test any applications the expect to run, be they custom, third-party, or even Microsoft-provided. You need to establish proper operation under this restrictive service model in a test environment, since by far the most common complaint of "hardened hosts" is that security measures "break" an application. This is often due to an application developer's assumptions about your particular server environment; developers tend to believe that every server is pretty much identical to factory defaults, but of course, you've just violated that assumption. Test, test, and test again before deploying these sorts of changes to your production environment.

Registry and File System ACLs

After you've finished configuring the default state for your services, the next two sections of the security template deal with establishing the default ACLs assigned to the Registry and the file system. Generally speaking, the defaults provided by Microsoft at the time of installation are appropriate for a secure build. However, some specific file system ACLs should be tightened to further enhance security. This is done through denying access to certain files and adding Object Access logging to others. Changing ACLs through the Security Editor is much like editing the security properties on the file system itself.

1. Highlight the **File System** entry, right-click in the right pane, and select **Add File...**.

2. In the resultant popup box (shown in Figure 13.9), you can either type a file or directory name or navigate to one. In this example, we're adding the POSIX subsystem executable.

Figure 13.9 Adding a File to the File System ACL Security Template

3. Press **Enter**, and you are presented with a normal security ACL configuration dialog box, illustrated in Figure 13.10. For POSIX.exe, we'll be changing the Everyone: Full Control ACL to **Everyone: Deny**. This will prohibit anyone, including LocalSystem and Administrators, from launching Posix subsystem commands.

Figure 13.10 Prohibiting Access to POSIX.exe

4. Click **Apply**. You'll be presented with a warning dialog box to confirm what you're about to do. Click **Yes**.

> **NOTE**
>
> The POSIX and OS/2 subsystems are installed by default in order for Windows 2000 to run some command-line applications originally written for these system architectures. However, since these subsystems are, for the most part, "tacked on" interfaces to the underlying kernels, applications written for them are generally considered not nearly as secure as their native counterparts. It's basically never a good idea to run these subsystems unless you know you are going to be using them, since doing so can open unexpected attack avenues. Thus, you will want to disable Everyone's rights to POSIX.exe, OS2.exe, OS2SRV.exe, and OS2SS.exe.

Repeat this process for each file you want to deny access to. Other good candidates include tftp.exe, arp.exe, net1.exe, and route.exe—all are all network-related commands that are commonly leveraged by attackers to either deliver their payloads (rootkits and other attack tools) or modify the server's normal behavior in the network.

Of course, some commands you'll want to keep on the system, but you'll want to keep an eye on their usage through auditing. Examples of these sorts of executables include cmd.exe, command.exe, net.exe, and telnet.exe. These commands tend to be in common enough usage by local administrators to justify their availability on the local server but not used so much that auditing their activities would put an undue strain on the system's Event Logging system.

To edit the SACLs on these commands, perform these steps:

1. As before, navigate to or enter the name of the file on which you'd like to define SACLs.

2. Remove the **Everyone** group by clicking the **Remove** button. (This does not actually remove "Everyone" from the ACL list but rather ensures that the normal ACLs are not overwritten by the security template.)

3. Click **Advanced** to open the advanced ACL editor.

4. Select the **Auditing** tab.

5. Click **Add**, and double-click **Everyone**.

6. In the Auditing Entry dialog box, check both the **Successful** and **Failed** boxes for **Traverse Folder/Execute File, Delete,** and **Change Permissions**.

7. Click **OK**, and close all the other windows by clicking **OK** again.

Repeat these steps for all the files and Registry keys you want to monitor.

Finally, one important default ACL to set right from the start is the top-level root directory of your data and log drives (in our example, drives D: and E:). These are created initially with the ACL of **Everyone: Full Control**, which is far too permissive for what is likely to be Internet-exposed data. At a minimum, set this to:

- **Administrators** Full Control

- **System** Full Control

- **Authenticated Users** Read (Remember, the "Internet User" is a member of Authenticated Users.)

Unfortunately, due to the number of default commands installed on Windows 2000 (we count well over 300 *.exe* commands in %windir%\system32 alone), it is all but impossible to describe the functions of each command in any sort of detail in a mere chapter on Windows 2000 security. Furthermore, virtually every organization has a different "style" and preferred command set for performing local administration.

One exercise that engineers might find useful to discover what their "operations baseline" looks like from a command perspective is to add SACLs on all *.exe* commands on the system drive of a production server and review that server's Security Event log to see which commands get accessed, how often, and by whom. Engineers can also compare the results of, say, a week's worth of activity to a list of system commands to discover which commands are never executed as part of normal operations.

Sadly, of those 300-plus commands, not one of them edits the SACLs on files. Thus, adding auditing (specifically, **Traverse/Execute: Success**) to each *.exe* is a daunting and tedious task. However, you can edit security policy templates directly with your favorite text editor. So, a quick-and-dirty method for applying auditing changes on a local system could be to perform the following:

1. Create a new, empty security template with the Security Template editor, and save it as **AUDITEXES.inf**.

2. Insert **[File Security]** at the end of the file with your favorite text editor.

3. From the command line, execute this command:

```
Dir /b /s %windir%\system32\*.exe >> auditexes.inf
```

4. Using your favorite text editor, take this list, and for each line that contains a file name under [File Security], modify it like so, including the quotes:

    ```
    "C:\WINNT\system32\FILENAME.EXE",0,"D:ARS:AR(AU;OICISA;WP;;;BU)",
    ```

    where *FILENAME.EXE* is the name of each command to audit. That cryptic information at the end is actually a text representation of the ACLs and SACLs to be set on the file. (This syntax, unfortunately, is extremely under-documented, and we have yet to find a reasonable reference to explain it. You'll just have to trust that this is right.)

5. Save the file, and apply the new policy as described in the next section. Watch your logs for a week or two of normal activity, and then institute a Deny and Audit policy that's reasonable for your site.

Applying the High-Security DMZ Template

Now that you've completed your security template, it's time to apply it to your server. First, let's import it into a security database:

1. On the left pane of the MMC you saved previously (**SECEDIT.msc**), right-click **Security Configuration and Analysis**, and select **Open Database…**

2. The default location for customized security databases is My Documents. This doesn't seem very appropriate, so use a full path name when naming your new database: **C:\WINNT\Security\HISECDMZ.sdb**.

3. Next, you are presented with the templates available to import. Double-click **hisecdmz.inf** to import it.

4. Finally, to apply the template, right-click **Security Configuration and Analysis** again, and select **Configure Computer Now…**

5. Some changes take effect immediately, such as File ACLs and Service start states, but many, such as actually applying the Disabled prohibition on services, need a reboot to update. So, when you're done, reboot your server.

Once you've rebooted, you will have a hardened Windows 2000 server that is reasonably safe to deploy within an Internet-facing DMZ. However, remotely managing it is now practically impossible. To remedy this, we'll install and configure two more services: Terminal Services and Telnet, the latter of which will be further hardened with IPSec.

> **WARNING**
>
> "Easy administration" should always be read with the subtext of "easy to target." The same methods legitimate administrators use to support their systems remotely can also be used by adversaries to remotely compromise those systems. The most secure method of administration is tying it to physical access of the device—but this becomes impractical for servers in distant locations or if you have more than one or two. Securing your methods of remote administration, therefore, is of paramount importance to ensure continued health and stability—for both you and your machines.

Remote Administration of DMZ Hosts

Since much of the native networking available to Windows 2000 has been disabled by the initial hardening procedures, we need to return some remote management functionality. Traditional remote management solutions provided by Microsoft tend to rely on the NetBIOS and Server Message Block (SMB) protocols, which communicate on TCP ports 135, 139, and 445 and UDP ports 137, 138, and 445. Also by default, these protocols transmit data in clear text, without any sort of encryption. This is bad news for remote connections over untrustworthy networks such as the Internet, where any device along the path between your console and your remote server can be logged and eavesdropped. Instead, we'll be exploring remote management with sufficiently strong encryption, using Terminal Services, which provides encryption natively, for remote console administration and Telnet wrapped with IPSec for command-line management.

Using Terminal Services for Remote Desktop Administration

Terminal Services allows for native, built-in remote desktop functionality with the added benefit of some very reasonable built-in encryption at the application level. Terminal Services is new to Windows 2000, and because of its inclusion, engineers no longer have to set up convoluted, error-prone, and usually less secure systems of remote console administration with third-party tools (as was the case with NT 4.0). Terminal Services is also highly configurable, as we'll see, and the 128-bit encryption it provides is generally safe enough to use over the Internet. Finally, the Remote Desktop Protocol (RDP) is extremely well supported by Microsoft, and its inclusion in Microsoft's later offerings of Windows XP and Windows 2003 bode well for its continued supportability.

Some organizations might feel a bit squeamish about offering Terminal Services for remote management over the Internet, since it effectively opens a logon prompt on the host's console to anyone who cares to take a whack at some password guessing. This concern has merit, but these same sites often also offer VPN services—which do pretty much the same thing.

WARNING

One problem with Terminal Services is that the encryption RDP provides does not make any attempt at mutual authentication; it is a simple stream cipher. So, if an attacker were able to impersonate your actual Terminal Server to you and tricked you well enough for you to provide your logon credentials, it's pretty much "game over." Although it sounds terrible, the likelihood of this actually happening is fairly minimal. An attacker would already need to take some level of control over your network, or the network hosting your Terminal Server, and perform some DNS, ARP, or other trickery in order to get you to believe his evil machine is really your Terminal Server. If he's gotten that far, you likely have bigger problems.

For what it's worth, many traditional VPN solutions, such as those based on L2TP, are also vulnerable to impersonation and man-in-the-middle attacks. Only systems that support mutual authentication (IPSec with certificate-based authentication, namely) are protected against such complex machinations.

There are some steps you can take to lessen the risks inherent in offering Terminal Services. For starters, you might want to build out a server in the DMZ that offers only Terminal Services and have remote, Internet-based administrators log on to this server, then establish Terminal Service connections to other hosts on the network. For the other machines in the DMZ, prohibit all inbound connection attempts on Terminal Services' default listening port, TCP 3389. Doing this is a relatively cheap and easy way to "fake" a VPN connection to perform server management.

Another option is to change the default listening port. To do this, edit the Registry value HKEY_LOCAL_MACHINE\System\CurrentControlSet\Control\Terminal Server\WinStations\RDP-Tcp\PortNumber to a nonstandard port. A good one is port 22—SSH's default listening port. By picking another well-known port, you can help disguise the true nature of the service from the perspective of a port scanner.

Then, on the client (i.e., your management station), export the connection information in the **Client Connection Manager** to a text file, edit the **Server Port** entry to match the port you just set, and reimport the file. (This process is covered in detail in Microsoft KB article 187623.)

Changing the default port, or limiting access to merely one server, will not fully conceal the server's existence, but it can at least defeat automated attacks (and less motivated attackers), since it will not conform to expected defaults. This is known as *security through obscurity*, a concept spoken of with some level of derision by the "security community." However, simply following a maxim of changing defaults can save a great deal of heartache inflicted by worms and viruses.

> **NOTE**
>
> For more information the RDP, you can find an in-depth article on Microsoft's site: www.microsoft.com/windows2000/techinfo/howitworks/terminal/rdpfandp.asp.

Installing Terminal Services

Installing Terminal Services is already half-way done—it's present on your system, and you can see it on a services list. However, it will remain disabled until it is installed through Control Panel:

1. On the desktop, navigate to **Start | Settings | Control Panel | Add/Remove Programs**.

2. Click **Add/Remove Windows Components**.

3. Scroll down until you see the **Terminal Services** check box, check it, and click **Next**.

4. The radio button for **Remote administration mode** is already selected, so click **Next**. This step allows up to two administrators to connect simultaneously to this server via Terminal Services. Note that this limit cannot be changed.

5. Wait a moment for Terminal Services to enable itself, and click **Finish**.

6. Reboot the server. (Windows 2000 cut out many of the reboots once required for NT 4.0, but there are still some unfortunate required reboots left.)

Configuring Terminal Services Securely

Once you've rebooted, log back in, and configure Terminal Services for a reasonable level of security. First, you'll want to create a local group of users who will be allowed to log in to this server via Terminal Services. By default, all Administrators are allowed this privilege, but remember, we want to limit the actions of the built-in Administrator account as much as possible. Go to the command line, and type the following commands:

```
net localgroup TSUsers /add
net localgroup joe_blow /add
```

Repeat the second command for each local Administrator you've created. (Again, this will also work for domain accounts, if you are member of a domain.)

In addition, remove the system-generated user account of TSInternetUser; it is not useful nor related to Remote Administration in this setting:

```
Net user TSInternetUser /delete
```

Next, configure Terminal Services itself:

1. Navigate to **Start | Programs | Administrative Tools | Terminal Services Configuration**.

2. Double-click **RDP-Tcp** in the right pane to open the configuration panel.

3. On the first tab, **General**, check the box for **Use Windows Standard Authentication**, and select **High** from the drop-down box for **Encryption Level**, as shown in Figure 13.11. This step ensures that all traffic to and from the server is encrypted with the RC4 stream cipher and a 128-bit key. While you cannot choose which cipher to use, RC4 is considered quite reasonable for this particular application. However, if you are nervous about using RC4 to protect administrative sessions, you can instead opt for encryption via IPSec.

Figure 13.11 RDP-Tcp Properties: General

4. Next, click the **Sessions** tab, check both available **Override user settings** boxes, and supply reasonable time limits, as shown in Figure 13.12. This step ensures that if a session is left idle or disconnected, it will not prevent other administrators from logging on to the server. Remember, only two Administrators can be logged on at a time. This limitation can be changed by purchasing licenses for Terminal Services in Application mode (and installing a Terminal Services License Server to keep track of them), but in reality, "only

two Administrators at a time" is a pretty good rule to ensure stability. After all, if you had more than two logged on, you'd be inviting disaster by having two people possibly making changes to the same files and systems.

Figure 13.12 RDP-Tcp Properties: Sessions

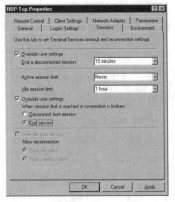

5. Click the **Permissions** tab, highlight **Administrators**, and click **Remove**. Next, click **Add**, and select the group you created previously, **TSUsers**. Grant this group **Full Control** rights by clicking the first **Allow** check box, as illustrated in Figure 13.13. Note that **SYSTEM** must also be granted the same full permissions to Terminal Services, since it is responsible for validating logon credentials.

Figure 13.13 RDP-Tcp Properties: Permissions

6. Finally, move to the **Client Settings** tab. The only function we allow here is **Clipboard mapping**, which is necessary for RDPClip to function. (We discuss this topic in more depth in the next section.) The rest will be disabled, as shown in Figure 13.14.

Figure 13.14 RDP-Tcp Properties: Client Settings

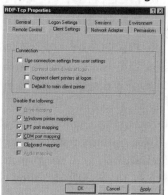

7. Click **OK** to commit these changes. They will take effect immediately upon the next Terminal Service connection, so there is no need to reboot.

Using Terminal Services for File Replication

Finally, since we've disabled the Workstation and Server services, file sharing has been disabled, so you need some way to copy files back and forth between your bastion host and your management station. For this, we have the Resource Kit utility, RDPClip. We do not want to install the entire Resource Kit on the DMZ server, since doing so opens up another set of useful tools for a potential attacker to increase and enhance his own access. Instead, download the RDPClip utility from Microsoft's FTP site, located at ftp.microsoft.com/reskit/win2000/rdpclip.zip. Unzip this file, and run the provided FXFRINST.bat on both the Terminal Services server and client. You can't quite drag and drop files between stations, but you can use Ctrl + C and **Ctrl + V** to copy files and directories. Unlike file transfers over SMB and NetBIOS, these transfers are protected with the same encryption provided by RDP for the rest of Terminal Services.

WARNING

The Resource Kits Microsoft publishes for its server platforms contain a plethora of useful tools, and we use a few of them in this chapter (RDPClip, IPSecPol, and so on). However, as we saw in the last section, ensuring that someone who has already owned our servers cannot use them for evil purposes can be a real pain—so instead of installing the entire thing and using tiny bits of it, we merely install only the components we need. Furthermore, Microsoft disclaims any and all support for Resource Kit tools and provides them "as is."

Using IPSec-Enhanced Telnet for Command-Line Administration

Although it's common in the UNIX world, Windows 2000 does not ship with its own SSH demon. Third-party software vendors (most notably SSH Communications Security and the GNU Cygwin project) can provide this functionality to Windows, but one of the goals of this chapter is to make do with Windows's on-board tool set. So, for a secure command-line administration solution, we use Telnet over IPSec. This IPSec configuration will is fairly basic, using a preshared key for authentication and the default cipher choices for the authentication and encapsulation protocols.

First, we need to configure Telnet. If you followed the guidelines for the services allowed by the hisecdmz policy, this part is practically done. The only change we need to make is to change the NTLM authentication piece.

First, navigate to **Start | Programs | Administrative Tools**, and click **Telnet Server Administration**. You will be presented with the screen shown in Figure 13.15, a dialog box that looks suspiciously like a command-line menu (not all Microsoft menus are pretty GUIs!).

Type **3** for **Display / change registry settings**, then **7** for **NTLM**, then **y** to confirm that you do want to change this setting. Next, type **0** to disable NTLM authentication, and type **y** again to confirm. Exit this menu by pressing **0**, then stop and start the Telnet service by typing **5**, then **4**. Finally, type **0** to exit the configuration menu.

Figure 13.15 An Unpretty Menu

Next, let's set up an IPSec policy to enforce encryption for our future Telnet sessions. However, rather than navigate through the approximately two dozen windows and four wizards to accomplish this task, we use the Resource Kit tool IPSECPOL.exe to create our basic IPSec policy. This tool can be downloaded from Microsoft's site at www.microsoft.com/windows2000/techinfo/reskit/tools/existing/ipsecpol-o.asp. Download and install this tool according to the instructions. This process installs, in the directory of your choice:

- IPSECPOL.exe (the command-line tool itself)

- IPSECUTIL.dll and TEXT2POL.dll (DLLs required by the tool)

- IPSECPOL_LICENSE.txt (the Microsoft license agreement)

- ipsecpol-d.htm and ToolDownloadReadme.htm (documentation for installation and use)

On the server, run the following command in the directory inn which you installed IPSECPOL.exe:

```
ipsecpol -f *+0:23:6 -a PRESHARE:"Secret Key!" -w REG -p SecureTelnetPolicy
    -r LocalPort23 -x
```

The first option, *-f *+0:23:6,* defines a filter for all traffic (*) coming to and from (+) the server's IP address (*0*) and port 23 (*:23*) over protocol 6, TCP (*:6*). The next option, *-a PRESHARE:"Secret Key!"*, defines the authentication method of a pre-shared key (*PRESHARE:*) and the value of that key (*"Secret Key!"*). The *-w REG* portion writes this policy to the local Registry, making it a static mode policy (rather than a dynamic mode policy, which would be lost on reboot), and *-p SecureTelnetPolicy -r LocalPort23* provide the name of the policy (*SecureTelnetPolicy*) and the rule (*LocalPort23*) we just defined. Finally, *-x* activates the policy immediately. All other values associated with this policy, such as the AH and ESP cipher selections, are left at default.

Now only clients that are both IPSec-aware and know the secret key can establish a TCP session with this server on port 23; your DMZ server will refuse any other kind of communication to this port. So, a similar command must be run on any clients you want to Telnet to this server:

```
ipsecpol -f 0+*:23:6 -a PRESHARE:"Secret Key!" -w REG -p SecureTelnetPolicy
    -r LocalPort23 -x
```

Here we have transposed the source and destination IP address aliases of 0 and *.

It's fairly obvious that this discussion is merely scratching the surface of IPSec and should be taken as only a casual introduction to Microsoft's implementation of the technology. This is due to the fact that so much of IPSec depends on other portions of your architecture and your overall, enterprisewide network. For example, if you have a Certificate Authority in your organization, you can use the far more secure CA-generated certificates for mutual authentication, rather than this easily guessable secret key.

For an in-depth look at Microsoft's implementation and configuration guidelines, refer to the step-by-step guide at www.microsoft.com/windows2000/techinfo/planning/security/ipsecsteps.asp.

Designing & Planning…

Using Windows Secure Shell

It appears that Windows is the only family of modern operating systems that does not ship with a free SSH implementation. This is really too bad, since the SSH standards provides for port tunneling, file copying, and remote command execution, all over TCP/22. In addition, its absence makes cross-administration of Windows from (or to) a Linux, BSD, or Solaris server much more inconvenient than it ought to be.

We've faked something similar with Telnet, but if you're looking for real SSH functionality, you have two options:

- Buy a third-party SSH server solution. The product suite from F-Secure, detailed at www.f-secure.com/products/ssh/, is perhaps the most comprehensive, complete, and easiest to administer and maintain, but it's also fairly pricey at about $800 a seat.

- Install a free implementation of SSH server. Virtually all the free SSH servers for Windows are based on the Cygwin Project's implementation, and until recently, most implementations required large chunks of the Cygwin environment. However, the OpenSSH for Windows package maintained by Michael Johnson of Claremont McKenna College (at http://lexa.mckenna.edu/sshwindows/) is an extremely stripped-down installation and requires as little of the Cygwin environment as possible.

Commercial solutions tend to be much better integrated with the Windows OS (authentication is seamless, for example) and tend to be better supported for that platform. However, they're expensive. Free solutions, are, well, free, but the support has traditionally been fairly dicey, especially since Microsoft appears so actively disinterested in the protocol.

As for the client side, a number of GUI and command-line-based SSH clients are available for Windows. The most popular today in the GUI space is Simon Tatham's PuTTY (available for download at www.chiark.greenend.org.uk/~sgtatham/putty/) and, again, the Cygwin SSH client for command-line interaction.

Vulnerability-Scan Your Host

The final step to finishing your secure foundation is to perform a quick "sanity check" by performing a basic vulnerability scan of your hardened host. There are quite a few automated vulnerability scanners on the market, some free, some not. One of the most popular is Nessus, free for use under the GNU Public License, written by Renaud Deraison and maintained by him and an active community of Nessus users.

Nessus ships as a client/server application. Sadly (or not, depending on your point of view), there is no Nessus server for Windows (yet). However, there is a fully featured Windows client, so one Nessus server can fulfill the vulnerability-scanning needs of several clients. This split architecture also helps contain your vulnerability-scanning traffic to just one source, which should make your IDS administrators happy. (Nessus can perform over 1200 security tests and is quite noisy from an IDS perspective.) Finally, the client/server communication can be secured using certificate-based, PKI encryption.

Details of installing and configuring the server component are a bit beyond the scope of this chapter, but after downloading the required components from nessus.org, it's as simple as

```
./configure ; make ; sudo make install
```

The Windows client (NessusWX) is similarly trivial to install, since it ships as a self-extracting installation binary.

Figure 13.16 is a screen shot of NessusWX's report on our sample server. Remember, we haven't installed any applications quite yet, but we have stripped out most of the functionality (attack vectors) default to Windows 2000 and re-added an IPSec-secured Telnet server and an installation of Terminal Services, modified to listen on the more innocuous port 22.

Figure 13.16 Nessus Report

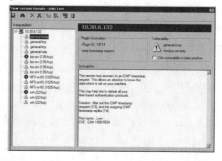

We can see here, at a glance, that there are some warnings about open ports, ICMP being fully available, and other relatively innocuous points. This is to be expected; after

all, although we cut out most Windows services, we did need to keep the Remote Procedure Call (RPC) service, which listens on port 135, and the Task Scheduler, which listens on the first available ephemeral port, port 1025. (This is a somewhat annoying "feature" of Task Scheduler; if we want to schedule jobs locally, we are forced to accept jobs remotely—with proper authentication, of course.) None of this is particularly surprising, given the work we put into planning our deployment.

The good news here is twofold. First, we have only 14 positive results, which is not too shabby for Windows, considering there's no firewall or other control mechanism between our scanner and our server. Second, and more obviously, we have no red "holes." This is great news—at least we know that between the time of installing the operating system and getting to the point where we're ready to install some applications, we haven't already lost the game by forgetting a critical hotfix, leaving some key management service enabled, or getting rooted in this short time. (The last concern might sound unlikely, but it does happen. Someone—not naming any names here—was building a test Windows server, left IIS enabled, and got hit with Nimda right after the first reboot. How annoying.)

One of the more flexible features of Nessus is that it doesn't tend to mind if services are listening on funny ports; Web servers on port 81 is a great example. However, we seem to have fooled it by dropping Terminal Services on port 22. Nessus is aware of Terminal Services, as long as it's found on port 3389 (and even warns sternly against using on the Internet, for fear of MITM attacks!). However, it just doesn't know what to make of it on TCP/22. It does, however, notice it's *not* SSH. In light of this, we're warned that his mystery service may be Adore SSH or Shaft, two common backdoor programs that also sit on TCP/22.

Nessus also seems to have completely ignored our encrypted Telnet service, since the Nessus server was missing our IPSec preshared key. There's not even a mention, in this default scan, that it's the only filtered port on the server. Nmap, the de facto port-scanning standard software by Fyodor of Insecure.org, would have called out this fact.

These are not a knocks against Nessus, mind you, since this behavior is completely expected. Plus, if we wanted to hunt down IPSec-filtered services or unerringly detect Terminal Services no matter what port it's listening on, we could, by writing a custom plug-in for the task. This user-controlled extensibility is perhaps Nessus's strongest feature.

However, we need to remember that vulnerability scanners, in general, are pretty good at finding common misconfigurations, common Web site SNAFUs, and even not-so-common Trojan horse applications. But they're mostly useful not in finding out things you don't know but in confirming things you already know. They can give hints and good guesses at what might be wrong with a server or network, but they should not be used blindly or religiously. After all, if vulnerability scanners were perfect, security engineers like your authors would be looking for work elsewhere.

Bastion Host Configuration

Now that you have a reasonably (some might say, highly) secure base server, it's time to finally make it do something. You just saw that from a vulnerability test, you can now ensure that hackers permeating your DMZ (who will do the same thing!) are not going to find much open. Since your server will operate in a DMZ, it's quite likely it will act as a Web server, a mail relay, or an FTP site. All these functions are serviced by Microsoft's flagship Internet product, Internet Information Services 5.0. These configurations are similar; in this section we take a look at each in turn, highlighting the differences.

Configuring IIS Servers for Web Access

Hosting a publicly accessible Web server is, far and away, the most common use of a DMZ Windows 2000 Server build. The sad fact, though, is that because Windows 2000 is shipped with IIS enabled by default and the default settings are so insecure, IIS servers out of the box don't often last more than an hour before they've been thoroughly compromised, broadcasting their weakness to anyone who cares to listen. Luckily, you've taken the time to actually plan your IIS deployment, and you won't be among the thousands of actively scanning Nimda hosts within minutes of operation. Let's get started.

Setting Up an Anonymous, Public Web Site

First, you need to install the basic components of IIS. Like Terminal Services, this is done by navigating to **Start | Settings | Control Panel | Add/Remove Programs** and clicking **Add/Remove Windows Components**.

Scroll down (one line) to the check box labeled **Internet Information Services (IIS)**. However, don't check it; this installs a lot of usually nonrequired components. Instead, merely highlight it, and click the **Details** button.

Since this server's role will be that of a mere Web server, scroll down to **World Wide Web Server**, and check its box. You will notice that as shown in Figure 13.17, the other required components, **Internet Information Services Snap-In** (the MMC for IIS) and **Common Files**, are also selected automatically.

Figure 13.17 Installing a Web Server Only

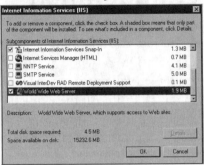

Click **OK**, then click **Next**, and IIS will begin installing. Since this is the first time IIS is installed, it's quite likely the installer will ask for your service pack source files, so be sure to have them handy. For this reason, we also need to apply the IIS-specific hot-fixes again at the end of this process. When you're done, click **Finish**, then click **Close**.

Next, we want to start the IIS MMC. To do so, navigate to **Start | Programs | Administrative Tools | Internet Services Manager**. You're presented with the basic IIS configuration panel. Click your server's name (shown in Figure 13.18 as **dmz-windows2000**), then **Default Web Site**. You'll notice that you have quite a few default files and applications there, all on your system partition—many of which offer current attack vectors for both worms and humans.

Figure 13.18 IIS's Default Web Site

First, stop the Web site by either clicking the **Stop** button (which resembles the Stop button on a VCR) at the top of the MMC, or delete the **Default Web Site** by right-clicking it and selecting **Delete**. And yes, you're sure, so click **Yes** when asked.

Now create a new, real Web site, where ultimately your content will go. First, you need to create a directory for it. This can be done quickly by clicking **Start | Run** and typing **cmd /c mkdir E:\www\public**, where *E:* is the drive where your application data should be located.

NOTE

The standard nomenclature of the top-level root directory is C:\InetPub\www-root. Of course, since we've become so "default-averse," you will want to consider using a different name for your Web root directory. The next killer worm could rely on this default to gain maximum exposure, defeat all your security measures, gain file system access using an 0day exploit, and totally trash the greater Internet—but your site will be safe and sound, thanks to your forethought of renaming your directory to something obscure. (*Note:* This is wishful thinking, but entirely possible; automated worms are notoriously bad at dealing with anything nonstandard.)

Next, right-click your server name, scroll to **New**, and select **Web Site**. This starts the Web Site Creation wizard. IIS 5.0's Web site creation process is remarkably simple—which is unsurprising, because virtually every feature is enabled by default. Remember, "Ease of administration" all too often means "Easy pickin's."

After clicking **Next**, the steps to creation are:

1. Give a description. **Public** will be fine, since this is a public Web site. Click **Next**.

2. Assuming that this is not a multihomed system, you don't want to change the default port, and this site has only one name, click **Next**.

3. In the **Path** field, enter the path to your Web site: **E:\www\public**. Keep the **Allow Anonymous access to this Web site** box checked. (Allowing anonymous connections is the whole point of this site.)

4. We assume you'll want to run Active Server Pages (*.asp) as part of your site, since this might be one of the main reasons for choosing IIS in the first place. Thus, you will keep the default access permissions of **Read** and **Run scripts (such as ASP)**. Click **Next**, and you're done.

Now, you have a brand-new site—one that's not quite empty. Notice that as shown in Figure 13.19, all the default virtual directories are still active.

Figure 13.19 Persistent Default Virtual Directories

We'll take care of those and a lot of other IIS security fine-tuning details right now, employing one of the most useful security tools Microsoft has produced in the past year: the IIS Lockdown Tool. But first, you'll want to stop the Web site again before the "Web worm du jour" sneaks into your private network and eats your secure server before you've completely hardened it. Again, click the **Stop** button or right-click the site name and select **Stop**.

The IIS Lockdown Tool

The IIS Lockdown tool is a comprehensive, scripted method that can be used to significantly enhance the security posture of your IIS site. It's currently at version 2.1 and is remarkably better than the first release. Among other annoyances, the first release had no Undo feature—so if you made a mistake, there was basically no way to restore a production site to the previous state. Ouch!

First, download the IIS Lockdown tool from the Microsoft site at www.microsoft.com/technet/security/tools/tools/locktool.asp. It is delivered as a compressed executable, much like a hotfix, so first, we'll extract it to a location that's relatively well protected, C:\WINNT\Security\Lockdown. Open a command prompt, and change directories to where you have saved

```
mkdir C:\WINNT\Security\Lockdown

iislockd.exe /T:C:\WINNT\Security\Lockdown /C
```

We can view the tool and, more important, the configuration .inf files in Explorer, as shown in Figure 13.20.

Figure 13.20 The IIS Lockdown Tool, Uncompressed

IIS Lockdown performs a number of other useful functions, which, like the Security Configuration MMC interface, obviates a good deal of "poking around" work we used to have to do to ensure an IIS server's inherent security.

In addition, the IIS Lockdown tool incorporates URLScan, which provides a filtering layer between the Web browser and the Web server. URLScan is the preferred mechanism for denying certain types of requests to your Web server—for example, with URLScan you can deny all WebDAV extensions or any URL that contains an ampersand (&). It also filters in the other direction; it can drop IIS's Server: header, for example, to aid in obfuscating your server brand and version, defeating automated "banner-grabbing" techniques designed to search for particular Web server platforms.

As you can see, there are many default server settings, and reading through them can give you a pretty good idea of the types of Web requests these services require. The most notable example is the default list of allowed verbs for Exchange 2000: *GET, HEAD, POST, OPTIONS, SEARCH, POLL, PROPFIND, BMOVE, BCOPY, SUB-SCRIBE, MOVE, PROPPATCH, BPROPPATCH, DELETE, BDELETE, MKCOL, UNSUBSCRIBE, SUBSCRIPTIONS, COPY, LOCK, UNLOCK, PUT, ACL, NOTIFY.* Clearly, Exchange 2000 wants to be able perform quite a bit of extended WebDAV content manipulation, and thus, it is not a service you should feel very comfortable with in your DMZ. Exposing this sort of data management functionality to the Internet is just asking for trouble.

Of course, we're not going to be happy with a default configuration, so let's create our own custom server type: a hardened ASP-serving IIS server, based on the Dynamic Web Server (ASP Enabled) profile.

Editing IISLOCKD.ini

IISLOCKD.ini is the "guts" of the IIS Lockdown tool, from which it gets its directives on what to allow and what to deny. To start editing the file, open **IISLOCKD.ini** with Notepad, and find the entry starting with **[dynamicweb]**. The elements are generally self-explanatory, and the defaults, in this case, are generally appropriate. We will change a few elements, though, as detailed in Table 13.2.

Table 13.2 Changed Elements in IISLOCKD.ini

Element	Details
Label="Hardened Dynamic Web server (ASP enabled)"	Changing the title reminds other administrators that you've edited the defaults for this server profile.
UrlScan_IniFileLocation= urlscan_hardened_dynamic.ini	Gives the location of the configuration file URLScan should use (described next).

Continued

Table 13.2 Changed Elements in IISLOCKD.ini

Element	Details
AdvancedSetup=Required	Steps us through the changes when we make them. This is basically a verbosity setting.
UninstallService=TRUE	In case we misclicked earlier (or are working with an existing installation), this element uninstalls non-HTTP services such as FTP, SMTP, and NNTP.

Save and close the file.

Editing URLSCAN_HARDENED_DYNAMIC.ini

Copy **URLSCAN_DYNAMIC.ini** to **URLSCAN_HARDENED_DYNAMIC.ini**. Like IISLOCKD.ini, this is the basic configuration file for URLScan, and we want to make the changes described in Table 13.3.

Table 13.3 Changed Elements in URLSCAN_HARDENED_DYNAMIC.ini

Element	Details
UseAllowExtensions=1	We know exactly what files to expect on our site. If, for example, we know we won't have *.py (Python) scripts, we won't put it in the AllowExtensions, and thus, if any show up (accidentally or maliciously) in the Web root, IIS will ignore them.
RemoveServerHeader=1	Eliminates the Server: banner the IIS server will return to clients. (This takes precedence over AlternateServerName).
UseFastPathReject=1	Perhaps a matter of personal preference, but some administrators don't want to fill up their IIS logs with bad access attempts. We're logging this activity anyway in URLScan's logs, and this sort of activity is more the job of an IDS than a production, content-providing server. Furthermore, this element also disables the URLScan response page—after all, there's not a lot of value in helping your attackers by explicitly telling them exactly what kinds of requests get scooped by URLScan.

Continued

Table 13.3 Changed Elements in URLSCAN_HARDENED_DYNAMIC.ini

Element	Details
AlternateServerName= Apache/1.3.6 (Win32)	Using this server name can mislead script kiddies into believing you are running one of the most ownable Web servers on the planet (or foul up your security administrator's automatic vulnerability scanner). Note that this effect is negated if you set the RemoveServerHeader=1 as described previously, though, so pick one or the other. Also note that Apache makes a fine Web server; this particular version was terrible, though.
[AllowExtensions] .asp .asa .htm .jpg .png	Include any filename extensions you plan to have on your site. This might be a very short list, but be sure to include all extensions you expect visitors to access. IIS will ignore any you miss here.
[DenyExtensions] .inf .js .pl .txt .dll ....etc.	Since we only allow a finite number of allowed extensions through AllowExtensions=1, this section will be ignored. But in the case of building a Web site where you're not sure what extensions should be allowed, at least you can call out some explicitly denied ones. You can fill this section with numerous extensions, but keep in mind that the more you name here, the longer URLScan is going to take to allow a *GET* request through. (Because of this performance hit, in almost all cases, you're better off sticking to AllowExtensions.)

Now you are ready to run IIS Lockdown. Follow these steps:

1. Start with double-clicking the program icon to start the wizard, and click **Next**.

2. Click the **I agree** radio button to accept the license, and click **Next**.

3. Scroll down, and select our new **Hardened Dynamic Web Server (ASP Enabled)**. Click **Next**.

4. Click **Next** when you're presented with the happily empty services list, shown in Figure 13.21.

Figure 13.21 IIS Lockdown: Disabling Services

5. Click **Next** to accept our default script maps, shown in Figure 13.22.

Figure 13.22 IIS Lockdown: Disabling Script Maps

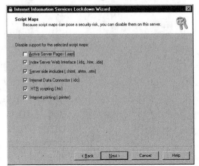

6. Click **Next** after reading the **Additional Security** panel, shown in Figure 13.23. Notice that not only are we blocking all cmd.exe access via URLScan and we're hosting our site off our system drive, but we're also blocking specific access by the Internet User account access to many system utilities—all executables found under %WINDIR%, or C:\WINNT. This added default ACL protection makes C:\WINNT\Security one of the best places to store your security tools, should you need to keep them on your production server.

Figure 13.23 IIS Lockdown: Additional Security

7.   Click **Next** to install URLScan, shown in Figure 13.24.

Figure 13.24 IIS Lockdown: Installing URLScan

8.   Click **Next** to confirm it all.

9.   Wait a minute or two while IIS Lockdown does its magic. Note that if you had accidentally installed any additional Web components, such as SMTP or FTP, the Windows Component wizard is initiated to uninstall them. Normally, this process requires no action on your part. Furthermore, this is the one function IIS Lockdown performs that cannot be undone. If you meant to keep FTP, you're out of luck—you'll have to reinstall it from the Windows Component wizard.

10.   After looking at the report, click **Next,** then click **Finish**.

You might have noticed that during the installation, you didn't interact with the wizard much more than clicking Next a few times and reading some screens. Although it's good to read along when security tools are performing scripted functions, if you plan to perform this task on a number of servers, you'll be happy to know to this can be sped up considerably by leaving **AdvancedSetup=** blank in IISLOCKD.ini. The process can be further automated for use in a batch file by specifying **UNAT-TENDED=TRUE**. To undo your change (which might be necessary during testing), either rerun IIS Lockdown or change **UNDO=FALSE** to **UNDO=TRUE** in IIS-LOCKD.ini when running it unattended. Note that the undo functionality cannot reinstall Windows Components in this way; you'll have to reinstall them yourself.

The URLScan Tool (New and Improved)

At the time of this writing, Microsoft maintains two different versions of URLScan: the one you just installed as part of the IIS Lockdown tool (currently 2.0) and the standalone version (currently 2.5). There aren't any known problems with the 2.0 version, but the 2.5 version does offer some extra functionality. To further confuse matters, URLScan version 2.5 comes in two distinct flavors: Baseline and SRP.

Let's summarize the differences. URLScan 2.5 has the added features of being able to define explicitly its logging directory and to allow only URL requests that are under a maximum length. In addition, the SRP version blocks requests that utilize chunked encoding; it also blocks uploads that are over 30MB. This upload limitation can be a real deal breaker for some sites, so keep this in mind if you're expecting large inbound files. Finally, these SRP enhancements are all or nothing, and you cannot turn them off through an .ini file setting.

If you know you won't be affected by these "enhancements," download the SRP version. Otherwise, get the baseline version. In either case, the installation procedure is the same.

Editing URLSCAN.ini (Again)

Unfortunately, we have to edit this configuration file and run URLScan again in order to reap the benefits of the new version. We trust the next version of IIS Lockdown will include this change:

1. Download **URLScan** from Microsoft: www.microsoft.com/technet/security/tools/tools/urlscan.asp.

2. Place the file in a new directory on your server, **C:\WINNT\Security\URLScan**.

3. Double-click the **URLSCAN.exe** program icon. You will get a message stating it was successful, so click **OK**.

4. Change directories to **C:\WINNT\System32\inetsrv\urlscan**, and open **urlscan.ini** in Notepad to make the following edits:

   - **LogLongURLs=** Change this to **1** to log extremely long URLs (up to 128k in length).

- **LoggingDirectory=** Set this to **E:\Logs\URLScan**, presuming you have an alternate log partition, as recommended during setup.

- **MaxURL=** The default for this is 16384 bytes (characters) long. If you know your URLs will be shorter, adjust this number accordingly. The same logic applies to the rest of the items in the **[RequestLimits]** category.

Final Configuration Steps

There are a few configuration items that IIS Lockdown and URLScan don't perform for us. Let's take care of these final touches now.

First, we want to create some logging directories on the partition dedicated to it. Using Explorer, create the directory **E:\Logs\URLScan** (where *E:* is the name of the nonsystem drive where you will be storing your log files). Next, right-click the site name **Public** to open the Properties, and on the first tab, **Web Site**, click the **Properties** button in the **Enable Logging** box, and direct IIS's logs to **E:\Logs**, as shown in Figure 13.25.

Figure 13.25 Logging Directory

Next, since this is an anonymous Web site, we want to ensure that only anonymous people are connecting. On the **Web Site Properties** panel (illustrated in Figure 13.26), click the **Directory Security** tab, and click the **Edit** button for the **Anonymous access and authentication control**. Uncheck the box for **Integrated Windows authentication**.

Figure 13.26 Authentication Methods

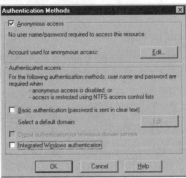

On the **Home Directory** tab, click the **Configuration** button for **Application Settings**, and remove any lingering cached script mappings, ending up with a pristine script mappings table, as shown in Figure 12.27.

Figure 13.27 Application Settings

Finally, on the **App Debugging** tab of the same panel, check the radio button for **Send a text error message to the client**. Many Web-based attacks rely on descriptive error messages being returned, which can give an attacker clues to weak points in the application. Verbose error messages should only be used during troubleshooting. Figure 13.28 shows a sample, nonverbose error message.

Figure 13.28 Nonverbose Error Messages

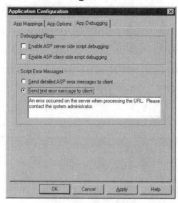

Now that your Web site is complete, you're almost ready to start dropping in your content and showing it off to the world—almost. Before doing so, be sure to reapply your latest IIS Cumulative hotfix. As of this writing, that's Microsoft Security Bulletin MS02-062, Q327696.

Reportedly, future hotfixes from Microsoft will not need to be reapplied between adding and removing programs, since Windows File Protection and the DLL cache will keep track of the latest versions. In the meantime, keep an eye on www.microsoft.com/technet/security/current.asp to stay abreast of the latest security fixes.

Setting Up a Secure Web Site

The primary reason for enabling HTTPS on a Web site is to establish a secure session between a client and a server in order to foil network-sniffing attempts at gleaning information about the session—usually, to protect secrets such as passwords and credit card numbers as well as sensitive content.

Setting up a secure Web server is practically the same procedure as setting up an anonymous Web server, with one important difference. Instead of (or in addition to) normal, port 80 HTTP traffic, your site is enabled on port 443 for HTTPS traffic as well. In order to enable this functionality, you must first obtain a certificate your users will trust. A number of trusted root authorities are available, such as VeriSign, Entrust, and Thawte.

To request a certificate from a certificate authority, open your Web site's **Properties**, and click the **Directory Security** tab. Next, click the **Server Certificate** button in the **Secure communications** box, and complete the **Web Server Certificate** wizard. Since this is a DMZ server, you are likely going to be requesting a certificate from a trusted third party, which means you need to prepare a cryptographic request to e-mail later.

Once your certificate is assigned to you (in the form of a *.cer file), you will import it in the same place.

Generally, if you are going to the trouble of getting a certificate assigned to your site, you will want to require encryption. Again, on the **Directory Security** tab, click the **Edit** button in the **Secure communications** box, and check the two top boxes, as shown in Figure 13.29.

Figure 13.29 Requiring Secure Communications

After you have imported and enabled your certificate, navigate back to the main **Web Site** tab, and fill in the box for the **SSL Port** with 443. (You are free to choose whatever port you like, just as you may choose any port for regular HTTP traffic, but all browsers default to 443 for HTTPS.)

A word of caution: Certificates are often viewed as a magical salve that heals all security wounds. This is not the case. The fact that the communication channel is secure means absolutely nothing about the security inherent in either end point of the conversation. In fact, criminal hackers love sites "protected" by SSL; very few sites require client certificates to validate the user to the server, and the SSL encryption makes Web site hacking very difficult to detect with traditional IDS implementations.

This is not to say you should abandon the idea of getting an SSL site if you plan to be trafficking in sensitive material. Do it, but know that the criminals will probably not bother trying to compromise your in-transit communications, since it tends to be easier to compromise a Web site in other ways, such as SQL injection, cross-site scripting, or other application-level weaknesses.

Configuring an IIS Server for FTP

The process of configuring an FTP site with IIS is virtually identical to that of configuring a Web site, at least initially. Again, navigate to **Start | Settings | Control Panel | Add/Remove Programs | Add New Windows Components | Internet Information Services (IIS) | Details**, just as you would for setting up a Web site. Instead of choosing World Wide Web (WWW) Server, though, choose **File Transfer Protocol (FTP) Server**. Wait a moment for the service to install, and again, launch the **Internet Configuration manager MMC**.

Just as you would configure a Web site, you administer your FTP site by right-clicking the **Default FTP Site** and selecting **Properties**. You will probably want to name the site something more descriptive, like **0day Warezzz** (or, in case you're not setting up a pirate software site, something a little more appropriate like **Public FTP**), but unlike IIS, you will not have to delete it and recreate it completely.

Again, we want to move the logging facilities off the system drive and onto a dedicated logs drive. On the first tab, **FTP Site**, click the **Properties** button in the **Enable Logging** box, and reset the log directory to **E:\Logs**. Also, for FTP logging we want to capture a little more information that what is tracked by default, so on the same panel, click the **Extended Properties** tab, and select the following check boxes: **User Name**, **Bytes Sent, Byte Received,** and **User Agent**. This sort of data can be useful in tracking open FTP-seeking bot networks.

> ## WARNING
>
> Much of Internet crime going on today is the trafficking of illegal data—called *warez*—which is almost wholly pirated software, music, movies, and adult content. Most of the storage sites for this criminal enterprise are poorly configured FTP sites. Furthermore, creating users to receive files over FTP of compromised hosts is a pretty common tactic, so related traffic would be the FTP scanners that attempt to log on using these well-known usernames. For a complete list of usernames, passwords, and other patterns to watch out for in your FTP, check out the most recent Snort IDS rules database, available from www.snort.org.

On the next tab, **Security Accounts**, unless you are requiring plain-text authentication, check the **Only Anonymous Connections** box. It is impossible to natively secure FTP logons without installing third-party SSH software or enforcing an IPSec policy between your server and clients.

For the **Home Directory** tab, create a directory on your data drive, **D:\ftp**, and set this as the root of your FTP site. If you want to allow write access (by checking

Write in the **FTP Site Directory** box), you need to assign IUSER_*computername* NTFS Write permissions on this directory as well. Generally, though, this is a bad idea. As we mentioned earlier, there are robot networks active on the Internet that probe for open FTP sites to traffic in illegal software and media.

The last tab is **Directory Security**, which is wholly concerned with maintaining IP address and subnet lists that you may allow or deny. (An identical tab is available in Web site Properties as well.) If you find yourself under attack from a specific site, this is a good place to block the attacker initially. However, it's usually more efficient to simply block the offending IP address or subnet at your border router.

Configuring an IIS Server for SMTP

Microsoft Exchange is a massively complex product that handles many, many aspects of messaging—mail, calendaring, meetings, instant messaging, NetMeeting, and the like— and complexity is the bane of security professionals. Keeping your DMZ profile as simple as possible will go a long, long way toward keeping your incident rate down.

That said, IIS as a standalone server providing SMTP relay services is an ideal method for separating an Exchange infrastructure from the perils of the Internet.

Essentially, IIS can act as a go-between for Internet-based mail users and internal Exchange users, ensuring that the Exchange infrastructure has no direct contact with the outside world. Setting up an SMTP relay for your Exchange domain is a straightforward process.

First, install the required components. Selecting **SMTP Service** from the **Windows Components | Internet Information Services (IIS)** menu will autoselect the other required components, as shown in Figure 13.30.

Figure 13.30 Selecting SMTP for Installation

Now follow these steps:

1. As before, first create the directories for logging and the site root directory on D: and E:. For SMTP, though, we also need D:\SMTP\Badmail.

2. Configure SMTP services by right-clicking **Default SMTP Virtual Server** and selecting **Properties**.

3. On the first tab, **General**, set logging by clicking the **Properties** button and changing the log file directory to **E:\Logs**. You will also want to set some logging properties, since none of the **Extended Properties** check boxes are enabled by default. At the very least, you should select **Date, Time, Client IP Address, User Name, Method, URI Stem,** and **Host**.

4. On the **Messages** tab, change the **Badmail directory** to **D:\SMTP\Badmail**. Now that basic configuration is out of the way, click **OK** to close the SMTP server's Properties.

5. On the right panel, add your domain's name to the **Domains** list by right-clicking and selecting **New | Domain**. This starts the New SMTP Domain wizard. Select the radio button for **Remote**, click **Next**, then type the domain in the box, with wildcards if required. (For example, *.mydomain.com* would be used to relay all mail for mydomain.com and all subdomains.)

6. Next, double-click the **Domains** icon, and right-click your domain's name. In this panel, check the option for **Allow incoming mail to be relayed to this domain**, and select the radio button for **Forward all mail to smart host**. Finally, enter the name of your site's Exchange mail server.

7. Restart the SMTP service for these changes to take effect.

Checklists

The checklist that follows is a summary of the steps taken in this chapter to ensure that the base Windows 2000 operating system provides a secure foundation for any DMZ-based application.

Windows 2000 Server Hardening Checklist

- Install Windows 2000 fresh (do not upgrade from NT 4.0).

- Commit separate disks or disk partitions for system, logs, and application data.

- Uncheck all optional components.

- Apply the latest service pack.

- Apply the latest appropriate hotfixes.

- Create user accounts, and add them to the local Administrator.

- Configure a high-security template through the Security Configuration Editor:

  1. Define a custom account lockout duration.

  2. Define an appropriate auditing policy.

  3. Define appropriate user rights.

  4. Define system security options.

  5. Define event log settings.

  6. Establish Administrators as a Restricted Group.

  7. Disable all unnecessary system services.

  8. Deny access to unnecessary system commands.

  9. Audit access to system commands.

- Apply the high-security template.

- Enable and configure Terminal Services for remote administration.

- Enable and configure Telnet remote administration.

- Enable and configure IPSec to encrypt Telnet sessions.

- Perform a vulnerability scan to confirm configuration is as expected.

IIS Hardening Checklist (WWW, FTP, and SMTP)

Once a secure foundation is established, the following steps are necessary to ensure that IIS 5.0, the most common DMZ service on Windows 2000, is resistant to attack.

For World Wide Web Service (HTTP)

- Install only the World Wide Web Publishing service.

- Immediately stop the service, because it installs enabled and running.

- Delete the default Web site.

- Create a new Web root directory on the application drive.

- Create a new Web site with the Internet Services Manager.

- Install the IIS Lockdown Tool.

- Modify the IIS Lockdown configuration file:

  1. Create a new, hardened profile.

2. Define the location of the URLScan configuration file.

3. Enable AdvancedSetup.

4. Enable UninstallService.

- Modify the URLScan configuration file:

  1. Enable UseAllowExtensions.

  2. Enable RemoveServerHeader (or AlternateServerName).

  3. Enable UseFastPathReject.

  4. Enable AlternateServerName (or RemoveServerHeader).

  5. List the allowed extensions for AllowExtensions.

  6. List the denied extensions for DenyExtensions (if required).

- Run the IIS Lockdown Tool:

  1. Uninstall the unnecessary services.

  2. Disable unnecessary script maps.

  3. Delete the default virtual directories.

  4. Disable IUSR access to system utilities.

  5. Disable IUSR write access to content directories.

  6. Disable WebDAV.

  7. Install URLScan.

- Install the latest URLScan version (2.5 or 2.5 SRP).

- Edit the URLScan configuration file (again):

  1. Enable LogLongURLs.

  2. Define a directory for URLScan logging on the log drive.

  3. Define a maximum character length for requested URLs.

- Define IIS's logging directory on the log drive.

- Define an authentication method (Anonymous only for anonymous WWW servers).

- Purge cached script maps.

- Enable a generic text error message for ASP errors.

- Reapply IIS hotfixes.

For World Wide Web Service (HTTPS)

- Follow the same steps for an anonymous HTTP site, as listed previously.

- Require SSL using 128-bit encryption.

- Import your server certificate.

- Enable SSL on port 443.

- Reapply IIS hotfixes.

For FTP Service

- Select FTP Service instead of WWW Service during the initial installation.

- As previously, install and run the IIS Lockdown Tool and URLScan.

- As previously, define site and logging directories on nonsystem drives.

- Enforce anonymous-only access, unless SSH or IPSec is used to protect user passwords.

- Reapply IIS hotfixes.

For SMTP Service

- Select SMTP Service instead of WWW Service during the initial installation.

- As previously, install and run the IIS Lockdown Tool and URLScan.

- As previously, define site and logging directories on non-system drives.

- Establish a relay to your organization's domain and Exchange server, if present.

- Reapply IIS hotfixes.

Summary

In this chapter, we learned that Windows 2000 Server is an extremely popular choice for deployment to Internet-facing networks. Despite Microsoft's poor reputation for security in such hostile environments, it's quite possible to secure Windows 2000 given some planning, forethought, and creative, nondefault configuration steps. "Change the defaults" is the mantra to live by when it comes to deploying Windows 2000, since relatively minor changes can have a large impact on the effectiveness of most automated, scripted attacks, such as Code Red, Nimda, and SQL Slammer.

In the actual deployment, we started with the configuration highlights of a base operating system, being careful to install and enable only the services we need and ensuring that we separate our data and applications from the core system. From there, we used the Security Policy Editor and the Security Configuration and Analysis management consoles to create a customized, highly secure template in order to further harden the OS by stripping down the out-of-the-box installation to the bare essentials. We also instituted some reasonable on-board logging, using the Event Logging service, to keep an eye on any "funny business" that might crop up in case of a failure in the network and other perimeter controls.

We then went over the fundamentals of remote management and ensured that our remote management strategies balanced the need to administer many Windows 2000 servers from a central location against the risk of attackers (human or machine-based) leveraging our remote access techniques against us.

Finally, we went through a sample installation of a typical Web server—by far the most common production use of a Windows 2000 Server in the DMZ—using the IIS Lockdown and URLScan tools, and we applied similar techniques to building a SSL-protected Web server, an anonymous FTP site, and an SMTP relay to handle Internet-based e-mail.

Solutions Fast Track

Configuring the Fundamentals

☑ Relying on network-based protective measures is not enough.

☑ A secure host is one that is running the minimum services and keeps a low "attack profile."

☑ Wherever it is practical, change the defaults!

Remote Administration of DMZ Hosts

☑ A poorly planned remote access management system can be used against you.

☑ Terminal Services is, in fact, good enough for most sites to perform system maintenance over the Internet. Careful planning and an understanding of the risk are critical, though.

☑ All administration should be performed with credentialed accounts tied to specific users. Eschew the effectively anonymous built-in Administrator account wherever you can.

Vulnerability-Scan Your Host

☑ Vulnerability scanning is useful for catching human error in implantation and for ongoing auditing of production installations.

☑ Many vulnerability scanners are available. All have their own strengths and weaknesses.

☑ Blind faith in vulnerability scanning is not an effective substitute for thoughtful planning.

Bastion Host Configuration

☑ Many weaknesses are trivial to exploit on a default installation of IIS 5.0, and an IIS server should be thoroughly configured before deployment to a DMZ.

☑ Tools such as IIS Lockdown and URLScan greatly ease the burden of building bastion hosts for the DMZ quickly and easily.

☑ A simple server is a secure server. Too much functionality drastically increases the likelihood that one function will be compromised. This places the entire environment at risk.

Checklists

☑ Use the checklists provided as a starting point to ensure that the base Windows 2000 operating system provides a secure foundation for any DMZ-based application, as well as to harden IIS.

Frequently Asked Questions

The following Frequently Asked Questions, answered by the authors of this book, are designed to both measure your understanding of the concepts presented in this chapter and to assist you with real-life implementation of these concepts. To have your questions about this chapter answered by the author, browse to **www.syngress.com/solutions** and click on the **"Ask the Author"** form. You will also gain access to thousands of other FAQs at ITFAQnet.com.

Q: Why is *J0eBl0w$* a bad password for a user named joe_blow?

A: Although the password does conform to common minimum requirements for password generation—characters from A–Z, a–z, 0–9, and punctuation—the pattern is obvious, since it's based on the username, substitutes zeros for o's, and merely tacks on the punctuation at the end. This pattern, naturally, makes the password easy to remember, but it's also comparatively easy to guess. And, of course, you're never supposed to write down your passwords or even see them as you're typing them and change them periodically. It's not an easy problem to solve. (We use Password Safe, available from SourceForge, and use mostly random passwords—but if our Password Safe password is ever compromised, we're in trouble.)

Q: If I disable Automatic Updates, how am I supposed to automatically update my servers when new hotfixes are released?

A: This, too, isn't easy. Microsoft's Systems Management Server is pretty good at delivering hotfixes, but it requires a fairly extensive SMS infrastructure, which, of course, requires access to your DMZ. Microsoft also provides Software Update Services, which ties into Automatic Updates. This at least saves you from having to traverse the Internet from the DMZ in order to retrieve fixes, by hosting hotfixes internally. There are also some third-party hotfix delivery tools, such as ConfigureSoft's Security Update Manager. In the end, though, large sites tend to write their own patch-management systems, since nothing on the market is particularly stellar.

Q: Why shouldn't I use the built-in Administrator account to perform regular work?

A: If we had our way, you would be able to disable and delete the local Administrator—in fact, this is a new feature in Windows 2003. Performing administrator functions as Administrator destroys a reasonable audit trail of the actions you take using this effectively anonymous account. If you make it a policy that Administrator is off-limits, you can at least use it as a sort of "honey account," since everything this account does will be suspicious.

Q: How am I supposed to watch the security event logs of all my heavily audited servers?

A: Offsite log management is another area Microsoft isn't particularly good at. There is no built-in method of routinely exporting system event data off the server to a central management station. Thankfully, though, SomarSoft's DumpEVT (free) and Hyena (not free) do a great job of faking it through text and database dumps, and Kiwi Enterprise's Kiwi Syslog Daemon enables Windows machines to talk syslog directly to UNIX logging stations. There are, of course, other products; shop around and experiment. It can be done.

Q: After installing IIS, don't I have to reinstall the latest service pack?

A: Not anymore. Microsoft's service packs now "check in," as it were, with the operating system, through updated configuration, cabinet, and catalog files to let the OS know where to get the latest versions of system files. Expect future hotfixes to act the same way, probably after SP4.

Q: If I really, really, don't want tftp.exe on my server, can't I just delete it?

A: You can try, but Windows File Protection will replace it in seconds. What you need to do is first delete it from %windir%\system32\dllcache, *then* delete it from %windir%/system32. Of course, if Microsoft includes it in any future hotfix or service pack, you'll get it back, which could be surprising.

Q: Seriously, no domains in the DMZ?

A: Okay, if you have perfect faith in all your border devices—firewalls, router ACLs, and the like—and they are always and forever configured flawlessly, you can probably get away with an Active Directory infrastructure in your domain. But the point of eschewing it in the first place is to (a) keep your host architecture simple and (b) isolate servers from one another in order to minimize the damage a hacker can do once he's breached your perimeter. If you need more justification, run the tool LSADump2, available at http://razor.bindview.com/tools/files/lsadump2.zip, sometime as the local System account, and get all the passwords to all the domain accounts that are running services on your domain member. (This is a long-known problem that Microsoft, so far, has refused to fix. Effectively, a local administrator can recover the passwords to all service accounts, even if they are domain credentials.) This sort of gross violation of account privilege separation is the reason to avoid any sort of domain architecture in the highly dangerous environment that is your DMZ.

Q: If I do everything in this chapter, will my hosts be perfectly secure from all attacks for all perpetuity?

A: No. "Security" is not a magical property you can imbue a machine, server, network, or system with and expect it to somehow stick. New vulnerabilities, exploits, and methodologies are constantly being discovered, refined, and implemented—sometimes by good guys, sometimes by bad guys, and sometimes by the vendors themselves. The "end of security" is not in sight today, so at the very least, you need to keep up on your patches and your service packs, and eventually, you will need to upgrade your servers when support for Windows 2000 is abandoned. Depressing? A little. But this constant, chaotic, and unpredictable change is what makes security engineering fun.

## Chapter 14

Hacking the DMZ

Solutions in this chapter:

- Reconnaissance and Penetration Testing

- Attacking the DMZ Hosts

- DMZ Hardening Checklist

☑ Summary

☑ Solutions Fast Track

☑ Frequently Asked Questions

Introduction

Warfare: For hundreds and thousands of years, civilized and uncivilized nations have waged combat with each other for good, bad, or indifferent reasons. In the technical world, it's much the same scenario. You need to plan your defense against the offense, which is the aggressor. The offense here is the attacker, the hacker, the script kiddie, or anyone else who wants to do harm to your company and its resources. Even unskilled attackers may attempt to probe your defenses no matter how fortified you may think they are. This chapter looks at the seriousness of the issue from all angles so that you can understand the importance of not only having a DMZ but properly securing it (which you have been learning how to do in the past 14 chapters).

In regard to this book, we must convey how to build a defense for your DMZ. The problem associated with building and maintaining a DMZ is simplistic; you are exposed to the public Internet. That single fact alone should be enough to alert you to the dangers of hosting services unsecurely, even within a protected public network segment such as a DMZ. To move back to our reference to modern warfare, to implement a proper security posture, you need to build your defenses. This entire book to this point has focused on just that—how to configure a DMZ properly with multiple technologies and how to securely deploy those technologies so that you do not leave back doors into your security infrastructure.

Now that you understand why we covered so much material on designing and configuring the DMZ, let's take a topical look at what an attacker could do to you if you do not take such protective measures. In this chapter we look at the offensive side and review some of the defense; from learning the offensive, you will learn how to build a better defense. It's always important to put on the "hacker hat" to test your own solution. In this chapter, that's exactly what you'll do. You will put on the security analysis hat and test what you have implemented so that you understand why it is so very important to lock down your DMZ and its contents.

In this chapter we look at the following:

- **Reconnaissance** We examine how attackers find out who you are, how they profile you, what services you have running, and the techniques used to probe your defenses. The information in this section is quite alarming; you will see that it is very simple to probe your network without expending much time or money. You will also be alarmed at how much information can be found about you and your company with a few online tools. Intelligence gathering is the most important part of successfully winning a war—and make no mistake, once attacked, you will be at war!

- **Testing** Next we take a look at actual penetration testing—trying to find the open holes and research ways to exploit those holes. We see how an attacker can easily find out the services you run, where you run these services, how to build a network map, and building a strategy to take the next step, which is to attack. So if you build up a defense, you must check it to make sure that it is secure.

- **Attacking** Lastly, we look at the attacks that will be used to penetrate the DMZ or cause havoc with the actual hosts and services available. Many times, it is quite impossible to actually penetrate a network segment, but you will see how weaknesses can be exploited quite easily once they're found with just a little research. In warfare, the strength of your opponent is matched only by your intelligence. Doing your research—finding the weaknesses and exploiting them—is how most battles are won.

In regard to these three areas, it is most important that you understand this whole methodology very clearly. This is the methodology that we hope you acquire after reading this chapter to apply to your own security assessment—assessing your own strength after building your DMZ. Again, this chapter is not meant to be a guide on how to hack someone else's DMZ but your own in hope of finding holes you might have missed. If you don't hack your DMZ, someone else will.

NOTE

The proper network-based terminology associated with this chapter is *foot-printing*—the art of profiling an organization based on reconnaissance techniques (which you'll learn in this chapter) to create a map of the organization's resources.

Before we get into the nuts and bolts, we must add a disclaimer: Please do not use the information contained within this chapter to cause harm to others; use it as a guide to help test your DMZ. This is not a hacking guidebook or a common security book. All solutions revolve around the DMZ. In addition, make certain that you gain permission from your senior management to conduct such tests on the network, especially if it is a live network. If you do decide to check out someone else's DMZ, remember, your IP address will probably be logged, so if you are not swift in your delivery (as from attacking via another machine or spoofing your address), it's very likely that you will be caught if you do not know what you're doing. Lastly, before we begin, we need to make it clear that by not checking your DMZ, you are likely to incur some costs down the road. If your network is penetrated successfully and you cannot catch the attacker, all damage done could be quite costly in time and resources, and you, your company, and the stockholders (if public) will be the bearers of the cost. This alone should be your motivation to at least perform the due diligence of "knocking on your own door" or simply "kicking the tires." Now let's begin.

Designing & Planning…

So, What Does It Cost?

Most folks don't realize how much a network penetration can cost. The dollar amount of damage that hacking causes has steadily increased over the past few years. According to the *CSI/FBI Computer Crime and Security Survey 2002* (www.gocsi.com), the total losses due to incidents such as viruses, fraud, DoS attacks, sabotage, and other computer crimes was $455,848,000—and it is predicted to rise. Other interesting statistics were the following:

- Seventy-five percent of the companies reported their Internet connection as the attack point.

- Thirty-four percent of the companies reported the intrusions to authorities. This finding was up from 16 percent in 1996. This figure will change significantly with new laws like the one in California requiring companies to report intrusions to customers.

- Forty percent of the companies reported detection of *internal* penetrations.

- Eighty-five percent of the companies reported virus attacks.

One of the rising statistics reflects the theft of transaction information. This report puts the number at 12 percent, which on the face sounds a bit low, but when you consider that 52 percent of the reporting companies have electronic commerce on their sites, it's no longer such a small number. With respect to the numbers in the report, you need to keep a few thoughts in mind. Even with such a small slice to build statistics on, the trends are clear and disturbing when you think about the companies that did not respond or weren't asked to participate.

The top security technologies used by most companies include:

- Physical security such as secured rooms
- Firewalls
- Antivirus software

Continued

- Access control

Technologies such as encryption and biometrics are not a large presence due to cost and a general lack of knowledge of the threats and solutions. One of the largest impediments to implementing technology for security is the perception that management does not yet appreciate that information has significant value to the business. The idea of information having more value than the company's building, assembly line, or even the people is a relatively new thought.

In recent years, the use of security audits, penetration testing, and overall awareness of security is increasing. With each new published attack or security breach, people become more aware of the issues. There has been significant debate in the security arena about publishing security information such as exploits and tools used. The general consensus is that with today's rapid-fire communications, hackers will have the information in a matter of days, so trying to keep the information under wraps is a disservice to people who are trying to protect networks and information.

Reconnaissance and Penetration Testing

A *penetration test* is a way to determine if you have left some doors open by accident. *Open doors* is a term used to describe services, back doors, lack of security, lack of auditing, or any other means to evade detection, penetrate, or exploit a device, segment, host, or service. An open door can really mess up your day after you invested an enormous amount of capital into your security infrastructure; an attacker is basically able to waltz right in without problem. In this section we take a solid look at how to penetration-test your DMZ with most of the same tools freely available to you (and your aggressors) on the Internet. We chose as many freeware tools to use as possible simply because it's easier (and more important) for you to learn how to duplicate these attacks with readily available tools. Some security assessment tools can be costly, and some of the freeware ones do the job just as well—at times, even better. Before we start testing, let's look at some fundamentals that you need to learn before you start your tests.

Defense in Depth

Before we begin our discussion on penetration testing, you should understand a simple concept about defense that will help you understand how a hacker thinks. *Defense in depth* is a term used to describe a multilayer security environment. In other words, just having a firewall installed is not enough, nor has it ever been. A firewall is necessary, but it should not be the only point of security you implement.

Take this scenario, for instance. Say that you are the security engineer for a medium-sized manufacturing company with three remote sites and an Internet connection in the core campus location. You have an Internet router and a PIX firewall implemented. You check logs and practice maintaining all updates on the firewall and the router. You ensure that the company is not hacked through the Internet connection by constantly keeping up with activity on both devices.

One morning when you come in to work, it's very apparent that something is wrong. Your Web server hosted on your DMZ segment off the PIX is toast. It is not responsive and you aren't sure why. You have checked the logs on the firewall and router, but nothing is showing up that alerts you to what might have happened. You then move to the Web server (which is running Solaris) to realize that had you set up auditing or IDS on the system itself, you might have been able to dig up some more clues. Worse yet, you realize that the administrator responsible for the server has not removed any extra software nor applied any security patches since the box was placed on the DMZ four months ago.

Scary? It shouldn't be, because this is a common occurrence. Let's break this scenario down—not to point fingers or find fault (we can see that the Web server administrator had not done his or her job and that the security engineer should have known about the possible holes in the Web server), but more to make this a learning experience. The first thing we see wrong here is that the security engineer was not involved with the security level set on the DMZ host and that the Web server administrator was not involved in hardening the server, using auditing, any host-based IDS, or service pack application. What's worse, the security personnel were not involved with other departments' security implementations, or possible holes in the system would have been found as soon as the server was placed in the DMZ. The last portion of fault here is directly placed on a lack of security beyond the firewall. This is lack of defense in depth. As we just mentioned, without taking a hard look at your systems and penetration testing them, you will not know that such holes are open, and worse yet, you could find that any security posture beyond the firewall is nonexistent. That is why defense in depth is so important to not only know, but also understand and follow closely to a near-religious fanaticism. You can see an example of defense in depth in Figure 14.1. Here you should not only use a firewall but also auditing, IDS, policies, ACLs, hardening, logging, and so on.

Figure 14.1 The Concept of Defense in Depth

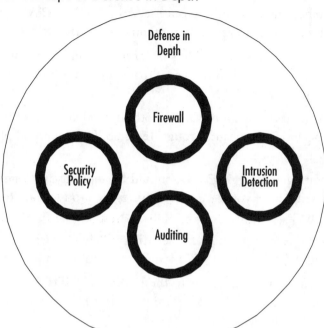

Defense in depth is a common sense-based approach to security. Defense in depth gives your security posture breadth as well as depth. Make sure this concept stays fresh in your mind as you perform your penetration testing. Make a list of what is missing from your environment. Here is a simple checklist to follow as you move through your testing:

1. Do I have an external router? If I do, does it use AAA? Do I have logging enabled? Is it secured from inappropriate access? Do I have ACLs in place to block traffic? Have I applied all the proper security patches? Have I followed the vendor (let's say it's Cisco) checklist in the appropriate chapter or on the appropriate Web site to harden this router?

2. Do I have a firewall in place? Is it controlling traffic as it should? Just like the router, is it patched, and does it have the proper security applied to it in the form of hardening?

3. Do I have IDS? Is it NIDS or HIDS? Do I have a network-based IDS? Are the signatures up to date? Does the IDS need patching and hardening? Do I have HIDS deployed on my DMZ hosts, regardless of whether I have a NIDS?

4. Am I using an internal router? Does it have the same attention applied to it as my external router did?

5. Are my hosts on my DMZ safe? Do I have auditing enabled? Are they hardened, patched, and up to the proper service pack levels? Am I using IDS? Have I gone through checklists to clean off any unneeded services?

6. Do I have any excessive protocols or services running on any device, as is common? Have I checked to ensure that once I did find unwanted services, I can safely remove them?

7. Have I secured access to the DMZ both in band and out of band, as well as physical access? This means through Telnet, SSH, dialup, and physical console access to any device.

8. Am I auditing and logging? (You should be auditing and logging on every DMZ-based device you have. Just about every product sold today has a logging feature.)

9. Does my infrastructure meet my security policies needs? Do I even have a policy, and if I do, is the DMZ addressed within it in anyway?

10. Have I secured internal threats to the DMZ and all its devices and hosts? (Remember, many attacks come from within.) Have I made certain that I can catch internal attacks as well?

This list is not complete; you could find other items you might want to place in it. Simply add them as you see fit. This is a good top-10 list to start with because these are some of the most general questions you can ask yourself when designing your DMZ.

> **NOTE**
>
> In this book we highlighted how to lock down Solaris on the DMZ, how to harden hosts, and how to implement all the solutions we mention in this chapter. As we hack, we will need to refer back to earlier chapters, where you were taught now to properly lock down these systems and check them.

Recon 101

As we move back into penetration testing, we break this section down into subsections dealing with each portion of the DMZ to make it easier for you to follow. You will find this layout throughout this chapter. We move external to internal, as illustrated in Figure 14.2. The external network is the dialup connections as well as the ISP-based Internet connection. Figure 14.2 shows a basic DMZ with an internal segment, an external segment, and a DMZ segment. We can penetration-test each section at a time so we have a standard process to follow. No matter whether you think this DMZ design is proper or not, that's not the point; you didn't build it because you are in the shoes of the hacker now. You are simply looking at someone else's design, and there could be design mistakes in here, which possibly makes more for you to exploit.

Figure 14.2 Penetration Testing the DMZ

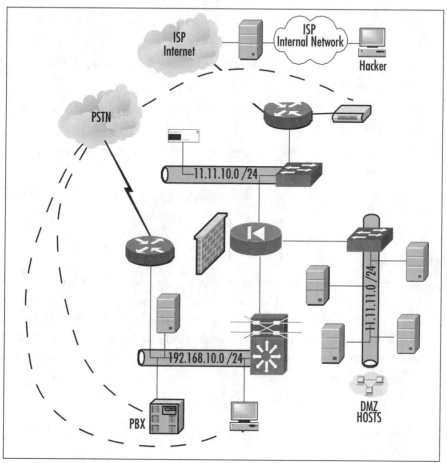

Now that you have a general idea of what the DMZ you attack will look like, let's take a look at how this map can be built remotely, and more important, how many tests you can do to find all this information out for yourself. Before we do that, remember that you want to gather as much information as possible, so pay very close attention to any details that can give you the following information about any particular company:

- Where the company is physically located and logically located (on the Internet)

- Any analog connections; these result in phones, fax, dialup lines, any out of band connectivity

- Any contact information online, in phone books, or elsewhere; people's names and phone numbers

- Companies that could be "connected" to the company you are profiling; business partners are key

- Any information you can glean on the company that results in a possible exploitation

Picking a Target

Your first and only target in penetration testing is your own network or that of a client. In this section, it should be clear that you are scanning your own network for vulnerabilities, not the network of an intended victim. We switch to the mind of the hacker here so that you can understand how the information-gathering process works. Before we start gathering information, we must choose a target. Attackers choose a victim network for a variety of reasons:

- They want to have fun. (Doesn't everyone?)

- There is a motive behind the attack (anger, monetary reasons, dismissal, personal vendetta).

- They want to see if they can beat the challenge the network represents.

Some of these reasons are common, but they all lead up to the same problem: attackers are coming after you for whatever reason they chose. Once the attacker has selected the target, the next step is to start gathering information. Let's look at this process in detail.

Basic Information Gathering

In the information-gathering phase, you will most likely start a written log to record all your findings and when you found each item. It's not wise to do everything at once, because if you simply "go for broke" on the first day, you will likely get caught. Most attackers do not attack a heavily fortified and maintained DMZ all at once; instead, they nibble on it here and there, checking out what defenses are in place. The information-gathering phase can be outlined by the following tasks:

- Start a log. Make sure you document all your findings and place the time and date in the log.

- Start with getting a domain name and an IP address in use by the company. Do a *whois* lookup.

- Mask your identity if possible. If it's not possible, try not to use your home PC or a system that can be tracked very easily. Most systems log your OS version and your IP address, so beware that this could happen.

- Once you have an IP or hostname, you can start a vulnerability scan on the range of IPs in use by the organization.

- Set up a network topology map for the external portion of the network as well as any hosts that reside on that segment.

- Start a vulnerability scan on all documented hosts.

- Try to match services to hosts. For instance, if you find a host on a DMZ segment with port 25 open, it could be an e-mail relay server. This is an assumption, but that is how you start to build your map.

- Try to find any exposure or any open services or vulnerabilities, and document these in detail. Use the Internet to find open holes through missing patches or service packs.

- Try out-of-band attacks to find open PSTN connections. War dialing is an option.

- Document all your findings, and make an assessment on where vulnerabilities lie and what you might be able to do to exploit them.

- When you have a basic network map in place, perform a masterful string of social engineering attacks to gather all other details you need.

- Start your next phase, which is to test each exploit without getting caught. Look at your log and start either developing the tools you need or acquiring them based on need.

Figure 14.3 shows a basic network map made from a light reconnaissance mission.

Figure 14.3 Basic Network Map Made from a Light Reconnaissance Mission

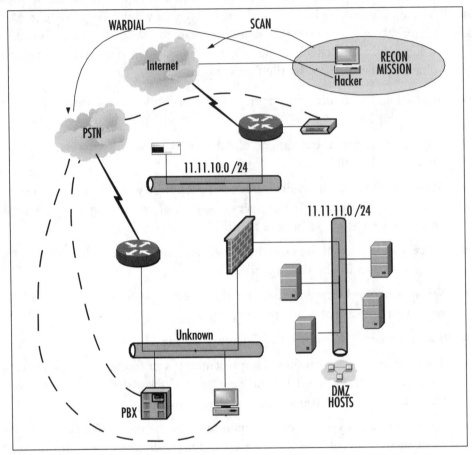

Basically, through scanning and mapping, we have the following information in our first map:

- A *whois* lookup provides us with an IP address to start with as well as a phone number.

- A vulnerability scan provides us with host types (DNS server, FTP server).

- A scan with a network-mapping tool shows us the whole IP range in use.

- War dialing has produced out-of-band connections through or past the DMZ.

So now that you have a basic understanding of how an attacker begins, let's take a look at how we built this map, the tools we used, and some detail on why.

> **WARNING**
>
> There is debate over whether port scanning and information gathering are illegal. In other words, if someone ran up to your house and knocked on your door to sell you something and realized that your door was ajar, no law is broken if the person doesn't do anything about it. However, if the person walked into your house through that open door, opened your fridge, and grabbed a cold one, the police could rightfully take me away. This theme holds true with information gathering. You can check things out, but if you do not belong there or you start to penetrate, you are breaking the law. Keep tabs on these laws for your own personal knowledge because network security and law enforcement are in flux, but as of today, its not a crime to skateboard nor knock on someone's door—yet.

Note that we don't cover wireless attacks in this chapter. Although access points (APs) can be found on many networks, its very uncommon for them not to be placed in such a high-risk area, so for the sake of complexity, we do not cover exposure of wireless technologies in this example. If you need to learn expose points on a WDMZ, refer to the relevant chapters of this book to research those areas.

The rest of this section covers the "how to" for the list we just went through. It is important that you really understand that this is not a race, and the slower you go, the more likely you will not be caught. Evading capture is very important to "winning" the intelligence war.

Whois Lookup

Information gathering always starts with the easiest way to get basic information—a general *whois* lookup. Basically, when you register a domain name online (which most companies do), you can use the following Web sites:

- www.whois.org
- www.networksolutions.com/cgi-bin/whois/whois

So, now that you know where to go, visit one of these URLs and pop in the domain name that you want to investigate. (Put in your own as well to check it out.) Figure 14.4 shows the *whois* lookup page.

Figure 14.4 The *Whois* Lookup Page

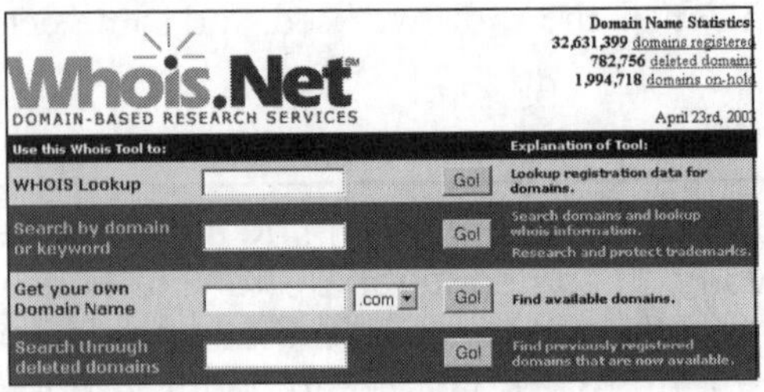

Let's keep this simple by picking a well-known domain that we know hosts its DNS servers on a DMZ segment as well as a domain name that we know will not be easily hacked or vulnerable. Novell.com is a good example. If you can penetrate Novell, you are pretty good, but we do not recommend trying it, because you will get caught unless you are an elite hacker. It is critical that you do a solid risk assessment of your target before you start your attack. As we said before, you could be caught, and hacking just isn't worth getting caught—as Kevin Mitnick found out when he was made an example of (www.kevinmitnick.com).

Once we run a lookup on the domain name www.novell.com, it is easy to see some very useful information, including company location, a personal contact, a phone number, a hostname, and an IP address:

```
Registrant:
Novell Inc. (NOVELL-DOM)
1800 South Novell Place
Provo
UT,84606
US
Domain Name: NOVELL.COM
Administrative Contact:
Wayne, Bruce  (BWS137)
bwayne@NOVELL.COM
Novell, Inc.
1800 South Novell Place
PROVO, UT 84606 US
801-861-2222
801-861-5556
Technical Contact:
Johnson, David N.  (DNJ4)
```

```
dnjohnson@NOVELL.COM
Novell Inc.
122 E 1700 S
PROVO, UT  84606-7379
US
801-861-2561 (801) 861-5556
Record expires on 21-Nov-2003.
Record created on 20-Nov-1989.
Database last updated on 23-Apr-2003 14:16:07 EDT.
Domain servers in listed order:
NS.NOVELL.COM            137.65.1.1
NS.UTAH.EDU              128.110.124.120
NS1.WESTNET.NET          128.138.213.13
```

Let's dissect this information for a moment. First, we can see that Novell has regis-tered the name. We can see that Novell is headquartered in Utah, which confirms what we know about the company. We always check the record expiration date first, just to see if the domain name is at least up to date. Then we move to record the phone number and then the IP addresses. We can see that there are three DNS servers here—a primary, a secondary, and a tertiary. Lastly, we have the name and e-mail address of a personal contact. The name cited is Bruce Wayne; this could be a Batman reference and distracter—listing a bogus contact like this is common, but at least we still have a name. Had this been an unprofessional company, you might be able to do more with the con-tacts via social engineering, but again, we chose this domain because it is known to be very hard to exploit.

We can start our social engineering, network-mapping, network vulnerability, and war-dialing assessments from this information alone. We now have an IP address to start with and a phone number to start dialing. Social engineering is also beneficial to get-ting needed information beyond what is listed here, but it warrants its own special sec-tion later in the chapter.

> **NOTE**
>
> If a company that you want to assess does not have a domain name (shame on them), you could use the phone book for that area to get general informa-tion or a contact number to start with.

Checking the Connection

Just because you did a *whois* lookup does not mean that you are on the right track. A *whois* lookup shows the provider that hosts your DNS and the IP addresses of the DNS servers. The way you can get a more granular set of information about whether this IP address is valid is to check it out with *ping* and *traceroute* tools. Do this securely using an Internet-based looking glass. You can visit one of these sites to use their tools online:

- www.traceroute.org/
- http://traffic.stealth.net/nph-trace.cgi

Basically, if you run a check on the IP addresses, you can garnish the following information. First, we *ping* it to see if it is a valid IP and in use (no need to chase something that isn't even in use):

```
Pinging 128.138.213.13 from jfk-engr-01.inet.qwest.net


64 bytes from ubu.Colorado.EDU (128.138.213.13): icmp_seq=0. time=59. ms
64 bytes from ubu.Colorado.EDU (128.138.213.13): icmp_seq=1. time=58. ms
64 bytes from ubu.Colorado.EDU (128.138.213.13): icmp_seq=2. time=59. ms
64 bytes from ubu.Colorado.EDU (128.138.213.13): icmp_seq=3. time=58. ms
64 bytes from ubu.Colorado.EDU (128.138.213.13): icmp_seq=4. time=58. ms
64 bytes from ubu.Colorado.EDU (128.138.213.13): icmp_seq=5. time=58. ms
64 bytes from ubu.Colorado.EDU (128.138.213.13): icmp_seq=6. time=58. ms
64 bytes from ubu.Colorado.EDU (128.138.213.13): icmp_seq=7. time=58. ms
64 bytes from ubu.Colorado.EDU (128.138.213.13): icmp_seq=8. time=58. ms
64 bytes from ubu.Colorado.EDU (128.138.213.13): icmp_seq=9. time=59. ms


----128.138.213.13 PING Statistics----
10 packets transmitted, 10 packets received, 0% packet loss
round-trip (ms)  min/avg/max = 58/58/59
```

You can also use the *traceroute* utility to get more information, such as the path that data travels to and from the DMZ in which the server may be kept:

```
Traceroute to 128.138.213.13 from atl-engr-01.inet.qwest.net


traceroute: Warning: ckecksums disabled
traceroute to 128.138.213.13 (128.138.213.13), 30 hops max, 40 byte
    packets
 1  205.171.21.214 (205.171.21.214)  0.718 ms  0.552 ms  0.433 ms
```

```
2    205.171.21.17 (205.171.21.17)   0.524 ms   0.531 ms   0.486 ms

3    205.171.8.154 (205.171.8.154)   16.081 ms   33.320 ms   26.080 ms

4    205.171.9.50 (205.171.9.50)   15.872 ms   15.869 ms   15.849 ms

5    205.171.209.114 (205.171.209.114)   17.178 ms   17.068 ms   17.047 ms

6    209.244.219.181 (209.244.219.181)   17.104 ms   17.002 ms   16.947 ms

7    so-5-0-0.gar2.Washington1.Level3.net (209.244.11.13)   17.374 ms
     17.378 ms

8    so-3-0-0.mp1.Denver1.Level3.net (64.159.1.113)   47.514 ms   47.517 ms
     47.494 ms

9    gigabitethernet10-0.hsipaccess1.Denver1.Level3.net (64.159.3.118)
     47.813 ms

10   209.245.20.26 (209.245.20.26)   47.546 ms   47.535 ms   47.661 ms

11   cuatm-frgp.Colorado.EDU (198.59.55.5)   48.606 ms   57.461 ms   48.535 ms

12   its-juniper-supb.Colorado.EDU (128.138.81.221)   49.030 ms   48.937 ms
     49.018 ms

13   ubu.Colorado.EDU (128.138.213.13)   49.392 ms   49.027 ms   49.099 ms
```

Use publicly accessible routers so that you have a device between yourself and the host you are checking out and doing reconnaissance on. A looking-glass router will be the host in the middle that is generally available and free to use over the Internet, as you can see in this section. Just be aware that if a company has disabled ICMP outbound from any device on the DMZ segment (this is highly advisable), it might not only stop ICMP-based attacks but also impede the reconnaissance phase of the attack. ICMP is used with both *pint* and *traceroute*.

NOTE

Often, a hacker will uses a host that he or she controls as a zombie to do this type of check. Just as a hacker will launch DoS attacks from zombies, they can also be used in the recon process.

Internal vs. Externally Hosted DNS

Now that you know you have a real IP address and it is valid, in use, and ready to be checked out more deeply via network mapping, let's first make sure that the IP address you are going to check out is actually the company you want to test, or an offsite, managed, or collocated solution that leads you to a provider instead of the company itself. Generally, companies design their infrastructures this way so that they do not have to invest many dollars in security solutions; they just outsource their e-mail, DNS, and Web server solutions to third parties and let them worry about them. You can either go after the sites, servers, and services at the provider, or you can stick to your intended plan to penetrate the DMZ at the local company. Either way, you can find out with the *whois* lookup. In the lookup, you will see information such as this:

```
Registration Service Provider:
Domain Name Systems as low as $10 domain name registrations
http://www.domainnamesystems.com
This company may be contacted for domain login/passwords, DNS/Nameserver
    changes, and general domain support questions.
```

That really says it all. As you can see, *whois* lookups are pretty informational, and what's funny about all this is, we haven't even run an attack or exposed ourselves at all—hence the reconnaissance mission!

Depending on how badly you want to tap into this network, you could eat a few bucks and set up an account with the same provider, then find out more about the internal structure of the hosting provider, but again, this is more for your knowledge. Let's get back on track to hacking your own DMZ to assess it. Now you have amassed quite a bit of information. Let's move on to the next possible information-gathering step: social engineering.

Social Engineering

If you are not good at social engineering or if you know little about it, you had better start learning now. Basically, social engineering is the art of deceptively lying to gain access to information that would normally not be disclosed. Social engineering is the biggest tool in your arsenal for information gathering. Normally, people at work are too busy or are uninformed about their professional conduct during business hours. Most people don't know what a security policy is, even though they might have signed one when they were hired. This is bad for you but good for the attacker on recon.

We have alluded to this attack quite a few times in this chapter; now it's time to explain why it is so useful. For one, it's been known for a long time that a hacker, quick on his feet and with the right speaking skills, can undermine your entire network security infrastructure with a simple phone call. He merely calls the company he would like to tap into, posing as a product vendor, and tries to get to the IT department to talk to the security staff members. As soon as he finds that there is no one in charge of security, he makes his first few assumptions:

■ They gave this information out freely; they must not know the dangers of social engineering. They must not have been told that this is dangerous.

- They don't have a security department or security staff. Well, maybe I can talk to one of the administrators or help desk staff on the phone to gather some more information.

- If I try to sell them an IDS system or firewall, they tend to tell me too much information right off the bat, such as "We already have a PIX firewall in place," "We don't need an IDS system at this time," or "We use SNORT for IDS and it works fine." Any information is good information, so this helps.

- I can also find out what their level of technical ability is by their general answers.

As a DMZ architect, you most likely work in engineering, architecture, or security, and if this is the case, its up to you to make sure that none of this information leaks out. We generally tell companies to ensure that any questions directly related to security are sent to a supervisor or the security staff on board. No answers or information are to be given out for any reason, no matter what. As a security analyst, you should have in your security policy a statement that no one (and we mean *no one*) is to divulge any meaningful information about the network over the phone.

NOTE

Some social engineering attacks, if done properly, can expose actual credentials on systems that are accessible over the Internet (such as Linux servers on the DMZ that can be reached via Telnet or SSH), and these are commonly the first to get blown off the map by attackers—all from a simple phone call.

Hiding Your Identity

Before you start any attack, it's important that you think about the company to pinpoint your location and your identity. Although companies cannot legally "hack you back," they can log the heck out of you and wait until you're nailed to reproduce those logs in court. This is a very common practice; the way around it is to mask your identity. In Figure 14.5, you can see that the attack is on a New York City (NYC) based company, and it appears to be originating from four different locations, all of which are in different countries. This is your first tip-off that your hacker is swift and making certain that zombies or remote control hosts are launching the attacks (passive or active) against you when in reality they are coming from someone sitting in the same city as you!

This is what the hacker is thinking. Now, as a white-hat security analyst, you need to ensure that your DMZ infrastructure has this level of auditing and logging enabled.

Make certain that you have logging turned on and you are auditing suspicious activity. Make certain you use IDS on mission-critical hosts and infrastructure.

Figure 14.5 Masking the Attack

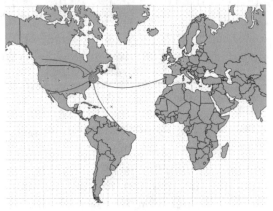

Remember, you need to be able to point the finger, but make sure that you are pointing the finger at the right person or organization. A serious hack attack on a DMZ-based system (like Yahoo.com's DoS takedown years ago) is done over time, not overnight.

Now that you have gathered enough information and understand the information-gathering process better, let's take a stab at finishing the network map so we can pin-point our hosts on the DMZ segment and start the identification process. In our next section, we look at scanning networks to add more identities to our network map.

Designing & Planning…

Penetration or Occupation?

Often you will wonder, do I want to merely pierce this DMZ and exploit it, or do I want to try to take over one of these hosts and sit and wait, to maybe take over the system and use it as a zombie in a DoS attack or to store warez? With the scan completed, you can adjust your penetration testing in a couple of ways. One way is to decide if this is a firewall test or a router test. Furthermore, you can decide to test applications such as Windows-based IIS. The penetration test is not just "Can I get to the firewall/IDS?"; but it also should cover whether you can use the ID of the device and become a *trusted*

Continued

node on the network to get further into the system. For example, if you can compromise a server in the DMZ, you can now launch a man-in-the-middle (MITM) exploit, where the network thinks the host is trusted when in reality you are sitting between two trusting hosts and capturing data. This allows you to possibly get the data you need to move further into the network.

Scanning Techniques

There are as many techniques to scan a network as there are tools. Most engineers find a couple of tools they like and become very proficient with them. You also have to know your tools and their limitations. One other rule is to never become fixated on a single method. Keep trying new methods of scanning and use different tools until you find the toolset that you like and are conformable with. Be careful where you scan your networks from as well. If you do it from your home PC, you will most likely get caught, depending on your ISP's rules. When most ISPs detect that scanning is occurring, they will shut down that account without first asking any questions. Some ISPs will do absolutely nothing at all.

A scanning program can use different methods of scanning the target. Some are a simple network sweep scanner and use the ICMP protocol. Others use certain features of the TCP/IP handshake against the target. You will see that you can scan using SYN or FIN packets, which are less likely to trip a scan detector. The way you can break the rules is to learn how the TCP protocol works. The TCP connection is a three-part handshake. You can see the normal three-way handshake illustrated in Figure 14.6.

Figure 14.6 A TCP Three-Way Handshake for a Normal Connection

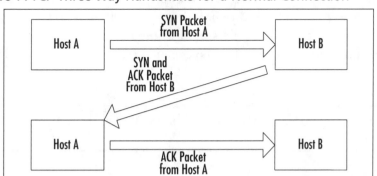

In the normal handshake, Host A sends a SYN packet to Host B. Host B responds with both a SYN and the ACK packets. Host A then returns an ACK packet, and the connection setup is completed. In the SYN scan or "half-open" connection scan, Host

A (a black hat) sends a SYN packet to Host B (target). Host B sends back the SYN-ACK response, and then Host A immediately sends an RST packet to reset the connection. Figure 14.7 shows a SYN scan handshake example.

Figure 14.7 A SYN Scan Handshake Example

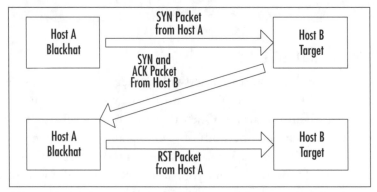

The SYN scan has a few advantages over the TCP connection scan. It never makes the full TCP connection so it doesn't show up in many logs; the SYN scan can be very fast relative to a three-way scan. The down side is that you might find that you launched an inadvertent DoS attack by the outstanding SYNs. Many scanner programs such as Nmap send an RST right after the SYN-ACK comes in to clear the connection. This is stealthier than the plain old TCP connection, but we can take it further. The next level of bending the TCP rules is to launch FIN packets against the target. The FIN packets instruct the TCP stake to tear down a connection, but there is no TCP connection—so what happens? The FIN packet arrives and if the port is open, the target responds with a RESET. If it is not open, there is no response. So, by breaking the three-way handshake, we have found a simple way to scan a system for open ports and not be tracked ourselves most of the time.

There are more scans like these, but these are the major ones you should be aware of.

> **NOTE**
>
> All the scans mentioned here can be done with the tools listed in this chapter, especially Nmap.

The easiest scan is to look for open ports such as 23 (TELNET), 25 (SMTP), 110 (POP3), and others. When a port like this is found to be open on the Internet, it's effectively an open door. In addition, never assume that you are the first one that has targeted this host. Look for exploits already present on the target. Depending on the scanning software you use, you can get just a simple report of ports open or very detailed information about the system itself.

When scanning a target, be aware that you yourself might be leaving fingerprints or triggering an alert. The scanners can trigger the alert by the amount of scanning they perform in a period of time or even by the fingerprint of the scanner software itself. The sample trace shown in Figure 14.8 is from Nmap running a scan using FIN packets. Even though this is a stealthy scan, if there is an IDS that looks for this type of traffic, it will see you.

Figure 14.8 Etherpeek Trace of Nmap Running a FIN Scan

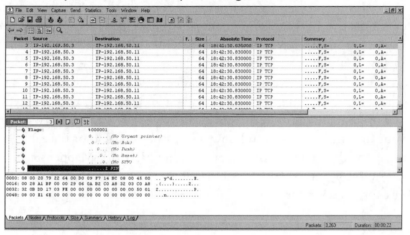

You can see that Nmap sends a group of packets with the FIN bit set. Then the response comes back from the target. This cycle repeats until Nmap has scanned all the requested ports. This shows up on a sniffer or IDS by a high number of FINs relative to SYNs, as shown in Figure 14.9.

Figure 14.9 High Number of FIN Packets Relative to SYN Packets

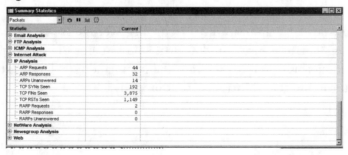

Network Mapping

Now that you have accumulated some decent information, you will want to start your assessment. We don't need to use a public domain (www.novell.com) anymore because it's not necessary; we did so before only to give you an idea what a hacker will do to find information about a target. Let's now direct our attention to attacking our own DMZ (as a hacker would) so that you can see that all your hardening efforts have paid off, and if they didn't, you will know.

Mapping a DMZ is quite simple. As long as you feel confident that you're not being monitored, you can continue to scan and search as much as you want. Again, it's common to do this in intervals so your presence is not noticed. You must assume that logs are not constantly checked. Larger companies most likely have a security staff on board, so you might want to steer clear of these types of companies as a hacker unless you are a pro, or you will most likely get caught. If you are a member of that staff, it's up to you to keep that fear alive. This book has covered many ways to do this besides hardening the servers, checking logs, and installing and working with honeypots. There are still many other methods to keep your security posture strong. Anyway, now that you have your initial IP address, you know it's up and pingable or traceable, so it's on to mapping the network segment. For this task we use Network Mapper, or Nmap, a free Windows and UNIX (Linux) based tool that allows you to map a network segment as well as check for open services.

Using Nmap

Nmap is an open-source utility for network exploration or security auditing. It was designed to rapidly scan large networks, although it works fine against single hosts. Nmap uses raw IP packets in novel ways to determine the hosts available on the network, the services (ports) they are offering, the operating system (and OS version) they are running, the type of packet filters or firewalls in use, and dozens of other characteristics. Nmap runs on most types of computers, and both console and graphical versions are available. Nmap is free software, available with full source code under the terms of the GNU GPL.

You can download Nmap from the insecure.org Web site: www.insecure.org/nmap/. Once you download and install it to your system, you can run it from a Linux system very easily from the command line. This next example lists the options you can use with Nmap to use it properly:

```
SSH Secure Shell 3.2.0
Last login: Wed Apr 16 15:45:57 2003 from 10.8.56.155
[root@SHIMONSKI root]# nmap
Nmap V. 3.00 Usage: nmap [Scan Type(s)] [Options] <host or net list>
```

```
Some Common Scan Types ('*' options require root privileges)
* -sS TCP SYN stealth port scan (default if privileged (root))
  -sT TCP connect() port scan (default for unprivileged users)
* -sU UDP port scan
  -sP ping scan (Find any reachable machines)
* -sF,-sX,-sN Stealth FIN, Xmas, or Null scan (experts only)
  -sR/-I RPC/Identd scan (use with other scan types)
Some Common Options (none are required, most can be combined):
* -O Use TCP/IP fingerprinting to guess remote operating system
  -p <range> ports to scan.  Example range: '1-1024,1080,6666,31337'
  -F Only scans ports listed in nmap-services
  -v Verbose. Its use is recommended.  Use twice for greater effect.
  -P0 Don't ping hosts (needed to scan www.microsoft.com and others)
* -Ddecoy_host1,decoy2[,...] Hide scan using many decoys
  -T <Paranoid|Sneaky|Polite|Normal|Aggressive|Insane> General timing
     policy
  -n/-R Never do DNS resolution/Always resolve [default: sometimes resolve]
  -oN/-oX/-oG <logfile> Output normal/XML/grepable scan logs to <logfile>
  -iL <inputfile> Get targets from file; Use '-' for stdin
* -S <your_IP>/-e <devicename> Specify source address or network interface
  --interactive Go into interactive mode (then press h for help)
Example: nmap -v -sS -O www.my.com 192.168.0.0/16 '192.88-90.*.*'
SEE THE MAN PAGE FOR MANY MORE OPTIONS, DESCRIPTIONS, AND EXAMPLES
[root@ SHIMONSKI root]#
```

You can also use a GUI-based client for Nmap, as shown in Figure 14.10. Either way, you now have a nice listing of the options available to you.

Figure 14.10 Using Nmap's GUI

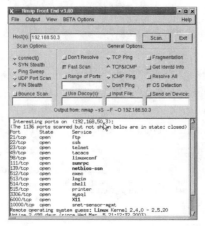

Now that you have Nmap installed and ready, let's check a scan of a host at 192.168.50.3. In this example we use a private IP address, but in your scan you will obviously be scanning a public range available over the Internet. Your DMZ will be using public IP addresses.

What comes from the port scan is *services identification*. This is the start of the gathering of information to find out exactly what the target might be (identification). This can be simple information such as the services that are running against the ports that are open or something like a TCP fingerprint, which takes a guess at what the OS is running as far as services and ports go. Every IP stack has a fingerprint, just as humans do, and there are tools that will match the fingerprints. These tools give you a better idea of what attacks or exploits might work against the target. In other words, let's say that you have a DMZ-based host running an e-mail relay service. This is very common in a DMZ segment, as we have learned in this book. More important, you have to understand that this is going to be a very large target for mass-mail spammers, and if you leave this hole open too long (an open e-mail relay), you could find yourself added to a blacklist of open relays like the one found in the Open Relay Database (www.ordb.org/faq/), and as a result you will have issues with companies that do not allow spam or don't want spam from you. Due to this possibility, you should try to hide a footprint that shows you are running an e-mail relay. You could start by scanning the host with Nmap (as the hacker would) and check to see if port 110 and port 25 are open. If they are, a hacker would attempt to Telnet to the port via the IP address to see what you are running:

```
Telnet 11.11.11.1 25
```

```
200 shimonski.rsnetworks.net GroupWise Internet Agent 5.5 Ready (C) Novell
```

This little footprint tells you a lot: that you can probably spam off your relay, and that your e-mail relay platform is currently Novell NetWare GroupWise Internet Agent (GWIA.NLM) running on the system. You can do this with any e-mail relay/system vendor if the port is open; it's up to you to secure the banner information from attackers. You could also only allow via ACL, Telnet access only via certain IP addresses. Regardless of what you choose, just remember that your scan with Nmap started it all. It opened the door so that you could see what services were running. It's up to you to then go to an active attack mode and start trying to access the systems.

This being said, it is important for you to check to see if you are running an open relay, if it is disclosing too much information about you, and more important (if you were a hacker), you would me very concerned about scanning the entire DMZ for hosts to see what services they are running, then exploit them if possible.

Run Nmap against your entire DMZ's IP range. Check the external IP address range and then go as far as you can go via the reconnaissance work you did earlier. An example of this attack from the hacker's perspective could look like this with Nmap:

1. The hacker first finds a company he or she would like to attack. This process is largely hit and miss, unless you have a company or individual in mind that you would like to personally attack. Once this is decided, the next step is to figure out what public IPs are in use for the organization. We have already taken care of these tasks.

2. The next step is to map the network. To do this, you need an IP address to start with. In this example, we use Cisco. Cisco of course has publicly accessible IP addressing because it has a Web site that can be reached via the Internet and seen within your Web browser. We already did this as well.

3. Next, choose the range (or single IP for a single host) and scan it with Nmap. In this example, we look at a host we scanned on the public Internet, checking a DMZ bastion host for vulnerabilities:

```
[root@SHIMONSKI root]# nmap -v -sS 10.0.0.1

Starting nmap V. 3.00 ( www.insecure.org/nmap/ )
Host  (10.0.0.1) appears to be up ... good.
Initiating SYN Stealth Scan against  (10.0.0.1)
Adding open port 3268/tcp
Adding open port 88/tcp
Adding open port 139/tcp
Adding open port 389/tcp
```

```
Adding open port 3372/tcp

Adding open port 1083/tcp

Adding open port 3269/tcp

Adding open port 25/tcp

Adding open port 445/tcp

Adding open port 80/tcp

Adding open port 135/tcp

Adding open port 443/tcp

Adding open port 1080/tcp

Adding open port 1029/tcp

Adding open port 3389/tcp

Adding open port 1026/tcp

Adding open port 636/tcp

Adding open port 464/tcp

Adding open port 53/tcp

Adding open port 593/tcp

The SYN Stealth Scan took 4 seconds to scan 1601 ports.

Interesting ports on  (10.0.0.1):

(The 1581 ports scanned but not shown below are in state: closed)

Port        State        Service
25/tcp      open         smtp
53/tcp      open         domain
80/tcp      open         http
88/tcp      open         kerberos-sec
135/tcp     open         loc-srv
139/tcp     open         netbios-ssn
389/tcp     open         ldap
443/tcp     open         https
445/tcp     open         microsoft-ds
464/tcp     open         kpasswd5
593/tcp     open         http-rpc-epmap
636/tcp     open         ldapssl
1026/tcp    open         LSA-or-nterm
1029/tcp    open         ms-lsa
1080/tcp    open         socks
1083/tcp    open         ansoft-lm-1
1433/tcp    open         ms-sql-s
```

```
3268/tcp      open          globalcatLDAP
3269/tcp      open          globalcatLDAPssl
3372/tcp      open          msdtc
3389/tcp      open          ms-term-serv
```

```
[root@SHIMONSKI root]#
```

Whoa, that's pretty shocking to see from a system running on the DMZ! A hacker could have a field day with this system. To be honest, to get this listing, we installed a Windows 2000 server, set it up to be scanned, and even with Service Pack 3 and all current security hotfixes up to the date it was scanned, it still showed me a lot. Windows on the DMZ is dangerous and should be watched very carefully for vulnerabilities. The whole point of this is, if a hacker were profiling our DMZ, he would basically figure out in about 3 seconds that we were running a Windows system on our DMZ and that it has a ton of open ports for him to play with.

For example, he can tell that we have SQL running from port 1433. This is instant death to your system because will soon be dealing with a SQL slammer problem. Furthermore, 3389 tells the hacker we are running terminal services, so of course he will try to set up a terminal server connection from the Internal network. He can also see we are running all NetBIOS services, so he can gather information about our system remotely. H can see our SMTP service is also running. He can relay off this system even if it isn't an e-mail relay. Yes, Windows systems by default (because they are running IIS by default) run the SMTP service through IIS. Refer back to Chapter 2, which discussed Windows-based services in the DMZ.

Designing & Planning…

What Services Should You Be Looking For?

When working on DMZs, you should always pay attention to a group of services that are the biggest culprits aiding a hacker's penetration and attack methodology. Make certain that when you are securing (or testing) DMZ-based services, you take a very close look at the following services and address them against all that you have learned reading this book:

Continued

www.syngress.com

- Login services:
    - Telnet -(23/tcp)
    - SSH -(22/tcp)
    - FTP -(21/tcp)
    - NetBIOS -(139/udp)
    - Rlogin -(512-514/tcp)

- NetBIOS on Windows:
    - Port 135 (tcp/udp)
    - Port 137 (tcp/udp)
    - Port 138 (udp)
    - Port 139 (tcp)

- X-Windows:
    - Ports 6000–6255 (tcp)

- Naming services:
    - DNS (53/udp)
    - LDAP (389/tcp/udp)

- Mail services:
    - SMTP (25/tcp)
    - POP (109-110/tcp)
    - IMAP (143/tcp)

- Web services:
    - HTTP (80/tcp)
    - SSL (443/tcp)
    - Common (8000,8080,8888/tcp)

- Small services:
    - Ports below 20 (tcp/udp)
    - Time (37/tcp 37/udp)

Continued

- Miscellaneous services:
  - TFTP (69/udp)
  - Finger (79/udp)
  - NNTP (119/udp)
  - Syslog (514/udp)
  - SNMP (161 tcp/udp)

- ICMP services:
  - Block inbound echo request
  - Block outbound echo replies
  - Block outbound time exceeded
  - Block outbound destination unreachable except "packet too big"

This wraps up our discussion of network mapping. To reiterate, you basically run through each host on the network, testing the system to see what services are running and if the host is alive so that you can map it on your log. After you use Nmap, your log should resemble the diagram shown in Figure 14.11.

Figure 14.11 Adding More Detail to Your Map

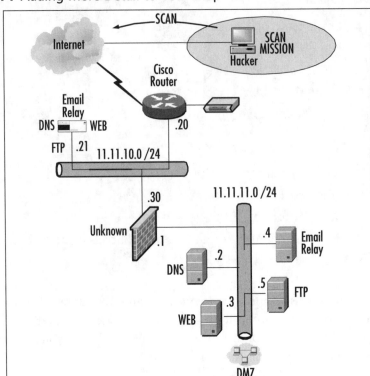

Now let's say that we have learned the following from penetration-testing our network, especially using Nmap. (See how easy it is to effortlessly map a network?):

- We are running a Cisco router. We found this out by running an XMAS tree attack on it through Nmap and crashing it. We also Telneted to it and were able to read the banner, where the engineer left the word *Cisco* in it. The banner also provided a company name.

- We saw a host on the 11.11.10.0 network with an IP address of 11.11.10.21. This host has a bunch of services open. We can't really tell what it is, maybe a Windows server, or "worse," it could be a trap. We can tell this because the single host with all services running like that could be a honeypot—in other words, the security personnel who work at this company are looking for us to tap on the door of .21 so they can see who we are. We will ignore this host; it's not worth our trouble and it is probably a trap.

- We can see that the network obviously has some form of firewall in place, but we can't tell what it is. Most firewalls by default are highly restrictive, we probably won't get far with this one.

- We can see our DMZ segment utilizing the 11.11.11.0 network, with active hosts on .2 through .5.

- From a scan of each system, we can see that each host is completely hardened, with only the following systems running specific services:

  - .2 is running DNS, port 53 is open.

  - .3 is running a Web site. This is obvious as seen through a browser.

  - .4 is running ports 25 and 110, telling us that it's an e-mail relay (we can Telnet to it).

  - .5 is running the FTP service, and we can check it with an anonymous login.

Now, this map might not be completely accurate as you scan, but we are not too far from the real map! See what we can learn with only a few tools and some time. Make sure you log all your new information before you move on.

Configuring & Implementing…

Ping Sweeping

If you have access to a Linux box, you can quickly see the hosts that are available on a segment. Simply move to a Linux prompt (if you have fping installed) and launch the tool against an IP range. You can create a text file to use with it as well. To get fping, download it from www.fping.com and install it on your Linux system. To create a text file, open the vi editor and create a file with your IP range in use. For example, if your DMZ hosts are 11.11.11.1-10, you can make the file like this:

```
11.11.11.1
11.11.11.2
11.11.11.3
11.11.11.4
11.11.11.5
11.11.11.6
```

Continued

```
11.11.11.7
11.11.11.8
11.11.11.9
11.11.11.10
```

Name the file *dmz.txt*. When you invoke fping, simply type the following:

```
[root@SHIMONSKI root]# fping -f dmz.txt
```

You will want to use fping because it is lightning-fast and you never have to wait; the tool just reads the file and responds quickly. You can use a tool like this to quickly scan the DMZ segment and check to see what hosts answer.

Now you have defined the first half of the topology map and documented most of the hosts that are readily available and the services they are running. You now need to scan the hosts for vulnerabilities. Vulnerability scanning is a little different. Vulnerability scanning takes your network map deeper because it allows you to check what's exploitable on each mapped device.

Vulnerability Scanning

Networking mapping is simply used to map out the topology. It can be argued that Nmap will be able to also show many vulnerabilities (which it can), but it is limited. A vulnerability scanner can also perform network mapping, so the lines pretty much blur. We separate the two techniques here because they are technically two different tools that provide different forms of information. A network mapper maps the network for you; a vulnerability scanner shows you open and unpatched services, among other things. In this example we look at two freely available scanners available on the Internet: Nessus and LANGuard.

Using Nessus

Once you have the system information, you can research the possible attacks or exploits that can be used against it. Nessus is a program that can run a set of exploits against a target in a nonintrusive way or with the intent to crash the system as part of the test. Nessus is a great scanner, even though it is free, as long as you know how to use it. In this section we look at how we can scan our DMZ (as a hacker would), looking for possible vulnerabilities. In Figure 14.12, you can see Nessus in use, showing the Nessus report of a host.

Simply plug the IP address into Nessus and let it check your host.

Figure 14.12 A Sample of a Nessus Report from Scanning a Cisco Router

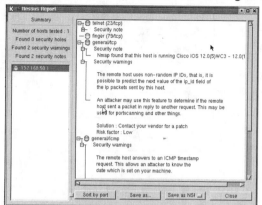

The Nessus Project aims to provide to the Internet community a free, powerful, up-to-date, and easy-to-use remote security scanner. A security scanner is software that audits remotely a given network and determines whether hackers might be able to break into it or misuse it in some way. Unlike many other security scanners, Nessus takes nothing for granted. That is, it will not consider that a given service is running on a fixed port—that is, if you run your Web server on port 1234, Nessus detects it and tests its security. It does not make its security tests regarding the version number of the remote services but attempts to exploit the vulnerability. Nessus is very fast and reliable and has a modular architecture that allows you to fit it to your needs. You can get Nessus free at www.nessus.org/intro.html.

LANGuard

LANGuard is another vulnerability scanner. In Figure 14.13, you can see that we scanned a DMZ host and were able to find quite a bit open here. The Windows 2000 host on the DMZ we scanned had IIS installed, and this is what it returned:

- An issue with SMTP running on this system. If you are not using it, it will become a spam relay immediately.

- FTP is running. We tested it and it was completely open for business.

- Terminal Services is running—very bad if not used.

- A Web server is running, but no site up and in use. This tells us that the server may be used for something else. Basically, it has IIS installed and running, but the administrator might not know that. Perfect for exploiting!

- There are also a few alerts. We can see where the vulnerability scanner's true strength comes in—showing where the common gateway interface (CGI) vulnerabilities are.

Figure 14.13 Viewing Windows 2000 Vulnerabilities with LANGuard

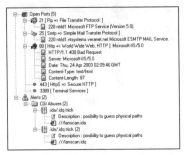

Basically, you can see that as we continue to test, you are getting deeper into the map, just as we planned. Our efforts to penetrate the DMZ might just pay off with all this reconnaissance. We have already started a map and populated it with a great amount of information. We know what hosts are where, what OSs they are running, what vulnerabilities that have exposed, and more.

At this point in the game, stealth and patience are virtues. We need to be stealthy in order to avoid tripping any IDS, and we need patience for working past these blocks to gather information that might be slow in coming.

Although penetration tests sound like and can be fun even while being serious, there are legal issues we must be very concerned about. The DMCA has cast a shadow across the land of security since, in the strictest sense of the law, writing about how a marker can bypass CD security is a violation of the DMCA's provisions. We do not purport to be legal experts and strongly suggest that before you do any testing, you consult an attorney and make sure you have a contract where the testing parameters are clearly stated and that the customer signs it. There have been cases in which someone has contracted for testing but does not really have the authority to approve security testing against a production network. The network engineer ends up in the middle trying to explain that he or she is not hacking the network for which they are under contract to run tests. As you might see, a situation can get very messy in a short period of time.

NOTE

Other available scanners that you can use include:

- Nessus, which is an exploit and vulnerability scanner
- Security Administrators Integrated Network Tool (SAINT)
- Cheops (pronounced *KEE-ops*), which is a network-mapping tool
- Netcat, which has been called the Swiss Army knife of network tools

- Whisker CGI Scanner
- Hunt Freeware sniffer with hijack capabilities
- Ethereal or other trace analysis tools such as NAI's Sniffer or Etherpeek
- A hex editor to make custom packets or to examine the results of a sniff
- A software emulator such as Virtual PC, which we use to run Linux concurrently with Windows
- A Telnet client such as Teraterm
- A war dialer such as THC-SCAN for those forgotten doorways in
- An SNMP string cracker like the one in Solarwinds

The SANS Top 20

Did you ever need help taking down systems? If you think like a hacker, you would appreciate sites like sans.org that very nicely puts up top 10 lists of common vulnerabilities seen in systems worldwide. We summarize the most commonly known and exploited ones here. These are the top vulnerabilities to Windows systems as reported by the FBI and SANS:

- **Internet Information Services (IIS)** IIS is highly vulnerable to attack (which most people know), but what they might not know is just how much vulnerability it really is prone to! Worse, it takes the top slot on the SANS list. IIS is prone to any attack not patched by you, the administrator, depending on what the exploit of the week is. Be very careful with IIS on the DMZ; make sure you pay close attention to it and very close attention to scanning it for yourself on a constant basis. Stay patched, remove default Web sites, samples, and remove connection to any APIs not in use.

- **Microsoft Data Access Components (MDAC) as well as Remote Data Services (RDS)** According to SANS, you need to worry about old unpatched systems running MDAC. MDAC has a component called RDS that runs with it. The flaw with RDS/MDAC is that remote users can easily run commands on the local system if they have administrative rights to the system. These are old exploits and have been patched, but due to lack of experience or knowledge (especially in the DMZ), you can easily find unpatched systems awaiting your command.

- **Microsoft SQL Server** According to SANS, the Microsoft SQL Server (MSSQL) application, when unpatched and unhardened, can be completely hacked. MSSQL exploits, issues, vulnerabilities, and hacks are well known, and there is much information available to aid you in securing such systems. Make certain that you cover these issues in your analysis and recon phase of your attack. DMZ hosts shouldn't be giving access to SQL information, so a bad design could be the culprit. If you need to promote DMZ access, you must lock down this product to the gills to avoid exploitation. The most common of the exploits are based on the service/port for SQL Server Port 1433 (MSSQL default port), also known to be constantly seen on the Internet from scanners. This tells you something—that need to scan your own systems and lock them down if you must expose them. Don't forget, it's not only SQL servers but also systems running the SQL Desktop Engine as well. (*Note:* SQL security is covered later in this chapter.)

- **NETBIOS and unprotected Windows Networking shares** The SMB protocol or the Common Internet File System (CIFS) are highly dangerous services to be running on the DMZ. These protocols allow for the manipulation of systems remotely (and very easily) and should be eliminated altogether whenever possible. The Nimda worm spreads extremely easily by discovering unprotected network shares and placing a copy of itself in them. To avoid such issues, you need to make sure you disable the service and file sharing when they're not needed. In addition, make sure that shares can be authenticated. You can also block ports 137-139 TCP and 137-139 UDP, as well as 445 TCP and 445 UDP.

- **Anonymous logon and null sessions** You need to check your Windows systems for anonymous logon ability and null session connection functionality. What this means is, we can run a *net use* command like so:

```
net use \\10.10.10.1\ipc$ "" /user:"" -
```

  and connect to the system. There is a Registry hack (visit the links to SANS) to fix this, but you still need to check your own systems (especially on the DMZ) for it.

- **LAN Manager authentication and weak LM hashing** According to SANS, LAN Manager (LM) support for Windows systems is old and outdated compared with newer authentication models such as NTLM and NTLMv2. Because by default Windows NT/2000/XP stores legacy LM hashes, you can still exploit the system. Since brute-force password cracking can be done remotely with a tool like Brutus (and others), you can be hacked within a week on trial and error.

- **General Windows authentication and accounts with no passwords or weak passwords** You need to develop a strong password policy. See the following Note for a long article on how to develop and implement good passwords.

- **Internet Explorer** If you use Microsoft Internet Explorer (IE), you need to have it patched and service packed to the latest levels. Although this doesn't have much to do with the DMZ hosts, it is still important to mention as part of the SANS list.

- **Remote Registry access** Improper permissions or security settings can permit remote Registry access. The Registry is pretty much the database for any Windows systems where all configuration settings are kept, among other things. Any damage to the Registry can result in a useless machine. Attackers can exploit this feature to compromise the system or form the basis for adjusting file association and permissions to enable malicious code—remotely! Make certain that on all systems where the Remote Registry service is allowable, you disable this service. The service is not really necessary, and because it exists in Windows systems, Windows DMZ hosts are susceptible to remote takeover if you leave it open.

- **Windows scripting host** According to SANS, the Windows Scripting Host (WSH) can be used to run Visual Basic script (VBScipt) exploits. Either patch systems to current levels or disable the WSH if you are not using it.

NOTE

For detailed information on how to create effective passwords, please visit IBM's online security library and read the following articles:

- **Introduction to password cracking** www-106.ibm.com/developer-works/security/library/s-crack/?dwzone=security
- **Creating effective passwords** www-106.ibm.com/developerworks/security/library/s-pass.html

---

If you are interested in what could be seen if someone knew you were running a UNIX-based system, there is a top 10 list for UNIX-based systems as well. We don't spend a lot of time reiterating what is already online for your viewing, so just be aware that with the right online research, you can keep finding more and more vulnerabilities, no matter what system you run—IBM mainframes, Oracle, Novell, and on and on. It is important to note that this list just gives hackers the idea of what to try on your system. It gives you a heads-up on what hackers have access to as far as information goes. Top vulnerabilities to UNIX systems as reported by the FBI and SANS include RPC vulnerabilities, many hacks to the Apache Web server, and attacks on all running services to include SNMP, FTP, Rlogin, LPD, Sendmail, and BIND.

Information gathering, reconnaissance, and stealth scanning don't all have to revolve around a tool like Nmap or Nessus. You can also use the Internet for plain old research. By running a check on any of these vulnerabilities on www.google.com, you can see how most of them are done—or better for you, the DMZ architect, how to save yourself from them!

This section of the chapter briefly described each vulnerability, but you can get more links to preventative maintenance by going directly to the SANS site at www.sans.org/top20.

Auditing and Logging Evasion

If you don't have auditing set up and logging enabled, you are basically missing out on some defense in depth! You should always enable logging on critical systems and audit specific events in particular. For example, you would definitely want to audit the erasing, deleting, or removing of an event log or an audit log on your host, no matter what type of host it is. If you are running a Windows system in your DMZ, you will want to ensure that you audit attempts to clear the event log. This is a solid indicator that you would not want to get caught with your hand in the cookie jar. Another point to mention is that the hacker's intention is to come into your public DMZ and penetrate or exploit it—undetected.

The whole point is, the hacker does not have the information as to whether you are or are not logging and auditing. Most hackers would think that you were, so they will be extra careful about what they do. Their true hopes lie with the fact that you won't check or monitor this log, and the hacker will be in and out undetected, even if you do check the logs once a week. Furthermore, if the hacker masked his or her identity, it will be truly hard to track, but you will at least know you were attacked, and the fact that the hacker hid their identity from you tells you that you are not dealing with a common script kiddie. Lastly, it tells you that you were prepared for the attack! This is what you have been learning how to do in this book. To sum this up, if a hacker finds out you are not logging or auditing, you are pretty much dead—and so are your systems.

Probing Analog Connections

As we wrap up our section on penetration testing, we move into the area of probing analog connections. We saved this topic for last because it is probably one of the most common exploits known to crack into networks, but most security analysts still have not cleaned out their networks of unauthorized modem use. Today, at any given company, we can find at least two or three answering modems from probes and tests. Not only do these analog lines answer, but often remote control or remote access services answer as well.

PC Anywhere is a common (old, but still common) application that many technicians set up and used years ago. There wasn't a big stir in the security world, so it wasn't common to have a PC Anywhere system running to allow administrators to remotely access their systems from home or on the road in case of emergency. In addition, many mainframes, PBX systems, and high-end pieces of equipment that are serviced from outside vendors also have modems connected to them to allow for remote entry and service. Often these passwords are very lame. We have some experience "shoulder surfing" with an onsite technician and being able to grab his credentials to dial in later and connect. Furthermore, other systems services by this vendor all had the same exact credential set. Not only is this upsetting, but it also caused us to change vendors due to this one's lack of security posture. In any case, you make the decisions as to how you want to handle your own vendors and staff, but be aware that this exploitation does exist and it is very easy to crack. If we can remotely attach to a mainframe, it's a great bet that we can use that as a springboard to other systems on the network. If we can remotely attach to a PBX, we can then perform a PBX fraud attack, where we can gather enough information about a system to dial in and use the company's PBX to make long distance calls.

What is even worse is that probing your analog lines, finding a connection, and exploiting it just bypassed your entire (costly) DMZ infrastructure. You can have all the firewalls and IDS in place you want, but it all means nothing when we can dial around it and enter your network undetected. Many networks (including Microsoft's network) have been exploited this way. You should consider your network the same way—and ensure that you have no way around your DMZ protection. For example, take a look at Figure 14.14.

Figure 14.14 Viewing the Probing of Dialup and Analog
Connections Around Your DMZ

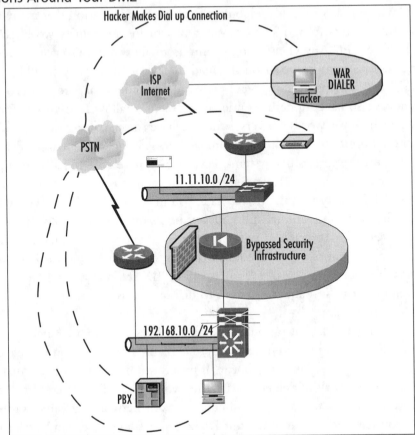

War dialing is your last check on the list for penetration testing. As you can see in the figure, it was pretty simple to get around the firewall. This is really the only way to get past your DMZ (if set up properly, as described in this book), and by probing analog lines, you can very easily and quickly break into a network undetected.

Now that you understand why probing analog lines can be a gold mine for attackers, let's take a look at exactly how a hacker is going to "war dial" you. Remember as we mentioned earlier in the chapter, in the information-gathering process, this is where you can find numbers (phone numbers) to start dialing and probing.

Designing & Planning…

Managed Router Fun

Have you ever wondered how easy it could be to tap into someone's Internet router? In Chapter 9, we covered in great detail the importance of locking down your routers and switching devices, especially those that are facing the Internet and are prone to attack. It might be even worse to know that if you are managing the router with a modem (connected to the routers aux port), you might be able to crack that router with a war dialer. We have been able to find routers on the Internet with a default password of *Cisco* (yes, it's true), and within seconds, we could own that device. Make certain that you check this very carefully.

War Dialing

War dialing is a forgotten hacking art form in the world of easy high-speed Internet access. However, in places like Eastern Europe where dialup access is still the primary method of connection, war dialing is alive and well. War dialing is nothing more than scanning a set of phone numbers, looking for an analog line accessible by modem that could lead to an answering device, which will then allow connectivity to a main net-work—undetected. Often this will be a weak link in the network's armor, because many systems administrators assume the scans will come in over the high-speed access points—hence all our discussions on the DMZ and how to fortify it. Another issue could be that the systems administrator doesn't know about the rogue modem that a user has installed on a system to make it easy to work from home. This is a common occurrence; it is pretty easy to bring in a modem to work, install it, and set up VNC or any other remote access tool to access it. To understand what war dialing is, watch *War Games,* the movie from the early 1980s in which the hero uses war dialing to find and hack into NORAD's war game computer. How many of us can recall the robotic voice saying, "Would you like to play a game?"

Many versions of commercial and freeware war dialer software are available. Some are easy and some are just crude hacks that someone put together in the dead of night and released. One of the better dialers is called THC-Scan www.pimmel.com/thcfiles.php3. Unlike many applications today, this one is still a DOS-based application, so it requires very little in resources to use. A decent commercial dialer is called ModemScan v5.3. For people that like to experiment or to take a drive down memory lane, there is ProComm Plus; you'll find directions to make it a very custom dialer at

http://home.mminternet.com/~barneshouse/haq.htm. You will find ProComm Plus
there and some very interesting scripts as examples. You can see an example of
ProComm Plus in use in Figure 14.15. You should know that ProComm Plus is not
necessarily a war-dialer utility, but it can be used as one. In other words, it's true purpose is to provide terminal access to routers, switches, PBXs, and so on.

Figure 14.15 The ProComm Plus Opening Screen

How does it work? The war-dialer software simply takes a block of numbers that
you provide (for example, a full block starting with 213-123-4500 and ending with
213-123-5000), dials all 500 numbers, and then logs those for which a computer
modem answers. Then you go through the logs and try the numbers that are flagged.
Some of the better software can be programmed to try certain command strings and
passwords to help filter out the phone numbers. Once you have dialed into the
modem, you could hack whatever host was answering the call. Often this is a workstation of some kind with minimal, if any, security.

> **NOTE**
>
> A war dialer can be set up at night and run over a period of time. You can
> sleep soundly while your war dialer diligently dials up and tries to connect to
> systems. You can check the logs later to see what numbers did answer and
> what they answered with. If you get a warning banner, it's a good bet that
> you just dialed into a router or switch.

Some of the war dialers are more sophisticated than the old DOS-based programs
like ProComm Plus and THC-SCAN. Phonesweep is a Windows-based application that
will let you set up four concurrent sweep sessions, capture data to Excel, or just log the
results. You can set up exclusions so you don't dial a number that might trigger a
warning about your activity. You can see an example of Phonesweep in Figure 14.16.
(Note that the numbers have been removed to hide the company's true identity.)

Figure 14.16 The Phonesweep History Screen

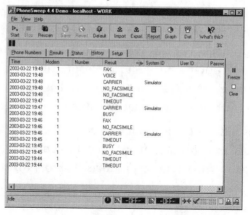

The second method of exploiting this type of attack is to war-dial a vendor of the target and use its system as the jump point. Many companies allow remote access to their networks for remote support. The target is trusting that the remote support staff has its security in place. Between the simple dialup lines to the installations of PC Anywhere and VNC, there are a multitude of ways to get in by the back door, springboarding from one system to another—trying to, again, hide your identity.

> **NOTE**
>
> For a highly granular and detailed explanation on war dialing, you can visit IBM's security site, which has an article on how to war-dial a network, if you still need to know more about it: www-106.ibm.com/developerworks/security/library/s-dial/?t=gr,lnxw06=WarDialing

In sum, it's important to always check your systems and your entry points and try to lock them down so they are not exploited through holes, back doors, or a lack of proper security.

Now that we have looked at all the penetration testing, reconnaissance, stealth scanning, and network mapping, we need to act on our acquired information. In the next section of the chapter, we look at how to really wreak havoc on your bastion hosts, routers, switches, firewalls, and anything else we can penetrate or exploit. Again, we need to make a few points very clear:

- This chapter is not about how to hack someone else's DMZ; it's a chapter on how to vulnerability-test and harden your own DMZ. In this book you have been taught how to secure your network devices and hosts. It's up to you now to test your work, as a hacker would, to see if you are vulnerable.

- This chapter's next section, "Attacking the DMZ Hosts," is really more vulnerability testing on your DMZ and its contents. We cover in detail what a hacker might do, but not all scenarios are covered. We could write an entire book on how to hack, but this is not a how-to-hack book. This is a how-to-check-your-DMZ-for-proper-security chapter in a book on securing and building enterprise DMZs. Keep this in mind as you continue, because it's very important that you know that this discussion is highly DMZ-centric.

- Every DMZ is different, with different contents, designs, traffic flows, and vendor products. For this reason, we have to generalize, but follow each section based on your own vendor products (Cisco, Nokia, or the like), and seek out more information as needed based on your own configurations.

NOTE

It should seem obvious, but it is important to mention that all this security and methodology are useless if you do not secure physical access to all your devices.

Attacking the DMZ Hosts

In this section we pass beyond the information-gathering phase of our project and enter the attack phase. In a DMZ, you must continue to think about how vulnerable you really are. In all reality, you have all your servers and systems available to anyone who wants to get at them because they're opened up on the firewall. It's up to you to secure them properly; it's up to you to ensure that you read through this book and perform due diligence in hardening your systems as much as possible, keeping up on them and working to keep them continuously secure and monitored. In this section we look at the most common targets and what a hacker might do to them if they're openly available. Common targets are DNS, e-mail, FTP, and Web services. We look at others, too, but these are the four most common (and commonly exploited) services available on the Web today.

DNS Exploits

Along with scanning ports, there are other ways to gather information on the target's network. An easy way to is to find the DNS servers. DNS servers are a very common and hackable target. Depending on the network's configuration, they can provide an excellent doorway into the network for MITM attacks. You can use a couple of tools that are on most systems. For Windows, the common tool is NSLOOKUP; for the Linux/UNIX world, the command *dig* is the preferred tool. Both tools are explained here.

In this example of the *dig* command (shown in Figure 14.17), we started with:

```
dig @<ipaddress or domain name of dns server>
```

Figure 14.17 Starting DiG on a Name Server

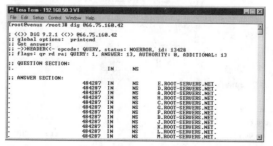

This command gave us is the contents of a DNS server. What we need is the DNS of a particular domain. So we modify the *dig* command a bit, as shown in Figure 14.18.

Figure 14.18 Querying the DNS for a Certain DNS Server IP Address

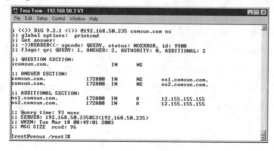

We can see in Figure 14.18 that when we run the query asking for the name servers (NS) of comsun.com, the public DNS server gives up its entries about comsun.com's name servers. We now have the IP addresses of comsun.com. To carry this a bit further, when we run the same query but with the argument of *any* instead of *ns*, we get a listing of *all* matching items to comsun.com in the DNS server. This means that if there are any mail servers in the DNS zone, we will get that information also. Now we can run the query against comsun.com directly and see if we can get a zone transfer from comsun.com to us.

If you know how to "dig," you can gather a lot of information about the network and its DNS infrastructure. Now that we have looked at what we can work with, let's start to formulate an attack on this host. You see a zone transfer in Figure 14.19.

Figure 14.19 Sample Zone Transfer Output

```
[root@venus msweeney]# dig @12.155.155.155 pacsun.com AXFR

; <<>> DiG 9.2.1 <<>> @12.155.155.155 comnsun.com AXFR
;; global options:  printcmd
comsun.com.         86400   IN    SOA    ns1.comsun.com. admin.comsun.com.
287 600 600 259200 86400
comsun.com.               900   IN    NS     ns1.comsun.com.
comsun.com.             86400 IN    NS     ns2.comsun.com.
comsun.com.             86400 IN    MX     10
commail.pacificsunwear.com.
comsun.com.             86400 IN    MX     20 commail2.comsun.com.
beach.comsun.com.       86400 IN    A      12.155.155.11
beach.comsun.com.       86400 IN    A      12.155.155.12
cache.comsun.com.       86400 IN    CNAME  p.mii.instacontent.net.
cwilliams.comsun.com.   86400 IN    MB     commail.comsun.com.
cwilliams.comsun.com.   86400 IN    RP     commail.comsun.com. .
images.comsun.com.      86400 IN    A      12.155.155.23
::output truncated::
```

You might be asking what good a zone transfer does us. The answer is that many DNS servers contain a great deal of good information—things like other name servers, e-mail records, Web servers, possible firewall listings, and servers and sometimes even workstations. This information can help you to build your network map of the target. Furthermore, it's not just a map of the network; we might get information on what the of box at a certain IP address. Often there are entries like *ntserver1* or *myxpbox* and so on. Now we have a better idea of what OS is on a certain IP address on the target network.

The last command we discuss that provides useful information is that if the DNS server is the Berkeley Internet Name Domain (BIND), we can get the version of the server. We can *dig* again and find this information pretty quickly, as shown in Figure 14.20. This information is beneficial because depending on the version of BIND, exploits could be associated with that particular version if it's unpatched.

Figure 14.20 Using DiG to Get the Version of BIND

Why do we care about the version of BIND? Because certain exploits work on different versions of BIND. The earlier versions are not very secure, and the BIND process runs as ROOT. So if you can gain access to the process, you can gain control of the BIND server as root. Let's take a closer look at BIND.

> **NOTE**
>
> There are two papers on the Internet (one for BIND 8 and one for 9) that should you standard procedures for BIND, how to lock it down, common exploits and so on. You can see them here:
>
> - www.boran.com/security/sp/bind_hardening8.html
> - www.boran.com/security/sp/bind9_20010430.html
>
> You'll find another general paper that n detail, everything about BIND: www.linuxjournal.com/article.php?sid=4198.

The BIND package is the most widely used implementation of DNS today. BIND allows you to locate a server on the Internet (or a local network) by using a hostname without having to know its specific IP address. The concepts of DNS should be mastered if you are going to be a DMZ architect or a security analyst responsible for DNS security, especially in the DMZ. Before we get into the issues directly related to DNS, you should know how DNS might sit in the DMZ. Figure 14.21 shows you a clear map of where DNS in your organization may sit.

Figure 14.21 Viewing DNS in Your DMZ

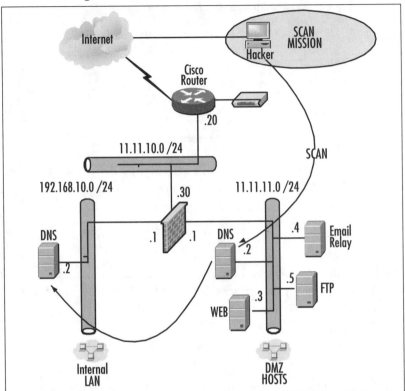

Consider the following: If you were a hacker, your intention would be to pollute the DNS on the internal LAN. This can be done by wreaking havoc with the DNS server on the DMZ, which is most likely a real name server, whereas the internal DNS server is most likely using an internal namespace with a forwarder out to the DMZ. We look more deeply into the attack in a moment, but you should be familiar with the placement of the DNS servers here and now. It is also important to note (since we are talking about BIND) that UNIX/Linux-based DNS servers are commonly used on the Internet, and if you are hosting your own name server, it's very common that your DNS server on your DMZ will also be using BIND. Most engineers would not be caught dead using Microsoft DNS servers on the Internet, because they are very easy to exploit, as you have seen in this book. So why is DNS such a massive target on your DMZ? There are many immediate answers, but here are some that you might not be aware of:

- If you take out a company's DNS server, you paralyze the organization's way of resolving IP to hostnames. This can take out just about every device on the network that uses DNS to communicate.

- You can pollute a company's DNS server with fake or incorrect information to either cause havoc or redirect users to lookalike sites where private information can be captured by an attacker. *DNS cache poisoning* is what it is called when a hacker replaces your "a" records with bogus information.

- If you are the administrator, you might not be aware of the myriad security upgrades available for your systems that are running the BIND daemon (called *named*). Hackers know that without the proper service pack levels of security fixes installed, you could be susceptible to a large number of attacks, buffer overflows, exploitations, and so on.

- You could be open to a DoS attack from Trojan implantation, unnecessary services, or configuration files. Hackers know that your DNS server is there from doing a lookup on it, they know its BIND, and they know they might be able to Telnet from that server to another.

- Not only could a compromised machine provide information about the organization to the attacker; it can also be used as a springboard for other attacks.

NOTE

Most newest and most common BIND attacks are:

- A DoS attack, covered in CERT Advisory CA-2002-15 (www.cert.org/advisories/CA-2002-15.html). With this DoS attack, a hacker can shut down the BIND daemon by sending certain packets to force an internal consistency check, which itself will cause the DoS.
- A buffer overflow attack, covered in CERT Advisory CA-2002-19 (www.cert.org/advisories/CA-2002-19.html). The DNS resolver libraries can be vulnerable, and when a hacker sends malicious DNS responses, they can execute arbitrary code or cause a DoS.

Now that you are comfortable with the attack patterns, the reason the attacks might take place, and what to look out for in your DMZ, let's take a look at more details that revolve around DNS security in and around the DMZ.

Designing & Planning…

What Is a Buffer Overflow?

Let's take a quick look in a little extra detail at the buffer overflow attack, since they are so very common, especially if you are a Microsoft shop. Exploiting the buffer overflow takes patience, knowledge, skill, and time. Hackers put a great deal of effort into the exploitation of buffers. You can think of a buffer as a place in memory that holds data for whatever reason you can think of. Often buffers are used to buffer the incoming data so that the system can manipulate it in sequence or when it has time, instead of a first-come, first-served system. You can either flood a buffer to make it unusable (this is a DoS attack), or you can try to manipulate it to raise privileges so that you can exploit the system as an elevated process. When developers code their applications, the components in some languages that do not properly validate input can easily be crashed and, in many cases, used to take control of a process. When we mention these components, we assume that on a Web-accessible platform (like a DMZ), your components can include CGI-based applications, scripts, libraries, drivers, and Web-based server components. It is important that you be familiar with this concept, so if you are still sketchy on the details and you would like to know more, you can visit the Cult of the Dead Cow (CDC) site to learn how to actually pull off a buffer overflow attack: www.cultdeadcow .com/cDc_files/cDc-351/page1.html.

General BIND Security

Before you start looking into granular detail, you need to know the version of BIND you are running. You can get this information by entering the following command:

```
[root@SHIMONSKI root]# named -v
BIND 9.2.1
```

Most systems use this command, which produces the version of BIND followed by three numbers, as shown in the example. The three numbers actually stand for the following: BIND 9 is the version of BIND. BIND 9.2 is the minor level of the version—in our case, BIND 9.2. BIND 9.2.1 represents the service pack level/patch level for that version of BIND. This version only has up to 1 as the patch level. It is important that you know this system, because the first thing a hacker will do in penetrating a system is assess the vulnerability of the server, and if he can get your BIND version, he can attack your server based on that version's known weaknesses. Some of the most common weaknesses your systems will be probed for or you should lock down include the following:

- Your first item of security should be to disable or remove BIND if you are not using it (disable the *named* daemon).

- If you are using BIND, you should check the version to make sure you are at the top patch level for your version. You should also run newer versions to take advantage of newer enhancements.

- To complicate automated attacks or scans of your systems, you can easily hide the *Version String* banner in BIND with a bogus one. You can do this by replacing the string information and version number in the *named.conf* file options statement.

- You should only permit zone transfers to secondary DNS servers in your domain. Disable zone transfers to parent or child domains instead by using delegation and forwarding.

- Disable recursion and glue fetching to defend against DNS cache poisoning.

- You can create what's called a *padded cell*. Doing so prevents a compromised *named* from exposing your entire system. You can accomplish this goal by restricting BIND so that it runs as a nonprivileged user in a *chroot()*ed directory.

NOTE

The document at the following URL describes installing the BIND 9 name server to run in a *chroot* jail and as a nonroot user to provide added security and minimize the potential effects of a security compromise: www.losurs.org/docs/howto/Chroot-BIND.html.

DNS Spoofing Attacks

DNS spoofing has become one of the most common attacks of late. The technique has been around for a few years, yet it is still a very viable method of attacking a DMZ-based host. It is estimated that two out of three DNS servers are improperly configured or the perimeter security is misconfigured. This was proven in the past year or so when Internet-based attackers took down DNS servers maintained here in the United States.

Another interesting statistic is that it's estimated that one–third of all DNS servers are spoofable.

What is a DNS spoof attack? The DNS spoof causes a DNS server to accept incorrect information from a different DNS server that has no authority to give out that bogus information. This type of attack can cause havoc since the targeted DNS server can route users to fraudulent Web sites or redirect e-mail to a rogue e-mail server. The beauty of this type of attack is that it can be a long time before someone notices that the DNS server has been spoofed. It might be as late as when the competition brings out a product very much like the one that the targeted company is selling. Another reason for hacking a DNS server is that many of the DNS servers running the older BIND code use *root* to run the *named* process.

New standards help close this hole, and some new DNS servers are not as vulnerable to this type of attack. Both UNIX and Windows DNS servers are vulnerable to spoofing.

Designing & Planning…

Attacking DMZ Hosts

Something to be aware of when you're trying to attack a target, you can easily knock yourself out by not understanding what the tool is doing. For example, in trying to run an Nmap scan against a target using a FIN scan, a local firewall was brought to its knees by filling up its cache with open connections. As a security analyst continuing to check your DMZ, be careful you don't hack yourself so badly that you cause an outage! You can see this gaffe in action in Figure 15.22.

Figure 14.22 FIN Scan Crashing Local Firewall Due to Cache Poisoning

03/08/2003 10:38:38.480	The cache is full; too many open connections; some will be dropped	192.168.1.2, 1037, LAN	63.251.224.177, 80, WAN
03/08/2003 10:40:08.816	The cache is full; too many open connections; some will be dropped	192.168.1.2, 1080, LAN	216.49.88.38, 80, WAN
03/08/2003 10:41:37.064	The cache is full; too many open connections; some will be dropped	192.168.1.2, 1104, LAN	63.251.224.177, 80, WAN
03/08/2003 10:42:52.928	The cache is full; too many open connections; some will be dropped	192.168.1.2, 1093, LAN	216.239.32.10, 53, WAN
03/08/2003 10:44:03.032	The cache is full; too many open connections; some will be dropped	192.168.1.2, 1093, LAN	216.239.36.10, 53, WAN
03/08/2003 10:45:05.512	Successful administrator login	192.168.1.2, LAN	192.168.1.251

SQL Attacks and Hacks

As we continue looking at attacking hosts on the DMZ, you should understand that it's not only DNS that's the target (although it's most commonly attacked), but databases are also high-profile targets. It is not uncommon to have another layer of security added on to your SQL servers (or any other database product) in the DMZ if they are in fact accessible. SQL servers used in this method, if you follow proper design structure, should never be accessible via the Internet, so when we talk about these hacks—attacking SQL in the DMZ—we are really talking about IIS servers, or other servers, running the SQL service on their systems whether they do or do not know it. The SQL Slammer showed us that we were highly vulnerable to attack on our DMZs and public Internet connection-based hosts. SQL Slammer wrought havoc and caused a lot of damage, so you can see that SQL security on the DMZ is paramount.

SQL Slammer, also known as W32.SQLExp.Worm, is in fact a worm that targets any system running either Microsoft SQL Server 2000 or Microsoft Desktop Engine (MSDE) 2000. We alluded to this concept earlier, when we mentioned administrators not knowing that SQL is running because they are using MSDE. The SQL Slammer worm sends 376 bytes to UDP port 1434, the SQL Server Resolution Service Port. The attack is a DoS attack, and this is because the worm sends so many packets to the system that it simply knocks it out of commission.

> **NOTE**
>
> You can find more information relating to the SQL Slammer worm on Microsoft's security site; look for Microsoft Security Bulletin MS02-039 and Microsoft Security Bulletin MS02-061.

As we continue to talk about securing your DMZ from attack, you should really watch SQL, if not for the SQL Slammer worm alone, but many other SQL-based vulnerabilities. You can configure firewalls and ACLs to black out traffic to help aid in the defeat of this worm. You can stop it by setting up your firewalls and ACLs to block the ingress UDP traffic to port 1434 from untrusted hosts as well as blocking the egress UDP traffic from your network to the destination port 1434.

SQL Security Design

One of the newer attack methods to breach a DMZ is to launch a simple buffer over-flow against a SQL server, which could be the back-end database for an e-commerce site or possible *N*-tier architecture solution. Often the SQL box is in the DMZ because trying to get SQL working through the firewall drives the administrator crazy (due to its complexity) and he or she gave up too soon. Hackers look for this vulnerability. Figure 14.23 shows you the general idea of what we're referring to. If you look at the load-balanced solution, your SQL cluster is secured because there is a whole separate layer of firewall protection in front of it. Now think of removing that firewall. You would then have SQL servers with public addresses available through the first firewall, whereas the second set is behind a dedicated firewall just for the SQL servers. Depending on your budget, risk assessment, security policy, and wanted/needed security posture, you can decide to place this however you see fit, but pay attention to why it is important to keep this extra-secure:

- Databases are a high-profile target because they generally contain transaction information, client information, or information usable by the attacker.

- Taking out a database, especially for an e-commerce site, is an immediate paralysis tool. The target Web site will be unable to obtain order information while its SQL servers are toast, so pay attention to this as you design your *N*-tier architecture, and make sure that you flag the need to have heightened security on your SQL-based systems.

Figure 14.23 Viewing a Clustered and Load-Balanced Solution in the DMZ

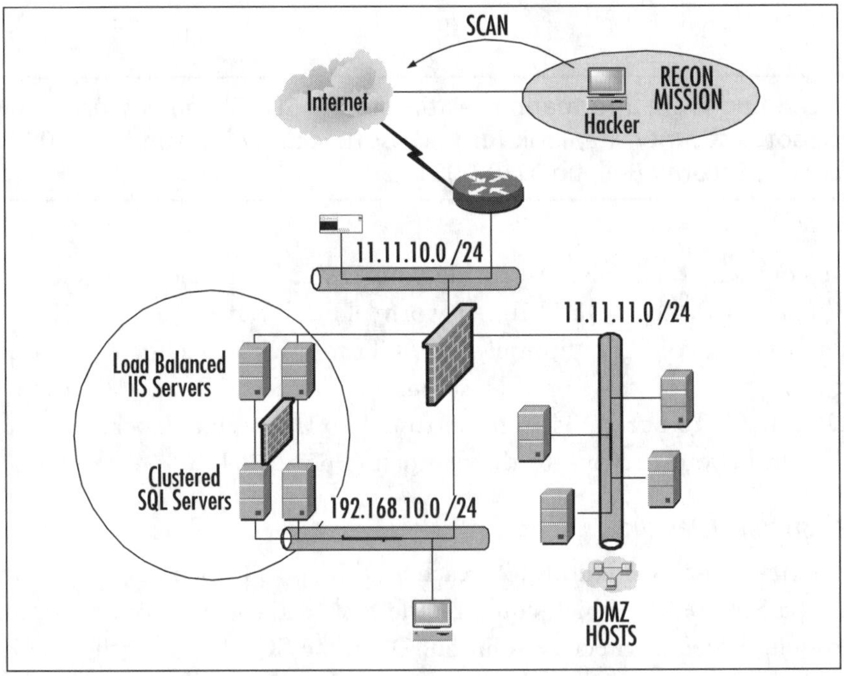

SQL Injection

SQL injection is the act of passing SQL code into an application that was not intended by the developer. Remember, applications were meant to do specific things, and it's up to the attacker (or you, the white hat) to test them. By injecting new code, you are performing the attack, which is a very common one, especially due to the fact that the target (DMZ-based hosts) are accessible to attacks from the Internet—if you have not configured your security properly.

You should also know that SQL injection attacks are possible not only on SQL servers but also Sybase, Oracle, and DB2 as well as SQL Server from Microsoft..You should also be aware that SQL injection is not necessarily the issue with the server or the application itself, but the actual coding procedures that take place on the system that allow access, such as poor input validation. Although the server itself might be secure, the application itself has probably not been given a very thorough security testing—and all coding procedures should always go through some form of quality assurance (QA) testing.

Now that we understand the background of the attack, let's look at SQL injection in more detail.

The SQL injection attack has its root in the way SQL works. (To any database administrators reading along, our apologies for keeping this part rather simplistic.) SQL is a language that allows us to manipulate a database of tables, rows, columns, and fields. The attack consists of a database and a way to connect to said database. We connect to the database using a user ID and a password. The weakest link is the authentication information. This where many of the opportunities for attack arise. Often the database is designed not with security in mind but with ease of programming and/or management uppermost. This means that simple passwords, null passwords, or poor error checking of the user ID and password are implemented or not checked. Table 15.1 is a starting point; it is not intended to be a complete list of default user IDs and passwords for common SQL servers. Most databases can be cracked with default credentials. Once someone has gained control, he or she can then follow up on the attack.

Table 14.1 Default User IDs and Passwords for Common SQL Servers

Name	User ID	Default Password
Oracle	Sys	Oracle
MySQL (win)	Root	Null
MS SQL Server	Sa	Null
DB2	Dlfm	ibmdb2
MS MSDE	Sa	Null

The indirect method of SQL injection works like this:

1. There is a Web page with a user login and password entry point. The attacker does not use a normal user ID in this attack. Instead, he uses something like:

    ```
    "bob'; update tbluses set password ='hackthis' where username='bob'
    ```

2. The entered password would be *n/a*. Since the error-checking code doesn't know what to do with this string, the SQL server sees this:

    ```
    "SELECT * FROM tblusers WHERE username= 'bob'; update tblusers set
        password='hackthis' where username='bob"
    ```

3. The SQL server then executes this command sequence and sets the password of *bob* to *hackthis*. Now the hacker simply returns to the login page and logs into the SQL server like any other user. The real power in this type of attack is when you combine it with a Trojan attack. Although SQL injection is not easy or fast, it can be very effective. The prized command to work with is a stored procedure called *xp_cmdshell*, which allows a command prompt to be run.

When you're using SQL injection, the code runs with whatever SQL Server context the application is configured to use. Unfortunately, due to lack of security policy in code development, mistakes, or lack of proper QA work, it is common to find an excessive level of privileges such as that delivered with the *sa* account or an account with database-owner privileges. In many cases, developers do this in order to avoid having to configure and maintain permissions for their database objects, which is the right way to do it but more time consuming and difficult.

If you look at the *sa* account, you can see that if an attacker is able to compromise this system, he can gain total control over the Microsoft SQL server. This allows for the highest level of privilege on the system. Not to scare you, but when we say *total* control over the highest level, we mean *total* control of the SQL Server with an operating system shell at the level of privilege of the MSSQLSERVER service while using the *xp_cmdshell* extended stored procedure. The attacker will have the ability to read, write, and mutilate all data stored on the SQL Server databases.

Now that you are familiar with the reasons that SQL could be vulnerable (especially on the DMZ), the reasons you must test for it, and what can be done against your systems if you don't test and secure it, let's look at the "how" of it.

QA is the key to stopping SQL injection attacks. With good code review, you can prevent many problematic attacks because you know that the code will not allow for the attacks to take place. Another method you could try to test for such vulnerabilities would be to disable error handling so that ODBC software and driver errors can be displayed, seen, and analyzed. Once you do this, you can test the string by simply using single quotes to see if you can get the application in use to fail. If you are able to make it fail, you have a problem. A failure is usually indicative of poor validation and corruption of the SQL string, which could lead to an exploit or an attack.

> **NOTE**
>
> For highly in-depth information on SQL attacks, especially injection attacks, please review the following sites and PDFs:
> - www.spidynamics.com/whitepapers/WhitepaperSQLInjection.pdf
> - www.nextgenss.com/papers/advanced_sql_injection.pdf
> - www.owasp.org

These are not the only SQL-based attacks there are, but they are the most important to look at because they are the most common attacks on the DMZ-based hosts. We left many out that are covered by patches, hotfixes, and antivirus updates because, as a DMZ architect (and as you have learned in all the hardening chapters), your systems on the DMZ should already be fairly locked down. This section covered issues that you might not have been aware of and need to test. Now let's take a look at e-mail-based attacks and prevention on the DMZ from an attacker's point of view.

E-Mail Attacks and Hacks

E-mail is universal among companies in today's connected world. It has become a mission-critical application, yet it is one of the most poorly protected applications on many networks. You might ask, "Why is it so common to run e-mail attacks when e-mail is such a high-risk application?" You would think that this platform would be the most secured item. This is not the case. We have compiled a short list of reasons that e-mail is so frequently exploited:

- E-mail systems are almost always accessible via the Internet. To get your e-mail to the Internet, you need to have a passage to and from the Internet. Not only that—you also have other e-mail services available that will allow your attacker to exploit a great many areas instead of focusing on just one area. For instance, an attacker can exploit SMTP and POP3.

- E-mail systems are not always well understood. It is our belief that an e-mail administrator needs to be a network engineer first. Others might disagree, but we explain our reasoning in the next bullet.

- Part of the lack of security on e-mail systems comes from overworked administrators who get the e-mail systems running and then leave them to go "fight other network fires"—or they simply maintain a system as is, without really checking for vulnerabilities on the current system. You could have an open relay with loads of spam being launched off your server, and if you didn't know any better, this would just continue indefinitely, whereas the source of origin for the attack is your relay's IP address on the DMZ.

Before we move any further, let's quickly look at what the e-mail system looks like from a DMZ perspective, as shown in Figure 14.24.

Figure 14.24 Viewing E-Mail Systems on the DMZ

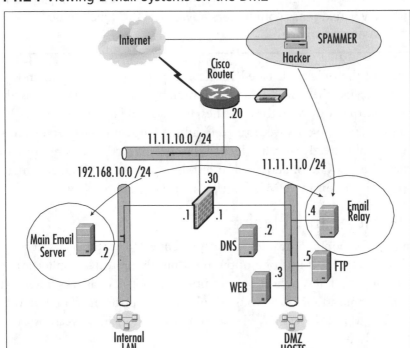

As you can see in Figure 14.24, you have an attacker looking to spam from your relay. Here is the breakdown:

■ The attacker will use a program, tool, or technique to probe your DMZ looking for the e-mail relay. Finding one is simple: Look for port 25 for SMTP and port 110 for POP3. Once you know this, you know that the system is functional for e-mail.

■ Next you have to try to relay off the server. This can be done in many ways, which we look at shortly. Once you know it is spammable, you just need to know exploit the system.

- Technically, if the hacker is not overzealous, the attack could actually go unde-tected, because if you don't know you have an open relay, you might miss the spam going through it. If the hacker pelts your system with data to relay, how-ever, you will see a slowdown (by checking the e-mail system's performance-monitoring tools), especially if the spam contains large attachments.

- A truly nasty hack would be if the internal server were compromised via the relay, as you see in Figure 14.24. It is quite possible that if defenses are not set properly, a hacker can actually open the door directly into your private intranet, so be very careful to lock down access at the firewall that divides the DMZ from the private internal network.

In Figure 14.24, you see an attacker on the Internet looking to use your system as an open relay. The hacker tests your system to see if it is in fact an open relay and then exploits it. You really have to know how STMP works to totally understand the hack. In order to do that, you have to know how to get into and test an e-mail system without a GUI, which you saw us do earlier in this chapter with the Novell e-mail relay on the DMZ. Here, we look at Novell by UNIX Sendmail as well as IIS from Microsoft. SMTP relays are exploitable on any platform that allows an open relay. SMTP mail runs over TCP port 25 and is present on virtually all UNIX machines as Sendmail and is present on many Windows machines if IIS has been installed or other popular applications—mostly without anyone knowing it (hence the vulnerability scan-ning). Spoofing e-mail is very simple. Take a look at the following examples:

```
#telnet <ip address or DNS name of email server> 25
HELO <anyhost@anydomainname>
MAIL FROM: <anyuser at anydomainname>
RCPT TO: <returnaddressofchoice at anydomainname>
DATA:
Your email goes here

.

quit
```

It was very common for e-mail servers to allow mail relaying as a rule. This has been tightened down in recent years, but many e-mail servers can be found that still will allow you to relay mail this way, or if they are misconfigured, which is also very common. Here is a real-world example with some minor editing using one of a major ISP's e-mail servers:

```
220 orngca-mls03.socal.XX.com ESMTP *** FOR AUTHORIZED USE ONLY! ***
HELO anydomain.com
```

```
250 orngca-mls03.socal.XX.com Hello XXXX-west-12-34-56-78.biz.XX.com
    [12.34.56.78], pleased to meet you

MAIL FROM: anyhost@mydomain.com
250 2.1.0 anyhost@mydomain.com... Sender ok

RCPT TO: blowthis@myhackdomain.com
250 2.1.5 blowthis@myhackdomain.com... Recipient ok

DATA
354 Enter mail, end with "." on a line by itself
this is a test
.
250 2.0.0 h2N0oRX19041 Message accepted for delivery
```

You can see that the ISP's SMTP e-mail server happily accepted the dummy
domain name and user we keyed in, and then it accepted the message for delivery.
Remember, exploits and attacks are not always the work of a C++ programmer
hacking up code to launch crafted packets at vulnerable servers, but at times, you might
find a person new to the security game looking for a testing ground—your e-mail
server.

Your e-mail server is very easy to lock down as well. In Figure 14.25, you can see
that just about any program or system you use will have a hardening feature built in.
We cover Novell in this chapter because we covered the hardening of Solaris and
Windows in the earlier portion of this book, so in this figure you can see that the
SMTP relay properties of the SMTP object in the GroupWise system allow you to dis-
able the use of your relay for spamming purposes.

Figure 14.25 Disabling Relaying on Your E-Mail Relay

We have now covered e-mail-relaying issues within the DMZ; you should have a new idea as to where you need to focus your analysis. An open relay, spamming problem, or any other disruption to your e-mail service is not good for your network or for your company once it winds up on a blacklist and cannot legitimately send and receive mail to certain protected domains. It is important that you test this; try to see if it is vulnerable yourself and close it up and patch it as needed.

You should know by now that we have not listed every single attack you could possibly see. This chapter is meant only to show you the DMZ in a different perspective, the way a potential hacker might see it. Often spamming is the most important thing that a hacker will do to your e-mail relay.

Other Attack Methods

Before we move on, we want to make something very clear: This chapter outlines a thought process between the attacker and you. You should both be thinking exactly the same, minus malicious intent on your side. There are many other attack methods to gain access to the DMZ and the network. Hacking via CGI script vulnerabilities is very common. Poorly configured cheap firewalls that are passing ports 135 through 139, which is used for Windows products, are very common. Web server sample pages that were not cleaned off the server before deployment are commonly found. Hosts without current service packs for both UNIX and Windows operating systems, or any other system for that matter, are often found in the DMZ. Even poor network architecture can help an attack if discovered. We have seen where dual-homed hosts are on the network on one side and on the Internet on the other side, bypassing the firewall completely. The best firewall in the world is useless at this point.

Here are samples of Web server log files that show a Linux Web server being tested by a clueless script kiddie. Notice that the attack is for a Windows-based Web server. This does nothing but annoy the sysop for a Linux box. As we said before, scope out the target before you try to attack it.

```
[error] [client 12.34.56.78] File does not exist: /apache/vhosts/xxxxxxxx
    .com/httpdocs/d/winnt/system32/cmd.exe

[error] [client 12.34.56.78] File does not exist: /apache/vhosts/
    xxxxxxxx.com/httpdocs/scripts/..%5c../winnt/system32/cmd.exe

[error] [client 12.34.56.78] File does not exist: /apache/vhosts/
    xxxxxxxx.com/httpdocs/_vti_bin/..%5c../..%5c../..%5c../winnt/system32
        /cmd.exe
```

```
[error] [client 12.34.56.78] File does not exist:/apache/vhosts/
    xxxxxxxx.com/httpdocs/_mem_bin/..%5c../..%5c../..%5c../winnt/system32
        /cmd.exe
```

The one line that shows the _vti_bin deserves special mention. The Microsoft product FrontPage uses server extensions to provide a lot of special (added) functionality. These FrontPage extensions provide a multitude of security holes to exploit the IIS server on which they are installed. Since the extensions are installed by default with IIS, it can make for an interesting time on the Internet.

Again, don't assume that these are the only exploits available or that you should test. For example, we covered in this book how to harden Solaris. Let's take a look at a simple Solaris exploit that you could find on the Internet with little effort. There is a very useful hack for the slightly older versions of Solaris version 8 and higher unless patched. It is a very simple hack of the buffer overflow type, which breaks the login binary. When it breaks, the hacker gets a prompt. Once she has the prompt, it is not much effort to get to be the root. This opens all kinds of possibilities, given that there are many Sparcs throughout the Internet. The process is very simple:

1. Open a Telnet session.
2. Set the TTYPROMPT to **abcdefg**.
3. Open the session to the targeted Sparc.
4. You might or might not get a prompt. Key in the bin and 65 **c** characters and spaces, then close it off with **/n**.
5. Press **Enter**. If you are lucky, bingo! A prompt appears like magic. See Figure 14.26 for the screen.

Figure 14.26 Hacking to the Command Line on a Solaris 8 Box

Again, this discussion is merely meant to show you the magnitude of information you need about vulnerabilities and hacking just to stay afloat on one platform, where DMZs are notoriously multiple platforms, different systems for different applications, and so on.

To wind up this section, we end with a few URLs that you can use to further investigate your DMZ and a checklist that can help you defend your DMZ and its publicly assessable hosts:

- To check out Open Source Security Testing Methodology Manual 2.0, visit www.isecom.org/projects/osstmm.htm.

- To read 50 ways to defeat your firewall and 50 ways to defeat your IDS, visit: www.all.net.

- A list of current exploits and hacks as well as various mailing lists about security and bugs can be found by visiting www.securityfocus.com/archive.

DMZ Hardening Checklist

This section lists the most common items you want to remember when you're testing your DMZ like a hacker. You can, of course, add to this list as you become more familiar with the process:

1. Turn off and remove unneeded services. By default, many operating systems install auxiliary services that are not critical, such as an FTP, Telnet, and Web. These services are avenues of attack if they're unused, unknown, or unpatched. If they are removed, attacks have fewer avenues of penetration.

2. If a threat arises, you need to contain the issue. In other words, if you have a system that is compromised, you need to isolate that system from the rest to contain the issue—much like containing in virus outbreak. Make sure that if you find something wrong or questionable, you do not leave it but instead isolate and address it immediately.

3. When you are running public services that can be accessible through the firewall to the public Internet, such as HTTP, FTP, mail, and DNS services, you need to make certain that every one of those systems is patched, service packed, hardened, and vulnerability tested.

4. Enforce a password policy. You should have a strong password set to a traceable username. The full set of credentials needs to be monitored in case they are compromised. Often you have service accounts in use on systems, and they are

manipulated after the password for them (often simplistic) is cracked and exploited.

5. You can set your e-mail system to block specific file attachments that are commonly used to spread viruses, such as *.vbs, *.bat, *.exe, *.pif, and *.scr files. Of course, you can extend this list, but these are the most common extensions for malware.

6. If you ever have an attack on a system (on the DMZ or exposed on the Internet), it's your safest bet to completely rebuild the system from scratch (reinstall the OS, drivers, and applications) and then reapply the backed-up data. It is never safe to just run a scan on the system or apply a new antivirus; it's always safest to rebuild the system—just in case.

Summary

Hacking the DMZ sounds like fun, doesn't it? Well, the true intention of this chapter was to teach you that getting your DMZ hacked is *not* fun. Even worse, it is downright costly if the exploits are devastating enough, which they usually are. Whenever you hear of large corporations' or enterprises' Web sites being taken down by hackers, it's a safe bet that the hosts were exploited through a DMZ environment. So, if all this protection is put in place, how does a hacker still crack though, usually undetected? To answer that question, this chapter we took a solid look at the two parts of any attack: reconnaissance and the actual attack that takes place.

Reconnaissance is the art of "scoping out the joint," or in technical terms, looking over what you want to analyze and possibly exploit, keeping a low profile—and hopefully not getting caught. Recon operations (as you learned in great detail in this chapter) are the frontrunner to the attack. It is critical that an attacker map out what will be attacked and then exploited for many reasons that you learned here. For one, the hacker does not want to get caught, so he places great importance on hiding his identity. Another common aspect of a recon mission is information gathering—enough so that you do not get caught gathering it and so that you have enough information to pull off the exploit. Although we did not add a "testing" section here in the chapter, don't forget that you, as the white-hat analyst, need to *test, test, test* all your systems for deployment and afterward on all DMZ-based systems.

The attack section mainly demonstrated that you can be *very* vulnerable, even with all the lockdown procedures you have implemented. We could have written a three-volume set on the number of vulnerabilities that can be exploited within a DMZ environment, but we listed the most common, why they are issues, how they are done, how to protect against them, and how to get more information about them. This section of the chapter was intended as an eye opener to alert you what a hacker will do to your hosts if they are not hardened. The list could have extended for hundreds of pages. Take what is listed in the chapter as a common ground that you should stand on, with a goal to continue to learn about the exploits already available and constantly look for new ones. Getting on lists such NTBugTraq and others that send you updates on vulnerabilities is one of the only ways to keep up with the amount of updates that come out each day, but generally, stay focused on the externally available hosts on your DMZ far more than you do your internal servers. Although the internal servers are at risk, the external, Internet-facing hosts are under far more probing and attack and should be addressed immediately within your own infrastructures and DMZs.

Solutions Fast Track

Reconnaissance and Penetration Testing

☑ When we perform *reconnaissance*, we look at how attackers find out who you are, how they profile you, how they learn the services you have running, and the techniques they use to probe your defenses. You can see that it is very simple to probe your network without expending much time or money. You also know how much information can be found about you and your company with a few online tools. *Intelligence gathering* is the most important part of successfully protecting your interests if you are a white hat or exploiting your systems as a black hat.

☑ Trying to find the open holes and researching ways to exploit those holes is called *penetration testing*. An attacker can easily find out what services you run, where you run them, how to build a network map, and build a strategy to take the next step, which is to attack. If you build a defense, you must check it out to make sure that it is secure. Make sure that penetration testing your DMZ is a high priority.

☑ In this chapter we took a topical look at the attacks that will be used to penetrate the DMZ or cause havoc with the actual hosts and services available. Often it is quite impossible to actually penetrate a network segment, but you will see how weaknesses can be exploited quite easily once they're found with just a little research. In warfare, the strength of your opponent is matched only by your intelligence and doing your research; finding your opponent's weaknesses and exploiting them is the way most battles are won. We looked at this topic in detail, and you should be able to test your DMZ for weaknesses so that you can stop the actual attacks that could result from these weaknesses.

☑ *Social engineering* is the art of lying or deceiving to gain access to information that would normally not be disclosed. Social engineering is the biggest tool in your arsenal for information gathering. Normally, people at work are too busy or are uninformed about their professional conduct during business hours. Most people don't know what a security policy is, even though they might have signed one upon being hired. It's been known for a long time that a hacker, quick on his feet and with the right speaking skills, can undermine your entire network security infrastructure with a simple phone call.

☑ It's important that before you start any attack, you consider that the company you assess, attack, or scan can pinpoint your location and your identity.

Although companies cannot legally "hack you back," they can log your activities and wait until you're nailed to reproduce those logs in court. This is a very common practice, so the way around this is to mask your identity.

☑ Network Mapper (Nmap) is an open-source utility for network exploration or security auditing. It was designed to rapidly scan large networks, although it works fine against single hosts. Nmap uses raw IP packets in novel ways to determine the hosts available on the network, the services (ports) they are offering, the OS (and OS version) they are running, the type of packet filters or firewalls in use, and dozens of other characteristics. Nmap runs on most types of computers, and both console and graphical versions are available. Nmap is free software, available with full source code under the terms of the GNU GPL.

Attacking the DMZ Hosts

☑ When considering the possibility of being attacked, it is up to you to secure your systems properly, ensure that you read through this book and did due diligence in hardening the systems as much as possible, and keep up on them and work to keep them continuously secure and monitored. Common targets are DNS, e-mail, and FTP and Web services. We looked at others, but these are the four most common (and commonly exploited) services available on the public Internet today.

☑ DNS attacks are very common. With a DMZ, you must continue to think about how vulnerable you really are. In reality, all your servers and systems are available to anyone who wants to get at them and opened up on the firewall. DNS is generally located in a DMZ, especially when companies host their own DNS servers. If you place one in your DMZ, you should know right away that it could become a target of attack.

☑ Along with scanning ports, you can gather information on the target's network in other ways. An easy way to is to find any company's DNS servers and exploit them for their information. DNS servers are a very commonly hackable target because much damage can be done as well as a great deal of information gathered through DNS exploitation. Depending on the configuration of the network, they can provide an excellent doorway into the network for MITM attacks. You can use a couple of tools that are on most systems. For Windows, the common tool is NSLOOKUP; for the Linux/UNIX world, the command *dig* is the preferred tool. Both tools are valuable and should be examined by you, the DMZ architect.

☑ DNS spoofing is a very common DNS attack. The technique has been around for a few years, yet it is still a very viable method of attacking a DMZ-based host. It is estimated that two out of three DNS servers are improperly configured or the perimeter security is misconfigured. Another interesting statistic is that it's estimated that one-third of all DNS servers are spoofable.

☑ Databases are also high-profile targets in the DMZ. It is not uncommon to have another layer of security added on to your SQL servers (or any other database product) in the DMZ if they are in fact accessible—like a second firewall or IDS. SQL servers, if you follow proper design structure, should never be accessible via the Internet, so when we talk about these hacks—attacking SQL in the DMZ—we are really talking about cases where improper design was followed, or worse, where Desktop SQL or a SQL server are running on a system without your knowledge. Having read this book, you couldn't possibly make this mistake now, since it could paralyze your company if a hacker found it.

☑ E-mail is universal among companies in today's connected world. It has become a mission-critical application, yet it is one of the most poorly protected applications on many networks. To get your e-mail to the Internet, you need to have a passage to and from the Internet. Not only that—you also have other e-mail services available that will allow your attacker to exploit a great many areas instead of focusing on just one area. E-mail systems are not always well understood. Make certain that you design your e-mail system properly, harden and patch where needed, and monitor for vulnerability because relays in the DMZ are huge targets for attackers and spammers.

DMZ Hardening Checklist

☑ When performing tests on your DMZ, follow the DMZ hardening checklist. Although it's not an exhaustive resource, it will provide you with an excellent starting point for your tests.

Frequently Asked Questions

The following Frequently Asked Questions, answered by the authors of this book, are designed to both measure your understanding of the concepts presented in this chapter and to assist you with real-life implementation of these concepts. To have your questions about this chapter answered by the author, browse to **www.syngress.com/solutions** and click on the **"Ask the Author"** form. You will also gain access to thousands of other FAQs at ITFAQnet.com.

Q: I had an open relay, and now I have a problem sending e-mail to certain organizations. I have been told that I am now "blacklisted." What is this, and what can I do about it?

A: Mailing lists have a long and venerable history on the Internet. Mailing lists are an excellent vehicle for distributing focused, targeted information to an interested, receptive audience. Consequently, mailing lists have been used successfully as a highly effective direct marketing tool. Unfortunately, mailing lists are also vulnerable to misuse through a variety of means. An all-too-common example is where an individual is subscribed to a high number of mailing lists and must take extraordinary measures to be removed. Furthermore, some marketers misuse mailing lists, often through a lack of knowledge about longstanding Internet customs and rules or because they attempt to apply direct paper mail methodology to the electronic realm. This practice is called *spam* or *spamming*, and as you have seen in this chapter and others, it is very common for these attackers to take advantage of you. If you run an open relay, you will be placed on a list of other systems that are known spammers, and you will not be able to send e-mail to certain organizations that opt to be a part of a blacklisting service. To correct this problem, all you need to do is contact the agency that blacklisted you (you will know because they will e-mail you first), then close the open relay and let them know. You will then be removed from the blacklist. For more information, visit http://mail-abuse.org/.

Q: I am having a problem with my DMZ-based e-mail relay and internal mail server. I am getting a ton of viruses all over my systems, and they are spreading. What can I do to stop the most common exploits from wreaking havoc on my e-mail systems?

A: You can set your e-mail system to block specific file attachments that are commonly used to spread viruses, such as *.vbs, *.bat, *.exe, *.pif, and *.scr files. Of course, you can extend this list, but these are the most common extensions for malware.

Q: I know that from auditing and logs, an attacker is trying to remotely crack my Web server password. It was easy for the attacker to get in and manipulate the system. Did I use too weak a password?

A: Enforce a password policy. You should have a strong password set to a traceable username. The full set of credentials needs to be monitored in case they are compromised. Often you have service accounts in use on systems and they are manipulated after the password for them (often simplistic) is cracked and exploited.

Q: My e-mail relay is set to open relay by default. Since it is set this way by default, is it OK to close it?

A: It was very common for e-mail servers to allow mail relaying as a rule. This has been tightened down in recent years, but many e-mail servers can be found that still allow you to relay mail this way. Or they could be misconfigured, which is also very common. You can leave it set as open, but you will have problems. You should always run a closed relay whenever possible, or you will be spammed eventually.

Q: My DMZ hosts were hacked last night. Three of the four servers have been completely wiped out and have to be rebuilt from scratch. When asked when the last time patches were applied, I wasn't sure what the consultant was talking about. We applied the service packs when the systems were put into service eight months ago.

A: When you are running public services that can be accessible through the firewall to the public Internet, such as HTTP, FTP, mail, and DNS services, you need to make certain that every one of those systems is patched, service packed, hardened, and vulnerability tested. Service packs, hotfixes, security updates, and patches come out on a almost daily basis. The fact that eight months went by when the systems were unattended is the reason that they were exploited; it was because the systems were neglected.

Q: I heard that doing vulnerability testing and trying to gain a list of information like OS versions is called *footprinting*. Is this right? I thought it was called vulnerability testing.

A: The proper network terminology associated with this chapter is *footprinting*. Footprinting is the art of profiling an organization based on reconnaissance techniques (learned in this chapter) to create a map of the organization's resources.

Q: I have a system that was penetrated last night. The system was left operating in the DMZ until morning so that the security team could look at it when they come in. Is that the proper procedure?

A: If a threat arises, you need to contain the issue then and there. In other words, if you have a system that is compromised, you need to isolate that system from the rest to contain the issue—much like contain a virus outbreak. Make sure that if you find something wrong or questionable, you do not leave it but instead isolate and address it immediately.

## Chapter 15

Intrusion Detection in the DMZ

Solutions in this chapter:

- **Intrusion Detection**

- **Repelling the Hacker**

- **CiscoSecure IDS**

- **Snort**

- **The Poor Man's IDS**

- **More IDS Deployment Strategies**

- **Lessons Learned**

☑ **Summary**

☑ **Solutions Fast Track**

☑ **Frequently Asked Questions**

667

Introduction

In order to defend against attacks, we must first define just what the threats are. A *threat* is an intentional or unintentional act against something of value. Put simply, a threat is something bad that might happen to the item of value. The item of value could be a router, a firewall, or data itself. A *vulnerability* is a point of weakness in the defenses of the items of value. An attack (whether a passive or an active attack) is the act of finding or acting on the vulnerabilities of a system.

Today the firewall has become something of a commodity and is sold virtually everywhere. The marketing of the firewall has caused an indirect problem: Many people who purchase this commodity think that by using the firewall out of the box, the job of securing their network is completed. The reality is that their job has just begun, and if the task of securing the network is not finished, the entire network is still at risk of compromise. In today's world of threats from worms, viruses, intentional attacks, industrial espionage, and worse, a firewall is not enough.

Still, people think, "Yes, my network is protected—I installed a firewall." The disturbing truth is that configuring the firewall is not very easy yet, even with the various Web and GUI front ends. You still have to have some knowledge of how packets travel across a network and what makes a good packet turn into a bad packet. In order to protect your network effectively, you need to know the basics of how IP should work and how IP can be twisted to nefarious purposes, such as the SYN and FIN scans we saw in Chapter 14.

With a misclick of the mouse or a press of the wrong button, your shiny new firewall could suddenly have a very large hole in it due to misconfiguration. Although it's not technically a hole, this term is the name we append to a vulnerability; it's a "hole" in the system. Hackers live for the misconfigured firewall, because it's often the easiest target to find and exploit. The biggest problem with the misconfigured firewall is the false sense of security it gives you while you are sitting there thinking life is good and your personal or business assets are secure. Even with a properly configured firewall, an attacker can still get past it in many ways. As we saw in Chapter 15, between the port 80 attacks, Unicode attacks, buffer overflows, SQL injection, and the like, there are many ways to get past a firewall. Now we can clearly see that using just a firewall and calling our network security done is very much a fallacy.

To help understand how to effectively protect our network, we need to view the network in a different way. With the firewall at the border, the network is much like an egg, with a hard shell on the outside but an inside that is soft, unprotected, and easily affected if attacked. Think about what happens to the egg when "attacked" (as when you crack it on the lip of a bowl): It breaks, and everything inside comes running out. By the time your supposedly secure data is leaking past the firewall, it is much too late.

We want our network to be more like an onion, with layers of defenses down to the last ring—which explains our defense-in-depth conversation from the last chapter. To this end, we use firewalls, IDS, honeypots, VLANs, ACLs, and applications such as antivirus programs or spyware detection programs like Spybot all together to provide a deep security posture. This posture allows us to not only secure out networks and systems from many different threats but to provide an "umbrella" of security methods to create the "onion." Along with the technology, we use a layered architecture of network design. We have the perimeter network defenses, then we move to the DMZ, incorporating the various resources that need to touch the Internet, such as Web, e-mail, and FTP servers. Behind those resources are more routers or firewalls and then the internal or protected network. But even on the protected network we use VLANs, more routers with ACLs, and physical security. In a well-defended network, the attackers should not get past the DMZ, which will minimize any damage the attacker can cause.

A firewall is the drawbridge of the castle. On one side of the drawbridge are the hordes of barbarians, and on the other side is the castle. You can raise or lower the drawbridge based on need, or in the case of a firewall, you can open or close ports. You can block packets based on IP address, protocols, or source. You can hide IP addresses by using NAT or filter frames based on MAC addresses. The newer firewalls sold today will act as proxies between IP addresses and offer a higher level of network protection than the firewalls of just a few years ago. Another thought here is that as time passes, the single role of the firewall slowly disappears, and we start to see many different solutions offered in a single product. For instance, most firewalls today are very modular and will perform firewall, VPN, and IDS services, all in one. With all this in mind, you should also be aware that firewalls do have their limits. Although the firewall can block a protocol, what do you do about an attack that is hidden inside of a permitted protocol such as HTTP? Enter the IDS.

Intrusion detection systems are a relatively new technology. They arrived on the scene in the mid-1980s or so and were mostly research projects or military projects. With the Internet becoming a critical part of daily life, IDS started to take a more active role in networks. Now IDS is a constantly evolving technology, sometimes ahead of the attacker and sometimes behind it. There are commercial versions of IDS, such as the older Cisco Netranger, which is now the Host and Appliance Sensor, and open source IDS systems such as Snort, which can be found at www.Snort.org. Along with the IDS come signature files and various graphical front ends and SQL databases for storing log files.

An IDS sensor works in simple terms, much like an alarm system for a house. It watches to see if anything trips the alarm, and if so, logs the event and sends the alarm to the systems administrator. The IDS watches the network traffic as it goes by and looks to see if it can match a signature. The IDS is a much more elegant solution to the problem of hidden attacks than the gross blocking of packets or protocols that the traditional firewall solution offers. The IDS does not work by itself, however; the IDS supplements the firewall's protection.

There are many obstacles to deploying an effective IDS solution. Problems range from report generation to where to place the sensor(s) or how to diminish the false positives that occur. The whole concept of the IDS is so important to the enterprise DMZ because, unlike the firewall, which is a relatively fixed defense, the IDS can be an active defense. The IDS can look for and find problems or attacks within a permitted protocol such as HTTP. The firewall cannot isolate the payload of the HTTP traffic; the firewall can only tell if the traffic is port 80 and if it is permitted based on parameters such as IP address, direction, or if the packet is a fragment, and some can go further by distinguishing whether the packet is a FIN without the first part of the IP handshake..

A new tool in the defense of your network's DMZ is the *honeypot*. The honeypot is the modern equivalent of the canaries that were used in mines to warn of dangerous gases that were unseen. In modern networks, the honeypot "sees" the unseen dangers of someone testing your network or actually attacking your network and alerts you —not by falling over dead like the canary but by alerts sent via technology such as e-mail and pagers.

A honeypot is nothing more than a server set up in the DMZ to act, look, and feel like a legitimate target. However, the honeypot can be a nasty surprise for the attacker, with behavior ranging from acting as the early warning system of the network to a sophisticated attack logger. The honeypot can give out faked replies while logging keystrokes and uploaded files for later analysis. What better way to know if you have someone knocking at the door than to have them ring a doorbell? In this chapter, we examine the intricacies of using a honeypot in the DMZ so that we are not only warned about an attack after the fact but we learn how to supply misinformation and even log the hacker's activities. These log files can play a very important part in deciphering how the attack took place and then building a defense against it. The logs can also provide legal forensic evidence about attempted attacks and provide a timeline of when the events took place.

A forgotten item in many security checklists is to look at the Web site content itself. Often programs and programmers insert company information and contact information into corporate Web pages. Along with phone numbers, names, and other personal information, you can often find directory information or even IP addresses if the link has been hardcoded by a lazy programmer. All this information can be of help to a would-be attacker. This information is very easy to cull from the Web site by "ripping," or stealing, the entire site to a local drive using any of a number of common utilities, such as Teleport Pro, which can found at www.tenmax.com/teleport/pro/home.htm, or HTTrack Website Copier, found at www.httrack.com. Once the site is on the local drive, the attacker can start to search for various strings in the code, such as contact, phone, name, or other information. You can easily correct this vulnerability through minor changes in the structure of Web page design and the thinking that goes into the coding of a Web page, keeping all references to company information out of the page. So even though it's a good programming practice to document your program with comments, in Web design this can be a very bad idea. Keeping the normal programming comments such as "Programmed by John Smith at ABC Company, Telephone 444.4444" out of the Web page can reduce the amount of social engineering that might take place. Comments such as "This is where the login authentication takes place" is not something you would want to flag for an attacker. The Web page should use soft links, not hardcoded links with IP addresses or even the full path if it can be avoided. You might laugh at these examples, but we have seen real-world programmers following good coding practices by inline documenting everything the Web page did. You don't want to give the attacker any freebies with your Web pages to aid his attack on your DMZ.

A different approach to network security is not really security but in the near future will become much more important to anyone with a server on the Internet. This approach is to run all program code through a quality assurance program to tighten up holes such as buffer overflows and SQL injection attacks. Within the DMZ, having secure code is of the utmost importance, since there is often interaction between a DMZ host and outside or untrusted users. Virtually all the vendors of the various operating systems have the same issues of buffer overflows. Some vendors have more flaws than others, but in the end, one flaw is one too many. For readers who might not have a good grasp of just what a buffer overflow is, let's take a quick look at the details of a buffer overflow attack.

In programming, various functions are performed in random-access memory (RAM). The program and the operating system allocate certain amounts of RAM for functions such as a buffer or a temporary data storage area or for the stack. This can be a fixed amount or a dynamic amount of RAM. A clever attacker can twist the process of how the application runs by forcing either the application or the operating system daemon or process to error out by exceeding the parameters the application set for the buffer space. In the case of the buffer, when the application has an error condition in the buffer space such that exceeding the string length for an input and the error handling code is poor or nonexistent, a few different results can occur. One is that the application crashes and hands control over to a command prompt. The classic example of this result is where a long, strange string is sent to a Microsoft IIS Web server and the Web server crashes and gives you a root prompt. A different result occurs when an attacker can literally reset the stack pointers to run code inserted into the buffer space. Now the application can be restarted and the new piece of code will be executed. As software complexity increases with each new release, the odds of poor programming practices leaving open these exploits increases. Already we have seen where Microsoft has thrown in the towel with Windows NT 4.0 and said that it cannot correct a current exploit, that the architecture will not allow Microsoft to fix the problem. We grant you that this decision could indicate that Microsoft does not really want to put in the effort on an older operating system, but it gives you insight to the magnitude of the problem of poorly written software.

Correcting this type of security breach will be a multidiscipline effort with the programmers, network engineers, and security officers all having to work together. For example, with distributed applications that use "personal" versions of SQL on the desktop, having bad code across the enterprise will certainly cause problems. All we need to do is to look at the recent SLAMMER worm attack and understand that the Microsoft SQL servers were not the only things at risk—every desktop that used the Microsoft SQL engine as part of a distributed application was at risk. Now instead of one or two doors for the attacker, he has many doors to choose from. So the threat is not only in the DMZ with the SQL servers; it migrates to the desktop. The bar for keeping the DMZ secure has just been raised a significant amount. In this chapter, you will learn how to make certain that publicly accessible DMZ hosts are locked down and secure.

As Edmund Burke (1729–1797) said, "Better to be despised for too anxious apprehensions than ruined by too confident security."

Intrusion Detection

Now let's look at our "burglar alarm," or IDS. There are two major types of IDS system. The first is called *host IDS*, or HIDS, and this is where the IDS will run on the host system, or quite simply, on the host itself. The HIDS system uses an agent to monitor the local host for changes in various files such as the Registry, log files, system files, kernel files, or other specified files. When a change is detected, the agent sends out an alarm, alert, or trap via pager, SNMP, or some other notification method. One well-known HIDS system called Tripwire is available in an open-source version or a commercial version.

The second major type of IDS is called *network IDS*, or NIDS, and consists of one or more remote sensors with a management node. The NIDS monitors traffic at wire speed and examines each packet in real time to look for a pattern match. One problem that should be readily apparent is trying to have the sensor keep up with today's gigabit speeds on the wire. Some NIDS systems offer different ways to filter out the massive quantity of traffic you would run into by examining every packet.

Some of the significant characteristics of HIDS and NIDS systems are:

- HIDS:
  - Detailed logging
  - Better at detecting unknown attacks
  - Fewer false positives
  - Each host needs an agent installed and configured

- NIDS:
  - Ease of deployment
  - Cost is generally lower
  - Managed by a single director or management station

When you think of intrusion detection, there are four primary types of data sources to consider.

- Network data packets
- Host details and system details
- Application log files
- Targeted data where the IDS looks for tampered data

Each type of data requires different handling. It's up to you to decide which type of data you need to see or track. The data type will drive, to an extent, the type of IDS system you deploy, or perhaps you'll deploy a mix of sensors. The optimal deployment would be multiple NDIS systems and HIDS installed on key hosts or using a HIDS-like Tripwire to watch key hosts. However, in the real world there is something called a budget that brings heartburn to the network engineer trying to protect his or her network. Personal experience shows that with some careful planning of budget dollars and utilizing resources such as open-source projects, you can protect your network very well with a mix of the two technologies. This way you can budget for the brand-name IDS such as Cisco for the primary IDS sensor and use a "free" product like Snort for the remaining internal sensors. Use a HIDS product like Tripwire to protect the server farm and infrastructure such as the routers and switches, and voilà—you have an effective layered defense that starts from the outside to the DMZ and down to the internal network resources. Given the quality of open-source applications such as Snort, there is no longer any excuse not to have an IDS system or even multiple sensors deployed.

As mentioned in the introduction, there are two primary types of intrusion detection. There is a third method called *network node intrusion detection*, or NNIDS, which is a hybrid of HIDS and NIDS. NNIDS is an agent-based system, but it views packets and runs an analysis against the packets. The difference between NIDS (where all packets are analyzed) and NNIDS is that NNIDS only looks at the packets destined for the host machine it is installed on and protecting. This allows the NNIDS to run very fast. The downside is that you have to install an agent on each host you want protected in this manner.

> **NOTE**
>
> One of the best-known names for looking for tampered data is a product called Tripwire, which can be found at www.tripwire.org. For a very cool poster that has exploits mapped to type and source, go to www.tripwire.com/files/literature/poster/tripwire_exploit_poster.pdf and find a plotter to print it.

An IDS deployment has two parts. One part is called the *sensor*, the other is the *management station* or *director*. The sensor is connected to the network and sniffs the packets as they go by. The management station controls the sensors and generates the various reports and alarms from a database of alarm data sent to it by the sensor. The sensor has two NICs, one attached to the target network and without an IP address. The lack of an IP address helps protect the sensor from attack. An even better way is to use a network tap on the target network to attach the sensor's monitoring interface. The tap allows you to monitor a full-duplex connection and prevent someone from attacking the sensor itself.

In Figure 15.1, we see a basic network tap schematic and the data flow between Network A and Network B. The tap is in between the two networks and provides a copy of both the transmitted data flow and the received data flow. The tap can be passive or active and allow the IDS to send TCP resets to an attacker.

Figure 15.1 Common Network Tap

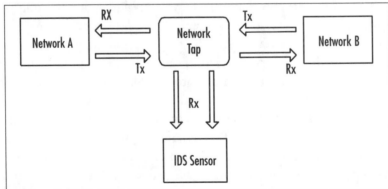

The second NIC is attached to the trusted network and allows communication between the sensor and the management station. The classic deployment of an IDS has the unnumbered port on the outside of the firewall and the management port on the DMZ or on the inside network. An IDS sensor can also be configured with the unnumbered port on a vendor segment and the management port on your trusted network. With enough resources, you can have multiple IDS sensors deployed on the network at the same time watching different areas of interest and each using a different rule set.

An IDS system works by using a sensor to see or Snort the raw data off the network or host. Then the IDS engine applies rules to the data to see if the data matches either normal activity or suspect activity, as shown in Figure 15.2. Once the match is made, the IDS sends an alert or writes the alert to a log file. The data that the IDS sensor looks for can be quite varied. It can be IP addresses, port numbers or types, strings in the packet payload, or certain combinations of hex with a particular offset in the packet. Due to this flexibility, the IDS sensor can see things that virtually nothing else on the network can see. If an attacker launches a port 80 HTTP attack, the firewall will most likely miss it, because it appears to be normal port 80 HTTP traffic. The IDS sensor, on the other hand, sees the possible attack, given that the proper rules have been enabled. The sensor sees the attack because the sensor looks at the entire packet and finds the match of the attack string being used.

Figure 15.2 Block Diagram Describing the Way IDS Works

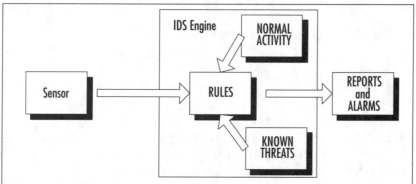

In order to effectively use IDS on your network, you first need to understand how TCP/IP works and the so-called three-way handshake. This three-way handshake is how the classic TCP connection is built up between the hosts. The bad news is that an attacker can take advantage of this handshake and manipulate its functionality into something else useful and informational, such as a hacking tool. We discussed how this could be done in some detail in Chapter 15. In this discussion, the question is, how do we find this altered handshake taking place? We can track this type of activity with an IDS system and the correct signature for the IDS sensor to use. In Figure 15.3, we see the normal three-way handshake for TCP/IP.

Figure 15.3 TCP/IP Three-Way Handshake

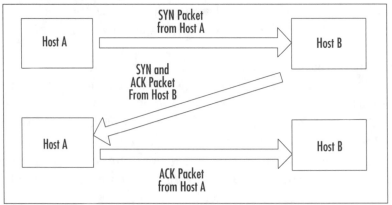

Designing & Planning…

Where to Put the IDS Sensor?

Many factors drive just where to place an IDS sensor. In the end, cost normally wins out. With that in mind, let's look at the most common places to use one or two IDS sensors. The first is to place the sensor right behind the perimeter firewall and LAN router. This is the network choke point for all traffic that passes in and out of the private network to the outside world. The second choice is to place the IDS sensor within the DMZ. This allows you to watch the exposed servers that face the outside world and look for attacks starting there. Since most attacks are directed against DNS, mail, and database servers and the like, this placement can be of high value. Remember, the IDS is observing traffic, looking for attack patterns against a signature database, regardless of whether you are using HIDS or NIDS. The point here is that if you place an IDS correctly, you will be able to observe malicious traffic quite easily, but if you misplace it, you might not capture or analyze anything of importance. The third and somewhat "argued over" placement is between the firewall and the border router. In many cases the border router is the gateway facing your network at the ISP side of the Internet connection.

Continued

This style of deployment directly exposes the sensor to the Internet, so care is needed n configuring the sensor so that you don't add a new security problem or issue when securing the DMZ in this manner. This is a perfect example of when to use a network tap, which we discuss in depth later in this chapter.

However, this placement gives a wealth of information as to what attacks are being launched and which actually make it through the firewall.

It is not enough to know the three-way handshake breakdown to effectively use an IDS system. You must also understand, at the very least and at a high level, the various attack methods and how you can make or modify signatures to protect your network against attack. As we saw in Chapter 15, all attacks are not apparent on the surface. Some are written into an HTML header or keyed in at the user ID and password prompt. A good signature will look for these types of attacks. Once the IDS is deployed, don't make the mistake of thinking your job is done—the job has just started.

Configuring & Implementing...

How to TAP for the IDS Sensor

There are a few ways to get the IDS sensor on the wire. In today's switched network designs, it becomes harder to get the IDS sensor to see all the needed traffic due to the way a switch functions when it forwards frames. In simple terms, a switch is really a collection of bridges and operates at Layer 2 of the OSI model. Each bridge or port is its own collision domain, but all the ports share the broadcast domain, since the broadcast domain is set by Layer 3 in the OSI model. The switch looks at the frame and decides which port or "bridge" the frame needs to be sent to. Unlike a hub, where all ports see all frames on the switch, only the port that needs to see the frame will have that frame sent to it unless the frame is a broadcast or the frame has been flooded to all ports. This brings us to our deployment problem with the IDS sensor. Since the IDS sensor needs to see all traffic, what shall we do?

We have a few options, depending on the type of switch and configurations. The first option is to configure the switch for port spanning or mirroring. This would copy each frame and send it to the port the IDS sensor was attached to. There are a few problems with this solution—such as you miss

Continued

half the traffic in a full-duplex link and the mirrored port might not be able to handle the aggregate traffic load.

An alternative choice is to use a device called a *network tap,* which is a T-type device that can allow the IDS to sit in the traffic flow from a bidirectional perspective, which can help lower false positives. In some cases the tap can be configured for receive (Rx) only for high security or bidirectional, where the IDS can send RST to clear connections transparently.

Now that you understand the underlying concepts of an IDS, let's start to look at how to deploy an IDS in a DMZ-based network. In this chapter we look at how to set up an IDS in a DMZ utilizing popular vendor-based solutions, including Cisco-based IDS and the freeware program called Snort.

Deployment of an IDS

There are six steps for the successful deployment of any IDS system:

1. Determine what network traffic you need to monitor with the IDS to protect assets.

2. Connect the sensors to the network where previously identified traffic will flow.

3. Run the sensors for a week or so with the default configuration. This allows you to build a baseline of alarms and traffic for analysis. This tool helps you decide which alarm is real and which is not and why not. For example, is there a network management software package on the wire that acts like a port scanner? Once you have analyzed the baseline traffic, you can adjust the signatures to reduce the false positives.

4. Analyze the alarm log and weed out the false positives by editing the signatures, editing the severity level, or disabling the alarm for that signature.

5. Implement response actions based on positive alarms such as sending a pager alert, using the IDS sensors to send a TCP reset packet, or shunning the source IP address.

6. Update sensors with current signatures based on the vendor's release of new signatures or as needed by adding custom signatures.

These six steps reflect a fair amount of work and thinking in order to successfully deploy IDS systems. Along with updating signature files, take the time to make a few minor adjustments to help beat the hacker who is looking to defeat the IDS sensor.

Take the interface that is sensing the traffic and remove the IP address or build a cable that is receive (Rx) only by clipping the transmit wires. If you are running Snort, be aware that some distributions will run Snort as root. This is very dangerous to your IDS's security and your network security if the IDS is breached. We delve into this topic in more detail when we discuss Snort later in this chapter.

The IDS must be able to see all the monitored traffic and be able to keep up with the data flow. A switched network can pose special problems, since each port of a switch is considered a network segment. A way around this is to use port mirroring or span commands.

Configuring & Implementing…

How to Configure Cisco Port Mirroring/Span for the IDS Sensor

There are many different vendors of network switches, but here we show you how to configure Cisco switches, since Cisco is arguably the biggest player in networking infrastructure. The goal is to have a VLAN or port mirrored to a single port for the IDS sensor to see the traffic. You do need to read the switch documentation because the procedure will vary slightly from model to model. Furthermore, there are some limitations, such as the number of VLANs that can be monitored or how many mirrors or span ports can be configured. For an excellent tutorial on Cisco *span*, see www.cisco.com/warp/public/473/41.html.

For a CatOS (COS) switch such as the Catalyst 4000, 5000, and 6000 series, our example spans VLAN 1 to module 6 port 2 and is Rx only:

```
Set span <source port>  <source VLAN> <direction>
switch (enable) set span 1  6/2 rx
```

For a Cisco IOS switch such as the 2900 series, our example is port Fa0/1, which will be monitoring traffic sent and received by port Fa0/5:

```
; enter destination port
Switch(config)#int fa0/1


; enter port to be monitored
Switch(config-if)#port monitor fastEthernet 0/5
```

Continued

> Note that the Catalyst 2900XL and 3500XL do not support *span* in receive direction only or in transmit direction only. You need to take care not to create a spanning tree loop. There are some additional caveats for the 2950 and 3550 switches from Cisco. Catalyst 2950 switches can have only one *span* session active at a time and can monitor only source ports, not VLANs. Catalyst 3550 switches can support up to two *span* sessions at a time and can monitor source ports as well as VLANs.

A third option is to use a network *tap*, a hardware device that splits a full–duplex connection into two separate streams. The same tap will in many cases only allow the traffic to be sent to the IDS sensor, although some taps, such as SecureNet IDS taps, can allow the sensor to send TCP resets back out into the datastream. The taps prevent a scanner from even seeing the MAC address of the NIC being used as the sensing port on the IDS sensor. This is an ideal method of attaching the IDS sensor to the DMZ, where attackers are certainly going to run various scans against the IP range in the DMZ. It's hard for the attacker to defeat something that they do not know is there watching them. There are several manufacturers of network taps. A few of the bigger names are Finisar at www.finisar.com, SecureNet at www.intrusion.com, and Shomiti at www.shomiti.net.

The basic network tap is a small box with three interface jacks on it and a power supply attachment. The tap itself can be for Ethernet, asynchronous transfer mode (ATM), and use copper or fiber optic interfaces. Inside is a circuit that will split the datastreams, and in many, if power is lost to the tap, failover to a pass–through configuration to keep the network connection from being broken. There are special IDS taps that block outbound traffic but allow the IDS to send a TCP reset packet as part of your layered DMZ defense. The taps can be rack mounted or they can be intended just to sit on a shelf in the rack.

At this point you might be thinking, "You just showed me how to monitor my traffic for free, and now you tell about something to buy. Why would I want to spend any money on this?" That's a fair question, but like many things in life, each of these tools has its place, and neither tool will do it all. Port mirroring does have the advantage of being cheap. It also might be able to view all the traffic, depending on the switch, and it certainly is easy to configure and use. However, the downside is that if you try to mirror a heavy traffic load, the switch might not be able to buffer all the mirrored traffic, and it might start to shed the excess frames.

A much more subtle issue is that when the packets go through the buffer, the timing is reset so you no longer have an accurate time reference point. On some switches, when the mirror is set up, it resets the ports, which, on a live network, can be problematic if you need to insert the sensor into the network during uptime. As we saw in the sidebar configuration notes, some switches will not allow you to set the data flow on the mirror to be Rx only, which can cause serious network issues if a mistake is made with the configuration. With a network tap, many of the "cons" fall by the way-side and no longer will give you heartburn. In the end, you need to look at your network and the infrastructure and make an informed decision as to the best solution for you and your organization's needs.

In order to see the traffic on the core of the network, it would be best if there were a way to see the traffic on the core switch backplane. Cisco has done just this with an IDS sensor module or blade for the Catalyst 6000 series switch. The Catalyst 6000 IDS module uses an embedded version of Windows and sees all traffic on the backplane of the switch. The IDS module uses two methods of capturing traffic to analyze. The first way is to use the switch's *span* feature that many of us use to capture traffic for a sniffer. The second is to use a VACL (also called a VLAN ACL). The VACL gets around the limitations of how many span ports you can have on a switch. One of the biggest benefits of the IDS module is that it can capture multi–VLAN traffic, whereas an appliance like the 4230 or a PC running Snort cannot. The IDS module can capture data at the full 100Mbps and a 64-byte size packet. This translates into that the switch can capture more than 100Mbps of traffic when the packet size exceeds 64 bytes, which your network most certainly will. The downside is that to implement the IDS module requires a very specific Catalyst switch configuration, which does not come cheap. In addition, the IDS module cannot track IP addresses or perform IP blocking the way the appliances can.

Figure 15.4 shows the classic deployment of an IDS system when you have a single sensor. The IDS sensor watches all the traffic on the Internet or unsecured side of the DMZ, and then you can compare what is making it through the firewall for possible corrective action.

Figure 15.4 Classic IDS Deployment

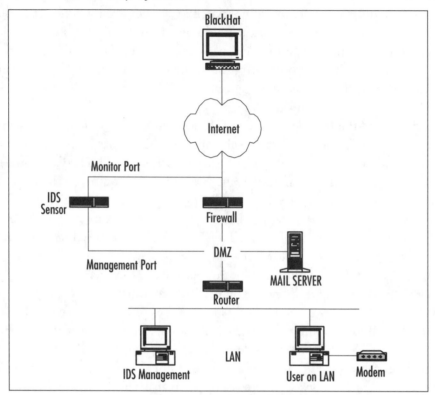

One of the possible corrective actions is to have the IDS tell the firewall to shun or block an IP address of an attacker. You would see the port scan starting on the Internet side, and then the IDS sensor, either directly or through a management station, would tell the firewall to block the IP address of whomever was scanning the firewall. In the case of a worm or HTTP attack, the IDS sensor would see the match of the signature and could have the firewall block the address, or the IDS could send a TCP reset to break the IP connection between the attacker and the Web server, SQL server, or other host. This type of deployment complements the protection that the firewall gives to the hosts in the DMZ. The firewall will pass a port 80 attack since it appears to be normal HTML traffic, so this type of deployment works well and fits into the layered defense model of network security.

In Figure 15.5, we see the results of not having an IDS sensor watching over the DMZ traffic. An attacker used the Unicode style of attack to get past the firewall and, from the Microsoft IIS Web server, get a directory listing of drive C:.

Figure 15.5 IIS Unicode Attack Via Port 80 and HTML Results

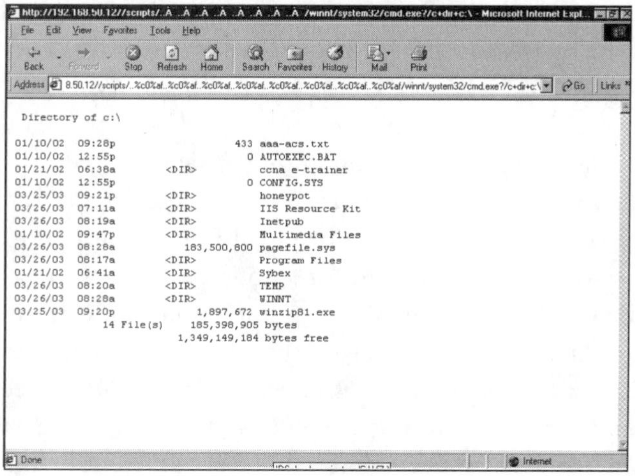

Many firewalls would not have even seen this attack coming, but many IDS would have spotted it by the Unicode signature. This successful attack has now given the attacker several pieces of information: He knows for sure that the server is an IIS box, he knows the directory structure, and by digging deeper, he could find out if the default IIS files are still there for even more exploits.

In Figure 15.6 we see a screen from an Etherpeek capture of a Unicode attack in progress.

Figure 15.6 Trace of HMTL Code Sent with Unicode Attack

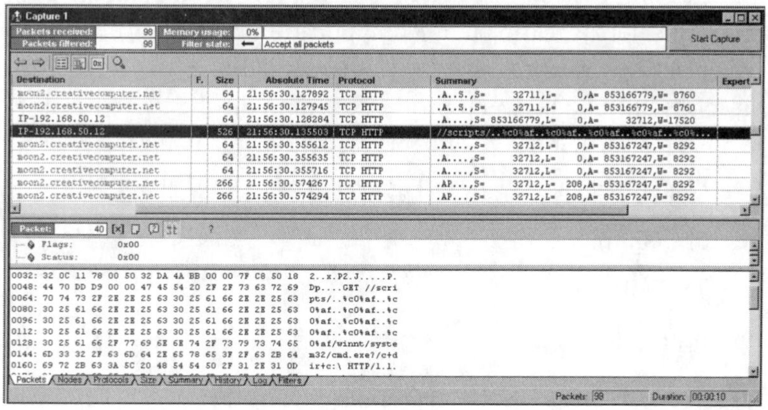

In this capture you can see the signature that the IDS sensor uses to identify the attack, even though it is buried in what appears to be normal HTML traffic, according to the firewall. The IDS scans the payload of the packet and matches the Unicode attack.

By contrast, if the IDS is placed on the inside leg of the firewall, the IDS sees only the traffic permitted by the firewall, and you will need an IDS for each leg of the firewall. So, if you have two DMZs and a LAN connection, you will need three network IDS sensors.

This type of deployment can be rather costly in terms of purchasing equipment, time to install the sensors, and time to configure the sensors. The rule of thumb to remember is that if you cannot see the traffic with a sniffer, the IDS will not see it, either. Knowing this, you might want to download Ethereal, a high-quality and free protocol analyzer, set it up, and run a test for a couple of weeks to baseline the traversing traffic. Based on the results of the captures you run, you can see if it is truly crucial to set up an IDS, since you might not be capturing much traffic at all. Another reason you might want to test the traffic is to see if you do in fact need to *span* or mirror the ports on your switch. In this chapter, we look at how to *span* ports on a Cisco switch, where it might be needed. If you have a different brand of switch, the commands probably differ from the Cisco syntax.

Normally there are two interfaces on an IDS sensor. One is for management, and the other is for the sensor to see the traffic. For example, on the Cisco 4230 IDS, the built-in NIC is the management interface and the additional NIC is the sensor interface. Snort can be used with a single NIC, but it is preferable to have two NICs installed.

When you're trying to use the *span* or port-mirroring functionality, remember that the commands differ between the Cisco product lines and those of other switch vendors. Some implementations limit the number of span ports you can have, and some limit whether you can monitor multi-VLAN traffic.

When you're tuning the sensor to reduce false positives, it can take a lot of time to sort out whether the alert is real or not. An application such as What's Up, which uses ICMP *ping* sweeps of the hosts to verify they are responding, can trigger the IDS sensor, since it looks like a *ping* sweep probe. You can edit the signature, filter out the traffic based on source or destination attributes, or go ahead and log it but ignore it.

Typical responses to the sensor having a match of a signature and traffic are:

- IP session logging
- Sending a TCP reset
- Shunning or blocking

Remember that you need to be sure about the positive match before you enable a response. For example, blocking on a port scan could prove embarrassing when the scan comes from your network manager trying to discover nodes on the network. On most IDS systems, the response can be enabled on a per-signature basis. Logging the IP addresses, although it doesn't provide much protection, does provide a way to build trends and to trip the alarm or notification. *Shunning* or blocking can buy time for you to enable a better defense against the attack. Some IDS systems can actually work with the routers and firewalls to dynamically adjust access lists based on matches to the various signatures.

Repelling the Hacker

One of the most common tools hackers use is Nmap. This knowledge helps you defend the DMZ, since you can look for certain characteristic signatures from Nmap. If the attacker uses the SYN switch, the pattern is easily seen from the IDS perspective, since they are crafted packets. If the attacker uses the older style of connect scanning, it is harder to tell if it is from Nmap, since the IP datagrams are built by the host operating system. You can still find clues based on Nmap itself. If you see an all-port scan and then a second scan of only the open ports, you can be pretty sure someone is running Nmap against your host. Keep this in mind as you check for attacks on your DMZ segment-based hosts. You could see a lot of scanning coming from the Internet, and you will want to make certain that nothing is open for a hacker to see, so you should be doing your own scans also, just to be safe.

Another tool to consider along with an IDS system is the honeypot. You can find an excellent source of material about honeypots and the Honeypot Project at www.tracking-hackers.com. For readers who have not heard of honeypots, think about the children's book character Winnie the Pooh and how he is always getting into the honeypot for the sticky sweet stuff inside. This is the premise of a honeypot server. It presents itself as a juicy-sweet and irresistible target to the hacker. Once the hacker has "tasted" the honeypot, he keeps coming back for more, and you get to see it all. For the network administrator or security officer, the real plus is that a honeypot is very cost effective. It doesn't have to be a megaserver to be effective; a leftover P150 with 128MB of RAM can work very well.

The honeypot server can sit in the DMZ and perform an interesting function. It does nothing at all; it's the laziest server possible. In reality, the honeypot provides a juicy target for aspiring hackers to start probing, and since the honeypot does nothing, when there is a probe against port 80 or port 25, it can be assumed that the probe is real. This greatly reduces the noise and false alarms that can occur in a busy DMZ on the traditional IDS. The honeypot can be anything from a simple application to a very sophisticated design, depending on the business's needs and wants. It can provide just an early warning that probes are taking place, or it can act as a logger of all keystrokes and other information. You can use this information to build custom filters or signature files for the IDS. Let's look at how to create a basic honeypot to be placed on your DMZ segment and examine the types of attacks and scans that can be used against it, as well as what to do when you catch someone probing your network services and resources. We start with Figure 15.7, which shows the basic deployment of a typical honeypot on the DMZ.

Figure 15.7 Basic DMZ Deployment of a Honeypot

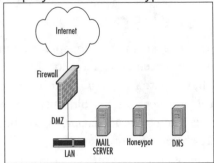

In this case, as we described earlier, the honeypot is not part of the network, so there should be no connections to it from legitimate network traffic. If there is a net-work connection, it can be assumed that a hacker has found it via some type of recon-naissance port scan or possibly from another form of passive attack, such as eavesdropping, where the name of the game is information gathering. The IDS might or might not have detected the port scan, so the honeypot has provided a backup method to alert you to the potential of a hacker knocking at the door. To make this concept clearer, a honeypot is not used *instead* of an IDS but *in addition* to the IDS sensor. If something is missed, you could record some poking and prodding on your honeypot, thus clueing you into the possibility of someone "hunting and pecking" your Internet-facing hosts for open services and known vulnerabilities.

One of the best honeypots to start with is Back Officer Friendly (BOF), which is a parody on the remote-control Trojan called Back Orifice. You can find BOF at www.nfr.com/products/bof/overview.shtml. It emulates several ports such as Telnet (23), SMTP (25), FTP (20 and 21), and others. When probed on these ports, BOF sends back fake replies and logs the interaction, allowing you to see if someone is knocking on your door. When it comes to your DMZ hosts, you must assess the need for this type of security product, because you most likely will be probed eventually.

A more sophisticated honeypot that can emulate 13 different operating systems and has a wealth of logging and tracking functionality is called Specter; it can be found at www.specter.com. Specter is a very sophisticated honeypot program that can appear to be a Windows 98, NT, 2000, or XP server. It can also seem to be a Linux, Solaris, Irix, or other UNIX style of box. For the kicker, it can appear to be a Macintosh running OS-X. In addition to the 13 different operating systems that it can emulate, Specter will monitor up to 14 ports. Specter has added an SSH trap and can use WHOIS to backtrack the attacker based on the IP address. You can set up Specter with false users, false Web pages, bogus e-mail, and other tantalizing tidbits to entice the would-be hacker to spend far too much time playing in the honeypot.

On the con side, Specter does not emulate IP stacks, so an Nmap scan shows the truth of the honeypot if the attacker takes time out from his excitement to find an open system to even scan the honeypot. Specter can also send its log files to a syslog server or to the local event log. You can also configure alerts that can be e-mailed or sent to a pager. Keep in mind that although Specter is a great honeypot, you still need to secure the OS you install it on. Specter does not secure the OS; that's up to you.

In the words of the philosopher Sun-Tzu, "Hold out baits to entice the enemy. Feign disorder, and crush him."

Honeypots in the DMZ

In this section we look at how to set up a honeypot with Specter. Again, it is crucial to your security posture that you harden and protect the DMZ segment as much as humanly possible, and setting up a honeypot offers you many strategic security options for doing so. Let's take a look at how a honeypot can be used.

Configuring a Honeypot for Your DMZ

One of the best locations for your honeypot is in the DMZ of your network. The honeypot is protected to a degree but gives enough back to the hacker to keep his interest away from other hosts on the DMZ. As we said before, what better way to find out there is a hacker than by having the hacker "ring the doorbell." Specter is easily installed, just like any other normal Windows application. Getting from start to working honeypot can happen in the range of 10 minutes. In Figure 15.8 we see the basic screen of Specter when we start to configure it.

Figure 15.8 The Initial Specter Screen

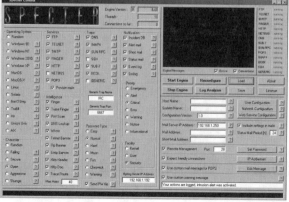

The authors of Specter assume that you know the basics of the operating system you are trying to simulate. Virtually everything is configurable. For example, you can configure how difficult the password should be. It can be easy, hard, or the best one, fun. We suppose that fun depends on one's point of view in this case. You can configure the various banners for things such as FTP or Telnet. You can turn on or off various services such as FTP, Telnet, SMTP, and things like SUB-7 or BO2K. This honeypot is not an interactive honeypot—in other words, the attacker does not get to play with the operating system. This makes a honeypot such as Specter relatively easy to deploy and run as you control exactly what the attacker can do. The downside is that you will not be able to recover interesting things such as root kits, e-mails, toolkits, or IRC chat logs.

To deploy Specter, you need a reasonably powered machine. The published guidelines call for a 450MHz PII processor and windows NT 4 Sp6a, Windows 2000 SP1, or Windows XP. Specter uses the normal Windows installer; once the product is installed, just start the honeypot. Each configurable parameter has a question mark (?) next to it; click it to get help if you need some explanation of the choice. You can remotely manage Specter, but that service is turned off by default, so you need to remember to enable it. The interface for remote management is virtually the same as if you were on the honeypot as a local user.

Specter offers an excellent remote alert function. This is one of the most valuable benefits of Specter, since the sooner you know the doorbell is ringing, the sooner you can stop the attacker. You can choose to have e-mails sent to you, pager alerts, log information to a syslog server, or have the information sent to the local event log. In Figure 15.9 we see a log entry that shows an FTP session starting. The attacker thinks that the password file was transferred to his machine.

Figure 15.9 A Specter Log File Screen

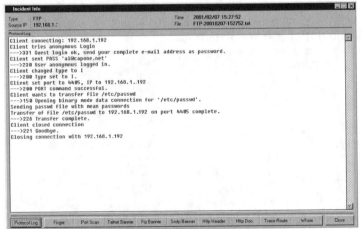

Specter or any other honeypot tends to work best on the DMZ or internal network. We already know that bad people are on the Internet, but we want to know who is poking around in our DMZ. For more details on honeypots and their use, see www.tracking-hackers.com for a good selection of resources and articles.

Now that we have learned how to implement a solid honeypot (and how to use it to find attackers), let's take a look at other types of hosts in the DMZ that you need to be concerned about, especially when dealing with HIDS.

Host-Based Intrusion Detection Systems

As we saw earlier in the chapter, HIDS are just what their name implies. The intrusion detection takes place locally on the host that's being protected. This can offer significant value to the intrusion detection process, but it also carries some issues.

Some of the value of HIDS is that the log files can be very detailed. You can see the actual results of an attack; the HIDS does not rely on signature files as much as the NIDS does, which can let the HIDS catch an unknown attack that the NIDS would have missed. Furthermore, the HIDS can catch an encrypted attack, since it would be decrypted at the host. All this good stuff comes with a price in the form of the possibility of high overhead on the host, the need to secure logging because many attacks will also change the log files, suspect logs if the attack was a success, the need to monitor each host, and possible cessation of monitoring due to a system crash.

The HIDS can watch for many different changes on the host, ranging from files being changed, time stamps, privileges changing, and deleting of data to system modifications. With any HIDS, you need to make sure that the log files have enough space to be stored. This is very important in Windows-based hosts because the default log file size is only 512Kb—far too small for any real security application. Given that disk space per megabyte is so cheap, there is no excuse for not having large log files. The rule of thumb is to have a week's worth of data in the log files. This means that you need to run a few baselines before turning the HIDS on as a production system. You need to determine the size the log files will be with normal traffic, then add to the number to account for any unexpected increase in activity such as might happen in an attack.

While we're speaking of log files, we want to discuss configuring the hosts monitored by HIDS with Network Time Protocol (NTP) clocking. If you need to analyze an attack spread over several hosts in the DMZ, you need to have all the log files on the some time standard so you can build an accurate timeline of the event. For legal purposes, the log file's timestamp must be in the Universal Coordinated Time format. Without an accurate timeline, deciphering and prosecuting an attack is much more arduous.

Some HIDS can gather information from hosts even if the software is not resident on the device. This feature can prove very useful in guarding your network infrastructure, such as the routers and switches—for example, if the router log files are configured to track exceptions to the access lists in place. This can provide an alarm that someone is knocking at the door or give insight into how the attack might have started. Even without a HIDS, the syslog functionality alone can be very helpful. With a combination of log severity level and facility levels, you can configure multiple entries on a syslog server such as Linux. For one thing, you could have two PIX firewalls and set up a custom directory for each PIX using the facility option of syslog. For analyzing the log file data, some excellent applications are available. One of the best is called Sawmill (www.sawmill.net). This application can read virtually any log file output and generate some excellent reports from the data. You can analyze your Web server log files, firewall log files, Cisco IDS log files, or Snort log files, just to name a few.

The world of HIDS holds a few major players and many minor players. Before you deploy a HIDS, you owe it to your sanity to do some research on which HIDS is the best one for your network design, risk factors, and budget. A few of the bigger names in HIDS are Tripwire, found at www.tripwire.com; Okena StormWatch, at www.okena.com; and Entercept, at www.entercept.com. Let's look at one of these products in a bit more detail.

Tripwire

Tripwire started life as an academic source project in 1992 and is UNIX based. It has morphed into a commercial project for both UNIX and Windows. A Linux version has been released as an open-source project and can be found at www.tripwire.org.

Tripwire, classified as a HIDS, provides an effective method to manage data and network integrity. It does not look at packets, the way a NIDS does; it watches the files and configurations of network nodes. To manage the nodes, Tripwire communicates with the various hosts and nodes on the network using Telnet/TFT, SSH/TFTP, or SSH/SCP. The information gathered is maintained in a database and used to make a baseline signature for each node. In Figure 15.10 we see the basic Tripwire screen showing nodes that are monitored.

Figure 15.10 Tripwire Node Manager

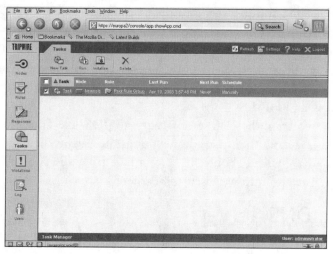

Tripwire is managed by an HTML interface, so the administrator can manage it from anywhere on the network. Tripwire's logging function is very sophisticated, with features ranging from basic reporting of alarms to the capability to quarantine evidence for forensic analysis. A very cool feature is that Tripwire can be configured to restore a changed node configuration either manually or automatically. This has some interesting possibilities for managing nodes in the DMZ. If someone were to attack and modify the configuration of a host/node in the DMZ, Tripwire can put back the old configuration as soon as it spots the change. In Figure 15.11 we see that Tripwire detected a change between the "startup configuration" of a router and the current "running configuration" of the same router.

Figure 15.11 Tripwire Detecting a Change in Configuration

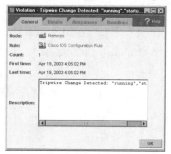

We can configure a rule that has Tripwire put the "baseline" image back onto the router automatically when a change such as this is detected. Of course, you would only want to do this to nodes that do not see very many changes in their configuration, but

you can set the rule to be manual in order to prevent Tripwire being overly helpful by overwriting changes that you just made to the to the node.

HIDS such as Tripwire can watch more than infrastructure nodes. They can monitor various file characteristics such as create time, last access time, user ID, file permissions, alternative datastreams, various Registry keys, and much more. Most HIDS such as Tripwire monitor both Windows and UNIX machines of various flavors such as AIX, Linux, Solaris, and HP-UX.

Ideally you would team the IDS sensors with a HIDS-like Tripwire for solid intrusion detection coverage and then use a honeypot as the early-warning system—the "doorbell" that we have talked about. Now we are getting closer to the "onion"-layered network defensive posture we discussed earlier.

Saving the DNS Server

In Chapter 15 we saw that the poor DNS server is one of the mostly likely targets in the DMZ for attackers to nail first. The reason is that most enterprise networks have a DNS server located on the DMZ segment, and with the number of attacks that can be launched on it, you will more than likely log some attempts on its life. Given how DNS works, you might think that all is lost and that protecting the DNS server in your DMZ is just about impossible—but nothing is further from the truth.

We can do several things to harden the DNS server against the malcontents of the Internet:

- Use the newest version of BIND, which is currently 9.2.2. You might also want to consider running a different DNS service such as *djbdns,* found at http://cr.yp.to/djbdns.html. This service is designed to be a hardened DNS service. Windows NT does offer a DNS service, but hardening a Windows NT DNS server takes quite a bit of work.

- Keep your patches up to date. Doing so is critical with all vendor products you are using in your DMZ, especially when the hosts deploying these services (such as DNS) are Internet facing and opened up to scanning by attackers.

- Restrict or authenticate zone transfers to prevent unauthorized release of your zone information, as we discussed in Chapter 15. Give no freebies to the wannabe hacker of your DMZ.

- Restrict DNS dynamic updates by using access lists to control exactly who can and cannot get the updates.

- Use the Split DNS architecture.

- Use the most secure method of updating your DNS server records.

- Make sure the firewall is configured correctly for DNS traffic on both TCP/UDP 53.

The two items that bring the most value to hardening of your DNS servers is the updated version of BIND and the split DNS architecture. The idea of a split DNS architecture is pretty straightforward; SANS has a good article explaining split DNS at www.sans.org/rr/firewall/DNS_sec.php. You will have two (or more) DNS file servers. One will be in the DMZ and offer public IPs; the second will be internal on the trusted network. One server will forward requests to the other.

When configuring the firewall, think about how DNS works, and make up access lists to help provide defense in depth. For example, if you have an internal DNS server, the only DNS server that should be asking for any information at all should be the DNS server in the DMZ. So, the ACL should deny all DNS traffic except for that server. Make sure that the attacker cannot use the *dig* or *nslookup* commands as we did in Chapter 15 to pull up the entire zone. You can accomplish this by using a feature called *xfrnets*, found in BIND versions 4.9.3 through 4.9.5. This feature allows you to edit the /etc/named.boot record and apply an access list to zone transfers by IP address. In BIND 8.1 or higher, this functionality is called *allow-query* and also applies an access list on DNS queries.

If we go back to Chapter 15, we also see that when you run the *dig* utility and ask for the version of BIND, as shown in Figure 15.12, you will get the DNS server to respond with the version of bind it is currently running. This gives the attacker a rather large clue as to how to begin to attack the DNS server. We want to hide that information from the attacker. It can be done, but it will take some effort on your part.

Figure 15.12 A DiG Query of BIND Version

```
[msweeney@venus msweeney]$ dig @66.75.160.41 version.bind txt chaos


; <<>> DiG 9.2.1 <<>> @66.75.160.41 version.bind txt chaos
;; global options:  printcmd
;; Got answer:
;; ->>HEADER<<- opcode: QUERY, status: NOERROR, id: 19939
;; flags: qr aa rd; QUERY: 1, ANSWER: 1, AUTHORITY: 0, ADDITIONAL: 0


;; QUESTION SECTION:
;version.bind.                   CH      TXT
```

Continued

Figure 15.12 A DiG Query of BIND Version

```
;; ANSWER SECTION:
version.bind.             0      CH      TXT      "9.2.1"


;; Query time: 27 msec
;; SERVER: 66.75.160.41#53(66.75.160.41)
;; WHEN: Sat Apr  5 07:08:32 2003
;; MSG SIZE  rcvd: 48
```

As you can see in Figure15.12, BIND happily gave out its version as 9.2.1 when we performed a *dig* query asking the server for the version. This information tells the attacker the version of BIND he needs to find an exploit for.

How do we get BIND to stop being so helpful to intruders? In Figure 15.13 we see the simplest way to stop BIND from this kind of helpfulness. We set an options substatement in BIND that gives back a string that we define in the version argument.

Figure 15.13 A Way to Stop Bind from Handing Out Its Version String

```
options {
     directory "/var/named";
     version "They stole it from us";
};
```

As you can see, with just a few simple fixes, you can deter any potential hacker who might want to compromise your DNS servers. Remember what the Greek philosopher Demosthenes said: "Small opportunities are often the beginning of great enterprises." We keep this statement in mind to resolve our DMZ concerns, where "small opportunities" to lock down vulnerabilities like this could be the beginning of a great (and secure) enterprise DMZ.

Implementing HIDS on Your DNS Server

Now that you understand why DNS services in the DMZ need to be secured (and you recall from other chapters of the book how to harden such systems), let's look at how to use HIDS on a DNS server in your DMZ. Since from reading this book you know many ways to test, attack, harden, and secure DNS, let's close it up in this chapter and cover how to perform intrusion detection on a DNS service in a DMZ.

Keeping the Web Server Serving

To keep your Web server from becoming a hacker's playground or to prevent hackers from showing off their newest graffiti or Web page manipulation skills, you need to pay attention to some simple rules while addressing security on a Web server in your DMZ.

As with the DNS server, keeping the Web server up to date on patch levels is of the utmost importance. For example, on Microsoft IIS servers, keeping current with Microsoft's patches and hotfixes can prevent virtually all the Unicode exploits we covered. Although sometimes it feels like there's an endless stream of hotfixes and patches, the fact remains that simply keeping the software up to date is one of the best ways to help keep your Web server from being hacked.

A second simple way to help harden the Web server is to disable *all* unneeded services and don't run too many things off a single box. Don't try to make a Web server also perform as a DNS server to save time and money. You will just buy yourself trouble in the long run. Other simple ways to help keep the hacker at bay: Either disable programs like FTP, command.com, and cmd.exe or rename them so that script kiddies end up getting discouraged and leaving your server alone, moving on to easier prey. A hacker will do sweeps of public IPs on the Internet looking for blocks that are assigned to specific companies. If a hacker scans, say, 1.1.1.1 through 1.1.10.255, he could find hundreds of IP addresses that are actively assigned to many systems either accessible from the Internet or sitting within a DMZ segment. If he cannot hack your server, he might very well move on to the next host standing by, maybe with more services or vulnerabilities available.

For the various flavors of UNIX/Linux, you should strongly consider downloading and running Bastille-Linux, which can be found at www.bastille-linux.org. Bastille-Linux attempts to harden your Linux installation and supports Red Hat, Debian, Mandrake, SuSE, and TurboLinux Linux distributions, along with HP-UX and Mac OS X.

For the Windows IIS server, it's an easy administrative tweak to rename the administrator account and disable the guest account on the Windows IIS servers. Although this will not prevent the expert hacker from finding the administrative account, it will deter those less talented hackers, and in the end, that's what we want. We want the hacker to go away to play on and exploit someone else's less protected server.

Never forget about passwords on any Web server, or any server for that matter. Always use strong passwords; choose nonword passwords so that basic dictionary attacks will fail. Use policies to lock out accounts after too many login failures to help discourage the would-be attacker.

Now that we have reviewed the reasons that Web services are so vulnerable, let's look at how to put the icing on your DMZ-cake and utilize HIDS on your Web services in the DMZ—the most likely target, and most common target, within the DMZ.

NOTE

Before we move on to applying intrusion detection and logging to your Web services, note that many organizations opt not to have a Web server on site. Instead, they place Web servers in an offsite location, remotely managed, outsourced, or colocated. If you have these types of solutions on your own corporate network, you should still ask your provider if services such as the ones listed in this chapter are applied and used. It is important to know this because often, depending on the provider, these services are not used. Many hacked Web sites are generally located on a third-party Web server on which a company might rent space. If you have your own server or one located elsewhere, ensure that your solution (wherever it is) is secured in the same ways listed here.

Configuring & Implementing...

Securing the E-Mail Relay with Intrusion Detection

In Chapter 14, we saw how a potential hacker could compromise your e-mail server in the DMZ to send spam or use the mail server as a relay. IDS can be a powerful tool in stopping this abuse of your e-mail server. In the following example, we have a scenario of an attacker wanting to DOS your e-mail server in the DMZ. By running an Nmap scan against your DMZ, the attacker has found that you have a Domino e-mail server running. You thought your network was safer than the average network since the e-mail server is not Exchange, but our wannabe hacker is not deterred. He does some research and finds an exploit for Domino that can either crash the server or possibly give him the ability to execute some code. All he needs to do is run a very long *rcpt to* command to start the buffer overflow (bugtraq:20010123). What our hacker doesn't know is that you are running an IDS via a network tap that hides the IDS from his scanning. Furthermore, you have a rule that looks for this type of attack. The rule, in a nutshell, looks for a string of any case over 800 characters following the *rcpt to* string. So our hacker tries to run his attack against your e-mail server, but the IDS sees the match and then sends a *TCP RST* to the hacker's IP address. This resets the hacker's TCP connection to your e-mail server, and poof! He is sitting there wondering why his connection to your e-mail server just dropped. This is just a sample of how an IDS can be configured to protect a certain host—in this case, the SMTP server—in the DMZ.

Continued

> The same IDS can also watch for an error condition that will alert you to someone who might be trying to relay mail through your server. Again, using Snort as the IDS, we would have a rule that looks for the string *smtp-relay-denied*. A match on this rule could be configured to send a page to alert you that someone is poking around on the e-mail server, or attempting to.

CiscoSecure IDS

Cisco IDS has gone through some changes recently. The older product, which was called NetRanger, has been deemed end of life (EOL), which simply means that support for it will no longer be kept up by the vendor as new products have replaced the older versions. NetRanger has been replaced by the 4200 series. A second choice is that you can get the Cisco IDS sensor on a blade for the Catalyst 6500 series switch. This offers some interesting potential, with access to the high-speed backplane of the switch versus tapping into a 10/100 port.

Until just a short while ago, the only way to manage the Cisco IDS sensor was to use the Cisco Secure Policy Manager (CSPM), which is a standalone product, or to use Ciscoworks. For some versions of the sensor, you can load the 3.1 version of the sensor software and get to a Web-based management screen of the sensor. This has changed again with the version 4.0 software for the IDS sensor. With version 4.0, you have the choice of managing the IDS sensor from the CLI, a Web browser, or Ciscoworks.

This chapter explains how to get a functional IDS in your DMZ, how to monitor it, and how to use the IDS logging functions, but we cannot cover the entire configuration of the IDS from the beginning of the installation. We do cover how to configure the IDS to make it operational and useful in your DMZ and network We look at filtering and signatures and how to edit these and generate reports.

When you start the CSPM application, you'll see the opening screen shown in Figure 15.14. This is the starting point for configuring the Cisco IDS sensor. In this example, we are configuring a 4230 sensor. The IDS blades in the 6500 series switch are configured in a different way. The switch has to be configured along with the sensor blade. We will concentrate on the external IDS for now.

Figure 15.14 Cisco Secure Policy Manager Startup Version 2.3.5i

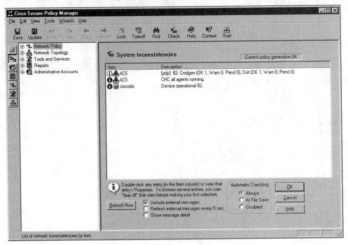

To configure or to change the sensor configuration, click the plus sign (+) next to the **Network Topology** menu. This opens the network node list and shows the nodes, including the sensors. Click the sensor you want to configure, and on the right side the various menus will appear. The first tab shown is Properties, but in Figure 15.15 we jump to the **Sensing** menu item. This screen shows us the active configuration that the sensor is using, the packet capture device or interface used, and whether IP Fragment Reassemble is enabled or not. The default is not to reassemble fragmented packets.

Figure 15.15 The Cisco Secure Policy Manager Sensing Tab

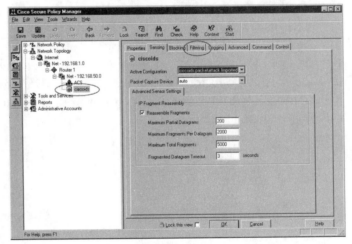

To make adjustments to the sensor to help reduce false positives, use the **Filtering** tab shown in Figure 15.16. This is where we tell the sensor to filter out certain signatures and IP addresses from the list of alarms.

Figure 15.16 Cisco Secure Policy Manager Sensor Filtering

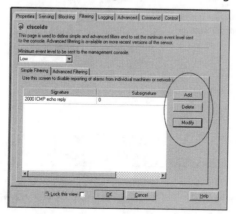

To edit this list, click the **Add** button to add a new exclusion or Modify to change an existing signature exclusion. In order to add the exclusion, we use the Create Filter option, as shown in Figure 15.17. You will choose the signature to exclude, the IP address, the mask, and whether it is a source or destination address.

Figure 15.17 Cisco Secure Policy Manager Sensor: Creating a Filter

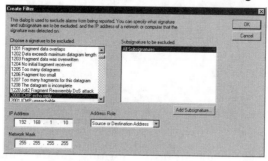

To make adjustments to the actual signatures, choose from the **Tools and Services** main menu, then choose **Sensor Signatures**, and then select the active signature configuration, as shown in Figure 15.18.

Figure 15.18 Cisco Secure Policy Manager Signature Menu Option

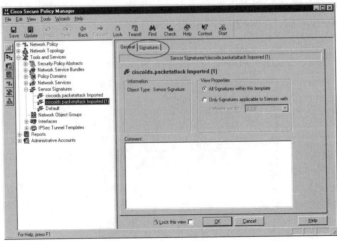

To see the various signatures used in this file, click the **Signatures** tab. You'll be presented with a choice of four tabs. The first is General Signatures, as shown in Figure 15.19.

Figure 15.19 Cisco Secure Policy Manager General Signatures Editor

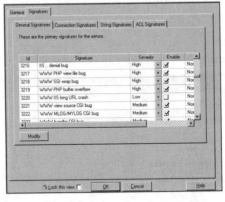

On this screen you can enable or disable various signatures and adjust the severity, depending on your network needs and activity. The signature can be modified by highlighting the signature and then clicking the **Modify** button on the lower left. Figure 15.20 shows the dialog box that will pop up. Any choice that doesn't apply to the signature is grayed out, such as TCP Reset shown in this figure. On this screen, we can adjust our signatures based on the needs of our DMZ hosts. For example, if you have one or more Web servers in the DMZ, any filter based on WWW signatures will be of interest to you, as will any IIS signatures if you have Microsoft IIS servers running. Of course, if you do not have IIS running, you can disable the IIS signatures to help reduce the false positives. If you find that in the course of normal business your sensor alarms on a certain signature too often, you can readjust the severity level from high to medium or low or disable it completely if needed.

Figure 15.20 The Signature Actions Dialog Box

The **Connection Signatures** tab lets us drill into the sensor signatures more deeply by focusing on connection-based signatures. In Figure 15.21 we see that we can enable signatures or change settings such as the port or type of connection. You can add, delete, or modify existing signatures based on your network's needs.

Figure 15.21 Cisco Secure Policy Manager IDS Connection Editor

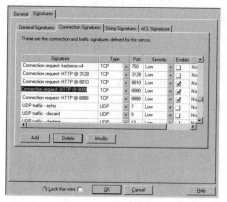

Next select the **String Signatures** tab. This is where we set up the signatures that look for certain strings in the packets. An example is trying to match the string signature of certain commands or keywords such as cmd.exe or a string like /etc/shadow. In Figure 15.22 we see where we can actually edit the string subsignatures to reflect exactly the string we are trying to match to. We can also adjust the direction to look, how often we should look for the string before we alarm on it, and the severity level. Again, based on the type of hosts in the DMZ, you can tune these parameters to reflect the actual type of host in the DMZ or segment of the network you're monitoring.

Figure 15.22 Cisco Secure Policy Manager IDS String Signature Editor

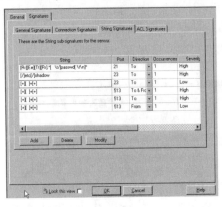

Now that configuration is completed, we need to save the changes before we move on to doing anything else. Saving can take a few minutes, depending on how many nodes are in the topology. This is also where you will find any errors in the topology configuration or configuration of the post office that the director and the IDS sensor use to exchange information and settings. Once you can complete the save without any errors, click the **Update** button. This adds all the changes to the database and allows the CSPM to generate the new configuration for the sensor. We need this new configuration information to be pushed out to the sensor; to do this, click the network topology and then choose the **Command** tab. When everything compiles correctly, you will see a screen similar to that shown in Figure 15.23.

Figure 15.23 Cisco Secure Policy Manager Command Screen

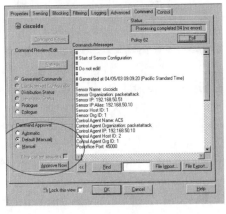

The default for CSPM is to have the approval as manual. This means that before the new configuration information is uploaded to the sensor, you must click the **Approve**

Now button. In the status screen in the upper-right corner, you can see that the new configuration is being sent to the sensor. You can save a copy of this configuration information by clicking the **File Export** button. Once the configuration is uploaded, the sensor will start to use the new rules and signatures.

Of course, all this setting of signatures is useless without some kind of reporting so that we can see the results from monitoring the network. CSPM provides several ways to get reporting information. The reports can be on demand or scheduled and can be in HTML format or text format.

Figure 15.24 shows where you select the reporting function from the Tools menu. The next selection is to choose between the on-demand reports or scheduled reports.

Figure 15.24 Cisco Secure Policy Manager View Reports Menu Option

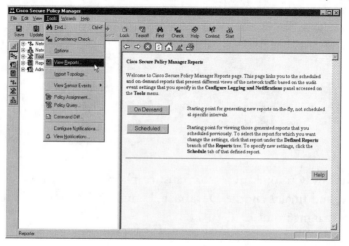

In Figure 15.25 we see the Intrusion Detection Summary report screen. We can select various times and dates, select the direction of the intrusion, specify a specific signature, or all of these actions and specify the sensors to query.

Figure 15.25 Cisco Secure Policy Manager Report Manager Screen

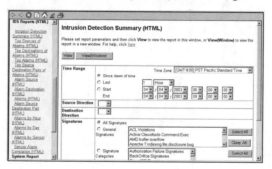

Figure 15.26 shows the results from the IDS Top Source report in text format. We see that the report shows the alarm level and the source address. It also tells us the details of each alarm.

Figure 15.26 Cisco Secure Policy Manager IDS Sensor Report

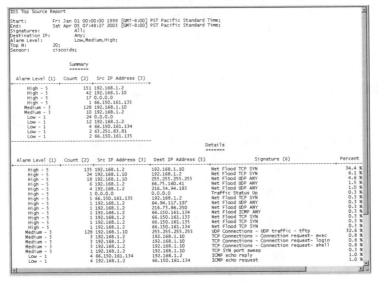

For a different way to pull up sensor statistics, choose **Tools,** then choose **View Sensor Events,** and finally, choose **Database**. Figure 15.27 shows the sequence of pulling the data straight from the database.

Figure 15.27 Choosing to View the Database

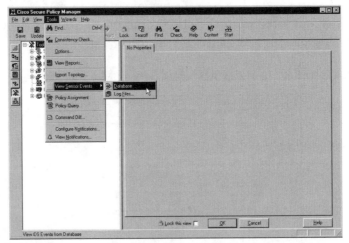

In Figure 15.28 we see the results of directly querying the database.

Figure 15.28 Database Query Results

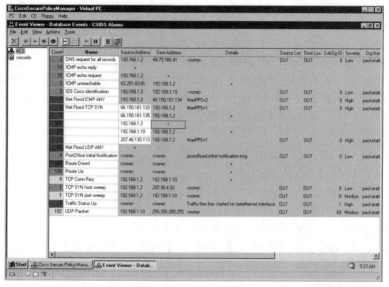

With the Cisco IDS sensor in place, you can access the reporting through a Web interface and HTML or in plain-text format. You can send the logging data to an FTP server for archiving and further analysis.

A very nice feature of the Cisco IDS is the Network Security Database, or NSDB. This is an HTML-based encyclopedia of network vulnerability information. Each alarm on the Cisco IDS is linked back to this database so you can click the alarm and get very detailed information about it.

Now that you've learned the basics of configuring the Cisco 4200 series of IDS sensors and how to manage the signatures, what can we do with it? The Cisco IDS is a relatively flexible sensor, especially with the newer 4.*x* software loaded on it. We can install the Cisco sensor with the monitoring port just in front of the firewall and the management port in the DMZ or push it back a bit and watch the DMZ with the sensor-monitoring port and have the management port on the trusted network. With the newer software, the sensor can be a standalone guardian without requiring a dedicated management station. We have a strong and well-supported solution that requires nothing more than a Web browser to manage it.

Snort

You have to love a program with the name Snort. This program is open source (it can be found at www.Snort.org), and there are few mail lists you can use to get support for it. Snort can be used as is, or you can use it with MySQL or add GUI interfaces to it. Whatever you choose, we show you how to use Snort effectively to defend your DMZ inexpensively. Formerly, when you installed Snort, you had to trudge through the installation, find the various dependencies, find the packages needed, install those packages, and a much later time, you would have the bare-bones IDS sensor running. We cover Snort's rules for signature matching and how Snort can use a few different formats for its log files.

Cisco has the name, but Snort has the price—it's *free*. When you are trying to protect your DMZ and conserve cash, free means a lot. But free in this case does not equate to a poor-quality product. Several companies have enhanced Snort with custom front ends and enhanced reporting functions.

One of the best ways to get a very clean packaged Snort with MySQL and a nice GUI interface is to download PureSecure from Demarc at www.demarc.com. The personal version is free and the commercial version is reasonably priced. We highly recommend getting the personal version, since it installs and configures Snort, Apache, and MySQL at one time for you. Figure 15.29 shows the opening screen you see as you log into a PureSecure host. Be warned that setting up the PureSecure IDS can take some time. On our test-bed PIII 800MHz unit, it took a bit more than one and a half hours. On the other hand, at the end of the install, the sensor started right up with no problems. We assume you already know how to install and use Snort, but in this section of the chapter, we show you how to implement a Snort solution in your DMZ for intrusion detection.

NOTE

For more information on Snort, you can read *Snort 2.0 Intrusion Detection* (Syngress Publishing, Inc.; ISBN 1-931836-74-4).

Figure 15.29 PureSecure, Showing an SMTP Overflow Attack

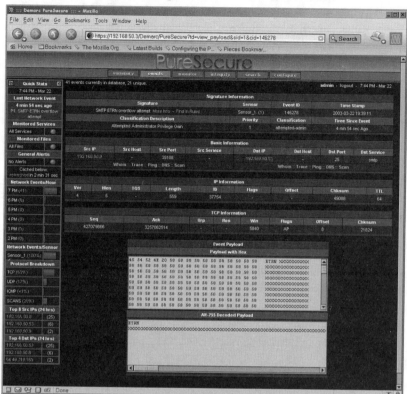

PureSecure gives a wealth of information up front without having to dig around for it. You get the signature match, sensor, timestamp, IP address information, and the event payload. There is even a miniviewer that can stay on the screen and give you a way to see the current events at a glance. PureSecure even has an automated rule update process.

As with the Cisco IDS sensor we just read about, Snort IDS sensors follow the same deployment rules. If Snort cannot see the traffic, it cannot protect your network. Snort can be placed in the DMZ in the same manner as the Cisco sensor—one leg in front of the firewall or in the DMZ and the second leg in the trusted network. Unlike the Cisco sensor, Snort functions with only a single NIC installed in the sensor. The management and the sensing are done through the same NIC. However, this is not recommended, because you should not place an interface on the network being watched with a live IP address. Doing so would provide the attacker with a tip-off that there was something on the wire, and we want to be stealthy—not to mention that if the attacker could compromise your IDS, that is one less alarm he needs to worry about while he does his dirty deeds in your DMZ.

When configuring Snort, you need to be aware that some Snort distributions or scripts run Snort as root. This is not good security practice. Dan Bernstein has a tool package called *daemontools* that can be found at http://cr.yp.to/daemontools.html; it can help prevent this situation if you're running Snort on Linux-based hosts.

To find detailed instructions on how to use Snort with daemontools, which we referred to earlier in the chapter, go to http://simonbs.com/Snort.html for the details of how to integrate the two. Once the assimilation has been completed, Snort will not run as root in the daemon mode (*-D*). Keep in mind that several versions of Snort are available, so always try to get the newest one, which, at this time, is 2.0. This version is a major rewrite of Snort and addresses a great many issues with versions 1.7, 1.8, and 1.9. Having the latest code is a much preferable security posture on something as critical as the IDS sensor sitting in your DMZ. Snort will run and sense with only a single NIC installed, but again, from a security perspective in the DMZ, this is not acceptable. Make sure to use *two* NICs for your Snort sensor. When configuring your Snort host, install SSH in order to provide a secure link from the sensor to a remote management or logging server. Make sure that all services such as FTP and X-Windows are disabled. We keep repeating: Leave no freebies for the would-be hacker of your DMZ.

Deploying Snort is no different than deploying any other NIDS, with one exception: It is one of the cheapest, so you can have a large number of sensors deployed around the network for a minimal amount of cash, covering places like the internal networks, the DMZ, and outside the DMZ. Combined with deployment of an HIDS such as Tripwire, Snort it is a very potent network defense against the wannabe hacker of your DMZ and network.

In Figure 15.30 we see how PureSecure and Snort detect a scan by Nmap over the network.

Figure 15.30 Nmap Scanning Detection by Snort

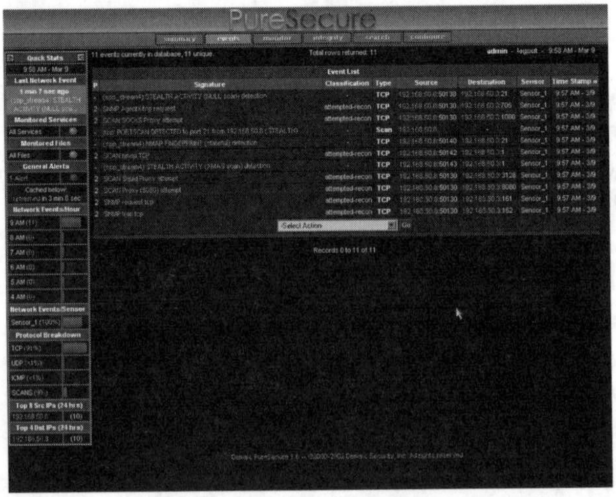

There are a variety of ways to manage Snort IDS sensors. An easy way to configure Snort is to use the Webadmin Snort plug-in found at http://msbnetworks.net/Snort/. Figure 15.31 shows a screen of the Snort IDS plug-in for managing Snort. From this plug-in we can set virtually all settings of Snort as well as the alerts and logging. We can also manage our rules for Snort from this tool.

Figure 15.31 The Webadmin Snort Tool

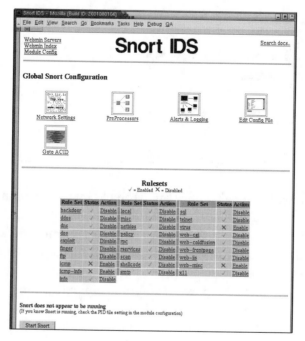

A very popular PHP-based front end for Snort is called Analysis Console for Intrusion Databases, or ACID, and can be found at www.andrew.cmu.edu/ ~rdanyliw/Snort/Snortacid.html. Many people use ACID for the GUI front end for Snort; and there is a great deal of documentation and other sources of information for tuning and working with ACID and Snort. Figure 15.32 shows the ACID front end for Snort.

Figure 15.32 The ACID Front End for Snort

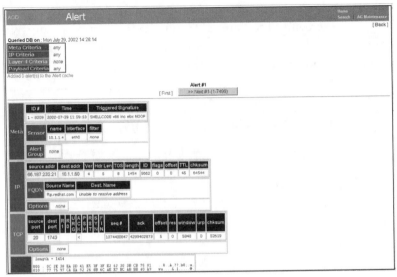

Snort can keep log files of alerts that are triggered by the established rules and the mode that Snort is running in. Snort can be run in a sniffer mode, packet-logging mode, or IDS mode. Sniffer mode gives you the header information and prints it to the screen. Packet-logging mode gives the entire packet and records it to disk. IDS mode catches the packets based on the rules.

The log files can be pretty verbose, or you can configure Snort to dump the logs in the *tcpdump* format, which can be played back for further analysis later. The log file output can also be XML, Syslog, full dumps (which can get *very* large), or to a database such as MySQL. These logs can provide quite a bit of information about exactly what is happening on the network. Since they can be tied to a specific IP address such as the one shown in Figure 15.33, which is tied to 192.168.50.2, the log files can make finding information relatively easy.

Figure 15.33 Snort Logs

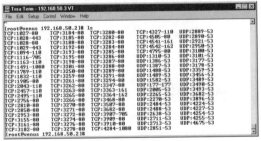

When you pick and read one of these log entries, there is information on what was seen, why it was logged, and the direction of the data flow, along with some packet information. In Figure 15.34 we have a sample of a DNS spoof that was caught and logged by Snort.

Figure 15.34 Sample of Snort Log Showing a DNS Spoof

```
[**] DNS SPOOF query response with ttl: 1 min. and no authority [**]
11/01-19:35:28.110783 192.168.50.235:53 -> 192.168.50.2:2889
UDP TTL:128 TOS:0x0 ID:14883 IpLen:20 DgmLen:80
Len: 60
=+=+=+=+=+=+=+=+=+=+=+=+=+=+=+=+=+=+=+=+=+=+=+=+=+=+=+=+=+=+=+=+=+=+=+=+=+
```

You can find tools to convert the log files to HTML for real-time publishing of the statistics. One excellent tool based on Perl, called Snortalog, can be downloaded from http://jeremy.chartier.free.fr/Snortalog/. This tool gives its output in either HTML or plain text. It works with all Snort log formats (syslog, full, and fast). Figure 15.35 shows the Snortalog Sample Report in ASCII.

Figure 15.35 Snortalog Sample Report in ASCII

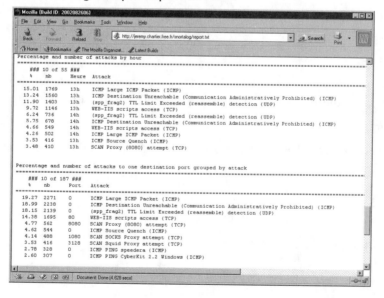

One of the joys of Snort is that you can write your own rules for it. Doing so is not really for the faint of heart, but it does have immense value. You can tweak an existing rule for your own purposes or come up with a completely custom rule based on your needs. As with the Cisco IDS, you can finely tune Snort in the DMZ to look for specific intrusions based on the hosts in the DMZ. You enable or disable rules, make rules with specific Boolean logic, IP addressing, ports, or specific strings. Snort.org has a comprehensive rule database online where you can search for a specific rule or find something close and then modify it to suit your needs. A second resource, which we prefer over Snort's database, can be found at http://whitehats.com. They have matched the rules with packet trace files and the research that accounted for the rule. It's a great way to see how and why a rule was coded in a certain manner. In Figure 15.36 we see a sample rule for Snort. Since Snort does not understand multiple lines, the rules consist of a single line.

Figure 15.36 Sample Snort Rule

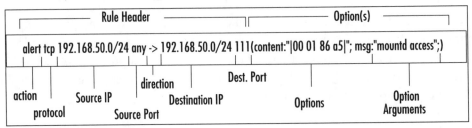

The text in the rule up to the first parenthesis is the *rule header:*

```
alert tcp 192.168.50.0/24 any -> 192.168.1.0/24 111 (......)
```

The first item is the *rule action.* In this example, it is *alert.* This is what Snort is supposed to do when Snort finds a match to this rule. There are three choices of action to choose from:

- **Alert** Generates an alert using the selected alert method and then logs the packet.

- **Log** Logs the packet.

- **Pass** Drops or ignores the packet.

The next item is the *protocol field:*

```
alert <protocol> 192.168.50.0/24 any -> 192.168.1.0/24 111 (......)
```

There are three protocols that Snort can watch for:

- tcp
- udp
- icmp

However, with future versions, this number will more than likely change.
Next in line is the *IP address field:*

```
alert tcp <IP address> 111 (......)
```

We can specify specific IP address, wildcard addresses using *any*, or a range of IP addresses using the CIDR block mask. This is where we specify a subnet mask by the slash (/) and then the number of bits to mask the address. An example is 192.168.50.0 /24, which translates to 255.255.255.0.

The final field before the parenthesis is the *port field*.

```
alert tcp 192.168.50.0/24 any -> 192.168.1.0/24 <port> (......)
```

We can specify a certain port, a range of ports, or any port.

- **1:1024** Tells the rule to use ports 1 to 1024.
- **:6000** Tells the rule to use any ports less than or equal to 6000.
- **400:** Tells the rule to use any ports greater than or equal to 400.

We can tell the rule to ignore something by using the *bang* or ! symbol. This tells the rule to do something to ports except what comes after the ! symbol.

In the rule we can tell Snort which direction to watch by using the *directional operator* (->) in the rule, or we can say "any direction" using the <> operator.

Since this chapter is not about writing rules for Snort, we leave the options to you to study. The options can be quite simple or very complex, with offsets and Boolean logic. For more detailed information on writing Snort rules, you can find the information in Syngress's book on Snort that we mentioned earlier in this chapter or by going to the Snort Web site.

Many Snort enhancements are available, ranging from graphical interfaces, signature generators, and log file analyzers to plug-ins. Snort can be one of the most valuable tools to protect your DMZ and network from intruders and attacks. For the price, Snort is one of the best bargains for network security and IDS systems.

The Poor Man's IDS

Until the advent of Snort and other open-source IDS, you had to be prepared to spend a significant amount of money on an IDS. Or perhaps you needed an IDS in the DMZ for a short amount of time, say to identify Kazaa or a suspected Web hack taking place or to look for a worm like CodeRed. What can you do with existing tools and not break the budget?

In many packet-sniffing tools, you can design and set up custom filters and then have the packet analyzer look for the match and trip an alarm. That way, you could have the analyzer running and checking for Kazaa, Back Oriface, various worm signatures, and so on. The signatures are pretty easy to come by at sites such as the Snort Web site rule database or the Snort signature mail list at http://lists.sourceforge.net/lists/listinfo/Snort-sigs. The signatures give you the details you need to look for in the packets. In the example in Figure 15.37, we can see the signature string for the worm CodeRed V2:

Figure 15.37 Signature of CodeRed V2 for Snort

```
alert tcp $EXTERNAL_NET any -> $HTTP_SERVERS $HTTP_PORTS (msg:"WEB-IIS
    CodeRed v2 root.exe access"; flow:to_server,established; uricontent:"
        /root.exe"; nocase; classtype:web-application-attack;
            reference:url, www.cert.org/advisories/CA-2001-19.html; sid:
                1256; rev:7;)
```

The part of the signature we are interested in is *uricontent: "/root.exe"*. This string is what we want our custom packet filter to look for. Depending on what exactly you want to look for, you might need to calculate the offset in the packet in order to tell the analyzer just where to look for the data. Some packet analyzers such as NAI Sniffer and Etherpeek let you use Boolean logic when you build the filter. These can be a real help with you want to find, say, FTP traffic but the FTP traffic is not on the expected port. You can use the custom filter to find all packets that contain FTP strings but *not* look at packets using the expected port 21. This way you could look for FTP commands as strings but filter out the normal FTP traffic on your network.

It's relatively easy to make a custom filter in Etherpeek. You start by selecting either **Edit** and then **Insert**, as shown in Figure 15.38, or right-clicking the filters and then choosing **Insert**.

Figure 15.38 Starting to Make a Custom Filter in Etherpeek

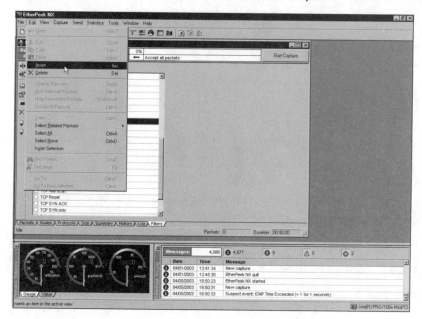

The Edit Filter dialog box appears, as shown in Figure 15.39.

Figure 15.39 Editing Etherpeek Filter Dialog Box

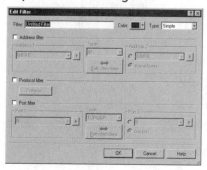

In this box, we need to click **Simple** and change it to **Advanced**. This will bring up the Boolean logic editor that we want. In Figure 15.40 we see that the title is Port 80 Attack Fingerprints. We use Boolean logic to look for four different strings that would signal a port attack on a Web server. To add another logic function, just click the **And** or the **Or** button.

Figure 15.40 Adding Boolean Logic Functions to Our Filter

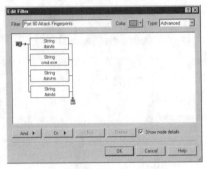

When we click the button, we are presented with a dialog box that asks on what we want to filter: ports, protocols, error, or string. Choose **string**, and then all you have to do is to type in the string and any offset that might be needed, as shown in Figure 15.41.

Figure 15.41 Adding a String to Custom Filter

Once you have completed our filter, it will be in the list of filters to choose from. Now all you do is click the box next to our filter to enable it, as shown in Figure 15.42, and start the capture. That's not too much trouble to make a custom filter for a poor man's IDS system, is it?

Figure 15.42 Enabling the New Custom Filter

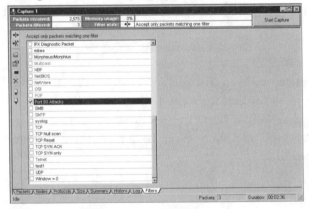

Network Time

A few extra points to know are that you need a plan for incident reporting and a plan for post mortem evaluations. If there will be legal action, you need to know the procedures on how to save evidence, copy log files, and report the incident. We saw in Chapter 15 that a way to beat the IDS and other security devices in the DMZ is to break into the DMZ slowly and then over a period time have the log files overwrite your tracks. In order to file a legal action, you need those log files, and they need to be complete and accurate. Given how cheap disk space is nowadays, there is not much excuse for not maintaining good log files. In order to aid in the tracking of the attack, a good timeline is needed. This becomes even more important when the attack might start with the DNS server in the DMZ and then jump to the Web servers or other DMZ hosts. Often the firewalls and IDS have internal clocks but they have not been set or have drifted. Correcting this normal drift of the time is where having an NTP server or atomic clock server is helpful. You can now have very accurate logs across multiple nodes on the DMZ or network using these types of technologies, and if the attack spanned hours or geographic locations, the accurate clock will of great help in the analysis of the attack.

More IDS Deployment Strategies

We saw early on the classic deployment of the typical IDS sensor just in front of the firewall. We also learned that we can have a host-based IDS system. But is that all there is to deployment of an effective IDS security model? Is this the best we can do? No; this is just the start of what we can do to protect our DMZ hosts and networks. In Figure 15.43 we see a mixed deployment of NIDS in the form of IDS Sensors 1 and 2 plus the mail server and the DNS server in the DMZ being protected by a HIDS system.

Figure 15.43 Mixed NIDS and HIDS Deployment

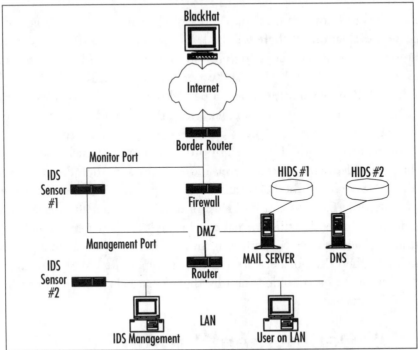

In this design, the IDS Sensor 1 monitors anyone who is at the Internet side of the firewall and starting to knock against it. This would be the first port scans against your network, for example. IDS Sensor 2 is positioned to watch Internet network traffic, which could be a certain segment, server farm, or the entire LAN looking for an internal attacker. As Chapter 15 showed us with the FBI report, often an attack is started on the inside of the network from someone who is trusted. In the DMZ, we have our mail server and our DNS server both protected by a HIDS. This guards our systems against an attack that might have slipped past the firewall and IDS Sensor 1. Remember, we want layered network defense, just like the layers of an onion, and here we have a good start at it. More layers would include the ACLs on the router between the DMZ and the LAN and would even include our password policies, server permissions, and so on.

As good as this design is, we can improve it even more, as shown in Figure 15.44. Remember our good friend the honeypot? Here we see a honeypot deployed in our DMZ.

Figure 15.44 Mixed NIDS and HIDS with the Honeypot

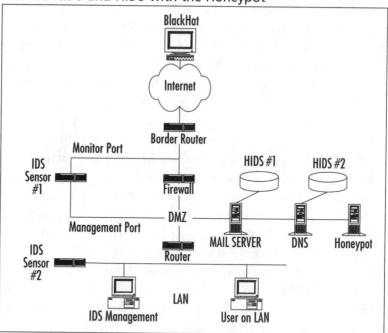

Now we really can have some fun with our network defense. We have the firewall to stop the average wannabe hacker. We have an IDS acting as the sentry, watching the front door to alert us to anyone who starts to find a way in. We have a DMZ to keep network-accessible hosts off our LAN. We have those DMZ hosts protected by a HIDS that monitors the hosts locally for any changes that might take place. We have now added the temptation of the honeypot, which we hope will keep the attacker's attention away from our real hosts and give us time to set up a defense, such as shunning his IP address, blocking his IP address, sending TCP resets, and logging his activities. On the LAN side, we have a NIDS watching for anyone who either gets past all the DMZ defenses or has started on the inside and is working his way out. We now have a layered defense configured for our DMZ and network.

Case Study

Our client, a company called Magic Potter, has a basic network installed and running. The IT staff at the company use a conventional design of a LAN with a DMZ separated by a firewall on either end of the DMZ. Within the DMZ they have their mail server, a primary and secondary DNS server, a SQL server and three Web servers. Their security officer, who is also their network administrator, Cisco geek, and desktop support technician, managed to convince her management that outside help was needed to bring up their network security standards to reflect the new threats she has been reading about in the industry trade magazines. We enter the company as security consultants. Like many IT departments, the budget is lean for this project, but after sitting down and discussing the current status of the network, future plans, support issues, and budget concerns, we assure our client that we can offer some reasonable solutions that won't break their bank too badly.

Magic Potter does not have the budget for a penetration test, but the security officer shows us the results of her own private audits using Nmap from her home PC against the company's firewalls. She has found a few holes in the firewall, but she is very concerned about the vulnerabilities highlighted, such as various Unicode attacks on the Web servers, and she asks us about something she heard about, called SQL injection attacks.

We take all this down and arrive back on site a week later with some recommendations to what Magic Potter can do to help tighten things:

1. We suggested that we or Magic Potter should service-pack all the servers in the DMZ to bring them up to current levels.

2. We suggested that they upgrade the DNS servers to BIND 9.22.

3. We suggested that they split the DNS servers into one server in the DNS and one on the internal network.

4. We suggest that they apply access lists on the firewalls to control zone updates to and from only certain IP addresses.

5. Since the budget is lean, we suggest that they use a Snort sensor in the classic deployment, with the monitoring port watching over the firewall facing the Internet.

6. We then suggest that they use the open source Linux version of Tripwire on the Web servers, the SQL server, and the one DNS server in the DMZ.

7. We suggest that the firewalls be configured to use only SSH and that all services not required on the Web servers and SQL server to be either removed or disabled. We also suggest that since the Web servers are Windows based, they

rename the cmd.exe file to something else to help defeat various HTTP attacks.

8. We suggest that all the severs and firewalls send log files back to a syslog server and that Magic Potter purchase Sawmill to build reports from the syslog files.

All of these suggestions would bring Magic Potter into a much improved defensive posture at a minimal cost to the IT department. None of the suggestions required special training or expensive class time in order to be effective. We did suggest that at a later time the company might want to consider a honeypot inside the DMZ to help keep intruders away from the production servers.

Lessons Learned

In the last two chapters we have covered an incredible amount of material about how to hack your DMZ, firewall, and network. Then we covered how to find the hacking, how to stop it, and how we might prevent it from happening again. The one thing that should stand out by now is that although firewalls are still a requirement on a network, the IDS is tremendous aid to protecting your network. You need to protect the DMZ and network in layers. No single silver bullet will protect the DMZ and network.

An important lesson that should be apparent by now is how important it is to have the different parts of the network correct architected and the equipment configured. Our mantra is, "Defaults are *not* your friend." You can have the best firewall in the world, but without defense in layers such as the DMZ, hardened routers, hardened servers, VLANs, and desktop security, in reality your defenses are very weak. The best defense is a good offense, and in this case the offense is having a solid network architecture, defense in layers, and current software patches in place. Network security is constantly evolving, and to stay current on the various threats requires some effort on your part; you need to stay abreast of current events in network security. This means reading some of the newsgroups, hit the magazines, and what the experts such as SANS and CERT are recommending for best practices.

We have seen that once the network defenses are breached, the attacker can cause all kinds of havoc on the network—from erasing files to stealing intellectual property. Part of the planning of a solid defense assumes the worst and that the attacker will make it past all the defenses in place and compromise something of value. You must include in your planning a business continuity plan that would be a backup strategy, server recovery plans, and how to handle the incident response, which can include legal issues such as evidence preservation. The following chapter will give you the tools and knowledge to be prepared for the day your network is compromised. We hope that with the knowledge gleaned from these preceding chapters you can make life as difficult as possible for the would-be hacker.

Summary

So you thought you were protected by the firewall? As we have seen in this chapter, to prevent unwanted visitors on our network we must take more sophisticated steps than simply installing a firewall. The lesson in Chapter 15 was that hackers are a very creative group of people, and it takes someone just as creative to effectively deter them from breaking a network.

There are several tools that are invaluable to the network engineer; one in particular, called the intrusion detection system or IDS, is our "big gun" in the arsenal of network defense. With the two types of IDS systems, the HIDS and NIDS, we can adjust our design to suit the network's needs and the level of protection we are looking for from the IDS. It's not a plug-and-play device, but the IDS is worth the time and effort it takes to install, configure, and learn because of what the IDS brings to the table in terms of network protection. With custom signatures, we can look for virtually anything on the network we need to see, and we can track it, tag it, and bag it with an IDS.

Not only can we use applications such as Snort or combination hardware/software such as the Cisco IDS solution to monitor our network, but we can reuse other tools such as the network analyzer. With custom filters, we can turn a packet sniffer into a poor man's IDS for that quick look that we might need. IDS such as the Cisco solution can actually monitor the IDS, routers, and PIX firewalls and then adjust the various rules and access lists on the fly to defeat attacks while they occur.

But for all the sophistication of an IDS, it means nothing without good reporting. We have to read the reports generated by our security devices in order to be aware of what is happening. We also need to understand what is normal for our network and what is abnormal. Along with the reporting comes the need to have an accurate timestamp on the logs. We can get this by using an NTP server or an atomic clock on our network. Everything should be synchronized to this timepiece so that the log files and reports all match up very nicely across the timeline.

To protect the DMZ and to have the DMZ protect the network is no small undertaking. It involves examining the network, all the way from the big-picture enterprise view down to the desktop and if the servers are locked away in a secure room.

Remember these words of Ovid (42 B.C.–17 A.D.): "We can learn even from our enemies."

Solutions Fast Track

Intrusion Detection

☑ There are two primary types of IDS. One is network based, or NIDS, and the second is host based, or HIDS.

☑ HIDS provide in-depth logging, are better at detecting unknown attacks, and have fewer false positives than NIDS. However, HIDS need to have an agent on each host.

☑ The NIDS has a lower overall cost since it is an appliance instead of an agent on each host. NIDS are generally easier and quicker to deploy than HIDS.

☑ To help the NIDS see all traffic, you can either mirror the switch ports or use a hardware device called a *network tap,* which is inserted into the network between two nodes for a T-type of connection.

☑ To use IDS effectively to protect your network and the DMZ, you should consider a mix of NIDS and HIDS.

Repelling the Hacker

☑ One of the easiest tools to help repel a hacker is to deploy a honeypot to distract him from your real systems.

☑ An effective DNS solution is to split the normal two DNS servers into one DNS server in the DMZ and the second on the internal network. Use ACLs to control the flow of zone information between them.

☑ Use a HIDS such as Tripwire to lock down and protect your DMZ hosts.

☑ One of the quickest and simplest fixes in the DMZ to help repel boarders is to keep all servers current on service packs and hotfixes.

☑ Follow best practices for setting up servers, such as hardening them, setting strong passwords, using SSH instead of Telnet, and other security-minded practices.

☑ Do not give away any information about your DMZ or hosts for free. Use various Web server-masking software, use options in BIND to change version strings, and don't use "gimme" names in the DNS server, such as myWindows2Kserver1.

CiscoSecure IDS

☑ The Cisco IDS sensor can be managed depending on code level by Ciscoworks, Cisco Secure Policy Manager (CSPM), or a Web browser.

☑ Using the CSPM, you can have reports in either HTML format or plain text, or you can send the log files to an FTP server.

☑ Cisco IDS sensors are available in an appliance form factor or in a module form factor for the Catalyst 6000 series switch.

Snort

☑ Snort is a freely available application and extremely flexible architecture. There are many log file analyzers, graphical front ends, interfaces to SQL databases, and rule generators.

☑ Snort rules consist of a single line of code that can set up filters based on IP addresses, port numbers, direction of traffic, search string, or offset within the packet.

The Poor Man's IDS

☑ A network analyzer such as Ethereal, Etherpeek, or NAI Sniffer can be used as a NIDS with custom filters.

☑ To build custom filters, you can find the various search strings, offsets, and other information from Snort rules.

☑ One of the easiest network analyzers to build custom filters for is Etherpeek due to the "cut and paste" function within the filter-building mechanism.

More IDS Deployment Strategies

☑ Never rely on a single IDS if running intrusion detection is so important. It might be important (based on your risk assessment) to run a combination of both HIDS and NIDS, depending on the need.

☑ An advanced strategy is based on the design of the DMZ: ACLs on the Internet router, AAA in use, auditing logging, a firewall, a honeypot, and last but not least, an IDS. Make sure you use NIDS where applicable, and where you can afford it, use HIDS on all DMZ hosts.

Lessons Learned

☑ Always stay current with your software patches and hotfixes to help protect your servers.

☑ To protect your DMZ, you need to use a layered approach, like an onion, instead of one hard layer like an egg, which is easily broken.

☑ You do not have to spend a lot of money in order to protect your DMZ and network. Many high-quality tools are available in open source.

Frequently Asked Questions

The following Frequently Asked Questions, answered by the authors of this book, are designed to both measure your understanding of the concepts presented in this chapter and to assist you with real-life implementation of these concepts. To have your questions about this chapter answered by the author, browse to **www.syngress.com/solutions** and click on the **"Ask the Author"** form. You will also gain access to thousands of other FAQs at ITFAQnet.com.

Q: Where can I find strings to build custom filters for my sniffer or rules?

A: Snort.org has one of the best databases for rules. You can look at the rule and find out exactly the string you need to filter or even the hex code and offset.

Q: I can only afford a single IDS. Where should I put it in my network?

A: The traditional deployment of a single IDS is to place the monitoring port in the DMZ and the management port in the trusted network. This way you can watch for anything that gets past the firewall's blocking. There is some debate as to whether this is optimal or the monitoring port should be on the Internet side of the firewall. Try them both and see what works best for your network.

Q: How can I keep my IDS from being "seen" on the network?

A: An easy way is to use an Ethernet cable with the transmit pairs cut so that the IDS only receives traffic. An optional but better method is use a network tap, which keeps even the MAC address of the IDS sensor from appearing on the network.

Q: Can I use more then one IDS sensor on a network?

A: Sure. In fact, it is highly recommended to use more than a single sensor to provide adequate protection.

Q: Can I mix both types of IDS on the segment, like my DMZ?

A: Yes. Best practices say that you should use a mix of NIDS sensors and HIDS agents to fully protect the hosts in the DMZ.

Q: How can my IDS sensor see full-duplex 10/100 traffic on my network?

A: The better choice is to insert a hardware device called a *network tap* into the full-duplex segment. Once you have done that, you can plug in the IDS sensor at will without disrupting the existing network connection.

Q: I don't have the budget for network taps. Is there anything else that will work to monitor all traffic on a segment?

A: Depending on your network hardware, you might be able to configure a span or a monitor port where the switch will copy all traffic you specify to a certain switch port into which the IDS sensor is plugged.

Q: Do I really need a honeypot on my DMZ?

A: No, you don't really need the honeypot. The DMZ will function fine without it, but you risk having one of your production servers become the center of attention from a hacker. It would be better to offer up the honeypot for the hacker to waste his time on than sacrifice your production server.

Index

Syngress: *The Definition of a Serious Security Library*

Syn·gress (sin-gres): *noun, sing.* Freedom from risk or danger; safety. See *security*.